THE REAL GUIDE

NEW YORK

New and Revised

S0-AXP-325

REAL GUIDE CREDITS

Series Editor: Mark Ellingham
Editorial: Martin Dunford, John Fisher, Jack Holland, Jonathan Buckley,
    Greg Ward, Richard Trillo
US Text Editor: Ellen Sarewitz
Production: Susanne Hillen, Kate Berens, Gail Jammy
Typesetting: Andy Hilliard

Thanks for this new edition to everyone at Real Guides, especially Andy Hilliard and Gail Jammy for typesetting; to Donald Suggs for invaluable gay updates; to Phil Cheeseman for last-minute clubbing notes; and to Darren Colby for his support and all-round good humor. Also to Daniela Marino of the State of New York Division of Tourism; Jules Brown; Tim Perry; Sally Ann Whittaker; Hank S. Fried; Syd Lazarus; Robert Fisher; Dorothy Vaghela; Roy Videen; Lola Lenzo; Bridget Bouch; Mog Greenwood; Caroline, Kate, and Margaret for the good company; and, last but not least, to Jeanne and Matthew for their dispatches from the Big City.

Many thanks also to those who wrote in with comments on, and corrections to, previous editions: Mike and Marilyn Miller, Laura Drazin Boyes, Eveline Thevenard, David McClelland, Penny Geary, R.G. Bowden, David Smith, Jane Lawrence, Hugh Duffy, A.E.M Oijen, Marion Butcher, Alexandre F. Stotz, A.E. Egerton, Brian Anderson, Sylvia Woods, Albert Hoffmann, Igor Pashutinski, Annette Grey, Adrienne Banks, Peter Morris, Damien Rea, Joyce Gold, Jackie Weinstein, Olga Happenin, Peter Smith, Helen Hill, the folks at the Mission, John Davies, Pablo Ramirez, Petri Pajulahti, Richard Connaughton, Yale Alexander, Rory Houston, Robin Katz, Jon Melnick, Ken Scudder, Henrietta O'Connor, Mark Flannagan, Jay Dixon, David Nicholls, Sarah Howell, David Smith, Andrew T. Irving, Bob Smith, Jon Lee, J. Jerrard Dinn, Millie Bastha, R. Audifredi, Andrew Bone, Cynthia Arnolds. Please keep writing!

Typeset in Linotron Univers and Century Old Style to an original design by Andrew Oliver.
Printed in the United States by R.R. Donnelley & Sons.

Illustrations in Part One and Part Three by Ed Briant; Basics illustration by Christina Brimage;
Contexts illustration by Sally Davies.

The publishers and authors have done their best to ensure the accuracy and currency of all the information in
New York: the Real Guide; however, they can accept no responsibility for any loss, injury, or inconvenience
sustained by any traveler as a result of information or advice contained in the guide.

Published in the United States by
Prentice Hall General Reference
A division of Simon & Schuster Inc.
15 Columbus Circle
New York, NY 10023

Library of Congress Cataloging-in-Publication Data

Dunford, Martin.
    The real guide. New York / written and researched by Martin Dunford and Jack Holland; with additional
    accounts by Phyllis Cohen . . . (et al.).
    384p. (The Real guides)
    Includes bibliographical references and index.
    ISBN 0–13–766668–3: $13.00
    1. New York (N.Y.)—Description—1981—Guide-books.
    I. Holland, Jack, 1959-. II. Title. III. Series.
F128.18.D86 1991
917.47'10443—dc20   91–18524
                                                                                                CIP

THE REAL GUIDE

NEW YORK
New and Revised

Written and researched by

MARTIN DUNFORD and JACK HOLLAND

With additional accounts by
Jeanne Muchnick and Matthew Yeomans

PRENTICE HALL TRAVEL

NEW YORK LONDON TORONTO SYDNEY TOKYO SINGAPORE

CONTENTS

Introduction viii

A hundred times I have thought, New York is a catastrophe, and fifty times: It is a beautiful catastrophe

Le Corbusier

INTRODUCTION

New York City is the most beguiling place there is. You may not think so at first—for the city is admittedly mad, the epitome in many ways of all that is wrong (and really drastically wrong) in modern America. But spend even a week here and it happens—the pace, the adrenalin takes hold, and the shock gives way to myth. Walking through the city streets *is* an experience, the buildings like icons to the modern age, to the excitement and violence of change, and above all to the power of money. And despite all the hype, the movie-image sentimentality, Manhattan—the central island and the city's real core—has massive romance: whether it's the flickering lights of the Midtown Manhattan skyscrapers as you speed across the Queensboro Bridge, the 4am half-life in Greenwich Village, or just wasting the morning on the Staten Island ferry. You really would have to be made of stone not to be moved by it all.

None of which is to suggest that New York is a conventional or a conventionally pleasing city. Take a walk in **Manhattan** beside Central Park, past the city's richest apartments (and they are *rich*) and keep walking, and within a dozen or so blocks you find yourself in the burnt-out degradation of the lower reaches of Harlem. The shock could hardly be more extreme. The city is constantly like that—nowhere in the Western world are there so many derelicts alongside so much glaring wealth. And the problems are increasing—racism, the drug trade, homelessness; for many, New York is a city on the brink, home to some of the world's most classic and vivid cases of urban blight and neglect. Whether you seek it or not, it's hard to not to become aware of this fast; indeed, in a perverse way, it's these tangible and potent contrasts that give New York much of its excitement.

But the city also has more straightforward pleasures. There are the different **ethnic neighborhoods** of Lower Manhattan, from Chinatown to the Jewish Lower East Side or—ever diminishing—Little Italy, or among the arts and gay

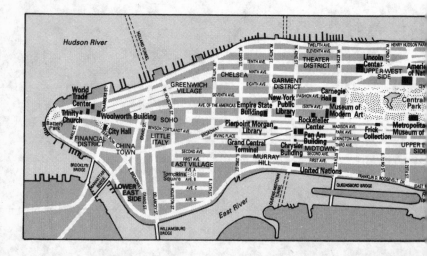

concentrations of SoHo and TriBeCa, Greenwich, and East Village. There is the **architecture** (the whole city reads like an illustrated history of modern design) of corporate Midtown Manhattan and the more residential Upper East and West Side districts. And there is the **art**, arguably unrivaled and affording infinite weeks of wandering in the Metropolitan Museum of Art and the Museum of Modern Art and countless smaller collections.

All of which is just the background. For, to enjoy and experience New York the greatest attraction of all, whether you're resident or visitor, is in the action. You can **eat** anything, cooked in any style; **drink** in any kind of company; sit through any amount of (or simply continuous) **movies**. The established arts—**dance**, **theater**, **music**—are superbly catered for, and though the contemporary **music scene** is lacking vitality or originality, New York's **clubs** are varied and exciting, if rarely inexpensive. And if you're into shopping or **consuming**, the choice is vast, almost numbingly exhaustive in this heartland of the great capitalist dream.

Bear in mind, also, that **upstate** New York is easily accessible from the city—worth escaping to if you're here for more than a couple of weeks. A short break on **Long Island** is perhaps the most tempting option: the traditional summer resort for New York's better-heeled society and for its artistically inclined, and with beaches that are among the best in the country. Or for more natural spectacle there is the wooded beauty of the **Hudson Valley** and the broad, sluggish majesty of the Hudson itself; see Chapter Eleven, "Out from the City," for more details.

Costs, climate, and when to go

Perhaps your biggest single problem in New York is going to be **money**, or rather how to hold on to what you have. **Accommodation** will be your biggest day-to-day expense, with rock-bottom double hotel rooms in Manhattan starting at $60–90 a night and even a basic YMCA bed going for around $30—though there are a few hostel options that work out cheaper. The **bottom line** for staying alive—*after this*—is around $20 a day, a figure which will of course skyrocket the more you eat out and party, although it is possible to eat out both well and cheaply. There are

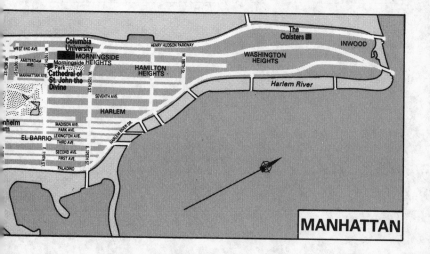

bargain **restaurants**—see Chapter Eight, "Drinking and Eating," for listings—where you'll be well fed for under $10, while the all-American breakfast will keep you going all day for around $5 and ubiquitous delis and pizza places provide the cheapest snacks for just a couple of dollars. Be warned, though, that in restaurants of all kinds you're expected to tip no less than fifteen percent. **Transport** costs also mount up fast, with flat fares of over a dollar for any Manhattan bus or subway journey—passes and season tickets don't exist.

Climate-wise, New York ranges from the stickily hot and humid in summer to well below freezing in January: winter and high summer (most people claim the city is unbearable in July and August) are the worst time you could come. Spring is gentler, if unpredictable, and usually wet; autumn is perhaps the best season; come at either time and you'll find it easier to get things done and the people more welcoming. For **clothing**, bring your warmest coats, longjohns and insulated underwear in January—and stout boots, hats and ear-muffs to combat the blizzards—and a good selection of t-shirts, shorts, and the like if you arrive in July. Whatever time of year you come, dress in layers: buildings tend to be absurdly overheated during the winter months and air-conditioned to the point of iciness in summer. Also bring comfortable shoes—you're going to be doing a lot of walking.

AVERAGE TEMPERATURES											
	JAN	FEB	MAR	APR	MAY	JUN	JUL	AUG	SEP	OCT	NOV	DEC
MAX (°F)	39	40	48	61	71	81	85	83	77	67	54	41
(°C)	4	5	8	16	21	27	29	28	25	19	12	5
MIN (°F)	26	27	34	44	53	63	68	66	60	51	41	30
(°C)	-3	-3	1	6	11	17	18	19	16	10	5	-1

For a full and up-to-the-minute rundown on weather conditions in NYC phone ☎976-1212.

GETTING THERE

BY AIR

New York is the hub of most North American air traffic so not surprisingly **flying** is the fastest, and usually the cheapest, way of getting there. **Shuttles** from the nearby centers of **Washington DC** and **Boston**, will set you back about $90 to $100, though from any point beyond, the cost is much more dependent on passenger volume than distance. As an example, bargain-basement one ways from the West Coast hover around $120, while the least expensive flight from Miami, half the distance, is about $95 during the same season. Prices fluctuate wildly depending on the time of year and whether there's a price war on, but historically you've been able to count on paying up to $170 one way in summer or around Christmas from California, or a slightly more advantageous $300 for a round-trip ticket. Regular fares—ie those booked 14 days in advance with a major airline—cost around $350 to $400.

The **main carriers** to call (there's little point in going through an agent initially; check newspaper ads instead) are *Air Canada, American, Delta, United, Pan Am, TWA,* and *USAir*. There is usually a discount on flying late at night on the so-called "red-eye" flights; fares tend to be uniform across the industry, whether there's a price war on or not, so the difference will be in service, not cost.

AIRPORTS

New York has three **airports**: **La Guardia**, in Queens about 8 miles from Manhattan, **John F.** Kennedy (**JFK International**), in Queens but 15 miles out, and **Newark**, actually in New Jersey 16 miles across the mouth of the Hudson River. La Guardia tends to handle a bare majority of domestic flights. Any flight continuing internationally— and this means most of TWA and Pan Am services—will go through JFK; many of the cut-rate services are required to land at slightly less convenient Newark. For details on the best options for getting from the various airports to the city, see "Points of Arrival" on p.29.

BY TRAIN

For those heading to New York City from within the same radius as the shuttle flights noted above, travel **by train** is a viable alternative, though not likely to be any cheaper. The best services are along the New England–New York–Washington D.C. *Metroliner* corridor; round-trip fares from Washington or Boston are around $90. There are also two daily trains linking Montreal with New York, and one each day with Toronto.

Although in theory it's possible to haul yourself **long-distance** from the West Coast, the Midwest, or the South, it's a slow trip (three-plus days from California). One-way tickets will be downright expensive as well, but they do allow **stop offs** (at full fare) and round-trip fares are often competitive. Current examples, both available only by booking well in advance are the "All Aboard" fare that gives a cross-country round trip with three stops for $339. A standard one-way fare is around $325.

Amtrak has realized that it can't compete with the airlines on the long-distance runs, so it has intelligently divided the US into several regions and offers extremely advantageous fares for travel within each **zone**; for a flat rate of a hundred-plus dollars you usually get unrestricted travel within the region for a couple of weeks, a month for somewhat more. If you're going to be doing a lot of visiting along the Eastern Seaboard, using New York as a base, it makes good sense to inquire about these specials. In New York City the information and reservations number is ☎212/736-4545; elsewhere look in the phonebook or dial ☎1 800/USA RAIL. VIA *Rail Canada* (☎204/949-1830 or ☎1 800/561–8630) may offer something advantageous other than a

COUNCIL TRAVEL IN THE US

Head Office: 205 E. 42nd St., New York, NY 10017; ☎212/661-1450

CALIFORNIA
2486 Channing Way, Berkeley, CA 94704; ☎415/848-8604
UCSD Price Center, Q-076, La Jolla, CA 92093; ☎619/452-0630
1818 Palo Verde Ave., Suite E, Long Beach, CA 90815; ☎213/598-3338
1093 Broxton Ave., Suite 220, Los Angeles, CA 90024; ☎213/208-3551
4429 Cass St., San Diego, CA 92109; ☎619/270-6401
312 Sutter St., Suite 407, San Francisco, CA 94108; ☎415/421-3473
919 Irving St., Suite 102, San Francisco, CA 94122; ☎415/566-6222
14515 Ventura Blvd., Suite 250, Sherman Oaks, CA 91403; ☎818/905-5777

COLORADO
1138 13th St., Boulder, CO 80302; ☎818/905-5777

CONNECTICUT
Yale Co-op East, 77 Broadway, New Haven, CT 06520; ☎203/562-5335

DISTRICT OF COLUMBIA
1210 Potomac St., NW Washington, DC 20007; ☎202/337-6464

GEORGIA
12 Park Place South, Atlanta, GA 30303; ☎404/577-1678

ILLINOIS
1153 N. Dearborn St., Chicago, IL 60610; ☎312/951-0585
831 Foster St., Evanston, IL 60201; ☎708/475-5070

LOUISIANA
8141 Maple St., New Orleans, LA 70118; ☎504/866-1767

MASSACHUSETTS
79 South Pleasant St., 2nd Floor, Amherst, MA 01002; ☎413/256-1261
729 Boylston St., Suite 201, Boston, MA 02116; ☎617/266-1926
1384 Massachusetts Ave., Suite 206, Cambridge, MA 02138; ☎617/497-1497
Stratton Student Center MIT, W20-024, 84 Massachusetts Ave., Cambridge, MA 02139; ☎617/497-1497

MINNESOTA
1501 University Ave. SE, Room 300, Minneapolis, MN 55414; ☎612/379-2323

NEW YORK
35 W. 8th St., New York, NY 10011; ☎212/254-2525
Student Center, 356 West 34th St., New York, NY 10001; ☎212/643-1365

NORTH CAROLINA
703 Ninth St., Suite B-2, Durham, NC 27705; ☎919/286-4664

OREGON
715SW Morrison, Suite 600, Portland, OR 97205; ☎503/228-1900

RHODE ISLAND
171 Angell St., Suite 212, Providence, RI 02906; ☎401/331-5810

TEXAS
2000 Guadalupe St., Suite 6, Austin, TX 78705; ☎512/472-4931
Exec. Tower Office Center, 3300 W. Mockingbird, Suite 101, Dallas,TX 75235; ☎214/350-6166

WASHINGTON
1314 Northeast 43rd St., Suite 210, Seattle, WA 98105; ☎206/632-2448

WISCONSIN
2615 North Hackett Ave., Milwaukee, WI; ☎414/332-4740

STA IN THE US

BOSTON
273 Newbury St., Boston, MA 02116; ☎617/266-6014

HONOLULU
1831 S. King St., Suite 202, Honolulu, HI 96826; ☎808/942-7755

LOS ANGELES
920 Westwood Blvd., Los Angeles, CA 90024; ☎213/824-1574
7204 Melrose Ave., Los Angeles, CA 90046; ☎213/934-8722

2500 Wilsrent Blvd., Los Angeles, CA 90057; ☎213/380-2184

NEW YORK
17 E. 45th St., Suite 805, New York, NY 10017; ☎212/986-9470;☎ 800/777-0112

SAN DIEGO
6447 El Cajon Blvd., San Diego, CA 92115; ☎619/286-1322

SAN FRANCISCO
166 Geary St., Suite 702, San Francisco, CA 94108; ☎415/391-8407

TRAVEL CUTS IN CANADA

Head Office: 187 College St., Toronto, Ontario M5T 1P7; ☎416/979-2406

ALBERTA
MacEwan Hall Student Center, Univ. of Calgary, Calgary T2N 1N4; ☎403/282-7687. 10424A 118th Ave., Edmonton T6G 0P7; ☎403/471-8054

BRITISH COLUMBIA
Room 326, T.C., Student Rotunda, Simon Fraser University, Burnaby, British Columbia V5A 1S6; ☎604/291-1204. 1516 Duranleau St., Granville Island, Vancouver V6H 3S4; ☎604/687-6033. Student Union Building, University of British Columbia, Vancouver V6T 1W5; ☎604/228-6890 Student Union Building, University of Victoria, Victoria V8W 2Y2; ☎604/721-8352

MANITOBA
University Center, University of Manitoba, Winnipeg R3T 2N2; ☎204/269-9530

NOVA SCOTIA
Student Union Building, Dalhousie University, Halifax B3H 4J2; ☎902/424-2054. 6139 South St., Halifax B3H 4J2; ☎902/494-7027

ONTARIO
University Center, University of Guelph, Guelph N1G 2W1; ☎519/763-1660. Fourth Level Unicentre, Carleton University, Ottawa, K1S5B6; ☎613/238-5493. 60 Laurier Ave. E, Ottawa K1N 6N4; ☎613/238-8222. Student Street, Room G27, Laurentian University, Sudbury P3E 2C6; ☎705/673-1401. 96 Gerrard St. E, Toronto M5B 1G7; ☎ (416) 977-0441. University Shops Plaza, 170 University Ave. W, Waterloo N2L 3E9; ☎519/886-0400.

QUÉBEC (Known as *Voyages CUTS*)
Université McGill, 3480 rue McTavish, Montréal H3A 1X9; ☎514/398-0647. 1613 rue St. Denis, Montréal H2X 3K3; ☎514/843-8511. Université Concordia, Edifice Hall, Suite 643, S.G.W. Campus, 1455 blvd. de Maisonneuve Ouest, Montréal H3G 1M8; ☎514/288-1130. 19 rue Ste. Ursule, Québec G1R 4E1; ☎418/692-3971

SASKATCHEWAN
Place Riel Campus Center, University of Saskatchewan, Saskatoon S7N 0W0; ☎306/975-3722

NOUVELLES FRONTIÈRES

In the United States
NEW YORK 12 East 33rd St., New York, NY 10016 ☎212/779-0600

LOS ANGELES 6363 Wilsrent Blvd., Suite 200, Los Angeles, CA 90048; ☎213/658-8955

SAN FRANCISCO 209 Post St., Suite 1121, San Francisco, CA 94108; ☎415/781-4480

In Canada
MONTREAL 800 East Blvd. de Maison Neuve, Montréal, Quebec (☎514/288-9942)

QUEBEC 176 Grande Allée Ouest, Québec, PQ G1R 2G9; ☎418/525-5255

---

straight fare from Quebec or Ontario; from elsewhere in Canada people usually fly in.

All Amtrak services, including trains from Canada, **arrive** at Penn Station, 33rd Street and Seventh Avenue; only local Metro North commuter trains use Grand Central Station at 42nd and Park Avenue. For information on both, see "Points of Arrival" in *The Guide*.

BY BUS

This is the most time-consuming and least comfortable mode of travel and, by the time you've kept yourself alive on the trip, is rarely the most economical. To add insult to injury, simple tickets are no longer the bargains they once were. **Greyhound** runs special deals from time to time, with round-trip fares across the country

starting at $70, but remember that even the shorter, more bearable trips cost only about $10 less than the train. In New York you'll arrive by bus at the **Port Authority Bus Terminal** (Eighth Avenue and 42nd Street; see "Points of Arrival" in *The Guide*.

GREEN TORTOISE

The alternative to Bus Hell is the famous, slightly counter-cultural, ***Green Tortoise***, which connects **Washington**, **Oregon**, and **California** with **New York** and **Boston** a dozen times a year between May and September. Their buses are comfortable and congenial, with tape-deck systems, ample mattresses to sack out on, and—usually—a very interesting mix of people. The 11–12-day trip costs $249 food extra and is actually a mini-tour, serpentining through various beauty spots of America, with plenty of stops for hiking, river-rafting, and hot springs.

Two routes are offered, a **northern one** via Reno, Idaho, Montana, Wyoming, South Dakota, Minnesota, Chicago, Indiana, Pennsylvania, and a **southern one**, via Los Angeles, the Mojave Desert, Arizona, New Mexico (plus Juarez), the Rio Grande country of Texas, New Orleans, and Appalachia. Round-trip itineraries are somewhat different so you wouldn't get bored doing it two ways; as the Tortoise's apt motto has it, "Nothing like your last bus ride!" They also run trips between Seattle and Los Angeles ($30 more for Pacific Northwest passengers going to New York), through the western national parks, to the highlights of California, to Alaska, and Baja.

DRIVEAWAYS

Potentially the cheapest legitimate way of getting to New York, not counting hitching, is to arrange for a **driveaway**, in which you deliver a car cross country for someone who, out of laziness or other good reasons, won't do it themselves. Look in your local Yellow Pages under "Automobile Transporters and Driveaway Companies."

The usual requirements stipulate that you have to be over 21, have a valid driver's license (and sometimes a clean record printout from your local DMV), and have anything between $100 and $200 and/or a credit card handy as a deposit (which raises the question of why you're not flying if you have that kind of cash or plastic handy . . .).

The deposit is refundable on arrival and theoretically there's nothing to pay on the way except gas—and motel overnights. But keep in mind that while it's accepted that you may want to see a bit of the country on the way, there are generally tight delivery deadlines—four to seven days is the norm—and if you're late without good reason you'll forfeit the deposit.

PACKAGES

Many operators run **all-inclusive packages** combining plane tickets and hotel accommodation with (for example) sightseeing, wining and dining, or admission to Broadway shows. Even if the "package" aspect doesn't thrill you to pieces, these deals can still be more convenient and sometimes even more economical than arranging the same thing yourself, providing you don't mind losing a little flexibility. With such a vast range of these packages available, it's impossible to give an overview—major travel agents will have brochures detailing what's on offer.

CUSTOMS: A NOTE FOR CANADIANS

Canadians visiting the US for stays of less than 90 days need only a **valid passport** to get into the country. However, stays of 90 days and longer require a **visa**, which must have been obtained in Canada.

Bear in mind that if you cross into the States in your car, trunks and passenger compartments are subject to spot searches by US Customs personnel, though this sort of surveillance is likely to decrease as remaining tariff barriers fall over the next few years. Remember, too, that Canadians are legally barred from seeking gainful employment in the US (see "Living and Working in NYC" later in this section).

INSURANCE AND HEALTH

If you need a doctor, look in the Yellow Pages under "Clinics" or "Physicians & Surgeons." If you have an accident, emergency medical services will get to you quickly, and charge you later, like anywhere else. For emergencies or ambulances, the number you should dial is ☎911 (or whatever variant may be on the information plate of the pay phone). For a mishap that doesn't require emergency treatment, try *Bellevue Hospital* (address below).

Your **health insurance** should cover you for any charges or costs; if you don't have any you can get adequate coverage either from a travel agent's insurance plan or from specialist travel insurance companies such as *The Travelers*. If you are unable to use a phone or if the practitioner requires payment up front, save all the **documents** to support a claim for subsequent reimbursal. Remember also that time limits may apply when making claims after the event, so **promptness** in contacting your insurer is highly advisable.

However, few, if any, of the above plans will cover you against theft while traveling, especially in a city with a reputation like New York's. **Renter's or homeowner's insurance** can compensate for this, as most policies will cover you for up to $500 in losses while on the road. If you have anything stolen, report it to the nearest police station (call ☎374–5000 for the address) and make a note of the precinct number. You'll be issued with a reference number to pass on to your insurance company, instead of the full statement usually required. Don't worry unnecessarily; these details should be enough to get your agent started.

EMERGENCY DENTAL TREATMENT
☎679-3966
After 8pm ☎679-4172

A final word about health: one of the most serious health problems affecting New York City is, of course, **AIDS**. Although the comparatively high number of HIV-positive cases has led to a more informed and open attitude to the virus than is the case in many other parts of the US, it still can't be stressed strongly enough that sex without condoms is wildly irresponsible.

HOSPITAL EMERGENCY DEPARTMENTS OPEN AT ALL TIMES

Bellevue Hospital, First Avenue and East 29th Street (☎561–4141).

St. Vincent's Hospital, Seventh Avenue at 11th Street (☎790–7000).

New York Hospital, East 70th Street at York Avenue (☎472–5454).

Mount Sinai Hospital, Madison Avenue at 100th Street (☎650–7171).

INFORMATION, MAPS, AND TOURS

For New York information and literature, particularly free guides and booklets, contact *I Love New York*, 1515 Broadway, New York City, NY 10036 (☎827-6250) or 1 Commerce Plaza, Albany, NY 12245 (☎518/474-4116), both of which you can only write to or telephone—no visits. Residents of New York State, New England, New Jersey, Pennsylvania, Delaware, Virginia, West Virginia, Ohio, Michigan (except area code 906), and Washington DC can call toll-free ☎800/CALLNYS.

Though much of their material concentrates on New York State, among the *I Love New York* info worth picking up is a comprehensive state-wide **map**, a glossy **Travel Guide** to each region of the state, a **booklet** on New York City listing useful addresses and details of all-inclusive packages, and leaflets listing restaurants, museums, and hotels.

Perhaps more useful—and obtainable across the counter once you're in New York—is the information from the **New York Convention and Visitors Bureau** at 2 Columbus Circle (Mon–Fri 9am–6pm, Sat & Sun 10am–6pm; ☎397-8222). They have up-to-date **leaflets** on what's going on arts-wise and otherwise, bus and subway maps, and information on hotels and accommodation—though they can't actually book anything for you. Their high-gloss *Big Apple Guide* is good, too, though the kind of information it gives—on restaurants, hotels, and sights—is also available in the many kinds of free magazines and guidettes like *Where*, *Broadway*, *Key*, and *The Guide*, which you can pick up all over the city. These appear in hotel foyers and the like and include complete (if superficial) rundowns on what's on in the arts, eating out and shops, and a host of ads that might just point you in the right direction.

We think our maps of the city should be fine for most purposes; **commercial maps**, like the *Rand McNally* plan of the city and all five boroughs ($1.95), fill in the gaps. Others include the tiny glossy *Streetwise* maps—neatly laid out and not expensive at around $3 from most bookshops—or *Fodor's Flashmaps*, a book of different New York maps for $7.95. If you're after a map of one of the individual Outer Boroughs try those produced by *Geographia* at $1.95, again on sale in bookshops—or, for Brooklyn, the free plan doled out by the borough's information booth in Cadman Plaza West.

A good **map shop**, if you have trouble finding any of these, is the *Complete Traveler*; see Chapter Seven for the details.

For **New York State maps**, the *I Love New York* production is more than adequate for most purposes; for something a little more detailed, *Rand McNally* publishes maps of specific regions.

TOURS

One way of getting a hold on New York is simply to climb up to the **observation deck** of one of its tallest buildings, most obviously the Empire State Building or World Trade Center. Of the two, the Empire State's position in the heart of Manhattan gives it the edge; see the guide for more details. Or you can enjoy the view of Lower Manhattan for free by simply walking across the **Brooklyn Bridge**. However, if you want more detailed background than this, or you have a specific interest in the city, there are all kinds of **tours** you can join, taking in the city from just about every angle, and by just about every means of transport available.

BUS TOURS

Apart from equipping yourself with a decent map, perhaps the most obvious way of orienting yourself to the city is to take a **bus tour**—something that's extremely popular, though frankly you'll find yourself swept around so quickly that you'll scarcely see anything. In recent years *Grayline* has cornered the market in bus tours. They have three terminals in Midtown Manhattan: on Eighth Avenue between 53rd and 54th streets (☎397-2600); on West 49th Street between Sixth and Seventh (☎869-5005); and at 166 West 46th Street (☎354-5122). Half-day tours, taking in the main sights of Manhattan, cost around $23, while a full day costs $32.50, bookable through any travel agent.

A more flexible alternative to a regular bus tour is the **Manhattan Neighborhood Trolley**, a refurbished trolley bus which between April and October runs daily from noon to 6pm around Lower Manhattan below Canal Street, taking in the major sights of the Financial District and around, Chinatown and Little Italy, and the Lower East Side. The bus starts at the South Street Seaport, and for the price of a $3.50 ticket you can get off when and where you like all day. There's a guide on board, and reservations are not required. For more details—and a timetable—call ☎677-7268.

HELICOPTER TOURS

If you have the money, a better and certainly a more exciting option is to take a look at the city from the air, by catching a ride on a **helicopter**. This is expensive, but is an experience you won't easily forget. *Island Helicopter*, at the far eastern end of East 34th St. (☎683-4575), and *Liberty Helicopter Tours*, at the western end of 30th St., near the Jacob Javits Convention Center (☎465-8905) offer flights starting at around $40. You can't book a place, but the helicopters take off throughout the day, seven days a week; just go down and stand in line—and bear in mind that in high season you may have quite a wait. One decision to make is whether to go by day or night; after doing one, you'll probably want to do the other.

TOURS ON WATER

Cheaper, if not nearly as breathtaking, is the **Circle Line Ferry** (☎563-3200), which sails all the way around Manhattan from Pier 83 at the far west end of 42nd St. between March and December. This is probably the most popular way of seeing the island at first, at least on a fair day, taking in everything from the classic soaring views of Lower Manhattan to the bleaker stretches of Harlem and the industrially blighted Bronx, and complete with a live wise-cracking commentary and on-board bar. It runs roughly twice a day in low season, almost hourly in the summer, and the three-hour voyage costs $16 (children under 12 $8).

Two further alternatives for seeing the city from the water are the **Seaport Line**, Pier 16 at the South Street Seaport (☎406-3434), which for $8 spends ninety minutes cruising around Lower Manhattan and the outlying islands, or for those not so loaded the regular **Staten Island ferry**, whose 45-minute journey to the city's remotest borough costs just 50¢ and lays on an equally staggering panorama.

WALKING TOURS

Walking tours, which allow you to get to know a specific part of Manhattan or the Outer Boroughs, are another matter. Usually led by experts, the range is considerable—some are general city strolls, others (like those of the Brooklyn Historical Society) devoted to one particular area. Detailed below are some of the most interesting: note that they don't all operate year-round, the more esoteric only setting up for a couple of outings at specific times of year. If you're interested, call in advance for the full schedules.

Art Tours of Manhattan, 63 E. 82nd St. (☎772-7888). Definitely the best people to go with if you're interested in first-hand accounts of the city's art scene, establishment and fringe. Tours include the galleries of SoHo, 57th Street, and Madison Avenue, as well as "hospitality" visits to an artist's studio, all guided by qualified—and entertaining—art historians.

Bronx County Historical Society, 3309 Bainbridge Ave., Bronx (☎881-8900). According to its fans, there really is enough in the Bronx to warrant a series of neighborhood tours, ranging from strolls through suburban Riverdale to furtive hikes across the desolate wastes of the South Bronx. Excellent value at about $5 per person.

Brooklyn Historical Society, 128 Pierrepont St., Brooklyn (☎718/624-0890). Walking tours of Brooklyn neighborhoods like Brooklyn Heights itself, Park Slope, Greenpoint, and plenty more. Cost around $8.

Central Park The *Urban Rangers* (☎427-4040) runs a varied selection of free educational walks throughout the year, as does the *Department of Parks and Recreation* at the Dairy (see Chapter Three; Tues–Sun 11am–4pm).

Harlem Gospel and Jazz Tours, 1457 Broadway (☎302-2594). Various tours of Harlem, ranging from Sunday morning visits to a Baptist church, to night-time affairs taking in dinner and a club. Professionally run and excellent value, with prices starting at $27 per person.

Joyce Gold, 141 W. 17th St. (☎242-5762). Sunday tours of Manhattan neighborhoods by an informed local author and historian. $10 per person.

Lower East Side Tenement Museum, 97 Orchard St. (☎431-0233). This museum organizes Sunday walking tours of the Lower East Side; prices around $10.

Municipal Arts Society, 457 Madison Ave. (☎935-3960). As the name implies, principally tours with an architectural or cultural slant, but no less enjoyable to the layperson for all that. Regular trips around Harlem, the Upper West Side, and other neighborhoods, as well as "hard hat" jaunts around construction sites for the *really* committed, and free Wednesday lunchtime tours—at 12:30pm—of Grand Central Station. Prices around $14.

Museum of the City of New York, Fifth Ave. at 103rd St. (☎534-1672). Sunday walking tours, six

months of the year, again around New York neighborhoods, Downtown and Midtown Manhattan and in Brooklyn. Prices a flat $6.

The 92nd Street Y, 1395 Lexington Ave. (☎996-1105). None better, offering a pot pourri of walking tours ranging from straight explorations of specific New York neighborhoods (like Park Slope Brooklyn or Harlem) to art tours, walking tours of political New York, or a pre-dawn visit to the city's wholesale meat and fish markets. Average costs are $8–12 per person, and the commentary is erudite and informative. Look out, too, for the Y's day excursions by bus to accessible parts of upstate New York, and their specialized location talks led by well-known writers and artists. All in all, an excellent and useful organization, whose brochure is well worth getting hold of.

The Penny Sightseeing Company, 1565 Park Ave. (☎410-0080). A black-run tour company that specializes in tours of Harlem, claiming to give an "honest view of Harlem as it is." Tour bus-based trips run on Tuesdays and Saturdays at 11am and cost $15; reservations are needed two days in advance. They also offer Harlem Gospel Tours that take in the rousing spiritual singing of a Baptist service: Thursdays at 10am, Sundays at 10:30am, reservations two days in advance, cost $17.

Prospect Park Environmental Center, Tennis House, Prospect Park, Brooklyn (☎718/788-8500). This group runs the same sort of range of tours as the Historical Society (above). Costs around $6 per person.

Queens Historical Society, 143–35 37th Ave., Flushing, Queens (☎718/939-0647). No actual walking tours as such, but if you write to them enclosing a SASE they'll send a free do-it-yourself walking tour of "historic" Flushing. How can you resist?

River to River Downtown Tours, 375 South End Ave. (☎321-2823). Individual and small group tours of Lower Manhattan by New York aficionado Ruth Alscher-Green. Individual prices are $35, or $50 for two people, for a unique two-hour tour spiced with gossip and anecdotal tidbits.

Sidewalks of New York, PO Box 1660 Cathedral Station, NY 10025 (☎517-0201). Quirkily designed walking tours covering all aspects of the city, from famous murder sites to celebrity homes. $10 per person, by appointment only.

THE MEDIA

NEWSPAPERS AND MAGAZINES

The Nineties have so far not been good to the New York print media, and the days are gone when New York could support twenty different **daily newspapers**. Today, only four remain, and all of these—the upscale *New York Times* (40¢) and the *New York Post* (40¢), *Daily News* (40¢), and *Newsday* (35¢)—are in various stages of disrepair, mainly due to decades of cynical and poor management and union abuses and restrictive practices. The decline of the papers at the lower end of the spectrum, especially, has been a sad spectacle. In September 1990, the *New York Post* was given a stay of execution when the staff accepted a pay cut of twenty percent to try and recover debts of some $25 million; barely a month later, the *Daily News* became embroiled in a dispute that saw the circulation of the paper drop by two-thirds, as it was blacked by newsstands and sold by homeless hawkers on the subway.

The New York Times is a national institution: it prides itself on being the "paper of record," and boasts "All the news that's fit to print." But the recent front-page coverage of Kitty Kelly's hatchet job on Nancy Reagan, and the Kennedy rape case, has dented its reputation considerably. It has solid, sometimes stolid international coverage, and places much emphasis on its news analysis, though its coverage of issues closer to home is much thinner, and few New Yorkers turn to the *Times* for purely local news. Each weekday there's a special section, such as a special sports section on Monday and a good weekend section on Friday. The Sunday edition ($1.50), available from early Saturday night over most of Manhattan, is a thumping bundle divided into eight or nine sections that could take you the whole day to read—though much of it is made up of advertisements.

Both the *Post* and the *Daily News* concentrate on local news, usually screamed out in banner headlines. Pre-strike, the **Daily News** was far and away the better of the two, renowned as a picture newspaper but with a fresh, energetic—and serious—with intelligent features and many racy headlines, most famous of which was their succinct summary of the President's attitude to New York during the crisis of the mid-1970s: "FORD TO CITY—DROP DEAD." Five months after

the strike began, the paper's owners, the *Chicago Tribune*, sold it to London publisher Robert Maxwell and the unions agreed to return to work. However, crippled by enormous debts and having lost most of its star writers, "New York's Hometown Newspaper," as it likes to call itself, is far from back on course.

The **New York Post** is the city's oldest newspaper, started in 1801 by Alexander Hamilton, though it seems to have been on its way out for the last twenty years. Known for its solid city news reporting, not to mention consistent conservative-slanted sermonizing, it is perhaps renowned most for its sensational approach to stories: "HEADLESS WOMAN FOUND IN TOPLESS BAR" is one of its more memorable headlines from the 1980s.

Newsday is essentially a Long Island newspaper which in recent years has attempted to corner part of the New York tabloid market, scoring some success with its strong Outer Boroughs coverage. Despite a rather ugly design, the paper is good on New York and international news, and is generally reckoned to have the city's best sports section (it even has a regular cricket column).

The other New York-based daily newspaper is **The Wall Street Journal** (75¢), in fact a national financial paper that also has strong national and international news coverage—despite an old-fashioned design that eschews the use of photographs. The only other daily newspaper is the ailing national **USA Today** (50¢), that places its emphasis on weather and news roundups rather than in-depth reporting—all in all an exceptionally dull read. You'll see it on sale throughout New York—though less often read. One of the newest newspapers on the city stands is the all-sport daily, **The National** (75¢), launched in 1990 and giving a good roundup of all sports.

THE WEEKLIES AND MONTHLIES

Of the **weekly papers**, the **Village Voice** (Thurs, $1) is the most widely read, mainly for its comprehensive arts coverage and investigative features. Originating in Greenwich Village, it made its name as a youthful, intelligent, vaguely left journal—the nearest the city ever got to "alternative" journalism. After a brief flirtation in the 1980s with Rupert Murdoch's News International group, the paper is now owned by pet-food mogul Leonard Stern, and, although it has grown a little mainstream over the last decade or so, it's still a good read—and the best pointer to what's on around town.

The other leading weekly, the glossier **New York** magazine ($2.25), has more comprehensive listings, and is more of an entertainment journal than the harder-hitting *Voice*. **The New Yorker** ($1.75), with its heavy 1930s design and high, almost pedantic literary style, features one of the best theater and gallery reviews available. The monthly **Details** ($2.50) is a high fashion glossy, good for getting the lowdown on the latest night-spots—and nightpeople—while the late Andy Warhol's **Interview** ($2.95) is, as the name suggests, mainly given over to interviews, as well as fashion. Perhaps the best, certainly the wackiest, most downtown-oriented alternative to the *Voice*, is **The Paper** ($2.50), a monthly which carries witty and well-written rundowns on New York City nightlife, restaurants, and all the current news and gossip. Look out also for the free weekly paper, *NY Press*, which has news and listings covering all aspects of city life.

BROADCAST TV STATIONS

2 WCBS (CBS)
4 WNBC (NBC)
5 WNYW (Fox)
7 WABC (ABC)
9 WWOR (Independent)
11 WPIX (Independent)
13 WNET (PBS)
31 WNYC (PBS)
41 UNIVISION (Spanish language)

RADIO

The **FM** dial is crammed with local stations of highly varying quality and content. If you possess a Walkman radio bring it, as skipping through the channels is a pleasure. Stations are constantly changing formats, opening up and closing down. **AM** stations aren't nearly so interesting, with just a few good talk shows among a sea of belting rock and lobotomized easy listening. For the most complete listings, see the *New York Times*.

FM RADIO STATIONS

WPLJ (95.5) Pop/rock/etc. One of many stations that focus (with numbing repetition) on the top thirty hits.

WRKS (98.7) Calls itself KISS 98FM. Aggressively poppy and urban.

WHTZ (100.1) Top Forty station.

WBLS (97.5) Soul and black pop, and, on Friday and Saturday night, two hours of rap, house, and great dance music.

WQXR (96.3) Staid commercial classical station.

WNYC (93.9) Adventurous classical music and the best morning news program—from 6am–8:30am.

WNCN (104.3) Reliable end-of-the-dial classical station.

WKCR (98.9) Excellent jazz.

WBAI (99.5) Non-profit-making independent station with an intelligent variety of features.

WXRK (92.3) Famous New Yorker Howard Stern insults and delights.

AM RADIO STATIONS

WOR 710 Worth dipping into for its interviews.
WINS 1010 All news.
WCBS All news.

WNYC 830 Good quality local talk station that uses regular news reports from National Public Radio (NPR) in Washington. Best shows are Morning and Weekend Edition on Sat and Sun, 8–10am.

MONEY AND BANKS

TRAVELERS' CHECKS

The best way to carry your money is in **travelers' checks**. The most widely recognized are *American Express* and *Visa*. The advantage of using the better-known checks is that they can be cashed in more places—shops, restaurants, and gas stations (don't be put off by "no checks" signs in windows; this only refers to personal checks). Order mostly $10 and $20 denominations (although lately the $10 ones seem to be an endangered species); you won't make many friends in stores where you pay for a five-dollar purchase with a fifty-dollar check. Note that almost all of the 24-hour Korean delis will cash small checks—a lifesaver if you run out of cash at 4am.

CREDIT OR AUTOTELLER CARDS

If you have a **Visa**, **Mastercard**, **Diners**, or **American Express** card you really *shouldn't* leave home without it. Almost all stores, most restaurants, and many services will take some kind of plastic. In addition, hotels and car rental companies will ask for a card either to establish your credit-worthiness, or as security, or both. And some people, even in these dark days for credit buying, sometimes treat cash with suspicion.

With *Mastercard* or *Visa* it is also possible to **withdraw cash** at any bank displaying relevant stickers; or with the correct card and a PIN (Personal Identification Number) you can use an automatic teller. *American Express* and *Diners*

Club cards, on the other hand, cannot generally be used to withdraw cash, but if you can find a *Citibank* branch and belong to *Diners Club*, you can cash personal checks. An *American Express* card will get you cash or enable you to buy travelers' checks at any *American Express* office (check the Yellow Pages) or, using your PIN number, you can operate the travelers' check dispensers at the airports. For Canadians, most credit cards issued by hometown banks will generally be honored in the US.

Thanks to relaxation in interstate banking restrictions, holders of **ATM** (automatic teller machines) cards from out of state may discover that their cards work in the ATMs of certain New York banks. For example *Security Pacific* cards from California are compatible with *Chase Manhattan* machines. Before you leave home, check with your bank to see if any such affiliations exist with West Coast institutions; not only is this method of financing you trip safer, but at only about a dollar per transaction it's more economical as well.

PHONE HOTLINES FOR LOST ATM/CREDIT CARDS AND TRAVELERS' CHECKS
American Express cards ☎800/528–2121
American Express checks ☎800/968–8300
Diner's Club ☎800/525–9150
Thomas Cook Checks ☎921–3800
Visa checks ☎800/227–6811

BANKS

Banking hours are usually Monday–Friday 9am–3/3:30pm, with some of the banks staying open later on Fridays. Major banks such as *CitiBank* and *Chemical Bank* will exchange travelers' checks for a standard fee (this may be waived if your home bank has an affiliate in New York).

Other **change facilities** such as those at airports may levy ruinous commission charges so it's wise to ask first. Also, American Express machines at airports and other locations will issue travelers' checks for card holders who know their PIN.

Outside of banking hours, try cashing checks at *Chequepoint*, 551 Madison Ave. at 55th St. (Mon–Fri 8am–6pm, Sat & Sun 10am–6pm; ☎980-6443), or *Freeport Money Exchange*, 132 W. 45th St.; 49 W. 57th St. (Mon–Fri 9am–6pm, Sat & Sun 10am–5pm; ☎1/800/223-6776).

EMERGENCIES

All else has failed. You're broke and far from home. Before you decide to jump off the Brooklyn Bridge, be aware that there are some alternatives to consider.

● Wire money from home to a NYC bank. This requires an understanding friend or relative (to take a collect call at the very least), and a wait of a day or two for the funds to clear.

● Sell some blood. (See "Working and living in NYC" below): you can get $12 for a pint.

● Approach the nearest Salvation Army branch or city shelter for accommodation and a frugal meal.

COMMUNICATIONS: TELEPHONES AND THE MAIL

PHONE CALLS

The New York area is so populous that several area codes are necessary. In New York City, the **212 code** covers just Manhattan and the Bronx; when calling within this area simply dial the seven digit number. Outside the area—long distance or to the outer boroughs of Queens, Brooklyn, etc,—dial **1** first, then the **area code** and **number**.

Where we've given phone numbers for areas outside Manhattan, you'll find codes are included. To check codes elsewhere, consult the phone book or dial the operator.

One of the more impressive features of new York life is that the **Payphones**, no matter how graffitied or otherwise unpromising, invariably work. The basic payphone **charge** for **local calls** (ie calls within the same area code) is 25¢, followed by top-ups of 10¢. To phone long distance, dial the number and a recorded message will cut in to demand enough money for the first three minutes.

Make good use of the Manhattan **White** and **Yellow Page phonebooks**—although they may be pretty dull or (literally) listless in your hometown, here they contain vital information. The **Blue Pages** (bound with the White Pages) are a directory of government agencies; the

AREA CODES AROUND MANHATTAN

Brooklyn, Queens, and Staten Island (1) **718**
Long Island (1) **516**
New Jersey (north) (1) **201**

New Jersey (south) (1) **609**
To phone Manhattan from these areas or anywhere else (1) **212**

SERVICE NUMBERS

Emergencies **911** for police, ambulance, and fire
Operator **0**
Information **411** (Manhattan)
1 555-1212 (local)

1 + (area code) + 555-1212 (numbers in other area codes)

For other **useful telephone numbers**—to find out the time, weather, etc.—see p.24.

Yellow Pages detail just about every business and service in the city, including delicatessens, groceries, liquor stores, pharmacies, physicians and surgeons by location, and restaurants by location *and* cuisine. It's also handy for finding bike and car rental firms—and just about anything legal that can be paid for. Look for it in most bars, hotel rooms, and lobbies and the larger post offices.

Many government agencies, car rental firms, hotels, airlines, and other nationwide companies have toll-free (800) information/reservation lines; if you're unable to find the one you need in the Yellow or White Pages you should dial ☎**800/ 555–1212**.

For other useful telephone numbers—to find out the time, weather, etc—see the "Directory" at the end of this chapter.

SENDING AND RECEIVING MAIL

In terms of efficiency the overloaded New York **mail** ranks a very poor second to its phone system. Even within Manhattan mail can take a few days to arrive and a letter to LA might take a week. Businesses use bicycle messengers as a matter of course.

You can **buy stamps** in shops, supermarkets, and from (usually non-functioning) vending machines, but the best place is the **post office**, of which there are many (see the box). Most New York offices open Monday to Friday 10am to 5pm;

only the larger ones are open Saturday 9am to 12pm. In Manhattan, the **main General Post Office** at Eighth Avenue between West 31st and 33rd streets is open Monday through Saturday around the clock for important services. Letters mailed from the General or Lexington Avenue branches seem to arrive soonest.

Especially within densely packed New York, omitting the **zip code** is tempting fate. For a map showing codes, see p.48.

GENERAL DELIVERY

If you want to send—or receive—something **general delivery**, have it addressed c/o General Delivery, General Post Office (see above for address).

To collect letters you'll need two forms of ID (preferably one with a photo). Mail will be kept for thirty days before being returned to sender, so make sure there's a return address somewhere on the envelope. If receiving mail at someone else's address. be sure your correspondents put "c/o (your host)" on the envelope, since without that you risk your mail being returned to sender by an overzealous postperson. By law a person's last name must appear on the box nameplate of a multi-unit apartment (this rule does not apply to single-family houses).

PARCELS AND PACKAGES

When **sending presents or personal effects** home, use United Parcel Service if you can—

MANHATTAN POST OFFICES

JAF Building, 421 Eighth Ave., NY 10001.
Knickerbocker, 128 E. Broadway, NY10002.
Cooper, 93 Fourth Ave., NY 10003.
Bowling Green, 25 Broadway, NY 10004.
Wall Street, 73 Pine St., NY 10005.
Church, 90 Church St., NY 10007.
Peter Stuyvesant, 432 E. 14th St., NY 10009.
Madison Square, 149 E. 23rd St., NY 10010.
Old Chelsea, 217 W. 18th St., NY 10011.
Prince, 103 Prince St., NY 10012.
Canal Street, 350 Canal St., NY 10013.
Village, 201 Varick St., NY 10014.
Murray Hill, 115 E. 34th St., NY 10016.

Grand Central, 450 Lexington Ave., NY 10017.
Midtown, 221 W. 38th St., NY 10018.
Radio City, 322 W. 52nd St., NY 10019.
Rockefeller Center, 610 Fifth Ave., NY 10020.
Lenox Hill, 217 E. 70th St., NY 10021.
FD Roosevelt, 909 Third Ave., NY 10022.
Ansonia, 1990 Broadway, NY 10023.
Planetarium, 127 W. 83rd St., NY 10024.
Cathedral, 215 W. 104th St., NY 10025.
Morningside, 232 W. 116th St., NY 10026.
Gracie, 229 E. 85th St., NY 10028.
Times Square, 340 W. 42nd St., NY 10036.
Yorkville, 1591 Third Ave., NY 10128.
Peck Slip, 1 Peck Slip, NY 10038.

cheaper, better, and less exigent than the US Mail. If you do elect to brave the post office regulations, show up with the box unsealed but otherwise ready to go and bring a roll of porous, paper-surface tape. With cellophane, Scotch, filament, or wax-paper-finish tape its unlikely that you'll be able to register or insure valuable articles.

For smaller, valuable documents (ie, for receiving the address book you forgot) you can rely on the post office's **certified or Express Mail** services, though nowadays it's trendy to use courier companies such as Federal Express or Airborne Express, some of which will make home deliveries/pickup and accept payment on the spot from non-account holders.

POLICE AND TROUBLE

The New York City Police ("New York's Finest") are for the most part approachable, helpful, and overworked. This means that asking directions gets a friendly response, reporting a theft a weary "Whaddya want me to do about it?" Each locality has a station, numbered at a precinct; to find out which is the nearest phone ☎374-5000. In emergencies phone ☎911 or use one of the outdoor posts that give you a direct line to the emergency services. Out of the city you may have to tangle with the State Police, which operates the Highway Patrol—and does so quite ruthlessly.

Regardless of how dangerous New York really is, it *feels* dangerous. Perhaps more than any other city in the world, a sense of nervy self-preservation is rife here: people make studied efforts to avoid eye contact, and any unusual behavior clears a space immediately: the atmosphere of impending violence is sometimes sniffable.

The reality is somewhat different. There *is* a great deal of crime in New York, some of it violent. But seven million people live in the city and as far as per capita crime rates go, Boston is more dangerous, as are Phoenix, Dallas, Washington, Atlanta, and half a dozen other cities. New York's tension doesn't automatically mean violence: as with any big city, anywhere, the main thing is to walk with confidence and to be streetwise: there are a few places and/or times that you really should avoid. Though crime can and does happen day and night it's unlikely you'll be robbed outside the Rockefeller Center at midday; Times Square at midnight is a different matter. Throughout the guide we've outlined places where you should be careful and those few to be avoided altogether, but really it's a case of

using your common sense; it doesn't take long to figure out that you're somewhere unsavory.

It is of course the murders that make the headlines: reassure yourself that ninety percent of victims are known to their killers, which is to say most killings are personal disputes rather than random attacks. A more real problem—and the subject of obsessive conversation among New Yorkers—is **street crime**, especially **mugging**. It's impossible to give hard and fast rules on what to do if you meet up with a mugger: whether to run or scream or fight depends on you and the situation. Most New Yorkers would hand over the money every time, and that's probably what you should do—indeed, keeping a spare $20 or so as "mugger's money," lest your attacker turn nasty at finding empty pockets, is common practice.

Of course the best tactic is to **avoid being mugged**, and there are a few simple points of mental preparation worth taking: *don't* flash money, jewelry, or your Rolex Oyster around; *don't* peer at your map (or this book) at every street corner thereby announcing that you're a lost stranger; even if you are terrified or drunk (or both) *don't* appear so; *never* walk down a dark side street, especially one you can't see the end of; and in the early hours stick to the curb side of the sidewalk so if approached it's easier to run into the road and attract the attention that muggers hate.

If **the worst** happens and your assailant is toting a gun or (more likely) a knife, play it calmly. Remember that he (for this is generally a male pursuit) is probably almost as scared as you and just as jumpy; keep still, don't make any sudden movements—and do what he says. When he's run off hail a cab and ask to be taken to the nearest police station: taxis rarely charge for this, but if they do the police are supposed to pay. Don't stand around on the street in a shocked condition—this is inviting more trouble. At the stations you'll get sympathy and little else; file the theft and take the reference (see "Insurance and Health") to claim your insurance back home.

WOMEN'S NEW YORK: PROBLEMS AND CONTACTS

In New York—as with any large, cosmopolitan city—you're likely to experience some level of sexual harassment. And you've probably heard enough about how manic and threatening the streets can appear. What you may find surprising is the sheer crassness of attitude displayed by many local men and, in a city where women outnumber men by a considerable ratio, the passivity with which some women accept this. On the positive side, the women's movement of the 1960s and 1970s has had a dynamic effect in New York (indeed on both American coasts). Women are much more visible in business, politics, and the professions. The attitudes around can equally well be more progressive and sophisticated, even if it's the negative that first and most powerfully catches your attention.

FEELING SAFE

It must be safe to travel around New York; New York women do it all the time. So runs the thinking, but the city does throw up unique and definite problems for women—and especially for women traveling alone and just getting to know this city. If you feel and look like a visitor, not quite knowing which direction to ride the subway, for instance, it's little comfort to know that New York women routinely use it on their own and late in the evening. What follows are a few points to bear in mind when beginning your explorations of the city: if they duplicate, in part, the comments on "Trouble" (above), no apologies.

The truth is you're more likely to feel unsafe than *be* unsafe—something that can lead to problems in itself, for part of the technique in surviving (and enjoying) New York is to look as if you know what you're doing and where you're going. Maintain the facade and you should find a lot of the aggravation fades away, though subtle hints are a waste of time and energy: if someone's bugging you, let them know your feelings loudly and firmly. Some women carry whistles, gas, and sprays, which, while pretty useless in the event of real trouble, can lend confidence and ward off creeps.

Harassment in the city is certainly worse for women than men—and it can be a lot scarier. But it's not always that different, at least in intent. You're far, far less likely to be raped than you are **mugged**. For a few ground rules on lessening chances of mugging, see "Trouble," but above all be wary about any display of wealth in the wrong place—if you wear jewelry (or a flashy watch) think about where you're walking before starting off for the day. If you are being **followed**, step off the sidewalk and into the streets as attackers hate the open. Never let yourself be pushed into a building or alley and never turn down an unlit, empty-looking street. If you're unsure about the area where you're staying, don't be reluctant to ask other women's advice. They'll tell you when they walk and when they take a bus so as to avoid walking more than a block; which bars and parks they feel free to walk in with confidence; and what times they don't go anywhere without a cab. Listen to this advice and merge it into your own experience. However, don't avoid parts of the city just through hearsay—you might miss what's most of interest—and learn to *expect* Manhattanites to sound alarmist ... it's part of the culture.

If you don't have much money, **accommodation** is important: it can be very unnerving to end up in a hotel that's one step up from a flophouse. Make sure that you have a hotel lobby that's well lit, the door locks on your room are secure, and the night porters seem reliable. If you feel uneasy, move. If you're staying for a couple of weeks or more, you might try one of the city's women-only long-term residences; for addresses of these, see "Staying On."

CRISIS/SUPPORT CENTERS

There are competent and solid support systems for women in **crisis**, or in need of **medical** or **emotional** support. At the following you can be assured of finding skilled, compassionate staff.

New York Women Against Rape (☎477-0819—or ☎777-4000 hotline). Crisis counseling, advocacy, and support groups for victims of rape or sexual abuse.

The Women's Counseling Project, c/o Barnard College Women's Center (see below) (☎854-3063). Referral service that can connect you with a range of medical agencies, including abortion and birth control, psychological health and alternative treatment services.

The Saint Mark's Women's Health Collective, 9 Second Ave. (☎228-7482). One of the foundations of the New York women's community, offering traditional and alternative medicine at sliding scale prices.

Women's Care Clinic, 235 E. 67th St. (☎734-5700). Handles all women's health needs for reasonable fees.

Identity House, 544 Sixth Ave. (☎243-8181). Psychological assistance and counseling.

OTHER FEMINIST CONTACTS

Three Lives, 154 W. 10th St. (☎741-2069). Though there is no longer a bookstore devoted specifically to women, this store has a good selection of books by and for women. Try also *A Different Light*, 548 Hudson St. (☎989-4850). Aside from books, you'll be able to pick up *Womanews*, the city's monthly feminist newspaper—a good read and reasonably comprehensive for feminist/lesbian events, readings, dances, and gatherings.

Barnard College Women's Center, Barnard College, 117th St. and Broadway (☎854-2067). Clearing house for information on women's organizations, studies, conferences, events, etc. They also maintain an extensive library collection of books, articles, and periodicals.

Women's International Resource Exchange (WIRE), 2700 Broadway (☎870-2783).

National Organization for Women, 9th Floor, 15 W. 18th St. (☎807-0721). The largest feminist organization in the US—active in abortion and lesbian rights and ERA agitation.

More Fire! Productions Apt. 16, 63rd E. 7th St. (☎533-7667); **WOW** (Women's One World Theater), 59 E. 4th St. (☎460-8067). Feminist theater groups. If you're interested, WOW welcomes visits (and foreign contacts).

Ceres, 91 Franklin St. (☎226-4725). Women's gallery.

See also the lesbian listings in "Gay and Lesbian New York" *below and the women's/lesbian bars and clubs detailed* in Chapter Eight.

GAY AND LESBIAN NEW YORK

Gay refugees from all over America and the world come to New York, and it's estimated that around twenty percent of New Yorkers (or at least Manhattanites) are lesbian or gay. The passage of the Gay Rights Bill has contributed to the high visibility of gay men and women in the community: NY's Governor and the city's Mayor, its City Council President and Controller, and the Manhattan Borough President all employ full-time liaison officers to gay and lesbian groups. So, too, does the Health Department in the midst of the catastrophic AIDS epidemic—a major problem which has further politicized an already outspoken community.

Greenwich Village is the traditional and most established gay neighborhood and it's here that you'll find most of the action—bars and nightclubs, bookshops, businesses, theater, arts, and contact/support groups. The **East Village**, too, has a growing scene, especially for younger, more politically active gays and lesbians. Other promising locales include the **East 20s and 30s**, **Chelsea** , and the **Upper West Side**.

You'll find all **bars and nightclubs** detailed in Chapters Seven and Eight: what follows are the more **community/resource** kind of listings. If you need to supplement these (and obviously space forbids a comprehensive New York gay guide) get hold of the **Gayellow Pages** ($3.95), available from either of the bookshops below. For up-to-the-minute info, check also *Outweek*, New York's provocative weekly news magazine for gay men, or *Womanews*, a monthly lesbian/feminist news sheet. Both, along with the more national *The Advocate*, are available from many newsstands or from one of the bookshops below.

LESBIAN AND GAY RESOURCES

CENTERS
Lesbian and Gay Community Services Center, 208 W. 13th St. (☎620-7310). Occupying a run-down high school, this has only been in existence since 1985, but already provides meeting space for over eighty organizations ranging from Gay Alcoholics Anonymous to a group for gay advertising executives. In addition to the numerous groups which have activities going all the time—from sports to political lobbying—the Center itself sponsors regular dances and other social events. Call the above number to see what's happening.

BOOKSHOPS
The Oscar Wilde Memorial Bookshop, 15 Christopher St. (☎255-8097). The first gay bookshop in America. Unbeatable.

A Different Light 548 Hudson St. (☎989-4850). Excellent selections of gay and lesbian publications. Open late throughout the week, and often hosts booksigning parties and readings.

HEALTH AND WELL BEING
Community Health Project, 208 W. 13th St. (☎675-3559). Low-priced gay clinic which can either treat or refer you.

Identity House, 544 Sixth Ave. (☎243-8181). Coming-out groups and counseling.

Lambda Legal Defense and Education Fund (☎995-8585). Legal referrals.

SAGE: Senior Action in a Gay Environment (☎741-2247). Advice and numerous activities for gay seniors.

RELIGION
There are numerous gay religious organizations in New York:

Beth Simchat Torah (☎929-9498). The gay synagogue.

Dignity (☎666-2531). Catholic.

Integrity (☎720-3054). Episcopal.

Metropolitan Community Church (☎242-1212). Protestant.

THEATER AND TELEVISION
There's always a fair amount of gay theater (and some TV) going on in New York: check the listings in *Outweek* and *The Village Voice*.

Stonewall Rep (☎675-1014). Mixed gay theater company.

Gay Cable Network. Broadcasts for two hours every Thursday from 10pm to 12:30am on channels 17 and 35.

EXCLUSIVELY FOR WOMEN

INFO/HELP
Lesbian Switchboard (Mon–Fri 6pm–10pm; ☎741-2610). Because no lesbian organizations receive any centralized funding, the community relies on the commitment of small groups of volunteers. One such group is the Switchboard—*the* place to phone for information on events, happenings, and contacts in the New York community.

ARCHIVES
Lesbian Herstory Archives (☎874-7232 for an appointment). Celebrated and unmissable.

RADIO
Lesbian Radio Show WBAI 99.5FM Tuesday 8:30pm. Issues and news for lesbians.

ACCOMMODATION
Womyn's Bed & Breakfast (☎794-8645). Phone for details of women-only rooms in central Manhattan.

See also Women's New York (above).

EXCLUSIVELY FOR MEN

INFO/HELP
Gay Switchboard (daily 10:30am–midnight; ☎777-1800). Help and what's on information.

RADIO

Gay Rap WBAI 99.5FM Wednesdays 9pm–10pm. Weekly program for and about the gay male community.

ACCOMMODATION

If you're looking for somewhere to rest your head that is specifically sympathetic to gays (or well located for the Village), here are a few more suggestions:

Chelsea Pines Inn, 317 W. 14th St. (☎929-1023). Well-priced hotel housed in an old brownstone on the Greenwich Village/Chelsea borders that offers clean, comfortable, attractively furnished rooms for $50–65 a double. Advisable to book in advance.

Longacre House, 317 W. 45th St. (☎246-8580). In the theater district. Singles start at $30.

See also Fire Island (Chapter Eleven).

WORKING AND LIVING IN NYC

Nobody ever says it's easy to live and work in New York City, New Yorkers especially—most of whom, when you broach the subject of prolonged residence, will talk obsessively about their jobs and salaries (assuming they have them), and where they live, or will live, or won't be living any more. Which should give you some idea of the nature of the competition for a good apartment address—definable to the street by most natives, in terms of money, social status, and mobility. Both work and rooms however are there, if you've got the energy, imagination, or just plain foolhardiness to pursue them.

The first order of business, especially for **temporary workers**, is finding out exactly what people do in New York—and how you can fit in. For ideas (and positions) check the Employment Want Ads in *The New York Times* and *Village Voice* and in the plethora of smaller neighborhood freebies available throughout the city.

Possibilities obviously depend on your own personal skills and inventiveness, but among the more general or obvious you might look at some of the following suggestions:

• **Restaurant work**. With over 25,000 restaurants in the city, this is perhaps the best bet, waiting tables, dishwashing, or even cooking, Experience helps, as does dropping by in person since most restaurants won't deal with you over the phone. And don't forget about **tending bar** in one (or more) of the city's thousands of watering holes: as in the restaurant biz, tips can be excellent.

• **Child-care, house-cleaning, dog-walking**. New Yorkers frequently advertise these tasks on notices posted in supermarkets and corner drugstores, healthfood shops, bus shelters, and on university and college bulletin boards.

• **Telemarketing/Market research**. Often not too choosey about whom they employ—though pay tends to be largely on commission basis, and hours tend to be ungodly to take advantage of discount calling rates.

• **Agency work**. *Travelers Aid* (158 W. 42nd St.; ☎944-0013) puts out a handy list of temp agencies seeking skilled and unskilled labor, though it's mainly directed at the homeless and those living on the streets. They usually require you to apply in advance and to arrive early (like 6am), but, if you're hired, some pay the same night.

• **Painting and decorating**. Hard work but good rates. Some agencies offer this kind of work—or you can hunt privately through friends and friends of friends.

• **Foreign language lessons**. If you've a language or two try advertising it on a noticeboard or in the *Voice*, etc. Rates can be good.

• **Artist's model**. Pass your name and a contact number around to the various independent studios or artists' hang-outs in SoHo or TriBeCa. Or try to reach the model booking directors at the art schools themselves.

• **Nightclub bouncer**. For those with physique—and a liking for the hours.

• **Blood donation**. A final, if slightly desperate, option for quick emergency cash. Check Yellow Pages for agencies or hospitals.

Whatever you do (or try to do), proceed with caution. Be selective, if you can. And don't enter into any sweatshop or slave labor type set-up if you're at all suspicious. If you're Canadian, be discreet—despite the lack of immigration formalities, and although you'll blend in well for obvious reasons, if you're caught working you'll be treated like any other illegal alien by the immigratiuon service and ridden out of town on a rail.

FINDING AN APARTMENT OR LONG-TERM ROOM

If work can be hard to find, wait till you start **apartment hunting**. Costs are outrageous. A one-room **Manhattan** apartment with bathroom and kitchenette in a reasonably safe neighborhood can start at $1000 a month, and even in traditionally undesirable parts of the city—the Lower East Side being the most recent and extreme example—gentrification (and property rentals) are proceeding apace. More and more, unless you have established New York friends (or intend to make some fast), the options are being restricted to commuting in from the Outer Boroughs, or even farther afield, from Jersey City, say, or Hoboken. It's a fact that the farther you get from Manhattan, the lower the rent . . ..

The best **source** for actually hearing about an apartment, or apartment room, is, as anywhere, word of mouth. On the media front keep an eye on the ads in the *Voice*, *The New York Times*, *New York Magazine*, and other publications: and if you're reading this before setting out for New York consider advertising yourself, particularly if you have an apartment on the West Coast to exchange. Try the **commercial and campus notice boards**, too, where you might secure a **temporary apartment-sit** or a **sublet** while the regular tenant is away.

Some of the city's many universities and colleges also provide **holiday vacancies**, especially in the summertime. For instance

Barnard College (Columbia University, 3009 Broadway, NY 10027; ☎854-8021) offers a variety of dormitory facilities to students, interns, and associates from the end of May through mid-August for under $500 a month: write well in advance as they're "selective" about who gets a room. During a similar period *New York University* has several hundred shared dorm rooms going for a fixed daily rate supplemented by meal plans.

Less satisfactory, perhaps, but a common fallback option are **long-stay hotels**. A number of these cater specifically for **single women on long stays**: *Allerton House*, 130 E. 57th St,. NY 10022 (☎753-8841), the *Martha Washington Hotel*, 29 E. 29th St., NY 10016 (☎689-1900), *Parkside Evangeline Residence*, 18 Gramercy Park South (☎677-6200), and *Katherine House*, 118 W. 13th St. (☎242-6566). The last two are by far the nicest, though each usually has a long waiting list—call ahead. Others, open to both women and men, include: the *West Side Y*, 5 W. 63rd St., NY 10023 (☎787-4400); the *International Student Hospice*, 154 E. 33rd St., NY 10016 (☎228-7470/4689)—students only for $25 a night; the *Chelsea Center* 511 W. 20th St., NY 10011 (☎243-4922)—$19 a head including breakfast; and the *International Student Center*, 38 W. 88th St., NY 10024 (☎787-7706)—just $10 per person. At most of these, costs range from nightly rates to weekly charges that vary depending on the facilities available; though bear in mind that most of the cheaper hotels offer reduced weekly rates. Contact the respective reservations managers.

Another, less likely source is **Travelers Aid**. Although they mostly deal with crime victims and (US) travelers stranded without funds, they may refer you to low-budget (or even free) temporary accommodation. The **New York Convention and Visitors Bureau** (2 Columbus Circle; ☎397-8222) can also be worth a call. They dole out a leaflet listing all reduced hotel rates.

Just possibly, you might also find it to your advantage to resort to one of the city's several **roommate finding agencies**. Oldest and most reliable of these is *Roommate Finders* (☎489-6862), a non-discriminatory but discriminating company. If you use one of the other agencies—and the *Voice* carries all their names, numbers, and descriptions—make sure you read the contract before any money changes hands or papers are signed.

Lastly, for the really organized, other viable accommodation alternatives include **homesteading**, **coop**, and **mutual housing associations**. These revolve around low-rent group occupation and renovation of often abandoned, city-owned buildings. It's the group element—and the commitment that entails—that marks this system as different from squatting. Each individual tenant contributes the particular skills at their disposal, as well as monthly dues that collectively support normal operating, maintenance, and repair costs. Various agencies designed to assist and protect coop groups and tenant associations have sprung up, providing legal assistance,

rehabilitation and repair loan pools, architectural services, tool lending, and so on: all very urban grass roots, community-oriented stuff. As for getting involved, in the words of one young homesteader it's a matter of "being in the street and seeing what's happening." Sound advice in any case, but for more direct information call the *Department of Housing Preservation and Development* (75 Maiden Lane, NY 10038; ☎806-8171) and ask about the *TIL (Tenant Interim Lease) Program*, or phone the *Urban Homestead Assistance Board* (40 Prince St., NY 10013; ☎226-4119) and inquire about *Self-Help Work Consumer Cooperative*. And good luck.

DIRECTORY

AIRLINES *Air Canada*, 1166 Sixth Ave. (☎869-1900); *Aer Lingus*, 122 E. 42nd St. (☎557-1110); *Air India*, 400 Park Ave. (☎407-1416); *American*, 100 E. 42nd St. (☎1/800/433-7300); *British Airways*, 530 5th Ave. (☎1/800/247-9297); *Continental Airlines*, 120 Broadway (☎319-9494); *El Al*, 850 3rd Ave. (☎768-9200); *Kuwait Airways*, 405 Park Ave. (☎308-5707); *North West Airlines*, 537 5th Ave. (☎736 1220); *Pan Am*, 600 Fifth Ave. (☎687-2600); *TWA*, 1 E. 59th St. and all over the city (☎290-2121); *United*, 100 E. 42nd St. (☎1/800/241-6522); *Virgin Atlantic*, 96 Morton St. (☎242-1330).

CAR PROBLEMS See "Out from the City."

COCKROACHES New York is familiarly known as "Roach City," and no wonder. The creatures infest every apartment or hotel, however luxurious, and it's no good imagining that a $300-a-night suite will ensure you're free of the things. It won't. Latest invention to deal with the problem is a spray said to render all roaches sterile.

CONSULATES *Australia*, 630 Fifth Ave. (☎245-4000); *Canada*, 1251 Sixth Ave. (☎768-2400); *Denmark*, 825 Third Ave. (☎223-4545); *Eire*, 515 Madison Ave. (☎319-2555); *Netherlands*, 1 Rockefeller Plaza (☎246-1429); *Sweden*, 825 Third Ave. (☎751-5900); *United Kingdom*, 845 Third Ave. (☎745-0202).

CONTRACEPTION Condoms are available in all pharmacies. If you're on the pill it's obviously best to bring a supply with you; should you run out, or need advice on other aspects of contraception, abortion, or related matters, contact the *Margaret Sanger Center*, 380 Second Ave. (☎677-6474), or the *Women's Counseling Project* at Barnard College (see "Women's New York").

DISABLED VISITORS Well provided for as far as public buildings (all refitted) and sidewalks (most are now ramped) go. Less so in terms of getting around: the subway is impossible unless you have someone to help you, while only the old "checker" cabs tend to be big enough for wheelchairs, and many cab drivers are unwilling to stop for anyone who looks likely to cause them problems. Buses are better, since the modern ones are fitted with a lowering platform which considerably eases getting on and off, and drivers are obliged to—and generally do—help out. Further information on New York City for disabled people can be had from the *Center for the Handicapped*, 52 Chambers St., Office 206 (☎566-3913).

DOGS Dog shit on the sidewalk is much less of a problem than it was, since it's now illegal not to clear up after your mutt. This law is firmly enforced, and wherever you go in the city you'll see conscientious dog owners scraping up after their pets with makeshift cardboard shovels and dumping the evidence in the nearest litter bin. So if you're doing your New York friend a favor and walking the dog, you know what to do.

DRUGS Though cannabis is now decriminalized in a few states—Alaska for example—it's most definitely not in New York and if you're caught with any you'll incur at least a $100 fine. Harder drugs are, of course, illegal, too, and so should be avoided. If anyone offers you a "nickel bag", they're not selling candy (probably not even selling drugs). The urgent whispers of the traders around Washington Square and many other parts of the city of "Sens, sens" are short for sensamilia (a particular type of marijuana)—though again whether that's what you'd actually end up with if you handed over any money is debatable.

EMERGENCIES For Police, Fire, or Ambulance dial ☎**911**.

ID Carry some at all times, as there are any number of occasions on which you may be asked to show it. Two pieces of ID are preferable and one should have a photo—passport and credit card are the best bets.

HOMELESSNESS Partly simply due to the lack of affordable accommodation, partly to a policy a few years back of releasing long-term mental patients into the community without any real policy of community care, you will be struck by the number of people living on the streets in New York—a population which seems to be ever-growing.

LAUNDRY Hotels do it but charge the earth. You're much better off going to an ordinary laundromat or dry cleaners, both of which you'll find plenty of in the Yellow Pages under "Laundries." Remember also that the YMCAs have coin-op washing machines.

LUGGAGE CONSIGNMENT Two of the most likely places to dump your stuff are Grand Central Station (42nd St. and Park Ave.) and Port Authority Bus Terminal (41st St. and Eighth Ave.). Grand Central's luggage department is open Monday–Friday 7am-8pm, Saturday & Sunday 10am–6pm, and charges $1 an item, $2 for a rucksack, $3 for a bike; and Port Authority's office is open daily 7am–12pm and has rates of 80¢ per item, $1.60 for a backpack.

LIBRARIES The real heavyweight is the central reference section of the New York Public Library on Fifth Ave. at 42nd St. (see Chapter Two). However, as the name suggests, while this is a great place to work and its stock of books is one of the best in the country and indeed the world, you can't actually take books out at the end of the day. To do this you need to go to one of the branches of the NYC Public Library (for a full list ask in the reference library) and produce proof of residence in the city.

LOST PROPERTY Things lost on buses or on the subway: *MTA Lost Property Division*, 370 Jay St., Brooklyn (☎718/625-6200). Things left behind in a cab: *Taxi & Limousine Commission Lost Property Information Dept.*, 211 W. 41st St. (☎869-4513). Otherwise, the nearest police station, particularly if you think they may have been stolen.

NOTICE BOARDS For contacts, casual work, articles for sale, etc. it's hard to beat the notice board just inside the doorway of the *Village Voice* office at 842 Broadway (near Union Square). Otherwise there are numerous notice boards up at Columbia University, or in the Loeb Student Center of New York University on Washington Square.

PUBLIC HOLIDAYS You'll find most offices, some stores and certain museums closed on the following days: January 1; *Martin Luther King's Birthday* (January 21); *President's Day* (third Monday of February); *Memorial Day* (last Monday in May); *Independence Day* (July 4); *Labor Day* (first Monday in September); *Columbus Day* (second Monday in October); *Veterans Day* (November 11); *Thanksgiving* (fourth Thursday in November); *Christmas Day* (December 25). Also, New York's numerous parades mean that on certain days—*Washington's Birthday*, *St. Patrick's Day*, *Easter Sunday*, and *Columbus Day*—much of Fifth Avenue is closed off.

SUBWAY GRAFFITI Once a major feature of the New York cityscape, there's been a campaign against subway graffiti over recent years that has left trains for the most part looking cleaner; indeed most of the trains are now no more graffitied than those of any other major city. Whether this is a good or bad thing, it certainly means subway stations are less colorful, though one thing is certain—most New Yorkers hated the graffiti and are glad to see the back of it.

SWIMMING POOLS See Chapter Six, "Sports, Kids, and Daytime Activities."

TAX Within New York City you'll pay an 8.25 percent sales tax on top of marked prices on just about everything but the very barest of essentials, a measure brought in to help alleviate the city's 1975 economic crisis, and one which stuck.

TIME Eastern Standard Time—three hours ahead of California, one hour ahead of Chicago, etc.

TELEPHONE SERVICES AND HELPLINES Crime Victims Hotline (☎577-7777—24 hours); Alcoholics Anonymous (☎683-3900); Drugs Anonymous (☎874-0700); Free Events (☎360-1333); Herpes Hotline (☎628-9154); Horoscopes (☎540-4444); Jokes (☎976-3838); Missing Persons Bureau (☎374-6913); Rape Hotline (☎267-7273); Restaurant Hotline (East Side: ☎838-7030/6644); West Side: ☎838-7430/6883); Road conditions (☎594-0700); Soap Opera reports (☎540-Ssenior citizen); Sleep (☎439-2992); Suicide Helpline (☎532-2400); Time (☎976-1616); Traffic report (☎830-7666); VD Hotline (☎226-5353); Weather (☎976-1212).

TERMINALS AND TRANSPORT INFORMATION Grand Central Terminal, 42nd St. and Park Ave. (☎532-4900); Amtrak (☎582-6875); Pennsylvania Station, 31st-33rd St. and Seventh-Eighth Ave. (☎868-8970); New Jersey Transit (☎201/460-8444); Long Island Railroad (☎718/217-5477); Port Authority Bus Terminal 41st St. and Eighth Ave. (☎564-8484); George Washington Bridge Bus Terminal, W. 179th St. and Broadway (☎564-1114); Greyhound bus office (☎635-0800).

TIPPING Bartenders and barmaids, cabbies, bellhops, skycaps, restroom attendants, and all other service personnel, will have their hand out for an expected gratuity. There isn't a way around this except to refuse all offers of help in public places—carry your own bags up to your room,

open all doors yourself, and most importantly, never accept handouts of aftershave or perfume in smart washrooms. You will suffer the opprobrium of being considered "cheap" by your friends as well as the spurned personnel, but it could save you a bundle.

TOILETS Bars and restaurants like to put casual users off with forbidding signs like "Restrooms for patrons only." This can be overcome with the right degree of boldness and lack of care for appearances—and if you're desperate you're not going to be that worried anyway. Among centrally located places you can steal into without feeling too guilty are the glossy Grand Hyatt Hotel; the Trump Tower, where there are public toilets on the Garden level; the Waldorf Astoria, where the Ladies is sumptuous in the extreme; the New York Public Library at 42nd St. and Fifth Ave.; and the Lincoln Center's Avery Fisher Hall and Library, both of which have several bathrooms.

TRAVEL AGENTS *Council Travel*, America's principal student/youth travel organization, has an office at 205 E. 42nd St. (☎661-1450) and deal in airline and other tickets, inclusive tours, car rental, international student cards, guidebooks, and work camps. Other agents you might try are *STA Travel*, 48, E. 11th St. (☎986-9470); *Nouvelles Frontières*, 19 W. 44th St. (☎764-6494); *Whole World Travel*, 17 W. 45th St. (☎986-9470).

TURKISH BATHS *Tenth Street Turkish Baths* 268 E. 10th St. (☎473-8806). Manhattan's longest-established Turkish bath, where you can use the steam rooms, pool, and get a massage for just $10.

TV SHOW TAPING AUDIENCES There are always free tickets on offer for certain TV game and chat shows, so if you want a look at your favorite host—or just feel like doing something goofy—inquire within NBC's Rockefeller Center studios on Fifth Avenue and there's a good chance you'll be offered some. If you're organized enough, you can write ahead for tickets at the address flashed at the end of your favorite New York-based sitcom or quiz show.

WHAT'S ON Any number of ways to pick up information. These include dropping into the *Convention and Visitors Bureau* (see above, p.8), which has up-to-date leaflets, buying *New York* magazine, the *New Yorker*, or *Village Voice*, or getting hold of one of several free weekly magazines you find in hotels (*Key*, *Where*, and *Broadway* are three) or the free weekly paper *NY Press*. If your appetite for absolutely fresh data still isn't sated, phone ☎360-1333 for a rundown of the day's cultural events.

WORSHIP There are regular services and masses at the following churches and synagogues: *Anglican Episcopal*: Cathedral of St. John the Divine, Amsterdam Ave. at 112th St. (☎678-6888); St. Bartholomew's, 109 E. 50th St. (☎751-1616); Trinity Church, Broadway and Wall St. (☎602-0872). *Catholic*: St. Patrick's Cathedral, Fifth Ave. at 50th St. (☎753-2261). *Jewish*: Temple Emanu-el, Fifth Ave. at 65th St. (☎744-1400). *Unitarian*: Church of All Souls, Lexington Ave. at 80th St. (☎535-5535).

PART TWO

THE

GUIDE

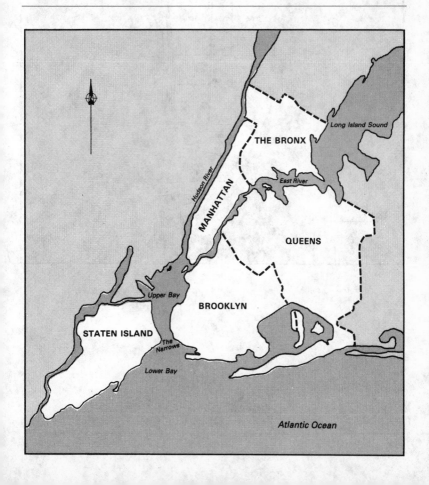

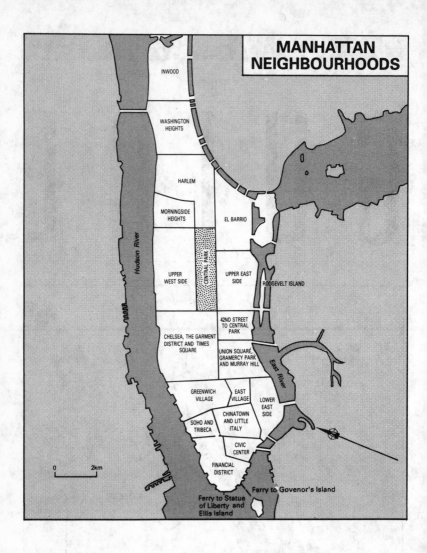

MANHATTAN NEIGHBOURHOODS

INWOOD

WASHINGTON HEIGHTS

HARLEM

MORNINGSIDE HEIGHTS

EL BARRIO

Hudson River

CENTRAL PARK

UPPER WEST SIDE

UPPER EAST SIDE

ROOSEVELT ISLAND

42ND STREET TO CENTRAL PARK

CHELSEA, THE GARMENT DISTRICT AND TIMES SQUARE

UNION SQUARE, GRAMERCY PARK AND MURRAY HILL

East River

GREENWICH VILLAGE

EAST VILLAGE

LOWER EAST SIDE

SOHO AND TRIBECA

CHINATOWN AND LITTLE ITALY

CIVIC CENTER

FINANCIAL DISTRICT

Ferry to Govenor's Island

Ferry to Statue of Liberty and Ellis Island

0   2km

POINTS OF ARRIVAL

AIRPORTS

La Guardia airport (☎718/476-5000), in Queens, handles the majority of **domestic flights**, and is the airport at which you're most likely to arrive. Some domestic flights arrive at either of New York's two **international airports**: Newark (☎201/961-2000) in New Jersey, and **John F. Kennedy (JFK)** (☎718/656-4520) in Queens.

Wherever you arrive, the cheapest and most straightforward way into Manhattan is by **bus**. The two Manhattan **bus terminals**, used by all airport buses, are Grand Central Station and the Port Authority Bus Terminal. For most hotels, **Grand Central** (at Park Ave. and 42nd St.) is the more convenient: well placed for taxis to midtown Manhattan and with a subway station if you're heading toward the east of the city. Bear in mind, also, that some of the larger midtown hotels—the Marriot Marquis, Hilton, etc—operate a free shuttle service to Grand Central. The **Port Authority Terminal**, on Eighth Ave. and 42nd St., isn't as good for Manhattan (there's a lot of humping luggage from bus to street), though you may find it handier if you're heading for the city's West Side (via the A train), out to New Jersey (by bus), or on to other parts of the country from the nearby Penn Station, 33rd Street and Seventh Avenue.

Taxis are the easiest option if you are in a group, or are arriving at an antisocial hour, but are otherwise an unnecessary expense; reckon on paying $20 from La Guardia, $30 plus from JFK, $40 or more from Newark. **Car and minivan services** (limos or minivan may be booked by phone rather than hailed) can also be expensive *from* the airports, but when leaving Manhattan (again especially as a group or in the early hours) may be a viable alternative. Prices are around $12 per person to La Guardia, $15 to JFK, $18 to Newark, but check with the company first. Any hotel will book a car for you, or there are listings in the Yellow Pages. Failing that, call *Gray Line Air Shuttles* on ☎757-6840. Finally, for those with money to throw around, a **helicopter ride** (around $60 plus tax), will deposit you within minutes at the East Side heliport (34th St. and First Ave.); call ☎800/645-3494 for more details.

For **general information** on getting from and to the airports, call ☎1/800/AIR RIDE.

JFK

Carey Buses These leave every thirty minutes (5am–12:30am) for the Port Authority Bus Terminal and Grand Central Station. Journey time is 35–75 minutes, the fare $9.50 one way. Details: ☎718/632-0500.

JFK Express bus/subway link There are a number of bus/subway links between JFK and Manhattan, all—at just the price of a subway token ($1.15)—much cheaper than a scheduled bus or taxi, though the only one that's really any use on arrival is the shuttle bus link which runs every ten minutes from each of the JFK terminals to Howard Beach station on the A line of the subway system, from where trains leave every twenty minutes (6am–1am), stopping at lower and midtown Manhattan subway stations. The journey time is at least an hour to central Manhattan. Further info on ☎718/330-1234.

*When you come to **leave**, remember that JFK is large and very spread out: if your terminal is last on the bus route (like TWA) you should allow an extra fifteen minutes or so to get there.*

NEWARK

Olympia Trails Airport Express Buses leave for Manhattan every twenty minutes (5am–1am), stopping at the World Trade Center and Grand Central and Penn stations. The journey takes twenty to forty minutes depending on the traffic; fare $7. Details: ☎201/964-6233, ☎201/354-3330, or ☎718/622-7700.

New Jersey Transit Buses run to the Port Authority Terminal every fifteen to thirty minutes (24hr.). Journey time thirty to forty minutes; fare $7. Details: ☎201/460-8444.

PATH Rapid Transit The cheapest option, though not by much, involving taking a shuttle Airlink bus to Newark's Penn Station, where PATH trains run to stations in Manhattan. $4 for the bus, $1 for PATH.

LA GUARDIA

Carey Buses leave every twenty to thirty minutes for Grand Central (6am–1am) and Port Authority (7:30am–10pm). Journey time 25–40 minutes; fares for both services are $7.50 one way. Details: ☎718/632-0500.

JFK TO LA GUARDIA

Carey Buses There's a non-stop service linking JFK and La Guardia airports between 6am and 11pm. Buses leave every thirty minutes and take 45 minutes; the fare is $9.50 one way.

ROCK-BOTTOM ALTERNATIVES

For those whose stay has left them financially embarrassed, there are a couple of cheaper alternative routes out from the city to JFK and La Guardia—though not really to Newark. They're real last resorts, however, and not options you'd want to consider for getting into New York City after a red-eye flight.

For **JFK**, the best thing to do is to simply take the JFK subway/bus link (see above). Failing that, take the **E** train to the Union Turnpike-Kew Gardens station and then catch the Q10 green bus (every ten minutes) to the airport: this will cost $1 for the subway, $1 for the bus and takes around ninety minutes. To get to **La Guardia**, take the **7** train to 82nd Street-Jackson Heights stop and a

Q33 bus to the airport: total $1.50. For **Newark**, your only real hope is to take the PATH train and bus link from Manhattan (see above), though this doesn't save much on the price of the regular bus ticket.

ARRIVING BY BUS OR TRAIN

If you're coming to New York by **Greyhound bus**, you will arrive at the Port Authority Bus Terminal (see above).

By **train**, you'll come in at either **Grand Central** or **Penn Station**. Grand Central takes arrivals from the Hudson Valley and other local Metro commuter trains. Trains from Long Island and New Jersey, Boston, Chicago, Washington, DC, Florida, the North and West US and Canada arrive at Penn Station.

See "Directory" in *Basics* for **more details** on the Port Authority and Grand Central terminals.

ORIENTATION

New York City comprises the central island of Manhattan along with four outer boroughs—Brooklyn, Queens, The Bronx, and Staten Island.

Manhattan, to many, is New York. And certainly, whatever your interest in the city, it's here that you'll spend most time, and, unless you have friends elsewhere, are likely to stay. Understanding the intricacies of Manhattan's layout, and above all getting some grasp of its subway and transport system (see the following section), should be your first priority. If at all possible, try to master at least some of the following before arrival—if needs be on the way there.

MANHATTAN'S LAYOUT

Despite its grid-pattern arrangement, **Manhattan** can seem a wearyingly complicated place to get around: blocks of streets and avenues, apparently straightforward on the map, can be uniquely confusing on foot and the psychedelic squiggles of the subway map impenetrably arcane. Don't let subways and buses overawe you, though, as with a little know-how you'll find

them efficient and fast. And if you're at all unsure, just ask—New Yorkers are the most helpful and accurate of direction givers and have seemingly infinite interest in initiating visitors into the great mysteries of their city.

From north to south **the island** of Manhattan is about thirteen miles long and from east to west around two miles wide. Whatever is north of where you're standing is **uptown**, whatever south **downtown**; east or west is **crosstown**. As far as **districts** go, there are three major divisions:

- **Downtown** (below 14th St.).
- **Midtown** (from 14th St. up as far as Central Park).
- **Upper Manhattan** (north of Central Park).

The **southern (downtown) part of Manhattan** was first to be settled, which means that its streets have names and that they're somewhat randomly arranged. **Uptown, above Houston Street on the East Side, 14th Street on the West**, the streets are numbered and follow a strict grid pattern. The numbers of these streets increase as you move north. Downtown, the main **points of reference** are buildings: the World

Trade Center and Woolworth Building are unmistakable landmarks. Uptown, just look out for the big north–south **avenues**. **Fifth Avenue**, the greatest of these, cuts along the east side of Central Park and serves as a dividing line between east streets (the "**East Side**") and west streets ("**the West Side**"). **House numbers** increase as you walk away from either side of Fifth Avenue; numbers on avenues increase as you move north.

ADDRESSES

Locations are easily pinpointed by giving the nearest intersection of avenue and street: the Chrysler Building for example is at Lexington Avenue and 42nd Street—"Lex and 42nd" in conversational shorthand. If you know the number of an address on an avenue it's possible to work out fairly precisely where the building is by referring to the plan of Manhattan printed on p.39. When walking, remember that east–west blocks are about twice as long as north–south blocks—and it's ten north–south blocks to the mile.

When **cycling, driving, or looking for a bus**, it's useful to know that traffic on **odd**-numbered streets runs from east to west, on **even**-numbered streets from west to east, and in both directions on major crosstown streets. Apart from Park, Broadway, and 11th (which are two-way), avenues run in alternate directions.

GETTING AROUND

THE SUBWAY

The **New York subway** is dirty, noisy, intimidating, and initially incomprehensible. But it's also the fastest and most efficient method of getting from A to B throughout Manhattan and the boroughs, which means that sooner or later you'll have to use it. Here are the basics. . . .

• Broadly speaking, **train routes** run uptown or downtown, following the great avenues and targetting in on the downtown financial district: crosstown routes are limited.

• Trains and their routes are identified by a **number** or **letter**. Though the subway is open 24 hours a day, most routes operate at certain times of the day only.

• There are two types of train: **Expresses**, which stop only at major stations, and **Locals**, which stop at every station. If your destination is an express stop, the quickest way to get there is to change from local to express at the first express station, either by walking across the platform or taking the stairs to another level.

• Any subway journey costs a **flat fare of $1.15** (rumored to be going up soon), bought in the form of a **subway token** from a token booth. There's no discount for buying several, but stocking up means less standing in line and they can be used for buses too. The best way to do this is to ask for a "ten-pack," which costs $11.50.

• **Subway maps** can theoretically be obtained from a token booth (at any subway station—though many run out), or, more reliably, from the concourse office at Grand Central; as a stopgap we've printed a map on pp.42–45. Take time to study it before you start—there are few on the platforms, it will make travel much easier, and prevent the sign saying "Tourist—Please Mug" that hangs around the neck of those who peer at maps on trains. If you're starting to panic or are hopelessly lost, phone ☎718/330-1234 and state your destination: they'll tell you the most direct route by subway or bus.

• **A special treat** is to stand right at the front next to the driver's cabin and watch stations hurtling by and rats fleeing along the track: the A train from 125th to 59th is best for this.

Perhaps the main source of confusion is the multiplicity of **line/train names**. The line names on the subway map will be recognized by most people, but the old line names (the IRT, the IND, and the BMT) are still very much in use, as are popular "direction names." Just to give one example: the West Side IRT, Broadway Local, Seventh Avenue Local, and Number 1 train are all the same thing.

The main lines and directions, however, are:

• **IRT** (Interborough Rapid Transport). Runs north and south on the west and east sides of Manhattan. Train numbers **1 (local), 2, and 3** all follow Broadway and Seventh Avenue on the West Side; numbers **4, 5, and 6 (local)** follow Lexington Avenue on the East Side. Number **7** runs from Grand Central out to Corona and Flushing in Queens.

• **Grand Central–Times Square Shuttle**. Connects the east and west sides of the IRT by going along 42nd Street.

• **L**. Connects the east and west sides of the IRT at 14th Street.

• **A and C (local)**. Follow Eighth Avenue through midtown Manhattan and cut through lower Manhattan to connect with Brooklyn.

• **N and R (local)**. Follow Broadway through Manhattan and connect with Brooklyn and Queens.

Lastly, **safety**. Everyone has different views on this and everyone, too, has their horror stories. Many are exaggerated—and the subway definitely feels more dangerous than it actually is—but it's as well to follow a few established rules:

• **At night** always try to use the center **cars**, as they are usually more crowded, and while you're waiting, keep to the area marked in yellow where you can be seen by the booth attendants (more subway crime occurs on the platform than in the trains).

• **By day** the whole train is theoretically safe, but *don't* go into empty cars if you can help it.

• Keep an eye on bags at all times, especially when sitting/standing **near the doors**, a favorite snatching spot.

BUSES

New York's bus system is a lot simpler than the subway, and a lot more frequent; you can also see where you're going and hop off when you pass anything interesting. Its one disadvan-

tage is that it can be extremely slow—at rush hour almost down to walking pace.

Bus maps, like subway maps, can be obtained from the main concourse of Grand Central. Again, we've printed a small-size one to tide you over.

A quick glance at the **routes** will reveal that they run along all the avenues and across major streets. There are three **types of bus**: **regular**, which stop every two or three blocks arriving at five- to ten-minute intervals; **limited stop**, which travel the same routes though stopping at only about a quarter of the regular stops; and **express**, which stop hardly anywhere, shuttling commuters in and out of the suburbs. In addition, you'll also find small private buses running in from New Jersey.

Bus stops are marked by yellow curbs and signs indicating bus routes, times (rarely accurate), and intersections. Buses **display their number, origin, and destination** on the front. If a bus arrives that isn't going the whole way to your intended destination ask for a **transfer** when boarding: this enables you to change to another service within one hour of the ticket's issue, a facility designed so that a single fare lets you make any one-way trip in Manhattan. It's always worth asking for a transfer when you get on a bus, just in case.

Anywhere in Manhattan the **fare** is $1.15, payable on entry with either a subway token (the most convenient way) or with exact change—the driver won't give you any, nor accept pennies or dollar bills.

Bus and subway information ☎718/330-1234 (daily 6am–9pm).
Lost and Found ☎625-6200.

TAXIS

Taxis are fairly inexpensive and worth considering if you're in a hurry or a group, or if it's late at night.

There are two types: **Medallion Cabs**, immediately recognizable by their yellow color and medallion on top, and **gypsy cabs**, unlicensed, uninsured operators who pick up business where the tourists arrive. Avoid gypsy cabs like the plague as they're rip-off merchants—their main hunting grounds are outside Grand Central and the East Side Airline Terminal on East 38th Street and 1st Avenue.

Up to **four people** can travel in an ordinary Medallion Cab, **five** in the chunky, old-fashioned *Checker* cab—though these are thin on the ground these days. **Fares** are $1.50 for the first eighth of a mile, 25¢ for each fifth of a mile thereafter. Basic charges rise by 50¢ after 8pm and all day Sundays, and by 100 percent if you're rich or foolish enough to take a cab outside New York City limits (eg to Newark Airport). Trips off Manhattan additionally incur toll fees (which the driver either asks you for at the time or pays and charges at the end of the trip).

The **tip** should be around fifteen percent of the fare; you'll get a dirty look (if not a nasty comment) if you offer less. Also likely to cause a problem is change: drivers don't like splitting anything bigger than a $10 bill, and anything bigger than $20 will produce invective.

Before you hail a cab, it's always a good idea to work out exactly where you're going and if possible the quickest route there, since New York taxi drivers don't always know the city very well (there's a large turnover of immigrant cabbies) and often speak little English. If you feel the driver doesn't seem to know your destination, don't hesitate to point it out on a map. An illuminated sign on top of the taxi indicates its availability; if the small lights on the side of the sign are lit, it means the cab is on radio call—and won't pick you up.

Officially there are certain **regulations** governing taxi operators. A driver can ask your destination only when you're seated—and must transport you (within the city limits), however undesirable your destination. Also, if you request it, a driver must pick up or drop off other passengers, open or close the windows, and stop smoking (they can also ask you to stop). If you have any **problems** with a driver get the license number from the right-hand side of the dashboard, or medallion number from the rooftop sign or on the print-out receipt for the fare, and phone the *NYC Taxis and Limousine Commission* on ☎302-8294. Should you leave something in a cab try the commission's **lost and found office**—☎869-4513.

DRIVING

In a word, don't. Car rental is expensive and parking almost laughably so. It's much better to keep your New York driving to upstate excursions (for more on which, including car rental addresses, etc., see Chapter Eleven, "Out From the City").

If you do need to drive, though, bear in mind NYC's particular **laws of the road**, which include compulsory seat belts for those in front, a 35-mph speed limit within the city, and the *alcotest* to weed out drunken drivers. When you can find somewhere to **park** don't do so within fifteen feet of a fire hydrant, and check which side of the street it's permitted: this alternates daily on many streets, so follow the signs or the crowds. Private parking is expensive, extremely so at peak periods, but it makes sense to leave your car somewhere legitimate: if it's towed away you'll need to liberate it from the **car pound** (☎971-0770): expect to pay around $100 and waste the best part of a day.

CYCLING

Pulling away from the lights on a bike in Manhattan can mean a replay of the Indy 500, and it's just about as dangerous. To enjoy it—and it can be a viable form of transport once you're confident enough—do as the locals and go for all possible rentable safety equipment: pads, a helmet, goggles, and a whistle to move straying pedestrians. Also, when you stop, be sure to chain your machine to something totally immovable if you'd like it to be there when you return.

Bike **rental** starts at about $4 an hour, $20 a day (more for racing models). You'll need two pieces of ID (driver's license and credit card) and a deposit (usually $100, though some firms will take your credit card details instead). The Yellow Pages have full listings of firms, but among good-value, central suppliers are:

Bikes in the Park, Loeb Boathouse, Central Park (☎861-4137). The best place to rent bikes to tour the park.

Metro Bicycles, 1311 Lexington Ave. (☎427-4450); 546 Sixth Ave. (☎255-5100); and other branches in Manhattan. One of the city's largest bike stores.

Midtown Bicycles, 360 W 47th St. (☎581-4500). Corner of Ninth Ave., useful for the West Side.

West Side Bicycles, 231 W 96th St (☎663-7531). Upper West Side store, again handy for Central Park.

WALKING

Few cities equal New York for sheer street-level stimulation, and getting around **on foot** is often the most exciting—and exhausting—method of exploring. Count on around fifteen minutes to walk ten north–south blocks—rather more at rush hour. And keep in mind that however you plan your wanderings you're going to spend much of your time slogging it out on the streets. **Footwear** is important (sneakers are good for

spring/summer; winter needs something more waterproof). So is **safety**: a lot more people are injured in New York carelessly crossing the road than are mugged. Pedestrian crossings don't give you automatic right of way unless the *WALK* sign is on—and even then be prudent.

FINDING A PLACE TO STAY

Accommodation in New York City is a major cost. The only way to cut it radically is to utilize every contact you have—however tenuous—in the city and the Tri-State area. Spend some of your time on a floor or two and suddenly the city, cost-wise at least, isn't all that different from any other. All that the recommendations below can do is cut a few corners . . . and steer you toward the better value places and the more interesting locations.

There aren't many alternatives at the **cheap** end of the market. The choice is between a room in a **YMCA/YWCA** (a *Y*, as they're known), the official New York YHA **youth hostel**, or one of a number of student-oriented long-stay hostels. The latter are the cheapest, with dormitory rooms for as little as $10 a night, though they are distinctly a last resort. The YMCAs charge around $45 a double (though one of them, the William Sloane, has dorm beds, too), while the official YHA hostel has dorm beds for $20 with breakfast.

Bed and breakfast is an increasingly popular (and inexpensive) option, staying in a New Yorker's spare room or better still subletting an apartment. Normally arranged through an agency, rates run at an average of about $60 a double, per night, $90 a night for a studio apartment.

Hotels, which do not normally include breakfast (or **NY City sales tax**, currently running at 8.25 percent), in their published rates, also start at around $60 a double, though at this end of the

scale they are rarely too enticing. If you want a place you won't dread going back to each evening, count on $80 and up, and even then be selective in where you choose; mid-range prices are around $120 for a double room.

Whether you decide to plump for a hostel or hotel, **booking ahead** is very strongly advised. At certain times of the year—Christmas and early summer particularly—you're likely to find *everything* (and we mean this) booked solid. You can book a room yourself, by calling direct to the hotel, (☎1–212 before the listed number if you're dialling from outside Manhattan), or by going through a specialist **travel agent**—which can sometimes work out cheaper (see "Getting There" in *Basics* for addresses); bear in mind, too, the possibilities of all-inclusive flight-and-hotel package trip, again detailed under "Getting There." There are also **booking services** that reserve rooms at no extra charge. Try either *Meegan's* (☎718/995-9292, from outside the city, ☎1/800/221-1235); or *Central Reservations* (☎1/800/356-1123).

For **accommodation outside the city limits**—on Long Island and up the Hudson Valley—see Chapter Eleven, "Out From the City."

THE HOSTELS

Chelsea Center Hostel, 511 W 20th St. (☎243-4922). Small, clean, and safe private downtown hostel, with prices from $16. A useful alternative for downtown New York, though you'll need to reserve in high season.

International House of New York, 500 Riverside Drive, NY 10027 (☎316-8400). Large well-equipped hostel with good clean dormitory accommodation for $25, and a few rooms for $55 single, $65 double. You need to be able to prove that you're a student to get a dormitory bed, but the management will be flexible if there's room to spare. Disadvantages are that the dorms (but not individual rooms) are only open from May 15 to August 20, and the sequestered site is up in Harlem. Write or phone for reservations.

International Student Center, 38 W 88th St. (☎787-7706). New York's bottom line, little more than a few grubby, roach-ridden dorms. Rates are around $10 a bed, phoning ahead is advised, and keeping an eye on your belongings essential (the dorms don't go in for the luxury of lockers for your gear).

International Youth Hostel, 891 Amsterdam Ave., at 103rd St. (☎932-2300). Opened in October 1989, with dormitory-style lodgings, this is the most decent cost-cutting alternative to the YMCAs, with beds for $19 per night and facilities including a restaurant, travel shop, and theater. Though large (480 beds), there's a good chance it'll be heavily booked, so phone well in advance.

THE YMCAS

William Sloane YMCA, 356 W 34th St. (☎760-5860). The largest of the YMCAs, with around 1500 rooms, a café, laundromat, and student travel shop. Cell-like rooms and surly management are the downside. Singles $33, doubles $47, more with individual bath. YHA members can also stay in bunk-bedded rooms for $17 a night, plus $5 key deposit.

Vanderbilt YMCA, 224 E 47th St. (☎755-2410). Smaller and quieter than the Sloane House, and neatly placed in midtown Manhattan, just five minutes' walk from Grand Central Station. Inexpensive restaurant, swimming pool, gym, and laundromat. Singles $34, doubles $44.

West Side YMCA, 5 W 63rd St. (☎787-4400). Well placed for the Upper West Side, Lincoln Center, and Central Park—and with a similarly impressive range of facilities. Singles $39, doubles $44.

For details of **long-stay residences**, particularly ones geared specifically to **women**, see "Staying On" in *Basics*. For details of hotels sympathetic to **gay and lesbian travelers**, see "Gay and Lesbian New York," also in *Basics*.

CAMPING

You won't save a great deal on any of the above options by **camping**. All of the campgrounds that could conceivably serve New York City are situated so far out as to make travel in and out a major cost. For the dedicated, though, these are the most accessible.

Old Bethpage, Claremont Road, Long Island. The nearest site to the city—a short way up Long Island. Prices range from $6–15 depending on tent size and numbers sharing.

East Islip, Hecksher State Park. Beautiful situation and easier to reach on public transit—on the Long Island Railroad from New York City's Penn Station. Prices around $10 for a tent and two campers.

BED AND BREAKFAST

Bed and Breakfast has taken off in a big way particularly in New York where Manhattanites need all the cash possible to pay their astronomical rent. For the visitor, it can be a good way of staying bang in the center of Manhattan at a reasonably affordable price. Don't expect to socialize with your temporary landlord/lady—chances are you'll have a room to yourself and hardly see them—and don't go looking for street signs or ads; all rooms—except for a few out in Brooklyn which advertize individually (see below)—are let out via official agencies.

Bed and Breakfast Network of New York, Suite 602, 134 W 32nd St., NY 10001 (☎645-8134). New and growing network with hosted singles for around $60, doubles $80–90; prices for un-hosted accommodation are slightly more, running to luxury multi-bedded apartments for $130. For an assured booking write at least a month in advance, though short-notice reservations are possible by phone.

Urban Ventures, PO Box 426, NY 10024 (☎594-5650). The first and largest registry in the city. Their budget double rooms go for $45 upward, "comfort range" rooms (with private bath) from about $65. You can rent an entire apartment—minus hosts from $95 a night. Book at least a month in advance; minimum stay is two nights.

New World Bed and Breakfast, 150 Fifth Ave., Suite 711, NY 10011 (☎675-5600). Most of the same options at around the same rates—double rooms for around $60.

Brooklyn B&Bs. If you don't mind staying off Manhattan, there are a number of bed and breakfasts out in Brooklyn that rent out rooms for favorable rates. Try from *Brownstone Bed & Breakfast* (☎1/718/857-0196); *Bed & Breakfast on the Park* (☎1/718/499-6115); *Foy House* (☎1/718/636-1492).

HOTELS

Most of New York's hotels tend to be in midtown Manhattan—which is as good a **location** as any. You'll find only a handful downtown. **Selections** below are divided into two price categories: "Inexpensive" (under $100 for a double) and "Moderate" ($100–180) and "Expensive" ($200 up)—this last a small and select grouping of really special places for which it's worth paying over the odds.

With almost any hotel room it's possible to **cut costs** slightly if you can fill a double with three or even four people: managements rarely mind providing an extra bed or two for an extra $20 or so. If you're staying long enough, you may also be able to pay a special **weekly rate**, maybe getting one night in seven for free. Some hotels, particularly those that see tourists as a major part of their revenue, also lay on special **weekend discounts** if you stay two nights or more, bringing prices down by as much as a third. One good thing: almost all NY hotels, even the scuzziest, have **TVs** in their rooms as a matter of course— so if you've spent all your money on a bed for the night you can always curl up in front of Johnny Carson . . .

For full hotel listings and prices, consult the New York Convention and Visitors Bureau leaflet, *Hotels in New York City*, available from their office (see "Information, Maps and Tours" in *Basics*).

INEXPENSIVE

Aberdeen, 17 W. 32nd St. (☎736-1600). Rather spartan rooms, but in a good location just off Fifth Avenue. Doubles from $85, quads from $115.

Carlton, 22 E. 29th St. (☎532-4100). Useful if you want to be a little farther downtown. $95 a night for doubles.

Carlton Arms, 160 E. 25th St. (☎679-0680). A strong contender for the city's latest Bohemian dosshouse, with a characterful location, eclectic interior decor by contemporary artists, and a clientele made up of Europeans, down-at-heel artists, and long-stay guests. Doubles around $50 make it one of the city's best bargains.

Chelsea, 222 W. 23rd St. (☎243-3700). One of New York's most noted landmarks, both for its aging neo-Gothic building and, more importantly, its long list of alumni, from Dylan Thomas to Bob Dylan and Leonard Cohen, to Sid Vicious, when it

was the scene of the final few days of a doomed punk icon and his girlfriend Nancy. It's still something of a haunt of musicians and art-school types, though its days of notoriety seem pretty much over. Indifferent doubles cost from $85, along with triples and quads.

Chelsea Inn, 46 W. 17th St. (☎645-8989). Nicely situated in the heart of Chelsea, not too far from the Village, and with double rooms for around $95.

Esplanade, 305 West End Ave. (☎874-5000). A good choice if you want to stay in a quieter, residential area within reach of the midtown attractions. Doubles around $100, suites for three to four people for not a lot more.

Excelsior, 45 W. 81st St. (☎362-9200). Upper West Side hotel situated across from the Natural History Museum in the heart of the liveliest stretch of the Columbus Avenue scene. Decently sized doubles cost around $90.

Herald Square, 19 W. 31st St. (☎279-4017). Cheap, well-placed midtown hotel, with spartan doubles from about $60.

Iroquois, 49 W. 44th St. (☎840-3080). Same block as the *Algonquin*, *Mansfield*, and *Royalton* (see below). Doubles $85–100.

Malibu Studios, 2688 Broadway (☎633-0275). Probably the best-value budget accommodation in the city. A fair step from the heart of things up at the Morningside Heights end of the Upper West Side, but adjacent to the 103rd St. stop on the 1 subway line, and within walking distance of plenty of restaurants and nightlife due to the nearby presence of Columbia University. Prices are $35 for a single room ($50 with bath), $50 for a double ($60 with bath), and $19–24 per person for a triple; all these prices drop if you stay for a week or more. Friendly management, too, though you'll need to book.

Mansfield, 12 W. 44th St. (☎944-6050). The real value alternative to both the nearby *Algonquin* and the *Royalton* (see below), with doubles hovering around $85, three-person suites at $100 or so.

Milburn, 242 W. 76th St. (☎362-1006). Welcoming and well-situated hotel in the heart of the Upper West Side that's in the course of being renovated. A few double rooms for $80– 100, one-bedroom suites (complete with kitchen) for a little over $100. Excellent value.

Pickwick Arms, 230 E. 51th St. (☎355-0300). For the price, one of the best deals you'll get in this part of town. Clean, reasonable doubles go for about $90.

Remington, 129 W. 46th St. (☎221-2600). About as near as this category of hotel gets to luxury. Good value, and certainly central, with doubles from $75.

New York Bed and Breakfast, 134 W. 119th St. (☎666-0559). Lovely old brownstone with nice rooms going for just $40 a double, the only drawback is the location, way uptown in El Barrio.

Stanford, 43 W. 32nd St. (☎563-1480). Good prices and location, just off Fifth Avenue, with doubles for around $90.

Washington Square, 103 Waverley Place (☎777-9515). One of very few truly downtown hotels, bang in the heart of Greenwich Village, and with double rooms at $90 up. Don't be deceived by the smart-looking refurbished lobby—the rooms are what you'd expect for the price.

Westpark, 308 W. 58th St. (☎246-6440). A centrally situated, if rather seedy budget hotel just off Columbus Circle. Doubles $80 and upwards.

MODERATE

Ameritania, 230 W. 54th St. (☎247-5000). Just opened, and superb value at $110 per night for beautifully furnished double-bedded rooms with private bath (singles $95). Mention *Real Guides* and this goes down to $90 per night (singles $69). Without question the best deal you'll find in this part of town.

Beekman Tower Hotel, 3 Mitchell Place (1st Ave. at 49th St.). An all-suite hotel with studios starting at around $185. For inexpensive luxury, get a single room and share it with a friend.

Best Western Woodward, 2190 W. 55th St. (☎247-2000). Newly renovated and handy for the Museum of Modern Art. Doubles from $85–105.

Beverly, 125 E. 50th St. (☎753-2700). Nicely furnished, comfortable rooms in an otherwise slightly rundown-looking building. Doubles cost around $140.

Chatwal Inn on Park Avenue, 429 Park Ave. South (☎532-4860). One of a popular Manhattan chain, with doubles starting at just over $100.

Edison, 228 W. 47th St. (☎840-5000). The most striking thing about this hotel is its size, with 1000 rooms at around $90 for a double, four-bedded rooms for just a little more. Good value, but often booked by tour groups.

Empire, 44 W. 63rd St. (☎265-7400). Unexciting hotel, recently refurbished with box-sized rooms, but handy for Lincoln Center and the Upper West Side. Doubles from $160 or so.

Gorham, 136th W. 55th St. (☎245 1800). Excellent value midtown hotel, handy for Central Park and with jacuzzis, cable TV, and a kitchen in every room. At around $120 a double, without doubt the best bargain in this part of town.

Gramercy Park, 2 Lexington Ave. (☎475-4320). Excellent downtown alternative, popular with Europeans. Doubles around $140 normally, though weekend special deals bring the price down to below $100.

Madison Towers, 22 E. 38th St. (☎685-3700). Clean accommodation in the heart of midtown. In summer rates dip down to $75 per night; otherwise prices average about $130 for a double.

Master Host Chatwal Inn, 132 W. 45th St. (☎921-7600). Good-value midtown choice, with double rooms for upward of $115, including breakfast.

New York Penta, 401 Seventh Ave. (☎736-5000). Just across from Penn Station and Madison Square Garden, the *Penta* is a vast, old-fashioned building equipped with every possible convenience. Doubles $160 plus.

Novotel, 226 W. 52nd St. (☎315-0100). Chain hotel large enough to offer a decent range of facilities, while small enough to avoid anonymity. Double rooms, comfortable without being extravagant, go for around $160 a night.

Paramount, 235 W. 46th St. (☎764-5500). A former budget hotel recently renovated by the *Morgan's/Royalton* crew and now not surprisingly one of the hippest places in town to stay, popular with a pop and media crowd, who come to enjoy an interior designed by French architect Philippe Starck and be waited on by the *Comme des Garçons*-adorned staff. Doubles aren't as pricey as you'd think—$140–190—and all have VCR.

President, 234 W. 48th St. (☎246-8800). Standard midtown hotel whose doubles, at $100–120 including breakfast, are excellent value.

Ramada Inn, 790 Eighth Ave. (☎581-7000). Midtown hotel that's a bit characterless and showing its age, although there's the bonus of a rooftop pool open during the summer months. Doubles around $120.

Roger Smith Winthrop, 501 Lexington Ave. (☎755-1400). Solid midtown hotel with doubles from $125.

Salisbury, 123 W. 57th St. (☎246-1300). For the location—at the very hub of the 57th Street shopping scene—not an overpriced hotel, and quite cosy too. Doubles around $120.

Shelburne Murray Hill, 303 Lexington Ave. (☎689-5200). Suite-hotel, with much the same deals as its sister hotel, the *Beekman*; otherwise, expect to pay $195 for a double-bedded suite.

Southgate Tower, 371 Seventh Ave. (☎563-1800). Large and rather atmospheric old place, like the above specializing in suites. Double rooms start at $135, suites at $165.

Surrey, 20 E. 76th St. (☎288-3700). Another elegant suite-only hotel, run by the same company as the *Southgate* and *Beekman* but a little more upmarket. Rates from $200.

Tudor, 304 E. 42nd St. (☎986-8800). Comfortable and convivial, and recently renovated. Doubles from about $200.

Viscount, 127 E. 55th St. (☎826-1100). Clean, safe hotel with mini-suites starting at $150.

Wales, 1295 Madison Ave. (☎876-6000). Almost in Spanish Harlem, though very definitely Upper East Side in feel. Fair prices and handy for the museums. Fairly recently refurbished elegant doubles range from about $125.

Wellington, Seventh Ave. at 55th St. (☎247-3900). Close to Carnegie Hall and handy for the Lincoln Center. A fair price for this stretch of town—doubles from $100.

Wentworth, 59 W. 46th St. (☎719-2300). Hard by Diamond Row and a stone's throw from the Rockefeller Center. Doubles $80 and up.

Wyndham, 42 W. 58th St. (☎753-3500). Pleasantly furnished if unspectacular hotel. Doubles start at $125 which, bearing in mind the area and quality of the hotel, is excellent value.

EXPENSIVE

Algonquin, 59 W. 44th St. (☎840-6800). New York's classic literary hangout, as created by Dorothy Parker and her Round Table associates, and perpetuated by Noel Coward, Bernard Shaw, Irving Berlin, and most names subsequent. Decor remains little changed; prices, if you've the $180 or so necessary for the cheapest double, compare very well with many much more mundane "moderate" places.

Marriott Marquis, 1535 Broadway (☎398-1900). The hotel as fantasy palace. Even if you can't afford to stay here (doubles start at $290), it's worth dropping by to gape at the split level atrium and to ride the glass elevators to NY's only revolving restaurant.

Morgan's, 237 Madison Ave. (☎686-0300). Created by the instigators of Studio 54 and the Palladium nightclub, this is self-consciously—and quite successfully—the chicest dosshouse in town. Discreet furnishings are by André Putnam, good-looking young staff clothed in Klein and Armani. At around $230 for the cheapest double room, you may not decide to join them, but for the price you do get a jacuzzi, a great stereo system, and cable TV in your room.

Plaza, 768 Fifth Ave. (☎759-3000). The last word in New York luxury, at least by reputation, and worth the money for the fine old pseudo French chateau building if nothing else. Doubles start at not much short of $300 and go sky-high. The place to stay if someone else is paying.

Royalton, 44 W. 44th St. (☎869-4400). Owned by the same management as *Morgan's*, the *Royalton* attempts to capture the market for the discerning style person, with more interiors designed by Phillippe Starck. It aims to be the *Algonquin* of the 1990s, and is as much a place to meet and be seen as to stay. Doubles from about $235.

Waldorf Astoria, 301 Park Ave. (☎355-3000). One of the great names among New York hotels, and newly spruced up, making it a wonderful place to stay if you can afford it or someone else is paying. Doubles go for around $200.

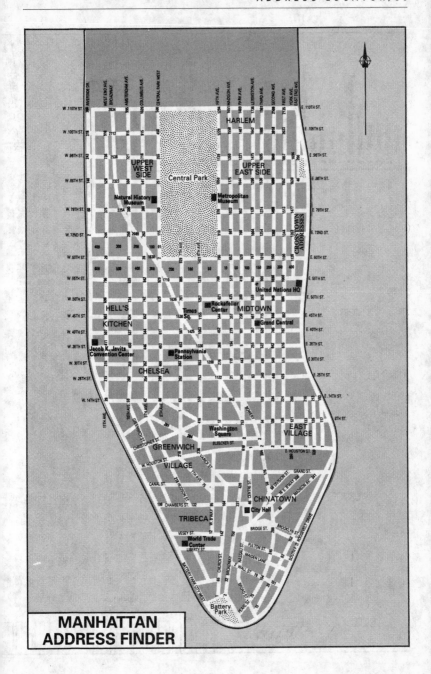

MANHATTAN
ADDRESS FINDER

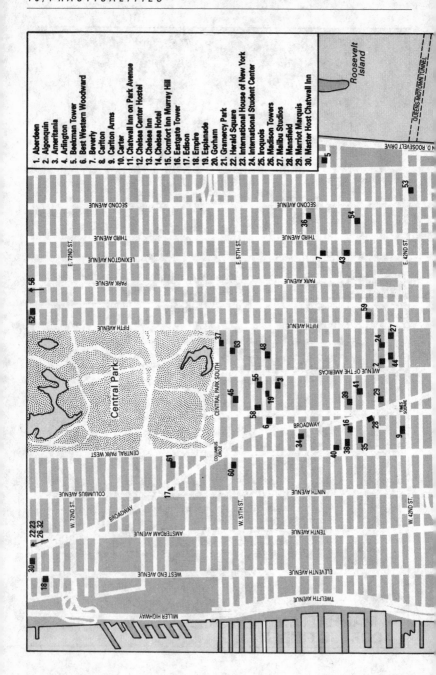

1. Aberdeen
2. Algonquin
3. Ameritania
4. Arlington
5. Best Western Woodward
6. Beekman Tower
7. Beverly
8. Carlton
9. Carlton Arms
10. Carter
11. Chatwall Inn on Park Avenue
12. Chelsea Center Hostel
13. Chelsea Inn
14. Chelsea Hotel
15. Comfort Inn Murray Hill
16. Eastgate Tower
17. Edison
18. Empire
19. Esplanade
20. Gorham
21. Gramercy Park
22. Herald Square
23. International House of New York
24. International Student Center
25. Iroquois
26. Madison Towers
27. Malibu Studios
28. Mansfield
29. Marriot Marquis
30. Master Host Chatwall Inn

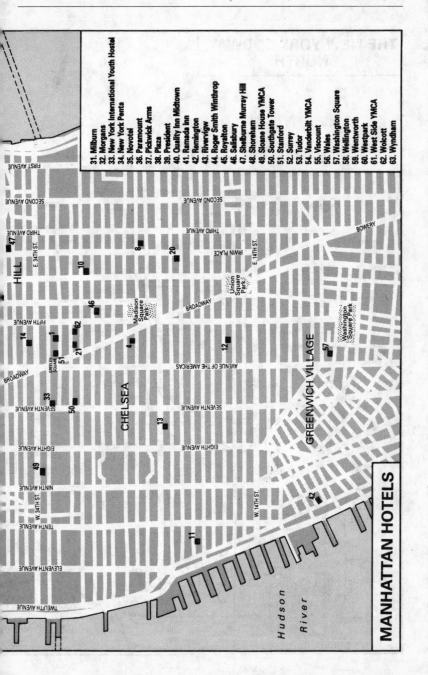

31. Milburn
32. Morgans
33. New York International Youth Hostel
34. New York Penta
35. Novotel
36. Paramount
37. Pickwick Arms
38. Plaza
39. President
40. Quality Inn Midtown
41. Ramada Inn
42. Remington
43. Riverview
44. Roger Smith Winthrop
45. Royalton
46. Salisbury
47. Shelburne Murray Hill
48. Shoreham
49. Sloane House YMCA
50. Southgate Tower
51. Stanford
52. Surrey
53. Tudor
54. Vanderbilt YMCA
55. Viscount
56. Wales
57. Washington Square
58. Wellington
59. Wentworth
60. Westpark
61. West Side YMCA
62. Wolcott
63. Wyndham

MANHATTAN HOTELS

THE NEW YORK SUBWAY: NORTH

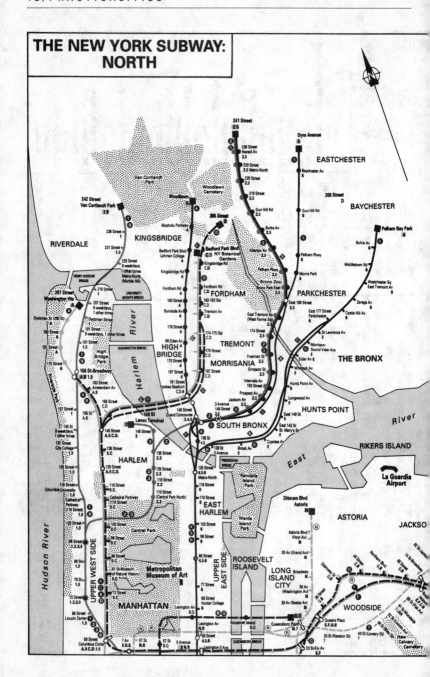

How to Use This Map

Transit Authority services operates 24 hours a day, but not all routes operate at all times. Train identification letters or numbers below station names on this map show the basic, seven-day-a-week service from 6 AM to midnight. A heavy letter or number at a station indicates that the route always operates and always stops at the station between 6 AM and midnight (**N.R S 1.2 7 9**). A light letter or number indicates that the route either does not operate at all times or sometimes skips the station

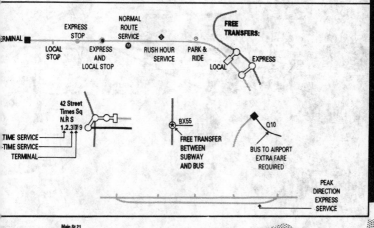

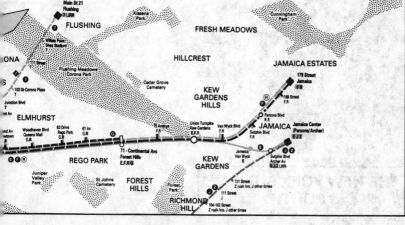

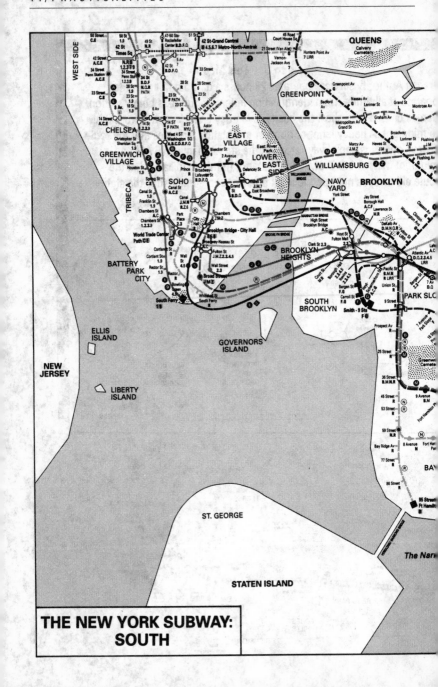

THE NEW YORK SUBWAY:
SOUTH

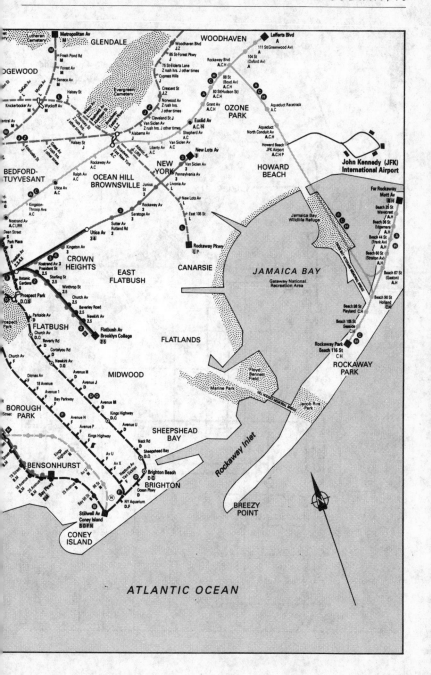

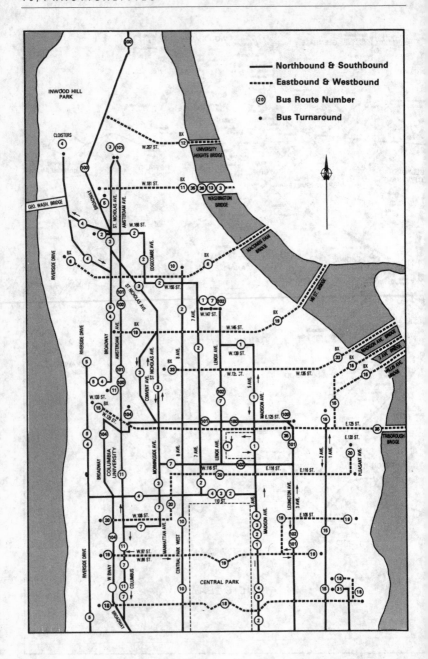

MANHATTAN BUS ROUTES

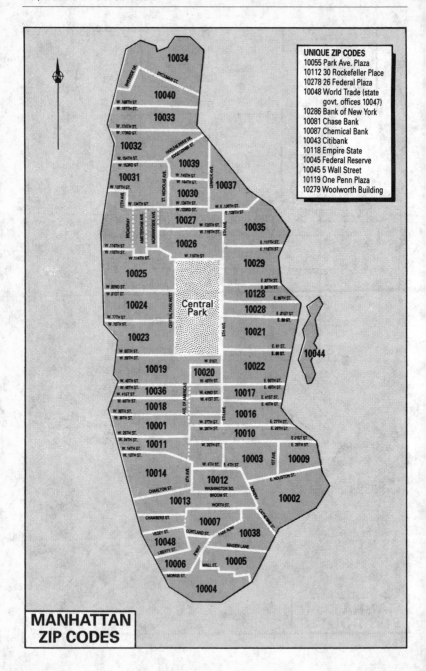

UNIQUE ZIP CODES
10055 Park Ave. Plaza
10112 30 Rockefeller Place
10278 26 Federal Plaza
10048 World Trade (state
 govt. offices 10047)
10286 Bank of New York
10081 Chase Bank
10087 Chemical Bank
10043 Citibank
10118 Empire State
10045 Federal Reserve
10045 5 Wall Street
10119 One Penn Plaza
10279 Woolworth Building

**MANHATTAN
ZIP CODES**

CHAPTER ONE

LOWER MANHATTAN

LOWER MANHATTAN harbors its extremes in close proximity. For some it's the most spectacular, most glamorous skyline in the world, for others a run down and seedy home. But whatever your final perspective, it is undeniably archetypal New York: an area that encompasses Greenwich and the East Village, Chinatown and Little Italy, and, at the skyscraper heart of things, the startling corporate identity of the Financial District.

As a prelude to neighborhood wanderings, the **Statue of Liberty** provides an obvious focus. Not so much for the vaunted symbolism (though this is hard to ignore) as for the views of southern Manhattan. This lower part of the island begins with the shoreline **Financial District**—Wall Street at its center—and then drifts, within half a mile, into the first of the city's ethnic districts. **Chinatown** is still solidly a community (often Chinese-speaking only) and seemingly oblivious to nearby real estate wealth. It's a part of the city well worth getting to know, not least for some astonishingly cheap lunchtime eating. **Little Italy**, adjacent, is in contrast an early warning of New York's irresistible tide—a quarter now largely overrun by slick cafés and restaurants.

Over to the west, quite different again in population and feel, are **SoHo** and **TriBeCa**, one-time industrial areas, now up-and-coming residential blocks and home to Manhattan's (and the world's) art scene. Farther north, a less radical shift, are traditionally politicized/literary **Greenwich Village** (touristy now but fun) and the **East Village**, which has taken on much of the Village's alternative/ arts/political mantle. All of which makes for enjoyable and rewarding walking and café browsing. Walk beyond, though, into the **Lower East Side**, and the riches fade fast—New York's very real poverty quite unhidden and not a little threatening.

At the end of each section in this and the subsequent two chapters, you will find listings of cafés, bars, and restaurants. These are laid out alphabetically for cross-referencing with the entries in Chapter Seven, Drinking and Eating.

The Harbor Islands

The tip of Manhattan island, and the enclosing shores of New Jersey, Staten Island, and Brooklyn, form the broad expanse of **New York Harbor**, one of the finest natural harbors in the world, and one of the things that persuaded the first immigrants to establish their first settlement here several centuries ago. It's an almost landlocked body of water, divided into the Upper and Lower Bay, some hundred miles square in total and stretching as far as the Verrazano Narrows— the narrow neck of land between Staten Island and Long Island. It's possible to appreciate it by simply gazing out from the promenade on Battery Park. But to

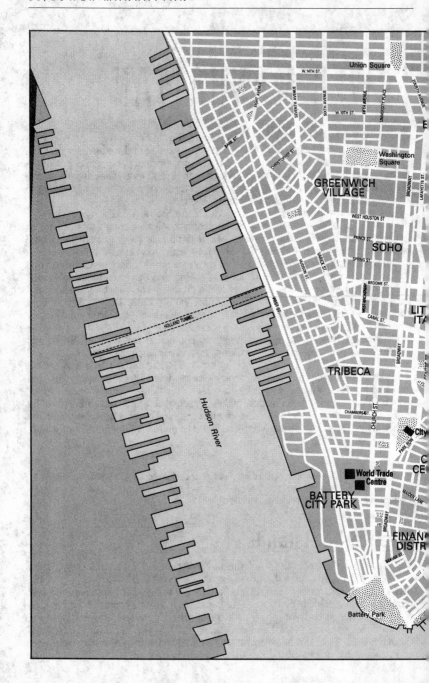

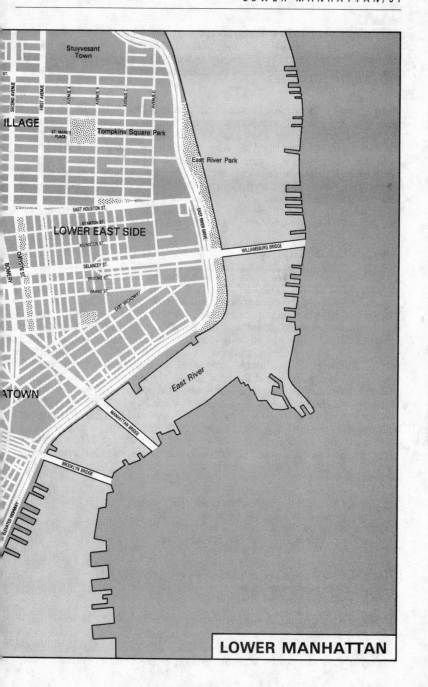

LOWER MANHATTAN

get a proper sense of New York's specialness, and to get the best views of the classic skyline, you should really take to the water. You can do this by taking a trip on the Staten Island Ferry, though the islands in the bay, notably Liberty and Ellis islands, provide far more compelling targets for a trip.

Practicalities

Ferries, run by *Circle Line*, go to both the Statue of Liberty and Ellis Island and leave from the pier in the Battery, every half hour in summer roughly between 9:15am and 5pm. The fare is $6 for the full round trip, half price for children (tickets from Castle Clinton). The last ferry you can feasibly take is at 3:30pm, and even then you couldn't see both islands. It's best to try and leave as early as possible, thereby avoiding the lines (which can be very long in high season, especially at weekends) and giving yourself enough time to explore both islands properly: Liberty Island needs a good couple of hours, and if the weather's fine and there aren't too many people, it can be a pleasant place to spend an afternoon; Ellis Island, too, demands two hours at least if you want to see everything.

The Statue of Liberty

Of all the many symbols of America, none has proved more enduring or evocative than the **STATUE OF LIBERTY**. This giant figure, torch in hand and clutching a stone tablet, has for a century acted as a kind of figurehead for the American Dream, and it's a measure of the global power of the United States that there is today probably no more immediately recognizable profile in existence. It's worth remembering, also, that the statue is—for Americans at least—a potent reminder that the USA is a land of immigrants: it was New York harbor where the first big waves of European immigrants arrived, their ships entering through the Verrazano Narrows to round the bend of the bay and catch a first glimpse of "Liberty Enlightening the World"—for them the end of their journey into the unknown and the symbolic beginning of a new life. Now, although only the very wealthy can afford to arrive here by sea these days, and a would-be immigrant's first (and possibly last) view of the US is more likely to be the immigration check at JFK airport, Liberty remains—notwithstanding US foreign policy—a stirring sight, Emma Lazarus's poem, written originally to raise funds for the statue's base, no less quotable than when it was written:

> *Here at our sea-washed, sunset gates shall stand*
> *A mighty woman with a torch, whose flame*
> *Is the imprisoned lightning, and her name*
> *Mother of Exiles. From her beacon-hand*
> *Glows world-wide welcome; her mild eyes command*
> *The air-bridged harbor that twin cities frame.*
> *"Keep ancient lands, your storied pomp!" cries she*
> *With silent lips. "Give me your tired, your poor,*
> *Your huddled masses yearning to breathe free,*
> *The wretched refuse to your teeming shore.*
> *Send these, the homeless, tempest-tost to me,*
> *I lift my lamp beside the golden door."*

The statue, which depicts Liberty throwing off her shackles and holding a beacon to light the world, was the creation of the French sculptor Frédéric

Auguste Bartholdi, crafted a hundred years after the American Revolution in recognition of fraternity between the French and American people (though it's fair to add that Bartholdi originally intended the statue for Alexandria in Egypt). Bartholdi constructed Liberty in Paris between 1874 and 1884, starting with a terracotta model and enlarging it through four successive versions to its present size, a composition of thin copper sheets bolted together and supported by an iron framework designed by Gustave Eiffel. The arm carrying the torch was exhibited in Madison Square Park for seven years, but the whole statue wasn't officially accepted on behalf of the American people until 1884, after which it was taken apart, crated up, and shipped to New York.

It was to be another two years before it could be properly unveiled: money had to be collected to fund the construction of the base, and for some reason Americans were unwilling—or unable—to dip into their pockets. Only through the campaigning efforts of newspaper magnate Joseph Pulitzer, a keen supporter of the statue, did it all come together in the end. Richard Morris Hunt built a pedestal around the existing star-shaped Fort Wood, and Liberty was formally dedicated by President Cleveland on October 28, 1886 in a flag-waving shindig that has never really stopped. The statue was closed a few years back for extensive renovation once more paid for by a fervently patriotic public—but now the whole thing is accessible again, opened in July, 1986 with more back-patting ceremonial to commemorate the statue's centennial. Fifteen million people descended on Manhattan for the celebrations, well over half a million of them piling into Central Park to hear a special Liberty performance by the New York Philharmonic.

You can today climb steps up to the crown, though the torch, to which there is a cramped stairway, is sadly to remain closed to the public. Don't be surprised if you find an hour-long line to ascend, though even if there is Liberty Park's views of the Lower Manhattan skyline, the twin towers of the World Trade Center lording it over the jutting teeth of New York's financial quarter, are spectacular enough.

Ellis Island

Just across the water, and just a few minutes on by ferry, sits **ELLIS ISLAND**, the first stop for over twelve million immigrants hoping to settle in the USA. The island, originally known as Gibbet Island by the English (who used it for punishing unfortunate pirates), became an immigration station in 1894, in order to cope with the massive influx of mostly southern and Eastern European immigrants. It remained open until 1954, when it was abandoned and left to fall into atmospheric ruin.

Up until the 1850s there was no official immigration process in New York. Then, the upsurge of Irish, German, and Scandinavian immigrants, escaping the great famines of 1846 and failed revolutions of 1848, forced the authorities to open an immigration center at Castle Clinton in Battery Park. By the 1880s widespread hardship in Eastern and southern Europe, the pogroms in Russia, and the massive economic failure in southern Italy forced thousands to flee the continent. At the same time, America was experiencing the first successes of its Industrial Revolution and more and more people started to move to the cities from the country. Ellis Island opened in 1894, just as America came out of a depression and began to assert itself on the world stage. News spread through Europe of what the New World could offer and immigrants left in their thousands.

The immigrants who arrived at Ellis Island were all steerage class passengers; richer immigrants were processed at their leisure on board ship. The scenes on the island were horribly confused: most families arrived hungry, filthy, and penniless, rarely speaking English and invariably overawed by the beckoning metropolis across the water. Con men preyed from all sides, stealing their baggage as it was checked and offering rip-off exchange rates for whatever money they had managed to bring. Each family was split up, men sent to one area, women and children to another, while a series of checks took place to weed out the undesirables and the infirm. The latter were taken to the second floor, the Registry Room, where doctors would check for "loathsome and contagious diseases" as well as signs of insanity. Those who failed medical tests were marked with a white cross on their backs and either sent to the hospital or put back on the boat. Steamship carriers had an obligation to return any immigrants not accepted to their original port, though according to official records only two percent were ever rejected, and many of those jumped into the sea and tried to swim to Manhattan rather than face going home. There was also a legal test, which checked nationality and, very importantly, political affiliations. The majority of the immigrants were processed in a matter of hours and then headed either to New Jersey and trains heading West, or into New York City to settle in one of the rapidly expanding ethnic neighborhoods.

By the time of its closure, Ellis Island was a formidable complex. The first building burned down in 1897; the present one was built in 1903, and there were various additions built in the ensuing years, hospitals, outhouses, and the like, usually on bits of landfill that were added to the island in an attempt to contend with the swelling numbers passing through. The buildings were derelict until the mid-1980s, since when the main, four-turreted central building has been completely renovated, reopening in 1990 as the **Museum of Immigration**. This is an ambitious museum, and tries hard to recapture some of the spirit of the place, with films and tapes documenting the celebration of America as the immigrant nation, although you can't help feeling that it might have been more memorable before the authorities got their hands on the place. Nonetheless some 100 million Americans can trace their roots back through Ellis Island, and for them especially it must be an engaging and instructive display. The huge vaulted Registry Room has been left bare, with just a couple of inspectors' desks and American flags, and leads on to a series of interview rooms and white-tiled corridors that also have been left suitably institutional, more reminiscent of prison or mental institution than a stepping stone to liberty. Each is illustrated by the recorded voices of those who passed through Ellis Island recalling their experience, along with photographs, thoughtful and informative explanatory text, and small artifacts—train timetables and familiar items brought from home. There are descriptions of arrival and the subsequent interviews, examples of questions asked and medical tests given; there are evocative photographs, too, of the building before it was restored, along with items rescued from the building and rooms devoted to the peak years of immigration; on the top floor one of the dormitories, used by those kept overnight for further examination, has been left almost intact.

Outside, the place has an eerie, unfinished feel, heightened by the derelict shell of what was once the center's hospital. On the fortified spurs of the island, names of immigrant families who passed through the building over the years are engraved in copper; paid for by a minimum donation of $100 from their descendants, this "American Immigrant Wall of Honor" helped fund the restoration.

Governor's Island

The last of the three small islands which lie just south of Manhattan, **GOVERNOR'S ISLAND** is home these days to the US Coast Guard and only visitable if you write first for a permit from the *USCG Support Center* (Governor's Island, NY 10004; ☎668-7255). In summer tours run quite regularly, the ferries are free, and it makes for a close-by escape from the city if you've an hour or two to spare. "Nowhere in New York is more pastoral," Jan Morris wrote of the island in *The Great Port*. Sights include a handful of colonial and nineteenth-century houses, and Fort Jay and Castle Williams—the former put up in 1789 by zealous and ever-vigilant revolutionary volunteers. Otherwise it's once again the views of downtown Manhattan that steal the show: from the peaceful, almost villagy environment of the island, more impressive than ever.

The Financial District

The skyline of Manhattan's **FINANCIAL DISTRICT** is the one you see in all the movies—dramatic skyscrapers pushed into the narrow southern tip of the island and framed by the monumental elegance of the Brooklyn Bridge. Heart of the nation's wheeler-dealering, this is the place where Manhattan (and indeed America) began—though precious few leftovers of those days remain, shunted out by big business eager to boost their corporate image with headquarters in the right places. Like every other commercial center, the Financial District has a nine-to-five existence: don't go expecting life out of these times or at weekends.

The Stock Exchange and the Wall Street Crash

The Dutch arrived here first, building a wooden wall at the edge of their small settlement as protection from pro-British settlers to the north. Hence the narrow canyon of today's **Wall Street** gained its name, and it's here, behind the thin neo-Classical mask of the **New York Stock Exchange**, that the purse strings of the capitalist world are pulled. From the **Visitors' Gallery** (Mon–Fri 9:15am–4pm; free) the exchange floor appears a melee of brokers and buyers, all scrambling for the elusive fractional cent on which to make a megabuck. Sit through the glib introductory film, though, and the hectic scurrying and constantly moving hiero-glyphs of the stock prices make more sense. Along with the film, there's a small exhibition on the history of the Exchange—notably quiet on the more spectacular screw-ups. The most disastrous, the notorious "Black Tuesday" of 1929, is mentioned almost in passing, perhaps because it was so obviously caused by the greed and short-sightedness of the money men themselves. In those days shares could be bought "on margin," which meant the buyer needed to pay only a small part of their total cost, borrowing the rest using the shares as security. This worked fine so long as the market kept rising—share dividends came in to pay off the loans, investors' money bought more shares. But it was, as Alistair Cooke put it, "a mountain of credit on a molehill of actual money," and only a small scare was needed to start the avalanche. When the market slackened punters had to find more cash to service their debts and make up for the fall in value of their stocks, which they did by selling off shares cheaply. A panicked chain reaction began, and on October 24 sixteen million shares were traded; five days later the whole

Exchange collapsed as $125 million was wiped off stock values. Fortunes disappeared overnight: millions lost their life savings, banks, businesses and industries shut their doors, unemployment spiraled helplessly. The Great Depression began. It says much for the safety nets that today surround the market's operations that the equally tumultuous crash of October, 1987 caused comparatively negligible reverberations.

Federal Hall and Trinity Church

The **Federal Hall National Memorial**, at Wall Street's canyon-like head, can't help but look a little foolish, a Doric temple that woke up one morning and found itself surrounded by skyscrapers. The building was once the Customs House, later a bank, but the exhibition inside (Mon–Fri 9am–5pm; free) relates the headier days of 1789 when George Washington was sworn in as America's first president from a balcony on this site. It was a showy affair for a great if rather pompous man: "I fear we may have exchanged George III for George I," commented one senator observing Washington's affectations. The documents and models of the event repay a wander, as does the daintily rotunded hall. Washington's statue stands, very properly, on the steps.

At Wall Street's other end, **Trinity Church** (guided tours at 2pm, daily) waits darkly in the wings, an ironic onlooker to the street's dealings. There's been a church here since the end of the seventeenth century, but this one in knobbly neo-Gothic went up in 1846, and for fifty years was the city's tallest building, a reminder of just how recently high-rise Manhattan has sprung up. It has much of the air of an English village church (Richard Upjohn, its architect, came from rural Dorset), especially in the sheltered **graveyard**, resting place of early Manhattanites and lunching office workers. A search around the old tombstones rewards one with such luminaries as first Secretary to the Treasury Alexander Hamilton.

Around Wall Street

Trinity Church is an oddity among its office building neighbors, several of which are worth nosing into. **One Wall Street**, immediately opposite the church, is among the best, with an Art Deco lobby in sumptuous red and gold that naggingly suggests a bankers' bordello. East down Wall Street, the **Morgan Guaranty Trust Building**, at no. 23, bears the scars of a weird happening of 1920. On September 16 a horse-drawn cart pulled up outside and its driver jumped off and disappeared down a side street. A few seconds later the cart blew up in a devastating explosion that knocked out windows half a mile away. Thirty-three people were killed (many literally blown to bits) and hundreds injured, but the explosion remains unexplained. One theory holds that it was a premeditated attack on Morgan and his vast financial empire; another that the cart belonged to an explosives company and was illegally traveling through the city. Curiously, or perhaps deliberately, the pock-marks on the building's wall have never been healed.

The most impressive leftover of the confident days before the Wall Street crash is the old **Cunard Building** at 25 Broadway, whose marble walls and high dome housed the steamship's booking office—hence the elaborate, whimsical murals of sea travel and nautical gods splashed all around. As the large liners gave way to jet travel, Cunard could no longer afford such an extravagant shop window. Its sorry fate today is to house a post office, one that's been fitted out with little feeling for the exuberant space it occupies.

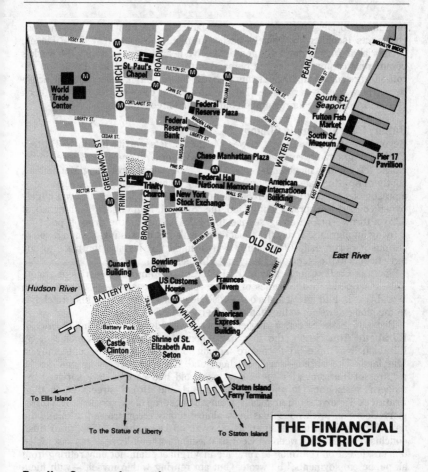

THE FINANCIAL
DISTRICT

Bowling Green and around

Broadway comes to a gentle end at the **Bowling Green**, a grassy oval used for the game by eighteenth-century colonial Brits on a lease of "one peppercorn per year." The encircling iron fence is an original of 1771, though the crowns that once topped the stakes were removed in later revolutionary fervor, as was a statue of George III, to be melted down and put to more practical use in cannonballs. Earlier still the green was the site of one of Manhattan's more memorable business deals, when Peter Minuit, first director general of the Dutch colony of New Amsterdam, bought the whole island from the Indians for a handful of baubles worth 60 guilders (about $25): but the other side of the story, the bit you never hear, was that these Indians didn't actually own the island; no doubt both parties went home smiling. Today the green is a spot for office people picnicking in the shadow of Cass Gilbert's **US Customs House**, which forms a grandiose plug to the south. With its back firmly to the sea the Customs House is a heroic monument to New York the port; four statues at the front represent the four continents (sculpted by Daniel Chester French, who also created the Lincoln Memorial in Washington DC), and the twelve near the top personify the world's commercial centers, all fixed in homage to the maritime market. Inside, on the rotunda, are some rumbustious murals by Reginald Marsh, celebrating the activities of New York's harborside. Take a look if you can—the murals have been closed for some time for restoration but are due to reopen soon.

Battery Park and Castle Clinton

Beyond the Customs House, Lower Manhattan lets out its breath in **Battery Park**, a bright and breezy space with **Castle Clinton** on one side. Before landfill closed the gap this nineteenth-century fort was an island, protecting Manhattan's southern tip—the battery of cannons providing its name. Later it found new life as a prestigious concert hall—in 1850 the enterprising P.T. Barnum threw a hugely hyped concert by soprano Jenny Lind, the "Swedish Nightingale," with tickets at $225 a throw—before doing service (pre-Ellis Island) as the drop-off point for arriving immigrants. Today the squat castle isn't that interesting, though if you're curious it's open daily (9am–5pm); bear in mind that it's also the place to buy ferry tickets to the Statue of Liberty and Ellis Island.

South of Castle Clinton stands the **East Coast Memorial**, a series of granite slabs inscribed with the names of all the American seamen who were killed in World War II. Fittingly, it looks out across New York Harbor, and this stretch has tremendous views out to the Statue of Liberty and Ellis Island.

Back on State Street, a dapper Georgian facade identifies the **Shrine of Elizabeth Ann Seton**, the first native-born American to be canonized. St. Elizabeth lived here briefly before moving to found a religious community in Maryland. The shrine—small, hushed, and illustrated by pious and tearful pictures of the saint's life—is one of a few old houses that have survived the modern onslaught. On the corner of Pearl and Broad streets is another, **Fraunces Tavern**, set dramatically against a backdrop of skyscrapers. The three-story Georgian brick house has been almost totally reconstructed to mimic the day of the incident that ensured its survival: on December 4, 1783, the British conclusively beaten, a weeping George Washington took leave of his assembled officers, intent on returning to rural life in Virginia: "I am not only retiring from all public employments," he wrote, "but am retiring within myself"—with hindsight a hasty statement as six years later he was to return as the new nation's President. The second floor recreates the simple colonial dining room where this took place—all probably as genuine as the relics of Washington's false teeth and hair in the adjacent museum. Admission is Monday to Friday, 10am to 4pm; $2.50, $1 students.

Along Water Street

Turn a corner by the tavern and you're on **Water Street**, in its southern reaches a thinned-out agglomeration of skyscrapers developed in the early 1960s when the powers-that-were took it into their heads that Manhattan's business was stagnating because of lack of room for growth and so tore down the Victorian brownstones and warehouses that lined the waterfront. They thus missed a vital chance to let the old give context to the new, and if you stand on the barren plaza of the **American Express Building** at 2 New York Plaza, you're a long way from feeling anything other than windswept and alone. But not all of Water Street's development is quite so faceless: turn east down Old Slip and a pocket-size palazzo that was once the **First Precinct Police Station** slots good-naturedly into the narrow strip, a cheerful throwback to a different era. A little to the south, off Water Street, is the **Vietnam Veterans' Memorial**, an ugly assembly of glass blocks etched with troops' letters home. While these are sad and occasionally moving, the memorial is unpleasantly shabby, reminiscent of an ill-kept municipal toilet.

Cross Water Street, take the next left to Pine Street and you'll find a skyscraper that's one of Manhattan's most joyful. In 1916 the authorities became worried that the massive buildings looming up around town would shield light from the streets, turning the lower and midtown areas into grim passages between soaring monoliths. The result of their fears was the first *zoning ordinance*, which ruled that a building's total floor space couldn't be any more than twelve times the area of its site. This led to the "setback" style of skyscraper, and the **American International Building** at 70 Pine Street is the ultimate wedge of Art Deco wedding cake: light, zestful, and with one of the best—and most overlooked—Deco interiors. Like other lobbies, no one minds you going in, and recent demolitions mean you can get a good view of the whole building—which might have been almost as well known as the Empire State or Chrysler Building had it been more visible. Almost opposite, I. M. Pei's gridiron **88 Pine Street** stands coolly formal in white, a self-confident and self-contained modern descendant.

Around the South Street Seaport

At the eastern end of Fulton Street the **South Street Seaport** comes girded with the sort of praise and publicity that generally augurs a commercial bland-out. In fact it's a likable project that's attempting to preserve one of Lower Manhattan's few surviving historic industrial areas. A fair slice of commercial gentrification was needed to woo developers, but the presence of a working fish market has kept things real in a way that should be a lesson for future emulators.

For a hundred years this stretch of the waterfront was New York's sailing ship port: it began when Robert Fulton started a ferry service from here to Brooklyn, and left his name on the street and then its market. The harbor lapped up the trade brought by the opening of the Erie Canal and, by the end of the nineteenth century, was sending cargo ships on regular runs to California, Japan, and Liverpool. Trade eventually moved elsewhere, though, and the blocks of warehouses and ship's chandlers, gradually and secretively being bought up by property speculators, were left to rot. Their rescue—by a historical monument order—was probably only just in time.

Regular guided tours of the Seaport run from the Visitors' Center at 207 Water Street, but the best place to start looking around is the market's so-called **Museum Block**, an assembly of upmarket shops hidden behind Water Street's hotchpotch of Greek Revival and Italianate facades. Adjacent is the **New Fulton Market**, which, despite outward appearances, went up in 1983. Essentially it's a food emporium, and if prices aren't bargain basement they're certainly within reach, especially for the eclectic variety of fast food on the second floor, which other than the nearby *Jeremy's Alehouse* (see Chapter Seven, "Drinking and Eating") is the best bet for a cut-price lunch. Across the way the cleaned-up **Schermerhorn Row** has the "English" North Star Pub at one end and the pricey *Sloppy Louie's* restaurant around the corner.

The elevated East Side Highway forms a suitably grimy gateway to the **Fulton Fish Market**, a rough building that wears its eighty years as the city's wholesale outlet with no pretensions. If you can manage it, the time to be here is around 5am (organized tours run each first and third Thursday; $10, reservations needed—☎669-9416) when buyers' trucks park beneath the highway to collect the catches, the air reeks of salt and seaweed, and there's lots of slimy things to step in. But it's invigorating stuff, a twilight world that probably won't be around that much longer—the adjacent **Pier 17 Pavilion**, a hypercomplex of restaurants and shops, could be one nail in its coffin. Next door, around piers 15 and 16, is the **South Street Museum** (daily 10am–5pm; $6 admission includes all tours, films, and visits), a collection of nimble sailing ships and chubby ferries slowly being refitted to former glories. In the summer, the schooner *Pioneer* will coast you around the harbor for an additional consideration, though unless sailing is your passion I'd skip the ships; better to freeload at the outdoor **jazz concerts** on Friday and Saturday evenings (8pm throughout July and August).

The Brooklyn Bridge

From just about anywhere in the seaport you can see one of New York's most celebrated delights, the **Brooklyn Bridge**. This is now just one of several spans across the East River—and the Gothic slabs of the bridge's gateways are dwarfed by lower Manhattan's skyscrapers. But in its day the Brooklyn Bridge was a technological quantum leap: it towered over the low brick structures around and for twenty years was the world's largest suspension bridge, the first to use steel cables, and for many more the longest single span. To New Yorkers it was an object of awe, the massively concrete symbol of the Great American Dream: "All modern New York, heroic New York, started with the Brooklyn Bridge," wrote Kenneth Clark, and indeed its meeting of art and function, of romantic Gothic and daring practicality, became a sort of spiritual model for the next generation's skyscrapers.

It didn't go up without difficulties. John Augustus Roebling, its architect and engineer, crushed his foot taking measurements for the piers and died of gangrene three weeks later; his son Washington took over only to be crippled by the bends from working in an insecure underwater caisson, and subsequently directed the work from his sick bed overlooking the site. Twenty workers died during the construction, and, a week after the opening day in 1883, twelve people were crushed to death in a panicked rush on the bridge's footway. Despite this (and innumerable suicides), New Yorkers still look to the bridge with affection: for the 1983 centennial it was festooned with decorations—"Happy Birthday Brooklyn Bridge" ran the signs—and the city organized a party, replete with shiploads of fireworks.

Whether the bridge has a similar effect on you or not, the view from it is undeniably spectacular. Walk across, near sunset if possible, from City Hall Park and don't look back till you're midway: the Financial District's giants clutter shoulder to shoulder through the spidery latticework, the East River pulses below and cars scream to and from Brooklyn. It's a glimpse of the 1990s metropolis, and on no account to be missed.

The Federal Reserve Bank

Back on the island, Fulton Street arcs right across Lower Manhattan with **Maiden Lane** as its southern parallel, an august and anonymous rollercoaster of finance houses, with **Nassau Street** linking the two in a downbeat precinct of discount goods and fast food. Where Nassau and Maiden Lane meet, Johnson and Burgees' toybox castle of **Federal Reserve Plaza** resounds like a witless joke over the original **Federal Reserve Bank**, whose fortressy walls supplied their post-Modernist idea. The loggia of the plaza isn't all bad though, and it's worth poking your head inside for the **Whitney Museum Downtown**, changing collections of modern American art—for more on which see Chapter Five, "Museums."

There's good reason for the Reserve Bank proper's iron-barred exterior: stashed eighty feet below the street are most of the "free" world's **gold reserves**—11,000 tonnes of them, occasionally shifted from vault to vault as wars break out or international debts are settled. It is possible—but tricky—to tour the piles of gleaming bricks; write to the *Public Information Department*, Federal Reserve Bank, 33 Liberty Street, NY 10045, or phone ☎720-6130 at least a week ahead, as tickets have to be posted. Upstairs, dirty money and counterfeit currency are weeded out of circulation as automated checkers shuffle dollar bills like unending packs of cards. Assistants wheelbarrow loads of cash around ("How much there?" I asked one: "$8½ million," he replied) and, as you'd imagine, the security is just like in the movies.

When you've unboggled your mind of high finance's gold you can see some of its glitter at **One Chase Manhattan Plaza** immediately to the south on Pine Street. Prestigious New York headquarters of the bank, its boxy International-style tower was the first in Lower Manhattan and brought downtown the concept of the plaza, an open forecourt at the entrance. Unfortunately Chase Manhattan's plaza has all the soul and charm of a parking lot, and even Dubuffet's *Four Trees* sculpture can't get things going.

Continue to the end of Cedar Street and you'll find the **Marine Midland Bank** at 140 Broadway, a smaller, more successful tower by the same design team, with a tiptoeing sculpture by Isamu Noguchi. More sculpture worth catching lies behind Chase Manhattan Plaza on **Louise Nevelson Plaza**. Here a clutch of Nevelson's works lie like a mass of shrapnel on an island of land: a striking ploy of sculpture in the urban environment.

Go back down Liberty Street to Church Street, and at **One Liberty Plaza** stands the **US Steel Building**, a threatening black mass all the more offensive since the famed **Singer Building** was demolished to make way for it. Ernest Flagg's 1908 construction was one of the most delicate on the New York skyline, a graceful Renaissance-style tower of metal and glass destroyed in 1968 and replaced with what has justly been called a "gloomy, cadaverous hulk."

The World Trade Center

Wherever you are in Lower Manhattan, two buildings dominate the landscape. Critics say the twin Ronson lighters of the **World Trade Center towers** don't relate to their surroundings and aren't especially pleasing in design—and spirited down to a tenth of their size they certainly wouldn't get a second glance. But the fact is they're *big*, undeniably and frighteningly so, and a walk across the plaza in summer months (closed in winter as icicles falling from the towers can kill) can make your head reel.

Perhaps the idea of so huge a project similarly affected the judgement of the Port Authority of New York and New Jersey, the Center's chief financier, which for several years found itself expensively stuck with two half-empty white elephants—which were quickly surpassed as the world's tallest building by the Sears Tower in Chicago. Now the Trade Center, whose towers are the best part of a five building development, is full and successful, as the bustling concourses and ritzy *Windows on the World* restaurant and, more affordably, the *City Lights* bar can vouch. With courage, a trip to the 107th floor **observation deck** of Two World Trade Center (daily 9:30am–9:30pm; $3.50) gives a mind-blowing view from a height of 1350 feet—over a quarter of a mile. From the open-air rooftop promenade (closed during bad weather) the silent panorama is more dramatic still: everything in New York is below you, including the planes gliding into the airports. Even Jersey City looks exciting. As you timidly edge your way around, ponder the fact that one Philippe Petit once walked a tightrope between the two towers: nerve indeed. Best time to ascend is toward sunset when the tourist crowds thin and Manhattan slowly turns itself into the most spectacular light show this side of the Apocalypse.

Straight across from the World Trade Center on Vesey Street and Broadway, **St. Paul's Chapel** comes from a very different order of things. It's the oldest church in Manhattan, dating from 1766—eighty years earlier than Trinity Church and almost prehistoric by New York standards. The church's architect was from London—St. Martin-in-the-Fields was his model—though his building seems quite American in feel, an unfussy eighteenth-century space of soap bar blues and pinks. George Washington worshiped here and his pew, zealously treasured, is much on show.

Battery Park City

The hole dug for the towers' foundations threw up a million cubic yards of earth and rock which were dumped into the Hudson to form the 23-acre base of **Battery Park City**. This, more than anything else, will change the character of the Financial District, with more office buildings and luxury apartments designed to turn the area into a place where the fortunate few can live as well as work. Originally, ten percent of the housing was to be set aside for low-income groups, but with the recession of the 1970s that plan was scrapped: now the city has promised to invest just under half of the $1 billion it will receive in profits back into housing schemes for the poor.

Architecturally, though, the Park is one of the better events of recent years: traditional themes are picked up throughout, and the whole scheme has a loose conformity that echoes much of the rest of Manhattan. Even before completion it was being lauded as the new Rockefeller Center. Using Rector Park as a starting-point, wandering through the gloomy Wintergarden (which often hosts lunch hour concerts in its huge indoor arboretum) and Dow Jones lobby, and provides a more sober view. A little piece of suburbia tacked onto the edge of the island and seemingly out of place with the rest of the city, Battery Park City has few shops, even fewer restaurants, and no traffic (one of its main selling points), and seems lost in some 1980s vision of a futuristic urban dream.

BARS *Jeremy's Alehouse.*
RESTAURANTS Budget *Harry's at Hanover Square, South Street Seaport Market, Wolf's Deli;* **Expense account** *Windows on the World.*

City Hall Park and the Civic Center

Broadway and Park Row form the apex of **CITY HALL PARK**, a noisy, pigeon-splattered triangle of green with the **Woolworth Building** as a venerable and much venerated onlooker. Some think this is New York's definitive skyscraper, and it's hard to disagree—money, ornament, and prestige mingle in Cass Gilbert's 1913 "Cathedral of Commerce," whose soaring, graceful lines are fringed with Gothic decoration more for fun than any portentous allusion: if the Trade Center towers railroad you into wonder by sheer size, then the Woolworth charms with good nature, and the famous lobby is one of the musts of the city. Frank Woolworth made his fortune from his "five and dime" stores—everything cost either 5¢ or 10¢, strictly no credit. True to his philosophy he paid cash for his skyscraper, and the whimsical reliefs at each corner of the lobby show him doing just that, counting out the money in nickels and dimes. Facing him in caricature are the architect (medievally clutching a model of his building), renting agent, and builder. Within, vaulted ceilings ooze honey-gold mosaics and even the mailboxes are magnificent. The whole building has a well-humored panache more or less extinct in today's architecture—have a look at the Citibank next door to see what recent years have come up with.

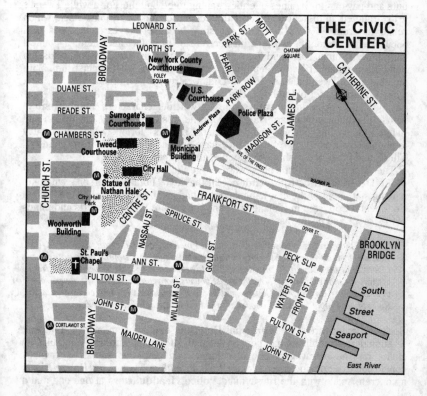

The Civic Center

At the top of the park, marking the beginning of the **CIVIC CENTER** and its incoherent jumble of municipal offices and courts, stands **City Hall** (Mon–Fri 10am–4pm). Finished in 1812 to a good-looking design that's a marriage of French Chateau and American Georgian, its first sorry moment of fame came in 1865 when Abraham Lincoln's body lay in state for 120,000 New Yorkers to file past. Later, after the city's 1927 feting of the returned aviator Charles Lindbergh, it became the traditional finishing point for Broadway tickertape parades given for triumphant baseball stars, astronauts, and, more recently, returned Iranian hostages. Inside it's an elegant meeting of arrogance and authority, with the sweeping spiral staircase delivering you to the precise geometry of the **Governor's Room** and the self-important rooms that formerly contained the **Board of Estimates Chamber**.

If City Hall is the acceptable face of municipal bureaucracy, the **Tweed Courthouse** behind is a reminder of a seamier underbelly of corruption. William Marcy "Boss" Tweed worked his way from nowhere to become chairman of the Democratic Central Committee at Tammany Hall in 1856, and by a series of adroit and illegal moves manipulated the city's revenues through his own and his supporters' pockets. He consolidated his position by registering thousands of immigrants as Democrats in return for a low-level welfare system, and by handouts and pay-offs to the lines of critics waiting to be bought. For a while Tweed's grip strangled all dissent (even over the budget for the Courthouse itself, which rolled up from $3 to $12 million, possibly because one carpenter was paid $360,747 for a month's work, a plasterer $2,870,464 for nine) until a political cartoonist, Thomas Nast, and the editor of the *New York Times* (who'd refused a half-million dollar bribe to keep quiet) turned public opinion against him. With suitable irony Tweed died in 1878 in Ludlow Street jail—a prison he'd had built when Commissioner of Public Works.

City Hall Park is dotted with statues of worthier characters, number one in whose pantheon is **Nathan Hale**. In 1776 he was captured by the British and hanged for spying, but not before he'd spat out his gloriously and memorably famous last words: "I regret that I only have but one life to lose for my country." These, and his over-swashbuckled statue, are his epitaph.

The same year and same place saw George Washington order the first reading of the **Declaration of Independence** in the city. Thomas Jefferson's eloquent, stirring statement of the new nation's rights had just been adopted by the Second Continental Congress in Philadelphia, and it no doubt fired the hearts and minds of the troops and people assembled.

> *We hold these truths to be self-evident, that all men are created equal, that they are endowed by their creator with certain unalienable rights, that among these are Life, Liberty and the pursuit of Happiness; that to secure these rights Governments are instituted among Men, deriving their just powers from the consent of the governed; that whenever any form of Government becomes destructive of these ends, it is the Right of the People to alter or abolish it, and to institute new Government . . ..*

Back on Center Street the **Municipal Building** stands like an oversized bureau, its shoulders straddling Chambers Street in an attempt to embrace or engulf City Hall. Atop, an extravagant pile of columns and pinnacles signals a frivolous conclusion to a no-nonsense building. Walk through and you reach **Police Plaza**, a concrete space with the russet-hued **Police Headquarters** at one end and a rusty-colored sculpture at its center. One side of the plaza runs down past the anachronistic neo-Georgian church of St. Andrews to the glum-gray **Foley Square** where, with some pomp, reside the United States and New York County **Courthouses**, grand though underwhelming buildings after what has preceded. The County Court is the more interesting and accessible (Mon–Fri 9am–5pm), its rotunda decorated with storybook WPA *murals* illustrating the history of justice. If there's time take a look, too, at the Art Deco **Criminal Courts Building** (known as "The Tombs" from a funereal Egyptian-style building that once stood on this site) on Center Street and the unapologetically modern **Family Court** across the way; but by and large civic dignity begins to fade north of here, as ramshackle electrical shops mark the edge of **Chinatown**.

Chinatown and Little Italy

With close on 100,000 residents (about half of New York's Chinese population), seven Chinese newspapers, around 150 restaurants, and over 300 garment factories, **CHINATOWN** is unique in that it's Manhattan's only truly thriving ethnic neighborhood, over recent years pushing its boundaries north across Canal Street into Little Italy, and sprawling east as far as the nether fringes of the Lower East Side.

On the face of things Chinatown is prosperous—a "model slum," some have called it—with the lowest crime rate, highest employment, and least juvenile delinquency of any city district. Walk through its crowded streets at any time of day, and every shop is doing a brisk and businesslike trade: restaurant after restaurant booming, displays of shiny squid, clawing crabs, and clambering bucketfuls of lobster, and all manner of exotic green vegetables, give this part of the city the feel of a land of plenty. The reason why lies with the Chinese themselves, who, even here, in the very core of downtown Manhattan, have been careful to preserve their own way of dealing with things, keeping affairs close to the bond of the family and allowing few intrusions into what is a still-insular culture. The one time of the year when Chinatown bursts onto the New York scene is during the Chinese New Year **festival** in January or February (see Chapter Six), when a giant dragon runs down Mott Street to the accompaniment of fire crackers, and the gutters run with ceremonial dyes.

The Chinese began to arrive in the mid-nineteenth century, following in the wake of a trickle of Irish and Italians. Most had previously worked out West, building railroads and digging gold mines, and few intended to stay: their idea was simply to make a nest-egg and retire to a life of leisure with their families (99 percent were men) back in China. Some, a few hundred perhaps, did go back, but on the whole the big money took rather longer to accumulate than expected, and so Chinatown as a permanent settlement began. Which is not to say that they were welcomed by the authorities. The Mafia-style Tong Wars, toward the end of the nineteenth century, made the quarter's violence notorious, and in 1882 the government passed an act forbidding entry for ten years to any further Chinese workers.

After the 1965 Immigration Act did away with the 1924 "National Origins" provision, a large number of new immigrants started arriving, many of whom were women. Within a few years the massive male majority had been displaced. At this time, Chinatown businessmen started to take advantage of the declining midtown

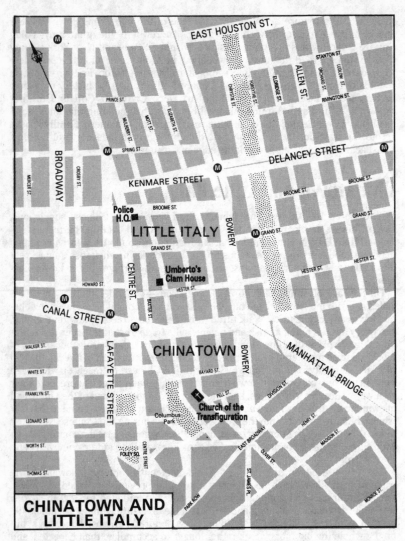

CHINATOWN AND LITTLE ITALY

garment business and made use of a new, large, and unskilled female workforce: they opened extensive garment factories and paid below minimum wages, which in turn enforced long hours. At the same time, many small restaurants opened up, spurred in part by the early 1970s western interest in Chinese food. Many of the working women had no time to cook, and frequented these restaurants to take food home for their families—hence the growth (and cheapness) of the restaurants. With the interest of the Wall Street crowd came fancier restaurants, more money, and greater investment in the area, which soon attracted more Asian money from overseas. Soon, Chinatown had an internal economy unlike any other new immigrant neighborhood in New York. Recently the community has swollen once again, with immigrants from Hong Kong anticipating the colony's uncertain future as it passes into the hands of the Chinese in 1997.

Today, beneath the neighborhood's blithely prosperous facade, sharp practices apparently continue to flourish, with traditional extortion, protection rackets, and non-union sweatshops. But the community is so concerned with being cloistered that you'd need long residence to detect any hint of it. And any kind of unpleasantness is certainly not directed toward the customer or tourist.

All of which is in any case academic, at least for most New Yorkers, who come to Chinatown not to get the lowdown on the Chinese but to eat. Nowhere in this city can you eat so well, and so much, for so little. **Mott Street** is the area's main thoroughfare and along with the streets around—Canal, Pell, Bayard, Doyers, and Bowery—hosts a positive glut of restaurants, tea and rice shops, and grocers. The different groups (all with different dialects) each tend to cluster in various sections of Chinatown: Fukienese on Division Street, Burmese Chinese on Henry Street, Chinese from Taiwan on Center Street, and the Vietnamese on East Broadway. The food is dotted all over; Cantonese cuisine predominates, but there are also many restaurants that specialize in the spicier Szechuan and Hunan cuisines, along with Fukien, Soochow, and the spicy Chowchou dishes. Anywhere you care to walk into is likely to be good, but if you're looking for specific recommendations (especially for lunchtime *Dim Sum*), some of the best are detailed in Chapter Eight, "Drinking and Eating."

The lure of Chinatown lies largely in this—eating and wandering among the exotica of the food and goods shops, and absorbing the neighborhood's vigorous streetlife—though there are a few interesting routes if you want to set structure to your explorations. Mott Street, again, is the obvious starting point, and you may want to detour from here to Mulberry Street, which runs parallel, and its flanking **Columbus Park**. Back on Mott there's the **Chinatown Museum** (see Chapter Five, "Museums and Galleries") at the far end, on the site of the district's first Chinese shop. Farther up, a rare building predates the Chinese intake, the early nineteenth-century **Church of the Transfiguration**; right from here the corner of Pell and Doyers streets was once known as "Bloody Angle" for its miserable reputation as dumping ground for dead bodies during the Tong Wars. Though rather less sinister now, it's still no place to linger—and really, once you've made this circuit (or at least a rough approximation of it), you've seen more or less all there is of Chinatown's nucleus. Moving on, stroll over the **Bowery** and wander the streets leading down to the projects that flank the East River, most of which are nowadays indigenous Chinese and where you'll encounter rather more local than tourist traffic. Then double back by way of East Broadway or Henry Street to where the **Manhattan Bridge**, its grand Beaux Arts entrance slightly ridiculous these days, mounts its assault on the East River. From here you could head north up Chrystie Street, which forms the nominal border between Chinatown and the Lower East Side, or west down Canal Street, back into the turmoil of Chinatown and the area known as Little Italy, long regarded as the hub of the city's considerable Italian community.

Little Italy

While many New Yorkers refuse to admit it, and many guidebooks continue to witter on about little old signoras and elderly men sitting on street corners sipping espresso, **LITTLE ITALY** is light years away from the solid ethnic enclave of old. It is also a lot smaller than it was, and the area settled by New York's huge nineteenth-century influx of Italian immigrants—who (like their Jewish and Chinese counterparts) cut themselves off clannishly to recreate the Old Country—is encroached upon a little more each year by Chinatown. Few Italians still live here and the restaurants (of which there are plenty) tend to have valet-parking and high prices. In fact, it is this quantity of restaurants, more than anything else, that gives Little Italy away: go to the city's true Italian areas, Belmont in the Bronx, or Carroll Gardens in Brooklyn, and you'll find very few genuine Italian eateries, since Italians prefer to consume their native food at home. It's significant, too, that when Martin Scorsese came to make *Mean Streets*—though the film was about Little Italy—it was in Belmont that he decided to shoot it.

But that's not to advise missing out on Little Italy altogether though. Some original delis and bakeries do survive, and there are still plenty of places to indulge yourself with a cappuccino and pricey pastry, not least *Ferrara's* on Grand Street, the oldest and most popular, with a vibrant street-life in summer. If you're here in September the **Festa di San Gennaro** is a wild, tacky, and typically Italian splurge to celebrate the saint's day, when Italians from all over the city turn up and **Mulberry Street**, Little Italy's main strip, is transformed by street stalls and numerous Italian fast-snack outlets. Of the **restaurants**, *Umberto's Clam House** on Mulberry Street remains most famed, not for the food but for the fact that it was the scene of a vicious gangland murder in 1972, when Joe "Crazy Joey" Gallo was shot dead while celebrating his birthday with his wife and daughter. Gallo, a big noise keen to protect his business interests in Brooklyn and as provenly ruthless as the rest of them, was alleged to have offended a rival family and so paid the price: the bullet holes from the slaying are still visible in the windows.

The mafia connection is still strong on these little streets—at least if you believe the papers it is. *SPQR* on Mulberry Street is the favored dining establishment of reputed mob boss **John Gotti**, the "Dapper Don" as he is known because of his penchant for fine suits. Gotti, a resident of Ozone Park, Queens, and scourge of the New York State Judicial System (he has been tried and acquitted three times for organized crime charges) is said to head the Gambino crime family, which along with the Gigante family, is reported to rule all mafia business in the city. New Yorkers have a love affair with the mob, and Gotti remains a firm crowd pleaser. On July 4 each year, he throws a massive Independence Day party in his Queens neighborhood openly flaunting a ban on unauthorized firework displays. Needless to say, no one has ever stopped him.

Slightly west of here, at the corner of Center and Broome streets and in striking counterpoint to the clandestine lawlessness of the Italian underworld, the old **Police Headquarters** rears grandiosely out of the gloom, a palatial neo-Classical confection meant to cow would-be criminals into obedience with a sky-scraping dome and lavish ornamentation. The police headquarters long since moved to a bland modern building in Civic Center, and the overbearing palace has been converted into upmarket condominiums—a sure sign of the times. Walk beyond Broadway and you're already in **SoHo**, like Chinatown a booming district bursting its borders from the farther side of Broadway.

---

*For full listings on *Umberto's* and the cheapest of Little Italy's other restaurants, see Chapter Eight.

CAFÉS AND TEA ROOMS *Café Roma, Ferrara.*
RESTAURANTS Chinese and Thai *Hee Sung Fung, Mon Bo, New Lin Heong, Nice Restaurant Nom-Wah, Phoenix Garden, Pongsri, Say Eng Look, Silver Palace, Sun Say Gay, Vegetarian Paradise, Wo Hop, Wonton Garden;* **Fish** *Umberto's Clam House;* **Italian** *Il Fornaio, Grotto Azzurra, La Luna, La Mela, Puglia.*

SoHo and TriBeCa

Since the mid-1960s, **SOHO**, the grid of streets that runs *So*uth of *Ho*uston Street, has meant art. Squashed between the Financial District and, farther north, Greenwich Village, it had long been a raggy no-man's land of manufacturers and wholesalers, but as the Village declined in hipness, SoHo was suddenly "in." Its loft spaces were ideal for cheap-rental studios, and galleries quickly attracted the city's art crowd, while boutique and restaurant hangers-on converted the ground floors. Like the Village, gentrification quickly followed—most of the artists left, the galleries stayed—and what remains is a mix of chi-chi antique, art and clothes shops, earthy industry, and high living. Today a loft in SoHo means money (and lots of it), but no amount of gloss can cover up SoHo's quintessential appearance, its dark alleys of paint-peeled factories fronted by some of the best cast iron facades in America, and indeed, the world.

Houston Street (pronounced *How*ston rather than *Hew*ston) marks the top of SoHo's trellis of streets, any exploration of which necessarily means criss-crossing and doubling back. **Greene Street** is as good a place to start as any, highlighted all along by the cast iron facades that, in part if not in whole, saved SoHo from the bulldozers. Their origins are nineteenth century, a time when the quarter fringed New York's liveliest street, Broadway marking a fashionable run of hotels, shops, and theaters, and the streets to the west a seamier backdrop of industrial and red light areas cheerfully known as "Hell's Hundred Acres."

The technique of **cast iron architecture** was utilized simply as a way of assembling buildings quickly and cheaply, with iron beams rather than heavy walls carrying the weight of the floors. The result was the removal of load bearing walls, greater space for windows, and, most noticeably, remarkably decorative facades. Almost any style or whim could be cast in iron and pinned to a building, and architects indulged themselves in Baroque balustrades, forests of Renaissance columns, and all the effusion of the French Second Empire to glorify SoHo's sweatshops. Have a look at **72–76 Greene Street**, a neat extravagance whose Corinthian portico stretches the whole five stories, all in painted metal, and at the strongly composed elaborations of its sister building at no. **28–30**. These are the best, but from Broome to Canal Street most of the fronts on Greene Street's west side are either real (or mock) cast iron. Ironically, what began as an engineering trait turned into a purely decorative one as stone copies of cast iron (you'd need a magnet to tell the real from the replicas) came into fashion. At the north east corner of Broome Street and Broadway the magnificent **Haughwout Building** is perhaps the ultimate in the cast iron genre. Rhythmically repeated motifs of colonnaded arches are framed behind taller columns in a thin sliver of a Venetian palace—and it's the first building ever to boast a steam-powered Otis elevator. In 1904 Ernest Flagg took the possibilities of cast iron to their conclusion in his **"Little Singer" Building** at 561 Broadway (at Prince Street), a design whose use of wide window frames points the way to the glass curtain wall of the 1950s.

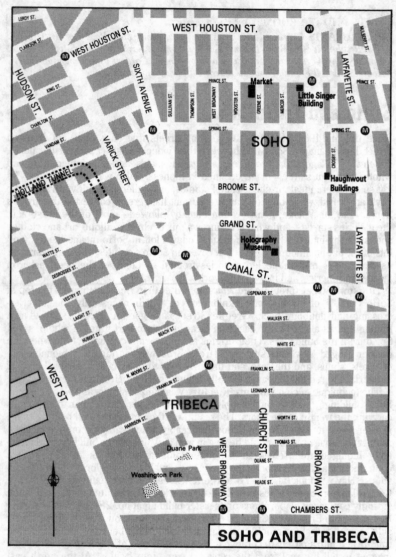

SOHO AND TRIBECA

SoHo celebrates all this architecture in Richard Haas's smirky **mural** at 114 Prince Street (corner of Greene Street), also the venue of one of SoHo's afforda- ble **markets** (there's another at the meeting of Spring and Wooster Street). Many, probably most, of the clothes and antique shops around are beyond reasonable budgets, though the junkier bric-a-brac places may provide a bargain—search around Wooster and Thompson streets, and see Chapter Seven, "Shopping" for details.

What you'll find in the innumerable **galleries** is similarly overpriced but makes for fascinating browsing, with just about every variety of contemporary artistic expression on view. No one minds you looking in for a while, and doing this is also a sure way of bumping into the more visible eccentrics of the area. Most of the galleries are concentrated on **West Broadway**, in a patch that likes to think of itself as an alternative Madison Avenue (though certainly not a lower-priced one any longer). They're generally open from Labor Day to Memorial Day Tuesday–Saturday 10/11am–6pm, Saturdays being most lively; for listings of galleries (and details of gallery tours) see Chapter Five, "Museums and Galleries" and pick up a copy of the *Art Now Guide* from (almost) any gallery. For a view of recent art outside the confines of SoHo, drop in on the **New Museum of Contemporary Art** at 583 Broadway between Prince and Houston streets (again, see Chapter Five).

Loosely speaking, SoHo's diversions get sleazier as you drop south. The revamped **Holography Museum** (see Chapter Five) at 11 Mercer is the last stop before SoHo hits **Canal Street** which links the Holland Tunnel with the Manhattan Bridge and forms a main thoroughfare between New Jersey and Brooklyn. This is SoHo's open bazaar, brash shop fronts loaded with fake Cartiers, dismembered torsos of electrical gear, books, cameras, records, and recently a budding pornographic video business that's been inherited from the sanitized Times Square district. Most people come here for the clothes places like the *Canal Jean Co.* at 504 Broadway between Spring and Broome streets and a host of others—but the army surplus and discarded technology stores crave most attention. Like the signs say it's all "as seen"—mainly trash, but good afford-able fun. As TriBeCa to the south skips up the social ladder it's reckoned that Canal Street will be "cleaned up"; which will be a pity.

TriBeCa

TRIBECA, the *Tri*angle *Be*low *Ca*nal Street, has caught the fall-out of SoHo artists, and retains a lived-in, worked-in feel. Less a triangle than a crumpled rectangle—the area bounded by Canal and Chambers streets, Broadway, and the Hudson—it takes in spacious industrial buildings whose upper layers sprout plants and cats behind tidy glazing, the apartments of TriBeCa's new gentry. Like "SoHo" the name TriBeCa was a 1960s invention to label the newly found scramble of warehouses that became such popular residential quarters. Bought while still abandoned, these apartments and lofts still resemble the former sweatshops they replaced, with clothes-hanging rails still running through the rooms; today they're approaching SoHo in status and price, and it's only a matter of time before TriBeCa becomes just another piece of juicy real estate.

Best place to get a feel of TriBeCa's old and new is **Duane Park** between Hudson and Greenwich streets, a tiny wedge of green trapped by old depots of egg and cheese distributors and new smart residential apartments, with the World Trade Center, Woolworth, and Municipal buildings peering over their shoulders. A block or two away, with less character but more space, there is also **Washington Park**, one of the few downtown patches you can stretch out in unin-timidated, looking up to views of the Trade Center and Woolworth Building.

At night TriBeCa seems completely deserted, save for the sound of footsteps echoing off the cobblestone streets and against the cast iron buildings for which the area is famous. TriBeCa used to shut when the Wall Street crowd went home, but the growth of Battery Park City has brought some chic restaurants into the neighborhood, while some of the traditional after-work bars now stay open much later. One notable newcomer at 375 Greenwich is the **TriBeCa Film Center**, a film production company owned among others by Robert De Niro, and accompanied by his ground-floor restaurant, the *TriBeCa Grill*, whose clientele often includes well-known names and faces from the film world.

BARS *La Jumelle, Luck Strike, Manhattan Brewery Company, Puffy's, Sporting Club.*
RESTAURANTS Budget *Brother's Bar B-Q, Ear Inn, Elephant and Castle, Prince Street Bar*; **American and Mexican** *Cinco de Mayo, Cupping Room Café, El Teddy's, SoHo Kitchen and Bar, Tennessee Mountain, TriBeCa Grill*; **Chinese and Thai** *Thai House Café*; **French** *Montrachet, Odeon*; **Indian and Middle Eastern** *Abyssinia*; **Italian** *Mezzogiorno*; **Vegetarian** *Spring Street Natural Restaurant.*

Greenwich Village

If you're a New Yorker, it's fashionable to dismiss **GREENWICH VILLAGE** (or "the Village" as it's most widely known). There's so much more happening in SoHo, people say; the East Village is *sooo* much more funky and real; TriBeCa will soon be where it's at; or farther uptown there's the Upper West Side . . .. And it's true that while the Bohemian image of Greenwich Village endures well enough if you don't actually live in New York, it's a tag that has long since ceased to hold genuine currency. The only writers that can afford to live here nowadays are copywriters, the only actors those that are starring regularly on Broadway, and as for politics—the average Village resident long since dismissed them for the more serious pursuit of making money. Greenwich Village is firmly for those who have Arrived. Not that the Village is no longer exciting: to a great extent the neighborhood still sports the attractions that brought people here in the first place. It's quiet, residential, but with a busy street life that lasts later than any other part of the city; there are more restaurants per head than anywhere else, and bars, while never cheap, clutter every corner. If interesting people no longer live in the Village, they do hang out here—Washington Square is a hub of aimless activity throughout the year—and as long as you have no illusions about the "alternativeness" of the place there are few better initiations into the city's life, especially at night.

Greenwich Village grew up as a rural retreat from the early and frenetic nucleus of New York City, first becoming sought after during the yellow fever epidemic of 1822 as a refuge from the infected downtown streets. When the fever was at its height the idea was mooted of moving the entire city center here. It was spared that dubious fate, and left to grow into a wealthy residential neighborhood that sprouted elegant Federal and Greek Revival terraces and lured some of the city's highest society names. Later, once the rich had moved uptown and built themselves a palace or two on Fifth Avenue, these large houses were to prove a fertile hunting ground for struggling artists and intellectuals on the lookout for cheap rents, and by the turn of the century Greenwich Village was well on its way to becoming New York's Left Bank. Of early Village characters, one Mabel Dodge was perhaps most influential. Wealthy and radical, she threw parties for the literary and political cognoscenti—parties to which everyone hoped, sooner or later, to be invited. Just about all of the well-known names who lived here during the first two decades of the century spent some time at her house on Fifth

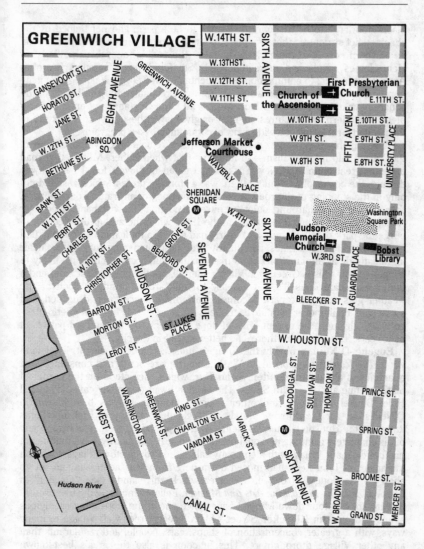

GREENWICH VILLAGE

Avenue, a little north of Washington Square. Emma Goldman discussed anarchism with Margaret Sanger, Conrad Aiken and T. S. Eliot dropped in from time to time, and John Reed—who went on to write *Ten Days That Shook the World*, the official record of the Russian Revolution—was a frequent guest.

Washington Square and Around

Best way to see the Village is to walk, and much the best place to start is its natural center, **Washington Square**, commemorated in a novel title by Henry James and haunted by most of the Village's illustrious past names. It is not an elegant-looking place—too large to be a square, too small to be a park, and not helped by the shacky toilet structures that group around its concreted center. But it does retain its northern edging of redbrick rowhouses—the "solid, honorable dwellings" of Henry James' novel—and, more imposingly, Stanford White's famous **Triumphal Arch**, built in 1892 to commemorate the centenary of George Washington's inauguration as President. James wouldn't, however, recognize the south side of the square now: only the fussy **Judson Memorial Church** stands out amid a messy blend of modern architectures, its interior given over these days to a mixture of theater and local focus for a wide array of community-based programs.

Most importantly, though, Washington Square remains the symbolic heart of the Village and its radicalism—so much so that when Robert Moses, that road paver of great chunks of New York City, wanted to plow a four-lane highway through the center of the square there was a storm of protest which resulted not only in the stopping of the road but also the banning of all traffic from the park, then used as a turnaround point by buses. And that's how it has stayed ever since, notwithstanding some battles in the 1960s when the authorities decided to purge the park of folk singers and nearly had a riot on their hands. You may find it a little threatening at times, particularly after dark when gangs of youths cluster intimidatingly at the junctions of its many paths. But, frankly, nothing's likely to happen to you (this is Greenwich Village after all, not the Lower East Side) and if things look hazardous it's just as easy to walk around. And, as soon as the weather gets warm, the park becomes sports field, dance floor, drug den, and social club, boiling over with life as frisbees fly, skateboards flip, and ghetto blasters crash through the urgent cries of dope peddlers and the studied patrols of police cars. Times like this there's no better square in the city.

Eugene O'Neill, probably the Village's most acclaimed resident, lived (and wrote *The Iceman Cometh*) at 38 Washington Square South and consumed vast quantities of ale at **The Golden Swan Bar**, which once stood on the corner of Sixth Avenue and West 4th Street. The Golden Swan (variously called The Hell Hole, Bucket of Blood, and other enticing nicknames) was best known in O'Neill's day for the dubious morals of its clientele, a gang of Irish hoodlums known as the Hudson Dusters. O'Neill was great pals with this lot and drew many of his characters from the personalities in this bar. It was nearby, also, that he got his first dramatic break, with a company called the Provincetown Players who on the advice of John Reed had moved down here from Massachusetts and set up shop on Macdougal Street, in a theater which still stands (see "Theater" in Chapter Ten, *The Performing Arts and Movies*). Follow **Macdougal Street** south, pausing for a detour down Minetta Lane (once one of the city's most prodigious slums) and you hit **Bleecker Street**—Main Street, Greenwich Village in many ways, with a greater concentration of shops, bars, people, and restaurants than any other Village thoroughfare. This junction is also the area's best-known meeting place, a vibrant corner with mock-European sidewalk cafés that have been literary hangouts since the beginning of this century. The **Café Figaro**, made famous by the Beat writers in the 1950s, is always thronged throughout the day: far from cheap though still worth the price of a cappuccino to people-watch for an hour or so. Afterward, you can follow Bleecker Street one of two ways—**east** toward the solid towers of Washington Square Village, built with typical disregard for history by NYU in 1958, or **west** right through the hubbub of Greenwich Village life.

West of Sixth Avenue

Sixth Avenue itself is mainly tawdry shops and plastic eating houses, but just the other side, across Father Demo Square and up Bleecker Street (until the 1970s an Italian open marketplace on this stretch, and still lined by a few Italian stores) are some of the Village's prettiest residential streets. Turn left on **Leroy Street** and cross over Seventh Avenue, where, confusingly, Leroy Street becomes St. Luke's Place for a block. The houses here, dating from the 1850s, are among the city's most graceful, one of them (recognizable by the two lamps of honor at the bottom of the steps) the ex-residence of **Jimmy Walker**, mayor of New York in the twenties. Walker was for a time the most popular of mayors, a big-spending, wise-cracking man who gave up his work as a songwriter for the world of politics, and lived an extravagant lifestyle that rarely kept him out of the gossip columns. Nothing if not shrewd, at a time when America had never been so prosperous, he for a time reflected people's most glamorous, big-living aspirations. He was, however, no match for the hard times to come, and once the 1930s Depression had taken hold he lost touch and—with it—office.

South of Leroy Street, the Village fades slowly into the warehouse districts of SoHo and TriBeCa, a bleak area where nothing much stirs outside working hours, and the buildings are an odd mixture of Federal terraces juxtaposed against grubby-gray rolldown entranced packing houses. There's a neatly preserved **row** from the 1820s on Charlton Street; the area just to its north, **Richmond Hill**, was George Washington's headquarters during the Revolution, later the home of Aaron Burr and John Jacob Astor. But those apart, you may just as well continue on up to Morton Street, which curves tranquilly round to Seventh Avenue a block north of St. Luke's Place.

Connecting with Seventh Avenue, **Bedford Street**, with Barrow and Commerce streets nearby, is one of the quietest and most desirable Village addresses. Edna St. Vincent Millay, the young poet and playwright who did much work with the Provincetown Playhouse, lived at no. 75½—said to be the narrowest house in the city, nine feet wide and topped with a tiny gable. Another superlative: the clapboard structure next door claims fame as the oldest house in the Village, built in 1799, but much renovated since and probably worth a considerable fortune now.

Farther up Bedford Street, past the former speakeasy **Chumley's** (see Chapter Seven, "Drinking and Eating"), recognizable only by the metal grille on its door, is **Grove Street**. There, if you've time, peer into one of the neighborhood's most typical and secluded little mews, **Grove Court**. Back on Seventh Avenue look out for **Marie's Crisis Café** (see *Gay bars* in "Drinking and Eating"), now a gay bar but once home to Thomas Paine, English by birth but perhaps *the* most important and radical thinker of the American revolutionary era, and from whose *Crisis Papers* the café takes its name. Paine was significantly involved in the Revolution, though afterward regarded with suspicion by the government, especially after his active support for the French Revolution. By the time of his death here, in 1809, he had been condemned as an atheist and stripped of citizenship of the country he helped found. Grove Street meets Seventh Avenue at one of the Village's busiest junctions, **Sheridan Square**—not in fact a square at all unless you count Christopher Park's slim strip of green, but simply a wide and hazardous meeting (the Mousetrap, some call it) of several busy streets.

Christopher Street

Christopher Street, main artery of the west Village, leads off from here—traditional heartland of the city's gay community. The Square was named after one General Sheridan, cavalry commander in the Civil War, and holds a pompous-looking statue to his memory, but it's better known as scene of one of the worst and bloodiest of New York's Draft Riots, when a marauding mob assembled here in 1863 and attacked members of the black community. It's said that if it hadn't been for the protestations of local people they would have strung them up and worse; as it was they made off after sating the worst of their blood-lust.

Not dissimilar scenes occurred in 1969 when the gay community wasn't quite as established as it is now. The violence on this occasion was down to the police, who raided the **Stonewall gay bar** and started ejecting its occupants—for the local gay community the latest in a long line of petty harassments from the police. Spontaneously they decided to do something about it: word went round the other bars in the area, and before long the Stonewall was surrounded, resulting in a siege which lasted the best part of an hour and ended with several arrests and a number of injured policemen. Though hardly a victory for their rights, it was the first time that gay men had stood up *en masse* to the persecutions of the police, and as such represents a turning point in their struggle, formally inaugurating the Gay Rights movement and remembered still by the annual **Gay Pride march** (held on the last Sunday in June). Nowadays, too, the gay community is much more a part of Greenwich Village life, indeed for most the Village would seem odd without it, and from here down to the Hudson is a tight-knit enclave— focusing on Christopher Street—of bars, restaurants, and bookshops used specifically, but not exclusively, by gay men. The scene on the Hudson itself, along and around West Street and the river piers, is considerably raunchier, and only for the really committed or curious (native New Yorkers, gay ones included, warn against going there at all), but this far east things crack off with the accent less on sex, more on a camp kind of humor. Among the more accessible gay bars, if you're strolling this quarter, are *The Monster* on Sheridan Square itself, *Marie's Crisis* on Grove Street (see above), and *Ty's*, farther west on Christopher Street; for full gay listings, see *Gay bars* in "Drinking and Eating."

North of Washington Square

At the eastern end of Christopher Street is another of those car-buzzing, life-risking Village junctions where Sixth Avenue is met by **Greenwich Avenue**, one of the neighborhood's major shopping streets. Hover for a while at the romantic Gothic bulk of the **Jefferson Market Courthouse**, voted fifth most beautiful building in America in 1885, and built with all the characteristic vigor of the age. It hasn't actually served as a courthouse for 40-odd years now, indeed at one time—like so many buildings in this city—it was branded for demolition. It was saved thanks to the efforts of a few determined Villagers, and now lives out its days as the local library. Walk around behind for a better look, perhaps pondering for a moment on the fact that the adjacent well-tended allotment was, until 1974, the **Women's House of Detention**, a prison known for its abysmal conditions and numbering among its inmates Angela Davis. Look out, also, for **Patchin Place**, a tiny mews whose neat gray terraces are yet another Village literary landmark, home to e e cummings for many years and at various times also to John Masefield, the ubiquitous Dreiser and O'Neill, and John Reed (who wrote *Ten Days that Shook the World* here).

Across the road, **Balducci's** forms a downtown alternative to its uptown deli rival, *Zabar's*, its stomach-tingling smells pricey but hard to resist. Nearby, **Bigelow's Pharmacy**, is possibly the city's oldest pharmacy and apparently little changed; and, south a block and left, **West 8th Street** is an occasionally rewarding strip of brash shoe shops and cut-price clothes stores. Up **West 10th Street** are some of the best preserved early nineteenth-century townhouses in the Village, and one of particular interest at **no. 18**. The facade of this house, which juts anglewise into the street, had to be rebuilt after the terrorist Weathermen had been using the house as a bomb factory and one of their devices exploded. Three of the group were killed in the blast, but two others escaped and remained on the run until just a few years ago.

For anyone not yet sated on architecture, a couple of imposing churches are to be found by following 10th Street down as far as the Fifth Avenue stretch of the Village, where the neighborhood's low-slung residential streets give on to some eminently desirable apartment buildings. On the corner stands the nineteenth-century **Church of the Ascension**, a small, light church built by Richard Upjohn (the Trinity Church architect), later redecorated by Stanford White and currently appealing desperately for funds to complete a much-needed restoration. Inside is a gracefully toned La Farge altarpiece and some fine stained glass but otherwise, unless the refurbishment is over, much of what you'll glimpse will be covered in brickdust and scaffolding. A block away, Joseph Wells' bulky, chocolatey-brown Gothic revival **First Presbyterian Church** is decidedly less attractive than Upjohn's structure, less soaring, heavier, and in every way more sober, with a tower said to have been modeled on the one at Magdalen College at Oxford University. To look inside, you need to enter through the discreetly added Church House (ring the bell for attention if the door's locked). Afterward you're just a few steps away from the pin-neat prettiness of **Washington Mews**.

BARS *Badlands* (gay), *Boots and Saddle* (gay), *Cedar Tavern, Chumley's, Crazy Nanny's* (lesbian), *Fifty Five, Jimmy Day's, Keller's* (gay), *Lion's Head, Marie's Crisis* (gay), *The Monster* (gay), *Pandora's* (lesbian), *Peculiar Pub, Ty's* (gay), *Scrap Bar, Uncle Charlie's* (gay), *White Horse Tavern*.

CAFÉS AND TEA ROOMS *Anglers and Writers, Caffé Dante, Café Le Figaro, Caffé Reggio, Peacock Caffé, Tea and Sympathy*.

RESTAURANTS Budget *Bagel Buffet BBQ, Campus Coffee Shop, Carmella's Village Garden, Corner Bistro, Ed Debevic's, Elephant and Castle, Fuddrucker's, Jimmy Day's, Little Mushroom Café, Riviera Café, Stromboli Pizza, Violet Café*; **American, Mexican, Latin and South American** *Bayamo, Benny Burritos, Caramba, Caribe, Casa Mexico, Cottonwood Café, Cowgirl Hall of Fame, El Coyote, Dave's Pot Belly, Great Jones Café, Gulf Coast, How's Bayou, Joe's Bar and Grill, Lupe's East LA Diner, Mary Anne's, Mesa Grill, Moondance Diner, The Pink Teacup, Royal Canadian Pancake Restaurant, Tortilla Flats*; **Chinese and Thai** *Thai House Café, Toons*; **French, Spanish and Greek** *Au Troquet, Café Español, Chez Brigitte, Delphi, El Faro, Florent, Quatorze, Spain*; **Indian** *Mamun's, Mitali West*; **Italian** *La Boheme, Arturo's Pizza, Cent' Anni, Cucina della Fontana, Cucina Stagionale, John's Pizzeria, Minetta Tavern, Pizzeria Uno, Ray's Pizza*; **Japanese** *Japonica*; **Fish and Seafood** *Jane's Seafood Café*; **Vegetarian** *Arnold's Turtle, Boostan, Eva's, Wholewheat 'n' Wild Berries*.

HOTELS Inexpensive *Riverview, Washington Square*.

The East Village

The **EAST VILLAGE** is quite different in look, feel and tempo to its western counterpart, Greenwich Village. Once, like the Lower East Side proper which it abuts, a refuge of immigrants and always a solidly working-class area, it became home to New York's non-conformist fringe in the earlier part of this century when, disenchanted and impoverished by rising rents and encroaching tourism, they left the city's traditional Bohemia and set up house here. Today the differences persist: where Greenwich Village is the home of Off-Broadway, the East Village plays stage to Off-Off, and rents, while rising fast as the district becomes chic-er and more sanitized, are about a third of what you'll pay farther west.

The East Village has seen its share of famous artists, politicos, and literati: W. H. Auden lived at 77 St. Mark's Place, the neighborhood's main street, and from the same building the Communist Journal *Novy Mir* was run, numbering among its more historic contributors Leon Trotsky, who lived for a brief time in New York. Much later the East Village became the New York haunt of the Beats—Kerouac, Burroughs, Ginsberg, *et al.*, who, when not jumping trains across the rest of the country, would get together at Alan Ginsberg's house on East 7th Street for declamatory poetry readings and drunken shareouts of experience. Later, Andy Warhol debuted the Velvet Underground; the Fillmore East played host to just about every band you've ever heard of—and forgotten about; and, more recently, Richard Hell noisily proclaimed himself the inventor of punk rock. Perhaps inevitably, a lot has changed over the last decade or so. Escalating rents have forced many people out and the East Village isn't the hotbed of dissidence and creativity it once was. But St. Mark's Place is still one of downtown Manhattan's more vibrant strips, even if the thrift shops and panhandlers and political hustlers have given way to a range of ritzy boutiques selling punk chic, and the area remains one of the city's most exciting enclaves.

Around Cooper Square

To explore the East Village best use **St. Mark's Place** as a base and branch out from there. Start at the western, more peopled end, between Second and Third avenues, where radical bookstores compete for space with offbeat clothiers, and, just beyond, young self-proclaimed priests of funky Manhattan chic mill around sucking on pizzas or gazing lazily at the mildewed items for sale at the unofficial flea market across the road on **Cooper Square**, a busy junction formed by the intersection of the Bowery, Third Avenue, and Lafayette Street. This is dominated by the seven-story brownstone mass of the **Cooper Union Building**, erected in 1859 by a wealthy industrialist as a college for the poor, and the first New York structure to be hung on a frame of iron girders. It's best known as the place where, in 1860, Abraham Lincoln wowed an audience of top New Yorkers with his so-called "might makes right" speech, in which he boldly criticized the pro-slavery policies of the southern states and helped propel himself to the White House later that year. For all its history, however, the Cooper Union remains a working college, with a well-respected architecture school, and it has recently and sensitively been restored to nineteenth-century glory with a statue of the benevolent Cooper just in front.

Just beyond, feeding through to Broadway, is **Astor Place**, named after John Jacob Astor and, for a very brief few years, just before high society moved west to

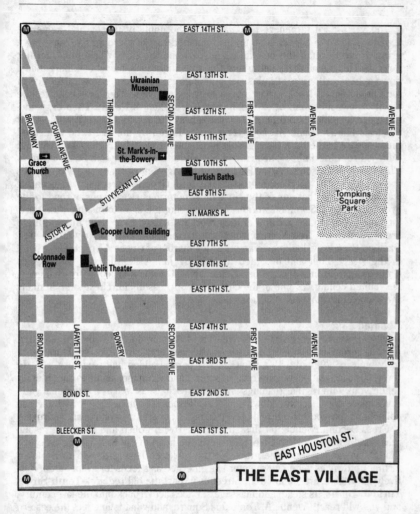

THE EAST VILLAGE

Washington Square, one of the city's most desirable neighborhoods. In the 1830s Lafayette Street in particular was home to the city's wealthiest names, not least John Jacob, one of New York's most hideously greedy tycoons, notorious for having won his enormous fortune by deceiving everybody right up to the President. When old and sick in his house here—no mean affair by all accounts but long since destroyed—it's said that although so weak he could accept no nourishment except a mother's milk, and so fat he had to be tossed up and down in a blanket for exercise, his greed for money was such that he lay and dispatched servants daily to collect his rents. The Astor Place **subway station**, bang in the middle of the junction, discreetly remembers the man on the platforms, its colored reliefs of beavers recalling Astor's first big killings—in the fur trade.

Today it's hard to believe this was once the home of money and influence, though. **Lafayette Street** is an undistinguished sort of thoroughfare, steering a grimy route through the no-man's land between the East Village, and, farther down, SoHo, and all that's left to hint that this might once have been more than a down-at-heel gathering of industrial buildings is **Colonnade Row**, a terrace of four monumental houses, now home to the Colonnade Theater. Opposite, the stocky brownstone and brick building is Joseph Papp's **Public Theater**, something of a legend as forerunner of Off-Broadway theater, and original venue of hit musicals like *Hair* and *A Chorus Line* and still run by the man who pioneered Shakespeare in the Park (see *Theater* in Chapter Ten, "The Performing Arts and Film"). From the Public Theater you can either follow Lafayette Street down to Chinatown, or cut down Astor Place and turn right into Broadway. Two minutes away, the **corner of Washington Place and Greene Street** is significant. It was here in 1911 that one of the city's most notorious sweatshops burned to the ground, killing 125 women workers and spurring the state to institute laws forcing employers to take account of their workers' safety. Even now, though, there are sweatshops in New York in which safety conditions are probably little better. Back on Broadway, look north and the lacy marble of **Grace Church** fills a bend in the street, built and designed in 1846 by James Renwick (of St. Patrick's Cathedral fame) in a delicate neo-Gothic style. Dark and aisled, with a flattened, fan-vaulted ceiling, it's one of the city's most successful churches—and, in many ways, one of its most secretive escapes.

Heading east

Walk east from here cross back over Third Avenue and you come to another, quite different church—**St. Mark's-in-the-Bowery**, a box-like structure originally built in 1799 but with a neo-Classical portico added half a century later. In the 1950s the Beat poets gave readings here, and it remains an important literary rendezvous with regular readings and music recitals, as well as a traditional gathering place for the city's down-and-outs, desperately hanging on to their can collections (passport to a frugal meal that night), or slumped half-dead on drugs.

Cross Second Avenue, on this stretch lined with Polish and Ukranian restaurants, and you're on **10th Street**, formerly the heart of the East Village art scene though nowadays very quiet, most of the galleries having moved to SoHo or farther uptown; as yet no new center has emerged as a focus for avant-garde, relatively affordable, art. Follow 10th Street east, past the old redbrick **Tenth Street Turkish Baths**, its steam and massage services active back into the last century, and you will reach Avenue A, Tompkins Square, and what is in effect the eastern fringe of the East Village.

Tompkins Square Park

Tompkins Square Park isn't one of the city's most inviting spaces but has long acted as a focus for the Lower East Side/East Village community and its reputation as the city's center for political demonstrations and home of radical thought. It was here in 1874 that the police massacred a crowd of workers protesting against unemployment, and here, too, in the 1960s that protests were organized and made themselves heard. The late Yippie leader Abbie Hoffman lived nearby, and residents like him, along with many incidents in the square and down St. Mark's Place (which joins the square on its western side), have given the East Village its maverick name.

Today Tompkins Square Park is the focus of dissent against the gentrification of the East Village and Lower East Side. From the mid-1980s, large chunks of real estate have been bought up, renovated, and turned into condominiums or co-ops for the new professional classes, much to the derision of the old squatters and new activists. Since 1988 the square has more or less been a shantytown for the homeless, known locally as **"Tent City,"** either sleeping on benches or under makeshift shelters on the patches of green between the paths. In the winter, only the really hardy or really desperate live here, but when the weather gets warmer the numbers swell, as activists, anarchists, and all manner of statement-makers descend upon this former army barracks from around the country, hoping to rekindle the spirit of 1988, the year of the Tompkins Square **riots**, when in August massive demonstrations led to the police—badge numbers covered up and nightsticks drawn—attempting to clear the park of people. In the ensuing battle, many demonstrators were hurt, including a large number of bystanders, and in the investigation that followed the police were heavily criticized for the violence that had occurred. Tent City remained and today is bigger than ever, the park almost useless to the public, though it's quite safe to walk through during the day. If you do, take a look at the small **relief** just inside the brick enclosure on the northern side, which shows a woman and child gazing folornly out to sea. It's a commemoration of a disaster of 1904, when the local community, then mostly made up of German immigrants, was decimated by the sinking of a cruise ship, the *General Slocum*, in Long Island Sound, with the death of around a thousand people.

BARS *The Bar* (gay), *Boy Bar* (gay), *Broome Street Bar, Continental Divide, Dan Lynch's, Downtown Beirut, Grassroots Tavern, Holiday Cocktail Lounge, McSorley's, NoHo Star, Sugar Reef, Temple Bar, The Tunnel Bar* (gay), *Vasac's*.
CAFÉS AND TEA ROOMS *Veniero's*.
RESTAURANTS Budget *Around the Clock, Astor Riviera, Khan's, Kiev, Life Café, 103rd 2nd, Phebe's, Second Avenue Deli*; **American, Latin, and South American** *Two Boots*; **Chinese and Thai** *Indochine*; **Indian and Middle Eastern** *Kyhber Pass, Mitali*; **Italian** *Cucina di Pesce*; **Japanese** *Chiaki, Dojo*; **Jewish, Eastern Europe, and German** *Christine's, Kiev Odessa, Ukrainian Restaurant, Vesalka*; **Fish and Seafood** *Pier Nine;* **Vegetarian** *Anjelica Kitchen, Vegetarian Paradise*.

The Lower East Side

I don't wanna be buried in Puerto Rico
I don't wanna rest in Long Island cemetery
I wanna be near the stabbing shooting
gambling fighting and unnatural dying
and new birth crying
So please when I die . . .
Keep me nearby
Take my ashes and scatter them thru out
the Lower East Side . . .

Miguel Piñero *A Lower East Side Poem*

The **LOWER EAST SIDE** is one of Manhattan's least changed and most unalluring downtown neighborhoods, a little-known quarter which began life toward the end of the last century as an insular slum for over half a million Jewish immigrants.

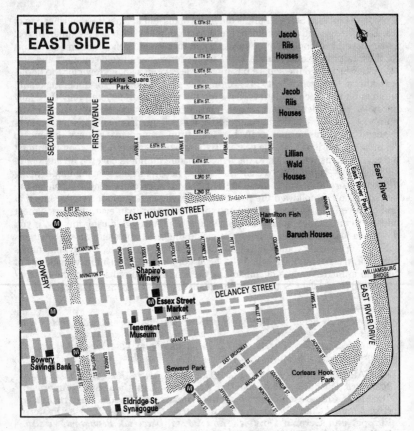

THE LOWER EAST SIDE

They came here from Eastern Europe via Ellis Island, refugees in search of a better life, scratching out a living in a free-for-all of crowded, sweatshop competition. Since then the area has become considerably depopulated, and the slum-dwellers are now largely Puerto Rican rather than Jewish; but otherwise, at least on the surface, little has visibly changed.

The area's lank brick tenements, ribbed with blackened fire escapes and housing rundown bargain basements, must have seemed a bleak kind of destiny for those who arrived here, crammed into a district which daily became more densely populated, and where low standards of hygiene and abysmal housing made disease rife and life expectancy horribly low. It was conditions like these which spurred local residents like Jacob Riis and, later, Stephen Crane, to record the plight of the city's immigrants in their writings and photographs, thereby spawning not only a whole school of realistic writing but also some notable social reforms. Not for nothing—and not without some degree of success—did the Lower East Side become known as a neighborhood where political battles were fought. Today the Lower East Side splits neatly into two distinct parts. **South of East Houston Street** is the most respectable: wholesomely seedy and much of it still firmly Jewish. **North of East Houston** is part cool Bohemia, abutting the East Village, but for the rest predominantly ruined and derelict, its houses either boarded up or serving as slum residences for the local Puerto Rican population.

South of Houston

This is the most explorable part of the Lower East Side—and the more rewarding. In the streets south of Houston, Jewish immigrants indelibly stamped their character, with their own shops, delis, restaurants, synagogues, and, latterly, community centers. Even now, with a broader ethnic mix, it feels uniquely Jewish and a place apart from the rest of Manhattan—geographically isolated, too, set out on the island's heel and served by few subway stations. If outsiders come here at all it's for the **bargain shopping**. You can get just about anything cut-price in the stores down here: clothes on Orchard Street, lamps and shades on the Bowery, ties and shirts on Allen Street, underwear and hosiery on Grand Street, textiles on Eldridge. And, whatever you're buying, people will if necessary still bargain down to the last cent. The time to come is Sunday morning, for the **Orchard Street Market**, when you'll catch the vibrancy of the Lower East Side at its best. Weekdays the stores are still there, and they're open, most of them, but far fewer people come to shop and the streets can have a forbidding, desolate feel, though the **Lower East Side Tenement Museum**, at 97 Orchard Street, is by far the best place to get the lowdown on the neighborhood's immigrant past—and present.

East Broadway used to be the Jewish Lower East Side's hub, though this is now almost exclusively Chinese. For the old feel of the quarter—where the synagogues remain active (many in the north of the area have become churches for the Puerto Ricans)—best explore north of here, starting with **Canal Street. The Eldridge Street Synagogue** is worth a look, in its day one of the neighborhood's grandest, though now the main doors of its formidable facade have been sealed shut and only the basement left for the sporadic get-togethers of a much-dwindled congregation. Carry on up Eldridge Street, though, and there is a little more activity: **Grand Street**, particularly, is lined with shops like the **Kossars Bakery**, at no. 367, whose hot fresh *bialys* are hard to resist.

Grand leads east, through housing projects to the messy **East River Park**—not one of the city's most attractive open spaces. Halfway down is the **Church of St. Mary**, elderly Jewish couples sitting on the benches outside, watching the world go by. The church bills itself as the oldest neo-Gothic building (1832) in the city, a dignified claim somewhat diminished by the sign adjacent, advertising the church's current crowd-puller of weekend bingo sessions.

Essex Street, north from here, leads to **Delancey**, horizontal axis of the Jewish Lower East Side, and to the **Williamsburg Bridge**—adopted as a shelter by New York's homeless, clustered below around oil drums, emerging occasionally to browbeat a motorist into risking their makeshift carwashes. Either side of Delancey sprawls the **Essex Street Covered Market**, worth a quick peep, with *Ratner's Dairy Restaurant*, one of the Lower East Side's most famous dairy restaurants, across the road. Farther up on Essex is the exotic culinary experience of *Bernstein's*, believe it or not, a kosher Chinese eatery. For more on the Lower East Side—and New York—Jewish food see Chapter Seven, "Drinking and Eating."

The atmosphere changes abruptly east of Essex Street. Here the inhabitants are mainly Latino, comprised largely of Puerto Ricans, but with a fair smattering of immigrants from other Latin and South American countries. Most of the Jews got rich long ago and moved into middle-income housing farther uptown or in the other boroughs, and there's little love lost between those that remain and the new inhabitants.

Today, much of the area east of Essex has lost the traditional Sunday bustle of Jewish market shopping and has been replaced by the Saturday afternoon Spanish chatter of the new residents shopping for records, cheap clothes, and loud electrical goods. **Clinton Street**, a mass of cheap Latino retailers, restaurants, and travel agents, is in many ways the central thoroughfare of the Puerto Rican Lower East Side. Otherwise, if you are here on a Sunday, check out the free wine tours and tastings at **Schapiro's Winery** at 124 Rivington Street (daily 11am–4pm, on the hour), the neighborhood's—and probably the city's—only kosher wine and liquor warehouse where wine is made on the premises. Afterward, head over to **Orchard Street**, again best on a Sunday when most of it becomes pedestrianized and filled with stalls selling off designer togs for hefty discounts. The rooms above the stores here used to house sweatshops, clothes factories so called since whatever the weather a stove had to be kept warm all the time for pressing the clothes when completed. The (reformed) garment industry moved uptown ages ago, but the buildings are little more salubrious now, slummy apartments at the end of dank unlit hallways occupied by poor, again mainly Latino, families.

At the top end of Orchard, East Houston Street forms the northern border of this part of the Lower East Side. The area just below East Houston Street has in recent years become a very desirable place to live for those hoping to escape the rising rents of the East Village while keeping in with the Village scene. Bars such as the *Ludlow Street Café* and *Max Fish* both on Ludlow Street, have helped expand the allure of the East Village arts and social scene south of Houston. But, as with all things fashionable in New York, they may well soon have upped and gone elsewhere

Walk east from here and it's for the most part burnt-out tenements interspersed with a scattering of Spanish-style grocery stores; to the west things aren't much better. The **Bowery** spears north out of Chinatown as far as Cooper Square on the edge of the East Village. This wide thoroughfare has gone through many changes over the years: it took its name from "Bouwerie," the Dutch word for farm, when it was the city's main agricultural supplier; later, in the closing decades of the last century, it was flanked by music halls, theaters, hotels, and middle-market restaurants, drawing people from all parts of Manhattan. Currently it's a skid row for the city's drunk and derelict, flanked by a long and demoralizing line of boarded-up shops and SRO hotels near which few New Yorkers venture of their own accord. If you do, it may be intimidating and uneasy, but rarely dangerous—the people who crash down here are mostly long past acts of physical violence. The one—bizarre—focus, certainly a must for any Lower East Side wanderings, is the **Bowery Savings Bank** on the corner of Grand Street. Designed by Stanford White in 1894, it rises out of the neighborhood's debris like a god, much as its sister bank on 42nd Street, a shrine to the virtue of saving money. Inside, the original carved check-writing stands are still in place, and the coffered ceiling, together with White's great gilded fake marble columns, couldn't create a more potent feel of security. An inscription above the door as you exit leaves you in no doubt: "Your financial welfare is the business of this bank." Quite so, but back on the Bowery, stepping over the drunks and avoiding the panhandlers, you can't help pondering what went wrong.

North of Houston

Cross East Houston Street and the Lower East Side takes on another mantle, veering from downbeat (but chic) Tompkins Square and the East Village to, farther east and in marked contrast, what ranks as one of the most serious and unchecked pieces of urban blight in Manhattan. Here the island bulges out beyond the city's grid structure, the extra avenues being named A to D, and the area, by its devotees, **Alphabet City** (*Loisada* to the Puerto Ricans). Until a very few years ago, this was a notoriously unsafe corner of town, run by drug pushers and the hoodlums that controlled them. People told of cars lining up for fixes in the street, and the rows of houses here were well-known safehouses for the brisk heroin trade. All of this was brought to a halt in 1983 with "Operation Pressure Point," a massive police campaign to clean up the area and make it a place where people would want to live. Which has to some extent happened, with crime figures radically down, although appearances remain much the same: the people who live here are poor Puerto Ricans; their houses, what's left of them, bombed-out shells among fields of flattened rubble, next to which gangs of tramps have erected makeshift shelters. Half the houses aren't lived in at all, and many are plastered with graffiti protesting their misuse ("Property of the People of the Lower East Side," some say). Come down here and you'll certainly be hassled, but—during the day at least—you're unlikely to be mugged. And it's worth a quick circuit around this part of the Lower East Side just to see how bad things can get through lack of effective city money or control. Oddly enough it's also the best illustration of the absurdity of the Manhattan housing issue: here there is astounding poverty, filth, even danger. Yet the area is in the process of a huge gentrification, and its apartments, though they may be next to some rat-infested ruin, are going for ever-rocketing rents.

Walking down Avenue A away from the park and down toward Houston street, there are, however, a number of good bars and restaurants, such as *Benny's Burrito* (4th Street and A), *Sophie's* (5th Street and A), and *Joe's* (6th Street between A and B). As you head east from A, the mood is far less relaxed. Avenue C is also known as "Avenue Loisaida" and is far less studenty and youthful than Avenue A and other points west. At Second Street and Avenue B, the **Gas Station** is a bizarre outdoor art gallery of customized junk—spray-painted telephone booths, chairs made out of fire hydrants, all very East Village. Also check out the *Nuyorican Poets' Café*, 236 East Third Street. Farther over, past Avenue D, are the East River housing projects, a good bet if you are a drug dealer but not recommended for the sensible tourist.

BARS *Joe's*, *Sophie's*.

RESTAURANTS **Budget** *Benny's Burrito*, *Bernstein-on-Essex*, *Grand Dairy Restaurant*, *Katz's Deli*, *Ratners*, *Sammy's Roumanian Restaurant*, *Triplet's Roumanian*, *Yonah Schimmel's*.

CHAPTER TWO

MIDTOWN MANHATTAN

You're likely to spend a fair amount of time in **MIDTOWN MANHATTAN**. It's here most of the city's hotels are situated, here, too, that you'll arrive—at Penn or Grand Central Station, or the Port Authority. And the area is in many ways the city's center. Cutting through its heart is **Fifth Avenue**, New York's most glamorous (and most expensive) street, with the theater strip of **Broadway**, an increasingly disreputable neighbor, just to its west.

The character of Midtown Manhattan undergoes a rapid and radical transformation depending on which side of Fifth you find yourself. **East** are the corporate businesses, a skyward wave that creates Manhattan's rollercoaster appearance. If you've any interest in architecture (or simply sensation) you'll want to stroll this sector, looking in and up at such delights as the **Chrysler**, **Citicorp**, and **Seagram buildings** and the magnificent **Rockefeller Center**. **Fifth Avenue** itself, and its fashion-oriented counterpart, **Madison**, should be experienced, too, if only to take measure of how much wealth a large number of Americans have accrued. And of course this is also a major museum strip, with the **Museum of Modern Art** and a host of lesser collections grouped together on **53rd Street** (see Chapter Five, "Museums and Galleries," for accounts of these).

West of Fifth Avenue, and in particular west of Broadway, the area takes a dive—both in status and interest. The **theater districts** are a natural entertainments focus, though these days more than a little sleazy, notwithstanding the fact that **Times Square**, the traditional center of sex shows and petty crime has recently undergone a multi-million dollar cleanup. **The Garment District** has a certain throwback interest as a nineteenth-century foil to the corporate skyscrapers across the way—and a startling nearby landmark in the **Empire State Building**. But the residential districts are frankly dull: **Chelsea** is long established but downbeat; **Clinton**, farther up the West Side, is gentrifying slowly but is still rough down by the West Side Highway; and **Murray Hill**, on the other side of town, has little to offer beyond some semi-elegant brownstones.

Fifth Avenue and East: Union Square to 42nd Street

Downtown Manhattan ends with 14th Street, which slices across the island from the housing projects of the East Side to the cut-price shops and eventually the meat-packing warehouses on the banks of the Hudson River. In the middle, where Broadway, Fourth, and Park avenues meet, is Union Square.

Union Square and north to 42nd Street

UNION SQUARE was once the elegant center of the city's theatrical and shopping scene, but was better known more recently as gathering point for political demonstrations. Up until the mid-1980s this was a seedy haunt of dope pushing and street violence, but it's much more inviting now, the spill of shallow steps enticing you in to stroll the paths, feed the squirrels, and gaze at its array of statuary—something no one would have dared do a few years back. As for the statues, they include an equestrian figure of George Washington, a Lafayette by Bartholdi (more famous for the Statue of Liberty), and, at the center of the park, a massive flagstaff base whose bas-reliefs symbolize the forces of Good and Evil in the Revolution.

The square itself is flanked by some good cafés and quite a mixture of buildings, not least the **American Savings Bank** on the eastern edge, of which only the grandiose columned exterior survives. The pedimented building just south of here is the former Tammany Hall, the once notorious headquarters of the Democratic Party, decorated with a Native American headdress, while the narrow building almost opposite was Andy Warhol's original Factory. The **Consolidated Edison** structure, off the southeast corner, the headquarters of the company responsible for providing the city with energy and those famous steaming manholes, is, with its campanile, an odd premonition of the Metropolitan Life Building a few blocks farther north. Inside, there's a museum devoted to the city's power supplies through the ages—strictly for energy buffs.

The stretch of **Broadway** north of here was known once as "Ladies' Mile" for its fancy stores and boutiques (*Lord and Taylor* started trading here), but notwithstanding a few sculpted facades and curvy lintels, it's now hard to imagine as an upmarket shopping thoroughfare. Turn right on East 20th Street for **Theodore Roosevelt's Birthplace** at number 28 (Wed–Sun 9am–5pm; $1)—or at least a reconstruction of it: a rather grim brownstone mansion that's not terribly exciting, just a few rooms with their original furnishings, some of Teddy's hunting trophies, and a small gallery documenting the President's life, viewable on an obligatory guided tour.

Past here Manhattan's clutter breaks into the ordered open space of **Gramercy Park**, a former swamp reclaimed in 1831. European in spirit, this is one of the city's best squares, its center clean, tidily planted, and, most noticeably, completely empty for much of the day—principally because the only people who can gain access are those rich or fortunate enough to live here. To the east **Peter Cooper Village** and **Stuyvesant Town** are perhaps the city's most successful examples of dense-packed urban housing, their tall, angled apartment blocks siding peaceful tree-lined walkways. It's worth knowing, though, that this is private not public housing, and the owners, Metropolitan Life, were accused of operating a color-bar when the projects first opened. Certainly, the contrast with the immigrant slums a little way downtown isn't hard to detect.

A block over, the land that makes up **Stuyvesant Square** was a gift to the city from its governor and, like Gramercy Park, the green space in the middle was modeled on the squares of London's Bloomsbury. Though partially framed by the buildings of **Beth Israel Medical Center** and cut down the middle by the bustle of Second Avenue, it still retains something of its secluded quality, especially on the western side. Here there's a smatter of elegant terrace, the strangely colonial-

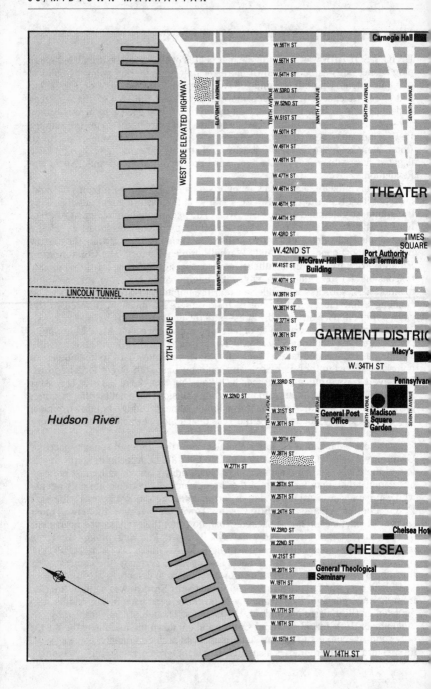

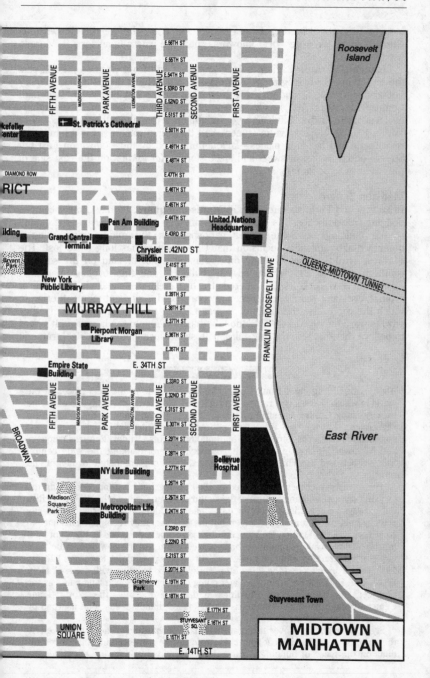

Roosevelt Island

FIFTH AVENUE
MADISON AVENUE
PARK AVENUE
LEXINGTON AVENUE
THIRD AVENUE
SECOND AVENUE
FIRST AVENUE

E.56TH ST
E.55TH ST
E.54TH ST
E.53RD ST
E.52ND ST
E.51ST ST
E.50TH ST
E.49TH ST
E.48TH ST
E.47TH ST
E.46TH ST
E.45TH ST
E.44TH ST
E.43RD ST
E.42ND ST
E.41ST ST
E.40TH ST
E.39TH ST
E.38TH ST
E.37TH ST
E.36TH ST
E.35TH ST

St. Patrick's Cathedral

kefeller
enter

DIAMOND ROW

RICT

ilding

Bryant Park

New York Public Library

Pan Am Building

Grand Central Terminal

Chrysler Building

United Nations Headquarters

QUEENS-MIDTOWN TUNNEL

FRANKLIN D. ROOSEVELT DRIVE

MURRAY HILL

Pierpont Morgan Library

Empire State Building

E. 34TH ST

East River

BROADWAY

FIFTH AVENUE
MADISON AVENUE
PARK AVENUE
LEXINGTON AVENUE
THIRD AVENUE
SECOND AVENUE
FIRST AVENUE

E.33RD ST
E.32ND ST
E.31ST ST
E.30TH ST
E.29TH ST
E.28TH ST
E.27TH ST
E.26TH ST
E.25TH ST
E.24TH ST
E.23RD ST
E.22ND ST
E.21ST ST
E.20TH ST
E.19TH ST
E.18TH ST
E.17TH ST
E.16TH ST
E.15TH ST

NY Life Building

Madison Square Park

Metropolitan Life Building

Bellevue Hospital

Gramercy Park

STUYVESANT SQ.

Stuyvesant Town

UNION SQUARE

E. 14TH ST

MIDTOWN MANHATTAN

looking **Friends' Meeting House**, and, next door, the weighty brownstone **Church of St. George**—best known as the place where financier J.P. Morgan used to worship.

Lexington Avenue begins its long journey north from Gramercy Park, past the lumbering **69th Regiment Armory**—site in 1913 of the notorious Armory Show which brought modern art to New York for the first time (see "Twentieth Century American Art" in *Contexts*)—to Manhattan's most condensed ethnic enclave, **Little India**. Blink and you might miss this altogether: most of New York's 100,000 Indians live in Queens and their only trace here is a handful of restaurants and fast-food places—far out-numbered by those down on East 6th Street—and a pocket of sweet and spice stores (*Kalyustan's*, on the east side of the street, is a good one).

Madison Square

Broadway and Fifth Avenue meet at **Madison Square**, by day a maelstrom of dodging cars and cabs, buses and pedestrians but, mainly because of the quality of the buildings and the clever park-space in the middle, possessing a monumentality and neat seclusion that Union Square has long since lost. The **Flatiron Building**, set daringly on a triangular plot of land on the square's southern side, is another famed city building, one that evokes images of Edwardian New York. Its thin tapered structure creates unusual wind currents at ground level, and years ago policemen were posted to prevent men gathering to watch the wind raise the skirts of women passing on 23rd Street. The cry they gave to warn off voyeurs—"23 Skidoo !"—has passed into the language. It's hard to believe that this was the city's first true skyscraper, hung on a steel frame in

---

SKYSCRAPERS

Along with Chicago and Hong Kong, Manhattan is one of the best places in the world in which to see **skyscrapers**, its puckered, almost medieval skyline of towers the city's most familiar and striking image. In fact there are only two main clusters of skyscrapers, but they set the tone for the city—the Financial District, where the combination of narrow streets and tall buildings forms slender, lightless canyons, and Midtown Manhattan, where the big skyscrapers, flanking the wide central avenues between the Thirties and the Sixties, have long competed for height and prestige.

The term "skyscraper" was coined in 1890 by one John J. Flinn, describing the evolving style of building in turn-of-the-century Chicago, since when the two cities have always been battling to produce the tallest building. It's uncertain which city actually built the first real skyscraper, but the first generally recognized instance in New York was the Flatiron Building on Madison Square, designed in 1902, not least for the obvious way its triangular shape made the most of the new iron-frame technique of construction that had made such structures possible. A few years later, in 1913, New York clinched the title of the world's tallest building with the sixty-story Woolworth Building on Broadway, later going on to produce such landmarks as the Chrysler and Empire State buildings, and, more recently, the World Trade Center—though the latter's status as world's tallest building was soon usurped by Chicago's Sears Tower.

Styles have changed over the years and have perhaps been most influenced by the stringency of the city's zoning laws, which early in the century placed restrictions on the types of building permitted. At first skyscrapers were sheer vertical

1902 with its full twenty stories dwarfing all the other structures around. Not for long though: the **Metropolitan Life Company** soon erected their clock tower on the eastern side of the square which put, height-wise at least, the Flatiron to shame.

Next door is the Corinthian-columned marble facade of the **Appellate Division** of the New York State Supreme Court, resolutely righteous with its statues of Justice, Wisdom, and Peace turning their weary backs on the ugly black glass New York Life Annexe behind. The grand structure behind that, the **New York Life Building** proper, was the work of Cass Gilbert, creator of the Woolworth Tower downtown. It went up in 1928 on the site of the original **Madison Square Garden**—renowned scene of drunken and debauched revels of high and Broadway society. This was the heart of the theater district in those days and the place where the Garden's architect, **Stanford White**, was murdered by Harry Thaw. White, a partner in the illustrious architectural team of McKim, Mead, and White, who designed many of the city's great Beaux Arts buildings, such as the General Post Office, the old Penn Station, and Columbia University, was something of a rake by all accounts, with a reputation for womanizing and fast living. His affair with Thaw's wife Evelyn Nesbit, a Broadway showgirl, had been well publicized—even to the extent that the naked statue of the goddess Diana on the top of the building was said to have been modeled on her. Millionaire Thaw was so humiliated by this that one night he burst into the roof garden, found White, surrounded as usual by doting women and admirers, and shot him through the head. Thaw was carted away to spend the rest of his life in mental institutions, and his wife's showbusiness career took a tumble: she resorted to drugs and prostitution somewhere in Central America.

---

monsters, maximizing the floor space possible from any given site but with no regard to how this affected the neighboring buildings, which more often than not were thrown into shade by the new arrival. In order to stop this happening the city authorities invented the concept of "air rights," putting a restriction on how high a building could be before it had to be set back from its base. This forced skyscrapers to be designed in a series of steps—a law most elegantly adhered to by the Empire State Building, which has no fewer than ten steps in all, but it's a pattern you will see repeated all over the city.

Due to the pressure on space in Manhattan's narrow confines, and the price of real estate, which makes speculatively building office blocks potentially so lucrative, the skyscrapers continue to rise, and it's always possible to see some slowly rising steel frame somewhere in the city. Traditionally the workers who brave the heights to work on the skyscrapers, lifting the girders into place and bolting them together, often bent into impossible positions, squatting or balancing on thin planks, are Native Americans, due to their unusual agility and remarkable head for heights. They still make up forty percent of such workers in New York, and even eighty floors up don't wear any kind of safety harness, claiming it restricts their movements too much.

As for the future, there seems to be almost no limit to the heights that are envisioned, the most notable plan being Donald Trump's bid to reclaim the tallest-building title for New York with a new structure on the Upper West Side well over a hundred stories high. Whether or not this comes off, it's certain that even in times of recession skyscrapers remain the "machines for making money" that Le Corbusier originally claimed they were.

So ended one of Madison Square's more dramatic episodes. Madison Square Garden has moved twice since then, first to a site on Eighth Avenue and 50th Street, finally to its present location in a grotesque drum-shaped eyesore on the corner of 32nd Street. There is, however, one reminder of the time when this was New York's theaterland—the **Episcopal Church of the Transfiguration** just off Fifth Avenue on 29th Street. This, a dinky rustic church set back from the street, brown brick and topped with copper roofs, has since 1870 been the traditional place of worship of showbiz people. It was tagged with the name "The Little Church Around the Corner" after a devout but understanding priest from a nearby church had refused to marry a theatrical couple and sent them here. It's an intimate building, furnished throughout in warm wood and with the figures of famous actors (most notably Edwin Booth as Hamlet) memorialized in the stained glass.

The Empire State Building

Farther up Fifth Avenue is New York's prime **shopping territory**, home to most of the city's heavyweight department stores. *Macy's* is just a short stroll away on Herald Square; filling the space between 38th and 39th Streets are the lavish headquarters of *Lord and Taylor* (see Chapter Seven, "Shops and Markets"). The **Empire State Building**—overshadowing by far the lure of such consumer items—occupies what has always been a prime site. Before it appeared this was home to the first Waldorf Astoria Hotel, built by William Waldorf Astor as a ruse to humiliate his formidable aunt, Caroline Schemmerhorn, into moving uptown. The hotel opened in 1893 and immediately became focus for city's rich—in an era, the "Gay Nineties," when "Meet me at the Waldorf" was the catchphrase to conjure with.* However, though the reputation of the Waldorf—at least for its prices—endures to this day, it didn't remain in its initial premises for very long, moving in 1929 to its current Art Deco home on Park Avenue.

Few would dispute the elegance of what took its place. The Empire State Building remains easily the most potent and evocative symbol of New York, and has done since its completion in 1931—well under budget and after just two years in the making. Soon after, King Kong clung to it and distressed squealing damsels while grabbing at passing planes; in 1945 a plane crashed into the building's 79th story; and most recently two Englishmen parachuted from its summit to the ground, only to be carted off by the NY police department for disturbing the peace. Its 102 stories and 1472 feet—toe to TV mast—make it the world's third tallest building, but the height is deceptive, rising in stately tiers with steady panache. Inside, its basement serves as an underground marbled shopping precinct, lined with newsstands, beauty parlors, cafés, even a post office, and is finished everywhere with delicate Deco touches. After wandering around you can visit the *Guinness World of Records Exhibition*—though, frankly, you'd be better advised to save your money for the assault on the top of the tower.

The first elevator, alarmingly old and rickety if you've previously zoomed to the top of the World Trade Center, takes you to the 86th floor, summit of the building before the radio and TV mast was added. The views from the outside walkways

---

*It was the consort of Mrs. Schemmerhorn Astor, Ward Macallister, who coined the label "The Four Hundred" to describe this lot. "There are only about four hundred people in fashionable New York society," he asserted. "If you go outside that number you strike people who are either not at ease in a ballroom or else make other people not at ease. See the point?"

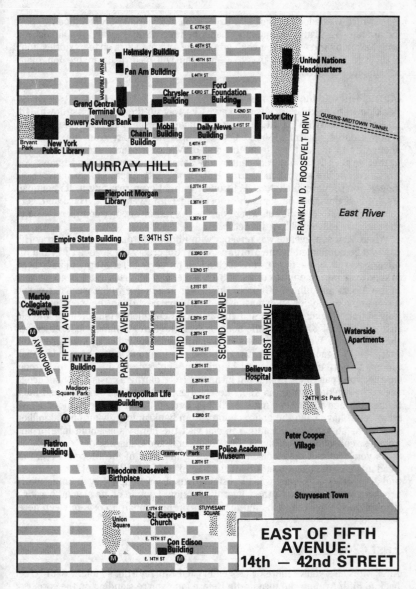

EAST OF FIFTH AVENUE: 14th — 42nd STREET

here are as stunning as you'd expect—better than the Trade Center since Manhattan spreads on all sides. On a clear day visibility is up to eighty miles, but given the city's pollution, on most it's more likely to be between ten and twenty. If you're feeling brave, and can stand the lines for the small single elevator, go up to the Empire State's last reachable zenith, a small cylinder at the foot of the TV mast which was added as part of a hare-brained scheme to erect a mooring post for airships—a plan subsequently abandoned after some local VIPs almost got swept away by the wind. You can't go outside and the extra sixteen stories don't really add a great deal to the view, but you will have been to the top (daily 9:30am–midnight; $3.50).

Murray Hill and the Morgans

Back down to earth, Fifth Avenue carves its way up the island. East down 34th Street lies **MURRAY HILL**, a tenuously tagged residential area of statuesque canopy-fronted apartment buildings, but with little apart from its WASPish anonymity to mark it out from the rest of Midtown Manhattan. Like Chelsea farther west, it lacks any real center, any sense of community, and unless you work, live, or are staying in Murray Hill, there's little reason to go there at all; indeed you're more likely to pass through without even realizing it. Its boundaries are indistinct, but lie somewhere between Fifth Avenue and Third and, very roughly, 32nd to 40th Street, where begins the rather brasher commercialism of the midtown office building district.

When Madison Avenue was on a par with Fifth as *the* place to live, Murray Hill came to be dominated by the **Morgan family**, the crusty old financier J.P. and his offspring, who at one time owned a clutch of property here. Morgan junior lived in the **brownstone** on the corner of 37th Street and Madison (now headquarters of the American Lutheran Church), his father in a house which was later pulled down to make way for an extension to his **library** next door, the mock but tastefully simple Roman villa that still stands and is commonly mistaken for the old man's house. (If you've read the book or seen the film *Ragtime*, you'll remember that Coalhouse Walker made this fundamental mistake when attempting to hold Pierpoint Morgan hostage). In fact, Morgan would simply come here to languish among the art treasures he had bought up wholesale on his trips to Europe: manuscripts, paintings, prints, and furniture. Here during a crisis of confidence in the city's banking system in 1907, he entertained New York's richest and most influential men night after night until they agreed to put up the money to save what could have been the entire country from bankruptcy, giving up $30 million himself as an act of good faith. You can visit the library's splendid interior and priceless collection; see Chapter Five, "Museums and Galleries."

As you continue up Madison Avenue the influence of the Morgans rears its head again in the shape (or at least the name) of **Morgan's Hotel** between 37th and 38th streets—the last word in ostentatious discretion, not even bothering to proclaim its presence with the vulgarity of a sign. Look in on its elegant bar for a drink if you've got the cash, and for details on how much it costs to sleep here, see p.38.

East 42nd Street

After Morgan's you've more or less exhausted Murray Hill, so follow 38th Street back to Fifth Avenue and turn north. Before long you're standing on the corner of **42ND STREET**, one of the few streets in the world to have an entire musical named after it. With good reason, too, for you *can* do anything on 42nd Street, highbrow or low, and it's also home to some of the city's most characteristic buildings, ranging from great Beaux Arts palaces like Grand Central Station to vulgar charge-card traps like the Grand Hyatt Hotel.

The New York Public Library

The **New York Public Library** (Central Research Library) on the corner of 42nd and Fifth is the first notable building on 42nd Street's eastern reaches: Beaux Arts in style and faced with white marble, its steps act as a meeting point and general hangout for pockets of people throughout the year. To tour the library either walk around yourself or take one of the **tours** (Mon–Sat at 11am & 2pm) which are free, last an hour, and give a good all-encompassing picture of the building. The main thing to see is the large coffered *Reading Room* at the back of the building. Trotsky worked here on and off during his brief sojourn in New York just prior to the 1917 Revolution, introduced to the place by his friend Bukharin, who was bowled over by a library you could use so late in the evening. The opening times are considerably less impressive now, but the library still boasts a collection among the five largest in the world, stored in eight levels beneath this room, which alone covers half an acre. And while Trotsky may have been, with hindsight, a far less prestigious customer than Karl Marx, the computerized technology, with which you can find a book and have it delivered in a matter of minutes, makes the reading room of London's British Library seem primitive by comparison.

Grand Central Station

Back outside, push through the crush crossing Fifth Avenue and walk east down Manhattan's most congested stretch to where Park Avenue lifts off the ground at Pershing Square to weave its way around the solid bulk of **Grand Central Station**. This, for its day, was a masterful piece of urban planning: after the electrification of the railroads made it possible to reroute trains underground, the rail lanes behind the existing station were sold off to developers and the profits went toward the building of a new terminal—constructed around a basic iron frame but clothed with a Beaux Arts skin. Since then Grand Central has taken on an almost mythical significance, and though with the insidious eating away of the country's rail network its major traffic is now mainly commuters speeding out no farther than Westchester County, it remains in essence what it was in the nineteenth century—symbolic gateway to an undiscovered continent.

You can either explore Grand Central on your own or take one of the free **tours** run by the *Municipal Arts Society* (see *Basics*); these leave from under the Kodak billboard every Wednesday at 12:30pm and are excellent. But for the efforts of a few dedicated New Yorkers (and, strangely enough, Jackie Onassis, whose voice was no doubt a godsend) Grand Central wouldn't be here at all, or at least it would be much uglified. For it was only deemed a National Landmark in 1978, after the railroad's plan to cap the whole lot with an office tower was quashed. The most spectacular aspect of the building is its size, now cowed by the soaring airplane wing of the Pan Am building behind but still no less impressive in the main station **concourse**. This is one of the world's finest and most imposing open spaces, 470 feet long and 150 feet high, the barrel-vaulted ceiling speckled like a Baroque church with a painted representation of the winter night sky, its 2500 stars shown back to front: "As God would have seen them," the painter is reputed to have remarked. It's a pity about the broad billboards, which can't help but obscure the enormous windows, but stand in the middle and you realize that Grand Central represents a time when stations were seen as appropriately dwarfing preludes to great cities. "A city within a city," as it has been called.

For the best view of the concourse climb up to the catwalks which span the sixty-feet-high windows on the Vanderbilt Avenue side; then explore the terminal's more esoteric reaches: places like the **Tennis Club** on the third floor, which used to be a CBS studio but now lets out court-time for a membership fee of around $2500 a year; and the **Oyster Bar** in the vaulted bowels of the station—one of the city's most highly regarded seafood restaurants, serving something like a dozen varieties of oyster and cram-packed every lunchtime with the midtown office crowd. Just outside is something that explains why the Oyster Bar's babble is not solely the result of the big-mouthed business people that eat there: you can stand on opposite sides of any of the vaulted spaces and hold a conversation just by whispering, an acoustic fluke that makes this the loudest eatery in town.

The Chrysler Building and around

Across the street, the **Bowery Savings Bank** echoes Grand Central's grandeur—like its sister branch downtown, extravagantly lauding the twin shibboleths of sound investment and savings. A Roman-style basilica, the floor is paved with mosaics, the columns are each fashioned from a different kind of marble, and, if you take a look at the elevator doors (through a door on the right) you'll see bronze bas-reliefs of bank employees hard at various tasks. But then, this kind of lavish expenditure is typical of the buildings on this stretch of 42nd Street, which is full of lobbies worth dropping inside for a glimpse as you're passing. The **Grand Hyatt Hotel** back on the north side of the street is a notable one, if nothing else probably the best example in the city of all that is truly vulgar about contemporary American interior design, its slushing waterfalls, lurking palms, and gliding escalators, representing plush-carpeted bad taste at its most meretricious.

The **Chrysler Building**, across Lexington Avenue, is a different story, dating from a time (1930) when architects carried off prestige with grace and style. This was for a brief while the world's tallest building*—until it was usurped by the Empire State in 1931—and since the rediscovery of Art Deco a decade or so ago has become easily Manhattan's best loved, its car-motif friezes, jutting gargoyles, and arched stainless steel pinnacle giving the solemn midtown skyline a welcome touch of fun. Chrysler moved out some time ago, and for a while the building was left to degenerate by a company that didn't wholly appreciate its spirited silliness, but now a new owner has pledged to keep it lovingly intact. The **lobby**, once a car showroom, is for the moment all you can see (there's no observation deck), but that's enough in itself, with opulently inlaid elevators, walls covered in African marble, and on the ceiling a realistic, if rather faded, study of work and endeavor, showing airplanes, machines, and brawny builders who worked on the tower.

Flanking each side of Lexington Avenue on the southern side of 42nd Street are two more buildings worthy of a studied walk past. The **Chanin Building** on the right is another Art Deco monument, cut with terracotta carvings of leaves, tendrils, and sea creatures. More interestingly, the design on the outside of the weighty **Mobil Building** across the way is deliberately folded so as to be cleaned automatically by the movement of the wind.

---

*Its designer, William Van Alen, indulged in a feud with an erstwhile partner who was designing a building at 40 Wall Street at the same time. Each was determined to have the higher skyscraper: Alen secretly built a stainless steel spire *inside* the Chrysler's crown; when 40 Wall Street was finally topped out a few feet higher than the Chrysler, Alen popped the 185 foot spire out through the top of the building, and won the day.

The Mobil Building fills the block as far as Third Avenue, across which, recently restored to pristine 1950s splendour, stands the **Horn and Hardart Automat**, "the last of a great breed," wrote Paul Goldberger, and which, until recently, still served up lukewarm ready meals out of chrome and glass drawers. Goldberger made inflated claims for the romance of this place, and in some ways he was right: it was the only remaining example of a fast food idea that used to be all over the city. At the time of writing it's uncertain whether the Automat will be preserved as the last remaining example in America, whether its interior will be stripped and sold off, or whether the whole thing will be moved to a museum.

East of here, beyond the deceptively modern headquarters of the **New York Daily News**—whose foyer holds blown-up prints of the paper's more memorable front pages—42nd Street grows more tranquil. And on the left, between Second and First Avenue, is one of the city's most peaceful spaces of all—the **Ford Foundation Building**. Built in 1967, this was the first of the city's long chain of atriums and is probably the best: a giant greenhouse gracefully supported by soaring granite columns and edged with two walls of offices from which workers can look down on to a sub-tropical garden which changes naturally with the seasons. It's astonishingly quiet: 42nd Street is no more than a murmur outside, and all you can hear is the burble of water, the echo of voices, and the clipped crack of feet on the brick walkways, mingled with the ripe smell of the atrium's considerable vegetation: all in all making for one of the great architectural experiences of New York City.

East to the United Nations Building

At the east end of 42nd Street, steps lead up to **Tudor City**, which rises behind a tree-filled parklet and with its coats of arms, leaded glass, and neat neighborhood shops, is the very picture of self-contained dowager respectability. Trip down the steps from here and you're plum opposite the building of the **United Nations**, which rose up after the last war on the site of what was once known as Turtle Bay. Some see the United Nations complex as one of the major sights of New York; others, usually those who've been there, are not so complimentary. For whatever the symbolism of the UN there can be few buildings that are quite so dull to walk round. What's more, the self-congratulatory nature of the (obligatory) guided tours can't—in the face of years of UN impotence in war and hunger zones the world over—help but grate a little.

For the determined, the complex consists of three main buildings—the thin glass-curtained slab of the **Secretariat**, the sweeping curve of the **General Assembly Building**, and, just between, the low-rise connecting **Conference Wing**. It went up immediately after the war and was finished in 1963, the product of a suitably international team of architects which included Le Corbusier—though he pulled out before the building was completed. Daily **tours** leave every half hour from the monumental General Assembly lobby (First Avenue at 45th Street; 9:15am–4:45pm; $5.50, students $3.50; ☎963-7713) and take in the main conference chambers of the UN and its constituent parts, foremost of which is the General Assembly Chamber itself, expanded a few years back to accommodate up to 179 member's delegations (though there are at present only 159). It's impressive certainly, but can't help but seem wasted on a body that only meets for a few months each year. Other council chambers, situated in the Conference Building, include the Security Council Chamber, the Economic and Social Council, and the Trusteeship Council. Once you've been whisked around all these, with the odd stop for examples of the many artifacts that have been donated to the UN by its various member states—rugs, paintings, sculptures, and so on—the tour is more or less over, and will leave you in the basement of the General Assembly Building, where a couple of **shops** sell ethnic items from around the world and a **post office** will sell you a UN postage stamp to prove that you've been here—though bear in mind it's only valid on mail posted from the UN.

BARS *Café Iguana, The Coffee Shop, Company* (gay), *Live Bait, Molly Malone's, Mumbles, Old Town Bar and Restaurant, Pete's Tavern, South Dakota* (gay).

RESTAURANTS Budget *Bagel Palace, Chez Laurence, Jackson Hole Wyoming, Reuben's, Sarge's, Scotty's Diner*; **American, Mexican, Latin, and South American** *America, Cinco de Mayo, El Rio Grande, Pete's Tavern, Union Square Café*; **Chinese** *Tina's*; **Italian** *Pasta Presto*; **Indian** *Curry in a Hurry, Madras Palace, Shaheen*; **Japanese** *Genroku Shushi, Yoshi*; **Vegetarian** *The Health Food Pub, Tibetan Kitchen*.

HOTELS/HOSTELS *Carlton, Carlton Arms, Gramercy Park, Madison Towers, Murray Hotel, Martha Washington* (women only), *Morgan's, Shelborne*.

The West Side: Chelsea, the Garment District, and Times Square

Few visitors bother with Chelsea and the Garment District, the two areas that fill the land between 14th and 42nd streets. Chelsea is a low-built surly seedy grid of tenements and row houses of so mixed a character as to be almost characterless. To the north, the Garment District muscles in between Sixth and Eighth avenues on 34th to 42nd streets taking in the dual monsters of Penn Station and Madison Square Garden. The majority of people who come here do so for a specific reason—to catch a train or bus, to watch wrestling, or to work in factories, and it's only a wedge of stores beween Herald and Greeley squares that attracts the out-of-towner.

Chelsea

CHELSEA took shape in 1830 when its owner, Charles Clarke Moore, laid out his land for sale in broad lots. Enough remains to indicate Chelsea's middle-class suburban origins, though in fact the area never quite made it onto the short list of desirable places to be. Stuck between Fifth Avenue and Hell's Kitchen, and caught between the ritziness of the one and the poverty of the other, Manhattan's chic residential focus leapfrogged Chelsea to the East 40s and 50s. These days the dreary facades quickly establish Chelsea's atmosphere of run down residentialism; the grid plan seems too wide, the streets too bare to encourage you to linger.

But that's not to say Chelsea doesn't have its moments. Moore donated an island of land to the **General Theological Seminary** on Chelsea Square at 20th Street and Ninth Avenue, an assembly of ivy-clad gothicisms seemingly dropped in from rural England. It's possible to explore inside—the entrance is via the modern building on Ninth Avenue—but the countrified feel is what makes it special, not any particular architectural feature.

During the nineteenth century this area, especially West 23rd Street, was a center of New York's theater district before it moved uptown. Nothing remains of the theaters now, but the hotel which put up all the actors, writers, and Bohemian hangers-on remains a New York landmark. The **Chelsea Hotel** has been undisputed watering hole of the city's harder-up literati for decades: Mark Twain and Tennessee Williams lived here, and Brendan Behan and Dylan Thomas staggered in and out during their New York visits. Thomas Wolfe assembled *You Can't Go Home Again* from thousands of pages of manuscript he had stacked in his room, and in 1951 Jack Kerouac, armed with a specially adapted typewriter (and a lot of Benzedrine) typed the first draft of *On the Road* non-stop on to a 120-foot roll of paper. In the 1960s the Chelsea took off again when Andy Warhol and his doomed protege Edie Sedgwick walled up here and made the film *Chelsea Girls* in (sort of) homage; Bob Dylan wrote songs in and about it, and most recently Sid Vicious stabbed Nancy Spungen to death in their suite, a few months before his own pathetic life ended with an overdose of heroin. With a pedigree like this it's easy to forget the hotel itself, which has a down-at-heel Edwardian grandeur all of its own and, incidentally, is an affordable place to stay and an interesting one to drink.

Sixth Avenue forms Chelsea's eastern perimeter, with the city's largest **antiques market** taking place at weekends in an open-air parking lot at the junction with 26th Street: open till 6pm, it's possible to find bargains amid the piles of overpriced junk (see Chapter Seven, "Shops and Markets"). The area around 28th Street is also Manhattan's **Flower Market**: not really a market as such, more the warehouses where pot plants and cut flowers are stored before brightening offices and atriums across the city. Nothing marks the strip and you come across it by chance, the greenery bursting out of drab blocks, blooms spangling shopfronts and providing a welcome touch of life to an otherwise dull neighborhood. For the record, West 28th Street was the original **Tin Pan Alley**, where music publishers would peddle songs to artists and producers from the nearby theaters. When the theaters moved, so did the publishers.

Greely Square and the Garment District

A few streets north, Sixth Avenue collides with Broadway at **Greeley Square**, an overblown name for what is a trashy triangle celebrating Horace Greeley, founder of the **Tribune** newspaper. Perhaps he deserves better: known for his rallying call to the youth of the nineteenth century to explore the continent ("Go West, young man!") he also supported the rights of women and trade unions, commissioned a weekly column from Karl Marx, and denounced slavery and capital punishment. His paper no longer exists (though one of its descendants is the bored traveler's last resort, the *International Herald Tribune*) and the square named after him is one of those bits of Manhattan that looks ready to disintegrate at any moment.

Across the way is **Macy's**, the all-American superstore. Until the mid-1970s Macy's contented itself by being the world's largest store (which it remains), then, in response to the needs of the maturing Yuppie (and Bloomingdale's success) it went fashionably and safely upmarket. Like all great stores it's worth exploring—there's an amazing food emporium plus a reconstruction of P. J. Clarke's bar in the basement—though leave all forms of spending power at home. Nearby, the thoroughly unlikable eight floors of the **Herald Center** attempt to add a little gloss to the street scene though, inside at least, they can't come near Macy's.

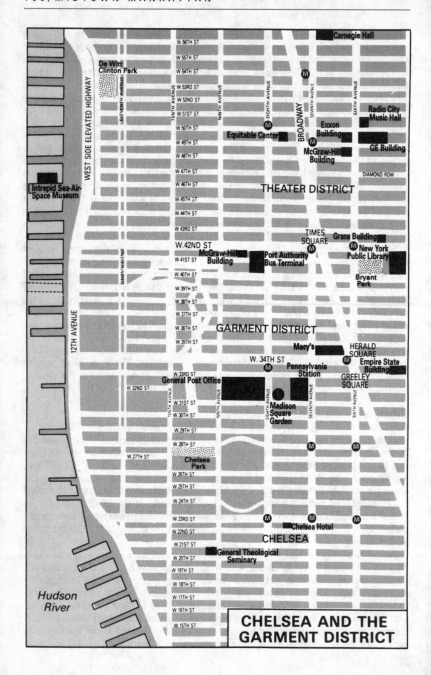

CHELSEA AND THE
GARMENT DISTRICT

In a way this part of Broadway is the shop window to the **GARMENT DISTRICT**, a loosely defined pool between 34th and 42nd streets and Sixth and Eighth avenues. From this patch three-quarters of all the women's and children's clothes in America are made, though you'd never believe it: outlets are strictly wholesale with no need to woo customers, and the only clues to the industry inside are the racks of clothes shunted around on the street and occasional skips of offcuts that give the area its look of an open-air rummage sale.

Around Madison Square Garden

The Garment District is something to see in passing: the unmissable landmark in this part of town is the **Pennsylvania Station** and **Madison Square Garden** complex, a combined box and drum structure that swallows up millions of commuters in its train station below and accommodates the *Knicks* basketball and *Rangers* hockey teams (along with their fans) up top. There's nothing memorable about Penn Station: its subterranean levels seem to have all the grime and just about everything else that's wrong with the subway, and to add insult to injury the original Penn Station, demolished to make way for this, is now hailed as a lost masterpiece. One of McKim, Mead, and White's greatest designs, it reworked the ideas of the Roman Baths of Caracalla to awesome effect: "Through it one entered the city like a god . . . One scuttles in now like a rat," mourned an observer. A whimsical reminder of the old days is the **Penta Hotel** on the corner of Seventh Avenue and 33rd Street: a main venue for Glenn Miller and other big swing bands of the 1940s, it keeps the phone number that made it famous—736-5000: under the old system PENnsylvania 6-5000, title of Miller's affectionate hit.

Immediately behind Penn Station the **General Post Office** is a McKim, Mead, and White structure that survived, a relic from an era when municipal pride was all about making statements—though to say that the Post Office is monumental in the grandest manner still seems to underplay it. The old joke is that it had to be this big to fit in the sonorous inscription above the columns—"Neither snow nor rain nor heat nor gloom of night stays these couriers from the swift completion of their appointed rounds"—a claim about as believable as the official one that the Manhattan postal district handles more mail than Britain, France, and Belgium combined.

The **Port Authority Terminal Building** at 40th Street and Eighth Avenue is another sink for the area: a Dantesque labyrinthine bus station. Coaches strain, waiting to escape the city to all points in America, and though initially confusing it's efficiently run. *Greyhound* leaves from here as do regional services out to the boroughs, and (should you arrive in the early hours) it's a remarkably safe place, station staff keeping the winos and weirdos in check.

Back to Broadway, and **Herald Square** faces Greeley Square in a headlong replay of the battles between the *Herald* newspaper and its arch rival Horace Greeley's *Tribune*. During the 1890s this was the **Tenderloin** area, dance halls, brothels, and rough bars thriving beside the Elevated Railroad that ran up Sixth Avenue. When the *Herald* arrived in 1895 it gave the square a new name and dignity, but it's perhaps best remembered as the square George M. Cohan said Hello to in the famous song. These days it wouldn't fire anyone to sing about it, saved only from unredeemed sleaziness by Macy's on the corner below.

Cross **42nd Street** and you find Broadway at its worst. The excitement and *élan* of the street's eastern section are gone, and all that's left is a clutch of squalid sex shops and porno movie theaters. Neither do things improve if you turn west: 42nd Street here is a sordid corner of prostitution and petty vice you'll do better to skip altogether—and that goes for much of Eighth Avenue north of 42nd. For years locals have lobbied for the neighborhood to be cleaned up, and with the recent attempts to sanitize Times Square it looks as though the days of the porn shops may be numbered. Unfortunately, market forces dictate that these shops won't disappear, but relocate—they've already begun to turn up on West Canal Street and in the Village, much to the alarm of the locals. For the moment, though, it's best to head straight on along 42nd Street, where at number 330 is the **McGraw-Hill Building**, a greeny-blue radiator that architects raved over: "proto-juke box modern," Vincent Scully called it. The lobby should be seen.

Clinton—aka "Hell's Kitchen"

Ninth Avenue makes amends of sorts for Eighth's unsavouriness, a long slash of ethnic delis and groceries of all kinds that come into their own in May when the **Ninth Avenue Food Festival** (see *Parades and Festivals* in Chapter Six) closes the run between 34th and 57th streets. This stretch down to the Hudson was once known as **Hell's Kitchen**, a descriptive name for one of New York's poorest and most violent areas. Impoverished Irish immigrants settled here, quickly followed by Greeks, Italians, and Latinos: by the end of the nineteenth century the tenements were the most overcrowded in the world, gangs roamed the garbage-filled streets, and the levels of disease and infant mortality were high. (It wasn't until 1867 that the city officially prohibited the roving herds of **pigs** that brushed with the better class of people on Broadway, and acted as a primitive method of removing the human waste that was dumped on the streets at night.) With the *Tenement Housing Act* of 1901 things started to improve, and since then the old tenements have been flattened and the area renamed as **Clinton** to hide its past. In 1977 **Manhattan Plaza** went up on 42nd and 43rd streets between Ninth and Tenth, in an attempt to draw the monied classes into the area. But prices were high and takers few for apartments irreparably sullied by nearby Times Square, and in a fit of innovation the buildings were let to actors, artists, and the like who could prove a low income and would enhance the theater district's "creative feel." Welfare families, needless to say, were deemed not to provide the right "class." Now Hell's Kitchen is gradually gentrifying against a background of ragged, multi-ethnic neighborhoods, at its center safe enough, but west of Ninth Avenue in the 40s and 50s bombed out and intimidating—a prelude to the out-and-out sleaze of the bars on the West Side Highway. There's no reason to go there, especially not at night, but if you do, be sure to take care.

Times Square

Eventually Broadway runs into **TIMES SQUARE**, a pinched strip that in its excess and brashness was for years a distillation of the city itself. Center of the Great White Way, it's been cleaned up recently, and it seems that its days as a venue of lurid enticements to sex shows alongside theaters only a touch more reputable are finally over. Traditionally, Times Square was the place where out-of-towners supplied easy pickings for petty criminals, drug dealers, and women working as prostitutes. You were more likely to be hassled here than anywhere in the city, and as the decline continued the municipal authorities were forced into action, forcing the sale of whole blocks, and spending billions of dollars to tear out the diseased heart of the Square. Now almost all of the peepshows and sex shops have gone, replaced by a massive new office development* and safely sanitized movie theaters and electrical shops. Much of the danger and a lot of the atmosphere have gone, too, but you should still be careful in the side streets off the square, though there's too much going on when the theaters empty to make street crime viable: at other times beware—and keep to the main drag.

Like Greeley and Herald squares, Times Square took its name from a newspaper connection when the *New York Times* built offices here in 1904. While the *Herald* and *Tribune* fought each other in ever more vicious circulation battles, the *NYT* took the sober middle ground under the banner "All the news that's fit to print," a policy that enabled the paper to survive and become one of the country's most respected liberal voices. **Times Tower**, the slim chip at the south end of the Square, was its original headquarters, though the paper itself has since crept around a corner to 43rd Street. Dotted around are some of Broadway's great theaters (see *Theater* in Chapter Ten, "The Performing Arts and Film")—and it's these last that add flavor to the scene—the clock-and-globe topped **Paramount Theater Building** at 1501 Broadway, between 43rd and 44th streets, is a favorite, and the **Lyceum**, **Shubert**, and **Lyric** each have their original facades. It's the nifty canvas and frame stand of the **TKTS**, the cut-price ticket shop, that immediately catches the eye though, selling tickets for shows that no one could otherwise afford. A lifelike statue of the doyen of Broadway people **George M. Cohan** looks on—though if you've ever seen the flick *Yankee Doodle Dandy* it's impossible to think of him other than as a swaggering Jimmy Cagney. Last word on the scene to Henry Miller from *Tropic of Capricorn*:

> *It's only a stretch of a few blocks from Times Square to Fiftieth Street, and when one says Broadway that's all that's really meant and it's really nothing, just a chicken run and a lousy one at that, but even at seven in the evening when everyone's rushing for a table there's a sort of electric crackle in the air and your hair stands on end like an antenna and if you're receptive you not only get every bash and flicker but you get the statistical itch, the quid pro quo of the interactive, interstitial, ectoplasmic quantum of bodies jostling in space like the stars which compose the Milky Way, only this is the Gay White Way, the top of the world with no roof and not even a crack or a hole under your feet to fall through and say it's a lie. The absolute impersonality of it brings you to a pitch of warm human delirium which makes you run forward like a blind nag and wag your delirious ears.*

The West Fifties

The **West 50s** between Sixth and Eighth avenues are emphatically tourist territory. Edged by Central Park in the north and the Theater District to the south, and with Fifth Avenue and the Rockefeller Center in easy striking distance, they've been invaded by overpriced restaurants and cheapo souvenir shops: should you want to stock up on *I Love New York* underwear this could be the place.

One sight worth searching out is the **Equitable Center** at 757 Seventh Avenue that's taken a branch of the **Whitney Museum of American Art** under its wing. The building itself is dapper if not a little self-important, with **Roy Lichtenstein**'s 68-foot *Mural with Blue Brush Stroke* poking you in the eye as you enter: best of all, look out for **Thomas Hart Benton**'s *America Today* murals (in the left-hand corridor), which dynamically and magnificently portray ordinary American life in the days before the Depression. For more the on Whitney collection, turn to Chapter Five, "Museums and Galleries."

---

*Under the leasing conditions imposed by the city, businesses renting these offices will have to allow neon signs and illuminated billboards on their walls—an attempt to retain the traditional feel of the Square.

Otherwise **Carnegie Hall**, an overblown and fussy warehouse-like venue for opera and concert at 154 West 57th Street, is the thing to see (Tchaikovsky conducted the program on opening night and Mahler, Rachmaninov, Toscanini, Frank Sinatra, and Judy Garland played here), and though it's dropped down a league since the Lincoln Center opened, the superb acoustics still ensure full houses most of the year. If you don't fancy or can't afford a performance, sneak in through the stage door on 56th Street for a look—no one minds as long as there's not a rehearsal in progress. Alternatively, tours are held on Tuesdays and Thursdays at 11:30am, 2pm, and 3pm; $6, $5 students; ☎903-9790 for more details.

A few doors down at no. 150, the **Russian Tea Room** (see Chapter Eight, "Drinking and Eating") is one of those places to see and be seen at, ever popular with in-names from the entertainment business. Reservations are needed for lunch and dinner, but to get an idea of the sumptuous red and gold interior, its totally un-Russian atmosphere and its astronomical prices, just order a sandwich.

Sixth Avenue

Sixth Avenue is properly named *Avenue of the Americas*, though no New Yorker ever calls it this: guidebooks and maps labor the convention, but the only manifestation of the tag are lamp post flags of Central and South American countries which serve as useful landmarks. If nothing else Sixth's distinction is its width, a result of the Elevated Railroad that once ran along here, now replaced by the Sixth Avenue subway. In its day the Sixth Avenue "El" marked the borderline between respectability to the east and disrepute to the west, and in a way it's still a dividing line separating the glamorous strips of Fifth, Madison, and Park avenues and the less salubrious western districts.

Running north from Herald Square, **Bryant Park** is the first open space, once again named after a newspaper editor—William Cullen Bryant of the *New York Post*, also famed as a poet and founding father of Central Park. Recently the park benefited from a civic cleanup, and secondhand bookstalls keep a truce with the dope dealers that lurk around. This is for the good, as Bryant Park is by design attractive—a bit straitlaced and formal perhaps, but more welcoming than many small parks. From here you can't miss the **Grace Building** which swoops down on 42nd Street, breaking the rules by stepping out of line with its neighbors, though with a showiness that rings sort of hollow—and which, in any case, is less well finished than its twin, the Solow Building, on West 57th Street. Much more approachable is the **American Radiator Building** (now the American Standard Building) on West 40th, its black Gothic tower topped with honey-colored terracotta that lights up to resemble a glowing coal—appropriate enough for the headquarters of a heating company.

One of the best things about New York City is the small hidden pockets abruptly discovered when you least expect them. West 47th Street between Fifth and Sixth is a perfect example: this is **Diamond Row**, a short strip of shops overflowing with wildly expensive stones and jewelry, managed by ultra-Orthodox Hasidic Jews who seem only to exist in the confines of the street. Maybe they are what gives the street its workaday feel—Diamond Row seems more like the Garment District than Fifth Avenue, and the conversations you overhear on the street or in the nearby delicatessens are invariably in Yiddish. The Hasidim are followers of a mystical sect of Judaism—the name means "Pious Ones"—and traditionally wear beards, sidelocks, and dark old-fashioned suits. A large contingent lives in Williamsburg and Crown Heights in Brooklyn.

By the time it reaches midtown Manhattan, Sixth Avenue has become a dazzling showcase of corporate wealth. True, there's little of the foyer glitz of Fifth or the razzamatazz of Broadway, but what *is* here, and in a way what defines the stretch from 47th to 51st streets, is the **Rockefeller Center Extension**. Following the earlier **Time & Life Building** at 50th Street three near-identical monoliths went up in the 1970s, and if they don't have the romance of their predecessor they at least possess some of its monumentality. Backing on to Rockefeller Center, by day and especially by night, the repeated statement of each building comes over with some power, giving the wide path of Sixth Avenue much of its visual excitement. At street level things can be just as interesting: the broad sidewalks allow peddlars of food and handbills, street musicians, mime artists, and actors to do their thing.

Across the avenue at 49th Street **Radio City Music Hall** has far greater rewards (for a description see the next section). Keep an eye open, too, for the **CBS Building** on the corner of 52nd Street: dark and inscrutable, this has been compared to the monolith from the film *2001* and, like it or not, certainly imposes a mysterious presence on this segment of Sixth Avenue.

The rack of streets below Central Park are home to some of the most opulent hotels, shops, and apartments in America, which means you spend a lot of time gaping at windows and gasping at prices. Best place to do both is along **57th Street**, where antiquarian bookstores and galleries crowd alongside the dyspeptic wealth of *Van Cleef and Arpels* (jewelry) and *Bergdorf Goodman* (jewelry and just about every other fashion that big money can buy). 57th Street has also recently overtaken SoHo as *the* center for upscale art sales, and galleries here are noticeably snottier than their downtown relations, often requiring an appointment for viewing. A couple that usually don't are the **Marlborough Gallery** (2nd floor, 40 West 57th) specializing in famous names both American and European, and the **Kennedy Gallery** (same building, 5th floor) which deals in nineteenth-century and twentieth-century American painting.

BARS *Chelsea Commons, Irish Pub, Kuklas, Landmark Tavern, Mickey Mantle's, Mulligan's Grill, Spike* (gay), *Town and Country* (gay), *Ye Olde Tripple Inn.*

RESTAURANTS Budget *J.J. Applebaum's Deli, Carnegie Deli, Empire Diner, Hard Rock Café, Jerry's Metro Delicatessen, Landmark Tavern, Market Diner, O'Reilly's, Wine and Apples*; **American, Mexican, Latin, and South American** *Arriba Arriba, Blue Moon Café, Cabana Carioca, Caramba Caramba, Harvey's Chelsea Restaurant, Joe Allen's, Miss Ruby's Café, Symphony Café, Via Brasil*; **Chinese and Thai** *Pongsri, Siam Inn*; **French, Spanish, and Greek** *The Ballroom, Bellevue, Café Un, Deux, Trois, Chantal Café, Hour Glass Tavern, La Bonne Soup, La Fondue, Man Ray, Peryali, Prix-Fixe, Rio Mar, West Bank Café*; **Indian and Middle Eastern** *Afghan Kebab*; **Italian** *Le Madri, Prego, Frank's*; *Supreme Macaroni Co., Trattoria dell'Arte*; **Jewish and Eastern European** *Lox Around the Clock, Grigori's Gourmet à la Russe*; **Expense Account** *Le Bernadin, Russian Tea Room, Sardi's.*

HOTELS/HOSTELS *Aberdeen, Algonquin, Ameritania, Best Western Woodward, Chelsea, Chelsea Inn, Chelsea Center Hostel, Edison, Gorham, Herald Square, Iroquois, Mansfield, Marriott Marquis, Master Host Chatwal Inn, Novotel, Paramount, President, Ramada Inn, Remington, Royalton, Southgate Tower, Stanford, Wentworth, William Sloane YMCA, Wyndham.*

Fifth Avenue and East: 42nd Street to Central Park

FIFTH AVENUE rolls on from 42nd Street with all the confidence of the material world. It's been a great strip for as long as New York has been a great city, and its name is an automatic image of wealth and opulence. Here that image is very real: all that considers itself suave and cosmopolitan ends up on Fifth, and the shops showcase New York's most opulent and conspicuous consumerism. That the shopping is beyond the power of most people needn't put you off, for Fifth rewards with some of the city's best architecture: the boutiques and stores are just the icing on the cake.

Fifth Avenue

The lower reaches of Fifth Avenue aren't really as alluring as the streets off. The only eye-catcher is the **Manufacturers Hanover Trust Bank** on the southwest corner of 43rd, an early glass 'n' gloss box that teasingly displays its safe to passers-by, a reaction against the fortress palaces of earlier banks.

Around the next corner, West 44th Street contains three New York institutions. The Georgian style **Harvard Club** at no. 27, easily spotted of an evening by the paparazzi hanging around outside, has interiors so lavish that lesser mortals aren't allowed to enter.

But it's still possible to enjoy the **New York Yacht Club**, its playfully eccentric exterior of bay windows molded as ships' sterns, and with waves and dolphins completing the effect of tipsy Beaux Arts fun. For years this was home of the America's Cup, the yachting trophy first won by the schooner *America* in 1851 and held here (indeed bolted to the table) until lost to the Australians amid much loss of face in 1984. Now though, for the time being at least, it's back in its place.

"Dammit, it was the twenties and we had to be smarty." So said Dorothy Parker of the group known as the Round Table who hung out at the **Algonquin Hotel** at no. 59, and gave it a name as *the* place for literary visitors to New York—a name which still to some extent endures. The Round Table used to meet regularly here, a kind of homegrown Bloomsbury group of the city's sharpest-tongued wits which had a reputation for being as egotistical as it was exclusive. Times have changed considerably, but over the years the Algonquin has continued to attract a steady stream of famous guests, most of them with some kind of literary bent, not least Noel Coward (whose table someone will point out to you if you ask politely), Bernard Shaw, Irving Berlin, and Boris Karloff. The bar is one of the most civilized in town.

West 47th Street or Diamond Row (for an account of which, turn back a page) is another surprise off Fifth Avenue, but the first building to strike out at street level is the facade of what was once **Charles Scribner & Son's bookstore** at 597 Fifth Avenue. Whatever happens to the premises, the black and gold iron and glass storefront that seems to have fallen from an Edwardian engraving will survive, having been given historic landmark status. If you're looking to browse through bargain books, **Barnes and Noble** across the Avenue offers no extras but good value.

Rockefeller Center

Central to this stretch of Fifth is a complex of buildings that, more than any other in the city, succeeds in being utterly self-contained and at the same time in complete agreement with its surroundings. Built between 1932 and 1940 by John D. Rockefeller, son of the oil magnate, **Rockefeller Center** is one of the finest pieces of urban planning anywhere: office space with cafés, a theater, underground concourses, and rooftop gardens work together with an intelligence and grace rare in any building then or now. It's a combination that shows every other city-centre shopping area the way, leaving you thinking that the snide aphorism— "that sinister Stonehenge of Economic Man"—was way off the mark.

You're lured in to the Center from Fifth Avenue down the gentle slope of the **Channel Gardens** (so named because they divide *La Maison Française* and the *British Empire Building*) to the **GE Building** (formerly the RCA Building, but renamed when General Electric took it over a few years ago), focus of the Center. Rising 850 feet, its monumental lines match the scale of Manhattan itself, though softened by symmetrical setbacks to prevent an overpowering expanse of wall. At its foot the **Lower Plaza** holds a sunken restaurant in the summer months, linked visually to the downward flow of the building by Paul Manship's sparkling *Prometheus*; in winter it becomes an ice rink, giving skaters a chance to show off their skills to passing shoppers. More ponderously, a panel on the eastern side relates John D. Rockefeller's priggish credo in gold and black.

Inside, the GE building is no less impressive. In the lobby José Maria Sert's murals, *American Progress* and *Time*, are a little faded but eagerly in tune with the 1930s' Deco ambience—presumably more so than the original paintings by Diego Rivera, which were removed by John D.'s son Nelson when the artist refused to scrap a panel glorifying Lenin. A leaflet available from the lobby desk details a **self-guided tour** of the Center, and while you can't reach the building's summit, a cocktail in the *Rainbow Room* restaurant on the 65th floor (see p.273) gives you Manhattan's best skyscraper view, especially at night, when helicopters hang like fireflies over the Financial District, and Central Park glitters to the north.

Among the many offices in the GE Building are the **NBC Studios**, and it's possible to tour these, (one-hour tours leave regularly, 9:30am–4:30pm Mon–Sat, reservations from the desk in the GE foyer first; $7.25; ☎664-4000) though if you're an American TV freak you'll do better to pick up a (free) ticket for a **show recording** from the mezzanine lobby, Room 48, or out on the street. The most popular tickets evaporate before 9am.

Just northwest of Rockefeller Center, at Sixth Avenue and 50th Street, is **Radio City Music Hall**, an Art Deco jewel box that represents the last word in 1930s luxury. The staircase is regally resplendent with the world's largest chandeliers, the murals from the men's toilets are now in the Museum of Modern Art, and the huge auditorium looks like an extravagant scalloped shell or a vast sunset; "Art Deco's true shrine" as critic Paul Goldberger rightly called it. Believe it or not Radio City was nearly demolished in 1970: the outcry this caused left it designated a National Landmark. To explore, take a tour from the lobby (Mon–Sat 10:15am–4:45pm, Sun 11:15am–4:45pm; $7; ☎632-4041).

North toward Central Park

A further bit of sumptuous Deco is the **International Building** on Fifth Avenue, whose black marble and gold leaf give the lobby a sleek, classy feel dramatized by the ritz of escalators and the view across Lee Lawrie's bronze *Atlas* out to

St. Patrick's Cathedral. Designed by James Renwick and completed in 1888, St. Patrick's sits bone-white in the sullied streets, and seems the result of a painstaking academic tour of the Gothic cathedrals of Europe—perfect in detail, lifeless in spirit. There's something wrong, too, in the way the cathedral slots ever-so-neatly into Manhattan's grid pattern; on the plus side, the Gothic details are perfect and the cathedral is certainly striking—and made all the more so by the backing of the sunglass-black **Olympic Tower**, whose exclusive apartments house notables like Jackie Onassis when she's in town.

North of 52nd Street Fifth Avenue's first floors quickly shift from airline offices to all-out glitz, *Cartier, Gucci*, and *Tiffany's* among many gilt-edged names. The window shopping is fine, but beware assistants, who seem to flip between the crawlingly obsequious and the downright rude according to how much they think you're worth. This isn't the case at **Steuben Glass**, 715 Fifth Avenue at 56th St., a showcase of delicate glass and Steuben crystalware perfectly displayed; nor **Nat Sherman's** at 711, tobacconist to the stars and purveyor of some lethal smokes (see Chapter Seven, "Shops and Markets" for fuller listings).

Just when you thought all the glitter had gone about as far as it could, you reach the **Trump Tower** at 57th Street, whose outrageously over-the-top atrium is just short of repellent—perhaps in tune with those who frequent the glamorous designer shops here. Perfumed air, polished marble paneling and a five-story waterfall are calculated to knock you senseless with expensive "good" taste: as it is even some of the security people look faintly embarrassed. But the building is clever, a neat little outdoor garden is squeezed high in a corner, and each of the 230 apartments above the atrium gets views in three directions. Donald Trump, the property developer all New York liberals love to hate, lives here, along with other worthies of the hyper-rich in-crowd.

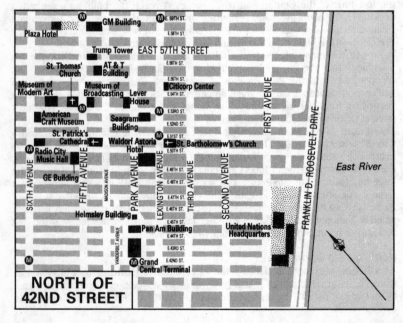

The antidote to all this is **F.A.O. Schwartz**, a block north at 745 Fifth Avenue at 58th Street, a colossal emporium of children's toys. Fight the kids off and there's some great stuff to play with—once again, the best money can buy. Across 58th, Fifth Avenue broadens to Grand Army Plaza and the fringes of **Central Park**.

Madison, Park, and Lexington Avenues

If there is a stretch that is immediately and unmistakably New York it is the area that runs east from Fifth Avenue in the 40s and 50s. The great avenues of Madison, Park, Lexington, and Third reach their richest heights as the skyscrapers line up in neck-cricking vistas, the streets choke with yellow cabs and office workers, and Con Edison vents belch steam from old heating systems. More than anything else it's buildings that define this part of town, the majority of them housing anonymous corporations and supplying excitement to the skyline in a 1960s build-em-high glass box bonanza. Others, like the new AT&T headquarters and Citycorp Center, don't play the game; and enough remains from the pre-box days to keep variety.

Madison Avenue

MADISON AVENUE shadows Fifth with some of its sweep but less of the excitement. A few good stores sit behind the scenes here, like *Brooks Brothers*, on the corner of East 44th Street, traditional clothiers to the Ivy League and inventors of the button-down collar, but Madison doesn't have quite the prestige of Fifth or Park. Between 50th and 51st streets the **Villard Houses** merit a serious walk past, a replay of an Italian palazzo (one that didn't quite make it to Fifth Avenue) by McKim, Mead, and White. The houses have been surgically incorporated into the Helmsley Palace Hotel and the interiors polished up to their original splendor.

Madison's most interesting buildings come in a four-block strip above 53rd Street: **Paley Park**, squeezed in a gap next to the Museum of Broadcasting (see Chapter Five, "Museums and Galleries") on the north side of East 53rd between Madison and Fifth is a tiny vest-pocket park complete with mini-waterfall. Around the corner the **Continental Illinois Center** looks like a cross beween a rocketship and a silo. But it's the new **AT&T Building** between 55th and 56th streets that has grabbed all the headlines. Another Johnson-Burgee collaboration, it follows the post-Modernist theory of eclectic borrowing from historical styles: a Modernist skyscraper sandwiched between a Chippendale top and a Renaissance base—the idea being to quote from great public buildings and simultaneously return to the fantasy of the early twentieth century. The building has its fans—especially for the lobby which contains Evelyn Longman's sculpture *The Spirit of Communication*, removed from the old AT&T headquarters downtown—but in the main the tower doesn't wholly work. Perhaps Johnson should have followed the advice of his teacher, Mies Van der Rohe: "It's better to build a good building than an original one." More info is on hand from the lobby attendants.

Less flamboyantly, the **IBM Building** next door at 590 Madison has a stylish enclosed plaza of plants, water and tinkling classical music, achieving the effect the Trump Tower aimed for and missed, and scoring much higher in the user-friendly stakes than AT&T. Across 57th Street, as the first of Madison's boutiques appear, the **Fuller Building** is worth catching—black and white Art Deco, with a fine entrance and tiled floor.

Park Avenue

"Where wealth is so swollen that it almost bursts," wrote Collinson Owen of **PARK AVENUE** in 1929 and things haven't changed much: corporate headquarters jostle for prominence in a triumphal procession to capitalism, pushed apart by Park's broad avenue that once carried railroad tracks. Whatever your feelings it's one of the city's most awesome sights. Looking south, everything progresses to the high altar of the **New York Central Building** (now rechristened the Helmsley Building), a delicate, energetic construction with a lewdly excessive Rococo lobby. In its day it formed a skilled punctuation mark to the avenue, but had its thunder stolen in 1963 by the **Pan Am Building** that looms behind. Bahaus guru Walter Gropius had a hand in designing this, and the critical consensus is that he should have done better. Headquarters of the ailing international airline, the profile is meant to suggest an aircraft wing and the blue-gray mass certainly adds drama to the cityscape, though whatever success Pan Am scores it robs Park Avenue of the views south it deserves and needs, sealing 44th Street and drawing much of the vigor from the surrounding buildings. Another black mark was the rooftop helipad, closed in the 1970s after a helicopter undercarriage collapsed shortly after landing, causing a rotor to sheer off and killing four arriving passengers, as well as injuring several people on the ground.

Despite Park Avenue's power, an individual look at most of the skyscrapers reveals the familiar glass box, and the first few buildings to stand out do so exactly because that's what they're not. Wherever you placed the solid mass of the **Waldorf Astoria Hotel** (between 49th and 50th) it would hold its own, a resplendent statement of Art Deco elegance. If you're tempted, it's a fraction cheaper than the comparable competition—$240 for a double. Crouching behind, **St. Bartholomew's Church** is a low-slung Byzantine hybrid that by contrast adds immeasurably to the street, giving the lumbering skyscrapers a much-needed sense of scale. As you'd imagine, every so often property developers wave a huge check under the church fathers' noses for the land rights: so far they've managed to resist. The spired **General Electric Building** behind seems like a wild extension of the church, its slender shaft rising to a meshed crown of abstract sparks and lightning strokes that symbolize the radio waves used by its original occupier, RCA. The lobby (entrance at 570 Lexington) is yet another Deco delight.

Among all this it's difficult at first to see the originality of the **Seagram Building** between 52nd and 53rd streets. Designed by Mies Van der Rohe with Philip Johnson and built in 1958, this was the seminal curtain-wall skyscraper, the floors supported internally, allowing a skin of smoked glass and whiskey-bronze metal (Seagram are distillers), now weathered to a dull black. In keeping with the era's vision, every interior detail down to the fixtures and lettering on the mailboxes was specially designed. It was the supreme example of Modernist reason, deceptively simple and cleverly detailed, and its opening met with a wave of approval. The plaza, an open plaza designed to set the building apart from its neighbors and display it to advantage, was such a success as a public space that the city revised the zoning laws to encourage other high-rise builders to follow the example. The result was the windswept anti-people places now found all over downtown and Midtown Manhattan, and a lot of pallid Mies copies, boxes that alienated many from "faceless" modern architecture.

Across Park Avenue McKim, Mead, and White's **Racquet and Squash Club** seems like a Classical continuation of the Seagram Plaza. More interesting is the

Lever House across the street between 53rd and 54th, the building that set the Modernist ball rolling on Park Avenue in 1952. Then, the two right-angled slabs that form a steel and glass bookend seemed revolutionary compared to the traditional buildings that surrounded it. Nowadays it's overlooked and not a little dingy.

Lexington Avenue and east

LEXINGTON AVENUE is always active, especially around the mid-40s, where commuters swarm around Grand Central and a well-placed post office on the corner of 50th Street. Just as the Chrysler Building dominates these lower stretches, the chisel-topped **Citicorp Center** (between 53rd and 54th streets) has taken the north end as its domain. Finished in 1979, the graph paper design sheathed in aluminum is architecture become mathematics, and now one of Manhattan's most conspicuous landmarks. The slanted roof was designed to house solar panels and provide power, but the idea was ahead of the technology and Citicorp had to content itself by adopting the distinctive top as a corporate logo. The atrium of stores known as *The Market* is also one of the city's best, with inexpensive food (try a *Healthwork's* salad) and live music at 6–8pm Saturdays, noon on Sundays. A more likable meeting of commerce, culture, and amiability you couldn't hope to find.

Hiding under the Center's skirts is **St. Peter's**, a tiny church built to replace one originally demolished to make way for the Citicorp. Part of the deal was that the church had to stand out from the Center—which explains the granite material. Thoroughly modern inside, it's worth peering in for sculptor Louise Nevelson's *Erol Beaker Chapel*, venue for Wednesday lunchtime jazz concerts, and a church hall-cum-theater with a reputation of being one of the city's most innovative.

The Citicorp provided a spur for the development of Third Avenue, though things really took off when the old Elevated Railroad that ran here was dismantled in 1955. Until then Third had been a strip of earthy bars and rundown tenements, in effect a border to the more salubrious midtown district. After the Citicorp gave it an "official" stamp of approval, office buildings sprouted, revitalizing the flagging fortunes of Midtown Manhattan in the late 1970s. The best section is between 44th and 50th streets—look out for the sheer marble monument of the **Wang Building** between 48th and 49th whose cross-patterns reveal the structure within.

All this office space hasn't totally removed interest from the street (there are a few good bars here, notably *P. J. Clarke's* at 55th, a New York institution—see Chapter Eight, "Drinking and Eating"), but most life, especially at nighttime, seems to have shifted across to **Second Avenue** on the whole lower, quieter, more residential and with any number of singles/Irish bars to crawl between. The area from Third to the East River in the upper 40s is known as **Turtle Bay** and there's a scattering of brownstones alongside chirpier shops and industry that disappear as you head north. Of course the UN Headquarters Building (see p.97) has had a knock-on effect, producing buildings like **1 UN Plaza** at 44th and First, a futuristic chess piece of a hotel that takes its design hints from the UN Building itself. Inside, its marbled, chrome-laden lobby is about as uninviting as any other modern luxury hotel. Should this be your thing, a double room will set you back a few hundred dollars; if not, just pray that all New York hotels don't end up like this.

First Avenue has a certain ragged looseness that's a relief after the concrete claustrophobia of Midtown Manhattan, and **Beekman Place** (49th–51st streets between First Avenue and the river) is quieter still, a beguiling enclave of garbled styles. Similar, though not quite as intimate, is **Sutton Place**, a long stretch running from 53rd to 59th between 1st and the river. Originally built for the lordly Morgans and Vanderbilts in 1875, Sutton increases in elegance as you move north and, for today's crème de la crème, **Riverview Terrace** (off 58th Street) is a (very) private enclave of five brownstones. The Secretary-General of the UN has a place here and the locals are choosy who they let in: disgraced ex-President Richard Nixon was refused on the grounds he would be a security risk.

BARS *Costello's, Green Derby, P.J. Clarke's, Shescape* (lesbian).

CAFES AND TEA ROOMS *Algonquin Oak Room, Citycorp Atrium.*

RESTAURANTS Budget *Stage Deli*; *Taste of the Apple*; **American, Mexican, Latin, and South American** *American Festival Café, Marvin Gardens, Popovers*; **French** *Brasserie, Les Sans Culottes, Magic Pan Creperie*; **Italian** *Rocky Lee, Trattoria*; **Japanese** *Hatsuhana*; **Fish and Seafood** *Goldwater's, Hobeau's, Oyster Bar*; **Vegetarian** *Au Natural, The Great American Health Bar*; **Expense Account** *American Festival Café, Le Bernadin, The Four Seasons, Lutèce, 21 Club, The Quilted Giraffe, The Rainbow Room.*

HOTELS/HOSTELS *Allerton House, Beekman Tower, Beverly, Chatwall Inn on Park Avenue, Pickwick Arms, Plaza, Roger Smith Winthrop, Tudor, Vanderbilt YMCA, Viscount.*

CHAPTER THREE

UPPER MANHATTAN

UPPER MANHATTAN begins above 57th Street, the corporate wealth of
Midtown Manhattan yielding abruptly to the smug residentialism of the
Upper East and West Sides. **Central Park** lies in between, the city's
back yard, where people come to play and jog or, in the summer months,
just stay sane, escaping the Midtown crowds in one of the most intelligent pieces
of urban landscaping anywhere.

The **Upper East Side** is at its most opulent in the mansions of **Fifth** and
Madison avenues, today taken over by the **Metropolitan Museum of Art** and
other of the city's great museums in what has become known as **Museum Mile**.
For the rest it's in part an elegant, mind-your-own-business residential area, a
scattering of historical attractions toward its periphery with, to the north, still
more or less identifiable, the old German neighborhood of **Yorkville**—the only
concession to ethnic presence.

The **Upper West Side** is a lot less refined, though it does have **Lincoln
Center**—carrying with it considerable cachet, as it hosts New York's most
prestigious arts performances. It is again predominantly residential, well heeled
on its southern fringe, especially along stretches of Columbus Avenue, though
considerably less so as you move north. At its top end, marked at the edge by the
monumental **Cathedral of St. John the Divine**, is **Morningside Heights**, an
area that is the last gasp of Manhattan's wealth before the decayed streets of
Harlem and—much farther east—its Latino counterpart **El Barrio**. Farther
north is **Inwood** and the city's least expected museum, the medieval arts collection at **The Cloisters**—for which see Chapter Five, "Museums and Galleries."

Central Park

"All radiant in the magic atmosphere of art and taste." So enthused *Harper's*
magazine on the opening of **CENTRAL PARK** in 1876, and though it's hard to be
quite so jubilant about the place today, few New Yorkers could imagine life without it. For whether you're into jogging, baseball, boating, botany, or just plain
walking, or even if you rarely go near the place, there's no question that it's
Central Park which makes New York a just-about-bearable place to live. For many
people here, it's their only contact with nature: they know it's spring because
Central Park is turning green; winter must be coming when the trees start losing
their leaves. Certainly, life without it would be a lot more unhinged.

Central Park came close to never happening at all. It was the poet and newspaper editor, William Cullen Bryant, who had the idea for an open public space back
in 1844, and he spent seven years trying to persuade city hall to carry it out, while
developers meanwhile leaned heavily on the authorities not to give up any valuable land. But eventually the city agreed and an 840-acre space north of the city

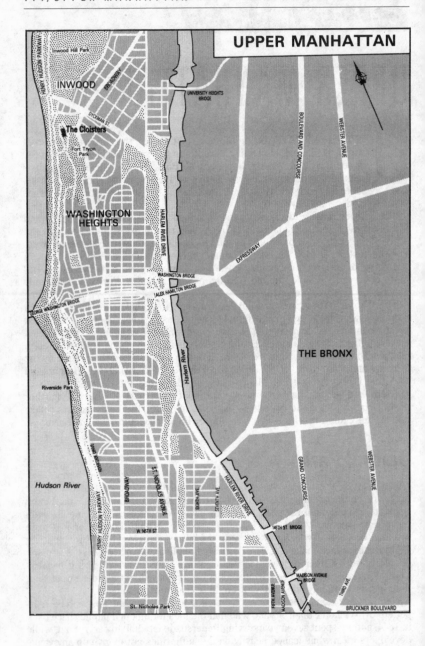

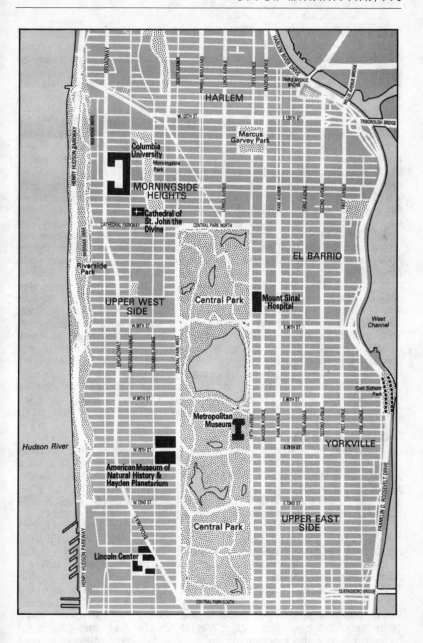

limits was set aside, a desolate swampy area then occupied by a shantytown of squatters. The two architects commissioned to design the landscape, Frederick Olmsted and Calvert Vaux, planned to create a rural paradise, a complete illusion of the countryside bang in the heart of Manhattan, which even then was growing at a fantastic rate. They also saw their scheme as a leveler, a democratic park where all would contribute "to the greater happiness of each . . . rich and poor, young and old, Jew and Gentile."

The park was finished in 1876, and opened with such publicity that Olmsted and Vaux were soon in demand as park architects all over the country. Locally they went on to design the Riverside and Morningside parks in Manhattan, and Prospect Park in Brooklyn. Working alone, Olmsted laid out the campuses at Berkeley and Stanford in California, and had a major hand in that most televised of American artificial landscapes—Capitol Hill in Washington DC.

Today, in spite of the advent of motorized traffic, the sense of disorderly nature Olmsted and Vaux intended largely survives, cars and buses cutting through the park in sheltered canyons originally meant for horse-drawn carriages. The skyline, however, has changed, buildings thrusting their way into view and detracting from the park's original pastoral intention. Worse still are Robert Moses' alterations, which turned large stretches of landscaped open space into paved playground. Lately, too, the success of Central Park has in a way been its downfall, for as the crowds have become thicker, so the park has become more difficult to keep up to scratch; its lawns have become muddied, the gardens weary-looking and patchy, and the quieter reaches, which the two architects imagined a haven of peace and solitude, sites of muggings and attacks on women. To their credit, the city authorities have since 1980 mounted a determined assault on all these evils, renovating large portions, upping the park's policing, and greenifying it at the expense of the softball fields and basketball nets. But it will be some time before Central Park is looking anything like its best.

There's not really much else to say: the attractions of Central Park depend on the time of year, and the thing to do is explore it for yourself—and check out possible events at the Visitors' Center (see below).

Getting around in the park

By far the best way is to rent a **bicycle** from either the *Loeb Boathouse* or *Metro Bicycles* (Lexington at 88th Street—see p.33). Both charge around $3 an hour plus deposit, a much better deal than the famed (and extortionate) **buggy rides** (about $15 for a half hour's trot). **On foot**, there's little chance of getting lost since one glance at the skyline should provide the clue to where you are. To know exactly, just find the nearest lamp post: the first two figures signify the number of the nearest street. As for **trouble**, should you run into anything serious don't resist, give up all you've got and make a dash for it. You should be all right during the day, though always be careful. After dark it's illegal to enter on foot, so if you want to look at the buildings of Central Park West lit-up, à la Woody Allen's *Manhattan*, fork out for a buggy.

The park divides easily in two: the area south of the reservoir, and the rest; most things of interest lie in the south. Entering here from Grand Army Plaza, the **Pond** lies to your left and to your right Central Park **Zoo** (April–Oct Mon–Fri 10am–5pm, Sat & Sun 10am–5:30pm; Nov–March Mon–Sun 10am–4:30pm; $1) recently reopened after extensive restoration. The zoo, whose collection is based on three climatic regions—the Tropic Zone, the Temperate Territory, and the

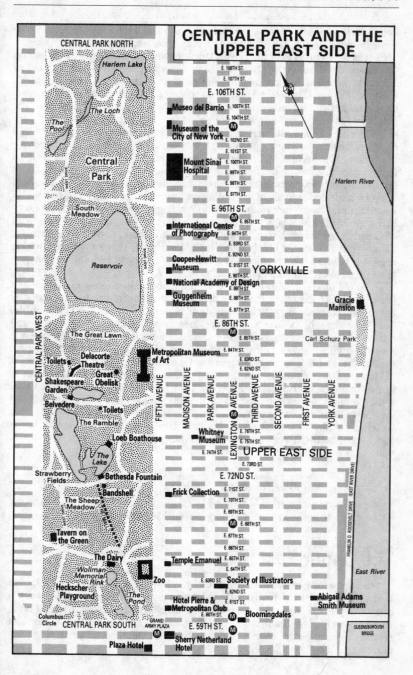

CENTRAL PARK AND THE UPPER EAST SIDE

CENTRAL PARK NORTH

Harlem Lake

The Loch

The Pool

Central Park

South Meadow

Reservoir

The Great Lawn

Delacorte Theatre

Toilets

Shakespeare Garden

Great Obelisk

Belvedere

Toilets

The Ramble

Loeb Boathouse

The Lake

Strawberry Fields

Bethesda Fountain

Bandshell

The Sheep Meadow

Tavern on the Green

The Dairy

Wollman Memorial Rink

Heckscher Playground

The Pond

Zoo

Columbus Circle

CENTRAL PARK SOUTH

GRAND ARMY PLAZA

Plaza Hotel

CENTRAL PARK WEST

FIFTH AVENUE

MADISON AVENUE

PARK AVENUE

LEXINGTON AVENUE

THIRD AVENUE

SECOND AVENUE

FIRST AVENUE

YORK AVENUE

FRANKLIN D. ROOSEVELT (EAST RIVER) DRIVE

E. 108TH ST.
E. 107TH ST.
E. 106TH ST.
E. 105TH ST.
E. 104TH ST.
E. 102ND ST.
E. 101ST ST.
E. 100TH ST.
E. 99TH ST.
E. 98TH ST.
E. 97TH ST.
E. 96TH ST.
E. 95TH ST.
E. 94TH ST.
E. 93RD ST.
E. 92ND ST.
E. 91ST ST.
E. 90TH ST.
E. 89TH ST.
E. 88TH ST.
E. 87TH ST.
E. 86TH ST.
E. 85TH ST.
E. 84TH ST.
E. 83RD ST.
E. 82ND ST.
E. 76TH ST.
E. 75TH ST.
E. 74TH ST.
E. 73RD ST.
E. 72ND ST.
E. 71ST ST.
E. 70TH ST.
E. 69TH ST.
E. 68TH ST.
E. 67TH ST.
E. 66TH ST.
E. 65TH ST.
E. 64TH ST.
E. 63RD ST.
E. 62ND ST.
E. 61ST ST.
E. 60TH ST.
E. 59TH ST.

Museo del Barrio

Museum of the City of New York

Mount Sinai Hospital

International Center of Photography

Cooper-Hewitt Museum

National Academy of Design

Guggenheim Museum

YORKVILLE

Gracie Mansion

Harlem River

Carl Schurz Park

Metropolitan Museum of Art

Whitney Museum

UPPER EAST SIDE

Frick Collection

Temple Emanuel

Society of Illustrators

Hotel Pierre & Metropolitan Club

Bloomingdales

Abigail Adams Smith Museum

East River

Sherry Netherland Hotel

QUEENSBOROUGH BRIDGE

Polar Circle—tries to keep caging to a minimum and the animals as close to the viewer as possible. It's an exciting and successful philosophy, and kids will love it.

First point to head for (unless you fancy a game of chess at the **Chess and Checkers Pavilion**) is the **Dairy**, a kind of Victorian gingerbread ranch building originally intended to provide milk for nursing mothers and now the park's **Visitors' Center** (Tues–Sun 11am–4pm), giving out free leaflets and maps, selling books and putting on sporadic exhibitions. There are two routes beyond. The first skirts the southern fringe of **Sheep's Meadow** past the **Carousel** (which kids can ride on for a pittance) to **Tavern on the Green**, actually planned as a sheep enclosure but now one of the city's most exclusive—and expensive—restaurants. The second, and more obvious, is north up the **Mall**, the park's most formal stretch, flanked by statues of an ecstatic-looking Robert Burns and a pensive Walter Scott, to the **Bandshell**, and, beyond that, to the terrace and sculpted birds and animals of the **Bethesda Fountain**. To your left, **Cherry Hill Fountain** provided a turnaround point for carriages, and has deliberately excellent views of the **Lake**, which sprawls a gnarled finger from here across the heart of Central Park. **Strawberry Fields** is just west of here, opposite the home of Yoko Ono in the Dakota Building on Central Park West. This is nothing special in itself, but is invariably crowded with those here to remember John Lennon (see "The Upper West Side and Morningside Heights").

To go out on the lake, **rent a boat** from the **Loeb Boathouse** on the eastern bank (April–Oct daily 9am–5pm; $20 deposit, $6 per hour); or cross the water by the elegant cast iron **Bow Bridge** and delve into the wild woods of **The Ramble**. Take care though, as The Ramble provides notorious cover for muggers and rapists. On the other side, **Belvedere Castle** is a mock medieval citadel recently renovated, giving views over the northern half of the park and mounting small exhibitions. Just below, the **Shakespeare Garden** holds, they say, every species of plant or flower mentioned in the Bard's plays, and the **Delacorte Theater** is venue for the annual *Shakespeare in the Park* festival. Across the **Great Lawn** stand **Cleopatra's Needle** (from the Heliopolis in Egypt and 3000 years old) and the **Metropolitan Museum of Art** (see Chapter Five, "Museums and Galleries"). Otherwise there's little beyond here—only the reservoir and, in the park's most northerly reaches, the **Conservatory Garden**. If you're planning on walking all the way to Harlem, this is a possible route.

Monthly park information ☎860-1809
Daily park information ☎397-3156
Urban Park Rangers ☎860-1351 (emergencies); ☎397-3080 (activities information)

The Upper East Side

A two-square-mile grid, scored with the great avenues of Madison, Park, and Lexington, the **UPPER EAST SIDE**'s defining characteristic is wealth—as you'll at once appreciate if you've seen one of the many Woody Allen movies set here. It's the **west** of this area that sets this tone; **east** of Lexington Avenue was until recently a working-class district of modest houses, though not surprisingly gentrification is quickly changing its character.

The west East Side—Fifth and Madison avenues

FIFTH AVENUE has been the haughty patrician face of Manhattan since the opening of Central Park attracted the Carnegies, Astors, and Whitneys to migrate north and build fashionable residences on the strip alongside. Gazing out over the park, most went up when neo-Classicism was the rage, and hence the original buildings—those that survive—are cluttered with columns and Classical statues. A great deal of what you see, though, is third or fourth generation building: through the latter part of the nineteenth century, fanciful mansions would be built at vast expense, to last only ten or fifteen years before being demolished for even wilder extravagances. Rocketing land values made the chance of selling at vast profit irresistible.

Grand Army Plaza is the introduction to all this, an oval at the junction of Central Park South and Fifth Avenue that marks the division between Fifth as shopping district and residential boulevard. It's one of the city's most dramatic open spaces, flanked by the extended chateau of the **Plaza Hotel**, with the darkened swoop of the **Solow Building** behind. Across the plaza, no one has a good word to say for the **General Motors Building** or its sunken plaza, especially since a much-admired hotel, the Savoy, was demolished to make way for it a few years back. Two more hotels, the high-necked **Sherry Netherland** and **Pierre** luxuriate nearby, mocked by the size of General Motors' marble clad monolith. Many of the rooms here have permanent guests—and they're not on welfare.

When **J.P. Morgan** and his pals arrived on the social scene in the 1890s, established society cocked a snook at the "new money" by closing its downtown clubs on Morgan and anyone else it considered jumped up. Morgan's response was the time-honored all-American one: he commissioned Stanford White to design him his own club, bigger, better, and grander than all the rest—and so the **Metropolitan Club** at 1 East 60th Street was born, an exuberant confection with a marvelously over-the-top gateway. Just the thing for arriving robber barons. On the corner of 65th Street America's largest reform synagogue, **Temple Emanuel**, strikes a more sober aspect, a brooding Romanesque-Byzantine cavern that manages to be bigger inside than it seems out. The interior melts away into mysterious darkness, making you feel very small indeed.

East 65th and most streets of the East 60s are typical Upper East Side, a neat mix of small apartment houses which, not as valuable or coveted as the mansions on the avenues, escaped demolition as land prices escalated. Even so they've always been salubrious places to live: 45–49 East 65th was commissioned by Sara Delano Roosevelt as a handy townhouse for her son Franklin, no. 142 belonged to Richard Nixon, and no. 115 is the US headquarters of the PLO. Quite a neighborhood.

Fifth Avenue's wall continues with Henry Clay Frick's house at 70th Street, marginally less ostentatious than its neighbors and now the tranquil home of the **Frick Collection**, one of the city's musts. This is the first of many prestigious museums that gives this stretch its name of *Museum Mile*. Along the avenue (or just off it) are the **Whitney** (modern American art), the **National Academy of Design**, the **Met**, the **Guggenheim Collection** (twentieth century painting housed in Frank Lloyd Wright's helter-skelter mustard pot), the **Cooper-Hewitt Museum of Design**, the **International Center of Photography** and, pushing farther north, the **Museum of the City of New York**. Enough to be going on with for a week at least; for listings see Chapter Five.

Take away Fifth Avenue's museums and a resplendent though fairly bloodless strip remains. **Madison Avenue**, especially above 62nd Street, is totally different, lined with top-notch designer clothes stores whose doors are kept locked, with security cameras to check you over before entry. **Park Avenue** is less developed and less extravagant yet still as stolidly comfortable—medium-rise apartment buildings in anonymous dark brick with a little ornament at ground level to prove the worth of their owners. The occasional building stands out, like the self-glorifying **Colonial Club** at 62nd Street, but the best feature is the view as Park Avenue coasts down to the New York Central and Pan Am buildings. Another landmark is the **Seventh Regiment Armory** between 66th and 67th streets, a Lego fortress bedecked with fairytale crenellations—yet just a little sinister all the same. It's the site of a winter antiques fair each January, a good opportunity to gape at the enormous drill hall inside, one that drew complaints from the locals not so long ago when it was used as a temporary shelter for the homeless.

The eastern East Side: Yorkville

Lexington Avenue is Madison without the class, firmly **EASTERN EAST SIDE**. As the west became richer, property developers rushed to slick up real estate in the east, seldom with total success. Subsequently, apartment buildings have been repartitioned to cater to the growing demand for single accommodation. Much of the East 60s and 70s now houses lone young upwardly mobile professionals wanting to play it safe with a conservatively modish address, as the number of singles bars on Second and Third Avenues gives away.

It's left to **YORKVILLE**, a German-Hungarian neighborhood that spills out from 77th to 96th streets between Lexington and the East River, to try and supply character. Much of New York's German community arrived after the failed revolution of 1848–9, to be quickly assimilated into the area around Tompkins Square before the opening of the Elevated Railroad forced a move uptown in the 1870s. The community here is greatly depleted, but the for or five block stretch south of 86th Street still has traditional German delicatessens like **Schaller and Weber** (1654 2nd Avenue between 84th and 85th streets) or **Bremen House** (218–220 East 86th between 2nd and 3rd avenues). Try also the baroque cakes and pastries at **Café Geiger** (206 East 86th) or a meal at **Ideal** (238 East 82nd between Second and Third avenues).

86th Street runs into a park named after **Carl Schurz**, a German immigrant who rose to fame as Secretary of the Interior under President John Quincy Adams and as editor of *Harper's Weekly*. It's a model park, a breathing space for elderly German speakers and East Siders escaping their minuscule apartments. The FDR Drive cuts beneath, giving uninterrupted views across the river to Queens and the confluence of dangerous currents where the Harlem River and Long Island Sound and Harbor meet—not for nothing known as **Hell's Gate**.

One of the reasons Schurz Park lacks the all-too-usual park weirdos is the high-profile security that surrounds **Gracie Mansion** at 88th Street nearby. Roughly contemporary with the Morris-Jumel Mansion (see "Washington Heights"), it has been much cut about over the years to end up as the official residence of the mayor of New York City—though "Mansion" is a bit overblown for what is a rather cramped clapboard house. The Mansion is open for walk-around **tours**, usually on Wednesday, though you need to book in advance (☎570-4751).

Across from the park and just below Gracie Mansion is **Henderson Place**, a set of old servants' quarters now transformed into luxury housing. Built in 1882 by John Henderson, a fur importer and real estate developer, the small Queen Anne style wooden and brick dwellings were constructed to provide close and convenient housing for servants working in the palatial old East End Avenue mansions, most of which have now been torn down. The servants' quarters now represent some of the most sought after real estate in the city, offering the space, quiet, and privacy that much of the city's housing lacks.

North of 86th Street, the mood begins to change rapidly as the bright turquoise facade of the diagonal housing projects on 97th and First signal the change as the streets become busier with the offshoots of **El Barrio**, the best-known part of New York's ever-expanding Latino community. Farther west, the elevated tracks of the 4, 5, and 6 Bronx-bound trains surface at Park and 96th, signaling the end of Park Avenue's old money dominance, while both Madison and Fifth retain their grandeur for only a few blocks more.

The streets south of Yorkville are again residential, mostly high-rise apartments of zero interest, in the main with little to lure you. On the southern perimeter, **Bloomingdale's** at 59th and Third is the celebrated, definitive American store for clothes and accessories, skillfully aiming its wares at the style-conscious and affluent (see Chapter Seven, "Shops and Markets"). And nearby, at 421 East 61st Street between York and First Avenue, is the **Abigail Adams Smith Museum** (Mon–Fri noon–4pm, Sun 1–5pm; $2) another of those eighteenth-century buildings that managed to survive by the skin of its teeth. This wasn't the actual home of Abigail Adams, daughter of President John Quincy Adams, just its stables, restored with Federal period propriety by the Colonial Dames of America as the dwelling house it became. In late years the Smith family fell on hard times, and there are interesting knickknacks from that era, including the simple dress poor Abigail had to make for herself. The contents are more engaging than the house itself and there's an odd sort of pull if you're lucky enough to be guided around by a garulously urbane Colonial Dame. The house is hemmed in by decidedly unhistoric buildings and overlooked by the **Queensboro Bridge**, which may stir memories as the 59th Street bridge of Simon and Garfunkel's *Feeling Groovy* or from the title credits of TV's *Taxi*. An intense profusion of clanging steelwork, it's utterly unlike the suspension bridges that elsewhere lace Manhattan to the boroughs; "My God, it's a blacksmith's shop!" was architect Henry Hornbostel's comment when he first saw the finished item in 1909.

Roosevelt Island

To get a view of and from the bridge, best way over is on the **aerial tramway** that connects with **ROOSEVELT ISLAND** across the water. For a subway token the trip is worth it in itself—and if you feel like exploring, Roosevelt Island rewards with some imaginative housing and eerie views. On paper this should long have been an ideal residential spot, but its history as "Welfare Island," a gloomy quarantine block of jail, poorhouse, lunatic asylum, and smallpox hospital, for years put it out of bounds to Manhattanites. The stigma only started to disappear in the 1970s when Johnson and Burgee's masterplan spawned the Eastview, Westwood, Island House, and Rivercross housing areas. The grim ruins remain—the octagonal **tower** at the island's north end is the insane asylum (it briefly housed Mae West after an unpalatably lewd performance in 1927), and to the south the **Smallpox Hospital** stands as a ghostly Gothic shell; currently both are off limits awaiting restoration. Maybe because no cars are allowed here, Roosevelt Island seems far away from New York City, a sort of post-Manhattan purgatory before the borough of Queens. Crossing back over the bridge gives a spine-tingling panorama of the city, the one Nick Carraway described in F. Scott Fitzgerald's *The Great Gatsby*.

> *Over the great bridge, with the sunlight through the girders making a constant flicker upon the moving cars, with the city rising up across the river in white heaps and sugar lumps all built with a wish out of non-olfactory money. The city seen from the Queensboro Bridge is always the city seen for the first time, in its wild promise of all the mystery and the beauty in the world . . . . "Anything can happen now that we've slid over this bridge" I thought; "anything at all . . . ."*

BARS *Astro's Turf, Border Café, Buckaroo's Bar and Roisserie, Drake's Drum, Hudson Bay Firm, Jim McMullen, JG Melon, Murphy's, Outback, Ruby's River Road Café and Bar, Rusty's, Bogart's* (gay), *Star Sapprent* (gay Asian).

RESTAURANTS Budget *Dallas Barbecue, Gray's, Little Mushroom Café, Madhatter, New Wave Coffee Shop, Papaya King, Rathbone's, Serendipity 3;* **American and Mexican** *Arizona 206, Brother Jimmy's BBQ, Caramba, El Pollo, El Sombrero;* **Chinese and Thai** *Pig Heaven, Sala Thai;* **French and Spanish** *Le Boeuf à la Mode, Café San Martin, Malaga, Le Refuge, Mme Romaine de Lyon, Le Steak, Voulez Vous;* **Indian** *Istanbul Cuisine, Uskudar;* **Italian** *Café Trevi, Carino, Contrapunto, Mezzaluna, Il Vagabondo, Via Via;* **Jewish, Eastern European, and German** *Café Geiger, Ideal Restaurant, Kleine Konditorei, Mocca Hungarian;* **Fish and Seafood** *Cockeyed Clams, Squid Roe;* **Vegetarian** *Living Springs, Greener Pastures, Zucchini;* **Expense Account** *Elaine's, Le Cirque.*

HOTELS *Wales.*

The Upper West Side and Morningside Heights

North of 59th Street, paralleling the spread of Central Park, Midtown Manhattan's tawdry west side becomes decidedly less commercial, less showy, and after Lincoln Center, fades into a residential area of mixed and multiple charms. This is the **UPPER WEST SIDE**, these days one of the city's most desirable addresses, though unlike its counterpart to the east of the park a neighborhood whose typical resident would be hard to pin down. The Upper West Side is an odd mixture of districts and faces: there's no shortage of money, as one glance at the statuesque apartment buildings of Central Park West will testify, but this exists alongside slum areas that, while they have been pushed north, have been little affected by any shifts in status.

First some **orientation**. The Upper West Side proper stretches west from Central Park as far as the Hudson River, and north from the bottom end of the park to Columbia University and Morningside Heights. Its main artery is Broadway, and generally speaking the farther you get away from here, to the east or west, the wealthier things become, until you reach either Central Park West or Riverside Drive. Sandwiched between these most prestigious of Manhattan addresses are enclaves of public housing, SRO hotels, and downbeat street hustle

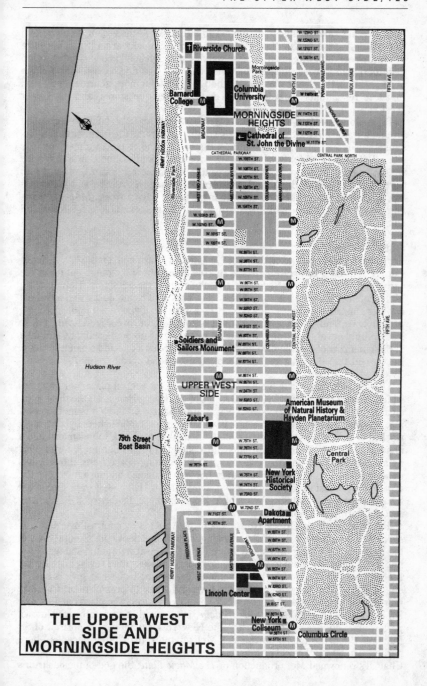

THE UPPER WEST
SIDE AND
MORNINGSIDE HEIGHTS

that increase the farther north you go, until, on Amsterdam Avenue and Columbus Avenue in the 100s (streets that in the blocks around the 70s have become irreparably yuppified), you're walking through solid and very poor Latino neighborhoods. These different lifestyles and incomes do co-exist—and for the most part happily. Give it a few years though, a handful more gourmet groceries, Japanese restaurants, sidewalk cafés, book and antique stores, and the Upper West Side may look quite different.

To explore, start at **Columbus Circle**, an odd cast of buildings grouped around a traffic circle at Central Park's southwest corner. Christopher Columbus stands uncomfortably atop a column in the center, and at the southern end, the city's *Department of Cultural Affairs* has recently found a home in a structure which, when it went up in 1965, was said to resemble a Persian brothel. From here the **NY Conventions and Visitors Bureau** gives advice and dispenses free leaflets and city, bus, and subway maps seven days a week (Mon–Fri 9am–6pm, weekends 10am–6pm), while upstairs houses exhibitions of local and community art.

Lincoln Center

Broadway sheers north from the circle to **Lincoln Plaza** and, on the left, **Lincoln Center for the Performing Arts**, a marble assembly of buildings put up in the early 1960s on the site of some of the city's most rancid slums. Home to the Metropolitan Opera Company and the New York Philharmonic, as well as a host of other smaller companies, this is worth seeing even if you're not into catching a performance, and the best way to do it is to go on an **organized tour**. These leave roughly every hour on the hour between 10am and 5pm each day, and take in the main part of Lincoln Center at a cost of $5.75 for a one-and-a-half hour tour. Be warned that they can get very booked up; phone ahead (☎769-7020 or 887-1800) to be sure of a place.

The complex itself pulls you in by way of its neat central plaza and fountain, which focuses on the grand classical forms of the Opera House. Of the three principal halls, Philip Johnson's **New York State Theater** on the left is most imposing, at least inside, its foyer serried with balconies embellished by delicately worked bronze grilles, and with a ceiling finished in gold leaf. Johnson also had a hand in the **Avery Fisher Hall** opposite, called in to refashion the interior after its acoustics were found to be below par. The seating space here, though, has none of the magnificence of his glittery horseshoe-shaped auditorium across the way, and the most exciting thing about Avery Fisher Hall is its foyer, dominated by a huge hanging sculpture by Richard Lippold, whose distinctive style you may recognize from an atrium or two downtown.

The **Metropolitan Opera House** (aka "the Met") is by contrast overdone, its staircases designed for the gliding evening wear of the city's elite. Behind each of the high windows hang **murals** by Marc Chagall. The artist wanted stained glass, but it was felt these wouldn't last long in an area still less than reverential toward the arts, so paintings were hung behind square-paned glass to give a similar effect. These days they're covered for part of the day to protect them from the morning sun; the rest of the time they're best viewed from the plaza outside. The left-hand one, *Le Triomphe de la Musique*, is cast with a variety of well-known performers, landmarks snipped from the New York skyline, and a portrait of Sir Rudolph Bing, the man who ran the Met for more than three decades—here garbed as a gypsy. The other mural, *Les Sources de la Musique*, is reminiscent of Chagall's renowned Met production of *The Magic Flute*: the god of music strums a lyre while a Tree of Life, Verdi, and Wagner all float down the Hudson River. As for performances, you'll find full details of what you can listen to and how to do it in Chapter Ten, "The Performing Arts and Film."

Each side of the Met broadens into two further piazzas, one centering on the **Guggenheim Bowl** where you can catch free summer lunchtime concerts, the other faced by the **Vivian Beaumont** and the **Mitzi E. Newhouse Theaters**. This latter square is mostly taken up by a pool, around which Manhattan office workers munch their lunch: while mid-pond reclines a lazy Henry Moore figure, given counterpoint at the edge by a spidery sculpture by Alexander Calder.

Whatever people say about the whys and wherefores of Lincoln Center, there can be little doubt of its impact on an area which before the 1960s was one of the city's most pitiful urban disasters. (It was here that the film of *West Side Story* was shot in 1960.) As well as creating an arts center, the scheme was an exercise in urban renewal, a grand plan intended to make this part of the Upper West Side a truly desirable neighborhood—which has succeeded remarkably well, even if in typical New York style it has in effect replaced a poor ghetto with a rich one and dumped the slum dwellers farther uptown. Up from Lincoln Plaza roads lead all ways, Broadway curving off north and Ninth Avenue becoming the increasingly sought-after **Columbus Avenue**. Not so long ago this, too, was run down; now its shops are being upgraded and its restaurants—and there are plenty, especially in the 60s and 70s—battle it out for the upwardly mobile custom of the local residents.

Central Park West—and John Lennon

A block east from Columbus Avenue, however, has always been well off—and as long as the monumental apartment buildings that line **Central Park West** continue to stand will remain so. Stroll down West 67th Street past the **Hotel des Artistes**, one-time Manhattan address of the likes of Noel Coward, Isadora Duncan, and Alexander Woollcott, and hang a left, following Central Park West as far as the junction of 72nd Street. More huge apartment buildings loom here, first the **Majestic**, yellow-brick and rectangular and topped with commanding twin towers; then, more famously, the **Dakota Building**, a grandiose German Renaissance-style mansion built in the late nineteenth century to persuade wealthy New Yorkers that life in an apartment could be just as luxurious as in a private house. Over the years there have been few residents here not publicly known in some way: big-time tenants included Lauren Bacall and Leonard Bernstein, and not so long ago the building was used as the setting for Polanski's film *Rosemary's Baby*. But most people now know the building as the former home of **John Lennon**—and (still) of his wife Yoko Ono, who owns a number of the apartments. It was outside the Dakota, on the night of December 8, 1980, that Lennon was murdered—shot by a man who professed to be one of his greatest admirers.

His murderer, Mark David Chapman, had been hanging around outside the building all day, clutching a copy of his hero's latest album, *Double Fantasy*, and accosted Lennon for his autograph—which he got. This was nothing unusual in itself—fans often used to loiter outside and hustle for a glimpse of Lennon—but Chapman was still there when the couple returned from a late-night recording session, and pumped five bullets into Lennon as he walked through the Dakota's 72nd Street entrance. Lennon was picked up by the doorman and rushed to hospital in a taxi, but he died on the way from a massive loss of blood. A distraught Yoko issued a statement immediately: "John loved and prayed for the human race. Please do the same for him."

Why Chapman did this to John Lennon no one really knows; suffice it to say his obsession with the man was symptomatic of his derangement. Fans may want to light a stick of incense for Lennon across the road in **Strawberry Fields**, a section of Central Park which has been restored and maintained in his memory through an endowment by Yoko Ono; trees and shrubs were donated by a number of countries as a gesture toward world peace. The gardens are pretty enough, if unspectacular, and it would take a hard-bitten skeptic not to be a little bit moved by the *Imagine* mosaic on the pathway and Yoko's handwritten note inviting passers-by to pay their respects.

Afterwards, keep on north up Central Park West, past the dull gray Beaux Arts slab of the **New York Historical Society**, which has a permanent museum (see Chapter Five, "Museums and Galleries"), and left by the **American Museum of Natural History**. Said to be the largest museum of any kind in the world, this fills four blocks with its bulk, a strange architectural melange of heavy neo-Classical and rustic Romanesque styles, that was built in several stages, the first by Calvert Vaux and Jacob Wrey Mould in 1872. For a full account of the museum and its exhibits, again see Chapter Five.

West to the Hudson

South of here West 72nd Street leads west to Broadway, where several streets meet in a busy, hustling riot of fast food joints and downgrade bars. This is officially named **Verdi Square**; unofficially, and rather more accurately, it's known as *Needle Park* (as in "Panic in . . ."), some say after the thin strip of gardens, others, less naively, because of its former function as a smack users' playground.

A short walk farther west brings you down to the Hudson River and West Side Highway, where you can see the old **Penn Railroad Yards**, abandoned for nearly two decades, though now earmarked for a new luxury housing project. Local residents, scared of yet another new influx of people into an already crowded and increasingly gentrified neighborhood, generated a storm of protest over this, but the plan currently looks set to go ahead regardless. North from here **Riverside Drive** weaves its way up the western fringe of Manhattan Island, the Upper West Side's second best address after Central Park West and flanked by palatial townhouses and towering apartment buildings put up in the early part of this century by those not quite rich enough to compete with the folks down on Fifth Avenue. **Riverside Park**, following for fifty blocks or so, provides a gentle break before the traffic hum of the Henry Hudson Parkway, landscaped in 1873 by Frederick Olmsted of Central Park fame.

A few blocks away, through the park and down the steps under the road, is a place few people know about: the **79th Street Boat Basin**, where a couple of hundred Manhattanites live on the water. It's one of the city's most peaceful locations, and while the views across to New Jersey aren't exactly awesome, they lift the spirits after the congestion of Manhattan proper. Across the canyon of West End Avenue, turn left at the junction of Broadway and 79th Street. Crossing 80th Street, the first thing you notice is another area landmark, **Zabar's**—the Upper West Side's principal and best foodie haven. Here you can find more or less anything connected with food, the first floor devoted to things edible, the second to cooking utensils and kitchenware, a collection which, in the obscurity of some of its items, must be unrivaled anywhere. What yuppie kitchen, for example, could do without a duck press?

The northern reaches

To the north, the Upper West Side gets rapidly seedy, merging into poor black and Latino neighborhoods where people hang out listlessly on street corners, hassling for small change. The transformation is sudden, but like so many districts of New York it's not entirely complete, and even here stately apartment buildings rub shoulders with SRO hotels, and always the spiked towers of the luxury **Eldorado Building** on Central Park West peak tantalisingly over the skyline.

A little farther up, the **Cathedral Church of St. John the Divine** rises out of the burned-out tenements, dumped cars and hustlers of the southern fringes of Harlem with a sure, solid kind of majesty—far from finished but already one of New York's main tourist hotspots, and on the itinerary of a steady stream of tour-bus parties throughout the season. The church was begun in 1892, to a Romanesque design that, with a change of architect, became French Gothic. Work progressed quickly but stopped with the outbreak of war in 1940 and has only resumed recently, fraught with funding difficulties and hard questioning by people who consider that, in such an impoverished area of the city, the money might be better spent on something of more tangible benefit. That said, St. John's is very much a community church, housing a soup kitchen and shelter for the homeless, studios for graphics and sculpture, a gymnasium, and (still to be built under the choir) an amphitheater for the production of drama and concerts. And the building itself is being undertaken by local Blacks trained by English stonemasons. Progress is long and slow: still only two-thirds of the cathedral is finished, and completion isn't due until around 2050—even assuming it goes on uninterrupted. But if this happens it will be the largest cathedral structure in the world, its floor space—at 600 feet long and at the transepts 320 feet wide—big enough to swallow both the cathedrals of Notre Dame and Chartres whole, or, as tour guides are at pains to point out, two full-size American football fields.

Walking the length of the nave, these figures seem much more than just another piece of American bravado. Though the cathedral appears a lot more finished here, it's not until you reach the crossing, where the naked stone has still to be encased in the milk-white marble of the choir, that you realize how far it is from completion. Here, too, you can see the welding of the two styles, particularly in the choir which rises from a heavy arcade of Romanesque columns to high, light Gothic vaulting, the dome of the crossing to be replaced by a tall and delicate Gothic spire. For some idea of how the cathedral as a whole will look, glance in on the gift shop, housed, for the moment, in the north transept, where there's a scale model of the projected design. Afterwards, take a stroll out into the cathedral yard and workshop, in which you can watch Harlem's apprentice masons tapping away at the stone blocks of the future—and finished—cathedral.

Columbia University and Morningside Heights

West out of the church toward Broadway is fringed by cheap restaurants, bars, and secondhand bookstores. No. 2911, between 113th and 114th streets is the **West End Café**, hangout of Kerouac, Ginsberg, and the Beats in the 1950s "one of those nondescript places," wrote Joyce Johnson, "before the era of white walls and potted ferns and imitation Tiffany lamps, that for some reason always made the best hangouts." It's little changed, and still serves the student crowd from **Columbia University**, whose campus fills seven blocks between Amsterdam and Broadway. This is one of the most prestigious academic institutions in the country, ranking among the Ivy League colleges and boasting a set of precincts laid out by

McKim, Mead, and White in grand Beaux Arts style. Of the buildings, the domed and colonnaded Low Memorial Library stands center stage at the top of a wide flight of stone steps, focus for demos during the 1960s. If you want to know more, guided **tours** leave regularly Monday to Friday from the information office on the corner of 116th Street and Broadway. For sustenance and great views of Manhattan, eat in the restaurant on the top floor of the Butler Library.

Across the road **Barnard College** is no less pastoral in feel, but was until recently, when Columbia removed their men-only policy, the school for women undergraduates. Just beyond, **Riverside Church** has a graceful French Gothic Revival tower, loosely modeled on Chartres and, like St. John's, turned over to a mixture of community center and administrative activities for the surrounding parish. Take the elevator to the 20th floor and ascend the steps around the carillon for some classic spreads of Manhattan's jagged skyline, New Jersey, and the hills beyond—and the rest of the city well into the Bronx and Queens. Take a look, too, at the church, whose open and restrained interior (apart from the apse, which is positively burdened with Gothic ornament) is in stark contrast to the darkened mystery of St. John the Divine.

Around the corner from the church is **Grant's Tomb**, a grubby, Greek-style memorial plastered with graffiti and surrounded by bizarre, reptilian, mosaic-covered benches. The Grant in question is General Ulysses S., Yankee Civil War hero and miserable failure as US President in the latter years of the nineteenth century. Perhaps not surprisingly, this memorial concentrates on the general's military successes rather than his term in the White House, the sarcophagi holding the general and his wife grandiosely based on that of Napoleon in Paris.

This area is known as **MORNINGSIDE HEIGHTS**, buffer zone for Harlem sprawling forbiddingly below, and with an academic, almost provincial air lent by its abundance of colleges and some swanky properties on Riverside and Morningside drives. **Morningside Park** was landscaped in 1887 by Frederick Olmsted, but it's never been especially appealing and is today a refuge of muggers and the dispossessed. If it's light it's quite feasible to walk north into Harlem; after dark you should turn south for the downtown crowds.

BARS *Augie's, Cannon's Pub, Dublin House, Emerald Inn, KCOU, Lucy's Retired Surfers, Oscar and Toni's, Racoon Lodge, The Saloon, McGlades.*

RESTAURANTS Budget *Amsterdam's, Dallas Barbecue, Diane's Uptown, EJ's Luncheonette, Flor De Mayo, O'Neal's, Taste of the Apple, Hot Dog King;* **American, Mexican, Latin, and South American** *All State Café, Arizona 206, Bahama Mama, Caramba, La Caridad, The Ginger Man, Los Panchos, Positively 104th St, Teachers, Third World Café, USA Border Café, Victor's Café, Vince and Eddies, West Side Storey, Yellow Rose Café;* **Chinese and Thai** *Empire Szechuan, Flor de Mayo, Hunan Balcony, Ollie's, Pez Dorado;* **French and Spanish** *Alcala, La Boite en Bois, Café Luxembourg, Poiret;* **Indian and Middle Eastern** *Asmara, At Our Place, The Blue Nile, Indian Kitchen, Mughlai, Zula;* **Italian** *Al Buon Gusto, Carmine's, Corrado, Ernie's, Genoa, Pizzeria Uno, Perretti, Presto, V&T Pizzeria, Vinnie's Pizza;* **Japanese** *Fujiama Mama, Lenge, Rikyu, Sakura;* **Jewish, Eastern European, and German** *Fine & Schapiro, Green Tree Restaurant;* **Fish and Seafood** *Coastal, Dock's Oyster Bar;* **Vegetarian** *Amy's.*

HOTELS/HOSTELS *Empire, Esplinade, Excelsior, International Student Center, International Youth Hostel, Malibu Studios, Milburn, Plaza, Salisbury, Wellington, Westpark, West Side YMCA.*

Harlem, Hamilton Heights and the North

HARLEM is the side of Manhattan that few visitors bother to see. Home of a declined and still declining black community, its name is synonymous with racial tension and urban decay, languishing under the bad reputation gained from riots of the 1940s, 1950s, and 1960s. Yet Harlem is more a focus of black conscious-ness and culture than out-and-out ghetto. And, perhaps because of its near-total lack of support from Federal and municipal funds (one example—there is no public high school here, the kids have to be shipped out), Harlem has formed a self-reliant and inward-looking community. For many Manhattanites, white and black, 110th Street is a physical and mental border not willingly crossed: but to understand New York, its problems and its strengths, it is necessary to under-stand—and explore—Harlem.

Harlem—hints and history

Practically speaking, Harlem's **sights** are too spread out to amble between. You'll do best to make several trips, preferably using one of the **guided tours** available (see "Information, Maps, and Tours" in *Basics*) to get acquainted with the area. Harlem's **problems** of poverty, unemployment, and attendant crime mean that foreign visitors, especially whites, can be soft targets for trouble. Though it's unlikely you'll be in any danger during the daytime, 125th Street, 145th Street, Convent and Lenox Avenues, and East 116th Street in Spanish Harlem are the places you're *least* likely be hassled—at night stick to the clubs only.

As the name suggests, it was the Dutch who founded the settlement of *Nieuw Haarlem*, naming it after a town in Holland. Until the mid-nineteenth century this was farmland, but when the New York and Harlem Railroad linked the area with Lower Manhattan it attracted the richer immigrant families (mainly German Jews from the Lower East Side) to build elegant and fashionable brownstones in the steadily developing suburb. When work began on the IRT Lenox line later in the century, property speculators were quick to build good quality homes in the expectation of seeing Harlem repeat the success of the Upper West Side. They were too quick and too ambitious, for by the time the IRT line opened most of the buildings were still empty, their would-be takers uneasy at moving so far north. A black real estate agent saw his chance, bought the empty houses cheaply and rented them to blacks from the run-down, midtown districts. Very quickly Harlem became black, while remaining home to a mix of cultural and social communities: the western areas along **Convent Avenue** and **Sugar Hill** were for years the patch of the middle classes and preserve traces of a well-to-do past. In the east the bulge between Park Avenue and the East River became **Spanish Harlem**, now largely peopled by Puerto Ricans and more properly called *El Barrio*—"the Neighborhood." In between live the descendants of West Indian, African, Cuban, and Haitian immigrants, often crowded into poorly maintained housing.

This cramping together of dissimilar cultures has long caused tensions and problems not easily understood by the downtown bureaucracy. Dotted around Harlem are buildings and projects that attest to an uneasy municipal conscience, which have not in any real sense solved the problems of unemployment and urban decay. Sometimes, among the boarded-up storefronts and vacant lots, it's hard to believe you're but a mile or two away from the charming and patrician Upper East Side.

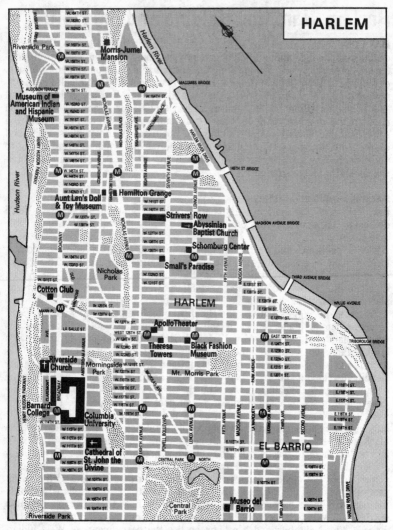

But there was a brief period when Harlem enjoyed a golden age. In the 1920s whites began to notice the explosion of black culture that had occurred here: jazz musicians like Duke Ellington, Count Basie, and Cab Calloway played in nightspots like the Cotton Club, Savoy Ballroom, Apollo Theater, and Small's Paradise; the drink flowed as if prohibition had never been heard of and the sophisticated set drove up to Harlem's speakeasies after the rest of the city had gone to bed. Maybe because these revelers never stayed longer than the last drink, they and history seldom recall the poverty then rife in Harlem, the harshness of scraping a living even before the Depression finally put paid to the revels of the few and decline drove middle-class blacks out of Harlem. One of the most evocative voices heard in the clubs those days was of Ethel Waters, who sang in the Sugar Cane Club:

> *Rent man waitin' for his forty dollars,*
> *Ain't got me but a dime and some bad news.*
> *Bartender give me a bracer, double beer chaser,*
> *Cause I got the low-down, mean, rent man blues.*

And today? As midtown real estate prices continue to rocket, new interest is being shown in sprucing up Harlem's residential dereliction. Unlike many "ghettos," the basic quality of the nineteenth-century houses here is excellent and ripe for renovation: what unsettles black activists is that 65 percent of the property in Harlem is owned by the City of New York, which assumed control after houses were abandoned by their owners. Mindful of historical precedent the downtown developers are viewed with suspicion, and renovation seen as a chance to attract young middle-class whites to the area and so signal the end of a black community that has won strength through long adversity. Others think that the arrival of whites would be a trickle at most, given the expense of renovation; and that integration in itself would be no bad thing. For Harlem, the future remains undecided . . ..

Around Harlem

125th Street between Broadway and Fifth Avenue is the working center of Harlem, a flattened, shell-shocked expanse punctuated by the occasional skyscraper. The subway throws you up here and the **New York State Office Building** on the corner of Seventh Avenue provides a looming modern landmark: commissioned after the last serious riots in 1968, it was intended to show the state's commitment to the support of the community, though really it's an intrusion on the earthy goings-on of 125th Street. Walk a little west from here and you reach the **Apollo Theater** at no. 253. Not much from the outside, despite a recent cleaning up, it was right into the 1960s the center of black entertainment in New York City and northeastern America: almost all the great figures of jazz and blues played here along with singers, comedians, and dancers. Since then it's served as a warehouse, movie theater, and radio station, and in its latest incarnation is the location for a weekly TV show, "Late Night at the Apollo." Across the way at 125th and Seventh Avenue the Theresa Towers office block was until the 1960s the **Theresa Hotel**. Fidel Castro was once a guest here, shunning midtown luxury in a popular political gesture.

125th Street rolls energetically eastward: turn right at Lenox Avenue and you enter the **Mount Morris Park Historical District** and at 201 Lenox the **Mount Oliphet Church**, an American version of a Roman version of what they thought a Greek temple looked like, and one of literally hundreds of religious buildings dotted around Harlem. The sombre, bulky **St. Martin's** at the southeast corner of Lenox Avenue and 122nd Street is among them, and both have been fortunate in avoiding falling into decay as church and community declined. Elsewhere the Mount Morris Park Historic District comprises some lovely **row houses** that went up in the speculative boom of the 1890s: take a look at the block on **Lenox Avenue** between 120th and 121st streets or the Romanesque **Mount Morris Park West** for the best. When a few years back, the city held a lottery to sell a dozen abandoned houses on Mount Morris Park there was an immediate outcry from the local people, who considered one of the prime slices of Harlem was being raffled off to faceless downtown concerns. A compromise was reached that ensured each prospective buyer who lived in Harlem would be entered three times, guaranteeing a 50-50 chance of a win. For these twelve houses, 2500 applications were received. Which is hardly surprising. Looking at Mount Morris Park West you can't help but feel that it, too, will go the way of Greenwich Village and the Lower East Side—the quality of building is so good, the pressures on Manhattan so great, it seems just a matter of time.

The former Mount Morris Park is now **Marcus Garvey Park**, taking its name from the black leader of the 1920s, and altogether a decidedly odd urban space. Ragged peaks block off views, meaning you never get an idea of the square as a unity, and the jutting outcrops contradict the precise lines of the houses around. At the top an elegant octagonal fire tower of 1856 is a unique example of the early warning devices once found throughout the city. Spiral your way to the top for a great view.

Seventh Avenue becomes **Adam Clayton Powell Jr. Boulevard** above 110th Street, a broad sweep pushing north between low-built houses that for once in Manhattan allow the sky to break through. Since its conception Powell Boulevard has been Harlem's main concourse, and it's not difficult to imagine the propriety the shops and side streets had in their late nineteenth-century heyday, though now they're a chain of graffiti-splattered walls and storefronts punctuated with demolished lots. At 135th Street and Powell Boulevard the new **Small's Paradise** is also a reminder of that era, taking its cue from the famous club of the 1920s where monied downtowners, gangsters, and bootleggers mingled with Small's dancing waiters to the sounds of jazz. The tradition is kept up in Friday and Saturday night jams and concerts; no cover and no minimum mean you can afford the car service back home—☎234-6330 for more details of this and who's on. When here during the day it's worth checking out the **Schomburg Center for Research in Black Culture** at 515 Lenox Avenue at 135th Street (Mon–Wed 10am–8pm, Fri 10am–6pm; ☎491-2200) for its exhibitions on the history of black culture in the US: see Chapter Five, "Museums and Galleries."

A few streets north at 132 West 138th Street is yet another church—though this one, the **Abyssinian Baptist Church**, is special not because it's architecturally interesting, but because of its long-time minister, the **Reverend Adam Clayton Powell Jr**. In the 1930s Powell was instrumental in forcing the mostly white-owned, white-workforce shops and stores of Harlem to begin employing the blacks who ensured their economic survival. Later he became the first black on the city council, then New York's first black representative in Congress—a career which came to an embittered end in 1967, when amid strong rumors of the misuse of public funds he was excluded from the House by majority vote. This failed to diminish his standing in Harlem, where voters twice re-elected him before his death in 1972. In the church there's a small **museum** to Powell's life, the scandal of course unmentioned, but a more fitting memorial is the Boulevard that today bears his name.

The Abyssinian Baptist Church is also famed for its revival-style Sunday morning **services** and a gospel choir of gut-busting vivacity. Usually all are welcome to join in, though it's discreet to phone ahead (☎862-7474). An alternative, and a viable one, is to join the Penny Sightseeing Company's **Harlem Gospel Tour** (Thurs 10am and Sun 10:30am; $17, reservations at least two days in advance from the address in "Information, Maps, and Tours" in *Basics*).

These days no one is going to make grandiose claims for Powell Boulevard, but cross over to 138th Street between Powell and Eighth Avenue (aka Frederick Douglass Boulevard) and you're in what many consider the finest, most articulate block of row houses in Manhattan—**Strivers' Row**. Commissioned during the 1890s housing boom, this takes in designs by three sets of architects—the best McKim, Mead, and White's north side of 139th, a dignified Renaissance-derived strip that's an amalgam of simplicity and elegance. Within the burgeoning black community of the turn of the century this came to be *the* desirable place for ambitious professionals to reside—hence its nickname. Maybe it's an indication of Harlem's future that despite the presence of Strivers' row there's been no knock-on effect on the wasteland all around; if streets like these can't trigger redevelopment, cynics argue, then what can?

El Barrio

From Park Avenue to the East River is Spanish Harlem or **EL BARRIO**, dipping down as far as East 96th Street to collide head on with the affluence of the Upper East Side. The center of a large Puerto Rican community, it is quite different from Harlem—the streets are dirtier, the atmosphere more intimidating. El Barrio was originally a working-class Italian neighborhood (a small pocket of Italian families survives around 116th Street and First Avenue) and the quality of building here was nowhere as good as that immediately to the west. In the early 1950s the federal government offered Puerto Ricans incentives to emigrate to the US under a policy known as "Operation Bootstrap" (so named for the theory that the scheme would help pull Puerto Rico up "by the straps of its boots" by reducing its overpopulation problem). But the occupants have had little opportunity to evolve Latino culture in any meaningful or noticeable way, and the only space where cultural roots are in evidence is **La Marqueta** on Park Avenue between 111th and 116th Streets, a five-block street market of tropical fruit and vegetables, sinister-looking meat and much shouting; brush up your Spanish and watch your change. To get some background on the whole scene **El Museo del Barrio** at Fifth Avenue and 104th Street (see Chapter Five, "Museums and Galleries") is a showcase of Latin American art and culture.

Hamilton Heights

The farther uptown you venture, the less like New York it seems. Much of Harlem's western edge is taken up by the area known as **HAMILTON HEIGHTS**, like Morningside Heights to the south a mixed bag of campus, garbage-strewn streets and slender parks on a bluff above Harlem. Just one stretch, the **Hamilton Heights Historic District** that runs down Convent Avenue to City College pulls Hamilton Heights up from the ranks of the unkempt mediocre. Years ago the black professionals who made it up here and to Sugar Hill farther north could glance down on lesser Harlemites with disdain: it's still a firmly bourgeois residential area—and one of the most attractive uptown.

But even if this mood of shabbiness around a well-heeled neighborhood is to your taste, there's little in the way of specific sights. The 135th Street St. Nicholas subway is as good a place to start as any, for up the hill and around the corner is Convent Avenue, containing the Heights' single historic lure—the house of Alexander Hamilton, **Hamilton Grange**.

Alexander Hamilton's life is as fascinating as it was flamboyant. An early supporter of the Revolution, his enthusiasm quickly brought him to the attention of George Washington, and he became the general's aide-de-camp, later founding the Bank of New York and becoming first Secretary to the Treasury. Hamilton's headlong tackling of problems made him enemies as well as friends: alienating Republican populists led to a clash with their leader Thomas Jefferson, and when Jefferson won the presidential election in 1801, Hamilton was left out in the political cold. Temporarily abandoning politics, he moved away from the city to his grange here (or rather near here—the house was moved in 1889) to tend his plantation and conduct a memorably sustained and vicious feud with **Aaron Burr**, who had beaten Hamilton's father-in-law to a seat in the US Senate and then set up the Bank of Manhattan as a direct rival to the Bank of New York. After a few years as Vice-President under Jefferson, Burr ran for the governorship of New York; Hamilton strenuously opposed his candidature and after an exchange of extraordinarily bitter letters, the two men fought a duel in Weehawken, New Jersey, roughly where today's Lincoln Tunnel emerges. Hamilton's eldest son had been killed in a duel on the same field a few years earlier, which may explain why, when pistols were drawn, Hamilton honorably discharged his into the air. Burr, evidently made of lesser stuff, aimed carefully and fatally wounded Hamilton. So died "the most restless, impatient, artful, indefatigable, and unprincipled intriguer in the United States" as President John Adams described him; you'll find his portrait on the back of a $10 note.

All of which is a lot more exciting than the **house** he lived in at 287 Convent Avenue (at 142nd Street, daily 9am–5pm; free), a Federal-style mansion today uncomfortably transplanted between a fiercely Romanesque church and an apartment building. It's probably only worth dropping in if visiting the wonderful **Aunt Len's Doll and Toy Museum** nearby—for which you'll need an appointment— see Chapter Five, "Museums and Galleries."

If you've just wandered up from Harlem, **Convent Avenue** comes as something of a surprise. Its secluded, blossom-lined streets have a suburban pleasance that's spangled with Gothic, French, and Italian Renaissance hints in the happily eclectic houses of the 1890s. Running south, the feathery span of the **Shepard Archway** announces **City College**, a rustic-feeling campus of collegiate Gothic halls built from gray Manhattan schist dug up during the excavations for the IRT subway line and mantled with white terracotta fripperies. Founded in 1905, City College made no charge for tuition, so becoming the seat of higher learning for many of New York's poor, and though free education came to an end in the 1970s, 75 percent of the students still come from minority backgrounds to enjoy a campus that's as warmly intimate as Columbia is grandiose.

Washington Heights

The change from Convent Avenue to Broadway is almost as abrupt as it is up from Harlem. Broadway here is a once-smart, now ragged sweep that slowly rises to the northernmost part of Manhattan Island, **WASHINGTON HEIGHTS**. Even from Morningside or Hamilton Heights the haul up is a long one: but the first two good stops are both easily reached from the number 1 train to 157th and Broadway or the A to 155th or 163rd. **Audubon Terrace** at 155th and Broadway is an Acropolis in a dead end, a weird, clumsy nineteenth-century attempt to deify 155th Street with museums tarted up as Beaux Arts temples. Easily the best of these is the **Museum of the American Indian**, but as you might expect from something so far out of town, it's little known and little visited. For a full account of each museum, see "Museums and Galleries."

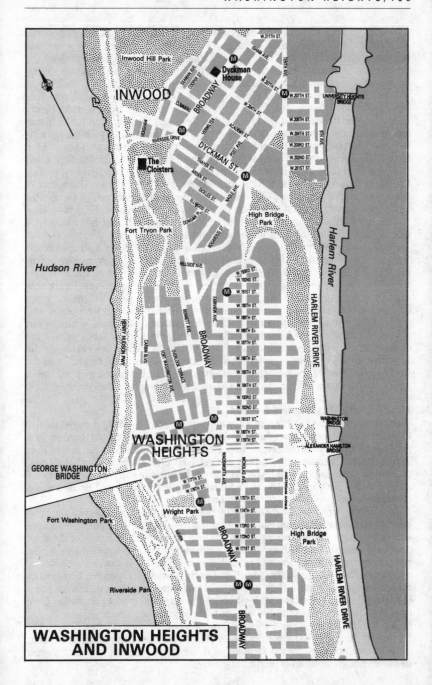

W.211TH ST.
ISHAM AVE.
TENTH AVE.
SEAMAN AVE.
COOPER ST.
Inwood Hill Park
Dyckman House
BROADWAY
W.207TH ST.
CUMMING
W.204TH ST.
INWOOD
W.207TH ST.
UNIVERSITY HEIGHTS BRIDGE
W.206TH ST.
9TH AVE.
W.205TH ST.
VERMILEA
ACADEMY ST.
W.204TH ST.
RIVERSIDE DRIVE
W.203RD ST.
POST AVE.
W.202ND ST.
DYCKMAN ST.
W.201ST ST.
The Cloisters
THAYER ST.
ARDEN ST.
High Bridge Park
SICKLES ST.
NAGLE AVE.
Harlem River
ELLWOOD ST.
Fort Tryon Park
DONGAN PL.
BOGARDUS ST.
HARLEM RIVER DRIVE
Hudson River
HILLSIDE AVE.
W.193RD ST.
W.192ND ST.
W.191ST ST.
FAIRVIEW AVE.
W.190TH ST.
W.189TH ST.
W.188TH ST.
BENNETT AVE.
W.187TH ST.
W.186TH ST.
HENRY HUDSON PKWY.
BROADWAY
W.185TH ST.
CABIN BLVD.
W.184TH ST.
OVERLOOK TERRACE
FORT WASHINGTON AVE.
W.183RD ST.
W.182ND ST.
W.181ST ST.
WASHINGTON
W.180TH ST.
WASHINGTON BRIDGE
W.179TH ST.
HEIGHTS
ALEXANDER HAMILTON BRIDGE
GEORGE WASHINGTON BRIDGE
W.177TH ST.
WASHINGTON AVE.
NICHOLAS AVE.
W.176TH ST.
Wright Park
W.175TH ST.
HARLEM RIVER DRIVE
Fort Washington Park
W.174TH ST.
W.173RD ST.
W.172ND ST.
BROADWAY
High Bridge Park
W.171ST ST.
HAVEN
Riverside Park
BROADWAY

**WASHINGTON HEIGHTS
AND INWOOD**

Within walking distance the **Morris-Jumel Mansion** (160th Street between Amsterdam and Edgecombe avenues, Tues–Sun 10am–4pm; $2) is another uptown surprise: cornered in its garden the mansion somehow survived the destruction all around, and today is one of the more successful house museums, its proud Georgian outlines faced with a later Federal portico. Inside, the mansion's rooms reveal some of its engaging history: built as a rural retreat in 1765 by Colonel Roger Morris, it was briefly Washington's headquarters before falling into the hands of the British. A leaflet describes the rooms and their historical connections, but curiously omits much of the later history. Wealthy wine merchant Stephen Jumel bought the derelict mansion in 1801 and refurbished it for his wife Eliza, formerly a prostitute and his mistress. New York society didn't take to such a past, but still, when Jumel died in 1832, Eliza married former Vice President Aaron Burr—she for his connections, he for her money. Burr was 78 when they married, 20 years older than Eliza: the marriage lasted for six months before old Burr upped and left, to die on the day of their divorce. Eliza battled on to the age of 91, and on the top floor of the house you'll find her obituary, a magnificently fictionalized account of a "scandalous" life.

From most western stretches of Washington Heights you get a glimpse of the **George Washington Bridge** that links Manhattan to New Jersey, and it's arguable that the feeder road to the bridge splits two distinct areas: below is bleakly run down, the biggest area of crack selling in the city, mainly to New Jersey residents making good use of the bridge; above, the streets relax in smaller, more diverse old-time ethnic neighborhoods of Jews, Greeks, Central Europeans, and especially the Irish, though a major Latino community has recently built up. A skillful, dazzling sketch high above the Hudson, the bridge skims across the channel in massive metalwork and graceful lines, a natural successor to the Brooklyn Bridge. "Here, finally, steel architecture seems to laugh," said Le Corbusier of the 1931 construction. To appreciate what he meant, grit your teeth and walk—Midtown Manhattan hangs like a visible promise in the distance.

The Cloisters Museum and Inwood

What most people pass through Washington Heights to visit, though, is **The Cloisters**, the Metropolitan Museum's collection of medieval art housed in a pastiche of medieval architecture, imported stone by stone from Europe in **Fort Tryon Park**. Unequivocally, this is a must (see the "Museums and Galleries" chapter for persuasion), and if you ride up on the subway you'll find an additional reward in the park itself, cleverly landscaped by Frederick Law Olmsted and a comfortable place to get lost for half an hour or so.

Fort Tryon Park joins Inwood Park by the Hudson River, and despite the presence of the Henry Hudson Parkway running underneath, it is possible to walk across Dyckman Street and into Inwood Park. The path up the side of the river gives a beautiful view of New Jersey, suprisingly hilly and wooded this far up river. Keep walking and you will reach the very tip of Manhattan, an area known as *Spuyten Duyvil*, "the spitting devil" in Dutch, nowadays Columbia University's Athletic Stadium. Inwood Park itself is wild and rambling, often confusing and a little threatening if you get lost. It was once the stamping ground for Indian Cave dwellers, but unfortunately, the site of their original settlement is now buried under the Henry Hudson Parkway. Inwood's single tourist attraction is the **Dyckman House** (4881 Broadway at 204th Street, Tues–Sun, 11am–5pm; free) an eighteenth-century Dutch farmhouse restored with period bits and pieces; pleasant enough, but hardly worth the journey.

RESTAURANTS American *Sylvia's Restaurant.*
HOSTELS *International House of New York.*

CHAPTER FOUR

THE OUTER BOROUGHS

Manhattan is a hard act to follow, and the four **OUTER BOROUGHS**—Brooklyn, Queens, The Bronx, and Staten Island—inevitably pale in comparison. They lack the excitement (and the mass money) of Manhattan's architecture; with a few honorable exceptions they don't have museums to compare with the Met or MoMA, nor galleries like SoHo's; and their life, essentially residential, is less obviously dynamic.

So why step off the island? The answer, perhaps, if you've just a few days in NYC, is "don't"—or at least only do so for the fun of returning on the **Staten Island Ferry**. But if you're staying longer, you will probably be more receptive to the boroughs' attractions, not least among them the chance to escape the sometimes stifling environment of Manhattan. And there are definite, if modest, attractions. **Brooklyn** offers the beautiful **Prospect Park**, salubrious **Brooklyn Heights**, and, for addicts of run down seaside resorts, **Coney Island**. **Queens**, scarcely ever visited by outsiders, has the bustling Greek community of **Astoria**. As for **Staten Island**, the ferry is its own justification. Whether you choose to take a look at the fourth borough, **The Bronx**, is a more ambivalent exercise. The area is ordinarily residential at its north end but the south, as any number of New York stories will attest, is Hard Territory, as desolate and bleak an urban landscape as you'll find anywhere.

BROOKLYN

> *Duh poor guy! Say, I've got to laugh, at dat, when I t'ink about him! Maybe he's found out by now dat he'll neveh live long enough to know the whole of Brooklyn. It'd take a guy a lifetime to know Brooklyn t'roo an' t'roo. An' even den, you wouldn't know it at all.*
>
> Thomas Wolfe *Only the Dead Know Brooklyn*

"The Great Mistake." So New York writer Pete Hamill summed up the 1898 annexation of his borough, and in a way, that's how most Brooklynites feel even today, traditionally seeing themselves as **Brooklyn** residents first, inhabitants of New York City a poor second. Though always the underdog to Manhattan, Brooklyn has a firm and individual identity, a definite feel which is embodied in a mass of urban folklore. The Brooklyn Dodgers, the accent, Woody Allen, Mel Brooks, Barbra Streisand: all, in one way or another, are unmistakably Brooklyn—and all to some degree sum up this most diverse of the New York City's boroughs.

If it were still a separate city Brooklyn would be the fourth largest in the United States, but until as recently as the early 1800s it was no more than a group of loosely associated towns and villages existing relatively autonomously from already thriving Manhattan across the water. It was with the arrival of Robert

Fulton's steamship service, linking the two, that Brooklyn began to take on its present form, starting with the establishment of a leafy retreat at Brooklyn Heights. What really changed the borough, though, was the opening of the Brooklyn Bridge, and thereafter development began to spread deeper inland, as housing was needed for the increasingly large workforce necessary to service a more commercialized Manhattan. By the turn of the century, Brooklyn was fully established as part of New York City, and its fate as Manhattan's perennial junior partner was sealed.

Brooklyn Heights is the most obvious—and justly the most visited—district, but that's as far as most people get. Yet there are other neighborhoods which are at least as picturesque, and in a way a lot more real. **Park Slope**, for example, has some of the city's best preserved brownstones, and Calvert and Vaux's **Prospect Park** is for many an improvement on their more famous bit of landscaping in Manhattan; **Coney Island** and **Brighton Beach** are worth the subway ride for their unique atmospheres if not as seaside resorts; and the **Brooklyn Museum** has a collection which can compete with anything on Manhattan. Basically, treat Brooklyn not as a suburb but as a separate city, and you begin to appreciate it.

Downtown Brooklyn: Brooklyn Heights, Atlantic Avenue, and South

BROOKLYN HEIGHTS is one of New York City's most beautiful and wealthy neighborhoods, and as such it has little in common with the rest of the borough. From the early eighteenth century on, bankers and financiers from Wall Street could live among its peace and exclusivity and imagine themselves far from the tumult of Manhattan, but still close enough to gaze across to the monied spires. Today the Heights are not far different, the original brownstones being assured protection back in 1965 when the Heights were made the first member of the New York Historical District scheme. Walking down the tree-lined streets, with their perfectly preserved rows and air of civilized calm, it's not hard to see why people want to live here. That is, though, give or take a handful of churches, all there is to see: students of urban architecture could have a field day, but for the rest of us there's little to do beyond wander and breathe in the neighborhood's peace.

Arriving from the Brooklyn Bridge

Assuming you're walking from Manhattan (and it really is the best way, for the views if nothing else), the Brooklyn Bridge is the most obvious place to begin a tour of the district. At its far end you'll find yourself in what's called the **Fulton Ferry District**. This, lurking under the glowering shadow of the Watchtower (world headquarters of the Jehovah's Witness organization), was where Robert Fulton's ferry used to put in, and during the nineteenth century it grew into Brooklyn's first and most prosperous industrial neighborhood. With the coming of the bridge it fell into decline, but now is on the way up again: its aging buildings are being slowly tarted up as loft spaces, and, down on the ferry wharf itself, a couple of barges—*Bargemusic* and the *River Café* (see Chapters Ten and Eight respectively)—entice die-hard Manhattanites across the bridge by night.

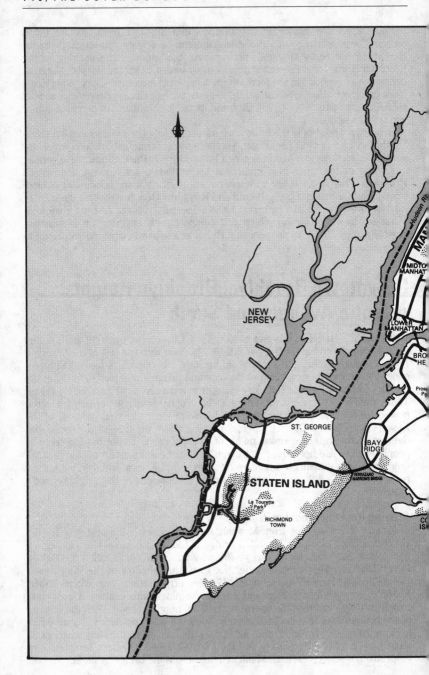

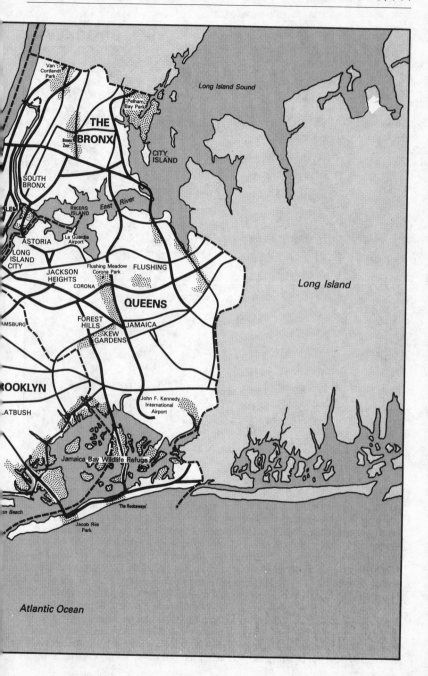

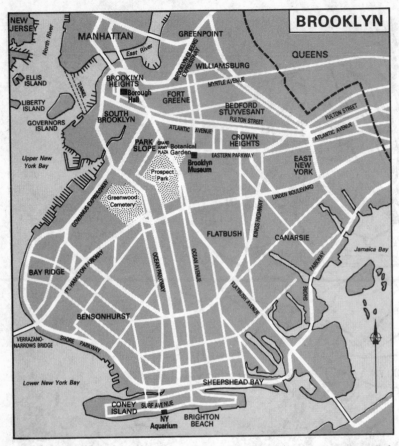

Camden Plaza West leads off beneath the elevated highway: follow this a little way, and a right up Henry Street will take you into the oldest part of Brooklyn Heights proper. Middagh Street holds the neighborhood's oldest house, number 24, dating from 1829 and built in the wooden Federal style—the "gingerbread" referring to its elaborately carved details. On the next street up, Orange, stands the **Plymouth Church of the Pilgrims**, a simple church that went up in the mid-nineteenth century and became the preaching base of **Henry Ward Beecher**, under whom it grew to be one of the country's most talked-about churches. Beecher—liberal, abolitionist, campaigner for women's rights—was a great orator: he held mock slave auctions here and used the money to buy slaves' freedom, and toured the country persuading the rich to give to charitable institutions. This brought the famous to his church, and Horace Greeley, Mark Twain, even Abraham Lincoln, all worshiped here on more than one occasion. Sadly, though, Henry Ward remains less known outside New York than his sister, Harriet Beecher Stowe, author of *Uncle Tom's Cabin*, since his later years were marred by an adultery scandal of which he was acquitted but never finally cleared in public esteem. The church is kept locked most of the time, so the only chance you'll get to see its barn-like interior is when there's a service on. No great loss.

The Esplanade and Pierrepoint Street

Clark Street leads down to the river and **The Esplanade** (called "The Promenade" by the locals), home of such as Norman Mailer (he lives in one of the creeper-hung palaces here) and with fine views of Lower Manhattan across the water. East is **Pierrepoint Street**, one of the Heights' main arteries and studded with delight-ful—and fantastic—brownstones. On the corner of Henry Street the **Herman Behr House** is a chunky Romanesque Revival mansion which has been, succes-sively, a hotel, brothel, Franciscan monastery (it was the brothers who added the horrific canopy), and currently private apartments. Farther down Pierrepoint, look in if you can on the **Church of the Saviour**, notable for its exquisite neo-Gothic interior, and, across the road, the **Brooklyn Historical Society**, which presents regular exhibits on the borough's social history. The society's walking tours of the Heights also leave from here (see "Information, Maps, and Tours" in *Basics*).

Montague Street and around

Head west, and you're on **Montague Street**, Brooklyn Heights' lively main thor-oughfare, lined with bars and restaurants and, surprisingly for such an exclusive district, with a workaday atmosphere that makes it one of New York's most pleas-ant thoroughfares. At the far end, on **Montague Terrace**, Thomas Wolfe lived for a while and wrote *Of Time and the River*. South of here are a couple of neat alley-ways, **Grace Court Alley** and **Hunts Lane**, not unlike those off Washington Square in Manhattan, and just below, **Joralemon Street**, traditionally a street of craftsmen and women rather than brokers and consequently holding houses decidedly less grand. The far end of Montague is known as "Bank Row"—downtown Brooklyn's business center—and leads on to what is in effect the borough's Civic Center, the end of the residential Heights signaled by the tall Art Deco buildings of Court Street. Across the road the sober Greek-style **Borough Hall** is topped with a cupola-ed belfry; to its left there's the massive **State Supreme Court** and Romanesque **post office**, next to which stands a bronze of Henry Ward Beecher. There's little to linger for, and the buildings are ugly, but stop off at the **Information Booth/TKTS Office** just in front for a map and Brooklyn information pack.

Beyond the civic grandeur **Fulton Street** leads east, principal shopping thor-oughfare for the borough as a whole and here pedestrianized into a characterless shopping precinct. There's another TKTS office, plentiful mainstream shops, and **Gage & Tollner**, Brooklyn's most famous restaurant that serves seafood and steaks in a setting determinedly left unchanged. If you can afford it—and the food doesn't come cheap—there are worse places to break for lunch.

Atlantic Avenue

South of Brooklyn Heights is **ATLANTIC AVENUE**, which runs from the East River all the way to Queens and is for a short stretch center to New York's Middle Eastern minority. There are some fine and reasonably priced Yemeni and Lebanese restaurants here and a good sprinkling of Middle Eastern grocery stores and bakeries. Try the **Damascus Bakery** for pitta bread, and the **Sahadi Importing Co.** at no. 187 for nuts, dried fruit, halva, and the like; and see Chapter Eight, "Drinking and Eating" for listings of the best restaurants.

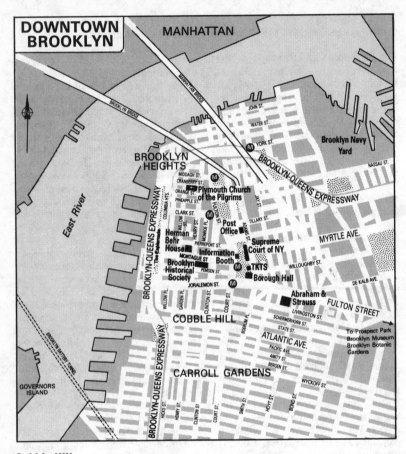

Cobble Hill

Crossing Atlantic Avenue, Cobble Hill, Carroll Gardens, and Boerum Hill, along with the old wharfing community of Red Hook, make up the area better known as South Brooklyn, a piece of land that juts out into Upper New York Bay. Of these three small districts (which adopted their historical names back in the 1960s to engender a sense of community spirit) **COBBLE HILL** is most elegant, its main streets—Congress, Warren, and Amity—a mixture of solid brownstones and colorful redbrick terraces, most of which have long been a haven of the professional classes. Really, the attraction is just in strolling along the streets, but there are a couple of features you may want to take in: Jenny Jerome, later Lady Randolph Churchill and mother of Winston, was born at **197 Amity Street** in a house now disfigured by aluminum windows and a modern rustic facing; and **Warren Place** is worth a quick peek for a tiny alley of laborers' cottages from the late nineteenth century—a shelter of quiet just a stone's throw from the thunder of the Brooklyn–Queens Expressway.

Carroll Gardens

Cobble Hill stops at De Graw Street, where the mood changes and the strong Italian community of **CARROLL GARDENS** begins. Originally a middle- and upper-class community of many nationalities, South Brooklyn received a massive influx of Italian dockworking immigrants who came in the early 1900s and settled in the area named after Charles Carroll, the only Roman Catholic signatory to the Declaration of Independence, Today, it remains staunchly Italian and is the first stop for many new Italian immigrants. **Court Street** is the main thoroughfare, lined with ubiquitous pizzerias, Italian pastry shops, and seafood restaurants. It's very family oriented, lower middle class, and far removed from the more famous Little Italy. The most bizzare sight in Carroll Gardens is the large number of religious shrines and statues that decorate the large gardens that give the neighborhood its name.

Red Hook

South of Carroll Street, the streets become distinctly seedy, with the elevated section of the Gowanus Expressway marking the beginning of **RED HOOK**, an old Irish and Italian community of dockworkers now largely idle following the demise of New York's docking industry. Most of the original immigrant groups left in the 1950s and 60s as the growing automation of the docking industry left Red Hook behind (vividly portrayed in the film and the notorious novel *Last Exit to Brooklyn*), most ships choosing instead to dock at modern facilities in New Jersey, where ships could be unloaded much more quickly—and cheaply. A small Italian contingent remains here and shares the now cheap housing with African-Americans and Latinos, many of whom live in the infamous Red Hook housing projects. While definitely not to be recommended for casual sightseeing, Red Hook is a testament to the ruthlessness of New York's development; one of the communities that helped build the city, and that has been left behind in its wake.

Red Hook is separated from the farther reaches of Brooklyn by the old Gowanus Canal, and only overcome by the elevated section of the F train, which rises out of the ground at Carroll Street, heading to Park Slope and ultimately Coney Island.

Boerum Hill

To the east of Cobble Hill, and south of Atlantic Avenue, is **BOERUM HILL**, less salubrious and less architecturally impressive than its neighbors and home to Italian- and Irish-descended families, and most recently a large Latino community. It's they who bring salsa music and dancing to the stoops of the neighborhood brownstones, and single room storefront social clubs are a common sight on Smith Street. Smith Street is also the site of one of Boerum Hill's gaudier attractions, the pastel green and silver of **J. Michaels department** store on the corner of Smith and Warren streets, a severe break with the more sober Greek Revival and Italianate Boerum Hill architecture.

RESTAURANTS *Gage & Tollner, Henry's End, Leaf 'n' Bean, Montague Street Saloon, Promenade, Slade's, Teresa's, Tripoli.*

Central Brooklyn: Fort Greene, Bedford-Stuyvesant, Crown Heights, and Park Slope

Just to the east of downtown Brooklyn sits **FORT GREENE**, named after Nathaniel Greene, a prominent general in the American Revolution, and long established as a strong multiracial community. Easily navigated by keeping an eye on the Williamsburg Savings Bank, Brooklyn's tallest building, Fort Greene also boasts America's oldest performing arts center at 30 Lafayette Avenue, the **Brooklyn Academy of Music**—BAM to its friends and one of the borough's most cherished institutions, playing host over the years to a glittering—and innovative—array of names.

At the northern tip of the neighborhood lies the **Brooklyn Naval Yard**, once one of the main sources of employment for Brooklyn workers, now a rather less impressive industrial park. Officially commissioned in 1801, it reached its peak in World War II, when over 70,000 men and women worked day and night building such famous battleships as the *Iowa*, *New Jersey*, and *Arizona*. The *USS Missouri* is still in use today. While Fort Greene remains strongly African-American in its make up, gentrification is creeping into the neighborhood and real estate values are increasing rapidly. At the moment the mix of neighborhood families and young professionals gives the area a pleasant feel: *Spike's Joint*, the movie merchandise and clothes store of film director and Fort Greene native Spike Lee is at 1 South Elliot Place, Brooklyn (☎718/802-1000), and for somewhere to eat, try the soul food at *Harper Valley* on Fulton Street near Greene Avenue.

Bedford-Stuyvesant
Immediately east of Fort Greene lies **BEDFORD-STUYVESANT**, originally one of the most elegant neighborhoods in the city, today one of the most badly neglected. Originally two separate areas, populated by both blacks and whites, the opening of the Brooklyn Bridge and later the construction of the A train brought a massive influx of African-Americans into the area. This led to increased hostility between the two groups, which in turn led to fighting. In the 1940s the white population left, and took with them funding for many important community services. This was the start of the decline of Bed-Stuy, as it has become colloquially known, and though it has suffered the all-too-usual problems of inner city neglect and drug dealing, today the African-American community here, the largest in the country, is desperately trying to stop Bed-Stuy's rot and take advantage of an architectural legacy of some of the best Romanesque revival Brownstones in the city.

Brownsville
Bedford-Stuyvesant's eastern neighbors of Bushwick, East New York, Brownsville, and East Flatbush have a similar story of generational ethnic development. In the early part of this century, **BROWNSVILLE** was notable for being a hotbed of prominent anarchists, Bolsheviks, and other political free thinkers. Emma Lazarus, author of the spirited inscription on the Statue of Liberty lived here, and in 1916, with over 150 prospective clients waiting outside its doors, the first birth control clinic in America opened here—only to be raided and closed nine days later by the vice squad, its founder, Margaret Sander, imprisoned for thirty days as a "public nuisance."

Williamsburg

North of Bedford-Stuyvesant and Fort Greene is **WILLIAMSBURG**, home of the huge landmark **Williamsburg Savings Bank** and immediately recognizable because of the large numbers of **Hasidic Jews** who live there. The men, dressed in black with long *payess* (earlocks) hanging from under their hats have been a common sight since the Williamsburg Bridge linked the area to the Lower East Side in 1903. Many of the Jews from that neighborhood left for the better conditions in Williamsburg, and during World War II a further settlement of Hasidim, mainly from the ultra-orthodox Satmar sect, established Williamsburg as an Jewish Center. At about the same time a large number of Puerto Ricans began to arrive here, and the two communities have coexisted in a state of strained tolerance ever since. Tensions boiled over in November 1990, with Latino residents accusing the police of favoritism toward the Jewish community. This was denied by the local 90th Precinct, but Jewish anger at the arrest of a Hasidic man on molestation charges brought over 300 Hasidim to the police station in late October, and a riot almost erupted.

The best place to start exploring Williamsburg is on **Lee Avenue**, the main shopping street, or the more residential **Bedford Avenue** that runs parallel. On either you'll see manifestations of the neighborhood's Orthodox Jewish character: *Glatt Kosher* delicatessens line the streets, signs are written in Yiddish, and the distinctive dress of the men especially gives the area the feel of being a throwback to some *mitteleuropa* town of the nineteenth century. If you do make it here, drop by the **Domsey Warehouse** at the end of South 9th Street for some of the cheapest clothes in the city: search long enough through the piles of coats and dresses and you're bound to find a bargain.

Crown Heights and Prospect Park

Fulton Street and Atlantic Avenue separate Bedford-Stuyvesant from **CROWN HEIGHTS**, New York's largest West Indian neighborhood, which bursts into life with an enormous carnival each Labor Day.

More interesting, though, is the route up Flatbush Avenue to **Grand Army Plaza**. This is where Brooklyn really asserts itself as a city in its own right—pure classicism, with the traffic being funneled around the central open space. It was laid out by Calvert and Vaux in the late nineteenth century, who designed it as a dramatic approach to their newly completed Prospect Park just behind. The triumphal **Soldiers, and Sailors' Memorial Arch**, which you can climb (spring and fall weekends only), was added thirty years later and topped with a fiery sculpture of Victory in tribute to the triumph of the North in the Civil War. On the far side of the square the creamy smooth **Brooklyn Public Library** continues the heroic theme, its facade smothered with stirring declarations to its function as fountain of knowledge, and with an entrance showing the borough's native son, poet Walt Whitman. Behind, there's the **Brooklyn Museum** (see Chapter Five, "Museums and Galleries") and the **Brooklyn Botanic Garden** (April–Sept Tues–Fri 8am–6pm, Sat & Sun 10am–4pm; Oct–March Tues–Fri 8am–4:30pm, Sat & Sun 10am–4:30pm).

This is one of the most enticing park spaces in the city, smaller and more immediately likable than its more celebrated rival in the Bronx, and making for a relaxing place to unwind after a couple of hours in the museum. Sumptuous but not overplanted, it sports a Rose Garden, a Japanese Garden, a Shakepeare Garden (laid out with plants mentioned in the bard's plays), and some delightful lawns draped with weeping willows and beds of flowering shrubs. There's also a conservatory housing, among other things, the country's largest collection of bonsai.

The Botanic Garden is about as far away from Manhattan's bustle as it's possible to get, but if you can tear yourself away there's also **PROSPECT PARK** itself. Energized by their success with Central Park, Olmsted and Vaux landscaped this in the early 1890s, completing it just as the finishing touches were being put to Grand Army Plaza outside. In a way it's better than Central Park, having more effectively managed to retain its pastoral quality, and though there have been encroachments over the years—tennis courts, a zoo—it remains for the most part remarkably bucolic in feel. Focal points include the **Lefferts Homestead**, an eighteenth-century colonial farmhouse shifted here some time ago and now open for tours from Wednesday to Sunday, the **Zoo** (though it's no better and no less cruel than Central Park Zoo), and the lake in the southern half. The **boathouse** has maps and information on events in the park (dance, drama, and music are performed in the bandshell most summer weekends) or you can pick up all kinds of park information on ☎718/788-0055.

Park Slope—and a note on Bensonhurst

The western exits of Prospect Park leave you on the fringes of **PARK SLOPE**, with some of New York's best preserved brownstones and, in an area currently building itself up as a serious rival to Brooklyn Heights, some of the city's fastest-soaring property prices. Main streets are **Seventh** and **Fifth avenues**, both of which share new shops for the recent incomers and long-established stores in almost equal proportion—though of the two Fifth is more downmarket, still supporting a solid Hispanic community.

Walk down Fifth Avenue, across the Prospect Expressway, and you reach **Greenwood Cemetery**: larger even than Prospect Park and very much the place to be buried in the last century if you could afford to splash out on an appropriately flashy gravestone—or better still mausoleum. Among the names buried here, Horace Greeley, politician and campaigning newspaper editor, lies relatively unpretentiously on a hill; William Marcy "Boss" Tweed, nineteenth-century Democratic party supremo and scoundrel, slumbers deep in the wilds; and the Steinway family, of piano fame, have their very own 119-room mausoleum. Look out also for the tomb of one John Matthews, who made a fortune out of carbonated drinks and had himself a memorial carved with birds and animals, some fierce-looking gargoyles, and (rather immodestly) scenes from his own life. You can stroll around the cemetery and find all this for yourself; or take a **guided tour** (see "Information, Maps, and Tours" in *Basics*).

BENSONHURST, to the south of Greenwood cemetery, merits a mention not for being a predominantly Italian area but for an incident that underlines the racism found in certain outlying parts of the city. In August 1989, Yusef Hawkins, a black boy of sixteen, wandered into the neighborhood looking to buy a bike. Surrounded by a gang of youths and mistaken for someone else, he was beaten and finally shot and killed. The incident brought to the surface racial tensions that had long been suppressed, and split the city in two. Rightly or wrongly, Bensonhurst will long be associated with racism in New York City.

RESTAURANTS *Aunt Sonia's, Aunt Suzie's, Cucina, Frost Restaurant, Once Upon a Sundae, 101, Sam's, Tartine.*

Coney Island and Brighton Beach

CONEY ISLAND, reachable direct from Manhattan on the B, D, F, or N subway lines, was for years where generations of working-class New Yorkers came to relax, at its height visited by 100,000 people a day who idled away their weekends indulging in beach-lounging, hot dogs, cotton candy, and strolls along the boardwalk. By the 1950s, however, the resort was past its best, and now, although plenty of people still flock here when the weather's fine, the good-time carefree atmosphere is long gone. Coney Island is today one of Brooklyn's—and New York's—poorest districts, predominantly Hispanic and with a pervasive atmosphere of menace through which even the police travel in groups of three. The amusement park is peeling and run down, until recently the boardwalk was cracked and broken, and *Nathan's*, Coney Island's once legendary and unique hot dog stand, now has franchises all over the city. But if you like run-down seaside resorts, there's no better place on earth.

The main street is **Surf Avenue**, above which run the gaudy subway trains on their way back to Manhattan. Weekdays here are a depressing sight—gangs of youths hanging around outside bars and souvenir-hung arcades that, whatever the weather, emit cringingly bathetic fairground music. The **beach** at least is beautiful, a broad clean swathe of golden sand, and it's not difficult to see what once made people flock here. But the rusting ironwork of the amusement park is an unwelcoming backdrop, and on hot weekends it's hard to find a space even now; dedicated swimmers would be better off aiming for Long Island.

Brighton Beach

Farther along, **BRIGHTON BEACH**, or "Little Odessa," is home to the country's largest community of Russian emigres, around 20,000 in all, who arrived in the 1970s following a relaxation of emigration restrictions on Soviet citizens entering the US. There's also a long-established and now largely elderly Jewish population. It's a livelier neighborhood than Coney Island, more prosperous, less defeated. But out of season the boardwalk, lined with melancholic elderly Slavs, can seem just as sad.

Things cheer up on **Brighton Beach Avenue**, the neighborhood main street which runs underneath the El in a hodgepodge of grocery stores and appetizing restaurants. Russian souvenirs are everywhere, and any number of groceries offer a range of possibilities for lunch—maybe some caviar or smoked fish from *International Food* at no. 249, as a topping to some pumpernickel. Or there's *Mrs Stahl's Knishes* on the corner of Brighton Beach and Coney Island Avenue, a remnant from more firmly Jewish days. **Sit-down food** is also readily available, though you'd be better off waiting until evening as it's then the restaurants really hot up, becoming a near parody of a rowdy Russian night out with loud live music, much glass clinking, and the frenzied knocking back of vodka. All very definitely worth a trip: see *The Outer Boroughs* in Chapter Eight, "Drinking and Eating."

Next stop on the D or Q subway line from Brighton Beach is **Sheepshead Bay**: not a place to go swimming (although you can swim at Manhattan Beach, a short walk away). At night the Bay is lively, especially along the main drag, **Emmons Avenue**, where the bars and restaurants along the waterfront make it a pleasant place to wander, especially in the afternoon or evening.

RESTAURANTS *Carolina, Gargiulo's, Jean's Clam Bar, Joe's, Nathan's Famous, Odessa, Primorski, Mrs Stahl's, Star of China.*

THE BRONX

The Bronx. There's no other part of New York about which people are so ready to roll out their latest and most gruesome horror stories. For this, the city's northernmost borough, represents in its decaying reaches one of the most severe examples of urban deprivation you're ever likely to see. But whatever they tell you in Manhattan, however many Bronx jokes you hear, it's not as unequivocally bleak as people would have you think. In fact, it's really only the South Bronx and a few isolated pockets which are in any way dangerous, and for the most part you can treat it much as you would any other part of New York.

The Bronx developed—and has since declined—more quickly than any other part of the city. First settled in the seventeenth century by a Swedish landowner named Jonas Bronk, like Brooklyn it only became part of the city proper at the turn of the last century. From 1900 onward things moved fast, and the Bronx became one of the most desirable parts of the city in which to live, its main thoroughfare, **Grand Concourse**, becoming edged with increasingly luxurious Art Deco apartment buildings—many of which, though greatly run down, still stand today. This avenue runs the length of the borough, and many places of interest lie on it or reasonably close by. Most people travel up for the **Zoo**, or bypass the greater part of the borough altogether for **Orchard Beach** or **City Island**. Other places besides these are worth seeing: the grotesqueries of **Woodlawn Cemetery** and smug **Riverdale** in the north; the **New York Botanical Gardens**—large enough to seem a really tangible escape from the city; and even the **South Bronx**, probably best experienced only as a passing cityscape from the relative comfort of the subway. This is easy to do, as the subway travels above ground after leaving Manhattan, cutting directly through the most cataclysmic of the South Bronx.

Yankee Stadium and the South Bronx

First stop on the subway after leaving Manhattan is **Yankee Stadium**, home of the New York Yankees and offering some of the best facilities for the sport in the country. The Yankees played in north Harlem before moving here in 1923, a move that was in part due to their most famous player ever, George Herman "Babe" Ruth, who joined the team in the spring of 1920 and went on to wear the uniform for the next fifteen years. It was the star quality of Babe Ruth, the original Bronx Bomber (as the team is now known), that helped pull in the cash to build the current stadium, which for a while was known as the "House that Ruth Built." Inside, Babe Ruth, Joe di Maggio, and a host of other Yankee heroes are immortalized in stone, but unless you're coming to watch a game (or, on occasion, be blessed—in 1965 and 1979 popes said mass here to over 50,000 New Yorkers), there's little reason to visit. (See "Sports" in Chapter Six for further details.)

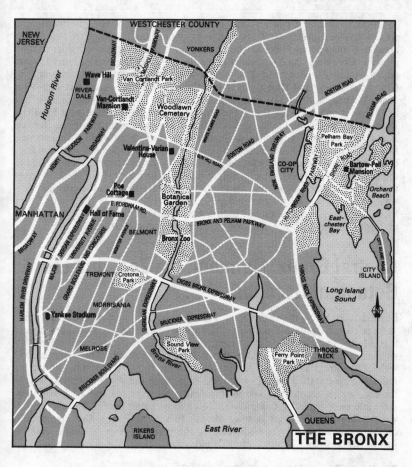

THE BRONX

To the north and west stretches the awful wasteland of the **SOUTH BRONX**, first part of the borough to become properly urbanized but now scarred by huge squares of rubble, leveled apartments sprawling between gaunt-eyed tenements, and with streets dotted with huddled groups of young blacks and Hispanics. The sense of hopelessness is overwhelming, and without a massive injection of money, and some encouragement to businesses and the white middle classes (all of which have long since moved way up or downtown) to come back with their cash, there are no signs that the South Bronx will ever get back on its feet. Carter promised to do something about this and did nothing, and Reagan's withdrawal of Federal support made things even worse. This is the place where a city's dispossessed have been shoveled up, dumped, and left to rot—and no one, not even those who live in other parts of the Bronx, would seem to care. Somehow, the South Bronx jokes you heard back in Manhattan fall a little flat when you experience the neighborhood for yourself.

Through all this, if you are on foot, the **Grand Concourse** still manages to shine with some level of sanity. Stray to either side, though, and you're getting into areas that most people—not all alarmists by any means—would consider dangerous. The Concourse itself contains the ever-busy **Bronx Supreme Court House**, where part of *The Bonfire of the Vanities* was filmed, and farther along at 1040 Grand Concourse and East 165th Street, the **Bronx Museum of Art** (Sat–Thur 10am–4:30pm, Sun 11am–4:30pm; $1) with changing displays of temporary exhibits, many oriented toward the Bronx. Carry on, and the junction with Fordham Road marks the beginning of the South Bronx's main shopping districts. Here on East Fordham and West Fordham Road are the main department stores and the focus of Saturday afternoon shopping. Fordham Road boasts every fast food franchise imaginable, complete with the necessary quota of homeboys checking out the territory. They would stand out were it not for the hundreds of families, street vendors, and barbecued-shrimp sellers that also vie for space on the crowded sidewalk. If you're seriously interested in seeing what the rest of the South Bronx looks like, a trip on the elevated 4 train down to Yankee Stadium gives a good view of the desolation—and will reinforce your wish to stay on the train.

Central Bronx: Belmont, the Zoo, and the Botanical Gardens

Beyond 180th Street the Bronx improves radically. Turn north up Arthur Avenue and you're in **BELMONT**, a strange mixture of tenements and clapboard houses that is home to by far the largest segment of New York's Italian community. It's a small area, bordered to the east by the Zoo and to the west by Third Avenue, and with 187th Street as its axis. And it's far enough away from Manhattan for the Italians to keep it their own. Few tourists come here, but if you're on your way to the zoo, amble through to see its pungent grocery stores and pork butchers, cafés and sweet-smelling bakeries. There's also no better part of the Bronx if you want to **eat**: choose from swanky *Mario's* (where Al Pacino shot the double-crossing policeman in *The Godfather*) or the pizzas at *Ann & Tony's*, both on Arthur Avenue. See Chapter Eight, "Drinking and Eating," for more details.

The Bronx Zoo and New York Botanical Gardens
Follow 187th to the end and you're on the edge of the park which holds **Bronx Zoo** (daily 10am–5pm, Sundays and holidays 10am–5:30pm; Fri–Mon $4.75, rest of the time a donation is sufficient), accessible either through its main gate on Fordham Road or a second entrance on Bronx Park South. This last is the entrance to use if you come directly here by subway (East Tremont Avenue stop).

The zoo is probably the only reason many New Yorkers from outside the borough ever visit the Bronx. Even if you don't like zoos, it's as good a one as any: the largest urban zoo in the United States, and one of the first to realize that animals both looked and felt better out in the open—something done artfully through a variety of simulated natural habitats. Visit in summer to appreciate it at its best (in winter a surprising number of the animals are still caged): one of the most interesting parts is the Wild Asia exhibit, an almost forty-acre wilderness through which tigers, elephants, and deer roam relatively freely, viewable from a monorail train ($1.25)—though this is only open from May to October. Look in also on the World of Darkness (a recreation of night, holding nocturnal species) and a simulation of a Himalayan mountain area, with endangered species like the giant panda and snow leopard. All in all a good focus for a day trip to the Bronx.

Across the road from the zoo's main entrance is the back turnstile of the **New York Botanical Gardens** (Tues–Sun 10am–5pm, last admission 4pm) which in their southernmost reaches are as wild as anything you're likely to see upstate. Farther north near the main entrance (Pelham Parkway subway) are more cultivated stretches and the *Enid A. Haupt Conservatory*, where you'll find eleven galleries of palms, ferns, cacti, and orchids in an airy iron-framed building of 1902. This costs $2.50, however, and unless you're especially keen is just as good from the outside. The gardens themselves are enormous enough to wander around for hours; guides are available from the shop in the *Museum Building*.

The Poe Cottage

Leave the gardens by their main entrance and walk west and you come eventually to the Grand Concourse and the **Poe Cottage**. This tiny white clapboard anachronism in the midst of the Bronx's bustle was Edgar Allen Poe's home for the last three years of his life, though it was only moved here recently when threatened with demolition. Poe came here in 1846 with his wife Virginia and her mother; Virginia suffered from tuberculosis and he thought the country air would do her good. Never a particularly stable character and dogged by problems, Poe was rarely happy in the cottage: he didn't write a great deal (only the short, touching poem, "Annabel Lee"), there was never enough money, and his wife's condition declined until she eventually died, leaving Poe with a distraught mother-in-law and a series of literary ambitions that never seemed to come off. He left the cottage for the last time in 1849 to seal the backing for his longest-running dream—his own literary magazine—but got entangled in the election furore in Baltimore, disappeared, and was eventually found weak and delirious in the street, dying in the hospital a few days later. What actually happened no one knows, and the house, with its few meager furnishings spread thinly through half a dozen rooms, tells you little more about the man. (Wed–Fri 9am–5pm, Sat 10am–4pm, Sun 1pm–5pm; $1.)

RESTAURANTS *Ann and Tony's, Il Boschetto, Dominick's, Mario's.*

North Bronx

The **NORTH BRONX** is the topmost fringe of New York City, and if anyone actually makes it up here it's to see **Woodlawn Cemetery** (subway Woodlawn), which is worth a stroll around if only to see how money doesn't necessarily buy good taste. This has for many years been the top people's cemetery, and like Greenwood in Brooklyn (see p.148) boasts some tombs and mausoleums which are memorable mainly for their hideousness. It's a huge place but there are some tombs which stand out: one Oliver Hazard Belmont, financier and horse dealer, lies in a dripping Gothic fantasy near the entrance, modeled on the resting place of Leonardo da Vinci in Amboise, France; F.W. Woolworth has himself an Egyptian palace guarded by sphinxes; while Jay Gould, not most people's favorite banker when he was alive, takes it easy in a Greek-style temple. And that's not all.

Pick up a guide from the office at the entrance and you can discover all kinds of famous names and disgusting mausolea.

West of the cemetery lies **Van Cortlandt Park**, forested and hilly (dangerous say some) and used in winter by skiers and tobogganers. Apart from the sheer pleasure of hiking through its woods, the best thing here is the **Van Cortlandt Mansion**, nestled in its southwest corner not far from the subway station. This is an authentically restored Georgian building, very pretty, and with its rough-hewn gray stone really rather rustic. During the Revolutionary Wars it changed hands a number of times, and was used as an operations headquarters by both the British and the Patriots. On the hills above, George Washington had fires lit to dupe the British into believing he was still here (he was in fact long gone), and it was in this house he slept before heading his victory march into Manhattan in 1783. Nowadays most of the rooms are open to the public, and kept up by the Society of Colonial Dames of America (Mon–Sat 10am–5pm, Sun noon–5pm; $2).

Immediately west rise the monied heights of **RIVERDALE**—one of the city's most desirable neighborhoods, and so far from the South Bronx in feel and income it might as well be on the moon. Venture up if you wish, but there's not a lot to see save **Wave Hill**, a small country estate donated to the city a couple of decades back and which in previous years was briefly home to Mark Twain and, later, Teddy Roosevelt. The grounds are botanical gardens, the nineteenth-century mansion a forum for temporary art installations, concerts, and workshops: a great idea, but a pity it couldn't have been in a part of the city that needed it more badly (daily 10am–5:30pm; greenhouses 10am–noon & 2pm–4pm; $2, students $1).

At the other side of the Bronx **Pelham Bay Park** leads to **Orchard Beach** and, linked by a short causeway, **City Island**. This, reachable by taking subway 6 to the end and a Bx12 bus, is something of an oddity in this part of town: a small fishing village whose main street is lined with fish and seafood restaurants and whose harbor is crammed with visiting yachtspeople. That it's so hard to get to is probably just as well . . ..

QUEENS

Of New York City's four outer boroughs, **Queens**, named after Catherine, wife of Charles II, is the most consistently ignored. Even Staten Island, across the water and barely considered part of the city at all, has something to offer, even if it's only the ferry that takes you there. But Queens, despite being considerably more accessible than Staten Island, a great deal larger than Brooklyn, and immeasurably safer than the Bronx, simply lacks enough cachet to make it a desirable place to live. People who live in Queens, the thinking seems to run, are either excruciatingly dull or just can't afford to live anywhere else.

Assuming you're still reading, it's worth pointing out that Queens isn't in fact so terrible. Just that architecturally it's more lower middle-class suburbs than tenements and brownstones, there are for the moment fewer immigrant areas than in either Brooklyn or the Bronx, and that if Queens has any historic buildings they tend to be clapboard. Do, however, check out Greek **Astoria**, for both its restaurants and foodstores and the film studios; **Jackson Heights**, which has the city's largest concentration of South Americans; and **Kew Gardens** and **Forest Hills**, which have any amount of yuppie chic—and tennis.

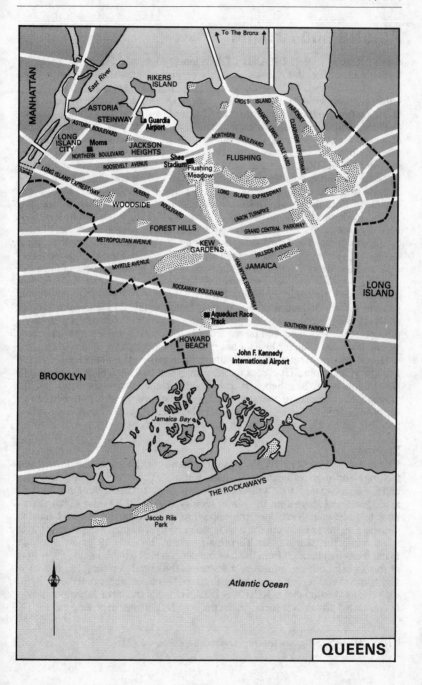

QUEENS

Astoria and Around

Bleak industrial **LONG ISLAND CITY** is most people's first view of Queens: it's through here that the subway cuts above ground after crossing over from Manhattan. Unless it's a weekend and you feel like browsing through the **Queens Plaza Flea Market** on the corner of Queens and Northern Boulevard, or the **Isamu Noguchi Museum** (see Chapter Five), there's no point getting off as there's nothing to see. This might change, as Long Island City is on the verge of being colonized by artists escaping extortionate Manhattan rents and taking over the disused loft spaces here. But it's not exactly SoHo yet, and for the present it's **ASTORIA** that makes it worth crossing the river, one of Queens' original communities and famous for two things: film making and the fact that it's the largest single concentration of Greeks outside Greece itself (Melbourne included). Until the **movie industry** moved out to the West Coast in the early 1930s Astoria was the cinematic capital of the world. Paramount had their studios here until the lure of Hollywood's reliable weather left Astoria empty and disused by all except the US Army—which was how it remained until recently when Hollywood's stranglehold on the industry weakened. The new studios here now rank as the country's fourth largest and, encouraged by the success of films like *The Wiz*, *Ragtime*, and others where the bulk of the filming was done in New York, are set for a major expansion. They're not open to the public at present, but you can visit the **Museum of the Moving Image** in the old Paramount complex at 34–31 35th Street, near Broadway, where there's an excellent display of posters, stills, sets, and equipment from both Astoria's golden age and more recent times. See Chapter Five for hours and a full description.

Greek Astoria stretches from Ditmars Boulevard in the north right down to Broadway, and from 31st across to Steinway Street. Between 80,000 and 100,000 Greeks live here (together with a substantial community of Italians) and the evidence is on display in a sizable quantity of **restaurants and patisseries** that repay a closer look. There's not a great deal else to see, but check out our restaurant listings in Chapter Eight before you write the area off.

Steinway

East of Astoria lies **STEINWAY**, a district that was bought up by the piano manufacturers and used as housing for their workers. These were mainly Germans and the area had for a time a distinctly Teutonic feel, but the community has long since gone, and apart from the **piano factory** (☎718/721-2600 for visits) there's little to keep you. Next door the noise-trap of **La Guardia Airport** handles domestic flights to and from the city. If you're lucky, you may find yourself traveling through the **Marine Air Terminal**, built in the early 1930s for the huge flying boats that took off from the lake outside. A small exhibit details the history of this stylish building, whose best feature is the mural depicting the history of flight, uncovered recently after being declared "Socialist" and painted over in the early 1950s. Just offshore, **RIKER'S ISLAND** holds the city's largest and most overcrowded prison. Not surprisingly, this isn't NYC's most appealing corner.

RESTAURANTS *Cyprus Taverna, Omonia Café, Roumeli.*

Jackson Heights, Flushing, Forest Hills, and Beyond

Next door to Steinway is the South American enclave of **JACKSON HEIGHTS**, a small and largely self-contained community of 150,000 or so Colombians, half as many Ecuadorians, and a good number of Argentinians and other South American peoples. The neighborhood first turned Hispanic in the 1960s, when huge influxes of people came over—many illegally—to find work and escape from the poverty and uncertain politics of their own countries, and it's now the largest South American contingent in the country. Tighter immigration controls, however, have radically cut the intake and the community here is now more or less static.

Eating-wise, there's no better part of Queens for exotic, unknown, and varied cuisines. Roosevelt Avenue and, running parallel, 37th Avenue between 82nd Street and Junction Boulevard, are the focus for the district, and along both streets you'll find Argentinian steakhouses, Colombian restaurants, and pungent coffee houses and bakeries stacked high with bread and pastries. See Chapter Eight for restaurant listings.

East of Jackson Heights you hit **CORONA**, its subway yards ringed by menacing barbed wire and patrolled by dogs to deter graffiti artists. A few steps away is **Shea Stadium**, home of the New York Mets. The Beatles, too, played here in 1965 (at that point far more successfully than the Mets—who have since however won two World Series), and the stadium, presumably in anticipation of further such events, has recently been upgraded with a giant video screen. For details on the Mets and when they play, see "Sports" in Chapter Six.

Shea went up as part of the 1964 World Fair, held in adjoining **Flushing Meadow Park**. This is now the site of the US Tennis Open Championships each summer, and boasts around 30 courts and seating for well over 25,000 people (again see "Sports"). The other side of the park, **FLUSHING** is a rather dull middle-income suburb which has picked up the tag "birthplace of religious freedom in America" for its role as secret Quaker meeting place during the seventeenth century, when anyone who wasn't a Calvinist was persecuted by the Dutch.

The Quakers met in the **Bowne House** which still stands, officially the oldest house in the city and open to the public on selected days of the week. It's a short walk from the Bowne Street subway station and if you're in Flushing you may just as well take a look. But be warned that the enthusiasm of the volunteers who show you around is not always mirrored by the excitement of the displays, which in the main consist of the drab furniture used over the years by the Bowne family; and, as symbolic centerpiece, the kitchen where the Quaker meetings took place. Outside stands **Kingsland House**, shifted here from its original site about a mile away and reputedly the first house in Flushing to release its slaves. All this and more is detailed in the Queens Historical Society's do-it-yourself walking tour of "Historic Flushing," for details of which see "Information, Maps, and Tours" in *Basics*. Or go to their headquarters in the Kingsland House itself.

Forest Hills and Jamaica Bay

On the other side of Flushing Meadow Park—and a long walk or a bus ride from Flushing—**FOREST HILLS** is perhaps choicest of Queens neighborhoods, home to Geraldine Ferraro and the West Side Tennis Club. This is snotty, a high-income suburb with a strong Jewish component, spectacularly expensive houses and a main street (Austin) of designer clothes stores and chi-chi restaurants. Top of the heap is **Forest Hills Gardens**, a pseudo Tudor village that is interesting not for what it is but for what it might have been, since it was built originally as housing for the urban poor until the rich grabbed it for themselves. Another "planned" neighborhood, **KEW GARDENS**, to the south, was at the turn of the century a resort popular with aging New Yorkers, complete with hotels, lakes, and a whole tourist infrastructure. All that has gone now but Kew remains, in a leafy and dignified kind of way, one of Queens' most visually enticing districts.

Just beyond is the city's other airport, **JFK International**, with to its right the wild, island-dotted indent of **JAMAICA BAY**—now an official wildlife refuge where you can observe around 300 species of birds, for free, seven days a week. Part enclosing the bay, the narrowing spit of **The Rockaways** is the largest beach in the country, stretching for 10 miles back toward Brooklyn—most of it lined by the boardwalk. At the far end **Jacob Riis Park** lays on another beach and assorted facilities, with **nude bathing** tolerated (if not officially allowed) in the eastern corner, haunt of predominantly gay naturists.

RESTAURANTS *Inti-Raymi, Las Americas, Carmichael's Diner and Cocktail Lounge, Chalet Alpina, La Pequena Columbia, Tierras Columbianas, Suzu.*

STATEN ISLAND

Until about twenty five years ago **Staten Island**, the common name for what's officially Richmond County, was isolated—getting to it meant a ferry trip or long ride through New Jersey, and daily commuting into town was almost an eccentricity. Staten Islanders enjoyed an insular, self-contained life in the state's least populous borough, and the stretch of water to Manhattan marked a cultural as much as physical divide. In 1964 the opening of the Verrazano Narrows Bridge changed things; upwardly mobile Brooklynites found cheap property on the island and swarmed over the bridge to buy their parcel of suburbia. And today Staten Island has swollen into tightly packed residential neighborhoods among the rambling shrubbery, endless backwaters of tidy look-don't-touch homes.

But most don't even see as much as this. Nine out of ten tourists who take the Staten Island ferry drool over the view and on arriving promptly turn back to Manhattan. What they miss are a couple of museums and a nerve-soothing break from the city, but that's about it: a few other bits and pieces lie scattered around but none is worth going out of the way for; thankfully either or both of the two museums repay the inland excursion.

The Ferry, the Jacques Marchais Center, and Richmondstown Restoration

The **Staten Island ferry** sails around the clock with half-hourly departures between 9:30am and 4pm, and is famed as New York's best bargain: for 50c (return) wide-angled views of the city and Liberty Island are yours, becoming

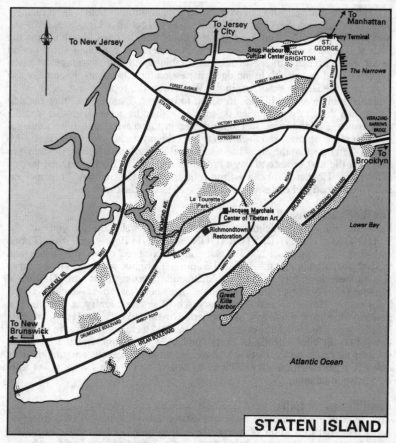

STATEN ISLAND

more spectacular as you retreat. By the time you arrive Manhattan's skyline stands mirage-like, filtered through the haze as the romantic, heroic city of a thousand and one posters. The Staten Island ferry terminal quickly dispels any romance: it's a dirty, disreputable sort of place, which serves as a novitiate for winos on their way to the Bowery. But if you're exploring the island it's easy enough to escape to the adjoining bus station and catch the 113 (connects with ferry so have exact change or a token ready as they're unavailable at the terminal) which cuts down and across to the two central museums. Along the way the **Verrazano Narrows Bridge** flashes its minimalist message across the entry to the bay, a slender, beautiful span that was, until recently, the world's longest at 4260 feet—so long that the tops of the towers are 4cm out of parallel to allow for the curvature of the earth.

The Jacques Marchais Center of Tibetan Art
In the middle of Staten Island's residential heartland the **JACQUES MARCHAIS CENTER OF TIBETAN ART** (May–Sept Wed–Sun 1pm–5pm; April, Oct, Nov,

Fri–Sun 1pm–5pm; $2.50; ☎987-3478 for additional summer hours) is an unlikely find; the bus drivers don't know it's there, so ask to get off at Lighthouse Avenue, walk up the hill and it's on the right at number 338. Jacques Marchais was the alias of Jacqueline Kleber, a New York art dealer who reckoned she'd get on better with a French name. She did, and combined with the advantages of a rich husband, used her wealth to indulge her passion for Tibetan art. Eventually she assembled the largest collection in the Western world, reproducing a *gompah* or Buddhist temple on the hillside in which to house it. Even if you know nothing about such things the exhibition is small enough to be accessible, with magnificent bronze Boddhistavas, fearsome deities in union with each other, musical instruments, costumes, and decorations from the mysterious world of Tibet. Give it time—after a while the air of the temple and its gardens is heady. Best time to visit is in the first or second week of October when the Tibetan harvest festival takes place: Tibetan monks in saffron robes perform the traditional ceremonies, and Tibetan food and crafts are sold. Phone ahead for the exact date.

The Richmondstown Restoration

Back on the main Richmond Road, a short walk brings you to the **RICHMONDSTOWN RESTORATION** (Wed–Fri 10am–5pm, Sat & Sun 1pm–5pm; $2, students $1.50), a gathering of a dozen or so old houses and miscellaneous buildings transplanted from their original sites and grafted on to the eighteenth-century village of Richmond. Starting from the **Historical Museum**, half-hourly tours negotiate the best of these—including the **Voorlezer's House**, oldest elementary school in the country, a picture-book **general store**, and the lovely, atmospheric **Guyon-Lake-Tyson House** of 1740. What brings it to life are the craftspeople using old techniques to weave cloth and fire pottery in kilns—in the summer conducted tours stop, and the costumed workers fill you in on the facts. It's all carried off to picturesque and ungimmicky effect in rustic surroundings: difficult to believe you're just twelve miles from downtown Manhattan.

Landfills and oil spills

To New Yorkers from other boroughs, Staten Island is mainly terra incognita. Ask most what they know of the smallest New York Borough and you get the reply "garbage"—the reason being that ninety percent of New York's **refuse**— some 100,000 tons *a week*—is dumped in Staten Island's Fresh Kills landfill. This is the largest landfill in the world, holding 2400 million cubic feet of garbage (twenty-five times the size of the Great Pyramid at Giza), and it's a claim to fame for which Staten Islanders feel strong resentment, not only because of environmental concern, but also because of the financial implications. They consider themselves as paying high taxes, only to be used by the city as a cheap dump. There's been much talk of Staten Island seceding from the city—something that may well be a popular cause on the Island, but which stands little chance of acceptance anywhere else. New York would lose a large amount in tax revenue from the many commuters who live on the Island, and would have to pay considerably more to dispose of its garbage.

A further reason Staten Islanders have become concerned over their environment has been the number of recent **oil spills**. The Island lies next to New Jersey's Perth Amboy, "armpit of the nation" and one of the largest refining centers in America, where spills are almost commonplace. These have continually polluted the Arthur Kill, once a favorite spot for local fishermen. Now, it's joked, the Kill produces the only crude cod liver oil in the US.

St. Georges

For the committed explorer the up-and-coming area of **St. Georges** (near the ferry terminal), is slightly more mixed than the firmly middle-income families farther inland. Good antique shops abound: try the **Edgewater Hall Antique Center**, a bank that's been refurbished as a shopping mall. About a mile and a half away in New Brighton is the Greek Revival pile of the **Snug Harbor Cultural Center**—former home for retired sailors that now houses the galleries and studios of the island's swelling artists' community. In summer the Metropolitan Opera and New York Philharmonic give concerts here—good music in intimate outdoor surroundings—and each weekend there are guided tours of the Center and nearby **Botanical Gardens** (March–Nov 2pm; free; ☎448-2500 for more info).

RESTAURANTS *Basilio Inn, La Fosse aux Loups, Just Omelettes, Tugs.*

CHAPTER FIVE

MUSEUMS AND GALLERIES

N ew York is not a city that lacks visual stimulation—and you may find there's enough on the streets without having to contemplate walking inside a museum. But you should at least be aware of what you're missing. For in the big two Manhattan museums—the **Metropolitan** and the **Museum of Modern Art**—there are few aspects of Western art left untapped. The Metropolitan, in particular, is exhaustive (mercilessly so, if you try to take in too much too quickly), with arguably the finest collection of European art anywhere in the world as well as superlative displays of everything from African artifacts to medieval sculpture. The Museum of Modern Art (MoMA) takes over where the Met leaves off, emphasizing exactly why (and how) New York has become the art capital of the world.

Among the other **major museums**, you'll find exciting collections of modern art and invariably excellent temporary shows at the **Whitney** and (when it reopens) **Guggenheim**, a wide array of seventeenth- and eighteenth-century paintings at the **Frick**, and—amid unexpectedly pastoral scenes a glorious display of medieval art out at **The Cloisters** in Fort Tryon. All of which should, if time permits, be seen. So, too, depending on personal interests and tastes, should some of the **lesser museums**, often quirkily devoted to some otherwise total obscurity. On a highly selective basis, highlights must include the **Pierpoint Morgan Library**, the **International Center for Photography**, the **Museum of the American Indian** (a neglected wonder of the city), and, for anyone less than enamored of current New York TV screens, the public archives of the **Museum of Broadcasting**.

Hours

Hours don't fall into any fixed patterns: many museums close on Mondays (and national holidays), opening into the early evening one or two nights a week. **Admission charges** are often high, occasionally softened for those with student ID cards, but happily, certain museums are free or much reduced one evening a

---

FREE MUSEUMS

The following museums are **free** at the stated times:

Tuesday Whitney (6–8pm), International Center of Photography (5–8pm), Cooper-Hewitt (5–9pm), Museum of American Folk Art (5:30–8pm), and National Academy of Design (5–8pm).

Thursday Museum of Modern Art (5–9pm pay what you wish).

To The Cloisters

To Audubon Terrace Museums

THE BRONX

NEW JERSEY

Schomburg Center

Black Fashion Museum

HENRY HUDSON PARKWAY

CATHEDRAL PARKWAY

W. 116TH ST.

W. 110TH ST.

E. 116TH ST.

E. 110TH ST.

LEXINGTON AVE.
FIFTH AVE.
MADISON AVE.
PARK AVE.
THIRD AVE.
SECOND AVE.
FIRST AVE.

Museo del Barrio

Museum of the City of New York

International Center of Photography

W. 97TH ST.

CENTRAL PARK

Cooper Hewitt Museum
National Academy of Design
Guggenheim Museum

The Metropolitan Museum of Art

American Museum of Natural History

New York Historical Society

Hudson River

E. 79TH ST.

W. 79TH ST.

Whitney Museum of American Art

Frick Collection

Center for African Art

Intrepid Sea, Air, Space Museum

W. 57TH ST.

Whitney at Equitable

Society of Illustrators

The Museum of Modern Art

Museums of American Folk Art and American Craft

E. 57TH ST.

ICP Midtown

TWELFTH AVE.
ELEVENTH AVE.
TENTH AVE.
NINTH AVE.
SCHUBERT AVE.
SIXTH AVE.
BROADWAY
FIFTH AVE.
PARK AVE.
THIRD AVE.
SECOND AVE.
FIRST AVE.

W. 42ND ST.

W. 38TH ST.

E. 34TH ST.

Whitney at Philip Morris

Pierpoint Morgan Library

Police Academy Museum

E. 23TH ST.

Forbes Gallery

W. 14TH ST.

BROADWAY

E. 14TH ST.

East River

QUEENS

Ukrainian Museum

E. 8TH ST.

CANAL ST.

Holography Museum

DELANCEY ST.

FRANKLIN D. ROOSEVELT DRIVE

Tenement Museum

Fire Dept. Museum

EAST BROADWAY

Whitney Downtown

BROOKLYN

MANHATTAN MUSEUMS

week. Otherwise you'll commonly find the "voluntary donation" system in opera-tion. This in theory means you're allowed to give as little or as much as you like to get in (hence enabling museums to keep their charitable status); in practice you'll need to be pretty hard-headed to give any less than the (not particularly low) recommended minimum.

THE MAJOR COLLECTIONS

The Metropolitan Museum of Art

Fifth Ave. at 82nd St. Subway #4, #5, or #6 to 86th St.–Lexington Ave. Tues–Thurs, & Sun 9:30am–5:15pm, Fri & Sat 9:30am–8:45pm, closed Mon. Admission by voluntary donation, suggested $6, $3 for students (includes admission to the Cloisters on the same day). Free conducted tours, "Highlights of the Met," daily; also highly detailed tours of specific galleries; recorded tours of the major collections $3.

The Met, as it's usually known, is the foremost museum in America. Its galleries take in over three-and-a-half million works of art and span the arts and cultures not just of America and Europe (though these are the most famous collections) but also of China, Africa, the Far East, and the Classical and Islamic worlds. Any kind of overview of the museum is out of the question: it demands many and specific visits, or, at least, self-imposed limits.

Broadly, the Met breaks down into five **major collections**: *European Painting, American Painting, Medieval Art, "Primitive" Art,* and *Egyptian Antiquities.* You'll find the highlights of these detailed below. Keep in mind, however, that there is much, much more for which space forbids anything other than a passing mention. Among the **"lesser" Met collections** are *Greek and Roman galleries* (second only to those in Athens), *Islamic art* (possibly the largest display anywhere in the world), a *Far Eastern gallery* (with a reconstruction of a Chinese garden, assembled by experts from the People's Republic), a *Musical Instrument Collection* (the world's oldest piano, of course, included), and what would, anywhere else, be seen as essential *Twentieth-Century Art galleries* (Picasso's *Portrait of Gertrude Stein* and Pollock's *Parsiphaë* are just two standouts).

There are two main **problems** in visiting, other than the obvious frustrations of size and time. The first is **scheduling**. Certain collections are open only on a rotating basis, so if you're intent on seeing anything less than the routine, phone ahead first (☎535-7710). The second difficulty is the piecemeal way the Met has developed. Its nineteenth-century multimillionaire benefactors were often as intent on advertising their own taste as on setting America on the cultural high-road, and their bequests often stipulated distinct and **separate galleries** for their donations. If you're interested in one particular period or movement of art you won't neccessarily find it all in the same place.

Initial orientation, despite this, is not too hard. There is just one main entrance and once within you find yourself in the **Great Hall**, a deftly lit neo-Classical cavern where you can consult plans, check tours, and pick up info on the Met's excellent lecture listings. Directly ahead is the **Grand Staircase** and what is for many visitors the single greatest attraction—the European Painting galleries.

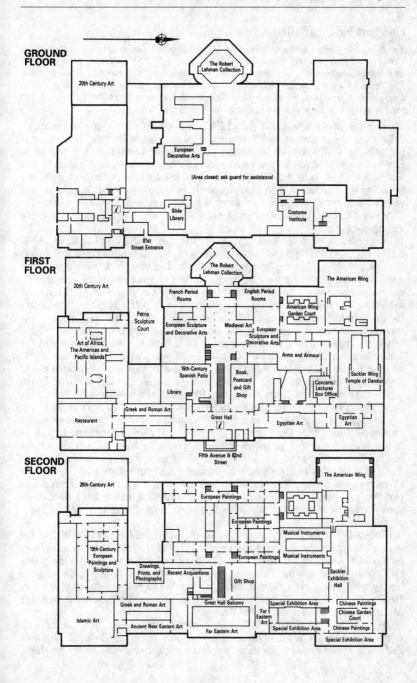

GROUND FLOOR

20th Century Art

The Robert Lehman Collection

European Decorative Arts

(Area closed; ask guard for assistance)

Slide Library

Costume Institute

81st Street Entrance

FIRST FLOOR

The Robert Lehman Collection

20th Century Art

French Period Rooms

English Period Rooms

The American Wing

Petrie Sculpture Court

European Sculpture and Decorative Arts

Medieval Art

American Wing Garden Court

European Sculpture and Decorative Arts

Art of Africa, The Americas and Pacific Islands

16th-Century Spanish Patio

Library

Book, Postcard and Gift Shop

Arms and Armour

Concerts/ Lectures Box Office

Sackler Wing Temple of Dendur

Greek and Roman Art

Restaurant

Great Hall

Egyptian Art

Egyptian Art

Fifth Avenue & 82nd Street

SECOND FLOOR

20th-Century Art

European Paintings

The American Wing

European Paintings

19th-Century European Paintings and Sculpture

Musical Instruments

Drawings, Prints, and Photographs

Recent Acquisitions

European Paintings

Musical Instruments

Gift Shop

Sackler Exhibition Hall

Greek and Roman Art

Great Hall Balcony

Special Exhibition Area

Chinese Paintings

Islamic Art

Ancient Near Eastern Art

Far Eastern Art

Far Eastern Art

Special Exhibition Area

Chinese Garden Court

Chinese Paintings

Special Exhibition Area

European Painting galleries

The Met's European Painting galleries divide in two parts. The initial rooms start with a scattering of Italian works, move into a small but fine English collection, then Northern and Italian Renaissance, and (probably the most significant) seventeenth-century Dutch. The André Meyer galleries *follow and are dominated by a tremendous core group of Impressionist paintings. Ideally, try to take in each half in separate bouts, separated at least by a break in the museum's café: these are large collections.*

Though the Met's **ENGLISH GALLERY** is essentially a prelude to the major collections, it's an unusually brilliant and elegant one. At its heart is a group of portraits by **William Gainsborough** and **Thomas Lawrence**, the two great English portrait artists of the eighteenth century. Gainsborough's *Mrs. Grace Dalrymple Elliott* is typical of his portrait style—an almost feathery lightness softening the monumental pose. Lawrence is best represented by his likable and virtuoso study of *Elizabeth Farren*, painted at the precocious age of 21, and by *The Calmady Children*, a much-engraved portrait that was the artist's own favorite among his works.

Beyond, and a drop back in time, are the **EARLY FLEMISH AND NETHERLANDISH PAINTINGS**, precursors of both the Northern and Italian Renaissance. Inevitably the first paintings are by **Jan van Eyck**, who is generally attributed with beginning the tradition of North European realism. There are two definitely accepted works—*The Crucifixion* and *The Last Judgment*—painted early in the artist's career and much like the minatures he painted for the Turin-Milan Hours; bright, realistic, and full of expressive (and horrific) detail. *The Annunciation* nearby is probably by Jan, too; its perspective is carefully if not totally accurately drawn, the Romanesque right-hand side of the portal and the Gothic left symbolizing the transition from Old Testament to New.

There's more allusion to things Gothic in **Rogier van der Weyden**'s *Christ Appearing to His Mother*, the apocryphal visit surrounded by tiny statuary depicting Christ's earlier and Mary's later life. It's one of the most beautiful of all van der Weyden's works, quite different in feel to van Eyck, with a warmth of design and feeling replacing the former's hard draftsman's clarity. This development is continued through the third great Northern Gothic painter, **Gerhard David**, as is the vogue for setting religious scenes in Low Countries settings. The background to David's exquisite *Virgin and Child with Four Angels* is medieval Bruges; in *The Rest on the Flight to Egypt* landscape features are added to by Low Country genre scenes. **Bruegel**'s *Harvesters*, one of the Met's most reproduced pictures, and part of the series of twelve paintings that included his (Christmas card familiar) *Hunters in the Snow*, shows how these innovations were assimilated.

Cutting left at this point brings you to the **SPANISH PAINTINGS** and the very different landscape of **El Greco**'s *View of Toledo*. This extraordinary picture—all brooding intensity as the skies seem about to swallow up the ghost-like town—is perhaps the best of his works anywhere in the world. Beside it is his *Portrait of a Cardinal*, and there is also **Velazquez**'s *Portrait of Juan de Pareja*—"All the rest are art, this alone is truth," remarked a critic of the piercing, somber portrait when it was first exhibited.

The **ITALIAN RENAISSANCE** is less spectacularly represented, but there's a worthy selection from the various Italian schools, including an early *Madonna and Child Enthroned with Saints* by **Raphael**, a late **Botticelli**, the crisply linear

Three Miracles of Saint Zenobius, and **Fra Filippo Lippi**'s *Madonna and Child Enthroned with Two Angels*. Among the **Mannerists**, best of the Italian collections, is **Bronzino's** *Portrait of a Young Man*. Turning right from the main galleries takes you to a smaller series of religious paintings: **Michele de Verona**'s handsome *Madonna and Child with the Infant John the Baptist*, very much in the fifteenth-century Italian tradition with a marmoreal surface bathed in soft light. Look out, too, for **Crivelli**'s *Pietà* and **Mantegna**'s rigid and sculptural *Adoration of the Shepherds*.

With the **Robert Altman Collection**, here cleverly jigsawed into the main gallery, a small number of Dutch works, including **Memling**'s *Tommaso Portinari and his Wife* and a *Mystical Marriage of St. Catherine*, prelude the main **DUTCH PAINTINGS** section. This, dominated by the major works of Rembrandt, Vermeer, and Hals, is the culmination of the main European galleries—and arguably the finest single group of paintings in the museum.

Vermeer, genius of the domestic interior, is represented by five works. *Young Woman with a Water Jug*, which hints at themes of purity and temperance, is a perfect example of his skill in composition and tonal gradation, combined with an uncannily naturalistic sense of lighting. *A Girl Asleep* is deeper in its composition—or at least appears to be, the rich fabric separating the foreground from the rooms beyond. Vermeer often used this trick, and you see it again in *Allegory of the Faith*, where the drawn curtain presents the tableau and separates the viewer from the lesson before him. Most haunting of all, however, is the great *Portrait of a Young Woman*, displaying the artist at his most complex and the Met at its most fortunate.

Vermeer's pictures show the domestic harmony of seventeenth-century Holland. **Hals'** early paintings reveal its exuberance. In *Merrymakers at Shrovetide* the figures explode out from the canvas in an abundance of gesture and richness. *Young Man and a Woman*, painted five years later, shows a more subdued use of color (though not vitality). As do the individual portraits, with their capturing of fleeting, telling pointers: step back from his *Portrait of a Man* or *Claes Kuyst Van Voorhout* and the seemingly careless strokes melt into a bravura statement of spirit.

The best of **Rembrandt**'s works here are also portraits. There is a beautiful painting of his common-law wife, *Hendrike Stoffjels*, painted three years before her early death—a blow that marked a further decline in the artist's fortunes. In 1660 he went bankrupt, and the superb *Self-Portrait* of that year shows the self-examination he brought to later works. A comparison between the flamboyant 1632 *Portrait of a Lady* and the warmer, later *Lady with a Pink* reveals his maturing genius.

In addition to these big three names, the Dutch rooms also display a good scattering of their contemporaries, most memorably **Pieter de Hooch**, whose *Two Men and a Woman in a Courtyard of a House* is his acknowledged masterpiece, with its perfect arrangement of line, form, and color. At the same time as de Hooch was painting peaceful courtyards and Vermeer lacemakers and lute players, **Adrian Brouwer** was turning his eye to the seamier side of Dutch life. When he wasn't drunk or in prison he came up with works like *The Smokers*, typical of his tavern scenes. Traditionally *The Smokers* is a portrait of Brouwer and his drinking pals—he's the one in the foreground, in case you hadn't guessed.

The André Meyer Galleries

David's sternly didactic *Death of Socrates*, **Turner**'s *Grand Canal, Venice*, and one of **Constable**'s *Salisbury Cathedral* paintings line the outer corridor of the André Meyer galleries. But once inside, you go straight to the heart of the collection, among a startling array of **IMPRESSIONIST AND POST-IMPRESSIONIST** art.

The display, fittingly, starts with **Edouard Manet**, the movement's most influential precursor yet in his early style, contrasting light and shadow with modulated shades of black, firmly linked in tradition with Hals, Velazquez, and Goya. The *Spanish Dancer*, an accomplished example of this style and heritage, was well received on Manet's debut at the Paris Salon in 1861. Within a few years, though, he was shocking the same establishment with *Olympia*, *Le Déjuner sur l'Herbe*, and the Meyer's striking *Woman with a Parrot*—the same woman model, incidentally, for all three paintings. Later his style shifted again as he adopted the Impressionist lightness of handling and interest in perception. He worked for a time with Renoir and Monet, a period of which *Boating* is typical, a celebration of the middle classes at play.

Claude Monet, who was influenced by Manet's early style before Impressionism, was one of the movement's most prolific painters. He returned again and again to a single subject to produce a series of paintings, each capturing a different moment of light or atmosphere. Three superb examples are on show here: *Rouen Cathedral*, *The Houses of Parliament from the Thames*, and *Poplars*—in which you can detect the beginnings of his final phase of near-Abstract Impressionism.

Cézanne's technique was very different. He labored long to achieve a painstaking analysis of form and color, something clear in the *Landscape of Marseilles*. Of his few portraits, the jarring, almost Cubist angles and spaces of *Mme. Cézanne in a Red Dress* seem years ahead of their time. Take a look, too, at *The Card Players*, whose dynamic triangular structure thrusts out, yet retains the quiet concentration of the moment. **Renoir** is perhaps the best represented among the remaining Impressionists, though his most important work here dates from 1878, when he began to move away from the mainstream techniques he'd learned working with Monet. *Mme. Charpentier and her Children* is a likable enough piece, whose affectionate if unsearching tone manages to sidestep the sugariness that affected his later work. Better, or at least more real, is his *Waitress at Duval's Restaurant*.

The Post-Impressionists, logically enough, follow, with **Gauguin**'s masterly *Ia Orana Maria*. The title, the archangel Gabriel's first words to Mary at the Annunciation, is the key to the work: the scene was a staple of the Renaissance, here it is transferred to a wholly different culture in an attempt to unfold the dense symbolic meaning, and perhaps also to voice the artist's feeling for the native South Sea islanders, whose cause he championed. *Two Tahitian Women* hangs adjacent, a portrait of his lover Tehura—skillful, studied simplicity.

Toulouse-Lautrec delighted in painting the world Gauguin went to Tahiti to escape. *The Sofa* is one of a series of sketches he made in Paris brothels. The artist's deformity distanced him from society, and he identified with the life of the prostitutes in his sketches—he also hated posed modeling, which made the bored women awaiting clients an ideal subject.

Courbet and **Degas**, too, are well represented. Courbet especially, with examples of every phase and period of his career, including *Young Ladies from the*

Village, a virtual manifesto of his idea of realism, and *Woman with a Parrot*, a superbly erotic and exotic work, and one that gave Manet the idea for his work of the same name. Degas constantly returned to the subject of dancers, and there are studies in just about every medium from pastels to sculpture. Unlike the Impressionists, Degas subordinated what he saw to what he believed, and his *Dancers Practicing* shows this—the painting is about structure, alluded to in the way the dancer on the right picks up the form of the watering can used to lay the dust in the studio. Also here is a vaguely macabre casting of his *Little Dancer*, complete with real tutu, bodice, and shoes.

All of which is little more than the surface of the André Meyer galleries. There's also work by **Van Gogh**, **Rousseau**, and **Seurat**, paintings from the **Barbizon School**, sculpture by **Rodin**, and a peripheral gallery of paintings that express the orthodox taste of the nineteenth century.

The Lehman Pavilion

The Lehman Pavilion was tacked on to the rear of the Met in 1975 to house the collection of Robert Lehman, millionaire banker and art collector. It breaks from the Met's usual sober arrangement of rectangular floor plans: rooms are laid out beside a brilliantly lit atrium, some in recreation of Lehman's own home.

More importantly, Lehman's enthusiasms fill the gaps in the Met's account of **ITALIAN RENAISSANCE** painting. This was his passion, and the heart of the collection centers around a small **Botticelli** *Annunciation*, an exquisite celebration of the Florentine discovery of perspective. From the Venetian school comes a sculptural *Madonna and Child* by **Giovanni Bellini** and two unaffected portraits by **Jacometto Veneziano**, as well as an unusual *Expulsion from Paradise* by the Sienese **Giovanni di Paolo**, in which an angel gently ushers Adam and Eve from Eden, while a Byzantine God points to their place of banishment.

Left of this core collection are works from the **NORTHERN RENAISSANCE**, highlighted by a trio of paintings by Memling, Holbein, and Petrus Christus. **Christus'** untypically large canvas of *St. Elegius*, patron saint of goldsmiths, shows an Eyckian attention to detail in its depiction of the saint's jewels and precious stones—a genre insight into the work of the fifteenth-century goldsmith. **Memling**, working around thirty years later, used a lighter palette to achieve the delicate serenity of his *Annunciation*, in which cool colors and a gentle portrayal of Mary and her attendant angels illuminate the Flemish interior. **Hans Holbein the Younger's** *Portrait of Erasmus of Rotterdam* was one of three he painted in 1523 that established his reputation as a portraitist. Elsewhere in the Lehman wing—and you could visit the Met rewardingly by limiting yourself just to these halls—are works by artists as diverse as El Greco, Ingres (the luminescent *Princesse de Broglie*), and Ter Bosch. But one painting that really stands out is **Rembrandt's** *Portrait of Gerard de Lairesse*: by all accounts de Lairesse was disliked for his luxurious tastes and unpleasant character, but mainly for his face—which had been ravaged by congenital syphilis.

As the Lehman wing moves toward the **nineteenth century and twentieth century** it loses authority, but there are minor works by major artists, including Renoir, Van Gogh, Gauguin, Cézanne, and Matisse. Have a look at **Suzanne Valadon's** *Reclining Nude*: Valadon is largely ignored today, and is best known as a model for Toulouse-Lautrec, Renoir, and Degas (who encouraged her to become a painter in her own right). But her boldly colored canvasses show her originality and also her influence on her son, **Maurice Utrillo**, whom she taught to paint as an attempt to wean him off the drink and drugs that were his downfall. Utrillo's *Rue Ravignon* here stands besides his mother's painting.

Twentieth-Century Art

Housed over two floors in the Lila Acheson Wallace Wing, the Met's **twentieth-century collection** is an enjoyable compact group of paintings, and fascinating viewing if you have an interest in the period. The first floor has a chronological installation of American and European Art from **1905 to 1940**, with paintings such as **Charles Demuth**'s *The Figure Five in Gold*, and **Picasso**'s *Portrait of Gertrude Stein* alongside works by Klee, Matisse, Braques, and Klimt. There's also a small design collection here, with changing pieces of furniture, ceramics, and (just about anything else) from the Met's collection.

The second floor contains European and American painting **from 1945 on**: **Pollock**'s masterly *Autumn Rhythm (Number 30)*, **Thomas Hart Benton**'s rural idyll of *July Hay*, **R.B. Kitaj**'s *John Ford on His Deathbed*, a dream-like painting of the director of westerns, and **Andy Warhol**'s final *Self-Portrait*, along with works by Max Beckmann, Roy Lichtenstein(*Painting Since 1945*), and Gilbert and George. On top of the Wallace wing is the **Cantor Roof Garden**, open in the summer to display contemporary sculpture against the dramatic backdrop of the New York skyline.

The American Wing

The American wing comes nearest to being a museum in its own right, and as an introduction to the development of fine and decorative art in America it's hard to fault.

Galleries—and most immediately a series of **furnished historical rooms**— lead off from the **Charles Engelhard Court**, a shrub-filled, restful sculpture garden enclosed at the lower end by the *Facade of the United States Bank*, lifted from Wall Street. Stepping through the facade would drop you in the **Federal Period Rooms** and the restrained neo-Classical elegance of the late eighteenth century. If you're approaching this section of the Met fresh, however, it's better to start at the third floor and work down to see the rooms in chronological order. You begin with the **Early Colonial period**, represented most evocatively in the Hart room of around 1674, and end with **Frank Lloyd Wright**'s *Room from the Little House, Minneapolis*, originally windowed on all four sides, in key with Wright's concept of minimizing interior–exterior division. On the second-floor balcony, an elegant accompaniment to all of this, be sure not to miss the iridescent Favrile glass of **Louis Comfort Tiffany**—Art Nouveau at its best.

THE COLLECTION OF AMERICAN PAINTINGS begins on the second floor with **eighteenth-century** works by **Benjamin West**, an artist who worked in London and taught or influenced almost all American painters of his day. *The Triumph of Love* is typical of his neo-Classical, allegorical works. More heroics come with **John Trumbull**, one of West's pupils, in *Sortie made by the Garrison of Gibraltar* and the full-blown Romanticism of *Washington Crossing the Delaware* by **Emanuel Leutzes**. This last shows Washington escaping the British army in the winter of 1776, historically and geographically inaccurate but nonetheless a national icon.

Early in the **nineteenth century**, American painters gained the confidence to move away from themes solely European. **William Sidney Mount** depicted genre scenes on his native Long Island, often with a sly political angle—as with *Cider Makers* and *The Bet*—and the painters of the **Hudson Valley School** apotheosized landscape in their vast lyrical canvases. **Thomas Cole**, the school's doyen, is represented by *The Oxbow*, his pupil **Frederick Church** by an immense *Heart of the Andes*—combining the grand sweep of the mountains with minutely depicted flora. **Albert Bierstadt** and **S.R. Gifford** continued to concentrate on the American West—their respective works *The Rocky Mountains, Lander's Peak*, and *Kauterskill Falls* have a near-visionary idyllism, bound to a belief that the westward development of the country was a manifestation of divine will.

Winslow Homer is allowed a gallery to himself—fittingly for a painter who was to influence greatly the late nineteenth-century artistic scene in America. Homer began his career illustrating the day-to-day realities of the Civil War—there's a good selection here that shows the tedium and sadness of those years—and a sense of recording detail carried over into his late, quasi-Impressionistic studies of seascapes. *Northeaster* is one of the finest of these, close to Courbet in its strength of composition and color.

The mezzanine below brings the Met's account of American art into the **twentieth century**. Some of the initial portraiture here tends to the sugary, but **J.W. Alexander**'s *Repose* deftly hits the mark—a simple, striking use of line and light with a sumptuous feel and more than a hint of eroticism. By contrast, there's **Thomas Eakin**'s subdued, almost ghostly *Max Schmitt in a Single Scull*, and **William Merritt Chase**'s *For the Little One*, an Impressionist study of his wife sewing. Chase studied in Europe and it was there that he painted his *Portrait of Whistler*. **Whistler** returned the compliment but destroyed the work on seeing Chase's (quite truthful) depiction of himself as a dandified fop—and in a teasing style that mimicked his own. Whatever Whistler's conceits, though, his portraits are adept: witness the *Arrangement in Flesh Color and Black: Portrait of Theodore Duret* nearby.

The reputation of **John Singer Sargent** has suffered its ups and downs over the years—he now seems to be coming back into fashion. There is certainly a virtuosity in his large portraits, like that of *Mr. and Mrs. I. N. Phelps Stokes*, the couple purposefully elongated as if to emphasize their aristocratic characters. *Padre Sebastiano* is a smaller, more personal response. The *Portrait of Madam X* (Mme. Pierre Gautreau, a notorious Parisian beauty) was one of the most famous pictures of its day: exhibited at the 1884 Paris salon, it was considered so improper that Sargent had to leave Paris for London. "I suppose it's the best thing I've done," he said wearily on selling it to the Met a few years later.

Medieval Art

You could—in theory at least—move straight on to the **MEDIEVAL GALLERIES** from the American wing. But this would be heavy going—and in any case you'd be missing out on a carefully planned approach.

This is the **corridor** leading in from the Great Hall, an entrance gallery that displays the sumptuous **Byzantine metalwork and jewelry** that J.P. Morgan donated to the museum in its early days. At its end is the main **sculpture hall**, piled high with religious statuary and carvings (a tremendous *St. Nicholas Saving Three Boys in the Brine Tub*) and split with a *reja* (altar screen) from Valladolid Cathedral.

Right from here the **medieval treasury** has an all-embracing—and magnificent—display of objects religious, liturgical, and secular. And beyond are the

Jack and Belle Linski galleries: Flemish, Florentine, and Venetian paintings, porcelains, and bronzes.

Dotted throughout the medieval galleries are later **period rooms**, paneled Tudor bedrooms, and Robert Adam fancies from England, florid Rococo boudoirs and salons from France, and an entire Renaissance patio from Velez Blanco in Spain. It's all a bit overwhelming, leaving you with the feeling that Morgan and his robber baron colleagues would probably have shipped over Versailles if they could have laid their hands on it.

The Egyptian Collection

"A chronological panorama of ancient Egypt's art, history, and culture," boasts the blurb to the Egyptian collection, and the display is certainly lavish. Brightly efficient corridors steer you through the treasures from the digs of the 1920s and 1930s, art and artifacts from the prehistoric to Byzantine periods of Egyptian culture.

The **statuary** is the most immediately striking of the exhibits, though after a while it's the smaller **sculptural** pieces that hold the attention longest. Figures like *Merti and his Wife* were modeled as portraits, but often carvings were made in the belief that a person's *Ka* or life force would continue to exist in an idealized model after their death. There's a beautifully crafted example in the *Carving of Senebi* in gallery 8; what was probably Senebi's tomb is displayed nearby. Also in this room is the dazzling collection of *Princess Sithathorunet's jewelry*, a pinnacle in Egyptian decorative art from around 1830 BC; the *Models of Mekutra's House* (around 1198 BC); and the radiant *Fragmentary Head of a Queen*, sensuously carved in polished yellow jasper.

At the end of all this sits the **Temple of Dendur**, housed in a vast airy gallery designed to give hints and symbols of its original site on the banks of the Nile. Built by the Emperor Augustus in 15 BC as an attempt to placate a local chieftain, the temple was moved here as a gift of the Egyptian people during the construction of the Aswan High dam—it would otherwise have been drowned. Sadly the gallery, rather than suggesting the empty expanses of the Nile, dwarfs what is essentially an unremarkable building, one that might be more engaging if you could explore inside. The temple needs a helping hand, and gets it at night, illuminated on a corner of Central Park with at least some of the mystery that's missing during the day.

The Michael C. Rockefeller Wing

Son of Governor Nelson Rockefeller, Michael C. Rockefeller disappeared during a trip to West New Guinea in 1961. The Rockefeller wing stands as a memorial to him, including many of his finds alongside the Met's comprehensive collection of art from Africa, the Pacific Islands, and the Americas. It's a superb gallery, the muted, reassuring decoration throwing the **"PRIMITIVE" ART** exhibits into sharp and often frightening focus. You don't need much knowledge of "Primitive" cultures to feel the intensity of the work here: the blackened *reliquary heads* from Gabon once contained the skulls of a family's ancestors and issued magical protection; the elegant spare lines of terracotta *heads* from Ghana find resonances in Modigliani portraits, and the rich geometry of the South American jewelry and ornaments, too, seems often startlingly contemporary.

The Museum of Modern Art

11 W. 53rd St. Subway E or F to Fifth Ave.–53rd St. Fri–Tues 11am–6pm, Thurs 11am–9pm, closed Wed; $7, students $4,Thurs 5–9pm pay what you wish.

Instigated in 1929, moved to its present permanent home ten years later, and in the mid-1980s extensively updated in a steel pipe and glass renovation that doubled its gallery space, **THE MUSEUM OF MODERN ART** (plain MoMA to the cognoscenti) offers probably the finest and most complete account of late nineteenth- and twentieth-century art you're likely to find. Basically, if you're in New York for any length of time and you want to catch some museums, MoMA has to be top of the list of places not to miss.

The museum's plan

The MoMA building is designed to ease you as effortlessly and easily as possible into the collections—and, with ultra-modern glass-enclosed landings and gliding escalators, it's an enjoyable place just to walk inside. On the **first floor** you'll find the usual pairing of restaurant and shop, as well as a video room and movie theater (pick up a leaflet for a rundown on what's currently showing), and, outside, a **sculpture garden** holding scattered works in rotation by the likes of Rodin and Matisse, alongside artifacts like an example of the curved Art Nouveau Paris metro sign. The museum proper begins upstairs, with the second and third floors devoted to the main **painting and sculpture galleries**, the fourth to **architecture and design**, and it's these, on the whole, that most people come to see. The roster of artists and major movements in these is, for the most part, fairly constant. However, apart from a few key works, paintings are changed regularly, and some of the pieces we've commented on below won't necessarily be up when you visit—though there will usually be something by the same artist in its place.

In addition to the three main sections, the museum also has galleries devoted to **photographs**, **prints**, and **drawings**, all of which give rotating displays of the museum's collections. The photographs, in particular, are marvelous—one of the finest, most eclectic collections around and a vivid evocation of twentieth-century America, from the dramatic landscapes of Ansel Adams to Stieglitz's dynamic views of New York and the revealing portraits of Man Ray.

Second floor Painting and Sculpture

Once on the second floor, **Cézanne**'s *Bather* of 1885, alongside other works by him, pulls you inside, leading on toward further **Post-Impressionists**—principally works by **Gauguin**, **Seurat**, and, most famously, **Van Gogh**, represented by *Starry Night*. In the third room are paintings by the Belgian James Ensor, by Redon and Bonnard, along with Rousseau's *The Dream*, painted in 1910, leading through to galleries devoted to works by the major Cubist painters, including a scattering of works by **Picasso** and **Braque**; and, most notably, Picasso's *Demoiselles d'Avignon of 1907*, a jagged, sharp, and, for its time, revolutionary clash of tones and planes which some hold to be the heralder (and initial arbiter) of Cubist principles—though **Derain**'s *Bathers* in the previous room may have equal claim to the title.

A room off to the left from this first Cubist gallery holds **Monet**'s *Water Lilies*, enormous, stirring attempts to abstract color and form which cover well over half their gallery's space, their swirling jades, pinks, and purples making it faintly like

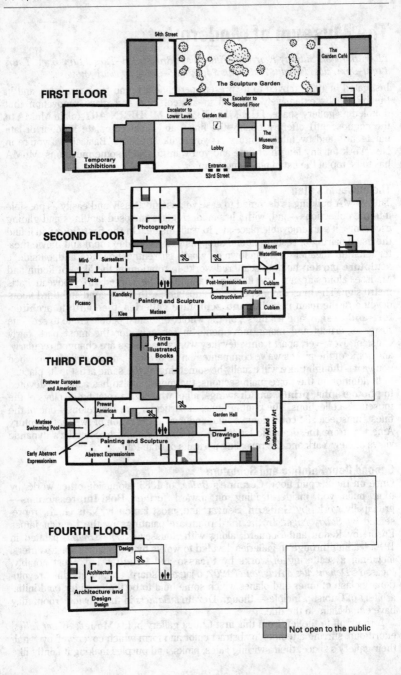

FIRST FLOOR

54th Street

The Garden Café

The Sculpture Garden

Escalator to Lower Level

Garden Hall

Escalator to Second Floor

Lobby

The Museum Store

Entrance 53rd Street

Temporary Exhibitions

SECOND FLOOR

Photography

Monet Waterlillies

Miró   Surrealism

Dada

Post-Impressionism   Cubism

Picasso   Kandisky

Futurism

Constructivism

Klee   Matisse

Painting and Sculpture

Cubism

THIRD FLOOR

Prints and Illustrated Books

Postwar European and American

Prewar American

Garden Hall

Matisse Swimming Pool

Painting and Sculpture

Drawings

Pop Art and Contemporary Art

Early Abstract Expressionism

Abstract Expressionism

FOURTH FLOOR

Design

Architecture

Architecture and Design   Design

Not open to the public

sitting in a giant aquarium. Otherwise continue straight through to the right to view some more **Cubist** canvases, later works mainly, taking in work by Leger, Picasso's *Three Women at the Spring* (1921), and *Three Musicians* from the same year, hung opposite Leger's jokier evocation of the same subject, painted in 1944.

Rooms encapsulating entire periods and movements follow, cursory glances but with a staggering quality of material. There are paintings by **Chagall**; Kirchner's *Dresden* and *Berlin* street scenes are the focus of a gallery devoted to the glaring realities of the **German Expressionists**; while the whirring abstractions of **Boccioni** are the mainstay of a room devoted to the **Futurists'** paeans to the industrial age. A further room takes in the work of **De Stijl**, principally **Mondrian**, following the artist's development from early limp Cubist pieces to later works like *Broadway Boogie Woogie*. This, painted in 1940 after he had moved to New York, reflects his love of jazz music—its short, sharp stabs of color conveying an almost physical rhythm.

Beyond here (past a staircase leading up to the next painting and sculpture floor), **Matisse** has a large room to himself, centering on the *Dancers* of 1909, and taking in other lesser-known works like his pudgy series of *Heads of Jeanette*, where straight Impressionism becomes, in the final head, no more than series of disfiguring lines and lumps. Look out, also, for the *Red Studio*, a depiction of Matisse's studio in France in which all perspective is resolved in shades of rusty red, and, if it's hung (which it's often not), *Le Bateau*. When this was first exhibited, MoMA had it hanging upside down for 47 days before noticing the mistake.

The next gallery holds paintings by **Klee**, some swirling canvases by **Kandinsky**, the smooth shapes of **Brancusi**'s sculpture, leading through to late works by **Braque** and **Picasso**: *Night Fishing at Antibes*, the *Seated Bather*, and the *Charnel House*—like *Guernica*, which used to hang here before it was removed to Spain's Prado, an angry protest against the horrors of war.

In contrast, a room on, are the brooding skies of **de Chirico**; a room containing works by Miro, notably his hilarious *Dutch Interior*, 1928; and a handful of dreamlike paintings by **Dali**, **Magritte**—*The Menaced Assassin*—**Delvaux**—*Phases of the Moon*—and **Balthus**: illogical scenes but disturbing in their clarity and undercurrents of eroticism. In Balthus' *The Living Room* the static poses of the adolescent girls and carefully positioned guitar hint at notions of sexual awakening; while his rather odd portrait of Dread, painted in 1936, shows the anxious artist in front of a half-dressed young girl.

Third floor Painting and Sculpture

The second Painting and Sculpture gallery continues chronologically and, perhaps inevitably, with a more American slant—**Andrew Wyeth**'s *Christina's World*, one of the best known of all modern American paintings, is often hung here, usually along with a couple of typically gloomy canvases by **Edward Hopper**—*House by the Railroad* and *New York Movie*: potent and atmospheric pieces which give a bleak account of modern American life. Contrast these with **Sheeler**'s *American Landscape*: "the industrial landscape pastoralized," a critic noted, and almost toytown in its neat vision of industrialization, in which nothing moves and all gleams neat and clean.

More abstract pieces follow: early Jackson Pollocks, **Gorky**'s Miro-like doodles, some neat satires by **Dubuffet**, and, at the end of the room, the anguished scream of **Bacon**'s *No. 7 from 8 Studies for a Portrait*. What many come here for, however, is to see the later paintings of the artists of the **New York school**—large-scale canvases meant to be viewed from a distance, as here, in large airy rooms. The paintings of **Pollock** and **de Kooning**—wild, and in Pollock's case textured, patterns with no clear beginning or end—mingle with the more ordered efforts of the Color Field artists and the later works of artists like **Matisse** and **Miro**. Matisse's work here is mainly paper cutouts, most striking the bold blue shapes of his *Swimming Pool* which the aging artist made to decorate the walls of his apartment in Nice. The work of the so-called **Color Field artists** is more vivid but emphasizes the importance of color in a similar way—their paintings, in **Barnett Newman**'s words, "drained of impediments of memory, association, nostalgia, legend, myth, and what have you": in short without anything but pure color, as in Newman's own *Vir Heroicus Sublimus*, sheer red and huge against the wall; in the radiating, almost humming blocks of color of the paintings of **Mark Rothko**; and, perhaps most palpably, in the sheer black canvases of **Ad Reinhardt**. **Robert Motherwell**'s *Elegy to the Spanish Republic*, one of a series of more than a hundred such paintings, is slightly different: color is less important, and the broad splashes of black are meant to hint at the rituals of the *corrida*, the shapes roughly reminiscent of the testicles displayed at the finale of a bullfight.

The last of the painting and sculpture rooms is in part made up of donations by Philip Johnson—**Pop Art** mainly, including **Jasper Johns'** *Flag*, a well-known piece in which the Stars and Stripes are painted on to newsprint, transforming America's most potent symbol into little more than an arrangement of shapes and colors. You might also see work by **Robert Rauschenberg** and **Claes Oldenburg**, though these galleries also regularly display **contemporary work** from the museum's permanent collection.

Fourth floor Architecture and Design

Architecture and design are, after painting and sculpture, MoMA's most important concern. The galleries on the fourth floor take in models and original drawings by the architects of key modern buildings—**Frank Lloyd Wright**'s *Falling Water*, projects by **Le Corbusier** and **Mies van der Rohe**. Further aspects of modern design are traced through the swollen glasswork of **Tiffany**, **Guimard**'s flowery Art Nouveau furniture, and, in addition to a couple of **Rietveld** chairs, a Rietveld buffet which looks as if it could do with a spot of Rietveld paint. There are also **chairs and other furniture** designed by Mies van der Rohe, Alvar Alto, and Henri van den Velde, some of which have been more successful examples of applied design than others. Look out, too—indeed you can't miss them—for the oversized items at the top of the escalator, notably a green Bell helicopter from 1945, poised delicately in the open space of the landing.

The Guggenheim Museum

Fifth Ave. at 89th St. Subway #4, #5, or #6 to 86th St. At time of writing closed undergoing restoration.

Indoor parking lot or upturned beehive? Whatever you think of the **GUGGENHEIM MUSEUM**, it's the building which steals the show. Frank Lloyd Wright's purpose-built structure, sixteen years in the making, caused a storm of controversy when it was unveiled in 1959, bearing little relation to the statuesque apartment buildings of this most genteel part of Fifth Avenue. Reactions, though Wright didn't live long enough to hear many, ranged from disgusted disbelief to critical praise and acclaim. And even now, though the years have given the building a certain respectability, no one seems to have entirely made up their mind, as the recent furore over the extension has proved. From 1990 to fall 1991 the museum was closed, undergoing a $55 million facelift of the original Lloyd Wright building that will open the whole space to the public for the first time. The extension, built behind the original building, and a little to the north, robs the spiral of some of its freestanding drama, but allows a much greater proportion of the collection to be on show at any one time.

Solomon R. Guggenheim was one of America's richest men, his mines extracting silver and copper—and a healthy profit—all over the USA. Like other nineteenth-century American capitalists the only problem for Guggenheim was what to spend his vast wealth on, so he started collecting Old Masters—a hobby he continued half-heartedly until the 1920s, when various sorties to Europe brought him into contact with the most avant-garde and influential of European art circles. Abstraction in art was then considered little more than a fad, but Guggenheim, always a man with an eye for a sound investment, started to collect modern paintings with fervor, snapping up wholesale the works of Kandinsky, adding items by Chagall, Gleizes, Leger, and others, and exhibiting them to a bemused American public in his suite of rooms in the Plaza Hotel. It's these works, enlarged with special purchases and the odd donation, which form the nucleus of the permanent collection. Don't, however, expect to see a great deal of it when you visit: most of the Guggenheim's space is these days devoted to temporary exhibitions of twentieth-century artists—a situation that will hopefully change with the completion of the extension.

Consequently, there's little you can say about the Guggenheim without predicting what's going to be on show. Rather it's the space itself which dominates—"one of the greatest rooms erected in the twentieth century," wrote Philip Johnson, and with justification: even if you hate the sight of the place from the outside it's hard not to be impressed by the tiers of cream concrete swirling overhead like spiraling bleached whales' ribs as you go in. Most of the temporary exhibits are shown in the circular galleries, and the best way of seeing them is to zip straight to the top of the building (by way of the crescent-shaped elevators) and mosey down the gentle slope. On the way, two galleries offer a representative sample of the Guggenheim's **Permanent Collection**: the first, on the **fifth floor**, giving a quick glance at the Cubists, Chagall, and, most completely, Kandinsky; the other, the **Tannhauser Wing**, offering a short resume of modern movements in European painting up to, roughly, the Fauves. Highpoints here are a handful of late nineteenth-century paintings, not least the exquisite Degas *Dancers* and other Post-Impressionists, Van Gogh's *Mountains at St. Remy* and some sensitive early Picassos.

The Frick Collection

1 E. 70th St. Subway #6 to 68th St.–Lexington Ave. Tues–Sat 10am–6pm, Sun 1–6pm, closed Mon; $3, students $1.50. Daily introductory talks (Tues–Fri) at 2pm; lectures on aspects of European art on Thurs at 3pm and Sat at 4pm; and weekly concerts of classical music: all for the price of the regular admission ticket—pick up a leaflet for details.

Housed in the former mansion of Henry Clay Frick, the **FRICK COLLECTION** is perhaps the most enjoyable of the big New York galleries, made up of the art treasures hoarded by Frick during his years as probably the most ruthless of

New York's robber barons. Vicious, uncompromising, and anti-union, Frick broke strikes with state troopers and was hated enough narrowly to survive a number of assassination attempts. However, the legacy of his self-aggrandizement—he spent millions on the best of Europe's art treasures—is a superb collection of works, and as good a glimpse of the sumptuous life enjoyed by New York's big industrialists as you'll find.

First opened in the mid-1930s, the museum has been kept largely as it would have looked when the Fricks were living there. It's in dubious taste for the most part, much of the furniture heavy eighteenth-century French, but the nice thing about it—and many people rank the Frick as their favorite New York gallery because of this—is that it strives hard to be as unlike a museum as possible. Ropes are kept to a minimum, and even in the most sumptuously decorated rooms there are plenty of chairs you can freely sink into. When weary, you can take refuge in the central enclosed courtyard, whose abundant greenery, fountains, and marble are arranged with a classical attention to order, and whose echoing serenity you'd be hard pushed to find anywhere else in the city.

The **collection** itself was acquired under the direction of Joseph Duveen, notorious—and not entirely trustworthy—advisor to the city's richest and most ignorant. For Frick, however, he seems to have picked out the cream of Europe's post-World War I private art hoards, even if the opening ensemble of the **Boucher Room** is not to twentieth-century tastes, decorated with succulent representations of the arts and sciences. Next along, the **Dining Room** is more reserved, its Reynoldses and Hogarths overshadowed by the one non-portrait in the room, **Gainsborough**'s *St. James's Park*: a subtly moving promenade under an arch of luxuriant trees—"Watteau far outdone," wrote a critic at the time. Outside there's more lusty French painting (Boucher again) and, in the next room, **Fragonard**'s *Progress of Love* series, which was painted for Madame du Barry in 1771—and rejected by her soon after.

Better paintings follow, not least of them **Bellini**'s *St. Francis*, which suggests his vision of Christ by means of pervading light, a bent tree, and an enraptured stare. **El Greco**'s *St. Jerome*, above the fireplace, reproachfully surveys the riches all around, and looks out to the South Hall where hangs one of Boucher's very intimate depictions of his naked wife—loaded with meaning—and an early **Vermeer**, *Officer and Laughing Girl*: similarly suggestive, and full of lewd allusions to forthcoming sex. In the opposite direction, the Library holds a number of British works, most notably one of **Constable**'s *Salisbury Cathedral* series, and in the North Hall hangs an engaging and sensitive portrait of the *Comtesse de Haussonville* by **Ingres**.

But it's the **West Gallery**, beyond here, that's the Frick's star attraction, and which holds some of its finest paintings. Two **Turners**, views of Cologne and Dieppe, hang opposite each other, both a blaze of orange and creamy tones; **Van Dyck** pitches in with a couple of uncharacteristically informal portraits of Frans Snyders and his wife—two paintings only reunited when Frick purchased them; and across the room **Frans Hals** reveals himself in a boozy and rare self-portrait. **Rembrandt**, too, is represented by a set of piercing self-portraits and (although serious doubt has recently been thrown on its authenticity) the enigmatic *Polish Rider*—more fantasy-piece than portrait. At the far end of the West Gallery **Whistler** shares the Oval Room with **Houdon**'s *Diana*, his portrait of fellow-artist *Rose Corder* posed to the point where she would have to faint before Whistler would stop painting. Past here, the East Gallery holds more paintings still, but more interesting is the tiny room on the other side of the West Gallery. This houses an exquisite set of Limoges **enamels**, mainly sixteenth century, as well as a collection of small-scale paintings that includes a *Virgin and Child* by **Jan van Eyck**—one of the artist's very last works, and among the rare few to have reached America.

The Whitney Museum of American Art

945 Madison Ave. Subway #6 to 77th St.–Lexington Ave. Closed Mon; Tues 1–8pm, Wed–Sat 11am–5pm, Sun noon–6pm; $5, students with ID free; also free for all Tues 6–8pm. Excellent—and free—gallery talks on Tues (1:30pm, 3:30pm, 6:15pm), Wed/Thurs/Fri (11:30am, 1:30pm, 3:30pm).

A gray-faced Brutalist arsenal designed by Marcel Breuer, the **WHITNEY's** oblique windows and cantilevered floors have an intimidating and suspiciously institutional air. Within, however, all such impressions are quickly dispelled. This is some of the best gallery space in the city and the perfect forum for the works that it owns—one of the preeminent collections of twentieth-century American art. It is also a superb exhibition locale and, like the Guggenheim, devotes much of its time and rooms to this end. The majority of Whitney exhibitions are given over to retrospectives and debuts of lesser-known themes—Ed Keinholz and sculpture of the New York School are a couple of recent examples. Every other year, though, there is an exhibition of a wholly different nature—the **Whitney biennial**—designed to give a provocative overview of what's happening in contemporary American art. It is often panned by critics but always packed with visitors; catch it if you can between March and June on odd-numbered years.

Gertrude Vanderbilt Whitney founded the collection in 1930 around works by Hopper, Thomas Hart Benton, George Bellows, and other living painters. Currently the gallery owns over 10,000 pieces of painting, sculpture, and photography by artists as diverse as Calder, Nevelson, O'Keefe, de Kooning, Rauschenburg, Le Witt, and Nam June Paik. The **Highlights of the Permanent Collection**, a somewhat arbitrary selection of the Whitney's best, are arranged by both chronology and theme. The works form a superb introduction to twentieth-century American art, best evaluated with the help of the gallery talks, designed to explain and orient the paintings and sculptures in their various movements.

Gertrude Whitney's taste tended toward **Realism**, and the paintings often tie in with the expectations of the genre. **George Bellows'** *Dempsey and Firpo*, though, is a sort of neo-Mannerist view of a boxing match, full of movement and flesh—"I don't know anything about boxing; I'm just painting two guys trying to kill each other," said Bellows. The collection is particularly strong on **Edward Hopper** (his works were bequeathed to the museum) and several of his best paintings are here: *Early Sun Morning* is typical, a bleak urban landscape, uneasily tense in its lighting and rejection of topical detail. The street could be anywhere (in fact it's Seventh Avenue) and, for Hopper, becomes universal.

As if to balance the figurative works that formed the nucleus of the collection, more recent purchases include much **abstraction**. **Marsden Hartley's** *Painting Number 5* is a strident, overwhelmed work, painted in the memory of a German officer friend killed in the early days of the Great War. **Georgia O'Keefe** called it "a brass band in a closet," and certainly her own work is gentler, though with its darknesses: *Abstraction* was suggested by the noises of cattle being driven to the local slaughterhouse. Have a look, too, at O'Keefe's flower paintings: verging on abstraction but hinting at deeper organic forms.

The **Abstract Expressionists** feature particularly strongly, with great works by high priests **Pollock** and **De Kooning**, leading on to **Rothko** and the **Color Field painters**—though you need a sharp eye to discern any color in **Ad Reinhard's** *Black Painting*. In a different direction, **Warhol**, **Johns**, and **Oldenburg** each subvert the meanings of their images. Warhol's silkscreened *Coke Bottles* fade into motif, Jasper Johns' celebrated *Three Flags* once again erases the emblem of patriotism, replacing it with ambiguity, and Claes Oldenburg's lighter-hearted *Soft Sculptures*, squashed toilets and melting engines, fall into line with his declaration, "I'm into art that doesn't sit on its ass in a museum." Finally, don't—you can't—miss **Ed Keinholz's** *The Wait*, perhaps the best macabre joke in town.

The Whitney also exhibits in three other galleries:

The Whitney at Philip Morris

120 Park Ave. Subway #4, #5, or #6 to Grand Central–42nd St.

Two sections: a small **Picture Gallery** (Mon–Sat 11am–6pm, Thurs 11am–7:30pm; free; gallery talks Mon, Wed, and Fri 12:30pm) with changing exhibitions on just about any (modern) theme you can think up. And a **Sculpture Court** (Mon–Sat 7:30am–9:30pm, Sun 11am–7pm; free) festooned with works: a great idea and a much better place to wait for a train than Grand Central across the street.

Whitney Museum at the Equitable Center

757 Seventh Ave. Subway B, D, or F to 50th St.–Sixth Ave. Mon–Fri 11am–6pm, Thurs 11am–7:30pm, Sat noon–5pm; Free. Gallery talks 12:30pm Mon, Wed, Fri.

Two collections of American art, one changed yearly, the other every couple of months. Expect striking works from big twentieth-century names like O'Keefe, Rothko, Hopper, and Johns—pick up the informative booklet for more details. Two things you can't miss: **Roy Lichtenstein's** 68-foot *Mural with Blue Brush Stroke*, facing you in the atrium as you enter, and in a corridor, **Thomas Hart Benton's** *America Today* murals, transferred here from the New School, which skillfully depict American life in the years before the Depression.

Whitney Museum Downtown

Federal Reserve Plaza. 33 Maiden Lane at Nassau St. Subway J, M, or R to Broad St. Mon–Fri 11am–6pm; free.

Five changing exhibitions of modern American art each year, with good free brochures and gallery talks.

The Cloisters

Fort Tryon Park. Subway 190th St.–Washington Ave.; also hourly direct shuttle bus from the Metropolitan Museum, June, July, & Aug, Fri & Sat; $5. Museum open March–Oct Tues–Sun 9:30am–5:15pm. Nov–Feb Tues–Sun 9:30am–4:45pm, closed Mon. Suggested *donation $6; $3 students (includes admission to Metropolitan Museum on same day). Free tours Tues–Thurs 3pm.*

High above the Hudson in Fort Tryon Park, **THE CLOISTERS** stands like some misplaced Gothic palazzo-cum-monastery. Which was presumably the desired effect. For this was the folly of collectors George Barnard and John D. Rockefeller, who in turn spent the early years of this century shipping over the best of medieval Europe that could be bought: Romanesque chapels and Gothic halls, transplanted brick by brick and now housing the best part of the Metropolitan Museum's **medieval collection**. If you're familiar with the type of buildings that have been cannibalized, then the place can't help but feel something of a golem, an assemblage of parts to make a caricatured whole. Nevertheless it is all undeniably carried off well, not without atmosphere, and in detail superb.

The best approach—from the 190th Street subway—is directly across the park; Rockefeller thoughtfully bought up the land on the other side of the river to preserve the views. Starting from the entrance hall, working counterclockwise, the collection unwinds in a loosely chronological order. First off is the simple monumentality of the **Romanesque Hall** made up from French remnants and the frescoed Spanish **Fuentiduena Chapel**, both thirteenth century and immediately inducing a reverential hush. They corner on perhaps the most charming of the four sets of cloisters here, those from **St. Guilhelm**, strong and busily carved capitals from thirteenth-century France. More or less contemporary, and again from France, is the nearby **Langon Chapel**, attractive enough in itself and enhanced by a twelfth-century **ciborium** that manages to be formal and graceful in just the right proportions, and protects an emotive **Virgin and Child** beneath.

At the center of the museum is the **Cuxa cloister**, from the twelfth-century Benedictine monastery of Saint Michel de Cuxa near Prades in the French Pyrenees; its capitals are brilliant peasant art, many carved with weird, self-devouring grotesque creatures. Pastiche additions to the scene are the gardens, planted with fragrant, almost overpowering, herbs and flowers, and (bizarrely in keeping) piped plainsong.

The museum's smaller **sculpture** is equally impressive. In the **Early Gothic Hall** are a number of carved figures, one a memorably tender and refined **Virgin and Child**, carved in England in the fourteenth century, probably for veneration at a private altar. The collection of **tapestries** is special, too, including a rare surviving Gothic work showing the **Nine Heroes**. The heroes, popular figures of the ballads of the Middle Ages, comprise three pagans (Hector, Alexander, Julius Caesar), three Hebrews (David, Joshua, Judas Maccabaeus), and three Christians (Arthur, Charlemagne, Godfrey of Bouillon). Five of the nine are here, clothed in the garb of the day (around 1385) against a rich backdrop. The **Unicorn Tapestries**, in the succeeding room, are even more spectacular—brilliantly alive with color, observation, and Christian symbolism.

Most of the Met's medieval paintings are to be found downtown, but one important exception here is **Campin**'s *Merode Altarpiece*. Housed in its own antechamber, this triptych depicts the Annunciation scene in a typical bourgeois Flemish interior of the day. On the left the donors gaze on timidly through an open door, to the right St. Joseph works in his carpenter's workshop; St. Joseph was mocked in the literature of the day, which might account for his rather ridiculous appearance—making a mousetrap, a symbol of the way the Devil traps souls.

Through the windows behind life goes on in a fifteenth-century marketplace, perhaps Campin's native Tournai.

With the first floor, you move into Gothic architecture. Or at least into a pseudo-Gothic chapel, built around the monumental **sarcophagus of Ermengol VII**, with its whole phalanx of family and clerics carved around to send him off. Two further cloisters are here to explore, along with an amazing downstairs **Treasury**. This is crammed with items, but two easily stand out: the **Belles Heures de Jean, Duc de Berry**, perhaps the greatest of all medieval illuminated Books of Hours, executed by the Limburg Brothers with dazzling genre miniatures of seasonal life; and the twelfth-century **altar cross** from Bury St. Edmunds in England, a mass of tiny expressive characters from Biblical stories. Finally, hunt out a minute **rosary bead** from sixteenth-century Flanders: enclosing a representation of the Passion, it seems barely possible it could have been carved by hand.

The American Museum of Natural History/Hayden Planetarium

Central Park West at 79th St. Subway C to 81st St.–Central Park West. Mon, Tue, Thur, Sun 10am–5:45pm, Wed, Fri, Sat 10am–9pm; free 10am–9pm Fri and Sat: otherwise suggested donation $4, Planetarium $5.

According to the *Guinness Book of Records*, this is the largest museum in the world bar none, and once you've traipsed the length of its aging exhibition hall and witnessed a fair number of its 34 million exhibits, you'll know it. Which is basically to say, be selective: anthropologists could have a field day here, but for anyone else a highly discriminating couple of hours should be ample.

The main entrance on Central Park West is the one to aim for, leaving you well placed for a loop of the more interesting halls on the second floor: principally intelligently mounted artifacts from Asia and Africa, backed up with informal commentary and given atmosphere with drums and ethnic music. These are sandwiched between dusty dioramas of the two continents' mammals. Upstairs there's a wilting array of dinosaurs, downstairs a static display of fish, both really only of interest to kids. Better to miss these altogether and check out the Hall of Meteorites instead: well laid out and including some strikingly beautiful crystals—not least the *Star of India*, the largest blue sapprent ever found.

The museum's astronomy department is installed in the adjacent **Hayden Planetarium**—accessible from the second floor of the Natural History Museum or from a separate entrance on 81st Street. Here you can view a variety of astronomical displays and gadgetry, hear Henry Fonda, Walter Kronkite, and assorted celebrities relate an impassioned tale of space endeavor, or watch a soporifically dull history of the universe (narrator Vincent Price) in the theater. All of which are cloyingly dull—and, again, primarily directed at children. You may instead prefer to fork out for the planetarium's **laser light shows**, held on Friday and Saturday evenings to provide visuals and sound for teenage stoners to freak out to their favorite Led Zep or Floyd tracks. If conventional New York nightlife is beginning to pale, well, it's always a thought . . . ..

SMALLER OR SPECIALIST MUSEUMS

Art and Visuals

Alternative Museum

17 White St. Subway #1 to Franklin St. Wed–Sat 11am–6pm, closed July & Aug; free.

Temporary exhibitions of contemporary art, emphasizing international developments. Well organized and adventurous, with displays supplemented by regular musical events and poetry readings. For information pick up their calendar, or give them a call—☎966-4444.

Asia Society Gallery

725 Park Ave. Subway #6 to 68th St.–Lexington Ave. Tues–Sat 11am–6pm, Sun noon–5pm; $2, Students $1.

Small permanent display of the Rockefeller collection of Asian art. Worth the admission fee if the accompanying temporary exhibition looks promising. Asia House also holds interesting performances/lectures/films/free events: ☎517-ASIA for details.

Bronx Museum of the Arts

1040 Grand Concourse, The Bronx. Subway #4 to 161st St.–Grand Concourse. Sat–Thurs 10am–4:30pm, Sun 11am–4:30pm; suggested donation $2.

Contemporary American art, none of any great note, plus changing exhibitions of Bronx-based artists.

The Brooklyn Museum

220 Eastern Parkway, Brooklyn. Subway #2 or #3 to Eastern Parkway–Brooklyn Museum. Daily 10am–5pm, closed Mon & Tues; $4, students $2. The museum's Gift Shop sells genuine ethnic items from around the world at not unreasonable prices.

When Judy Chicago's *Dinner Party* was exhibited here back in the early 1980s, the Brooklyn Museum had people lining up all the way around the block. Since then it's reverted to its former obscure status: a museum good in its own right but doomed to stand perpetually in the shadow of the Met. Which is a pity, for it's a likable place, and—together with a visit to the adjacent Botanical Garden, not to mention Prospect Park, just beyond—a good reason for forsaking Manhattan for an afternoon.

It does, however, need considerable selectivity, for in terms of size this is most certainly a major museum, with five floors stacked with exhibits. The highlights, depending on your personal interests, are likely to include the **ethnographic department** on the first floor, containing arts and applied arts from Oceania and the Americas, **the classical and Egyptian antiquities** on the third floor, and the excellent and evocative **American Period Rooms** on the fifth floor, which includes interiors and houses removed intact from elsewhere in Brooklyn, decorated with period furniture and other features. Be sure, too, to look in on the

American and European Picture Galleries on the top story. Here there are lots of eighteenth-century portraits, including one of George Washington by Gilbert Stuart; bucolic canvases by William Sidney Mount, alongside the heavily romantic paintings of the Hudson River School, not least the Catskills scenes of Thomas Cole and Frederick Church and Albert Bierstadt's *Storm in the Rocky Mountains*—a vast painting which established his reputation as a landscape artist. Later galleries display later paintings, notably by Eastman Johnson and John Singer Sargent, especially Johnson's curious *Not at Home*, leading right up to twentieth-century work by Charles Sheeler and Georgia O'Keefe. There's also a handful of works by European artists—Degas, Cézanne, Toulouse-Lautrec, Monet, Dufy, among others—though not including anything approaching their best work.

City Gallery

2 Columbus Circle. Subway A, B, C, or D to 59th St.–Columbus Circle. Mon–Fri 10am–5:30pm; free.

Funded by the city, this is a showcase gallery for NYC artists and community-based arts associations. Exhibitions change monthly.

Fashion Moda

2803 Third Ave. at 147th St. Subway #2 or #5 to Third Ave.–149th St. Tues–Sat 2–7pm; free.

"Fashion Moda is impossible to define because by definition we have no definition." Which goes some way to explaining what you're likely to see here: anarchic and always surprising temporary expositions of art that are a positive attempt to break with the at times chic safety of the Manhattan art scene. Its siting in the worst of the South Bronx's urban decay is deliberately intimidating, but if you can get someone to drop you on the doorstep, Fashion Moda's exhibitions rarely fail to entertain.

Forbes Galleries

62 Fifth Ave. Subway #4, #5, or #6 to Union Square, or F to 14th St.–Sixth Ave. Tues, Wed, Fri, & Sat, 10am–4pm; free.

The world's largest collection of Fabergé Easter Eggs, along with 500 toys boats and 12,000 toy soldiers—among the late Malcolm Forbes' favorite playthings.

Grey Art Gallery

33 Washington Place. Subway R to 8th St. Tues & Thurs 10am–6:30pm, Wed 10am–8:30pm, Fri 10am–5pm, Sat 1–5pm; free.

Display gallery of NYU's art department, mounting exhibitions of variable quality throughout the year. The permanent collection, when on display, is known for its post-1940s American works.

IBM Gallery of Science and Art

Madison Ave. at 56th St. Subway E or F to Fifth Ave.–53rd St. Tues–Sat 11am–6pm; free.

Unfairly ignored, this basement gallery exhibits more art than science—and sometimes a cross-over.

International Center of Photography

1130 Fifth Ave. Subway #6 to 96th St.–Lexington Ave. Tues noon–8pm, Wed–Fri noon–5pm, Sat–Sun 11am–6pm; $3, students $1.50. Free on Tues after 5pm.

Founded and directed by Cornell Capa, brother of Robert, the ICP exhibits on photography in all its aspects. The Center's permanent collection features most of the greats—Cartier-Bresson, Adams, Kertesz, Eugene Smith—and in addition there are usually three temporary shows on at any given time. At least one of these is bound to be worthwhile, often featuring the city's most exciting avant-garde and experimental work. Overall, an excellent adjunct to MoMA's static collection.

ICP Midtown

77 W. 45th St. (International Paper Plaza). Subway B, D, or F to 47th–50th St.-Rockefeller Center. Mon–Fri 11am–6pm, Sat noon–5pm; free.

Smaller, changing exhibitions of photographs from the main collection.

Isamu Noguchi Garden Museum

33–37 Vernon Boulevard, Long Island City, Queens. Saturday shuttle bus from Asia Society every hour on the half hour 11:30am–3:30pm, $5 round trip; call ☎718/721-1932 for more info. Museum open April–Nov Wed and Sat 11am–6pm; suggested donation $2.

A comprehensive collection containing over 250 stone, metal, and wood sculptures, on the site of the studio of **Isamu Noguchi** (1904–88). Noguchi was born in Japan and came to the US at the age of 14, later studying under Brancusi in Paris. His sculpture and designs for gardens can be seen throughout America: if you admire his work, then the collection here will knock you out.

Museum of the Moving Image

35th Ave. at 36th St., Astoria, Queens. Subway R to Steinway St. Tues–Fri noon–4pm, Sat & Sun noon–6pm; $5, students $2.50; film and exhibition information ☎718/784-0077.

Relatively new exhibition on film, TV, and video, housed in part of the once-more functioning Astoria studios, which are used by Woody Allen and the Cosby Show among others. Part of the museum is given over to temporary exhibitions—the first floor and third floor—while the second floor holds a permanent exhibition devoted to the development of the media through the ages. Along with posters and wonderfully kitsch movie souvenirs from the 1930s and 1940s are screenings designed to explain the technical development of an art form that, to millions around the world, defined America. You can listen in to directors explaining sequences from famous movies; watch fun short films made up of well-known clips; add your own sound effects to movies; and view original sets and costumes. There's also a wonderful, mock-Egyptian pastiche of a 1920s movie theater designed specially for the museum and actually used for showings of kids' movies and TV classics. Excellent and enthralling, though a shame it couldn't have been larger. See also *Astoria* in Chapter Four, "The Outer Boroughs."

National Academy of Design

1083 Fifth Ave. Subway #4, #5, or #6 to 86th St.–Lexington Ave. Tues noon–8pm, Wed–Sun noon–5pm; $2.50, students $2. Free Tues 5–8pm.

Samuel Morse founded the National Academy of Design along the lines of London's Royal Academy, and though 1083 Fifth Avenue is less grandiose than Burlington House, similarities remain: a school of fine art, exclusive membership, and regular exhibitions which, as you'd imagine, are usually (though not exclusively) American. There's a tradition that academicians and academics give a work of art on their election here: associates a self-portrait, academicians a "mature work." One hundred fifty years' worth of these pictures are now held by the Academy and form the mainstay of the Selection from the Permanent Collection—varied throughout the year but always with a strong slant toward portraiture.

Icing on the cake is the building itself: a faintly snotty Beaux Arts townhouse donated to the Academy by the husband of sculptor Anna Hyatt Huntingdon; her *Diana* gets pride of place below the cheerful rotunda.

New Museum of Contemporary Art

583 Broadway. Subway N or R to Prince St., or #6 to Spring St. Wed, Thurs, Sun noon–6pm, Fri–Sat noon–8pm; $3.50, students and artists $2.50.

Regularly changing exhibitions by contemporary American and international artists. Offbeat, eclectic, and worth checking out. Pick up the museum's calendar for details on current and forthcoming exhibits and lectures.

The Pierpoint Morgan Library

29 E. 36th St. Subway #6 to 33rd St.–Park Ave. Tues–Sat 10:30am–5pm, Sun 1–5pm, closed Sun in July & Aug; pay what you wish, suggested $3, students $1.

Built by McKim, Mead, and White for J. Pierpoint Morgan in 1917, this gracious Italian-style nest, feathered with the fruits of the omnivorous financier's trips to Europe, is one of New York's best small museums—though many of the exhibits are changed regularly so it's difficult to say precisely what you'll see.

The focal points are two main rooms, reached along a corridor usually lined with a fine assortment of **Rembrandt prints**. The first room you come to, the **West Room**, served as Morgan's study and has been left much as it was when he worked here, with a carved sixteenth-century Italian ceiling, a couple of paintings by Memling and Perugino, and, among the few items contemporary with the building, a desk custom-carved to a design by McKim. There's a portrait of J.P.'s father over the fifteenth-century Florentine fireplace, and a portrait of J.P. Junior on the far wall, swathed in the academic finery of an honorary University of Cambridge degree conferred in 1919. Through a domed and pillared hallway from here lies the **East Room** or library, a sumptuous three-tiered cocoon of rare books, autographed musical scores, and various trinkets culled from European households and churches. In a changing exhibit, there are original manuscripts by Mahler (the museum holds the world's largest collection of his work); a Gutenburg Bible from 1455 (one of 11 surviving); the only complete copy of Thomas Malory's *Morte d'Arthur*; as well as literary MS of everyone from the letters of Vasari and George Washington to works by Keats and Dickens. All in all a fascinating display.

Roerich Museum

319 W. 107th St. Subway #1 to 110th St.–Broadway. Tues–Sun 2–5pm; free.

Nicolas Roerich was a Russian artist who lived in India, was influenced by Indian mysticism, and produced strikingly original paintings. A small, weird, and virtually unknown collection.

Society of Illustrators' Museum

128 East 63rd St. Subway #4, #5, or #6 to 59th St.–Lexington Ave. Mon–Fri 10am–5pm, Tues 10am–8pm; free.

Changing selections from the Society's permanent collection of illustrations—wartime propaganda to slick contemporary ads, with all manner of cartoons and drawings between. The exhibitions center on theme or illustrator—designed primarily for aficionados but always accessible, well mounted, and topical.

City History

Fraunces Tavern

54 Pearl St. Subway #4 or #5 to Bowling Green. Mon–Fri 10am–4pm $2.50, students $1; free on Thurs.

Odds and ends from the Revolutionary era housed agreeably in a historic building; see *The Financial District* in Chapter One, "Lower Manhattan."

Museum of Bronx History

3266 Bainbridge Ave., The Bronx. Subway D to 205th St.–Bainbridge Ave. Mon–Fri 9am–5pm by appointment, Sat 10am–4pm, Sun 1–5pm; $1.

Bronx-related artifacts from pre-Colonial times to the Depression.

Museum of the City of New York

Fifth Ave. at 103rd St. Subway #6 to 103rd St.–Lexington Ave. Tues–Sat 10am–5pm, Sun 1–5pm; suggested donation $4, students $2.

Spaciously housed in a purpose-built neo-Georgian mansion on the fringes of Spanish Harlem, this gives a competent if unexciting rundown on the history of the city from Dutch times to the present day. Paintings, furniture, and a slide show—plus the museum runs Sunday walking tours of New York neighborhoods (see "Information, Maps, and Tours" in *Basics*).

The New York Historical Society

Central Park West at 77th St. Subway #1 to 79th St. Tues–Sun 10am–5pm; $3, Tues pay what you wish.

More a museum of American than New York history, but another site well worth keeping an eye on for its temporary exhibitions, and with a permanent collection that rewards a visit in its own right. Focus of this are the paintings of **James Audubon**, the Harlem artist and naturalist who specialized in lovingly detailed watercolors of birds—all very similar, and unless you're a keen ornithologist, not exactly attention-grabbing. Other galleries hold a broad sweep of **nineteenth-century American painting**: principally portraiture (a slobbish Aaron Burr, the picture of Alexander Hamilton that found its way on to the $10 bill) and Hudson River school landscapes (among them Thomas Cole's famed and fanatically pompous *Course of Empire* series). More rewarding is the glittering display of **Tiffany glass**, providing an excellent all-embracing view of Louis Tiffany's attempts "to provide good art for American homes." On a more historical note, and for a small additional fee, you can look around the museum **library**, which boasts such diverse items as the original Louisiana Purchase document and the correspondence between Aaron Burr and Alexander Hamilton that led to their duel. All in all an interesting museum, and one often overlooked.

Queens Museum

Flushing Meadows-Corona Park. Subway #7 to Willets Point–Shea Stadium. Tues–Sat 10am–5pm, Sun noon–5:30pm; $2, students $1.

Primarily worth the trip for its one and only permanent item: an 18,000-square-foot model of the five boroughs of New York City, spectacularly lit, constantly updated and originally conceived for the 1964 World's Fair by Robert Moses. Great fun if you know the city well, and useful orientation if you don't.

Community and Ethnic

Center for African Art

54 E. 68th St. Subway #6 to 68th St.–Lexington Ave. Tues–Fri 10am–5pm, Sat 11am–5pm, Sun noon–5pm; $3, students $2.

Changing exhibitions of the best of traditional African art. An eye-opener compared to the static/junky collections that are usually found.

The Museum of the American Indian

Audubon Terrace, 3753 Broadway at 155th St. Subway #2 to 157th St.–Broadway. Tues–Sat 10am–5pm, Sun 1–5pm. $3, students $2.

Far and away the finest of the Audubon Terrace collections, this languishes up in Harlem almost totally ignored. When a few of its prize exhibits were shown downtown for a couple of weeks, more people went to look than turned up at the museum that year. Don't follow this pattern, for you'll miss out on a superb and fascinating assemblage of daily artifacts from almost every tribe native to the Americas. Ordinarily this might sound a little overpowering, but the display here is skillful and backed up with an intelligent range of informational aids. Highlights include assorted scalps, the personal knickknacks of Sitting Bull and Geronimo, shrunken human figures from Ecuador, and some amazing Inuit scrimshaw. There's also a very reasonably priced museum shop selling various authentic items. It's planned to move the whole collection to Washington DC: catch it while it's still here.

Museo del Barrio

1230 Fifth Ave. Subway #6 to 103rd St. Wed–Sun 11am–5pm; suggested donation $2, students $1.

Literally "the neighborhood museum," this place was founded in the 1960s by a group of Puerto Ricans from Spanish Harlem who wanted to educate their children and remind them of their roots. Now, although the emphasis remains largely Puerto Rican, the museum has come to embrace the whole of Latin America, with five major loan exhibits of paintings, photographs, and crafts each year. Supplementary events include talks, summer concerts, and kids' puppet theater—all free.

Chinese Museum

8 Mott St. Subway N or R to Canal St. Mon–Sat 10am–6pm, closed Sun.

A hoard of Chinese costumes, Buddhas, and religious accoutrements located at the end of a sleazy amusement arcade (which itself includes a devastatingly cruel contraption caging a "live, dancing chicken"). A neat stop on any tour of Chinatown were it not for the fact that it's open only to groups of eight or more.

The Hall of Chinese History

246 Bowery, between Prince & Huston streets. Daily 10am–4pm; $5.

Exhibition of life-size terracotta warriors and horses of the Qin dynasty are the high spot of this collection of Chinese art across the ages.

Hispanic Museum

Audubon Terrace (see Museum of the American Indian, above). Tues–Sat 10am–4:30pm, Sun 1–4pm; free.

Inevitably this is overshadowed by the adjacent Museum of the American Indian, but it's worth sticking your nose around the door of the Hispanic for the chocolate terracotta interior, a scattering of Spanish masters, and, best of all, the joyful *Murals of Spain* by Joaquin Sorolla y Bastida.

Schomburg Center for Research in Black Culture

515 Lenox Ave. at 135th St. Subway #2 or #3 to 125th St.–Lenox Ave. Mon–Wed noon–8pm, Thurs–Sat 10am–6pm; free.

Thought-provoking exhibitions of documents, art, photos, and sculpture that detail the history of blacks in the US.

Studio Museum of Harlem

144 W. 125th St. Subway #2 or #3 to 125th St.–Lenox Ave. Wed–Fri 10am–5pm, Sat 1–6pm; $2, students $1.

Exhibitions of contemporary (and often local) art, photography, and sculpture.

Lower East Side Tenement Museum

97 Orchard St. Subway F to Delancey St.–Essex St. Tues–Fri 11am–4pm, Sun 10am–3pm; free. The museum also organizes Sunday walking tours of the Lower East Side, usually starting between noon and 2pm. Call ☎431-0233 for a program.

Housed in a former tenement building, this museum aims to present a complete picture of immigrant history in New York, especially lower Manhattan, through a variety of changing temporary exhibitions on its first floor. The two galleries show photos and community-based exhibits (importantly not just concentrating on the Jewish history of the area), while the upstairs rooms have been preserved more or less as they were when the house was occupied by numerous immigrant families earlier this century. This part is currently closed to the public, but there are plans to develop it as a "living history" display, with people occupying the evocatively decayed rooms—unlived in since the 1930s—in authentic costume. An earnest and sympathetic attempt to document the immigrant experience—well worth a visit if you're in the area.

Ukrainian Museum

203 Second Ave. Subway #4, #5, or #6 to Astor Place. Wed–Sun 1–5pm; $1, students 50¢.

Situated in the heart of the Ukrainian East Village, there's little to entice outsiders into this small collection. On two tiny floors, it divides itself between recounting the history of immigration to the US from the Ukraine and showing (more interestingly) ethnic items from the Ukraine itself. Look out for the hand-painted Easter eggs or *pysanky*—a craft that's still kept up since, according to Ukrainian folklore, when production ceases the world will end.

Crafts, Fashion, and Design

American Craft Museum

40 W. 53rd St. Subway E or F to Fifth Ave.–53rd St. Wed–Sun 10am–5pm, Tues 10am–8pm; $3.50, students $1.50, free Tues 5–8pm.

A showcase of modern crafts chosen by the American Craft Council. Bright, brash, and good fun.

Museum of American Folk Art

Columbus Ave. at 66th St. Daily 9am–9pm; free.

Changing exhibitions of traditional handicrafts with the emphasis on the domestic; could be just the place if the splendors the Met offers aren't your scene.

Black Fashion Museum

155 W. 126th St. Subway #2 or #3 to 125th St.–Lenox Ave. Mon–Fri noon–8pm; phone ☎666-1320 for an appointment; suggested donation $2.

It's on the premise that the contribution of the black fashion designers has gone largely unrecognized that the Black Fashion Museum organizes its exhibits, a wide variety of costumes designed and made by blacks from the eighteenth century on. The third floor has a quirky group of robes and gowns, including a slave dress of finely stitched cotton, and Mary Todd Lincoln's velvet inaugural gown designed by Elizabeth Keckley, a freed slave. The Lenox site, sadly, makes for specialist interest only.

Cooper-Hewitt Museum

2 E. 91st St. Subway #4, #5, or #6 to 86th St.–Lexington Ave. Tues 10am–9pm, Wed–Sat 10am–5pm, Sun noon–5pm; $3, free Tues 5–9pm.

When he decided to build on what was then the unfashionable end of Fifth Avenue, millionaire industrialist Andrew Carnegie asked for "the most modest, plainest and most roomy house in New York." And that's nearly what he got—a series of wood-paneled boxes too decorative to be plain, too large to be modest. But they provide good gallery space today for the Cooper-Hewitt collection of design, shown off here in three floors of changing exhibitions. Themes vary so check what's on first—the Cooper-Hewitt is as good as its exhibitions, which tend to be excellent.

Others

Museum of Broadcasting

1 E. 53rd St. Subway E or F to Fifth Ave.–53rd St. Tues–Sat noon–5pm; suggested $4, $3 students. Tues noon–8pm; pay what you wish. Phone ☎752-4690 for details of lectures by artists and directors.

An archive of American TV and radio broadcasts, unusual for its accessibility to the public and whose excellent card reference system allows you to trace 1950s comedies, old newsreels, and other oddities. Be warned though that there are only a couple of dozen video consoles, and someone before you may well be getting down to a day's worth of "I Love Lucy." Arrive, if possible, at opening.

Museum of Holography

11 Mercer St. Subway #6 to Canal St.–Lafayette St. Daily, 11am–6pm; $3.

Since a recent revamp, an interesting collection of holographic images from around the world, and "an international center for the understanding and advancement of holography" as a science. Also has changing exhibitions of artists working in holograms, as well as detailing the many practical uses of holographic images.

New York City Transit Exhibit

Old Subway entrance at Schermerhorn St. and Boerum Place, Brooklyn. Nearest subway Borough Hall. Mon–Fri 10am–4pm; entry by subway token ($1.15).

Subway cars from the turn of the century, artifacts and ephemera connected with the world's largest underground railroad. Cheap and engaging, even for non-enthusiasts, and made all the better by being housed in a disused subway station.

Police Academy Museum

235 E. 20th St. Subway #6 to 23rd St.–Park Ave. Mon–Fri 9am–3pm; free.

A collection of memorabilia of the New York Police Department, the largest and oldest in the country. It's used to inculcate reverence for the force in young cadets, and just about recommends itself to anyone not wildly interested in law and order. Really, it's not about crime or punishment so much as the personal effects of New York's Finest: night sticks, uniforms, photos, and the like. There's a copper badge of 1845 worn by the sergeants of the day, earning them the enduring nickname of "coppers." If you're into firepower, search out the tommy gun in a violin case—original gangster issue.

Commercial galleries

Art, and especially contemporary art, is big in New York: a fact reflected in the number and variety of **private galleries**. Even if you have no intention of buying, many of these are well worth seeing. Broadly they fall into three main areas: along **Madison Avenue** in the 60s and 70s for antique works and the occasional (minor) old master; **57th Street** between Sixth and Park avenues for contemporary big names; and **SoHo** for whatever is currently fashionable (until a couple of years ago the East Village scene held much of the more exciting—and cheaper—work, but it's pretty well dead today). A few of the more exclusive places are invitation only, though one of the best ways to see the galleries is with *Manhattan Art Tours* (see "Information, Maps, and Tours" in *Basics*), which runs excellent and informed conducted tours. Incidentally, if your budget can't stand the prices, the shops of the larger museums are the best places to go for cards, prints, and posters (for which see Chapter Seven, "Shops and Markets").

Below are listed some of the more interesting options in the main Manhattan locations. Opening times are roughly Tuesday–Saturday 11am–6pm, and the best time to gallery-hop, especially in SoHo, is Saturday, or wherever you spy an opening. These are identifiable by the crowds and are generally free for those with enough bluff.

SoHo Galleries

A.I.R. Gallery, 63 Crosby St. (☎966-0799). Women's co-op exhibiting work by members and others.

DIA Art Foundation, 141 Wooster St. (☎473-8072). Non-profit organization which commissions and exhibits works by new artists. Always worth a look.

The Drawing Center, 35 Wooster St. (☎219-2166). Specializes in oversized painting/sculpture/construction.

Dyansen Gallery, 122 Spring St. (☎226-3384). Contemporary painting and sculpture, plus an Erté sculpture collection.

Edward Thorp, 103 Prince St. (☎431-6880). Mainstream figurative painting.

49th Parallel, 4th Floor, 420 West Broadway (☎925-8349). Canadian art; sponsored by the Canadian Government.

Jay Gorney Modern Art, 100 Greene St. (☎966-4480). Hosts many group shows.

John Weber, 3rd Floor, 142 Greene St. (☎966-6115). Conceptual, Minimal and highly unusual works.

Leo Castelli, 2nd Floor, 420 West Broadway (☎431-5160). One of the original dealer/collectors, instrumental in aiding the careers of Rauschenberg and Warhol. Big names at big prices.

Louis Meisel, 141 Prince St. (☎677-1340). The place to find out what Abstract Illusionism looks like. Meisel claims to have invented the term, along with Photorealism, also well in evidence here.

Mary Boone, 420 and 417 Broadway (☎431-1818). Leo Castelli's protege, specializing in up-and-coming European and American artists.

O.K. Harris, 383 West Broadway (☎431-3100). A lively, unpredictable gallery run by Ivan Karp, champion of Superrealism. One of the first SoHo galleries.

Paula Cooper, 155 Wooster St. (☎674-0766). Minimal and Abstract works, and much more.

SoHo Center for Visual Artists, 114 Prince St. (☎226-1995). Non-profit exhibition gallery sponsored by the Aldrich Museum, Connecticut.

Sonnabend, 3rd Floor, 420 West Broadway (☎966-6160). Across-the-board painting, photography, and video.

Sperone Westwater, 2nd Floor, 142 Greene St. (☎431-3685). Flashy European and American painting.

Vorpal, 411 West Broadway (☎777-3939). Chiefly the tedious conundrums of Max Escher's prints.

Galleries elsewhere

Blum-Helman, 20 W. 57th St. (☎245-2111). Blum-Helman mounted the first Andy Warhol exhibition and has since gone on to promote both new and existing American art.

Jordan Volpe Gallery, 958 Madison Ave. (☎570-9500). Specialties include the American Arts and Crafts movement, the furniture of Gustav Stickel, Rookwood Pottery, and Louis Tiffany lamps.

M. Knoedler, 19 E. 70th St. (☎794-0550). Very highly reputed gallery specializing in European Old Masters and some of the best-known twentieth-century American artists.

Marlborough Gallery, 40 W. 57th St. (☎541-4900). Another internationally renowned gallery that shows some of the best British and American artists.

Nature Morte, 204 E. 10th St. (☎420-9544). One of the few survivors of the pretty much defunct East Village scene.

Robert Miller, 41 E. 57th St. (☎980-5454). Twentieth-century American art.

Pace Gallery, 32 E. 57th St. (☎759-7999). Well-known gallery that holds a large stock of modern American artworks.

For details of **museums specifically for kids**, see Chapter Six, "Sports, Kids, and Daytime Activities."

SPORTS, KIDS, AND DAYTIME ACTIVITIES

When you've had your fill of the city's big museums, and the glitz of Manhattan superstores and skyscrapers begins to pall, there are countless ways of filling your time. The most obvious perhaps are **sports**, which include the usual spectator activities as well as ample opportunities for the full gamut of participatory activities: in a city full of people neurotic about health and fitness there are any number of gyms and places to work out, and places to play organized sports abound.

Less athletically, or if you have a bored child in tow, there are carriage rides in Central Park, ice and roller skating in Central Park among other places, even a place to play with model trains. We've also detailed other listings for those traveling with **kids** in this chapter, including stores and museums of specific interest for children. Among other daytime activities, we've included the best of New York's **festivals and annual events**, useful for timing a visit around, along with details of **swimming pools** and a full list of the best of the city's **beaches**—worth bearing in mind when the sometimes excruciating August heat and humidity get too much.

SPORTS AND OUTDOOR ACTIVITIES

Sports are big business, which is to say that for all spectator sports financial considerations come first. The Brooklyn Dodgers, New York's official baseball team, deserted their home town as long ago as 1957, and every other professional team intermittently threatens to do the same. Yet New Yorkers are themselves highly sports-conscious: the city's newspapers devote a great many pages to the subject, as do the TV stations, which cover most of the regular season games and all of the post-season matches in the big four team sports—**football**, **baseball**, **basketball**, and **hockey**. If you want to watch a game, bear in mind that tickets can be hard to find and don't come that cheap. Remember, also, that bars—like, for example, the *McCann* chain—are a good alternative to actually being there, especially those (often known as sports bars) with a special kingsize screen.

Participation sports aren't cheap either—unless you're prepared to **swim** (either at the local pools or the borough beaches) or **jog**, still one of the city's main obsessions. If you play soccer, there are plenty lots of pick-up games on the Great Lawn in Central Park on summer Sundays. Other participatory sports, and all **fitness** fads, cost a lot of money, and many New Yorkers are members of private health clubs in order to cut costs. For anyone interested, these places fill sizable sections of the city's Yellow Pages.

Watching

In this section we've included details of each of the main **spectator sports** in New York followed by a section detailing the locations and ticket prices.

Baseball

Baseball is America. No other sport generates as much interest in the US over the whole season, and nothing else compares with the tradition and mystique that surround this still essentially parochial and small-town game. Watching a game, even if it's not your home team, can at least be a pleasant day out, drinking beer and eating hot dogs in the sun: tickets are not too expensive and the crowds usually friendly and sociable.

Teams and tickets
New York's two baseball teams still play in the city: the **Yankees** at Yankee Stadium in the Bronx and the Mets at Shea Stadium in Flushing, Queens. **Tickets** for both stadiums are around $10, though you can get *bleacher* seats for about half that.

Football

Home teams are the **Jets** and the **Giants**, both of whom deserted New York for the Meadowlands Sports Complex in New Jersey. On recent form, there is no contest—the Giants are the 1991 Superbowl champions; the Jets haven't won anything in years. The cheapest tickets are $8, though these can be tough to get. If you don't manage to get any, don't worry too much: at least two games are shown on TV every Sunday afternoon, with another on Monday night during the season.

Basketball

Basketball is perhaps the most popular American game to be played outside the US; it's also by far the most athletic of American team sports, and the most grace-ful to watch. The game is non-stop action conducted at a blistering pace. Until the 1950s the sport was all-white: in the last thirty years or so, however, it has been dominated by a succession of black athletes—Dr. J., "Magic" Johnson, Kareem Abdul Jabbar, and, currently, Michael Jordon, all of whom are big crowd-pullers.

The basketball season begins in October and runs until the first week of July, when the championships take place. The two New York teams are the **Knickerbockers** (Knicks), who play at Madison Square Garden, and the **Nets**, at the Meadowlands Sports Complex in New Jersey. Tickets are not too expen-sive at $10–15—well worth it to watch the Knicks in the company of committed fans like Woody Allen and Mike Tyson. College basketball is also hugely popular, and worth watching if you can catch it on TV. The college season culminates in the divisional play-offs and final in the two weeks of "March Madness."

Hockey

Hockey provides an excuse for getting a bunch of guys to beat the hell out of each other for the benefit of the paying public. However, while it is a violent sport, certainly, and some players are without doubt chosen mainly for their punching ability, there's a fair amount of skill involved, too—the speed the action takes place at is, without question, phenomenal. The two New York teams are the Rangers, who play at Madison Square Garden, and the less purely New York Islanders, who play out at the Nassau Coliseum on Long Island. There's also a New Jersey team, the Devils, who play at Meadowlands.

Tennis

The **American Open Championships**, held in Queens each September at the National Tennis Center, Flushing Meadows (☎718/592-8000), is the top tennis event of the year. The Flushing complex is perhaps most renowned for the at times excruciating noise of jets taking off and landing at nearby La Guardia Airport, although this is due to become less of a problem in years to come since Mayor Dinkins, an avowed tennis fan, has ordered the planes to be rerouted during the championships. Ticket prices for the big matches are, however, astronomical and need to be booked well in advance. Madison Square Garden also boasts annual international tennis matches in the form of the Virginia Slims tournament, held each year at the end of November.

Soccer

Thanks mainly to the South and Latin American communities of Queens, and the Italian areas of the Outer Boroughs and New Jersey, **soccer** is enormously popular in New York. However, apart from the odd British game shown on the Sports cable channels, most of the soccer shown on TV is confined to the Spanish-language stations—usually every Sunday on channels 31 and 41. No professional soccer is actually played in the New York area, though if you're desperate to see a game, decent quality college matches are played out at Rutgers University in New Jersey. Plans have been made for New York to be one of the host cities for the 1994 World Cup, but it seems likely that games will actually be played in New Haven, Connecticut.

Cricket

Bizarre though it may seem, there is a thriving and long-established **cricket** community in the New York area, dating back to the late nineteenth century and the formation of the Staten Island Cricket Club—where, on summer Sunday afternoons, the sound of leather upon willow can be experienced. Likewise Van Cortlandt Park in the Bronx is the weekly setting for the New York Cricket League, which is particularly popular with the Indian, Pakistani, and West Indian populations here. It is claimed, in fact, that there are around a million cricket players in the US, and American enthusiasts are trying hard to expand the popularity of the game: a match in New York in September 1990, when an England XI played the West Indies, drew some 15,000 supporters.

Horse racing

There are two major **race tracks** in the New York area, the **Aqueduct Race Track**, ("The Big A") in Rockaway, Queens, and **Belmont**, Long Island—home to the Belmont Stakes, which, along with the Kentucky Derby and Preakness, is one of the big three races of the year (the "Triple Crown").

Meetings take place at the Aqueduct between January and May, and June and July. It is possible to get there on a special A train from 42nd St. with a ticket that includes grandstand admission. More details on ☎718/330-1234. Belmont can be reached on similar all-inclusive tickets from Penn Station on the Long Island Railroad. Details on ☎516/739-4200. It's open May to June and August to October.

Also popular is **harness racing**. The main local racetrack is the **Roosevelt Raceway**, Westbury, Long Island (inclusive subway/bus tickets again from Penn Station; full details on ☎516/222-2000), at which races take place at various times throughout the year—check the papers for details. The **Meadowlands Complex** also has races from January to August, starting at 8pm in an enclosed stadium.

To **place a bet** anywhere other than the race track itself you'll need to find an **OTB—Off Track Betting**—office. There's one at Grand Central Station, otherwise there are plenty of others around the city—see the Yellow Pages for specific addresses. Hours are Monday to Friday 9am–5pm, Saturday 9am–3pm.

Wrestling

Wrestling, held regularly at Madison Square Garden, is perhaps the least "sporting" of all the sports you can watch in New York, more of a theatrical event really, with a patriotically charged, almost salivating crowd cheering on all-American superheroes against evil and distinctly un-American foes. Bouts start with a rendition of the *Star-spangled Banner*, after which the action—a staged affair between wrestlers with names like Hulk Hogan and the Red Devil—takes place to a background of jingoistic roars, the red-blooded American spirit invariably winning the day. For details of bouts, call Madison Square Garden direct.

Tickets and venues

Tickets for most events can be booked ahead with a credit card, through the Ticketmaster, Chargit, or Teletron numbers, and collected at the gate, though it's cheaper—and of course riskier for popular events—to pick up tickets on the night. If all else fails, try *Mackey's* at 234 W. 44th St. (☎840-2800), a ticket agency for all sports events, or simply catch the action on the big screen in a sports bar.

The main locations

Madison Square Garden Center, W. 33rd St. and Seventh Ave. (☎563-8300; credit card reservations on ☎307-7171 or ☎516/888-9000 or ☎201/507-8900). Subway #1, #2, #3, to 34th Street Penn Stadium. Box office open Sept–June Mon–Sat 10am–8pm, Sun 11am–7pm.

Meadowlands Sports Complex, Off routes 3, 17, and NJ Turnpike exit 16, East Rutherford, New Jersey (☎201/935-3900; credit card reservations on ☎201/507-8900 or ☎307-7171). Regular buses from Port Authority Bus Terminal on 42nd St. and 8th Ave. Box office open for all arenas Mon–Sat 10am–6pm, Sun noon–5pm.

Nassau Coliseum, Hempstead Turnpike, Uniondale, New York (☎516/794-9300; credit card reservations on ☎307-7171 or ☎516/888-9000). Long Island Railroad to Hempstead, then bus N70, N71, or N72 from Hempstead bus terminal, one block away. Box office open daily 10:30am–5:45pm.

Shea Stadium, 126th St. at Roosevelt Ave., Queens (☎718/507-8499; credit card reservations on ☎307-7171). Subway number 7, direct to Willets Point/Shea Stadium Station. Box office open Mon–Fri 8am–6pm, Sat & Sun 9am–5pm. Dress warmly in fall and winter as Shea is a windy icebox.

Yankee Stadium, 161st St. and River Ave., The Bronx (☎293-6000; credit card reservations on ☎307-7171 or ☎516/888-9000); subway C, D, or #4 direct to 161st Station. Stick with the crowds when you leave—it's not a good neighborhood. Box office open Mon–Fri 9:30am–5pm and during evening games.

Sports Bars

Kuklas, 220 W. 31st St. (☎268-7937).

Mickey Mantle's, 42 Central Park South (☎688-7777).

Rusty's, 1271 Third Ave. (☎861-4518).

Rusty Staub's, 575 Fifth Ave. (☎682-1000).

Sporting Club, 99 Hudson St. (☎219-0900).

Participating

For those energetic enough to try them, the following section details most of the **sports-related activities** possible within the city limits, along with listings of **beaches** for less athletic types.

Jogging

Jogging is still the number one fitness pursuit: the number of yearly coronaries in Central Park, the most popular place, probably runs well into double figures. A favorite circuit in the park is around the Receiving Reservoir; just make sure you jog in the right direction—counterclockwise. The East River Promenade and almost any other stretch of open space long enough to get up speed are also well jogged.

If, rather than bust your own guts, you'd prefer to see thousands of others do so, the **New York Marathon** takes place on the third or fourth Sunday of October. Two million people turn out each year to watch the 16,000 runners complete the 26-mile course, which starts in Staten Island, crosses the Verrazano Narrows Bridge, and passes through all the other boroughs before ending up at the Tavern on the Green in Central Park. To take part you need to apply for an entry form from the *New York Road Runners Club*, 9 E. 89th St. (☎860-4455).

Roller and ice-skating . . . and tobogganing

In winter, the freezing weather makes for good **ice-skating**, while in summer **roller-skating** is popular on the paths in Central Park and specifically the north-west corner of the Sheep Meadow; also at Riverside Park and even the smaller open spaces. **Tobogganing** is another popular winter activity, up on the slopes of Van Cortlandt Park in the Bronx; phone ☎543-4595 to see if the snow's thick enough.

Skating venues

Lasker Rink, 106th St., Central Park (☎397-3106). The lesser-known ice rink in Central Park, way up toward the Harlem end. Much cheaper than the Wollman Rink, though less accessible, and the neighborhood isn't great. Avoid at night. Open Mon–Thurs 10am–9:30pm, Fri & Sat 10am–11pm. Admission $2.50 plus $2 for skate rentals.

Rockefeller Center Ice Rink (☎757-5730). Without doubt the slickest place to skate, though you may have to stand in line and it's pricier than anywhere else. Open Mon–Thurs 9am–10pm, Fri & Sat 9am–midnight, Sun 9am–10pm. Admission $8 plus $4 for skate rentals.

Skyrink, 450 W. 33rd St. (☎695-6555). Centrally located indoor rink, high up a Midtown Manhattan skyscraper. Mon–Thurs 8:30am–10:15pm, Fri–Sat 8am–11pm. Admission $6.50 plus $2.50 for skate rentals.

Wollman Rink, 64th St., Central Park (☎517-4800). Lovely rink, where you can skate to the marvelous, inspiring backdrop of the lower Central Park skyline—incredibly impressive at night. Open Mon 9am–5pm, Tues–Thurs 10am–9:30pm, Fri–Sun 10am–11pm. Admission $5 plus $2.50 for skate rentals.

Billiards and snooker

Aside from bars and nightclubs, the new thing to do in the evening in Manhattan is play **pool**, not in dingy halls but in gleaming bars where well-heeled yuppies mix with the regulars. **Snooker** fans will also find a few tables.

The Billiard Club, 220 W. 19th St. (☎206-7665). A pool club with a nice, vaguely European atmosphere and a small bar serving soft drinks and cappuccinos.

Chelsea Billiards, 54 W. 21st St. (☎989-0096). A casual place with both snooker and pool tables. Refreshments from machines.

Society Billiards, 10 E. 21st St. (☎529-8600). More of a bar than a straight pool hall, but fun nonetheless.

Tekk Billiards, 75 Christopher St. (☎463-9282). Basic, no-frills pool hall. Open 24 hours.

Horse riding and carriage rides

Carriage Rides, Central Park South, between Fifth and Sixth Ave. For some, the ideal way to see Central Park, and some carriages are willing—with a little persuasion—to take you farther afield. Not cheap, though—around $25 for half an hour. Every day, all day, until the late evening.

Claremont Riding Academy, 175 W. 89th St. (☎724-5100). For riding in Central Park, this place rents ponies by the hour for $27. Saddles are English-style; lessons $30 per half hour.

Jamaica Bay Riding Academy, 7000 Shore Parkway, Brooklyn (☎718/531-8949). Trail riding, with western-style saddles, around the eerie landscape of Jamaica Bay. Very much the more atmospheric riding alternative, and a little cheaper than Claremont at $17 for 45 minutes' ride; lessons $40 an hour.

Bowling

Bowlmor Lanes, 110 University Place (☎255-8188). Long-established and large bowling alley with a bar and shop. Open Sun–Thurs 10–1am, Fri & Sat 10–4am. Price $3 per game per person, plus 75¢ shoe-rental.

Health and fitness: pools, gyms, and baths

Carmine St. Pool, Clarkson St. and Seventh Ave. (☎397-3107). You have to be a member to use this pool and gym; it only costs $1 but you need to prove you're living in New York, and provide a passport-sized photo. Mon–Fri evenings only.

East 54th St. Pool, 342 E. 54th St. (☎397-3154). Good-size indoor pool; annual membership just $2. Exercise classes, too. Open afternoons and evenings only Mon–Fri, all day until 5pm Sat & Sun.

Exercise Exchange, 236 W. 78th St. (☎595-6475). Aerobics and other exercise classes for around $10 a class—no membership required. Open Mon–Fri 9am–7pm, weekends 9am–4pm.

Sutton Gymnastics and Fitness Center, 440 Lafayette St. (☎533-9390). One of the few gyms in New York where you don't have to be a member to use the facilities. Gymnastics and exercise classes for around $18. Open Mon–Fri all day, for adults, and at weekends for kids.

Tenth Street Turkish Baths, 268 E 10th St (☎674-9250). An ancient place, something of a neighborhood landmark and still going, with steam baths, sauna, and pool, as well as exercise rooms, whirlpool, massage, etc. A restaurant, too. Admission $15, access to the various facilities extra. Open daily 9am–10pm; men only Sun & Thurs; women only Wed; co-ed Mon, Tues, Fri & Sat.

West 59th St. Pool, W. 59th St. and West End Ave. (☎397-3159). Two pools, one indoor and another outdoor. Open Mon–Sat, afternoons and evenings only; admission free.

Boating

Loeb Boathouse, Central Park (☎517-4723). Row boats to hire between April and October, daily 9am–6pm. Rates are $6 an hour plus $20 deposit.

Beaches

Few visitors come to New York for the **beaches**, and those New Yorkers with money tend to turn their noses up at the city strands, preferring to move farther afield to Long Island, just a couple of hours away and much better (see Chapter

Eleven "Out from the City"). But the city's beaches, though often crowded, *are* a cool summer escape from Manhattan and most are also just a subway token away.

Brooklyn

Coney Island Beach (at the end of half a dozen subway lines: fastest is the D train to Stillwell Avenue). After Rockaway (see below), NYC's most popular swimming spot, jam-packed on summer weekends. The Atlantic here is only moderately dirty and there's a good, reliable onshore breeze.

Brighton Beach (D train to Brighton Beach). Technically the same stretch as Coney Island, but less crowded and given color by the local Russian community (pick up on ethnic snacks from the boardwalk vendors).

Manhattan Beach (D train to Sheepshead Bay Road, walk to Ocean Avenue and cross the bridge). Small beach well used by locals.

Queens

Rockaway Beach (A and C trains to any stop along the beach). Forget California. This seven-mile strip is where New Yorkers—up to three quarters of a million daily in summer—come to get the best surf around. Best beaches are at 9th St., 23rd St., and 80-118th Sts.

Jacob Riis Park (IRT #2 train to Flatbush Avenue, then Q35 bus). Good sandy stretches, the western ones used almost exclusively by a gay male crowd.

The Bronx

Orchard Beach (Subway train #6 local to Pelham Bay Park, then Bx12 bus). Lovingly known as "Horseshit Beach"—and in any case less easy to get to than the rest.

Staten Island

Great Kills Park (Bus 103 from Staten Island Ferry Terminal). Quiet and used by locals.

Wolfe's Pond Park (Bus 103 to Main Street Tottenville, at Hylan and Cornelia). Packs in the crowds from New Jersey.

PARADES AND FESTIVALS

The other big daytime activities in New York, and often worth timing your visit around, are its **parades** and street **festivals**. The city takes these, especially the **parades**, very seriously. Almost every large ethnic group in the city holds an annual get-together, often using Fifth Avenue as the main drag; the events are often political or religious in origin, though now are just as much an excuse for music, food, and dance. Chances are your stay will coincide with at least one: the following list is roughly chronological—for more details and exact dates of parades, phone ☎397-8222. As you might expect, New York's **festivals** are concentrated in the spring and summer, tending to tie in with ethnic holidays and religious observances. We've included those that take place in Manhattan: for further details, exact dates, and lists of events in other boroughs, phone ☎755-4100.

Parades

The big celebration—and undoubtedly New York City's most famous—is the **St. Patrick's Day Parade**, held on the weekend nearest March 17. Celebrating an impromptu march through the streets by Irish militiamen on St. Patrick's Day, 1762, it has become a magnet for every Irish band and organization in the US and Ireland, which in recent years has meant increasing political overtones, with Noraid and Sinn Fein out in full force. Most of the city lines the route up Fifth Avenue from 44th to 86th Street, and general dementia runs especially high in Irish bars—should you find yourself in one, steer clear of politics. Perhaps the best vantage point is St. Patrick's Cathedral, where the Bishop of New York greets the marching pipes and bands.

The **Greek Independence Day Parade** (March 25) isn't as long or as boozy, more a patriotic nod to the old country from floats of pseudo-classically dressed Hellenes. When Independence Day falls in the Orthodox Lent, the parade is shifted to April or May. It kicks off from Fifth Avenue to 49th Street. Also in April is the **Easter Parade** (Fifth Avenue between 49th and 59th streets), an opportunity for New Yorkers to dress up in outrageous Easter bonnets.

Martin Luther King Jr. Memorial Day (May 17) marks a procession along Fifth Avenue from 44th to 86th Street to celebrate his work for equal rights for blacks. Of several Puerto Rican celebrations in the city, the largest is the **Puerto Rican Day Parade** (first Sunday of June), three hours of bands and baton twirling from 44th to 86th Street on Fifth Avenue, then across to Third. **July 4** in New York is marked by **Macy's fireworks display**—visible all over lower Manhattan but best seen from Riverside Park between West 80th and West 105th streets from around 9:30pm on. More local shindigs can be found just about everywhere else.

The **Gay Pride March** on the last Sunday in June commemorates the Stonewall riots of 1969 (see Chapter One)—a well-attended celebration of gay rights running south from Columbus Circle. The **Steuben Day Parade** is the biggest German-American event, taking place on the third weekend of September. Baron von Steuben was a Prussian general who fought with Washington at Valley Forge, which is as good an excuse as any for a costumed parade in his honor from 61st to 86th Street and Fifth Avenue. The **Columbus Day Parade** on or around October 12 is, after St. Patrick's Day, the city's largest binge, commemorating the day the Italians put America on the map. **Halloween** is celebrated on October 31 in a chase through Greenwich Village culminating at Washington Square. On the fourth Thursday in November, **Macy's Thanksgiving Parade** runs from 79th Street down Central Park West to Columbus Circle, afterwards down Broadway to Herald Square, with lots of bands, celebrities, and giant balloons.

Fifth Avenue gets seasonal trimming at **Christmas**, especially in the last two Sundays before Christmas week: Rockefeller Center lights up its Christmas tree in the first week of December and decorates Channel Gardens, so beginning the festivities. On the two Sundays before Christmas, Fifth Avenue is closed to traffic, with entertainment on the streets. **New Year's Eve** is traditionally marked by a mass gathering on Times Square where the last seconds of the year signal drunken but good-natured revelry in the cold.

Festivals

The festival year kicks off with **Chinese New Year**, a noisy, colorful occasion celebrated around Mott Street in Chinatown on the first full moon after January 21. Dragons dance in the street, firecrackers chase away evil spirits, and the chances of getting a meal anywhere in Chinatown are slim; phone ☎267-5780 for further details.

In May the **Ukrainian Festival** fills a weekend on East 7th Street between Second and Third avenues: marvelous Ukranian costumes, folk music, and dance plus authentic foods. At the Ukranian Museum (12th Ave. and 2nd St.) there's a special exhibition of *pysanky*—traditional hand-painted eggs; ☎228-0110 for festival details. The same area witnesses some celebrations of a different sort on Labor Day, in the last week of September, when **Wigstock** takes place in Tompkins Square Park—an essentially transvestite festival, with many different singing and dancing acts performing on the bandstand throughout the day.

The highspot of May is the **Ninth Avenue Festival** which closes the Avenue between 34th and 57th for the weekend, giving you the chance to graze your way along the strip of delis and restaurants that come out on to the street with their wares. Smaller, though perhaps more interesting, are the **Fiestas de Loisa Aldea** on the second weekend of July, miniature versions of the great Fiestas de Santiago Apostol (Festival of St. James the Apostle) in the town of Loisa Aldea, Puerto Rico. Following mass at the Church of San Pueblo at Lexington and 117th, separate processions of women, men, and children each carry a statue of the apostle to the footbridge at 102nd St. and East River Drive to Ward's Island. Look out for the *Vejigante*, the animal-headed creature covered with horns who symbolizes the devil, and the *Caballero*, a sixteenth-century Spanish nobleman. After the procession there's a festival of Latin music, dance, and salsa on Ward's Island, with plenty of Puerto Rican food: try the *pasteles* (spicy meat pies wrapped in a plantain), washed down with *coquito*, a drink made from eggs, coconut cream, and rum. Also, check out the **Fiesta Folklorica**, an all-singing, all-dancing spectacle that fills Central Park on the last Sunday in August, and the Lower East Side's **Loisada Street Fair**, traditionally held on the last weekend in May.

The city's two Italian festivals are well publicized: the **Festival of St. Anthony**, held in early June, is a two-week celebration on Sullivan Street from Spring to West Houston Street, culminating in a procession of Italian bands, led by a life-size statue of the saint carried on the shoulders of four men. More popular, and with great street stalls, is the **Festival of San Gennaro**, patron saint of Naples, held along Mulberry Street in Little Italy for ten days during the week of September 19. Highspot is a procession of the saint's statue through the streets, donations of dollar bills pinned to his cloak.

From early July to late August the **Summer Festival** has outdoor concerts and plays in Central Park, Rockefeller Center, and the South Street Seaport, many of which are free: phone ☎669-9430 for a daily roundup. Also running from mid-July to August is Lincoln Center's **Mostly Mozart** festival, which starts with a free outdoor performance and continues in a series of cut-price concerts in Avery Fisher Hall: phone ☎874-2424 for more details. One of the most popular summer events is the series of **concerts** given by the New York Philharmonic in **Central Park** and other parks throughout the boroughs, all for free: ☎669-9430 for a schedule of times and places.

NEW YORK'S PARADES AND FESTIVALS

Jan	*Chinese New Year*	Chinatown
March 17	*St. Patrick's Day Parade*	Fifth Ave.
25	*Greek Independence Day Parade*	Fifth Ave.
April	*Easter Day Parade*	Fifth Ave.
May	*Ninth Avenue Food Festival*	
	Ukranian Festival	East 7th St.
17	*Martin Luther King Jr. Memorial Day Parade*	Fifth Ave.
last weekend	*Loisada Street Fair*	
June	*Puerto Rican Day Parade*	Fifth Ave.
	Festival of St. Anthony	Sullivan St.
	Indian Festival	Central Park
	Lower East Side Jewish Spring Festival	East Broadway
	Tompkins Square Art Festival	
last Sun	*Gay Pride March*	from Columbus Ave.
July 4	*Independence Day Celebrations*	
	New York Summer Festival of Theater and Music	
	Mostly Mozart Music Festival	Lincoln Center
	Japanese Oban Festival	Riverside Park
	Fiestas de Loisa Aldea	Lexington Ave.
Aug	*Fiesta Folklorica*	Central Park
Sept	*Steuben Day Parade*	Fifth Ave.
	Festival of San Gennaro	Little Italy
Oct 4	*Pulaski Day Parade*	Fifth Ave.
12	*Columbus Day Parade*	Fifth Ave.
31	*Halloween*	Greenwich Village
Nov	*Macy's Thanksgiving Day Parade*	Broadway
Dec	*Rockefeller Center Christmas Tree Celebrations*	
31	*New Year' Eve*	Times Square

Central Park Mall (72nd St. entrance) sees the **Indian Festival** in June or July: Indian music and dance, sari stalls, and lots of Indian snacks. The biggest of the Jewish festivals is the **Lower East Side Jewish Spring Festival** (second Sunday in June) on East Broadway between Rutgers and Montgomery streets, featuring *glatt kosher* foods, Yiddish and Hebrew folk singing, and guided tours of the Jewish Lower East Side. Another religious-based occasion—and one of New York's prettiest—is the **Japanese Oban Festival**, which takes place at Riverside Park Mall at West 103rd Street in the early evening of the Saturday closest to July 15. Slow, simple dancing in the lantern-hung park make this well worth catching.

KIDS' NEW YORK

Believe it or not, New York can be a great place to visit with **children**. It's a visual, noisy, friendly place, and while the physical environment can be trying on the nerves of parents, chances are the kids will love it. Just walking around the streets, watching the street musicians, climbing the skyscrapers, taking a helicopter ride, or a trip on the Circle Line ferry, may be entertainment enough—and you should certainly do at least some of these things, both for your own entertainment and theirs. But as a supplement to the many and varied attractions that will appeal to kids and grown-ups alike, we've detailed below a number of ideas that are especially useful if you're traveling with children—listings of the best **museums** (together with a checklist of others that may be of interest, detailed in the "Museums and Galleries" chapter); **shops** catering specifically for kids; as well as details of visiting **circuses**, **puppet shows**, and **children's theaters**. We've also given addresses of **babysitters** for when you could use some time to yourself.

Museums, galleries, and other sights

Though the majority of New York **museums and galleries** have at least something of interest to kids, the following places boast attractions that will probably evoke more than dutiful enthusiasm.

Aunt Len's Doll and Toy Museum

6 Hamilton Terrace at 141st St. ☎281-4143. Phone first for an appointment, donation appreciated.

"Aunt Len" is a scholarly and charming retired schoolteacher whose collection of 3000-plus dolls and teddy bears is amusing and interesting—and made all the more so by her infectious enthusiasm.

Brooklyn Children's Museum

145 Brooklyn Ave. Subway #3 to Kingston Ave.–Eastern Parkway. Mon–Fri 2–5pm, Sat–Sun 10am–5pm, closed Tues; $2, kids $1.

Participatory museum stacked full of scientific and natural artifacts with which to play. Fun for both children and adults.

Children's Museum of Manhattan

314 W. 54th St. Subway C or E to 50th St.–Eighth Ave. Tues–Sun 11am–5pm; children and adults $4.

Another participatory museum centering on science and nature exhibits. Primarily directed at ages up to 12 years.

Con Edison Energy Museum

145 E. 14th St. Subway #4, #5, or #6 to 14th St./Union Sq. Tues–Sat 10am–4pm; free.

Imaginative, interactive museum that makes the best possible entertainment out of its subject—the generation of electricity. Sponsored by the company responsible for all those clouds of steam billowing out onto the Manhattan streets.

Fire Department Museum

278 Spring St. Subway C or E to Spring St. Tues–Sat 10am–4pm; $3, kids 50¢.

An unspectacular but pleasing homage to New York City's firefighters, and indeed firepeople everywhere. On display are fire engines from the last century (hand-drawn, horse-drawn, and steam-powered), helmets, dog-eared photos, and a host of motley objects on three floors of a disused fire station. A neat and endearing display.

Infoquest Center

AT&T Building, 550 Madison Ave. Subway E or F to Fifth Ave. Wed–Sun 10am–6pm, Tues 10am–9pm; free.

Hands-on museum of science sponsored by AT&T that puts the emphasis on participation in its descriptions and representations of the state of the art in modern technology, including computers, holograms, videos, as well as future developments. Fascinating for slightly older kids; fun for adults, too.

Intrepid Sea-Air-Space Museum

Far western end of 46th St. at Pier 86. M42 crosstown bus. Wed–Sun 10am–5pm; $4.75, cildren $2.75.

This worn-out aircraft carrier had a distinguished history, including hauling Neil Armstrong and co. out of the ocean following the Apollo 11 moonshot. Today it holds a celebration of the nation's military might of the very worst kind—fighter planes clustered with bombs and emblazoned with "World's Greatest Dad" stickers, prototype models for the evil-looking B-1B fighter-bomber housed in a cavernous ship that reeks of gunmetal and regimented sweat.

New York Aquarium

W. 8th St. and Surf Ave., Coney Island. Subway D, N, or R. Daily 10am–4:45pm; summer weekends 10am–5:45pm; $4.75.

First opened in 1896, the aquarium in Coney Island is the kind of place your New York friends used to be taken when they were kids, and it's still going strong, with fish and invertebrates from the world over. Mostly it's a series of darkened halls full of tanks containing creatures of various sizes from the deep, but there are also open-air shows of marine mammals several times daily, as well as a new educational hall, with crashing waves, a mock-up of a salt marsh and other marine environments, tanks of baby sharks and turtles, not to mention a (rather sad) whale exhibit. There's also a soon-to-be-opened sea cliff exhibition, with basking walruses and seals. Worth planning a trip out to Coney Island around.

New York Hall of Science

47–01 111th St., Corona, Queens. Subway #7 to 111th St. Wed–Sun 10am–5pm; $2.50 adults, kids $1.50.

This relatively new museum has the latest in technological displays, with hands-on exhibits that make it more fun for kids. Not worth a special trip if you've already done the Infoquest Center (see above), but certainly meriting a visit on the way out to nearby Shea Stadium.

OTHER MUSEUMS KIDS MIGHT LIKE

The following **museums**, at least in part, will also appeal to kids. For detailed accounts of them, see Chapter Five, "Museums and Galleries."

American Museum of Natural History/Hayden Planetarium *Central Park West at 79th St. Subway C to 81st St.–Central Park West. Mon, Tue, Thur, Sun 10am–5:45pm, Wed, Fri, Sat 10am–9pm; free 10am–9pm Fri and Sat: otherwise suggested donation $4, Planetarium $5.*

Museum of the American Indian *Audubon Terrace, 3753 Broadway at 155th St. Subway #2 to 157th St.–Broadway. Tues–Sat 10am–5pm, Sun 1–5pm. $3, children $2.*

Museum of Broadcasting *1 E. 53rd St. Subway E or F to Fifth Ave.–53rd St. Tues–Sat noon–5pm; suggested $4, children $3. Tues noon–8pm; pay what you wish. Phone ☎752-4690 for details of lectures by artists and directors.*

Museum of the City of New York *Fifth Ave. at 103rd St. Subway #6 to 103rd St.–Lexington Ave. Tues–Sat 10am–5pm, Sun 1–5pm; suggested donation $4, children $2.*

Museum of the Moving Image *35th Ave. at 36th St., Astoria, Queens. Subway R to Steinway St. Tues–Fri noon–4pm, Sat & Sun noon–6pm; $5, students $2.50; film and exhibition information ☎718/784-4777.*

New York City Transit Exhibit *Old Subway entrance at Schermerhorn St. and Boerum Place, Brooklyn. Nearest subway Borough Hall. Mon–Fri 10am–4pm; entry by subway token ($1.15).*

Queens Museum *Flushing Meadows–Corona Park. Subway #7 to Willets Point–Shea Stadium. Tues–Sat 10am–5pm, Sun noon–5:30pm; $2, students $1.*

See also **Bronx Zoo**, detailed on p.152, and **Central Park Zoo**, p.116.

Staten Island Children's Museum

Snug Harbor, 1000 Richmond Terrace, Staten Island. Winter Wed–Fri 1–5pm, Sat & Sun 11am–5pm; summer Tues–Fri 11am–5pm, closed Mon; $2.

Part of the Snug Harbor Cultural Center development, this is a good way to round off a trip on the Staten Island ferry, reachable on a trolley bus from the ferry terminal. There are many hands-on exhibits, covering subjects like the environment and technology, puppets and toys, with the emphasis on participation and learning.

Stores: toys, books, and clothes

Big City Kites, 1201 Lexington Ave. (☎472-7148). Manhattan's largest and best kite store, with a huge range.

Bodyscapes, 20 W. 22nd St. (☎243-2414). One-off designer jumpsuits and the like for kids—which sounds expensive but prices are in fact quite reasonable.

Books of Wonder, 64 Hudson St. (☎645-8006). Excellent kids' bookstore, with a great story-hour, too.

Children's Closet, 1324 Second Ave. (☎772-3779). Good, first-stop place to look for reasonably priced children's clothes.

Citykids, 130 Seventh Ave. (☎620-0120). A tiny store that sells clothes to the "discerning child," alongside toys and other kiddy-related items.

Dinosaur Hill, 302 E. 9th St. (☎473-5850). Small store downtown selling a range of handmade toys, as well as clothes up to age five.

Dolls and Dreams, 1421 Lexington Ave. (☎876-2434). All kinds of dolly paraphernalia, from antiques to modern, from around the world.

Eeyore's Books for Children, 222 Broadway (☎362-0634); 25 E. 83rd St. (☎988-3404). Not the only specialist children's bookstore in Manhattan but easily the best, with a broad selection of titles and storytelling sessions on Sunday mornings and Monday afternoons.

Enchanted Forest, 85 Mercer St. (☎925-6677). A marvelous shop that hides its merchandise—stuffed animals, puppets, masks, and the like—partly in the branches of its mock forest. Worth taking any child to, whether or not you intend to buy.

Kids Kids Kids, 436 Sixth Ave. (☎533-3523). Small but original and friendly children's clothes store—quite affordably priced.

Penny Whistle Toys, 1283 Madison Ave. (☎369-3868); 448 Columbus Ave. (☎873-9090); 132 Spring St. (☎925-2088). Shop selling a fun, imaginative range of toys that deliberately eschews guns and war accessories.

Polk's Hobby Shop, 314 Fifth Ave. (☎279-9034). Model planes, trains, and automobiles, some remote-controled. For kids or grown-up enthusiasts.

Red Caboose, 16 W. 45th St. (☎575-0155). Another shops specializing in models, but concentrating on trains and train sets.

F.A.O. Schwarz, 767 Fifth Ave. (☎644-9400). Showpiece of a nationwide chain sporting three floors of everything a child could want.

Second Childhood, 283 Bleecker St. (☎989-6140). Toys dating back to 1850, with a wide assortment of miniatures, soldiers, and lead animals.

Storyland, 1369 Third Ave. (☎517-6951). Small but well-stocked kids' bookstore. Readings and other events on Sunday lunchtimes.

Toy Park, 112 E. 86th St. (☎427-6611). Well-stocked general toy store that's a possible alternative to *F.A.O. Schwarz*—though not nearly as much fun.

For **sporting items**, see Chapter Seven, "Stores and Markets."

Other activities: theater, puppet shows, and circuses

The following is a highly selective roundup of other activities, particularly cultural ones, that might be of interest to young children. Bear in mind that you can—as always—find out more by checking the pages of Friday's *Daily News* or *New York Times*; or take a look at *New York* magazine or the *Village Voice*, which also sometime list children-oriented events. Note, too, that stores like *Macy's* and *F.A.O. Schwarz* often have events for children—puppet shows, story-hours, and the like—not to mention the better children's bookstores, most of which regularly have storytelling sessions (see above).

Barnum & Bailey Circus, Madison Square Garden (☎563-8300). This large touring circus is usually in New York between April and June.

Big Apple Circus, Lincoln Center (☎391-07670). Small circus which performs in a tent behind Lincoln Center, from late October to early January. Tickets $10–45.

Hans Christian Andersen statue, Central Park, 72nd St. entrance. Regular storytelling sessions, appropriately held next to the figure of the Danish writer. Saturdays 11am–noon, between June and September.

Manhattan Raceway, 893 Broadway (☎673-4100). The largest model railroad tracks in America, apparently, where kids and adults manipulate cars around the track. Open daily until 2am; prices around $5 for half an hour.

Museum of the Moving Image, 35th Ave. at 36th St., Astoria, Queens (☎718/784-0077). Showings of kids' films and TV classics in a marvelously over-the-top old-style movie palace, decorated in fancy pseudo-Egyptian style. Showings are usually held Tues to Fri at lunchtime, and lunchtimes and afternoons on Sat and Sun. Call for program details.

On Stage Children, 413 W. 46th St. (☎666-1716). Children's theater company that mounts around four productions a year, between fall and early May. Performances take place at weekends, usually Saturday; phone for details.

Puppet Playhouse, 555 E. 90th St. (☎369-8890). Puppet theater that puts on regular shows at weekends. Seasons run October to May—call for a schedule; reservations only.

Swedish Marionette Theater, Central Park, 79th St. entrance (☎988-9093). Another puppet theater, housed in a former Swedish school building that was brought to New York in the last century, and putting on regular performances between late September and early June. Again, tickets must be reserved in advance, and again performances usually take place on weekends.

BABYSITTING

All of the following offer **babysitting services**, with approved sitters. Fees range between $6 and $10 an hour, depending on the age of your child (kids under a year old generally cost more), plus a sum to cover transportation. As always, call for the full picture. Be sure, in all cases, to reserve well in advance—at the latest the day before you need the sitter, if possible.

Babysitters Guild, 60 E. 42nd St. (☎682-0227).

Babysitters Association, 610 Cathedral Parkway (☎865-9348).

Gilbert Childcare Agency, 115 W. 57th St. (☎757-7900).

CHAPTER SEVEN

STORES AND MARKETS

New York is consumer capital of the world. Its **stores** cater to every possible taste, preference, creed, or perversity, in any combination and in many cases at any time of day or night—and, as such, they're as good a reason as any for visiting the city. To enjoy them to the full you obviously have to have money, and lots of it, but even if you can't afford to buy, the city's shop windows, department stores, gourmet groceries, ethnic and oddity stores are still there for the browsing.

As in most large cities, New York stores are concentrated in specific neighborhoods, so if you want something particular you invariably know exactly where to head. The most mainstream shopping territory is **Midtown Manhattan**, where you'll find department stores, big-name clothes designers, and branches of the larger chains. **Downtown Manhattan** plays host to a wide variety of more offbeat stores: small boutiques, secondhand bookstores and almost pedantically specialized stores, selling nothing but candles or a hundred different types of caviar. **Uptown**, the Upper East Side is an upscale continuation of Midtown Manhattan, with, on Madison especially, a greater concentration of exclusive clothiers and antique and art dealers—a concentration that doesn't extend to the other side of the park, where the **Upper West Side** has a quite different personality and an array of off-the-wall stores that can compare to anything in SoHo or the Village. Bear in mind, too, that New York's **ethnic** enclaves have some of the city's most exciting and colorful places to shop, and—the Outer Boroughs included—some of its most specialized. For full details on specific shopping neighborhoods, see the relevant sections of this chapter.

When to shop, how to pay

Most parts of the city are at their least oppressive for shopping early weekday mornings, and at their worst around lunchtime and on Saturdays. There are few days of the year when everything closes (though really only Thanksgiving, Christmas, and New Year's Day), and many shops, including the big midtown department stores, regularly open on Sundays. Remember, however, that certain (usually ethnic) communities close their shops in accordance with religious and other holidays: don't bother to shop on the Lower East Side on Friday afternoon or on Saturday, for example, though places there are open on Sunday. By contrast, Chinatown is open all day every day, while the stores of the Financial District follow the area's nine-to-five routine and for the most part are shut all weekend.

Hours in Midtown Manhattan are roughly Monday–Saturday 9am–6pm, with late closing on—usually—Thursdays; downtown shops tend to stay open later, at least until 8pm and sometimes until about midnight; bookstores especially are often open late. Unless we've stated otherwise the stores listed follow broadly these hours.

As far as **payment** goes, credit cards are as widely accepted as you'd expect: even the smallest of shops will take *Visa, American Express, Mastercard,* and *Diners Club*; many department stores also have their own credit cards. Travelers' checks are a valid currency, too, though you may have to provide ID. Finally, wherever you're shopping, be careful. Manhattan's stores, crowded frenzied places that they are, are ripe territory for **pickpockets and bag-snatchers—** keep a firm eye on your belongings.

Department stores and malls

In *Saks, Bloomingdale's,* and other stores less familiar beyond the east coast, New York has some of the great **department stores** of the world. However, the last few years have seen a number of the better established stores close down, while others have gone upmarket, making them less places to stock up on essentials, and more outlets for designer clothes and chi-chi accessories, full of concessions on the top-line names. If you want to buy something in a hurry without turning it into a major New York shopping experience, you'd often do better to use a more specialized shop; if, on the other hand, you are on the look out for a specific item, especially clothes, a department store might be a good first stop. During sale-times—and there is always a sale somewhere—you may well find some excellent bargains; visit on and around holiday periods and watch the newspapers.

Manhattan also has a number of **shopping malls**, some of them housed in conversions of older premises, whose anodyne locations are on occasion reasonable places to browse—though they're not at all what New York does best. The larger and more important ones are listed below.

Department stores

Alexander's, 731 Lexington Ave. (☎593-0880); 4 World Trade Center Plaza (☎466-1414); and other branches in the Outer Boroughs. Often the same goods you'll find in more pretentious stores (designer "labels" minus the labels) but at much lower prices. If you're looking for something at *Lord & Taylor's* or *Bloomingdale's*, check out *Alexander's* first—you may turn up a bargain.

Barney's, 117 Seventh Ave. (☎929-9000). Though a genuine department store, Barney's actually concentrates on clothes, particularly men's, with the emphasis on high-flying, up-to-the-minute designer gear, alongside a relatively new womenswear department. If you've the money, there's no better place in the city to look for clothes. A smaller branch is at 225 Liberty St. in the World Financial Center mall (☎945-1600).

Bergdorf Goodman, 754 Fifth Ave. (☎753-7300). The name, the location, the thick carpets, and discreetly hidden escalators—everything about Bergdorf's speaks of its aspirations to be New York City's most gracious department store. Lucky that most of the folk who shop here have purses stacked with charge cards—the rustle of money would utterly ruin the feel. Recently restored to its former glories with many new contemporary designers.

Bloomingdale's, 1000 Third Ave. (☎355-5900). New Yorkers are proud of *Bloomie's*: somehow it's an affirmation of their status, their sense of style, and they not surprisingly flock here in droves. You may not be so impressed. It has the atmosphere of a large, bustling bazaar, packed full with concessions to perfumiers and designer clothes. It's certain, though, that whatever you want, *Bloomie's* is likely to stock it.

Henri Bendel, 712 Fifth Ave. (☎247-1100). Now in its new and very elegant Fifth Avenue location, *Bendel's* is and always has been deliberately more discreet in its approach than the biggies, with a name for exclusivity and top-line modern designers. One of Manhattan's most refined shopping experiences.

Lord & Taylor, 424 Fifth Ave. (☎391-3344). The most establishment of the New York stores, and to some extent its most pleasant, with a more traditional feel than *Macy's* or *Bloomingdale's*. Though no longer at the forefront of New York fashion, it's still good for classic designer fashions, household goods, and accessories, and the more basic items.

Macy's, Broadway at 34th St. (☎695-4400). Quite simply, the largest department store in the world, with two buildings, two million square feet of floor space, ten floors (four for women's garments alone), and around $5m gross turnover every day. It's also these days a serious designer fashion rival to *Saks* and *Bloomingdale's*. Wander around even if you don't want to buy: you'll be sprayed with the latest fragrances from France or Beverly Hills, smeared with virulent lipsticks, and fed on tasters in the basement foodhall. If you see only one of the city's large department stores, it should really be this.

Saks Fifth Avenue, 611 Fifth Ave. (☎753-4000). The name is virtually synonymous with style, and, although *Saks* has retained its name for quality, it has also updated itself to carry the merchandise of all the big designers. In any case, with the glittering array of celebrities that use the place regularly, Saks can't fail.

F.W. Woolworth. Good value for essentials like stationery and underwear, etc: ten branches dotted around Manhattan. Check the phone book for addresses.

Shopping malls

A&S Plaza/Herald Center, Sixth Ave. and 33rd St. Perhaps because of its location right oppposite *Macy's*, this large, mirror-fronted and rather glitzy shopping center has never really been a success, a pedestrian string of stores in what resembles nothing so much as a small-town shopping precinct. Unless there's a specific store you want, or you want to pig out at the various ethnic nosh counters in the food hall, you're better off in *Macy's*.

Pier 17, South Street Seaport. Again, not quite the shopping experience it would like to be, although it has a more interesting selection of shops than the chainstores of A&S Plaza, in a more sensitively converted location.

Trump Tower, Fifth Ave. and 56th St. The gaudiest and most expensively meritricious of the Manhattan malls, with a range of exclusive boutiques set around a deep, marbled atrium that mark it out as a tourist attraction in itself.

World Financial Center, Battery Park City. Centering on the huge, greenhouse-like Winter Garden, this is worth a visit just for a look at the development as a whole, and it has a handful of intriguing stores. On the other hand, it's out of the way if you're only shopping.

Pharmacies and drugstores

There's a **pharmacy or drugstore** on every corner in New York, and during the day at least it shouldn't be too difficult to find one. If you can't, the Yellow Pages has complete listings of places selling medicine and toiletries, listed under "pharmacies." Most pharmacies are open roughly Monday to Saturday 9am to 6pm, though many also open on Sunday in busy shopping or residential neighborhoods. Some of the better or more specialized pharmacies are listed below, along with a selection of those that stay open longer in case of need.

Everywhere

Duane Reed. A chain of drugstores which has cornered the market on discount OTC medicine, toiletries, cigarettes, and basic stationery across much of Manhattan, especially midtown. Check the phonebook for the nearest location.

McKay. Another drugstore chain, though with far fewer branches than *Duane Reed*. Again, exact locations in the phonebook.

Lower Manhattan

Bigelow Pharmacy, 414 Sixth Ave. (☎533-2700). Established in 1832, this is one of the oldest pharmacies in the city—and that's exactly how it looks, with the original Victorian fittings still in place. Open seven days a week.

Kiehl Pharmacy, 109 Third Ave. (☎475-3400). Another ancient pharmacy but with a stock more in keeping with its age, including herbs, roots, dried flowers, and spices.

Tak Sun Tong, 11 Mott St. (☎374-1183). Herbal Chinese remedies: snake skin, shark's teeth, and the like.

Midtown Manhattan

Caswell-Massey Ltd., 518 Lexington Ave. (☎755-2254); 21 Fulton St. (☎608-5401). The oldest pharmacy in America, and a national chain, selling a shaving cream created for George Washington and a cologne blended for his wife, as well as more mainstream items.

Edward's Drug Store, 225 E. 57th St. (☎753-2830). General pharmacy open seven days a week.

Freeda Pharmacy, 36 E. 41st St. (☎685-4980). Kosher drugs. Closed weekends.

Martin's Drugstore, 451 Third Ave. (☎680-5230). Open until 10pm, 8pm weekends.

Westerly Pharmacy, 911 Eighth Ave. (☎247-1096). Open seven days.

Upper Manhattan

Alexander Pharmacy, 1751 Second Ave. (☎410-0060). Open seven days.

Arnowitz Pharmacy, 1551 York Ave. (☎737-3305). Open seven days.

Jaros Drug Inc., 25 Central Park West (☎247-8080). Open seven days.

Plaza Pharmacy, 1657 Second Ave. (☎879-3878). Open daily until midnight.

Star Pharmacy, 1540 First Ave. (☎737-4304). Open seven days.

Tower Pharmacy Inc., 1257 Second Ave. (☎838-1490). Open seven days.

Windsor Pharmacy, 1419 Sixth Ave. (☎247-1538). Open until midnight seven days a week.

24-HOUR PHARMACY

Kaufman, 557 Lexington Ave. (☎755-2266).

Food and drink

Food—the buying as much as consuming of it—is a New York obsession. Nowhere do people take eating more seriously than Manhattan, and there's no better place to shop for food. Where to buy the best bagel, who stocks the widest—and weirdest—range of cheeses, are questions that occupy New Yorkers a disproportionate amount of time. The shops themselves are mouth watering, and even the simplest corner deli should be enough to get your tastebuds jumping; more sophisticated places, gourmet or specialty shops for example, will be enough to make you swoon.

The listings below, while comprehensive, are by no means exhaustive. Wander the streets and you'll no doubt uncover plenty more besides. If you're after **drink**, remember that you can only buy liquor—ie anything stronger than beer—at a specialist liquor store, and that you need to be 21 or over to do so.

Supermarkets, delis, and groceries

For the most **general food requirements**, there are a number of **supermarket** chains which turn up all over the city. *Big Apple*, *Sloan's*, and *Grand Union* you'll find pretty much everywhere; *D'Agostino* and *Gristedes* tend to appear in the classier neighborhoods. In addition, many of the **department stores** listed above—principally *Macy's* and *Bloomingdale's*—have food halls. **At night**, there's the *Food Emporium*, which opens 24 hours a day at most of its Manhattan branches (see the phone book for locations).

On a smaller scale, there are **delis and groceries**—the latter usually run by Koreans—which sell basic food and drink items, as well as sandwiches and coffee to go, and sometimes hot ready meals and the chance to dip into a copiously provided salad bar. You should never have to walk more than a couple of blocks to find one, and most, especially those owned by Koreans, are open late or all night; for specific locations see the Yellow Pages.

Gourmet stores

Gourmet stores are essentially a step up from delis, gloriously stocked places, selling innumerable edibles in a super-abundant environment that will make your taste buds jump. In general—though not exclusively—they supply the more gentrified neighborhoods with their most obscure (and more mainstream) objects of desire.

Balducci's, 424 Sixth Ave. (☎673-2600). This is the long-term, non-Jewish, downtown rival of *Zabar's* (see below), a family-run store that's no less appetizing—though some say it's slightly more expensive.

Dean & Delucca, 560 Broadway (☎431-1691). One of the original big neighborhood food emporia. Very chic, very SoHo, and not at all cheap.

Fairway, 2127 Broadway (☎595-1888). Long-established Upper West Side grocery store that for many locals is the better value alternative to *Zabar's*. They have their own farm on Long Island, so the produce is always fresh, and their range in some items is enormous.

Fine & Schapiro, 138 W. 72nd St. (☎877-2874). Long established, with excellent, principally kosher meals to go and renowned sandwiches and cold meats. Also a restaurant—see Chapter Eight.

Grace's Marketplace, 1237 Third Ave. (☎737-0600). Gourmet deli offspring of *Balducci's* that is a welcome addition to the Upper East Side food scene. An excellent selection of just about everything.

Russ & Daughters, 179 E. Houston St. (☎475-4880). Technically, this store is known as an *appetizing*—the original Manhattan gourmet shop, set up at the turn of the century to sate the homesick appetites of immigrant Jews, selling smoked fish, caviar, pickled vegetables, cheese, and bagel. This is one of the oldest.

Schaller & Weber, 1654 Second Ave. (☎879-3047) and other stores in the Outer Boroughs. Culinary heart of the Upper East Side's now sadly diminished German-Hungarian district of Yorkville, this shop is a riot of cold cuts, salami, and smoked meat. Not for vegetarians.

Silver Palate, 274 Columbus Ave. (☎799-6340). Tiny gourmet shop whose products and recipe books helped revolutionize New York's takeout food business. If you can afford it, there's no better place for a ready-made exotic picnic.

Zabar's, 2245 Broadway (☎787-2000). The apotheosis of New York food-fever, *Zabar's* is still the city's most eminent foodstore. Choose from an astonishing variety of cheeses, cooked meats, and salads, fresh baked bread and croissants, excellent bagel, and cooked dishes to go. Upstairs stocks implements to help you put it all together at home. Not to be missed.

Specialty foodstores

Along with the gourmet shops and delis are a number of stores that specialize in one item only. We've listed the best or most extraordinary of them below.

Bakeries and patisseries

Damascus Bakery, 56 Gold St., Brooklyn (☎718/855-1456). Syrian bakery, long established, with the city's best supply of different pitta breads, as well as a dazzling array of pastries.

The Erotic Baker, 582 Amsterdam Ave. (☎362-7557). The name says it all really, and if you're imagining all kinds of crusty phalluses and full frontal crutch arrangements, you'd be absolutely right. If you've got something special in mind you'll need to order it a day or two in advance.

Ferrara, 195 Grand St. (☎226-6150). Little Italy café-patisserie with branches in Milan and Montreal.

Fung Wong, 30 Mott St. (☎267-4037). Chinese pastries.

HBH Pastry Shop, 29–28 30th Ave., Astoria, Queens (☎718/274-1609). Greek pastry shop selling *baklava* plus numerous less well-known Balkan goodies. Sit-down café, too.

H&H Bagels, 2239 Broadway & 1551 Second Ave. (☎595-8000). Open 24 hours, seven days a week, this is the reputed home of New York's finest bagel.

Hungarian Pastry Shop, 1030 Amsterdam Ave. (☎866-4230). Though a long way from Yorkville, and not actually run by Hungarians, this place is good either for an afternoon snack or to finish a meal nearby. Popular with Columbia students.

Kleine Konditorei, 234 E. 86th St. (☎737-7130). Yorkville German patisserie with a restaurant serving all manner of honest, stolid Teutonic fare.

Kossar's, 367 Grand St. (☎473-4810). Jewish baker specializing in *bialys*.

Moishe's, 181 E. Houston St. (☎505-8555); 115 2nd Ave. (☎673-0708). New York's most authentic Jewish bakery.

Veniero's, 342 E. 11th St. (☎674-7264). Century-old Italian style patisserie.

Vesuvio, 160 Prince St. (☎925-8248). SoHo's most famous Italian bakery.

Yonah Schimmel's, 137 E. Houston St. (☎477-2858). Specialists in home-made *knishes*, with a variety of fillings (kasha, potato, cheese, etc), which you can either take away or consume on the premises. Even if you've tried the *knishes* sold by street vendors and didn't like them, it's worth giving this place a go. *Yonah's knishes* taste nothing like the mass-produced kind.

Zaro's, Grand Central Station. Croissants, bagel, and all good things. Good place to stop for a breakfast on the go.

Zito's, 259 Bleecker St. (☎929-6139). Long-established downtown Italian baker, renowned for its fine round *pane di casa*. Open every day.

Cheese and dairy

Alleva Latticini, 188 Grand St. (☎226-7990). Italian cheesery and grocery.

Ben's Cheese Shop, 181 E. Houston St. (☎254-8290). Next door, and a nice complement to, *Russ & Daughters* on the Lower East Side. The greater part of the cheese sold here is still made on the premises.

Cheese of all Nations, 153 Chambers St. (☎732-0752). Cheese from all over the world. Upstairs, a small restaurant serves substantial cheesey lunches for around $5, and there's a plentifully stocked wine cellar to help wash it all down.

Cheese Unlimited, 240 Ninth Ave. (☎691-1512). The name says it all.... A huge variety of cheeses.

Di Paolo, 226 Grand St. (☎206-1033). A wide array of different cheeses, including fresh varieties made on the premises.

Joe's Dairy, 156 Sullivan St. (☎677-8780). Family store that's the best bet for fresh mozzarella.

Ideal Cheese Shop, 1205 Second Ave. (☎688-7579). A fine uptown cheese emporium.

Fish and seafood

Caviarteria, 29 E. 60th St. (☎759-7410). Mainly caviar—over a dozen varieties—and a stock of smoked fish and patés.

Citarella, 2135 Broadway (☎874-0383). Upper West Side store selling a huge variety of fish and seafood, and with a wonderful bar serving prepared oysters, clams, and the like to take away. Great, artistic window displays, too.

Murray's Sturgeon Shop, 2429 Broadway (☎724-2650). Another popular Upper West Side haunt, this place specializes in smoked fish and caviar.

Petrossian, 182 W. 58th St. (☎245-2214). This well-known shop imports only the finest Russian caviar, alongside a range of other gourmet products—smoked salmon and other fish mainly—as well as high-priced implements to eat it all with. Quite the most exclusive place to shop for food in town, and with a restaurant attached to complete the experience.

Health food, vegetarian, and spice shops

Aphrodisia, 282 Bleecker St. (☎989-6440). For herbs and spices only, this place is hard to beat.

Brownies, 91 Fifth Ave. (☎242-2199). New York's first health food store and still one of the best in town.

Commodities, 117 Hudson St. (☎334-8330). Huge new health food store.

General Nutrition Center, The city's largest health food chain (check the phonebook for addresses), though often the individual downtown health shops are rather better.

Good Earth Foods, 1334 First Ave. (☎472-9055); 167 Amsterdam Ave. (☎496-1616). Not cheap but one of the best-equipped health food outlets in the city. Has a worthy juice and food café.

Gramercy Natural Food Center, 387 Second Ave. (☎725-1651). Best known for its fish, poultry, and organic dairy products.

The Health Nut, 2611 Broadway (☎678-0054) and other Manhattan locations. Good general health food and macrobiotic chain.

Prana, 125 First Ave. (☎982-7306). Wholefood shop, again expensive.

Vitamin Quota, 1039 Second Ave. (☎751-3920). Health food supermarket. Location also at 1645 Second Ave. (☎734-0333).

Whole Foods in SoHo, 117 Prince St. (☎673-5388). Health food supermarket, open daily with a very wide selection.

Ethnic Foods

Not surprisingly, you'll find the best ethnic foodstores in the areas where those communities live. Try the following:

BRITISH
Myers of Keswick, 634 Hudson St. (☎691-4194), is the place to find such treasures of British cuisine as Marmite, pork pies, and the like.

CHINESE
The best Chinese supermarket in Chinatown is *Kam-Man*, 200 Canal St. (☎571-0330). A marginally cheaper alternative, though with a greatly reduced selection, is *Chinese American Trading*, 91 Mulberry St. (☎267-5224).

GREEK
Astoria in Queens is the best source of Greek specialties—try *Kalamata Foods*, 38-01 Ditmars Boulevard (☎718/626-1250), or *Titan Foods*, 25–50 31st St. (☎718/626-7771).

INDIAN
Kalustyan's, 123 Lexington Ave. (☎685-3451), is the best of the small gang of food-eries that makes up the tiny Little India district of Manhattan. Failing that, *Spice and Sweet* is just up the block at no. 135 (☎683-0900), *Foods of India* across the street at 121 Lexington Ave. (☎683-4419).

ITALIAN
Carroll Gardens in Brooklyn or the Italian district of Belmont in the Bronx have many authentic Italian stores. More accessibly, you could visit the *Alleva Latticini* or *Di Paolo* (see above under "Cheese"), or the *Italian Food Center*, 186 Grand St. (☎925-2954)—all in Little Italy.

JEWISH
There are still many places down on the Lower East Side that specialize in Jewish and kosher foods, although Jewish cuisine tends to appear all over the city. See the "Gourmet shops" listings for some suggestions.

MIDDLE EASTERN
Although much depleted, there are still a handful of Middle Eastern stores on Atlantic Avenue in Brooklyn, not least the *Damascus Bakery* (see p.143). In Manhattan, try *Tashjian*, 123 Lexington Ave. (☎683-8458).

LATIN/SOUTH AMERICAN
The best neighborhoods to try are East Harlem (El Barrio), where *La Marqueta* (see p.133) is a riot of good things, and Jackson Heights in Queens, where you could try *La Constancia*, 95–05 Roosevelt Ave. (☎718/476-1876).

Ice cream
Two chains have monopolized the city's appetite for ice cream between them: **Baskin-Robbins**, which has about half a dozen outlets spread between Wall St. and Harlem, and the considerably better **Haagen-Dazs**, which trades from about ten locations across Manhattan; again, the phonebook has details.

While their ice cream is reasonable, and comes in myriad different flavors, there are a few smaller operators which real ice cream freaks swear by. Of these **Steve's** (444 Sixth Ave.; 145 Second Ave.; 286 Columbus Ave.), **Ben & Jerry's** (1 Herald Square; 327 Sixth Ave.; 41 Third Ave.) and **Frusen Gladje** (29 E. 8th St.; 349 Sixth Ave.; 170 Spring St.) all have their vehement defenders; and the **Chinatown Ice Cream Factory**, 65 Bayard St. (☎608-4170), elicits the most bemused reactions, since it's the only place that serves up mango, green tea, and lychee flavors.

Candy, nuts, and chocolates
Bazzini, 339 Greenwich St. (☎227-6241). Fabulous selection of nuts in all shapes and sizes. A wide selection of candy, too.

David's Cookies, A chain with numerous branches all over the city (see the phonebook for exact locations) selling excellent cookies.

Economy Candy, 131 Essex St. (☎254-1531). Best of a bunch of unpretentious Lower East Side stores selling tubs of candy, nuts, and dried fruit. Another branch at 108 Rivington St.

Elk, 240 E. 86th St. (☎650-1177). A Yorkville candy store selling Yorkville-style candies—rich and marzipaned.

Godiva, 701 Fifth Ave. (☎593-2845). This renowned Belgian chocolatier has branches all over Manhattan—all unbeatable for satisfying anyone's chocolate craving.

Li-Lac, 120 Christopher St. (☎242-7374). Delicious chocolates hand made on the premises since 1923. One of the city's best treats for sweet teeth.

Mutual, 127 Ludlow St. (☎673-3489). Another Lower East Side candy store, this time specializing in dried fruit.

Teuscher, 620 Fifth Ave. (☎246-4416); 251 E. 61st St. (☎751-8482). The truffles of this Upper East Side store are renowned.

Treat Boutique, 200 E. 86th St. (☎737-6619). Six different kinds of home-made fudge and a broad selection of dried fruit and nuts.

Tea and coffee

Gillies 1840, 160 Bleecker St. (☎614-0900). America's oldest coffee store.

McNulty's, 109 Christopher St. (☎242-5351). Coffee, and a wide selection of teas.

Porto Rico, 201 Bleecker St. (☎477-5421). Best for coffee, and with a bar for tasting.

The Sensuous Bean, 68 W. 70th St. (☎724-7725). Mostly coffee, with some tea.

Liquor stores

Prices for all kinds of **liquor** are controled in New York State and vary little from one shop to another. There are, however, a number of places which either have a particularly good selection or where things tend to be a touch less expensive. It's those which are listed here. Bear in mind there's a state law forbidding the sale of strong drink on Sundays, when all liquor stores are closed.

Manhattan liquor stores

Acker Merrall & Condit, 160 W. 72nd St. (☎787-1700). Holds a very wide selection of wine from the USA, especially California. Open until 11:30pm.

Astor Wines and Spirits, 12 Astor Place (☎674-7500). Manhattan's best selection and most competitive prices.

Beekman Liquor Store, 500 Lexington Ave. (☎759-5857). Good, well-priced midtown alternative to *Astor*.

Columbus Circle Liquor Store, 1780 Broadway (☎247-0764). Ditto for uptown.

Cork & Bottle, 1158 First Ave. (☎838-5300). Excellent selection; deliveries, too.

Garnett Wine & Liquor, 929 Lexington Ave. (☎772-3211). Another good value liquor store.

Maxwell Wine & Spirits, 1657 First Ave. (☎289-9595). Upper East Side liquor store that opens until midnight at weekends.

Morrell & Co, 535 Madison Ave. (☎688-9370). One of the best selections of good value wine in town.

Schapiro's, 126 Rivington St. (☎674-4404). Kosher wines made on the premises. Free tours of the cellars, with wine tasting, Sunday 11am–4pm on the hour.

Schumer's, 59 E. 54th St. (☎355-0940). Stays open until midnight Friday and Saturday, and will also deliver.

Sherry-Lehman, 679 Madison Ave. (☎838-7500). New York's premier wine merchant.

Spring Street Wines, 187 Spring St. (☎219-0521). Well-stocked SoHo liquor store.

Markets

New York doesn't really to go in for **markets** in a big way: those that there are are mostly highly organized, wholesale-only affairs with retail stores attached, or simply neighborhoods devoted to a specific items. Street markets on the other hand can't compare with those in Europe.

Flea markets, junk, and bargains

Flea markets have yet to catch on in the States, though New York has more outlets than most American cities for old clothes, antiques, and suchlike, as well as innumerable odd places—parking lots, playgrounds, or maybe just an extra-wide sidewalk—where people set up now and then to sell their wares, and groups of streets where stores and stalls devoted to specific items sell at discount rates. Below is a rundown of likely locations, but bearing in mind that it's illegal to sell anything in the street without a license, the more impromptu affairs may have disappeared by the time you read this.

Lower

Greenwich Village Flea Market, PS 41, Greenwich Ave. at Charles St. About seventy outdoor booths full of everything you've ever needed. Open Saturday noon–7pm.

Canal West Flea Market, 370 Canal St. The bargain basement of New York flea markets, with clothing for as little as $1.50 an item. Open Saturdays and Sundays 7am–6pm.

Tower Market, Broadway between W. 4th St. and Great Jones St. Lots of new, craftsy stalls, selling woven goods from South America, New Age paraphernalia, and the like. Saturdays and Sundays 10am–7pm.

Midtown

Bryant Park Crafts Show, 42nd St between Fifth and Sixth Ave. Crafts market with antique jewelry and the usual range of collectibles. Friday noon–7pm.

Upper

Antique Flea and Farmers Market, PS 183, E. 67th St. between First and York Ave. Usually about 150 stalls of fresh food, odd antiques, and needlework. Saturday 10am–6pm.

Yorkville Flea Market, 351 E. 74th St. Just a small market, with a regular location in the Jan Hus Presbyterian Church. Saturday 9am–4pm, June to August.

Local specialties

Besides regular organized markets, there are a number of Manhattan neighborhoods which are worth visiting simply for the specialties they are devoted to, usually sold at discount prices, not to mention the odd impromptu sidewalk market. **Orchard Street**, main artery of the Jewish Lower East Side, is worth a trip for its cheap clothes stores, especially on Sunday when it's pedestrianized. Lively, vibrant, and bulging with of bargains, it attracts people from all over the city. The rest of the **Lower East Side** is similarly well stocked with discount items all week: **Allen Street**, just below Houston, is good for shirts and, especially, ties; sections of **Grand Street** are given over to hosiery, underwear, fabrics, and linens; while the shops on the **Bowery** below Houston sell mainly lamps and lighting fixtures—above Houston, catering and kitchen items. Across town, **14th Street** is a good place to pick up discount household wares; the stores of **Canal Street** between Sixth Avenue and Lafayette Street, farther south, are stacked high with obscure electrical items, fake designer watches, pirate tapes, and cassette recorders.

On a less organized basis, **Cooper Square**, in summer at least, is usually lined with people squatting in front of pieces of old carpet piled high with junk and the clutter of various Manhattan attics and closets. Nearby, on and around St. Mark's Place and on **First Avenue** from around 12th Street down to Houston, there are numerous secondhand clothing stores. Across in SoHo the emphasis is more upscale, small markets selling new sweaters and handmade jewelry, like that on the corner of **Spring and Wooster Street**, and on **Prince and Greene Street**.

Finally, the **Flower District**, in west Manhattan on Sixth Avenue between 26th and 30th Street, has the city's largest concentration of plants and flowers. If you can't find what you want here, be it houseplant, tree, dried, cut, or artificial flower, then it's a fair bet it's not available anywhere else in New York.

Block fairs

Look out, too, for neighborhood **block fairs**. Organized by the local tenants' association, these are like urban village fairs, cropping up most frequently in August and giving residents the chance to turn out their unwanted junk. They're advertised locally, on notice boards and in newspapers, and depending on the neighborhood it can be well worth going along. The kind of thing that counts as unwanted junk on Madison Avenue might be someone else's idea of treasure. More significantly, block fairs are a good way of getting a taste of real, neighborhood New York, beyond the sirens and skyscrapers.

Food markets

Perhaps the best market in Manhattan dedicated specifically to food is **La Marqueta**, on Park Avenue between 111th and 116th Street in the heart of El Barrio, which sells candy, spices, vegetables, fruit, and all things Latin American. The few ranks of stalls along **Ninth Avenue** between 37th and 42nd Street sell foods from just about every country that has any kind of ethnic representation in New York, however small—a market that in mid-May blossoms into the **Ninth Avenue Festival**, when the length and breadth of the avenue is taken up with foodstalls; see "Parades and Festivals," Chapter Six. You can buy most types of food at the **Essex St. Covered Market**, as well as gaudy jewelry, cheap lace, and wigs, though the market has hit hard times of late and is now more a refuge for down-and-outs than a serious place to shop. If you're up early enough (5am—see "Information, Maps, and Tours" in *Basics*) the daily **Fulton fish market** is a lively affair; for New York's freshest fish at any time of day (though of course the earlier the better), use the market's retail store at 18 Fulton St. (☎952-9658).

Greenmarkets

Early risers might also want to visit one of the city's **greenmarkets**, which open early morning on a couple of days a week at about a dozen locations over Manhattan principally to sell fruit and vegetables. These are run by the city authorities, roughly between June and November, and act as a forum for market gardeners and small farmers from Long Island or the Hudson Valley who come into New York to sell their produce direct. Many of them close down at lunchtime (though the Union Square market continues all day), so get there in the morning to be sure of seeing anything.

WHERE TO FIND GREENMARKETS

Greenmarket locations vary, but you should find one at the following places on at least one day a week. Further information on ☎566-0990.

World Trade Center Tuesday and Thursday.

Southbridge Towers between Beekman and Pearl St. Saturday.

City Hall Friday.

St. Mark's-in-the-Bowerie Tuesday.

Independence Plaza at Greenwich and Harrison St. Wednesday and Saturday.

Tompkins Square Saturday.

Union Square Wednesday, Friday, and Saturday.

57th St. and Ninth Ave. Wednesday and Saturday.

67th St. between First and Second Ave. Saturday.

87th St. between First and Second Ave. Saturday.

102nd St. at Amsterdam Ave. Friday.

Clothes and fashion

Dressing right is important in Manhattan, though you may find that clothes are more about status here than fashion. Although New York may lead the rest of the country fashion-wise, compared to Europe it can sometimes seem pretty staid. If you are prepared to search the city with sufficient dedication you can find just about anything, but it's **designer clothes** and the snob values that go with them that predominate. **Secondhand clothes**, here referred to as "vintage" or "antique" clothing, have gained cachet of late but the "vintage" or "antique" label tends to make them ridiculously overpriced. Basically, if you want *real* second-hand stuff go to a thrift shop.

For secondhand and/or trendy clothes the best **place to look** is downtown, and particularly the East Village and parts of SoHo; for jeans, especially Levis,

Orchard Street is as good a place as any. Designer items, from the better known international designers, can be found on Fifth Avenue, in Saks, Bloomie's, and so on, and along Madison Avenue in the 60s and 70s. The Garment Center—basically the blocks between Sixth and Seventh avenues in the 30s—can be a good place to pick up designer clothes at a discount. There's an office here for every women's garment retailer and manufacturer in the country, and though some are wary of selling to individual, non-wholesale customers, you can pick up some enviable bargains if you have enough chutzpah, carry cash, and are ready to walk; again, check the phonebook for possibilities. Bear in mind, too, that many **department stores** stock as good a selection of the (more mainstream) designer fashions as you're likely to find.

New and designer clothes

Agnes B, 116 Prince St. (☎925-4649); 1063 Madison Ave. (☎570-9333). Great designs, now at two Manhattan branches.

Banana Republic 205 Bleecker St. (☎473-9570); and branches at Lexington Ave. and 59th St., Broadway and 87th St. and South Street Seaport. Expensive clobber for the chic traveler: boots, bags, designer safari suits, etc.

Betsey Johnson, 130 Thompson St. (☎420-0169). SoHo outlet of the New York designer. Functional clothes at almost affordable prices.

Brooks Brothers, 346 Madison Ave. (☎682-8800). Something of an institution in New York, priding itself on its non-observance of fashion and still selling the same tweeds, gaberdines, and quietly striped shirts and ties it did fifty years ago. It's a formula that seems to work.

Burberry's, 9 E. 57th St. (☎371-5010). If you're still not sure how to identify a yuppie, take a look at the clothes they sell here.

Canal Jean Co., 504 Broadway (☎226-1130). Enormous warehouse of a store sporting a prodigious array of jeans, jackets, t-shirts, hats, and more, new and secondhand. Young, fun, and reasonably cheap.

Capezio, 1650 Broadway (☎245-2140); 136 E. 61st St. (☎758-8833); 177 Macdougal St. (☎477-5634). Basically dancewear, although the Village branch now sells a range of New York's best designers. Not especially cheap, but some nice stuff.

Charivari. The city's fastest-growing designer fashion empire. Branches for men at 2339 Broadway and 85th St. (☎873-7242); for women at 2315 Broadway and 83rd St. (☎873-1424); for all at 257 Columbus Ave. (☎787-7272) and 18 W. 57th St. (☎333-4040).

Cignal, 79 Fifth Ave. (☎645-4330). Fashionable, moderately pricey, garments for men and women. Another branch at the World Trade Center.

Comme des Garçons, 116 Wooster St. (☎219-0660). Manhattan shop of the pricey Japanese designer.

CP Company, 680 Fifth Ave. (☎956-4690). Relatively new store selling well-made casual wear from European designers.

Dave's Army & Navy Store, 779 Sixth Ave. (☎989-6444). Good place to buy Levis; prices from $25.

Patricia Field, 10 E. 8th St. (☎254-1699). Vaunted as Manhattan's most inventive clothes store, Pat Field's was one of the first NYC vendors of "punk chic," and has since blossomed into one of the few downtown emporia that yuppie uptowners will actually visit.

Gucci, 685 Fifth Ave. (☎826-2600). Manhattan's swankiest clothes store.

Tommy Hilfinger, 284 Columbus Ave. (☎769-4910). Brand new fashions for the yuppie man-about-town. Expensive.

Parachute, 11 Wooster St. (☎925-8630). Pricey SoHo.

Paul Smith, 108 Fifth Ave. (☎627-9770). New Manhattan branch of the stylish British menswear designer.

Paul Stuart, Madison Ave. at 45th St. (☎682-0320). Classic men's garb, not unlike *Brooks Brothers* but with more style.

Trash 'n' Vaudeville, 4 St. Mark's Place (☎982-3590). Great clothes, new and "antique," in the true East Village spirit.

Unique Clothing Warehouse, 726 Broadway (☎674-1767). *Canal Jean*'s rival in the affordable youth clothes market—and there's not much to choose between them. In the t-shirt corner you can create your own design with a set of permanent, washable paints and a plain shirt.

Urban Outfitters, 628 Broadway (☎475-0009). A very good range of stylish clothing at reasonable prices.

Antique and secondhand clothes

Antique Boutique, 712 Broadway (☎460-8830). Self-proclaimed "largest and best vintage clothing store in the world."

Cheap Jack's, 841 Broadway (☎777-9564). Large vintage clothing store.

Exchange Unlimited, 563 Second Ave. (☎889-3229). Upscale thrift shop that puts up-to-the-minute style within most budgets.

Love Saves the Day, 119 Second Ave. (☎228-3802). Probably the only one of Manhattan's vintage clothes stores that could be described as anything like cheap.

Memorial Sloan Kettering Thrift Shop, 1440 Third Ave. (☎535-1250). Good thrift store with a fairly contemporary selection of clothes and tons of other bits and pieces.

Reminiscence, 74 Fifth Ave. (☎243-2292). Funky secondhand clothes for men and women. Quite inexpensive.

Richard Utilla, 244 E. 60th St. (☎737-6673). 1930s to 1950s clothing, and tons of bargains a bit *too* authentic for the average New Yorker.

Discount clothing

Bolton's, Designer clothes at vast reductions. Locations include: 19 E. 8th St. (☎475-9457); 53 W. 23rd St. (☎924-6860); 1180 Madison Ave. (☎722-4419); 225 E. 57th St. (☎755-2527); 27 W. 57th St. (☎935-4431); 2251 Broadway (☎873-8545).

Century 21, 12 Cortlandt St. (☎227-9092). A full-grown department store with designer brands for half the cost, a favorite among budget yet label-conscious New Yorkers. Only catch—no dressing rooms.

J.Crew, 203 Front St. (☎385-3500). South Street Seaport discount store housed in a former longshoremen's hostel and selling subtly updated classic garments in a rainbow of colors at easy-to-pay prices.

Daffy's, 111 Fifth Ave. (☎529-4477). A funkier version of *Loehmann's* (see below).

Gabay's, 225 First Ave. (☎254-3180). Over-ordered, flawed, or returned goods from the upscale midtown department stores. Well worth a rummage.

Orva, 166 E. 86th St. (☎369-3448). Discount fashion clothing and shoes for women. Great bargains.

Labels for Less, The name says it all—a chain selling discount designer labels for women. Branches at 639 Third Ave. (☎682-3330); 130 W. 48th St. (☎997-1032); 130 E. 34th St. (☎689-3455); 1302 First Ave. (☎249-4800); 186 Amsterdam Ave. (☎787-0850).

Loehmann's. New York's best-known store for designer clothes at knockdown prices. No frills, no refunds, no exchanges, but people still flock here with almost religious fervor. Next time you're deep in designer labels on Fifth Ave. in the 50s, bear in mind that most of the garments probably came from *Loehmann's*. Branches at: 19 Duryea Place, Brooklyn (☎718/469-9800); 60-06 99th St., Rego Park, Queens (☎718/271-4000); 9 West Fordham Rd., the Bronx (☎543-6420).

S&W, 165 W. 26th St. (☎924-6656). American designer sportswear at considerable discounts.

Finishing touches: shoes, hair, glasses

The best place to go for a **haircut** in New York City is the *Astor Place Haircutters* at 2 Astor Place (☎475-9854), where people stand in line outside while a doorman calls names from a clipboard. It's by no means Vidal Sassoon, but they'll do any kind of style, and, most importantly, don't cost the earth—around $10 (plus tip) for a straight cut, which by NYC standards is extremely cheap. Give your name to the doorman on arrival, and however long the line seems you should be seen in under half an hour. If you don't fancy *Astor* bear in mind that anywhere else will cost around $25.

As for **shoes**, for bargains the greatest concentration of shops is on West 8th Street between Fifth and Sixth avenues in the Village. If it's designer labels you're after you'll have to head way uptown—on and around Fifth Avenue in the 50s.

Glasses are considerably cheaper here than in Europe. If you break yours, or simply need a new pair to go with the new Armani outfit, try taking a look at the vast array at *Cohen's Optical*, 117 Orchard St. (☎674-1986). Nicaragua's Daniel Ortega supposedly spent $3000 here on a pair of bulletproof ones.

Books

Books are just one more thing of which there's a fantastic selection in New York. New or secondhand, US or foreign, there's little which isn't available somewhere. If there's a particular book you want to look at, but not buy, don't forget the New York Public Library at 42nd Street and Fifth Avenue.

General interest and new books

B. Dalton, A nationwide chain (now owned by *Barnes & Noble*—see below), and overall the city's best-stocked and most reliable bookstore for general titles, with a main branch in Manhattan at 666 Fifth Ave. (☎247-1740); others at 109 E. 42nd St. (☎490-7501); 396 Sixth Ave. (☎674-8780).

Barnes & Noble, New Yorkers feel cheated if they pay full price for anything: here they can pick up new hardbacks and paperbacks for a fraction of their published price. Branches at 105 Fifth Ave. (☎807-0099); their sale annexe opposite; Rockefeller Center; 56 W. 8th St.; Third Ave. and 47th St.; 57th St. and Seventh Ave.; Third Ave. and 59th St.; Broadway at 73rd St.; 45th St. and Broadway; 86th St. near Lexington Ave.; and at Penn Plaza. Many more in the Outer Boroughs.

Book Forum, 2955 Broadway (☎749-5535). Good on politics, poetry, and academic subjects.

Books and Co., 939 Madison Ave. (☎737-1450). Delightful bookshop with a literary bias and information on readings, events, etc.

Brentano's, 597 Fifth Ave. (☎826-2450). Housed in the fine old Scribner's bookstore, and continuing the tradition of good service and stock in elegant surroundings.

Coliseum Books, 2771 Broadway (☎757-8381). Large store, good on paperbacks and academic books.

Doubleday, An excellent general bookstore. Main branches at 245 Park Ave. (☎984-7561), and, larger, at 724 Fifth Ave. (☎397-0550). Otherwise in the Citicorp Center on E. 53rd St. (☎765-6500).

Endicott Booksellers, 450 Columbus Ave. (☎787-6300). Believe it or not, this place was here before the arthouse gang colonized Columbus, and it certainly tries hard to give the impression it has been here since the city began, providing helpful service and a wonderful range of titles.

Gotham Book Mart, 41 W. 47th St. (☎719-4448). The former owner of this store, Frances Stelloff, who died recently, made her name as patron of authors like Henry Miller, James Joyce, and Gertrude Stein in the 1920s, and needless to say, the shop still enjoys a legendary reputation. Good on drama and theater publications, and excellent for the more obscure literary stuff. A notice board downstairs advertises readings and literary functions, and a gallery has sporadic exhibitions.

Papyrus, 2915 Broadway (☎222-3350). New and used titles, especially good on political and radical literature.

Shakespeare & Co., 2259 Broadway (☎580-7800). New and used books, paper and hard cover, neatly located to capture the Upper West Side yuppie trade.

Spring Street Books, 169 Spring St. (☎219-3033). SoHo's most wide-ranging and pleasant bookshop, good on paperbacks, magazines, and newspapers, from home and abroad, as well as books.

Three Lives, 154 W. 10th St. (☎741-2069). Excellent, consciously literary bookstore that has an especially good selection of books for and by women, as well as general titles.

Secondhand books

Argosy Bookstore, 116 E. 59th St. (☎753-4455). Unbeatable for rare books, and also sells clearance books and titles of all kinds, though the shop's reputation means you may well find mainstream works cheaper elsewhere.

Bryant Park. Secondhand bookstalls Monday–Friday whenever the temperature hits 40°F or more. Excellent bargains if you're prepared to rummage.

Burlington Bookshop, 1082 Madison Ave. (☎288-7420). Secondhand and new books.

Gryphon Bookshop, 2246 Broadway (☎362-0706). Used and out of print books, records, CDs.

Pageant Book & Print Shop, 109 E. 9th St. (☎674-5296). Large selection of secondhand books and prints.

Ruby's Book Sale, 119 Chambers St. (☎732-8676). Civic Center's other used bookstore, dealing especially in paperbacks and ancient dog-eared magazines. Excellent value.

Strand Bookstore, 828 Broadway (☎473-1452). With around eight miles of books and a stock of over two million, this is the largest book operation in the city—and one of few survivors in an area once rife with secondhand book stores. As far as recent titles go, you can pick up review copies for half price; more ancient books go for anything from 50¢.

Special interest bookstores

New York has a good number of stores **specializing** in books on one particular area, from travel and art to more arcane subjects. The list below is fairly selective.

Travel

The Complete Traveler, 199 Madison Ave. (☎679-4339). Manhattan's premier travel bookstore, excellently stocked, secondhand and new.

Travelers Bookstore, 22 W. 52nd St. (☎664-0995). Small but well-stocked store that's a serious and friendly rival to *The Complete Traveler.*

New York Bound Bookshop, 50 Rockefeller Plaza (☎245-8503). Most city bookstores are copiously stocked with books about New York, but this one specializes in them, especially rare and out-of-print editions, alongside maps, photographs, and memorabilia.

Art and architecture

Wittenborn Art Books, 1018 Madison Ave. (☎288-1558). Probably the best stocked art bookshop in the city, new and antiquarian.

Urban Center Books, 457 Madison Ave. (☎935-3592). Architectural book specialists.

Photography, cinema, and the theater

A Photographer's Place, 133 Mercer St. (☎431-9358). Lovingly run bookshop specializing in all aspects of photography.

Applause Books, 211 W. 71st St. (☎496-7511). Books on the theater and cinema.

Drama Bookshop, 723 Seventh Ave. (☎944-0595). Theater books, scripts, and publications on anything to do with drama.

Crime

Foul Play, 10 Eighth Ave. (☎675-5115). Books for mystery and detective mavens.

Murder Ink, 271 W. 87th St. (☎362-8905). The first bookstore to specialize in mystery and detective fiction in the city, it's still the best, billed as stocking every murder, mystery, or suspense title in print, and plenty out.

Mysterious Bookshop, 129 W. 56th St. (☎765-0900). Run by a columnist from *Ellery Queen* magazine; especially good on used and out-of-print titles.

Sci-fi and comics

Forbidden Planet, 821 Broadway (☎473-1576). Science fiction, fantasy, and horror fiction and comics.

Science Fiction Shop, 163 Bleecker St. (☎473-3010). New and used science fiction records and books.

Language and foreign

Liberation Bookstore, 421 Lenox Ave. (☎281-4615). Works from Africa and the Caribbean.

Librairie de France/Libreria Hispanica/The Dictionary Store, 115 Fifth Ave. (☎673-7400). Massive complex housing New York's French and Spanish bookstores, a dictionary store with over 8000 dictionaries of more than 100 languages, and a department of teach-yourself language books, records, and tapes.

Rizzoli, 31 W. 57th St. (☎759 2424); 454a W. Broadway (☎674-1616). Manhattan branches of the prestigious Italian bookstore chain and publisher, specializing in European publications, with a good foreign newspaper and magazine selection.

Mind and body

East West Books, 78 Fifth Ave. (☎243-5994). Bookstore with a mind, body, and spirit slant.

Esoterica, 61 Fourth Ave. (☎529-9808). New Age Californiana (but not psychedelia).

Quest, 240 E. 53rd St. (☎ 758-5521). New Age books.

Samuel Weiser Inc., 132 E. 24th St. (☎777-6363). Occult and oriental books: witchcraft, eastern religions, satanism, and spiritualism.

Radical, feminist and gay

Revolution Books, 13 E. 16th St. (☎691-3345). New York's major left-wing bookshop and contact point. Books, pamphlets, periodicals, and information on current action and events.

St. Mark's Bookshop, 12 St. Mark's Place (☎260-7853). Probably the largest and best-known "alternative" bookstore in the city, with a good array of titles on politics, feminism, and the environment, literary criticism and journals, as well as more obscure subjects. Good postcards, too, and one of the best places to get hold of radical and art New York magazines. Open late.

A Different Light, 548 Hudson St. (☎989-4850). Excellent gay/lesbian bookstore, as well as a center for contacts and further information.

Oscar Wilde Memorial Bookshop, 15 Christopher St. (☎255-8097). Principally a gay men's bookstore.

> For listings of **children's bookstores**, see Chapter Six, "Sports, Kids, and Daytime Activities."

Miscellaneous

The things listed below don't fit easily into any of the previous categories. They're either shops which might be interesting to visit simply for themselves; or they sell items which are cheaper in New York than at home; or they're places which deserve a mention just for being weird.

Antiques

You'd be pretty crazy to come to New York to go **antiquing**—prices are outrageous. But if you do, the cheapest place to browse is in Brooklyn, along Atlantic Avenue between Hoyt and Third Street. For just looking, there are any number of snotty antique stores on Madison Avenue in the 60s and 70s. What follows is a highly selective rundown of the most interesting places in the city.

American Hurrah, 766 Madison Ave. (☎535-1930). Aged Americana mainly: furniture, quilts, paintings, and bric-a-brac. A wonderful selection but prohibitive prices.

Annex Antiques Fair, Sixth Ave. at 26th St. (☎243-5343). A huge range of stalls set up here at weekends, 9am to 5pm, to sell a range of antiques and memorabilia. Good for browsing, even if you're not looking for anything in particular. Admission $1.

Antique Arts & Ends, 83 Wooster St. (☎925-9470). Antique Wurlitzer jukeboxes, one-armed bandits, roulette wheels, and neon signs.

Depression Modern, 150 Sullivan St. (☎982-5699). A lesson in how to make money out of other people's junk.

Manhattan Art and Antiques Center, 1050 Second Ave. (☎355-4400). Around seventy shops and stalls in all, ranged over three floors and stocking a vast assortment—everything from American quilts to Oriental ceramics.

Urban Archeology, 285 Lafayette St. (☎431-6969). Large-scale accessories and furniture mainly American turn-of-the-century, so authentic that the shop hires them for film sets.

Art supplies

Arthur Brown Inc., 2 W. 46th St. (☎575-5555). America's largest art suppliers, with a pen department that claims to stock every pen in the universe.

Lee's Art Shop, 220 W. 57th St. (☎247-0110). All the artist needs under one roof. Framing, too.

New York Central Art Supply, 62 Third Ave. (☎473-7705). Suppliers to New York artists for four generations.

Pearl Paint Company, 308 Canal St. (☎431-7932). Five floors of artists' supplies including one for house painting. Another contender for title of the country's largest art shop.

Sam Flax, Artists' supplies store with branches at 15 Park Row (☎620-3040); 25 E. 28th St. (☎620-3040); 55 E. 55th St. (☎620-3060); 747 Third Ave. (☎620-3050); and 12 W. 20th St. (☎620-30380).

Ethnic crafts

General The *United Nations Gift Center*, in the basement of the UN Building on 1st Ave. (☎754-7700), and the excellent *Brooklyn Museum Shop* (see p.183), both sell a variety of crafts from different nations.

American
The *Museum of American Folk Art* on Lincoln Square (☎496-2966), stocks American crafts and applied arts, though little that can't be found cheaper elsewhere. For Native American crafts, try *The Common Ground*, 50 Greenwich Ave. (☎989-4178), which has jewelry, rugs, pottery, and sculpture.

Chinese
There are numerous places in Chinatown to buy Chinese and Oriental knick-knacks; try *Orienthouse*, 242 Broadway (☎431-8060), or *Quons, Yuen, Shing and Co.* on Mott St.

Irish
The *Irish Pavilion*, 130 E. 57th St. (☎759-9040) stocks all manner of things made in Ireland.

Japanese
Japanese Craft Shop at E. 6th St. and Second Ave.

Mexican/Latin American
Buena Dia, 108 W. Houston St. (☎673-1910); *Putamayo*, 857 Lexington Ave. (☎734-3111) .

Music, records, and electrical equipment

Record stores
If you're after anything fairly mainstream, branches of the **Sam Goody** chain (motto "Goody's got it") make a good first stop; addresses in the phonebook.

Tower Records, too, at 692 Broadway and 1965 Broadway, is great for most new records, tapes, CDs, and videos. For anything more specialized, or if you're just into browsing, try the selections below.

Bleecker Bob's, 118 W. 3rd St. (☎475-9677). This long-established record store specializing in punk and new wave has sadly become something of a tourist rip-off. Avoid.

CBGB Record Canteen, 313 the Bowery (☎677-6455). New wave and alternative music.

Colony Record & Tape Center, 1619 Broadway (☎265-2050). Printed sheet music and hard-to-find records.

Dayton's, 799 Broadway (☎254-5084). Rare records, old reviewers' copies, and deleted show and film soundtracks.

Footlight Records, 113 E. 12th St. (☎533-1572). *The* place for show music—everything from Broadway to Big Band, Sinatra to Merman. A must for record collectors.

The Golden Disc, 239 Bleecker St. (☎255-7899). Jazz, rock oldies, blues, and gospel.

House of Oldies, 35 Carmine St. (☎243-0500). Just what the name says—oldies but goldies of all kinds.

HMV, 2081 Broadway, at 72nd St. (☎721-5900). Manhattan branch of the newly arrived British chain. Also at 86th St. and Lexington Ave.

J&R Music World, 23 Park Row (☎732-8600). Good discounts; J&R's jazz and classical section is a few doors away at no. 33.

Record Mart in the Subway, near the N train in the Times Square subway station (☎840-0580). One of the best places in the city to find Caribbean—not to mention Central and South American—music. A knowledgeable staff, too; good browsing for the enthusiast.

Second Coming, 235 Sullivan St. (☎228-1313). The place to come for heavy metal and hard-core punk.

Sounds, 20 St. Mark's Place (☎677-3444). New and used records.

Vinyl Mania, 60 Carmine St. (☎691-1720). This, and two other branches on Carmine St., is where DJs come for the newest, rarest releases, especially of dance music. Hard-to-find imports, too, as well as homemade dance tapes.

Musical instruments

New York's heaviest concentration of musical instrument stores is located on one block of W. 48th St. between Sixth and Seventh Ave.: **Manny's**, at 156 (☎819-0576), and **Alex** at 164 (☎765-7738), are the best known in a row of many. A treat for guitar lovers, though harder to get to, is **Mandolin Brothers** at 629a Forest Ave. on Staten Island (☎718/981-8585), which has one of the world's best collection of vintage guitars.

Electrical equipment and cameras

The best place for discount shopping is on Seventh Avenue a little north of Times Square in the 50s, where there are countless stores selling cameras, stereo equipment, radios, and the like; for **cameras**, anywhere, especially in Midtown Manhattan from 30th and 50th streets between Park and Seventh avenues. You'll be offered different prices depending on whether you buy the equipment with or without a guarantee (ask for the price with to prevent any misunderstanding), and it's no use going into a shop without an *exact* idea of the model you want.

In all cases the best advice is to shop around, as prices vary wildly—hard-nosed bargaining is *de rigueur*, and you should be prepared for rudeness followed by a rapid drop in price when you walk on someone's "best offer." Remember, too, that you'll usually get a better price for cash than plastic.

You could also simply try one of the chains, among the best of which is *47th St. Photo*, at 67 W. 47th St. (☎398-1410), and other branches around Manhattan.

Prints, posters, and cards

Eurotrash, 301 Columbus Ave. (☎787-9119). Great selection of posters, old and new.

The Fourth Street Card Shop, 177 W. 4th St. (☎675-5465). Marvelous collection of postcards and greetings cards.

Postermat, 37 W. 8th St. (☎228-4027). Reproduction posters.

Poster Originals, 924 Madison Ave. (☎861-0422). Original (and as such expensive) prints from the States and Europe.

Metropolitan Museum of Art, Fifth Ave. (☎570-3726). Considering the size and breadth of the museum, its shop is disappointing: a fair selection of mainstream art books, posters, cards, and general paraphernalia.

Museum of Modern Art Shop, 11 W. 53rd St. (☎708-9700). The city's largest collection of modern art books, cards, and posters.

Untitled, 159 Prince St. (☎982-2088); 680 Broadway (☎982-1145). Art books, posters, and the world's largest selection of postcards.

Sports, games, and outdoors

Athlete's Foot, 500 Fifth Ave. (☎575-1680) and many other Manhattan locations. Jogging gear at affordable prices.

Herman's, 135 W. 42nd St. (☎730-7400); 845 Third Ave. (☎688-4603); 110 Nassau St. (☎233-0703); 39 W. 34th St. (☎279-8900). Sporting goods chain that has an excellent range of equipment, clothing, and footwear.

Hudsons, 97 Third Ave. (☎473-7320). Good-value camping equipment.

Modell's, 200 Broadway, 280 Broadway, 243 W. 42nd St. and 111 E. 42nd St. (☎962-6200). Army surplus and outdoor equipment plus straight sporting items.

Paragon, 867 Broadway (☎255-8036). Giant bargain-priced sports good store.

Tents and Trails, 21 Park Place (☎227-1760). Three floors of camping and hiking equipment.

US Athletics, 34 E. 8th St. (☎260-0750); 757 Third Ave. (☎832-1750); 500 Fifth Ave. (☎575-1680); and other branches all over Manhattan. The place to buy *Nike* and *Converse All-Star*, with a great selection of both.

Victor Fliegelman, 315 W. 39th St. (☎868-9155). Century-old family business supplying most Manhattan games shops and selling direct to the public at wholesale prices.

Village Chess Shop, 230 Thompson St. (☎475-9580). Every kind of chess set for every kind of pocket. Usually packed with people playing. Open until midnight.

For **toy shops**, both new and antique, see Chapter Six, "Sports, Kids, and Daytime Activities."

Trivia and oddities

Dapy Inc., 232 Columbus Ave. (☎877-4710). Assorted gadgets, novelties, and other useless gifts. Second location at 431 West Broadway (☎925-5082).

Gallery of History, 255 Liberty St., in the World Financial Center's Winter Garden, Battery Park City (☎945-1000). Come here just to look, at a range of documents autographed by the influential and famous, mounted with photos and explanatory plaques in elegant frames. Items include a legal document prepared by the Revolutionary War traitor Benedict Arnold—a snip at $11,990; Rollings photographs for just $3295; and Albert Einstein's first treatise on relativity, retailing for a mere $1,250,000.

Hammacher Schlemmer, 147 E. 57th St. (☎421-9000). Established in 1848, and probably New York's longest-running trivia store. Unique items, both practical and whimsical.

J&R Tobacco Corp., 11 E. 45th St. (☎869-8777). Self-proclaimed largest cigar store in the world, with an enormous—and affordably priced—range including all the best-known (and some not so known) brands—except Havanas.

The Last Wound-Up, 290 Columbus Ave. (☎529-4197). Wind-up toys of every shape and size. Other branches at South Street Seaport, Herald Center, and on Broadway at 19th St.

Maxilla & Mandible, 453 Columbus Ave. (☎724-6173). Animal and human bones for collectors, scientists, or the curious. Worth a visit even if you're not in the market for a perfectly preserved male skeleton.

Merrimack Publishing Corp., 85 Fifth Ave. (☎989-5162). Victorian repro toys, decorations, greetings cards, etc, as well as all sorts of useless and trivial items—wind-up toys, yo-yos, and the like. Good for presents.

Mythologies, 370 Columbus Ave. (☎874-0774). Sells a gamut of weird—and useless—items.

Only Hearts, 386 Columbus Ave. (☎724-5608). Everything heart-shaped.

Pipeworks & Wilke, 16 W. 55th St. (☎956-4820). Specialists in all kinds of pipe, including handmade and antique versions.

The Sharper Image, 4 W. 57th St. (☎265-2550). Novelty items for yuppies—talking alarm clocks, funny-shaped phones, and the like.

Star Magic, 743 Broadway (☎228-7770). Out of this world space-age gifts—crystals, celestial maps, books, cards, and records.

Think Big!, 390 West Broadway (☎925-7300). Oversized everyday items for the giant in your life.

CHAPTER EIGHT

DRINKING AND EATING

There isn't anything you can't find to **eat** in New York. The city has more restaurants per head than anywhere else in the States, and New Yorkers not only dine out all the time but take their food incredibly seriously, devoting long hours of discussion to the study of different cuisines, new dishes, and new restaurants—which can find themselves received with all the fervor of a second coming. As you stroll through the heavenly odors that emanate from the city's delis, bagel stores, Chinese restaurants, and popcorn palaces, it's hard not to work up an appetite.

As for **drinking**, there are many different kinds of bars, ranging from ordinary neighborhood locals, sometimes Irish, and invariably pretty much male-only territory, to larger, designer hangouts that are often the last word in Manhattan fashion.

Budget food: breakfast, lunch, and snacks

The cheapest place to eat any kind of meal, wherever you are in New York, is a **coffee shop** or a **diner.** For some reason, these are invariably run by Greeks (thus explaining why the standard takeout coffee cup is invariably decorated with a picture of the Parthenon), and they serve filling breakfasts, burgers, sandwiches, and basic fare from a usually enormous menu, which often includes good-value lunchtime specials, either at formica-topped tables or around a counter on stools. Prices are around $5 for a heavily garnished burger and fries, $5–8 for anything more elaborate, making coffee shops in general the choice for a filling lunch on a budget—though, brightly lit and fairly basic, they're not really places you'd want to eat dinner.

Breakfast
Although most hotels serve breakfast of some kind, it works out much less expensive to go out to a coffee shop for the first meal of the day. Most coffee shops do special deals up until 11am, allowing you to eat and drink until you're full for under $5. Figuring high on **breakfast menus** are sausages and bacon, along with eggs, waffles, and pancakes. Be prepared for a snappy interrogation as to how you want your eggs, and be ready to snap back with your preference.

Lunch and snacks
Aside from coffee shops, most **restaurants** in New York open at lunchtime, when you tend to get the better deals, either because there's a set menu or because prices are simply cheaper.

Some of the best lunchtime deals can be had in **Chinatown**, where you can get a massive plate of meat with noodles or rice for around $5 or less, or, if you're feeling a little more adventurous, feast at a dim sum restaurant for $7–8. Dim sum (literally "your heart's delight") consists of small dishes that you choose from a moving cart and pay for at the end, according to the empty dishes in front of you. For the inexperienced (and dim sum is not recommended to vegetarians) there's an element of chance, since Chinatown waiters tend not to speak English, and the dishes themselves are often unrecognizable until the first bite. But duckwebs aside, it's mostly pretty accessible fare (see the lists that follow for some of the standards).

Another option for lunch—and one that's not just limited to Manhattan—is to get a **sandwich to go** from a **deli**. Once again, be prepared for a rapid-fire question and answer session with the assistant, who will not only ask which kind of bread you want—white, wholewheat, rye, or french (in which case ask for a "hero" or a "sub")—but also whether you want mayo, lettuce, or anything else. New York sandwiches are custom-built and constrained only by your imagination, so bear in mind the size of the thing you're creating; if you hear them say "full house" it means you've ordered everything. You can expect to pay around $5 for a sandwich, but it is almost a meal in itself.

For **quick snacks**, many delis also do ready-cooked hot meals. Street **vendors** (most concentrated on Lower/Midtown Manhattan) sell hot dogs, pretzels, and knishes, or for around $1.50 you can get a slice of **pizza** (*Ray's* is the most widespread and reliable New York City chain). Additionally, there are of course the regular and familiar **burger chains**, such as (in descending order of quality) *Wendy's, Burger King,* and *McDonald's,* as well as a host of other less ubiquitous fast-food franchises.

Bar food and bargains

Just about every New York **bar** serves food of one kind or another, and you'll find a substantial—and inevitable—cross-over between our "Bars" and "Budget eats" sections. Even in the lowliest bar there's a good chance they'll cook you at least a burger or a plate of potato skins, and many places offer a full menu, particularly the more aspiring Irish hangouts. Though bars open late (see below), their kitchens are usually closed by 12pm.

In the **ritzier bars**—basically in Manhattan—there are almost invariably hot **hors d'oeuvres**, laid out between 5pm and 7pm Monday to Friday. For the price of a single drink (it won't be cheap) you can gorge yourself silly on pasta, seafood, chilli, or whatever. Remember, though, that the more you look like an office-person (it's for them, after all, that the hors d'oeuvres are put out) the easier you'll blend in with the free-loading crowds. Some places even demand you wear a tie.

Bars which serve serious food are detailed along with restaurant **listings** later in this chapter, as are some sources of hot hors d'oeuvres. For convenience in locating a nearby place on a walk around the city, they are also cross-referenced by area in the Manhattan and Outer Boroughs chapters.

Coffee, tea, soda

Coffee is drunk widely in New York and is usually fresh and good, served black or "regular" (with cream or milk, in contrast to other parts of the States where "regular" coffee is black coffee); caffeine-free coffee is available pretty much everywhere—ask for *Sanka* or simply "de-caff." You can get coffee "to go" in most delis, and in restaurants coffee is often served "ad lib," ie you can keep asking for refills at no extra charge. **Tea** is becoming more popular, and will normally be served straight or with lemon; if you want milk request it, and specify whether you want it hot or cold.

Soda comes in caffeine-free versions as well. These are drunk in three sizes: small (large), regular (bigger), and large (practically a bucket).

Restaurants

What follows is simply an introduction to the food you're likely to eat, and to peculiarly New York procedures of eating and paying for it. Specific **restaurant recommendations** follow, and you'll again find lists for cross-reference at the end of each section in the Manhattan and Outer Boroughs chapters.

Ethnic cusines

In New York City, at least, so-called American food inevitably fades into the background when you're confronted with the startling variety of different **ethnic cuisines**. Among them, none has had so dominant an effect as **Jewish** food, to the extent that many Jewish specialties—bagel, pastrami, lox and cream cheese—are now considered archetypal New York. Others retain more specific identities. **Chinese** food, available not just in Chinatown but all over Manhattan, is most frequently (and familiarly) Cantonese, though many restaurants also serve the spicier Szechuan and Hunan dishes. Chinese prices (see above) are usually among the city's lowest. **Japanese** food is generally expensive—the Eighties craze and still plentiful, in particular *sushi* (raw fish), served as much for the aesthetic arrangement as for the taste, which you'll either love or hate. Other Asian cuisines include **Indian**, becoming more widespread, and a broad and increasing sprinkling of **Thai**, **Korean**, and **Indonesian** restaurants, all of which tend to be pricier than Chinese but not prohibitively so.

Closer to home, **Irish** food dominates the city's bars, with corned beef, shepherd's pie, and Irish stew. **Italian** cooking is also widespread, and not terribly expensive, especially if you stick to pizza; as is **Spanish**, whose huge seafood dishes can make an economical night out for those in a group. **French** restaurants are fairly expensive on the whole, particularly so of late with the cultish popularity of *nouvelle cuisine*, although there is an increasing number of bistros and brasseries turning out authentic and reliable French nosh for very attractive prices.

More realistically, a whole range of **Eastern European** restaurants—Russian, Ukrainian, Polish, and Hungarian—serve well-priced filling fare. **Greek** food is easy to find in most parts of the city (especially, of course, in the Greeks' own quarters) and is usually edible and affordable. Finally, you'll also find **Tex-Mex** restaurants everywhere (though not at its best in New York City); it's honest grub by any standards, and as variable as you might expect, although you always get plenty and there are no extras to push up the bill.

Other sundry places include **Cuban-Chinese** and **Kosher-Chinese** hybrids, and any number of **vegetarian** and **wholefood** eateries to cater to any taste or fad. The key is to keep your eyes peeled and to be adventurous. Eating is *the* great joy of being in New York, and it would be a shame to waste it on the familiar.

Brunch

Brunch can also be a good value deal, and is something of a New York institution, usually served at weekends between noon and 4pm, and sometimes including a free cocktail with your meal—though the places that offer often this serve the worst food. Lox and cream cheese on a bagel, steak and eggs, and eggs benedict are favorite brunch items. See p.254 for recommended brunch venues.

GLOSSARY OF ETHNIC FOOD TERMS

MEXICAN

Arroz	Rice, usually prepared in tomato sauce
Burritos	Folded tortillas stuffed with re-fried beans or beef, and grated cheese
Chiles rellenos	Green chilies stuffed with cheese and fried in an egg batter
Enchiladas	Soft tortillas filled with meat and cheese or chilli and baked
Fajitas	Soft flour tortillas served with a shrimp, chicken, or beef dish to wrap inside
Frijoles	Re-fried beans, ie mashed fried beans; a yuppie fave
Guacamole	A thick sauce made from avocado, garlic, onion, and chile
Margarita	*The* cocktail to drink in a Mexican restaurant, made with tequila, triple sec, lime juice, and limes, and blended with ice to make slush. Served with or without salt
Mariscos	Seafood
Menudo	Soup made from a cow's stomach, said to be a cure for hangovers
Nachos	Tortilla chips topped with melted cheese
Salsa	Chilies, tomato, and onion and coriander, served in varying degrees of spiciness
Tacos	Folded, fried tortillas, stuffed with chicken, beef, or (occasionally) beef brains
Tamales	Corn meal dough with meat and chili, wrapped in a corn husk and baked
Tortillas	Corn dough pancakes used in most dishes
Tostada	Fried, flat tortillas, smothered with meat and vegetables
Quesadilla	Folded soft tortilla containing melted cheese

JEWISH

The Jewish faith allows two types of restaurant: those in which meat can be eaten and those where dairy products can be consumed. The two types of cooking can't be mixed. This section includes some Russian and Ukrainian dishes, which, though occasionally spelled differently on menus, are often much the same.

Bagel	Ring-shaped roll, boiled first then baked
Blintz	Crepe filled with cheese or fruit and eaten with sour cream
Borscht	Beet soup
Challah	Egg bread, eaten traditionally as part of the Friday evening Sabbath meal
Falafel	(Middle Eastern). Deep fried spiced chickpea balls.
Glatt kosher	Type of cuisine and restaurant catering to the diet of ultra-orthodox Jews
Kasha	Cracked buckwheat cooked until tender and served with soup or as a side dish
Knaidel	Meat dumpling. Also *matzo balls*
Knish	Pastry filled with cheese, meat, potato, fruit, or anything else
Kreplach	Noodle shells filled with *kasha*, meat, potato, etc.
Kugel	Potato or noodle pudding
Lox	Smoked salmon
Matzo	Flat unleavened bread eaten all year round but particularly at Passover
Pareve	Term for "neutral," ie something which can be eaten with meat or dairy food
Pirogen	Baked dough parcels filled with potato, meat, or cheese
Schmaltz	Chicken fat
Tzimmes	Literally "a mixture." Casserole of meat, vegetables, and fruit

GREEK

Baklava	Very sweet, flaky pastry made with nuts and honey	Moussaka	Baked eggplant dish, topped with a cheese sauce
Dolmades	Vine leaves stuffed with rice and meat	Pastitsio	Lamb pie topped with macaroni
Feta	Crumbly white cheese made with ewe's milk	Souvlaki	Shish kebab
		Spanakopita	Spinach pie
Gyro	Ground lamb	Stifado	Lamb stew
Horta	Salad, often dandelion leaves	Taramasalata	Creamed cod roe, olive oil, and lemon juice
Kasseri	Rubbery cheese made with ewe's milk	Tiropita	Cheese pie
Kokeretsi	Grilled lamb innards	Tzatziki	Yoghurt with garlic and cucumber

JAPANESE

California Roll	Mild tasting sushi with a slice of avocado	Sake	Strong rice wine, drunk hot
		Sashimi	Thinly sliced raw fish eaten with soy sauce or *Wasabi*
Gyoza	Meat and vegetable dumplings		
Karagei	Fried chicken	Sushi	Raw fish wrapped up in rice in seaweed. See *sushi* list below
Larmen	Noodles in spicy broth		
Negimayaki	Sliced beef with scallions	Tempura	Seafood and vegetables deep-fried in batter
Okonomi	Literally "as you like it," usually used with regard to sushi when choosing the topping		
		Tonkatsu	Deep-fried pork with rice
		Wasabi	Hot green horseradish sauce

Sushi/sashimi

Anago	Sea eel	Maguro	Tuna
Chirashi	Mixed fish on rice	Nigiri	Rice topped with fish
Ebi	Shrimp	Tai	Red snapper
Ikura	Salmon roe	Tekka (maki)	Tuna with rice rolled in seaweed (nori)
Kappa (maki)	Cucumber with rice and seaweed		
		Toro	Extra meaty part of the tuna

CHINESE

Cantonese Szechuan/Hunan

Cantonese	Szechuan/Hunan	
Chow	Chao	Stir-fried
Daofu	Doufu	Bean curd
Fun, fon	Fun	Rice
Gai, gee	Ji	Chicken
Har, ha	Xia	Shrimp
Siu	Shao	Roasted
Jyu yuk	Zhu rou	Pork
Ngow yuk	Niu rou	Beef
Opp, opp	Ya	Duck
Ow	Zha	Deep-fried
Yu	Yu	Fish

Dim Sum (Cantonese)

Bao, bau	Bun (generally steamed)
Cha Siu Bao	Steamed bun filled with sweet cubes of roast pork
Chow fun	Fried flat rice noodles
Chow mai fun	Fried rice vermicelli
Har Gow	Steamed shrimp dumplings
Jook	Congee, or rice gruel
Kow, gow	Dumplings
Lo Mein	Stir-fried noodles
Mai fun	Rice noodles
Tong mein	Soup noodles
Wonton, won ton	Thin-skinned dumplings filled with fish, usually served in broth

ITALIAN

Cacciatore	"Hunter's style"—cooked with tomatoes, mushrooms, herbs, and wine	**Pasta**	
Calzone	Pizza folded in half so the topping is inside	*Cannelloni*	Large pasta rolls, stuffed with ground meat and tomato and baked
Alla Carbonara	Sauce made with bacon and egg	*Cappelleti*	"Little hats" stuffed with chicken, cheese, and egg
Alla Veneziana	Cooked with onions and white wine	*Cappelli d'angeli*	"Angel's hair," very fine pasta strands
Alfredo	Tossed with cream, butter, and cheese	*Fettucini*	Flat ribbons of pasta
Al forno	Cooked in the oven	*Fusilli*	Pasta spirals
Posillipo	Tomato cooked with garlic, Neapolitan style	*Gnocchi*	Pasta and cheese dumplings
Puttanesca	Literally "whore style," cooked with tomatoes, garlic, olives, capers, and anchovies	*Linguine*	Flat pasta noodles, like *Fettucini*
		Manicotti	Squares stuffed with cheese; ravioli are the same only with meat
		Tortellini	Rings of pasta stuffed with either spiced meat or cheese
Zabaglione	Dessert of beaten egg yolks, sugar, and marsala	*Vermicelli*	Very thin spaghetti
		Ziti	Small tubes of pasta, often baked with tomato sauce

Service, tipping . . . and home deliveries

Whatever you eat, **service** everywhere will be excellent, since not only is the notion of customer service deeply engrained into the American psyche, but the system of **tipping**, whereby you double the figure on the bill for tax (just over 8 percent) to work out the minimum tip, can make the staff almost irritatingly attentive. There's no way around this: if you either refuse or forget to tip there's little point in going back to that restaurant again. As far as actual **payment** is concerned, many—although by no means all—restaurants take credit/charge cards (if you use one you'll find a space left for you to write in the appropriate tip); travelers' checks are also widely accepted (see *Basics*, "Money and Banks").

If you're not in the mood to get dressed up or fight the crowds, you might consider having **food delivered** to your hotel or host's home. Many pizza and most Chinese places offer this service for free if the order exceeds a given minimum and you're within a reasonable distance—though you should, of course, tip the bearer.

Drinking

Bars generally open from mid-morning (around 10am) to the early hours—4am at the latest, when they have to close by law. As for prices, in a basic bar you'll be paying $2–2.50 for a glass of draft beer, $3–4 a bottle, although in a swankier and/ or more fashionable environment, or in a singles joint, this may go up to $4–5 a glass or more. Detailed **listings** and recommendations again follow, and can be cross-referenced by area in the Manhattan and Outer Boroughs chapters.

Specific **savings on drinking** can often be made in the larger bars by ordering quart or half-gallon pitchers of beer, which represent a considerable discount on the price per glass. Look out, too, for "Happy Hour" bargains (usually 60 minutes stretched somewhere between 5 and 7pm) and "twofers" (two-for-the-price-of-one deals). Also, avoid bars or clubs that offer "free drinks for ladies"—they tend to be cattle markets or worse.

What to drink

When you've made your choice of bar, the problem is deciding **what to drink**. If you care about beer, imported ones like Canadian *Molsen*, Mexican *Dos Equis*, and the familiar European varieties (*Heineken*, *Lowenbräu*) are widely available, though also substantially more expensive. If price is a problem, then bear in mind you can walk into any supermarket and buy beer at around $1 a can.

Don't neglect Californian **wines**, since not only can they be very good, they're also fairly inexpensive at around $7–8 for a bottle in a liquor store, less than this if you buy a so-called "jug wine"—basically the rawest, lowest quality wine there is. If you're looking for something reasonably decent, try the varieties from the Napa or Sonoma valleys, just north of San Francisco, which between them produce some of the country's best quality wines. New York State also produces wine, though less reliably than California. French and Italian wines come more expensive, but they're still by no means costly. In all cases, however, wine does demand a better-filled wallet when in a restaurant or bar: expect 100 percent mark-up on the bottle.

As for **hard liquor**, there are a number of points of potential confusion. First bear in mind that whether you ask for a drink "on the rocks" or not, you'll most likely get it poured into a glass full to the brim with ice; if you don't want it like this ask for it "straight up." If you ask for *whiskey* you'll be given *bourbon*, of which the most common brands are *Old Grandad* and *Jim Beam* (not *Jack Daniels* since it's not made in Tennessee)? If you want Scotch or Irish whiskey you have to ask for them by nationality or brand name.

Cocktails are popular, especially during happy hours and weekend brunch (see above). The standards are listed below, but really varieties are innumerable, sometimes the specialty of a single bar. With any names you come across, experiment—that's half the fun. Look out, too, for something called **jello-shots**: they're served in the livelier bars and restaurants and are Jello basically, only made with vodka instead of water, and thus something of a peculiar way to get drunk.

COCKTAILS

Bacardi	white rum, lime, and grenadine	Manhattan	vermouth, whiskey, lemon juice, and soda
Black Russian	vodka with coffee liqueur, brown cacao, and Coke	Margarita	tequila, triple sec, and lime (or strawberry) juice
Bloody Mary	vodka, tomato juice, tabasco, worcestershire sauce, salt, and pepper	Mimosa	champagne and orange juice
		Mint Julep	bourbon, mint, and sugar
		Pina Colada	dark rum, light rum, coconut, cream, and pineapple juice
Daquiri	dark rum, light rum, and lime, often with fruit such as banana or strawberry	Screwdriver	vodka and orange juice
		Tequila Sunrise	tequila, orange juice, and grenadine
Harvey Wallbanger	vodka, galliano, orange juice	Tom Collins	gin, lemon juice, soda, and sugar
Highball	any spirit plus soda, water, or ginger ale	Vodka Collins	vodka, lemon juice, soda, and sugar
Kir Royale	champagne, cassis	Whisky Sour	bourbon, lemon juice, and sugar
Long Island Iced Tea	gin, vodka, white rum, tequila, lemon juice, and Coke	White Russian	vodka, white cacao, and cream

Buying your own alcohol, you need to find a liquor store—you won't get anything apart from beer in a supermarket, just one of New York State's complex **licensing laws**. Other laws worth keeping in mind are that you have to be over 21 to consume alcohol in a bar or restaurant (and you'll be asked to provide evidence if there's any dispute); that it's against the law to drink alcohol on the street (which is why you see so many people furtively swigging from brown paper bags); and that you can't buy booze, other than beer, anywhere on a Sunday.

MANHATTAN

It's in **Manhattan**—and more specifically Lower Manhattan (ie below about 23rd St.)—that you're likely to spend most time **drinking and eating**. Many of the city's better bars are situated in this part of town, as well the majority of the cheaper (and ethnic) restaurants. We've divided Manhattan into four main sections—"Bars," "Cafés and Tea Rooms," "Budget eats," and "Restaurants"— although you can generally eat in any of these, including most bars. For drinking only, you'll find some of the bars listed here (music and gay-oriented places, most obviously) cross over into the "Nightlife" chapter that follows, both in terms of feel and often escalating prices. Just in case you have a sudden 4am urge for bagel and cream cheese, **24-hour** eateries, coffee shops, and delis are also detailed at the end of this section.

Bars

The **bar scene** in New York City is a varied one, with a broader range of places to drink than in most American cities, and prices to suit most pockets. At the bottom end of the scale, the cheapest watering-holes you'll find, all over the city, are roughish places, sometimes Irish in name and ownership—convivial enough, though difficult ground for women on their own. In addition to these, there are more mixed hangouts, varying from some of the long-established haunts in Greenwich Village to newer, louder, and more deliberately stylish places that spring up—and die out—all the time in the downtown neighborhoods. Bars with some kind of theme are particularly big right now. Finally there are also bars, known as "singles bars," many of which concentrate around Midtown Manhattan on the east side, which New Yorkers tend to use to pick up a member of the opposite (or same) sex. Expect prices to be hiked up greatly anywhere like this.

Selections below are personal favorites. The potential choice, obviously, is a lot wider—below 14th Street it's hard to walk more than a block without finding a bar—and takes in the whole range of taste, budget, and purpose. (Bear in mind that many places double as bar and restaurant, and you may therefore find them listed not here but under "Budget eats" or "American Restaurants.") The best hunting grounds in Lower Manhattan are Greenwich Village, the East Village, and SoHo; there's a good choice of midtown bars—though here bars tend to be geared to an after-hours office crowd and (with a few notable exceptions) can be pricey and rather dull; uptown, the Upper West Side, between 60th and 85th streets along Amsterdam and Columbus, has a good array of bars and restaurants.

Hours of opening are generally mid-morning through to 1am or 2am; some stay open later but by law all must close by 4am. Bar kitchens usually stop operating around midnight or a little before. Wherever you go, even if you just have a drink you'll be expected to **tip**: the going rate is roughly ten percent of the bill or 50¢ for a single drink.

Groupings—as with the restaurant reviews that follow—are by the three main chapter divisions (Lower, Midtown, and Upper). For ease of reference, however, all specifically **gay and lesbian** bars are gathered together in a single section on p.246.

Almost everywhere

Blarney Stone. Chain of Irish (and essentially male-only) bars with branches all over Manhattan. Nothing too wild, and often filled with downbeat drunks slumped into their whiskey, but the city's cheapest drinks and some decent value food.

McAnn's. Another Irish chain serving affordable booze and a broad selection of food. Their biggest, best (and for women most accessible) branch is the E. 45th St. basement, between Fifth and Madison.

Lower Manhattan

Broome Street Bar, 363 West Broadway (☎925-2086). A popular and long-established local haunt, these days perhaps more restaurant than bar, serving reasonably priced burgers and salads in a dimly lit setting. A nice place just to nurse a beer, too, especially when footsore from SoHo's shops and galleries.

Café Iguana, 235 Park Ave. South (☎529-4770). Late-night frenzied bar that was once perhaps a hip place to drink downtown. Nowadays it's strictly singles territory.

Cedar Tavern, 82 University Place (☎929-9089). Legendary beat and artists' meeting-point in the 1950s and now a cosy bar with food—burgers for around $4 and other entrées $6 up – and well-priced drinks. Summertime you can sit and eat in their covered roof garden.

Chelsea Commons, 24th St. and Tenth Ave. (☎929-9424). Not only a personable bar but a great place to eat—outside meals for under $8. Very much a local hangout.

Chumley's, 86 Bedford St. (☎675-4449). Not easy to find, and with good reason—this place used to be a speakeasy and is obviously so well known now it doesn't need to advertise its presence. High on atmosphere and with a good choice of beers and food from around $8. Arrive before 9pm to be sure of one of the battered tables—at which, incidentally, James Joyce put the finishing touches to *Ulysses*.

Continental Divide, 25 Third Ave. (☎529-6924). Casual bar with a Western theme. Occasional live bands.

Downtown Beirut, 158 First Ave. (☎777-9011). Mega-sleaze East Village punk bar with music, live and recorded. Jukebox vintage 1977–79. Another branch—Downtown Beirut II—at 157 Houston (☎614-9040), which repeats much the same formula.

Fanelli, 94 Prince St. (☎226-9412). SoHo's oldest established bar, cosy and informal. Food—homecooked, unpretentious fare—weighs in at $5–7.

Fifty Five, 55 Christopher St. (☎929-9883). Almost next door to the more renowned *Lion's Head*, but cheaper, and with a great jazz jukebox and regular performances of live jazz.

Grassroots Tavern, 20 St. Mark's Place (☎475-9443). Basement bar at the center of the East Village hum: not expensive, and with a good oldies jukebox and two dartboards.

Holiday Cocktail Lounge, 75 St. Mark's Place (☎777-9637). Offbeat Village Bar that attracts a mixed bag of customers. Quite safe, but Bohemia with an edge nonetheless.

Joes, E. 6th St. between Aves. A & B (no phone). Cheap beer and pool table in a seedy East Village setting.

La Jumelle, 55 Grand St. (☎941-9551). Just down from the *Lucky Strike* in SoHo (see below), and similar in many ways, though perhaps a tad trendier at the moment, and used by a younger crowd. Popular with Europeans.

Lion's Head, 59 Christopher St. (☎929-0670). Small bar in the heart of the Village, traditionally patronized by a literary clientele that has plastered its book covers all over the walls. Nothing too alternative, but a lively place for a drink, especially at weekends. Food, too—burgers, steaks, etc; on busier evenings you might need to eat to get a table.

Lucky Strike, 59 Grand St. (☎941-0479). Convivial bar/bistro patronized by a mixed bunch of young and middle-aged SoHo-ites. Food served out back (nothing special and not cheap), and DJs on Friday, Saturday, and Sunday nights, when the scene can be buzzing—though it's really best at lunchtime, when it's less frenetic.

Manhattan Brewery Company, 42 Thompson St. (☎219-9250). Started by an Englishman with an eye to a money-spinner, this cavernous bar-restaurant brews and sells its own English-style beer and doles out simple food at okay prices. A hectic, crowded place, patronized by the after-hours office bunch.

McSorley's, 15 E. 7th St. (☎473-9148). New York City's longest-established watering-hole, so it claims, and a male-only bar until just over a decade ago. These days it retains a saloon look, with a youthful gang indulging themselves on the cheap strong ale. There's no trouble deciding what to drink—you can have beer, and you can have it dark or lite.

NoHo Star, 330 Lafayette St. (☎925-0070). Laid-back NoHo ("North of Houston") bar decorated by its artist clientele and serving an unusual mix of Chinese and American food.

Peculier Pub, 145 Bleecker St. (☎353-1327). Popular local bar whose main claim to fame is the number of beers it sells—over 200 in all and examples from any country you care to mention.

Puffy's, 95 Hudson St. (☎766-9159). Small, funky TriBeCa bar with lunchtime food, very cheap booze, and a great jukebox.

Scrap Bar, 130 W. 3rd St. (no phone). Built on the site of the folk club where Bob Dylan had his first residency, a small punky bar with loud music and an interesting clientele.

Sophie's, E. 5th St. at Ave. A (no phone). Beers for a dollar a shot make this East Village bar popular, especially with ex-pat Brits.

Sporting Club, 99 Hudson St. (☎219-0900). Sports-oriented bar with a large electronic screen to keep up with the action.

Sugar Reef, 93 Second Ave. (☎477-8754). High-spirited East Village bar with flaming tropical decor, forty different varieties of rum, and bopping waiters that's among Manhattan's hottest spots. You should expect to wait if you want to sample the Caribbean food, which goes for $10–15.

Temple Bar, 332 Lafayette St. (☎925-4242). Small, elegant bar serving champagne and, some claim, Manhattan's best Martinis to a self-consciously Beautiful Bunch. Very much a place to people-watch.

Vazac's, 108 Ave. B (☎473-8840). Known as "Seven and B" for its location on the corner of Tompkins Square, this is a popular East Village hangout, with an extremely mixed crowd, that's often used as a sleazy set in films and commercials—perhaps most famously in the film *Crocodile Dundee*.

White Horse Tavern, 567 Hudson St. (☎243-9260). Convivial and inexpensive Village bar where Dylan Thomas supped his last before being carted off to hospital with alcohol poisoning, and where today you can buy burgers, chilli, and the like for around $5. Bareboards Bohemia, little changed, apart from the excellent jukebox, since Dylan fell off his barstool.

Midtown

The Coffee Shop, 29 Union Square West (☎243-7969). A former coffee shop turned trendy bar and restaurant that at time of writing was very much *the* place to be seen. Still with the curvy counter and barstools of the old coffee shop, the bar is a nice place to hang out at any time; the noisy adjacent restaurant, complete with booths, serves vaguely Caribbean-style food—a little over-priced at around $12 an entree but not bad, and there's cheaper stuff as well, making it a decent alternative for lunch.

Costello's, 225 E. 44th St. (☎599-9614). Journalists' bar once, legend has it, frequented by Ernest Hemingway. Busy early evening. Food in the restaurant out back starts at around $10.

Green Derby, 978 Second Ave. (☎688-1250). Just opposite *Murphy's*, this tries hard to be Irish through and through. Basically, though, a singles hangout, convivial if not especially cheap.

Irish Pub, 839 Seventh Ave. (☎664-9531). As the name suggests, a straightforward, no-nonsense boozer with a long bar in a neighborhood that needs just that.

Kuklas, 220 W. 31st St. (☎268-7937). Sports bar handy for watching games if you have been unlucky in the line for tickets at nearby Madison Square Garden. Does reasonably priced food, too.

Live Bait, 14 E. 23rd St. (☎353-2400). Cajun bar/restaurant run by the same people as the *Coffee Shop* (see above), and popular with the after-office crowd. Not the place for a quiet drink.

Mickey Mantle's, 42 Central Park South (☎688-7777). Bar that's entirely given over to sports, with numerous TV screens showing different events, and even a video library of sports tapes. Decent food—burgers, squid, and good desserts.

Molly Malone's, 287 Third Ave. (☎725-8375). Comfortable Irish bar with solid, if unexciting, food.

Mulligan's Grill, 857 Seventh Ave. (☎246-8840). There's nothing particularly stunning about this place, except that it offers a welcome and affordable escape from the costlier reaches of theaterland, both for drink and food.

Mumbles, 603 Second Ave. (☎889-0750). Casual, friendly, and cosy bar in which people gather to watch the seasonal sport. Mixed, neighborhood crowd.

Murphy's, 977 Second Ave. (☎751-5400). Irish bar which attracts the midtown singles set. Drinks are costly but food less so—a rare and useful standby in this part of town.

Old Town Bar and Restaurant, 45 E. 18th St. (☎473-8874). One of the oldest bars in the city, and a favorite with publishing types, models, and photographers from the surrounding Flatiron district. High on atmosphere, and with an excellent, if standard, menu of chilli, burgers, and the like.

Pete's Tavern, 129 E. 18th St. (☎473-7676). Convivial watering-hole and former speakeasy that claims to be the oldest bar in New York, opened in 1864—though these days it inevitably trades somewhat on its history. The restaurant serves American-Italian food, but the burgers are reputedly excellent.

P.J. Clarke's, 915 Third Ave. (☎759-1650). One of the city's most famous watering-holes, this is a spit-and-sawdust alehouse with a not-so-cheap restaurant out the back. You may recognize it as the location of the film *The Lost Weekend*.

Ye Olde Tripple Inn, 263 W. 54th St. (☎245-9849). Basic Irish bar that serves inexpensive food at lunchtimes and early evening. A useful place to know about if you're after affordable food in this part of town.

Upper

Augie's, 2751 Broadway (☎864-9834). One of the more interesting places on this stretch of Broadway, downbeat and unpretentious, and favored by local jazz fans for its live music from 10pm onward. Also has inexpensive snacks and food.

Border Café, 244 E. 79th St. (☎535-4347). Friendly neighborhood hangout good for satisfying cravings for frozen margaritas. A down-to-earth place despite its upscale location. Also at 2637 Broadway, though not as lively.

Buckaroo's Bar & Rotisserie, First Ave. and 74th St. (☎861-8844). *The* place to mingle with thirtysomethingish Upper East Siders, with a good selection of fruit-based drinks, including jello-shots, and a pool table out back where you can lounge for hours. The food is pretty decent as well—great chicken wings for under $4 and fine burgers for around $7.

Cannon's Pub, Broadway and 108th St. (no phone). Big, brash, and above all loud bar that is a getaway spot for rock freaks and serious drinkers on this corner of the Upper West Side. Unvarying selections of West Coast soft rock make it the antithesis of the East Village.

Drake's Drum, 1629 Second Ave. (☎988-2826). Easy-going pub selling burgers, fish and chips, etc, for under $10.

Dublin House, 225 W. 79th St. (☎874-9528). Brash Irish bar with a young crowd, good jukebox, and inexpensive drinks. Definitely recommended if you're up this way.

Emerald Inn, Columbus Ave. between 69th and 70th St. (☎874-8840). Amiable pub with food.

Hudson Bay Firm, 1454 Second Ave. (☎861-5683). Neighborhood bar that offers occasional all-you-can-eat specials.

KCOU, 430 Amsterdam Ave. (☎580-0556). Straightforward upscale bar with jukebox. Not expensive, despite appearances.

Lucy's Retired Surfers, 503 Columbus Ave. (☎787-3009). Day-glo painted, surf-board-decorated bar with killer cocktails. Inevitably popular with Upper West Side yuppies, and with a restaurant out back.

Jim McMullen, 1341 Third Ave. (☎861-4700). Upper East Side bar usually crammed with the Beautiful People of the neighborhood.

Oscar and Toni's, 2662 Broadway at 101st St. (☎222-0242). A neighborhood bar that's popular with locals, especially students from nearby Columbia.

Outback, 1668 Third Ave. (☎996-8117). Bar with an Aussie theme. Always hopping....

Racoon Lodge, 480 Amsterdam Ave. (☎874-9984). Simple bar with cheap drinks. Also on the East Side at 1439 York Ave. (☎650-1775).

Ruby's River Road Cafe & Bar, 1754 Second Ave. (☎348-2328). Home of the famous jello-shots, and a fun bar with a Cajun café in the back.

Rusty's, 1271 Third Ave. (☎861-4518). Small bar, good for burgers and brew, that's run by an ex-Mets player and has the sporting paraphernalia to match—including a big screen TV to watch the action. Another branch—known as *Rusty Staub's*—at 575 Fifth Ave. (☎682-1000), where the food is probably better.

The Saloon, 1920 Broadway (☎874-1500). Large bar/restaurant with a vast menu. Bonuses include outside seating, and waiters serving on roller skates. Good for brunch.

Gay and Lesbian bars

New York's **gay men's** bars cover the spectrum: from relaxed, mainstream cafés to some very heavy numbers indeed, although the scene has quietened down a lot since the early 1980s; the recommendations below are geared firmly toward the former. Most of the better established places are in **Greenwich Village**, with the **East Village** and **Murray Hill–Gramercy Park** areas (the east 20s and 30s) up-and-coming, the East Village having a more lesbian—and more political—identity. Things tend to get raunchier farther west as you reach the bars and cruisers of the West Side Highway and meat-packing (literally—this is not gay slang) districts, both of which are hard-line and, at times, dangerous. For further listings and details, see the weekly *Outweek*.

Lesbian and **women-only** bars are, in comparison, thin on the ground, often operating only on one or two nights a week at one of the gay men's bars. *Womanews*, as well as *Outweek*, can be a useful supplement for listings and events.

Mainly for men

Greenwich Village

Badlands, 388 West St. (☎741-9236). One of the most popular and most enjoyable Village bars, especially in summer.

Boots and Saddle, 76 Christopher St. (☎929-9684). Middle-of-the-road leather action. A little sleazy.

Keller's, 384 West St. (☎243-1907). Lively West Village bar that draws a mostly black male crowd.

Marie's Crisis, 59 Grove St. (☎243-9323). Well-known cabaret/piano bar popular with gay men, and featuring old-time singing sessions on Friday and Saturday nights. Often packed, always fun.

The Monster, 80 Grove St. (☎924-3558). Large, campy bar with a drag cabaret, piano, and video.

Ty's, 114 Christopher St. (☎741-9641). Relaxed but convivial.

Uncle Charlie's, 56 Greenwich Ave. (☎255-8787). Bar attracting a young, main-stream gay crowd.

Elsewhere

The Bar, 68 Second Ave. (☎674-9714). Neighborhood bar for the East Village. Relaxed, pool table.

Bogart's, 320 E 59th St. (☎688-8534). Piano bar with a wide mix of custom.

Company, 365 Third Ave. (☎532-5222). Glittering decor and clientele to match.

South Dakota, 405 Third Ave. (☎684-8376). One of the friendliest spots in the city, and with excellent food. Recommended.

Spike, 120 Eleventh Ave. (☎243-9688). Another very popular leather bar.

Star Sapprent, 400 E. 59th St. (☎688-4710). New York's only gay Asian bar; gets going late on weekend nights.

Town and Country, 656 Ninth Ave. (☎307-1503). Clientele reflects the neighbor-hood—Hispanic/Irish. Unpretentious and downscale.

The Tunnel Bar, 116 First Ave. (☎777-9232). Formerly a leather bar, this estab-lishment increasingly caters to a younger, more activist-oriented gay male crowd.

The Works, 428 Columbus Ave. (☎799-7365). Laid-back theme bar. Cool and pleasant and about the only option for this part of town.

Mainly for women

Crazy Nanny's, 21 Seventh Ave. (☎366-6312). Yuppie-oriented, rather stylish lesbian bar.

Pandora's, 70 Grove St. (☎242-1408). Formerly known as the *Grove Club*, this legendary lesbian dive—small, tacky, and overpriced, has a devoted following.

Cafés and Tea Rooms

In addition to regular bars, New York has a number of **cafés and tea rooms**, which don't always serve alcohol but concentrate instead on providing fresh coffee and tea, fruit juice, and pastries and light snacks, and sometimes complete meals. Many of the more long-established cafés are downtown, congenial places with a European emphasis; indeed they're often determinedly Left Bank in feel (like the grouping at the junction of Bleecker and Macdougal streets) and perfect for lingering or just resting between sights. The smarter midtown **hotels** are good places to stop for tea, too, if you can afford the prices they charge for the fake English country house atmosphere they often try to contrive. Failing that, if all you want is a cup of something hot and a pastry, most of the larger **depart-ment stores** have coffee shops.

Algonquin Oak Room, 59 W. 44th St. (☎840-6800). The archetypal American interpretation of the English drawing room. Good for afternoon teas.

Anglers & Writers, 420 Hudson St. (☎675-0810). Village café serving a daily afternoon tea between 3pm and 6pm, as well as decent American fare—soups and desserts are just one specialty. A good place to just have a coffee, a snack, or a full meal.

Boathouse Café, Central Park Boating Lake—72nd St. entrance (☎517-2233). Peaceful retreat from a hard day's trudging around the Fifth Avenue museums, and with great views of the famous Central Park skyline.

Caffé Dante, 79 Macdougal St. (☎982-5275). A morning stop for many locals since 1915. Good cappuccino, double espresso, and caffé alfredo with ice cream. Often jammed with NYU students and teachers.

Café Le Figaro, 184 Bleecker St. (☎677-1100). Former Beat hangout during the Fifties and the ersatz Left Bank at its finest. Good views of the Bleecker Street hubbub, and excellent snacks and sandwiches, too.

Caffé Reggio, 119 Macdougal St. (☎475-9557). One of the first Village coffee houses, dating back to the 1920s, usually crowded and with tables outside for people-watching.

Café Roma, 385 Broome St. (☎226-8413). Old Little Italy *pasticceria*, ideal for a drawn-out coffee and pastry. Try the homemade Italian cookies, and the gelato counter out back.

Citicorp Atrium, Lexington Ave. and 53rd St. Again, a good place to stoke up after a hard morning's tramp around the midtown sights.

Ferrara, 195 Grand St. (☎226-6150). The oldest and best-known of all the Little Italy coffee houses, also with outside seating in summer.

Peacock Caffé, 24 Greenwich Ave. (☎242-9395). Puccini arias as background music to accompany rich desserts and *Café Royale*—coffee with whipped cream.

Tea and Sympathy, 108 Greenwich Ave. (☎807-8329). Self-consciously British tea room, serving an afternoon High Tea full of traditional Brit staples like jam roly-poly and treacle pudding, along with shepherd's pie, fish cakes, etc.

Veniero's, 342 E. 11th St. (☎674-4415). East Village bakery and almost century-old institution that sells wonderful pastries and has some seating in the back.

Budget eats

Bars are often the cheapest places to eat in New York, but they're by no means the only budget option. Any number of **diners**, **coffee shops**, and **burger joints** will serve you straight American food for $5–7, and many **delis** do hot takeout meals as well as snacks and bumper sandwiches. We've also included here the New York institution of **happy hour hors d'oeuvres**, one of the city's best scams if you're on a tight budget, when hors d'oeuvres are laid out around 5–7pm in numerous midtown bars and restaurants, all consumable for the cost of a drink. There is also a list of places to eat **brunch**, where many restaurants compete for custom by spreading a special well-priced brunch—sometimes including a free cocktail or even unlimited champagne thrown in with the cost of your meal.

For **further cheap eating options**, be sure to look also at the places detailed in the following "Restaurants" section. Although Chinese and East European food, and of course pizza, are perhaps the only cuisines that are reliably cheap almost everywhere, there are some good bargains to be found in every category.

Burgers, delis, and diners

Most of the listings that follow are for **diners** or basic **café-restaurants**, many of which tend to serve standard dishes (burgers, steak, and seafood) for under $10, plus drinks and tip, as well as a selection of the more interesting **delis** that offer sit-down meals.

Lower Manhattan

Around the Clock, 8 Stuyvesant St. (☎598-0402). Centrally situated East Village restaurant serving crepes, omelettes, burgers, and pasta at reasonable prices. Open 24 hours.

Astor Riviera, 452 Lafayette St. (☎677-4461). Inexpensive East Village 24-hour restaurant serving a broad coffee shop menu.

Bagel Buffet, Sixth Ave. at 8th St. (☎477-0448). Wide selection of spreads and good value bagel salad platters for around $5. Open 24 hours.

Boxer's, 190 W. 4th St. (☎929-8942). Dimly lit bar-restaurant serving some of the most inexpensive food and drink in the city—solid American fare for under $10.

Brother's Bar-B-Q, 228 W. Houston St. (☎727-2775). Downbeat SoHo diner serving some of the best barbecued food east of the Mississippi. The mashed potatoes and collards are not to be missed. Cheap, too—two people can eat generously for around $20.

Campus Coffee Shop, 31 W. 4th St. (☎228-1460). Old-established café usually packed with students from nearby NYU. Excellent breakfast bargains before 11am.

Carmella's Village Garden, 49 Charles St. (☎242-2155). Cheap café serving omelettes, pasta, and the like for $5 up.

Corner Bistro, 331 W. 4th St. (☎242-9502). Somewhat dark and dingy pub with cavernous cubicles and healthy servings of burgers, beer, and desserts for reasonable prices. Long-standing haunt of West Village literary and arty types.

Dave's Pot Belly, 98 Christopher St. (☎243-9614). Friendly all-night restaurant with inexpensive food in very large helpings. The desserts are easily enough for two.

Ed Debevic's, 661 Broadway (☎982-6000). A wacky retro diner—a landmark in Chicago—that recently opened in New York to rave reviews. Features a Forties-style bar, a "bomb shelter" party room, and a Sixties-style coffee shop. Staff are dressed like greasers, prom queens, cheerleaders, and the like, and the food is basic American fare—meatloaf, fried chicken, wets (french fries with gravy), etc.

Ear Inn, 326 Spring St. (☎226-9060). Arty kind of place, with cheap food (all under $10) and a good jukebox. Live folk and country music on Tuesday nights.

Elephant and Castle, 68 Greenwich Ave. (☎243-1400). Old Village favorite serving well-priced food and drink. Also another location at 183 Prince St. (☎260-3600).

Empire Diner, 210 Tenth Ave. (☎243-2736). With its gleaming chrome-ribbed art deco interior this is one of Manhattan's original diners, still open 24 hours and still serving up plates of simple food. The food is very average, but the place is a beauty.

Fuddrucker's, 87 Seventh Ave. South (☎255-9349). Burger restaurant imported from Texas, and serving suitably giant-size burgers and other down-home food. Outdoor seating when it's warm enough.

Harry's at Hanover Square, 1 Hanover Square (☎425-3412). Bar that gets into its stride when the floor traders come in after work. Great burgers.

Khan's, 23 Third Ave. (no phone). A Mongolian barbecue restaurant (sic) which offers lunch specials for $4.50 and all-you-can-eat dinner deals for a mere $8.95. Strictly carnivores only.

Life Café, 343 E. 10th St. (☎477-8791). Peaceful and long-established East Village haunt right on Tompkins Square that hosts sporadic classical and other music concerts. Food is sandwiches, Tex-Mex, or vegetarian—plates all around $6–8.

Little Mushroom Café, 183 W. 10th St. (☎242-1058). Fish, pasta, and omelettes at $5–12. One of the cheaper places along this stretch of the Village, catering to a mixed gay/straight crowd. Bring your own booze from the deli opposite. Also with an uptown location at 1439 Second Ave. (☎988-9006).

Phebe's, 361 Bowery (☎473-9008). Reasonable food—including weekend brunch and a three-hour "happy hour" during the week. Open till 4am—a regular off-off Broadway hangout.

Prince Street Bar, 125 Prince St. (☎228-8130). SoHo bar and restaurant used by the local arthouse clique. Broad array of different foods, and, for the area, not terribly expensive.

Riviera Café, 225 W. 4th St. (☎242-8732). Central Village restaurant serving acceptable food at low prices. In the 1960s this was definitely the place to be seen.

Second Avenue Deli, 156 Second Ave. (☎677-0606). The East Village rival to *Katz's* (see p.269), serving up marvelous burgers, pastrami sandwiches, and other deli goodies in ebullient, snap-happy style.

South Street Seaport Market, east end of Fulton St. The market's third-floor selection of fast-food chains are among the least expensive places to eat in the area.

Spring Street Market, 111 Spring St. (☎226-4410). Wonderful deli. The best sandwiches downtown.

Stromboli Pizzeria, 112 University Place (☎255-0812). Excellent thin crust pizzas—a good place for a quick slice.

Violet Café, 80 Washington Square East (☎529-5428). Coffee shop-cum-restaurant popular with NYU students. Best for inexpensive sandwiches and breakfasts.

Wolf's Delicatessen, 42 Broadway (☎422-4141). Classic New York deli that makes a good place for lunch in between seeing the sights of the Financial District.

Midtown

J. J. Applebaum's Deli, 34th St. at Seventh Ave. (☎563-6200). Huge and excellent deli with two sit-down floors. Good for refortifying after *Macy's*.

Bagel Palace, 36 Union Square (☎673-0452). Bagel topped with just about anything, plus a hundred different omelettes.

Carnegie Deli, 854 Seventh Ave. (☎757-2245). This place is known for the size of its sandwiches—by popular consent the most generously stuffed in the city, and a meal in themselves. The chicken noodle soup is good, too. Not cheap, however, and the waiters are among New York's rudest.

Chez Laurence, 245 Madison Ave. (☎683-0284). Well-placed little patisserie that makes great cheap breakfasts, decent lunches—and good coffee at any time of the day.

Hamburger Harry's, 145 W. 45th St. (☎840-0566). Sister to the downtown edition but more refined. Some claim its burgers are the best in town.

Hard Rock Café, 221 W. 57th St. (☎489-6565). Burger restaurant that for some reason continues to pull celebrity New York, or at least the odd rock star. Full to bursting most nights, especially at weekends, but only the famous can book ahead—everyone else stands in line outside. The food ain't bad, but only really worth it if you've a teenager in tow.

Harold's, 150 E. 34th St. at Lexington and Third Ave. (☎684-7761). Decent American food that's reasonably priced—quite a find for this part of town. Has outdoor seating in summer.

Jackson Hole Wyoming, 521 Third Ave. (☎679-3264); 1633 Second Ave. (☎737-8788). Midtown burger chain with a reputation for obscenely large burgers. Good value for dyed-in-the-wool carnivores.

Jerry's Metro Delicatessen, 790 Eighth Ave. (☎581-9100). Large deli restaurant with a huge choice of sandwiches, omelettes, and burgers, etc. Good breakfasts, too, which is handy given the Times Square vicinity location.

Landmark Tavern, 626 Eleventh Ave. (☎757-8595). Long-established Irish bar/restaurant popular with the midtown yuppie crowd. Good food, and huge helpings.

Market Diner, 572 Eleventh Ave. (☎244-6033). The ultimate 24-hour diner, chrome-furnished and usually full of weary clubbers filling up on breakfast. A good place to refuel early evening, too.

New York No.1 Delicatessen, 104 57th St. (☎541-8320). Enormous art deco restaurant, renowned for its pastrami and corned beef, and handy for those suffering from midtown shopping fatigue. Good breakfasts, too.

O'Reilly's, 56 W. 31st St. (☎684-4244) Classy Irish pub/restaurant with standard American dishes at $6-12. Good value for this part of town.

Reuben's, 244 Madison Ave. (☎867-7800). Busy midtown diner that makes a fine and filling haven in between the sights and shops of Fifth Avenue.

Sarge's, 548 Third Ave. (☎679-0442). Large coffee shop serving enormous portions of deli grub. Open 24 hours a day.

Scotty's Diner, 336 Lexington Ave. (☎986-1520). Conveniently placed midtown diner, close to Grand Central Station and the Empire State Building. Solid diner food, good breakfasts until 11am, and a friendly Spanish owner.

Stage Deli, 834 Seventh Ave. (☎245-7850). Another reliable all-night standby, and long-time rival to the *Carnegie Deli*, above.

Taste of the Apple, 1000 Second Ave. (☎751-1445). Home of the over half-pound burger, and some very fair prices for this part of town. Also at 283 Columbus Ave. (☎873-8892).

Wine and Apples, 117 W. 57th St. (☎246-9009). A kind of hybrid Greek-Hungarian diner with meals priced from $5–8 and inexpensive booze. A life-saver in this part of town.

Upper

Amsterdam's, 428 Amsterdam Ave. (☎874-1377). Bar-restaurant serving burgers, ribs, and the like for less than $10. Downtown branch at 454 Broadway (☎925 6166).

BBQ, 27 W. 72nd St. (☎873-2004); 1265 Third Ave. (☎772-9393); 21 University Place (☎674-4450); 132 Second Ave. (☎777-5574). A real-live budget option for this part of town, just off Central Park, though the Upper East Side branch has a better reputation. Excellent barbecue chicken and burgers for $5–$8, chilli for less. Whichever branch you try it'll be crowded, however, and the service can be poor, to say the least.

Diane's Uptown, 249 Columbus Ave. (☎799-6750). Fast, substantial burgers, and handy for *Ben & Jerry's* ice cream next door.

EJ's Luncheonette, 433 Amsterdam Ave. (☎873-3444). Newly opened diner that does its best to look old, with mirrors, booths upholstered in turquoise vinyl, and walls adorned with Fifties photographs. Unpretentious American food which includes pancakes in many guises and banana splits to die for. Expect long lines for the brunch served on Sunday.

Flor de Mayo, 2651 Broadway (☎595-2525). Very cheap, very popular Cuban-Chinese restaurant with coffee shop decor and lots of food, though not much for vegetarians—spicy chicken, Cuban-style steaks, etc. You can eat well for around $10.

Gray's Papaya, Broadway at 72nd St. (no phone). Two all-beef hotdogs and a papaya juice for just $1.65. A New York experience. No ambience, no seats, just good cheap grub.

Madhatter, 1485 Second Ave. (☎628-4917). Casual pub serving decent burgers and other simple food.

JG Melon, 340 Amsterdam Ave. (☎874-8291); 1291 Third Ave. (☎744-0585). Decent burgers and fries in a casual pubby environment make these places among Upper Manhattan's most desirable places for cheap eats.

O'Neal's, 48 W. 63rd St. (☎581-3770). Handily placed opposite Lincoln Center, and with burgers, chilli, and the like for $5–10.

New Wave Coffee Shop, 937 Madison Ave. (☎734-2467). A fairly standard coffee shop in most respects except for its status as something of a venue for celebrities—Dustin Hoffmann, Mary Tyler Moore, even Tony Bennett are said to be regulars when they're in town. Whatever the truth of this, the food is above-average diner grub, and it's handy for the museums. It's also a nice cheap option for those who have just blitzed with their credit card in the nearby Madison Avenue designer clothing emporia.

Papaya King, 179 E. 86th St. (☎369-0648). By general—and *New York Times*—consent, the best hotdogs in the city.

Rathbones, 1702 Second Ave. (☎369-7361). Opposite *Elaine's* (see "Expense account") and an excellent alternative for ordinary humans. Take a window seat and watch the stars arrive, and eat for a fraction of the price. Burgers, steak, fish for under $10—and a wide choice of beers.

Serendipity 3, 225 E. 60th St. (☎838-3531). Cheap, long-established daytime eatery and ice cream parlor serving up hearty comfort food to a young clientele. The frozen hot chocolate is out of this world.

BREAKFAST: COFFEE SHOPS AND DINERS

You rarely have to walk more than a block or two in Manhattan to find somewhere that serves **breakfast**: there are coffee shops and diners all over town serving up much the same array of discounted specials before 11am. But when you're desperate for a shot of early morning coffee, the following checklist should help you avoid traipsing too far from wherever you happen to be staying. You'll find full reviews, where appropriate, elsewhere in this chapter; otherwise just expect a regular Greek-run coffee shop.

LOWER

Astor Riviera, 452 Lafayette St. (☎677-4461).

Campus Coffee Shop, 31 W. 4th St. (☎228-1460).

Life Café, 343 E. 10th St. (☎477-8791).

Odessa, 117 Ave. A (☎473-8916).

Triumph, 148 Bleecker St. (☎228-3070).

Village Inn, 169 Bleecker St. (☎533-0823).

Violet Café, 80 Washington Square East (☎529-5428).

Waverley, 385 Sixth Ave. (☎675-3181).

ZZZ, 60 University Place (☎777-7370).

MIDTOWN

Astro, 101 W. 55th St. (☎489-6284).

Brooks, 330 Fifth Ave. (☎997-1030).

Chez Laurence, 245 Madison Ave. (☎683-0284).

Grand Central, Grand Central Terminal, 42nd St. (☎883-0009).

Jerry's Metro Delicatessen, 790 Eighth Ave. (☎581-9100).

Lantern, 209 E. 42nd St. (☎867-2760).

New York No.1 Deli, 104 57th St. (☎541-8320).

Penn Garden, 150 W. 31st St. (☎736-0293).

Red Flame, 67 W. 44th St. (☎869-3965).

UPPER

New Wave, 937 Madison Ave. (☎734-2467).

Tramway Coffee Shop, 1143 Second Ave. (☎758-7017).

Utopia, 267 Amsterdam Ave. (☎873-6233).

Venus Coffee Shop, 1051 Second Ave. (☎759-5597).

Happy hours and free food

Happy hour hors d'oeuvres are essentially a midtown phenomenon—and the hour(s) in question are generally 5 to 7pm, Monday to Friday only. Since the idea is to draw in well-heeled clientele, just out from their offices, you'll do well to dress in similar fashion, though the places listed below are all pretty accessible as long as you perform with confidence and don't too obviously clear the tables. The cost of a regular drink or cocktail at any should work out around $3. For happy hour devotees, there are additional possibilities in addition to those below: just check out the more upscale midtown bars and hotels.

Biff's Place, Marriott Hotel, 525 Lexington Ave. (☎288-6894). One of the most popular happy hours, with excellent hors d'oeuvres disappearing rather quickly. Don't arrive much after 6pm.

BRUNCH BARGAINS

Weekend brunch is a competitive business in New York, and the number of restaurants offering it is constantly expanding. Selections below (most of which are covered in more detail under "Restaurants") all do a good weekend menu, sometimes for a price that includes a free cocktail or two—though offers of freebies are to be treated with suspicion by those more interested in the food than getting blitzed. Above all, don't regard this as a definitive list. You'll find other possibilities all over Manhattan, especially on the east side of Midtown Manhattan, and places are opening up all the time—check the magazines and freesheets for the latest and best alternatives.

The Cupping Room Café, 359 W. Broadway (☎925-2898).

Ellen's Stardust Diner, 1377 Sixth Ave. (☎307-7575).

Elephant and Castle, 68 Greenwich St. (☎243-1400).

EJ's Luncheonette, 433 Amsterdam Ave. (☎873-3444).

Joe's Bar & Grill, 142 W. 10th St. (☎727-1785).

Landmark Tavern, 626 Eleventh Ave. (☎757-8595).

Leaf 'n' Bean, 136 Montague St. (☎718/855-7978).

Lola, 30 W. 22nd St. (☎675-6700).

Lox Around the Clock, 676 Sixth Ave. (☎691-3535).

Marmalade Park, 222 E. 39th St. (☎687-7803).

Los Panchos, 71 W. 71st St. (☎874-7336).

The Pink Teacup, 42 Grove St. (☎807-6755).

Royal Canadian Pancake Restaurant, 145 Hudson St. (☎219-3038).

The Saloon, 1920 Broadway (☎874-1500).

Sarabeth's Kitchen, 1295 Madison Ave. (☎410-7335).

Teachers, 2271 Broadway (☎362-4900).

Cheese Cellar, 125 E. 54th St. (☎758-6565). Convivial pub with lots of hot hors d'oeuvres.

Cheshire Cheese, 319 W. 51st St. (☎765-0616). Filling German fare.

Jimmy Weston's, 131 E. 54th St. (☎593-8800). Wide selection of food, though pricier than usual drinks. Men must wear jacket and tie.

Ryan McFadden's, 800 Second Ave. (☎599-2226). A long-established hangout of *Daily News* reporters and ex-pats. Always crowded and fun.

Sam's Restaurant, Equitable Center, 152 W. 52nd St. (☎582-8700). Upscale restaurant owned by Margaux Hemingway and her husband that serves free pizza and other specials during happy hour.

Top of the Sixes, 666 Fifth Ave. (☎757-6662). No better place to freeload really. Hot hors d'oeuvres every evening, Monday to Friday, and some great views over Manhattan.

Trattoria, first floor of the Pan Am Building, E. 45th St. (☎661-3090). Pasta, pizzas, and antipasti in relatively unintimidating surroundings. Recommended.

20 West, 27 W. 20th St. (☎924-0205). Complementary buffet from 5pm until 8pm that's one of the best freebies in town. Formerly known as *Chevy's*.

Whaler Bar, Madison Towers Hotel, 22 E. 38th St. (☎685-3700). Casual atmosphere with a large choice of cheese and veggie dishes.

Restaurants

New York's ethnic make-up is at its most obvious and accessible in the city's **restaurants**. Somewhere in Manhattan you can eat just about any world cuisine—and often a lot better than you'd find in its natural habitat. Don't, however, make the mistake of assuming ethnic food is necessarily inexpensive. Often it's not. You pay Manhattan's highest prices in the better Italian, French, and Japanese eateries; Greek and Spanish food, too, often works out expensive, and really only Chinese, Jewish, and East European (and sometimes Mexican) are dependably low-budget. (One other thing to bear in mind is that these days many of New York's better ethnic restaurants are in the Outer Boroughs.) **Selections** below shouldn't break the bank—most serve entrees at $10 or under (some well under), and at lunchtime you'll often find special deals or set menus—though we have tried to include the *best* of Manhattan's restaurants as well as the cheapest. The listings which follow are by country of origin, with closing sections on *Fish and seafood*, *Vegetarian and wholefood*, and, last (and in many cases least), *Expense account*.

American, Latin, and South American

Grouped together for simplicity, these are all filling and good value options. Regional **American** restaurants can be fairly sedate but will always be generous, and some serve interesting regional variations; similarly with **Mexicans** and **Tex-Mex** restaurants—though they're usually livelier hangouts serving cocktails. Watch out, also, for Manhattan's **Brazilian** restaurants, which are gaining in popularity—and numbers.

Lower

Bayamo, 704 Broadway (☎475-5151). Chino-Latino food, served in vast portions at moderate prices—around $15 for an entree. Try the stir-fried duck with chili and beans.

Benny's Burritos, 113 Greenwich Ave. (☎633-9210). Huge burritos with all kinds of fillings, and speedy, amiable service. Cheap too. Now with a branch in the East Village at 4th St. and Ave. A.

Caramba 684 Broadway (☎420-9817); 918 8th Ave. (☎245-7910); 1576 3rd Ave. (☎876-8838); 2567 Broadway (☎749-5055). Once one of the more fashionable places to eat around town, now firmly declasse. Combination Mexican platters go for around $8—after which, washed down by one of their notorious Margaritas, you're unlikely to be able to manage much more.

Caribe, 117 Perry St. (☎255-9191). A funky Caribbean restaurant filled with a leafy jungle decor and blasted with reggae music. Fairly spicy food, washed down with wild tropical cocktails make it the place for a fun night out. Cash only.

Casa Mexico, 557 Hudson St. (☎366-4893). Village restaurant serving solid Tex-Mex grub for $6 and over. Firmly average food, but on a Saturday night it may be the only place to get a table around these parts if you haven't booked.

Cinco de Mayo, 349 W. Broadway (☎226-5255). SoHo Mexican restaurant with authentic food and wild ambience. With another midtown branch at 153 E. 53rd St., in the Citicorp Building (☎755-5033).

Cottonwood Café, 415 Bleecker St. (☎924-6271). Noisy Village restaurant with almost exclusively young custom, mainly NYU students. Texan cuisine (chicken, chops, okra, and mash)—good, filling, and not over priced at $6 up. Live music every night (except Sunday) from 10:30pm.

Cowgirl Hall of Fame, 519 Hudson St. (☎633-1133). Down-home barbecue at affordable prices. Try the fried chicken.

El Coyote, 774 Broadway (☎ 677-4291). Texas-style food at low prices.

The Cupping Room Café, 359 W. Broadway (☎925-2898). Absurdly quaint American restaurant serving good wholesome food to occasional jazz and the odd tarot or palm reader on selected evenings. Brunches are best, with fresh baked breads and muffins, though you'll probably need to wait. Recommended.

Great Jones Café, 54 Great Jones St. (☎674-9304). Blackened redfish, great burgers, molasses cornbread, beer, and Cajun martinis in an intentionally anonymous-looking neighborhood restaurant.

Gulf Coast, 489 West St. (☎206-8790). Affordable Cajun specialties in a Fifties honky-tonk setting. Crowded, good bar, with a rousing rock 'n' roll jukebox.

How's Bayou, 355 Greenwich St. (☎925-5405). Great margaritas, Cajun food, and real mashed potatoes make this TriBeCa eatery well worth a visit. Cheap, too.

Jerry's Restaurant, 101 Prince St. (☎966-9464). American-French restaurant with an upscale diner type atmosphere that's become one of SoHo's trendier spots lately. Casual and good for people-watching. Moderate prices. Another branch—*Jerry's 103*—in the East Village at 103 Second Ave. (☎777-4120).

Joe's Bar & Grill, 142 W. 10th St. (☎727-1785). Bistro-type restaurant serving a wide array of dishes for $10–15 on average. Choices range from broiled tuna, "painted" duck, meat loaf, and others, as well as a variety of bar snacks—burgers, club sandwiches, etc. A little pricey for what you get.

Lupe's East LA Diner, 110 Sixth Ave. (☎966-1326). Very laid-back, hole-in-the-wall restaurant serving great beer and burritos. Good fun, and cheap.

Mary Ann's, 116 Eighth Ave. (☎633-0877). Good value Tex-Mex food, most for under $10, also available from a branch in the East Village at 300 E. 5th St. (☎475-5939).

Mesa Grill, 102 Fifth Ave. (☎807-7400). At time of writing this was definitely the restaurant of the moment, serving unique Southwestern fare at uniquely high prices. Full of publishing and advertising types doing lunch.

Moondance Diner, 80 Sixth Ave. (☎226-1191). Flashy and loud, popular with a would-be Bohemian crowd. Burgers, sandwiches, and great apple pancakes.

The Pink Teacup, 42 Grove St. (☎807-6755). Soulfood restaurant in the heart of the Village. Cheap and filling.

Royal Canadian Pancake Restaurant, 145 Hudson St. (☎219 3038). A memorable restaurant serving numerous kinds of vast—and delicious—pancakes, with fillings ranging from lager to white chocolate and almond to berries and bananas. Come hungry. A perfect place for Sunday brunch, though come later (after 3pm) when the crowds have gone.

SoHo Kitchen and Bar, 103 Greene St. (☎925-1866). Smart burger-pizza-pasta place frequented by local gallery-goers. Average food, moderately priced, and supplemented, if you so wish, by a fine list of wines and beers—though experimenting with this inevitably makes it less of a reasonable option.

El Teddy's, 219 W. Broadway (☎941-7070). Eccentrically decorated restaurant that serves good Mexican food and superb margaritas. Try fried tortillas wrapped around spicy chicken for hors d'oeuvres. Entrees run $10–15.

Tennessee Mountain, 143 Spring St. (☎431-3993). Though situated in the heart of SoHo, this is a very un-SoHo-like restaurant, serving huge portions of barbecued meat and fish for $10–15. Good value if you're hungry.

Tortilla Flats, 767 Washington St. (☎243-1053). Cheap Tex-Mex Village dive with great margaritas and a loud jukebox.

TriBeCa Grill, 375 Greenwich St. (☎941-3900). Part-owned by Robert de Niro, people come here for a glimpse of the actor when they should really be concentrating on the food—fine, French-American cooking at around $25 per entree. The setting is nice, too, a large airy eating area around a central Tiffany bar (rescued from the legendary Upper East Side singles' hangout, *Maxwell's Plum*). Well worth the money.

Two Boots, 37 Ave. A (☎505-5450). East Village restaurant serving pizzas with a Cajun flavor—crawfish and jalapeno peppers are common toppings. Main dishes, too, follow the same bias, spicy pasta and seafood options mainly. Not at all expensive.

Midtown

America, 9 E. 18th St. (☎505-2110). Enormous restaurant with menu to match. Very yuppie, very New York; have a drink at the bar and watch the scene.

American Festival Café, Rockefeller Plaza, Fifth Ave. at 50th St. (☎246-6699). For the views, at least, there's no better place to sample regional American cooking—everything from Louisiana catfish to Mississippi mud pie. A nice place to warm up after a spin on the skating rink, immediately outside—though it doesn't come at all cheap.

Arriba Arriba, 762 Ninth Ave. at 51st St. (☎489-0810). The less frenetic alternative to *Caramba*.

Blue Moon Café, 150 Eighth Ave. (☎463-0560). Standard Mexican food at moderate prices. Hockey fans may be interested to know the restaurant is owned by the NY Rangers.

Cabana Carioca, 123 W. 45th St. (☎581-8088). Fun, colorfully decorated Brazilian restaurant that's a great place to try out Brazilian specialties, like *fejiada* (black bean and meat stew), washed down with fiery *caipirinhas*. And portions big enough for two make it reasonably inexpensive, too.

Ellen's Stardust Diner, 1377 Sixth Ave. (☎307-7575). Fifties-style restaurant serving traditional American food.

Harvey's Chelsea Restaurant, 108 W. 18th St. (☎243-5644). Long-established but essentially mediocre restaurant that serves better snacks at its congenial bar than it does complete meals.

Joe Allen's, 326 W. 46th St. (☎581-6464). Tried and tested formula of check tablecloths, cosy bar-room feel, and reliable American food.

El Rio Grande, 160 E. 38th St. (☎867-0922). Long-established Murray Hill Tex-Mex place with a gimmick: you can eat Mexican or, if you prefer, Texan, by simply crossing the "border" and walking through the kitchen. Personable and fun—and the margaritas are earth (and brain) shattering.

Speed Limit 55, 154 W. 26th St. (☎645-8476). Merging of American and Japanese cooking, with tempuras and various dishes in teriyaki and soy sauces. Self-consciously modern decor, too, with minimal furnishings, videos, and waiters dressed as NYC cops. From about $8.

Symphony Café, 950 Eighth Ave. (☎397-9595). Situated between Carnegie Hall and Lincoln Center, it's not surprising to find a restaurant with a "symphony" theme. The food is nouvelle Americaine, the surroundings pleasant, and in summer you can sit outside. Moderately priced, too.

Union Square Café, 21 E. 16th St. (☎243-4020). A relatively new addition to the Manhattan quality dining scene, but a successful one, notching one of the city's best reputations for modern American food in no time. Not at all cheap—prices average $100 for two—but the California cuisine, not to mention the stylish, bustling environment, is a treat.

Via Brasil, 34 W. 46th St. (☎997-1158). Excellent, though pricey, Brazilian food. Not much for under $10.

Upper

All State Café, 250 W. 72nd St. (☎874-7883). An interesting mixture of American and French food from $7 to $15 makes this a popular Upper West Side hangout. Seating is limited, and it closes at 11:30pm; get here early to be sure of a table.

Arizona 206, 206 E. 60th St. (☎838-0440). Intriguing southwestern decor and food, though it doesn't come cheap, and the service is erratic. The next-door café section is cheaper, serving essentially the same food in smaller quantities.

Bahama Mama, 2628 Broadway (☎866-7760). Caribbean food in a soulful atmosphere. Fish and beef predominate and there's a wide array of cocktails. Meals run $13–16.

Brother Jimmy's BBQ, 1461 First Ave. (☎545-RIBS). Casual, fun barbecue restaurant whose motto is "Pig Out!." Quite a happening bar scene, too.

La Caridad, 2199 Broadway (☎874-2780). Something of an Upper West Side institution, a tacky little hole-in-the-wall doling out plentiful and cheap Cuban-Chinese food to hungry and (usually) waiting customers. Bring your own beer, and don't expect polite service.

Caridad Restaurant, 4311 Broadway (☎928-4645). Not to be confused with the Upper West Side restaurant of (almost) the same name, this places serves mountains of Dominican food at cheap prices. Try the *mariscos* or seafood, specialty of the house and eaten with lots of *pan y ajo*, thick slices of French bread, broiled with olive oil and plenty of garlic. Be sure to go feeling hungry.

The Ginger Man, 51 W. 64th St. (☎399-2358). The food is fairly middling at this long-time Lincoln Center haunt. But it's a pleasant, active place to eat, and at lunchtime at least you might spot a big name from across the road. Moderately priced.

Los Panchos, 71 W. 71st St. (☎874-7336). Moderate Tex-Mex restaurant serving a good-value weekend brunch. Tables outdoors in summer.

Marvin Gardens, 2274 Broadway (☎799-0578). Standard American fare for $7 up, and a nice bar.

El Pollo, 1746 First Ave. (☎996-7810). Fast food Peruvian-style chicken restaurant, serving rotisserie chicken flavored with a variety of spices to eat in or take out. Delicious—and very cheap.

Popovers, 551 Amsterdam Ave. (☎595-8555). Excellent uptown eatery whose dishes (American/wholefood) come served with a popover—a sort of dyspeptic brioche from the Midwest.

Positively 104th St., 2725 Broadway (☎316-0372). Basic but good American food, with excellent steaks and a friendly atmosphere, make this a good choice for this part of town. Reasonably priced, too.

Sylvia's Restaurant, 328 Lenox Ave. at 125th St. (☎996-0660). Legendary southern soulfood restaurant in Harlem. Go early on Wednesday night and get free tickets for amateur night at the Apollo.

Teacher's, 2271 Broadway (☎362-4900). Pasta and fish for about $6. Nice atmosphere and a useful notice board. Good brunch.

Third World Café, 700 W. 125th St. (☎749-8199). If Paul Simon's *Rhythm of the Saints* were a restaurant, it would be this one—a fantasy jumble of Cajun, Indian, and Caribbean spices. It serves sweet potato fries and black-eyed peas, Brazilian *picadillo*, and southern barbecue, in entrees running about $8 each, to a background plump with the music of Bob Marley and Hugh Masekela. Not the best neighborhood late at night, especially if you're alone, but worth it for the fun atmosphere and fantastic food.

USA Border Café, 2637 Broadway (☎749-8888). A good Tex-Mex menu with meals for $9–13 and regular live music. The going gets lively later on.

Victor's Café, 240 Columbus Ave. (☎595-8599). Cuban food at moderate prices on Columbus's central restaurant strip.

Vince & Eddie's, 70 W. 68th St. (☎721-0068). Slightly pseudo country-style American restaurant serving grub like your grandmother used to cook—hearty, wholesome, and delicious. Moderately priced.

West Side Story, 700 Columbus Ave. (☎749-1900). A wide range of American-style food, and ultra-friendly management, although the white tile booths are hard to cope with. But at $8–12 for an entree, there's little to complain about.

Yellow Rose Café, 450 Amsterdam Ave. (☎595-8760). As the name suggests, meaty Texan food. Burgers, ribs, and steaks from $5–15.

Chinese, Thai, and Vietnamese

Chinese cuisine provides one of the city's best bargains, particularly if you pick up on dim sum and other lunchtime specials. As far as areas go, Chinatown not surprisingly has the highest restaurant concentration, but there's another good contingent in the Upper West Side 90s. More expensively, **Thai** food has become more prevalent of late, the city's latest food fad, and you'll find Thai restaurants springing up all over Manhattan, not to mention the odd **Vietnamese** or **Korean** restaurant.

Lower

Hee Sung Feung ("HSF"), 46 Bowery (☎374-1319). Renowned dim sum restaurant where you choose what you want from a moving cart. An adventure for the uninitiated, though compared to London or Hong Kong the food isn't terrific.

Indochine, 430 Lafayette St. (☎505-5111). Not the kind of place you go to save money, more to lap up the elegant surroundings and authentic Vietnamese food ... and maybe spot a minor celebrity or two.

Mon Bo, 65 Mott St. (☎964-6480). Bright cheerful Cantonese serving incapacitating rice and noodle dishes for around $5, more exotic fare for just a little more.

New Lin Heong, 69 Bayard St. (☎233-0485). *Mon Bo*'s sister restaurant—and similarly substantial.

Nice Restaurant, 35 E. Broadway (☎406-9776). Vast restaurant especially good for dim sum. Usually crowded, particularly on Sundays.

Nom-Wah, 13 Doyers St. (☎962-6047). Reliable Cantonese restaurant, good for dim sum.

Phoenix Garden, 46 Bowery Arcade (☎233-6017). Hidden from the tourists but well known to New Yorkers for the quality and authenticity of its (Cantonese) food. Great value.

Pongsri, 106 Bayard St. (☎349-3132). Thai restaurant that's a popular lunchtime choice with local businesspeople for its extensive and good-value lunch menu—rice and noodle combos a specialty. A massive menu in the evenings, and Thai beer. A second branch at 244 W. 48th St. (☎582-3392).

Say Eng Look, 5 E. Broadway (☎732-0796). Good value Shanghai restaurant that'll tailor your meal to fit your budget. Just tell them how much you can afford and they'll do the rest. They rarely miss.

Siam Square, 92 Second Ave. (☎505-1240). Small restaurant serving excellent Thai food for very reasonable prices. Fine service, tacky decor.

Silver Palace, 50 Bowery (☎964-1204). Another basically dim sum restaurant.

Sun Say Gay, 220 Canal St. (☎964-7256). An obvious Chinatown lunchtime choice, serving up huge plates of meat and rice for around $3.

Thai House Café, 151 Hudson St. (☎334-1085). Small, friendly TriBeCa Thai restaurant, popular for its well-priced and authentic food. Beer and wine only.

Toons, 417 Bleecker St. (☎924-6420). Higher prices than the *Thai House Café*, but with a lower-lit, more intimate atmosphere. A Thai community favorite.

Vegetarian Paradise, 48 Bowery (☎571-1535). Delicious vegetarian Chinese food at low prices. $5 buys enough for two.

Wo Hop, 17 Mott St. (☎962-8617). Noodle shop used by local Chinese. Inexpensive.

Wong Kee, 113 & 117 Mott St. (☎226-9018/966-1160). Good cheap, reliable Cantonese.

Wonton Garden, 52 Mott St. (☎966-4886). Chinatown's cheapest noodles. Good for a quick lunch stopover.

Midtown

Fortune Garden, 209 E. 49th St. (☎753-0101). Unusual combination of Chinese food and live jazz, though you come more for the music and ambience than the food, which isn't cheap.

Siam Inn, 916 Eighth Ave. (☎489-5237). Unpretentious restaurant serving averagely priced Thai fare. Try the masaman curry.

Tina, 249 Park Ave. South (☎477-1761). Good Chinese in an area not known for its Chinese restaurants.

Upper

Empire Szechuan, 2581 Broadway (☎666-0555); 193 Columbus Ave. (☎496-8778). Szechuan food from $6.

Hunan Balcony, 2596 Broadway (☎865-0400). Hunan-style food from $6.

Ollie's, 2315 Broadway (☎362-3712); 2957 Broadway (☎932-3300). Downscale Upper West Side Chinese café that serves marvelous noodles. Not, however, a place to hang about.

Pig Heaven, 1540 Second Ave. (☎744-4333). Good value Chinese restaurant decorated with images of pigs. Not surprisingly, the accent is on pork.

Sala Thai, 1718 Second Ave. (☎410-5557). Restaurant serving lots of hot and spicy Thai food for under $15 a head.

French, Spanish, and Greek

French restaurants tend to trade on their names in New York: those that are good know it and make you pay accordingly, although a handful have slipped through with value-for-money intact. Downtown, in Greenwich Village especially, you'll find a number of enjoyable **Spanish** and **Greek** restaurants, not too expensive most of them—though the best place in the city for Greek food is Astoria out in Queens (see the Outer Boroughs section).

Lower

Café Español, 172 Bleecker St. (☎353-2317). Hole-in-the-wall restaurant serving sumptuous Spanish fare for $10–15 a plate. Try the *Mariscada*—a filling seafood dish that can easily feed two.

Chez Brigitte, 77 Greenwich Ave. (☎929-6736). Tiny restaurant that fits only eleven, but with an all-day roast meat dinner for under $10 as well as other bargains from a simple menu.

Delphi, 109 West Broadway (☎227-6322). Accommodating Greek restaurant with good menu, great portions and unbeatable prices. The antipasti and fish are excellent value at $5–10 or there's kebabs and the like from $2.50. Best Manhattan choice for bargain Greek eating.

El Faro, 823 Greenwich St. (☎929-8210). A dark, lively restaurant, where garlic smells from the kitchen and the look of the food at the next table (it's that cramped!) are guaranteed to stir any appetite. You can't go wrong with the paella or the seafood in green sauce. Moderate prices, too, and you can share most main dishes.

Florent, 69 Gansevoort St. (☎989-5779). Ultra-fashionable bistro on the edge of the meat-packing district that serves good French food, either a la carte or from a *prix fixe* menu ($16.95, $14.95 before 7:30pm). Coffee shop decor; excellent food and decent service; always busy. They also serve weekend brunch.

La Luncheonette, 130 Tenth Ave. (☎675-0342). Parisian-style bistro serving good quality French food, though in an unfortunately downbeat and out-of-the-way location. Don't go too late at night.

Montrachet, 239 W. Broadway (☎219-2777). Nouvelle cuisine food in a relaxed unpretentious setting. A good choice for a treat.

Odeon, 145 W. Broadway (☎233-0507). Very long-established restaurant serving Mediterranean-style food to a still largely chic clientele. Entrees go for around $15, and on the whole are well worth it.

Provence, 38 Macdougal St. (☎475-7500). Very popular SoHo bistro that serves excellent food but—at around $16 up for an entree—ain't that cheap. A nice place for a special occasion, though, with a lovely airy eating area, and a garden.

RESTAURANTS WITH OUTSIDE SEATING

The following is just a brief rundown of restaurants which regularly have outside seating in summer. Many Manhattan restaurants, especially in the Village and on the Upper East and West Sides, put at least a few tables out on the sidewalk when the weather gets warm.

American Festival Café, Rockefeller Plaza, Fifth Ave. at 50th St.

Boathouse Café, Central Park.

Boostan, 85 Macdougal St.

Caffé Reggio, 119 Macdougal St.

The Coffeeshop, 29 Union Square West.

Empire Diner, 210 Tenth Ave.

Fuddrucker's, 97 Seventh Ave. South.

103 2nd, 103 Second Ave.

Pete's Tavern, 302 Bleecker St.

Poiret, 474 Columbus Ave.

Provence, 38 Macdougal St.

The Saloon, 1920 Broadway.

Spring Street Natural Restaurant, 62 Spring St.

Symphony Café, 950 Eighth Ave.

White Horse Tavern, 567 Hudson St.

Quatorze, 240 W. 14th St. (☎206-7006). Good quality French restaurant at very reasonable prices.

Rio Mar, 7 Ninth Ave. (☎243-9015). A welcoming Spanish restaurant that serves low-priced and authentic food, albeit in a fairly downbeat setting. Recommended.

Spain, 113 W. 13th St. (☎929-9580). Budget prices and large portions are the prime attractions of this cosy Spanish restaurant. Order the paella and split it with a friend.

Au Troquet, 328 W. 12th St. (☎924-3413). Romantic Village haunt that has an authentic Parisian feel. Good food, moderately priced.

Midtown

The Ballroom, 253 W. 28th St. (☎244-3005). Long-established Chelsea tapas bar that's good both for snacks and for a full feed. Also one of the city's classiest cabaret and comedy spots; see Chapter Ten, "The Performing Arts and Film."

Bellevue, 496 Ninth Ave. (☎967-7850). French bistro with upscale coffee shop decor and decent food. The neighborhood, however, isn't that great—don't go too late.

Brasserie, 100 E. 53rd St. (☎751-4840). Always more highly regarded for its 24-hour opening policy than its food, and perhaps rightly so, although its hearty French staples have improved of late, if the atmosphere hasn't.

Café Un, Deux, Trois, 123 W. 44th St. (☎354-4148). French brasserie-style restaurant close to Times Square serving fair-to-middling food. Crayons for table-top doodling while you wait for your order. $10–20.

Chantal Café, 257 W. 55th St. (☎246-7076). Homey little bistro.

Hourglass Tavern, 373 W. 46th St. (☎265-2060). Tiny midtown French restaurant—around eight tables in all—which serves an excellent value two-course *prix fixe* menu for just $11.50. Choose between two hors d'oeuvres and half a dozen or so entrees—a small range that guarantees good cooking. The gimmick is the hourglass above each table, the emptying of which means you're supposed to leave and make way for someone else; in reality they seem to last more than an hour, and they only enforce it if there's a line.

La Bonne Soupe, 48 W. 55th St. (☎586-7650). Traditional French food at reasonable prices. Steaks, omelettes, snails, and fondues from $6.

La Fondue, 43 W. 55th St. (☎581-0820). Fondues for under $10.

Man Ray, 169 Eighth Ave. (☎627-4220). Affordably priced French food in a sleek setting.

Periyali, 35 W. 20th St. (☎463-7890). Greek food that's a notch above the average in a cheerful Mediterranean setting.

Prix-Fixe, 18 W. 18th St. (☎675-6777). A relative newcomer to the New York restaurant scene, but another that has fast established a reputation for good food. Its *prix fixe* menu for just over $20 a head is excellent value.

Les Sans-Culottes, 1085 Second Ave. (☎838-6660). Wonderful food served in massive portions. One of the best deals in town.

West Bank Café, 407 W. 42nd St., Manhattan Plaza (☎695-6909). Some French, some American, all delicious and not as expensive as you'd think—$7 and up.

Upper

Alcala, 349 Amsterdam Ave. (☎769-9600). Upper West Side Spanish bar-restaurant where you can either enjoy the terrific tapas and wine at the bar or indulge on the more pricey restaurant.

Le Boeuf à la Mode, 539 E. 81st St. (☎249-1473). Family run neighborhood spot that boasts good, homestyle cooking in an authentically handsome Parisian atmosphere. Expensive, though.

La Boite en Bois, 75 W. 68th St. (☎874-2705). Rustic, moderately priced Lincoln Center bistro that has good country French food.

Café San Martin, 1458 First Ave. (☎288-0470). One of the city's best Spanish restaurants at very affordable prices.

Café Luxembourg, 200 W. 70th St. (☎873-7411). Trendy Lincoln Center area bistro that packs in (literally, some say) a self-consciously hip crowd to enjoy its first-rate contemporary French food. Not too pricey—two people can eat for $50 or so.

Malaga, 406 E. 73rd St. (☎737-7659). Intimate Spanish restaurant frequented by locals. Good, wholesome food at decent prices.

Mme. Romaine de Lyon, 29 E. 61st St. (☎758-2422). The best place for omelettes: they've got 550 at lunch and dinner features an expanded non-omelette menu.

Poiret, 474 Columbus Ave. (☎724-6880). A trendy and fun—and reasonably inexpensive—French bistro with excellent food and outside seating in summer. A nice place for brunch, too.

Le Refuge, 166 E. 82nd St. (☎661-4505). Intimate and deliberately romantic old-style French restaurant situated in an old city brownstone. Expensive; save for special occasions.

Le Steak, 1069 Second Ave. (☎421-9072). Choose between steak-frites or swordfish-frites at this Upper East Side bistro—beautifully cooked and moderately priced. Dinner only.

Voulez Vous, 1462 First Ave. (☎249-1776). Decently priced Upper East Side French bistro.

Indian, Middle Eastern, and African

The two best places to look for **Indian** food in New York are in Midtown Manhattan, along Lexington Avenue between 28th and 30th streets, and (much cheaper) in the East Village, on the block-long stretch of 6th Street between First and Second avenues—the latter one of the city's best budget eating places. Other than a handful of places serving pitta-related snacks, **Middle Eastern** food is rather thinner on the ground in Manhattan, though budget **African** restaurants are becoming increasingly common.

Lower

Abyssinia, 35 Grand St. (☎226-5959). Ethiopian restaurant, ethnically furnished and popular with a youthful crowd. A good array of vegetarian dishes.

Ghandhi, 345 E. 6th St. (☎614-9718). One of the best and least expensive of the E. 6th Street Indian restaurants.

Khyber Pass, 34 St. Mark's Place (☎473-0989). Afghan food, which if you're unfamiliar is filling and has plenty to offer vegetarians (pulses, rice, eggplant are frequent ingredients). Excellent value for around $7. No liquor license.

Mamun's, 119 Macdougal St. (☎674-9246). Inexpensive snack bar and takeout serving felafel, kebabs, and suchlike.

Mitali, 334 E. 6th St. (☎533-2508). More expensive than the other 6th Street Indians, but well worth it, and still at half the price of spots farther uptown. Another branch across town, **Mitali West**, at 296 Bleecker St. (☎989-1367).

Midtown

Afghan Kebab, 764 Ninth Ave. (☎307-1612). A casual neighborhood restaurant with little decor and few tables, but excellent and inexpensive chicken, lamb, and beef kebabs. Bring your own beer or wine. Another branch across the street on the corner of Ninth and 50th St.

Annapurna, 108 Lexington Ave. (☎679-1284). Good value northern Indian restaurant.

Curry in a Hurry, 130 E. 29th St. (☎889-1159). Fast and inexpensive—eat for around $5.

Darbar, 432 W. 56th St. (☎432-7227). One of the best and most reasonable Indian restaurants in town.

Madras Palace, 104 Lexington Ave. (☎532-3314). One of few places serving South Indian cuisine. Around $10.

Shaheen, 99 Lexington Ave. (☎683-2139). Good, caféteria-style meals for around $5.

Upper

Asmara, 951 Amsterdam Ave. (☎749-9614). African restaurant serving a variety of curried meat dishes, along with a few vegetarian alternatives, eaten with chapti-like *injera* bread. Very cheap, and, although rather gloomy, the neighborhood is quite safe.

At Our Place, 2485 Broadway (☎864-1410). Middle Eastern cuisine at its best and least expensive, and including an extensive vegetarian menu. Most dishes around the $6 mark.

Blue Nile, 103 W. 77th St. (☎580-3232). Ethiopian restaurant, where the food is served on a communal tray at low tables. Eat with your fingers using soft, flat *injera* bread. The food consists of rich meat stews and lentil and vegetable concoctions washed down with sharp African beer. Entrees priced around $10.

Istanbul Cuisine, 303 E. 80th St. (☎744-6903). Basic-style restaurant where you can eat home-style Turkish food at what must be close to Turkish prices. Crowded, but great value.

Mughlai, 320 Columbus Ave. (☎724-6363). Uptown, upscale Indian with prices about the going rate for this strip—$10–15.

Uskudar, 1405 Second Ave. (☎988-2641). Authentic Turkish cuisine at a rather spartan Upper East Side joint. Great prices—reckon on $25 or so for two.

Zula, 1260 Amsterdam Ave. (☎663-1670). High quality and inexpensive ($7 up) Ethiopian food that's popular with the folk from Columbia. Spicy chicken, beef, and lamb dishes mainly, though a few veggie plates, too.

Italian ... and pizzas

Little Italy is the most obvious location for **Italian** food, though much of the area is aimed at tourists these days and consequently can be pricey: pick with care. For the real thing it's again best to head out to the Outer Boroughs—Belmont in the Bronx or Carroll Gardens in Brooklyn—or content yourself with pizza, either from *Ray's* (or a similar snack joint), or a regular sit-down restaurant.

Everywhere

Ray's Pizza. The city's most ubiquitous pizza chain, with branches all over Midtown (and other districts) Manhattan. Reckon on a dollar or so for a slice, $8 and up for the whole thing.

Lower

Arturo's Pizza, 106 W. Houston St. (☎475-9828). Excellent entrees around $10, coal-oven pizzas big enough to share for a little less. While-you-eat entertainment includes live music. Convivial, if not the cheapest feed in town.

La Boheme, 24 Minetta Lane (☎473-6447). Bright and amiable, if cramped, restaurant in the heart of the Village with pasta, pizza, and meat and fish dishes for $12–15. Good food, and nice in the summer when they open the big French doors to the street.

Cent' Anni, 50 Carmine St. (☎989-9494). Small Village restaurant serving delicious, and not overpriced, Florentine food.

Cucina della Fontana, 368 Bleecker St. (☎242-0636). From the outside this place looks like a normal bar, but out the back there's a plant-filled atrium where you can eat fine Italian food. Mussels, fish, pasta all excellent.

Cucina di Pesce, 87 E. 4th St. (☎260-6800). Excellent Italian seafood restaurant.

Cucina Stagionale, 275 Bleecker St. (☎924-2707). Enormously popular restaurant, sister to *Cucina di Pesce*, with most dishes at around $6. Expect to wait in line, and bring your own wine—there's no license.

Il Fornaio, 132a Mulberry St. (☎226-8306). Cheerful, bright tiled Italian restaurant with good lunch deals—fine calzone and pizza for $4. Affordable and decent southern Italian cooking, too—Italian stews and the like.

Grotta Azzurra, 387 Broome St. (☎925-8784). Busy Little Italy institution that serves substantial homecooked southern Italian food.

John's Pizzeria, 278 Bleecker St. (☎243-1680). No slices, no takeouts, but one of the city's best (thin crust) pizzas. Be prepared to stand in line. Another uptown branch at 408 E. 64th St. (☎935-2895).

La Luna, 112 Mulberry St. (☎226-8657). Surrounded by the valet-parked limos and eating palaces of Little Italy, this must be one of the city's cheapest Italian restaurants: honest and unassuming in every way, from the vast peasant portions of pasta they serve to the gruff Brooklyn manner of the waiters and the fact that you have to walk through the kitchen to sit down. If you like Italian food and are budgeting, a must.

La Mela, 167 Mulberry St. (☎431-9433). Old-established Little Italy restaurant serving food in huge portions.

Mezzogiorno, 195 Spring St. (☎334-2112). Bright, trendy SoHo Italian restaurant that's as much a place to people-watch as eat. A little overpriced, but a good and inventive menu, including excellent pizzas for around $12 (in the evening only available after 9pm), great salads and carpaccio—thinly sliced raw beef served in various ways. Sister restaurant is *Mezzaluna*—see below.

Minetta Tavern, 113 Macdougal St. (☎475-3850). One of the oldest bars in New York, decorated with murals showing Greenwich Village as it was in the 1930s, and with a restaurant out back turning out Italian food that's worth the extra cost

Puglia, 189 Hester St. (☎226-8912). One of Little Italy's more affordable restaurants, where they cut costs and sharpen the atmosphere by sitting everyone at the same long trestle tables. Consistently good food, consumed loudly and raucously.

Pizza Piazza, Broadway at W. 10th St. (☎505-0977). Generously filled deep pan pizzas in various sizes on wholewheat crusts. Good desserts, too.

Pizzeria Uno, 391 Sixth Ave. (☎242-5230). Solid value pizzas but again frequent lines. It's a good idea to book. Also at 432 Columbus Ave. (☎595-4700).

Ray's Pizza, 465 Sixth Ave. (☎243-2253). Long-time rival to *John's*, and not to be confused with the chain you see all over the city. Thick crusts.

Midtown

Frank's, 431 W. 14th St. (☎243-1349). Long-established Italian-American restaurant with pasta dishes from $5 up.

Le Madri, 168 W. 18th St. (☎727-8022). Named after the Italian "mothers" who work in the kitchen, this Tuscan restaurant has taken its place among the city's very best Italians since its opening in 1989. On the pricey side, but worth it. Try and get a table in the patio out back—if you can get one at all.

Pasta Presto, 613 Second Ave. (☎889-4131). Fast-paced inexpensive pasta joint. Other branches at 93 Macdougal St. (☎260-5679); 37 Barrow St. (☎691-0480); 959 Second Ave. (☎754-4880).

Prego, 1365 Sixth Ave. (☎307-5775). Pasta joint with a wide choice of generously ladled dishes for about $7 but an off-puttingly bathroom-like interior. Not for the hungover—and no liquor license either. Fill up and move on.

Rocky Lee, 987 Second Ave. (☎753-4858). Not the most amiable environment, but the thin crust pizzas here get rave reviews.

Supreme Macaroni Co., 511 Ninth Ave. (☎502-4842). A pasta shop with a small restaurant attached.

Trattoria, Pan Am Building, 200 Park Ave. (☎661-3090). Slightly characterless midtown Italian whose rather average food is best appreciated at lunchtime or during its regular evening happy hour.

Trattoria dell'Arte, 900 Seventh Ave. (☎245-9800). One of the nicest new restaurants to open in this part of Manhattan for years, with a gorgeous airy interior, excellent service, and marvelous food. Great, wafer thin crispy pizzas, decent and imaginative pasta dishes for around $15, and a mouth-watering antipasto bar—all eagerly patronized by an elegant out-to-be-seen crowd. Book.

Upper

Carino, 1710 Second Ave. (☎860-0566). Family-run Upper East Side Italian, with low prices, friendly service, and good food. Two can eat for under $25.

Carmine's, 2450 Broadway (☎362-2200). Large Upper West Side restaurant that has (justifiably) made something of a name for itself over the past year or so for its combination of decent (and decently priced) home-style Southern Italian food, in mountainous portions (be careful not to over-order), and the noisy, convivial atmosphere it's served in. If you're in a group of six or more you can book; otherwise be prepared to stand in line for at least thirty minutes—it's very popular.

Contrapunto, 200 E. 60th St. (☎751-8616). More than twenty fresh pastas daily at this friendly, shopping neighborhood restaurant. Reasonably priced as well.

Corrado, 1373 Sixth Ave. (☎333-3133). Northern Italian eatery with a breezy decor and great pasta. Moderately priced.

Ecco-la, 1660 Third Ave. (☎860-5609). Unique pasta combinations at very moderate prices make this place one of the Upper East Side's most popular Italians. If you don't mind waiting, though, a real find.

Ernie's, 2150 Broadway (☎496-1588). Casual, extra-large Upper West Side Italian, serving staple, affordable Italian food.

Genoa, 271 Amsterdam Ave. (☎787-1094). Very small, very authentic Italian restaurant. Cheap, dark, and always crowded. Expect to wait for a table.

Mezzaluna, 1295 Third Ave. (☎535-9600). Sister restaurant to the SoHo eatery, *Mezzogiorno*, this claims to be the place that introduced *carpaccio* to Manhattan. Whatever the truth of that, the food here is fine (great pizzas, inventive pastas), though the environment doesn't really justify the moderate-to-high prices.

Perretti, 270 Columbus Ave. (☎362-3939). Neighborhood Italian with below average prices.

Presto, 2770 Broadway (☎222-1760). An inexpensive Italian that's not bad for its pasta dishes—huge platefuls for around $9.

Café Trevi, 1570 First Ave. (☎249-0040). Casual Italian restaurant serving good food that doesn't cost the earth.

Il Vagabondo, 351 E. 62nd St. (☎832-9221). Southern Italian food in a casual setting that includes the restaurant's own *bocci* court.

V&T Pizzeria, 1024 Amsterdam Ave. (☎663-1708). Check-tableclothed pizzeria near Columbia that draws a predictably college-age crowd. Good, though, and very inexpensive.

Via Via, 1294 Third Ave. (☎535-9600). Popular Upper East Side Italian, with a wide choice of brick oven pizzas, decent stand-by pasta dishes, and carpaccio. A downtown branch at 560 Third Ave. (☎573-6093).

Vinnie's Pizza, 285 Amsterdam Ave. (☎874-4332). Some say the best, cheesiest pizzas on the Upper West Side. Cheap, too.

Japanese

When sushi arrived on the scene a few years back, **Japanese** food took off in a big way, and it's still one of the city's most popular cuisines. It tends to be expensive, however, many of the restaurants in the pricier reaches of Midtown Manhattan. But if you know where to go it is possible to experiment reasonably cheaply.

Everywhere

Dosanko. Chain of fast-food restaurants serving Japanese food at prices that everyone can afford. The food isn't the best in the city, and the surroundings are pure McDonald's, but there's no better way to try Japanese food if you're on a shoestring.

Lower

Chiaki, 396 Third Ave. (☎696-4920). New wave Japanese in art deco surroundings.

Dojo, 24 St. Mark's Place (☎674-9821). Popular East Village hangout, with reasonably priced vegetarian and Japanese food in a brash, fun environment. One of the best value restaurants in the city, and certainly one of the cheapest Japanese menus you'll find.

Japonica, 90 University Place (☎243-7752). Some of the freshest sushi in the city, at some of the most reasonable prices. Saturday and Sunday brunch deals are excellent—big plates of sushi or sahimi (teriaki, too), with salad and beer or plum wine for around $12 a head. Be prepared to stand in line after 7pm.

Midtown

Genroku Sushi, 365 Fifth Ave. (☎947-7940). Sushi and other Japanese-Chinese food. You pick what you fancy off a moving conveyor belt.

Hatsuhana, 17 E. 48th St. (☎355-3345); 237 Park Ave. (☎661-3400). Every sushi lover's favorite sushi restaurant, now with two branches. Not at all cheap.

Yoshi, 9 E. 17th St. (☎989-2938). Reasonably cheap Japanese restaurant. Good tempura and huge bottles of Sapporo.

Upper

Fujiama Mama, 467 Columbus Ave. (☎769-1144). The West Side's best—and most boisterous—sushi bar, with hi-tech decor and loud music.

Lenge, 200 Columbus Ave. (☎799-9188). Decent Japanese restaurant, averagely priced.

Rikyu, 210 Columbus Ave. (☎799-7847). A wide selection of Japanese food, including sushi made to order. Inexpensive lunches and earlybird specials make this place a bargain.

Sakura, 2298 Broadway (☎769-1003). Another highly elegant sushi bar.

Jewish, East European, and German

The city's large **Jewish** community, most of whom originated in Eastern Europe, means that kosher restaurants (serving dairy and non-dairy menu) are found all over town, with Manhattan's highest concentration on the Lower East Side. They cover all price ranges, but usually represent good, and very filling, value—as do the various and consistently delicious **Polish**, **Hungarian**, and other **Central European** restaurants.

Lower

Bernstein-on-Essex, 135 Essex St. (☎473-3900). Small Jewish restaurant serving orthodox menu and (believe it or not) kosher-Chinese food.

Christine's, 208 First Ave. (☎505-0376). Long-standing Polish coffee shop, one of several such places in the area—great soups, blintzes, and pirogi.

Grand Dairy Restaurant, 341 Grand St. (☎673-1904). Unpretentious restaurant with well-priced kosher food.

Katz's Deli, 205 E. Houston St. (☎254-2246). Cafeteria-style or sit down and be served. The pastrami or corned beef sandwiches, doused with mustard and with a pile of pickles on the side, should keep you going for about a week.

Kiev, 117 Second Ave. (☎674-4040). Eastern European dishes and burgers. Great and affordable food at any time of the day or night.

Odessa, 117 Ave. A at Tompkins Square (☎473-8916). The scramble for a seat may put you off, but the food here—a filling array of dishes from the Caucasus— and prices (under $5 for a meal) are impressive. Coffee shop decor, loud, plastic, and brightly lit—not the sort of place to chew the fat.

Ratner's, 138 Delancey St. (☎677-5588). Massive dairy restaurant, crowded at all times of the day. High on atmosphere though on the pricey side. Recently re-opened after renovation.

Sammy's Roumanian Restaurant, 157 Chrystie St. (☎673-0330). Surrounded by the boarded-up storefronts of Chrystie Street, *Sammy's* is some indication of just how far the Upper East Side is swayed by a restaurant's reputation. The food, if you've $25 or so to burn for a full meal, is undeniably a treat, though most people come for the raucous live music.

Triplet's Roumanian, 11–17 Grand St. (☎925-9303). Noisy neighborhood restaurant that's like crashing a loud Jewish wedding. A guaranteed blast.

Ukrainian Restaurant, 140 Second Ave. (☎529-5024). An East Village institution, still serving staggering portions of Slav fare for under $10. Very popular, though large enough to cope.

Veselka, 144 Second Ave. (☎228-9682). Ukrainian-Polish eatery that offers fine homemade borscht for $3.

Yonah Schimmel's, 137 E. Houston St. (☎477-2858). Knishes, baked on the premises, and some wonderful bagel. Unpretentious and patronized by a mixture of wrinkled old men wisecracking in Yiddish and—on Sundays especially—young uptowners slumming it while they wade through the *Sunday Times*.

Midtown

Grigori's Gourmet à la Russe, 315 W. 54th St. (☎246-6341). Russian deli that's half takeout, half small café, open for lunch or an early dinner. Closed by 7pm.

Lox Around the Clock, 676 Sixth Ave. (☎691-3535). Blintzes, bagel, and, of course, lox, in a trendy, noisy environment. Good for brunch. Open 24 hours.

Upper

Café Geiger, 208 E. 86th St. (☎734-4428). Famed German eatery in Yorkville. Around $7–14.

Fine & Schapiro, 138 W. 72nd St. (☎877-2721). Long-established Jewish deli that's open for lunch and dinner and serves delicious old-fashioned kosher fare— an experience that's getting harder to find in New York. See "Shops and Markets."

Ideal Restaurant, 238 E. 86th St. (☎535-0950). The genuine Germanic item: a small luncheonette serving wursts, sauerkraut, and suchlike in huge portions for paltry prices.

Kleine Konditorei, 234 E. 86th St. (☎737-7130). German patisserie and restaurant serving all manner of solid Teutonic food.

Mocca Hungarian, 1588 Second Ave. (☎734-6470). Homey restaurant serving hearty portions of Hungarian comfort food—schnitzel, goulash, and chicken paprikash, among others. Moderately priced, but be sure to come hungry.

Fish and seafood

Budget **fish restaurants** are a rarity in the city, sepcially since the area around the downtown fish market was dolled up into the South Street Seaport. However, fish and particularly seafood remain something New York does extremely well, and a couple of the places listed below are among its most unmissable culinary treats—though, with a couple of notable exceptions, they rarely come at all cheap.

Lower

Jeremy's Alehouse, 254 Front St. (☎964-3537). Once a waterside sleaze bar in the shadow of the Brooklyn Bridge, *Jeremy's* fortunes changed with the development of the nearby South Street Seaport. However, it still serves well-priced pint mugs of beer and excellent fish fresh from the adjacent Fulton St. market, as well as burgers. Expect to spend $10 in total.

Jane Street Seafood Café, 31 Eighth Ave. (☎242-9237). A cosy New England-style seafood restaurant with moderate prices and friendly service. Something of a neighborhood favorite.

Pier Nine, 215 Second Ave. (☎673-9263). Good, reasonably priced fish and shellfish dishes, many with an oriental flavor.

Umberto's Clam House, 129 Mulberry St. (☎431-7545). As renowned for its role as famous Mafia execution spot as for the food. Cooking, though, is good— seafood, hot, medium, or mild, and always delicious. See Chapter One, "Lower Manhattan," for more.

Vincent's Clam Bar, 119 Mott St. (☎226-8133). Little Italy restaurant serving cheap seafood dishes—clams, mussels, and squid.

Midtown

Goldwater's, 988 Second Ave. (☎888-2122). Fish dishes in huge portions for $10–15 a head.

Hobeau's, 882 First Ave. (☎421-2888). Excellent fresh fish and seafood for very reasonable prices—$8 and up.

Oyster Bar, Grand Central Terminal (☎490-6650). Wonderfully atmospheric old place, down in the vaulted dungeons of Grand Central, where midtown office workers stop for lunch. Fish, seafood, and of course oysters, though none of it exactly budget rated—reckon on $20 or more. If you're hard up, settle for the clam chowder with bread—delicious, ample, and around $3—or great creamy bowls of pan roasted oysters or clams for around $10.

Upper

Coastal, 300 Amsterdam Ave. (☎769-3988). Fresh fish and a yuppie to-the-max crowd eating it. Good and moderately priced nonetheless. Dinner only.

Dock's Oyster Bar, 2427 Broadway (☎724-5588); 633 Third Ave. (☎986-8080). Some of the freshest seafood in town at these popular uptown restaurants. The Upper West Side is the original and tends to have the homier atmosphere—though both can be noisy.

Squid Roe, 300 E. 77th St. (☎249-4666). Fine fresh fish for moderate prices make this a good uptown alternative.

Vegetarian and wholefood

Surprisingly, exclusively **vegetarian** restaurants are a rarity in New York, although most places serve fish and poultry along with meatless dishes, and unless you're in a real carnivore's haven it's unusual to find a menu that doesn't have something completely meat-free.

Lower

Anjelica Kitchen, 300 E. 12th St. (☎228-2909). Good quality vegetarian with various daily specials. Cheap, too. Patronized by an artistic and fashion crowd.

Boostan, 85 Macdougal St. (☎533-9561). Intimate Village vegetarian: good food, and you can take your own booze. Inexpensive.

Eva's, 11 W. 8th St. (☎677-3496). Healthy food in a coffee shop setting. Nice grub, speedily served, and very cheap.

Spring Street Natural Restaurant, 62 Spring St. (☎966-0290). Pricier and not wholly vegetarian but very good. $9 and up.

Vegetarians' Paradise, 48 Bowery (☎571-1535). East Village vegetarian Chinese—pricier than ordinary downtown Chinese restaurants but still pretty reasonable. Another location at 144 W. 4th St. (☎260-7049), near Washington Square.

Whole Wheat 'n' Wild Berries, 57 W. 10th St. (☎677-3410). Gourmet health-food and vegetarian specials, including fresh fish, pasta dishes, salads, and home-made soups.

Midtown

Au Natural, 1043 Second Ave. (☎832-2922). Not strictly vegetarian but plentiful portions of healthful food.

Everything Yoghurt, 954 Third Ave. (☎688-5757). Much as the name suggests, and with branches at 11 Fulton St. and 1 Herald Square.

The Great American Health Bar, 35 W. 57th St. (☎355-5177); 15 E. 40th St. (☎532-3232); 2 Park Ave. (☎685-7117); 55 John St. (☎227-6100). This Manhattan chain comes well praised, but in reality the food can be rather bland and uninviting. Committed veggies only.

Health Pub, 371 Second Ave. (☎529-9200). Vegetarian restaurant in light, airy café setting. Not especially cheap, but the food will appeal to veggies and meat-eaters alike.

Tibetan Kitchen, 444 Third Ave. (☎679-6286). Vegetarian food from the Himalayas—at just $3 up. Bring your own drink. Closed Sundays.

Upper

Amy's, 2888 Broadway (☎666-1100). Healthful fast food: veggie burgers, quiches, and pitta sandwiches.

Greener Pastures, 119 E. 60th St. (☎832-3212). Kosher healthy food.

Living Springs, 116 E. 60th St. (☎319-7850). All-you-can-eat lunch buffet for $7. Vegetarian entrees, salads, wholegrains, steamed vegetables, and fruit. Takeout too.

Zucchini, 1336 First Ave. (☎249-0559). Reliable and healthy vegetarian restaurant.

Expense account

Should you win the lottery or have rich relatives, New York has some superb restaurants to choose from, most of them serving **French-tinged** American food or **nouvelle cuisine**. Go expecting to pay anywhere from $75 a head, dress up, and phone first.

Aquavit, 13 W. 54th St. (☎307-7311). Superb Scandinavian food—pickled herring, salmon, even reindeer—in a lovely atrium restaurant. A real treat.

Le Bernadin, 155 W. 51st St. (☎489-1515). Renowned as perhaps the best place in New York to eat fish, for which the chef has received rave reviews. However, to enjoy both that and the clubby teak decor of this place you have to reserve months in advance. And it's one of the city's most expensive restaurants, of any kind. Not for the dilettante eater.

Le Cirque, 58 E. 65th St. (☎794-9292). This place is widely thought of as the city's top-rated restaurant. Very orchestrated, *very* expensive, and honored by such names as Liza Minelli, Richard Nixon, and Ronald Reagan. Not for the likes of us.

Elaine's, 1703 Second Ave. (☎534-8103). Remember the opening shots of Woody Allen's *Manhattan*? That was Elaine's, and today her restaurant is still something of a favorite with New York celebrities—though it's hard to see why. If you want to star-gaze there's no better place to come; if you're hungry or watching the pennies, go somewhere else.

Four Seasons, 99 E. 52nd St. (☎754-9494). Housed in Mies van der Rohe's Seagram Building, this is one of the city's most noted restaurants, not least for the decor, which includes murals by Picasso, sculptures by Richard Lippold, and interior design by Philip Johnson. The food isn't at all bad either, and there's a relatively inexpensive pre-theater menu—around $40—if you want to try it.

RESTAURANTS WITH VIEWS

This is a brief rundown of—mainly Manhattan—restaurants that draw many people just for their views or location. Some of the restaurants are covered in more detail in other sections (primarily "Expense account"); where they're not, it's worth bearing in mind that the quality of the views will almost invariably be reflected in the size of your bill.

Marriot Marquis, 1535 Broadway (☎398-1900).

Nirvana, 30 Central Park South, 15th floor (☎486-5700).

The Rainbow Room, RCA Building, 65th floor (☎632-5100).

River Café, 1 Water St., Brooklyn (☎718/522-5200).

Tavern on the Green, Central Park West and 67th St. (☎873-3200).

Top of the Sixes, 666 Fifth Ave., 39th floor (☎757-6662).

The Water Club, 500 E. 30th St. (☎683-3333).

Windows on the World (and City Lights Bar), 1 World Trade Center, 107th floor (☎938-1111).

World Yacht Cruises, Pier 62, W. 23rd St. (☎929-7090).

Gotham Bar & Grill, 12 E. 12th St. (☎620-4020). This restaurant serves marvelous American fare in an airy, trendy setting. Generally reckoned to be one of the city's truly best restaurants; and it's at least worth a drink in the bar to see the beautiful people drift in.

Lutece, 249 E. 50th St. (☎752-2225). Once rated as the best restaurant in the country, and still well up there with the best of the places that New Yorkers (those that can afford it) will kill to get a table at. Again, big bucks and best dress.

The Quilted Giraffe, 955 Second Ave. (☎593-1221). Nouvelle cuisine at astronomical prices: don't leave home without your credit card, and, if you're a man, a tie.

The Rainbow Room, RCA Building, 65th floor (☎632-5100). The city's best views, most overpriced food, and tackiest entertainment. Early evening, though, you might find it worth the price of a cocktail to take in the city skyline in comfort. Once again, Sunday best only.

River Café, 1 Water St., Brooklyn (☎718/522-5200). You probably won't be able to afford the food, but for the price of a drink you can enjoy the best view of the Lower Manhattan skyline there is. Try brunch—it's the best bargain.

Russian Tea Room, 150 W. 57th St. (☎265-0947). There's hardly a better place to eat in the city if you want to spot a celebrity, and rates are perhaps not as high as in the city's top French dining spots; plus it's easier to get a table at short notice. The wonderfully garish interior makes eating here a real occasion, too, though choose carefully on the rather over-rated menu, and stick to the old favorites—the blinis are among the city's best, as is the chicken kiev.

21 Club, 21 W. 52nd St. (☎582-7200). Though its days when the likes of Dorothy Parker regularly dined here are long over, this remains a stylish, power-broking restaurant, and is enormously popular despite its high (some might say through the roof) prices.

Windows on the World, World Trade Center, 107th floor (☎938-1111). The views, obviously, are the main attraction. But if you have money to burn the food's good, too, and the wine cellar is said to be among the best in New York. A nice venue for Sunday brunch.

24-HOUR EATS

This is simply a list for **late night** – and mainly budget-constrained—hunger. For details, either check the listings in the "Budget eats" and "Restaurants" sections, above, or assume they serve a straight coffee shop menu.

If you're nowhere near any of the addresses below, don't despair. There are numerous additional all-night delis (for takeout food), and in most neighborhoods of the city you'll also find at least one 24-hour Korean grocery—good for most food supplies.

LOWER

Around the Clock, 8 Stuyvesant St. (☎598-0402).

Astor Riviera, 454 Lafayette St. (☎677-4461).

Bagel Buffet, Sixth Ave. at 8th St. (☎477-0448).

Dave's Pot Belly, 98 Christopher St. (☎243-9614).

Empire Diner, 210 Tenth Ave. (☎243-2736).

Florent, 69 Gansevoort St. (☎989-5779).

Kiev, 117 Second Ave. (☎674-4040).

Triumph Restaurant, 148 Bleecker St. (☎228-3070).

Waverley Restaurant, 385 Sixth Ave. (☎675-3181).

West Side Diner, W. 31st and Ninth Ave. (☎560-8407).

MIDTOWN

Brasserie, 100 E. 53rd St. (☎751-4840).

Gemini Diner, 641 Second Ave. (☎532-2143).

Lox Around the Clock, 676 Sixth Ave. (☎691-3535).

Sarge's Deli, 548 Third Ave. (☎679-0442).

Stage Deli, 834 Third Ave. (☎245-7850).

Market Diner, 411 Ninth Ave. (☎695-6844); 572 Eleventh Ave. (☎244-6033).

UPTOWN

La Caridad, 2199 Broadway (☎874-2780).

Gray's Papaya, 2090 Broadway (☎799-0243).

Green Kitchen, 1477 First Ave. (☎988-4163).

H&H Bagels, 2239 Broadway (☎595-8000).

Tramway Coffee Shop, 1143 Second Ave. (☎758-7017).

THE OUTER BOROUGHS

If you decide to explore the **Outer Boroughs**, food could be as good a motivation as any. The ethnic communities here have for the most part retained close character—and their restaurants are similarly authentic, generally run by and for the locals. All of New York's ethnic groups are well represented, and you can eat more or less anything: **Brooklyn** has some of New York's best West Indian and Italian food, not to mention its most authentic Russian restaurants; **Queens** holds the city's biggest Greek and South American communities; while Belmont in the **Bronx** is one of the best places in the city to eat authentic Italian cuisine.

Brooklyn

Downtown Brooklyn, Brooklyn Heights, and Atlantic Avenue

Gage & Tollner, 372 Fulton St. (☎718/875-5181). Old-fashioned seafood restaurant that's long been part of the downtown Brooklyn eating scene. Not as expensive as it looks, and serving great crab cakes.

Henry's End, 44 Henry St. (☎718/834-1776). Varied menu with a wide selection of seasonal dishes, appetizers, and desserts. Popular with Brooklyn Heights locals, and normally crowded. Don't expect it to be all that cheap either.

Leaf 'n' Bean, 136 Montague St. (☎718/855-7978). Exotic coffees and teas plus excellent homemade soups, and, on weekends, brunch for about $10. Outdoor seating when it's fine.

Montague Street Saloon, 122 Montague St. (☎718/522-6770). Burgers and salads for under $10.

Promenade, 101 Montague St. (☎237-9796). Greek diner in the heart of Brooklyn Heights with a massive menu and good lunch specials for $5-7.

Slade's, 107 Montague St. (☎718/858-1200). Moderately priced burgers, salads, and Sunday brunch specials—and a big screen TV.

Teresa's, 80 Montague St. (☎718/797-3996). Large portions of Polish home cooking—blintzes, pirogi, and the like—make this a good lunchtime stop for those touring Brooklyn Heights.

Tripoli, 160 Atlantic Ave. (☎718/596-5800). Lebanese restaurant serving fish, lamb, and some vegetarian dishes for a low $8 or so.

Central Brooklyn

Aunt Sonia's, Eighth Ave. at 12th St. (☎718/965-9526). Eclectic menu featuring everything from Caribbean to Thai to Italian to traditional American. Entrees for around $10.

Aunt Suzie's, 247 Fifth Ave., Park Slope (☎718/788-3377). Neighborhood Italian serving decent food for as little as $10 a person. Not a restaurant to drive from Manhattan for, but if you're in the area, it's one of the best-value places around.

Cucina, 256 Fifth Ave. (☎718/230-0711). Homey Italian restaurant serving fine food for affordable prices.

Frost Restaurant, 193 Frost St. (☎718/389-3347). Williamsburg neighborhood Italian serving moderately priced food.

Once Upon a Sundae, 7702 Third Ave. (☎718/748-3412). Turn-of-the-century ice cream parlor.

101, 101 Fourth Ave. (☎718/833-1313). Eclectic Italian restaurant with a lively bar. A great neighborhood haunt.

Sam's, 238 Court St., Cobble Hill (☎718/596-3458). Long-established restaurant that serves standard Italian fare at very reasonable prices.

Tartine, 426a Seventh Ave. (☎718/768-2764). Wonderful French bistro with inexpensive prices and an outdoor garden in summer.

Coney Island and Brighton Beach

Carolina, 1409 Mermaid Ave., Coney Island (☎718/714-1294). Inexpensive, family-run Italian restaurant that's been around forever. Great food, great prices.

Gargiulo's, 2911 W. 15th St. (☎718/266-4891). Large, noisy family-run Coney Island restaurant famed for its large portions of hearty Neapolitan grub. Cheap.

Jean's Clam Bar, 2123 Emmons Ave. (☎718/646-9285). Inexpensive and lively seafood restaurant on Sheepshead Bay's main drag.

Joe's, 2009 Emmons Ave. (☎718/646-9375). Medium-priced Sheepshead Bay restaurant that's well worth the trip from Manhattan to sample.

Nathan's Famous, Surf and Stillwell Ave. (☎718/266-3161). New York's most famous hotdogs (and most other American snacks). Not the ultimate in gastronomy but legend nonetheless.

Odessa, 1113 Brighton Beach Ave. (☎718/769-2869). Excellent and varied Russian menu at unbeatable prices.

Primorski, 282 Brighton Beach Ave. (☎718/891-3111). Perhaps the best of Brighton Beach's Russian hangouts, serving up a huge menu of authentic Russian dishes at absurdly cheap prices—entrees around $5—though you may have problems communicating what you want to the waiting staff, most of whom barely speak English. Lively, too, with live music in the evening.

Mrs. Stahl's, 1001 Brighton Beach Ave. (☎718/648-0210). Long-standing Brighton Beach knishery.

Star of China, 2901 Bragg St. (☎718/615-2080). Reliable Chinese alternative to Sheepshead Bay's seafood.

The Bronx

Belmont

Ann and Tony's, 2407 Arthur Ave., corner of 187th St. (☎364-8250). Good pizzas.

Il Boschetto, 1660 E. Gun Hill Rd. (☎379-9335). Pricey, but the entrees and fresh pasta are worth it.

Dominick's, 2356 Westchester Ave. (☎822-8810). All you could hope for in a Belmont Italian: great atmosphere, wonderful food, and low(ish) prices.

Mario's, 2342 Arthur Ave. (☎584-1188). Pricey but very impressive cooking, enticing even die-hard Manhattanites out to the Bronx.

Queens

Astoria

Cyprus Taverna, 29–19 23rd Ave. (☎718/728-9561). Authentic Greek neighborhood restaurant.

Omonia Café, 32-20 Broadway (☎718/274-6650). Good Greek food at affordable prices.

Roumeli, 33-04 Broadway, between 33rd and 34th sts. (☎718/278-7533). Excellent Greek—a little upscale but very popular locally.

Jackson Heights

Inti-Raymi, 86-14 37th Ave. (☎718/424-1938). Unpretentious restaurant serving substantial, low-priced Peruvian food.

Las Americas, 93-09 37th Ave. at 90th St. (☎718/458-1638). Colombian cakes, pastries, and full meals. Good for inexpensive lunches.

La Pequena Columbia, 83-27 Roosevelt Ave. (☎718/478-6528). Literally "Little Colombia," this place ladles out heaped portions of seafood casserole, pork, and tortillas. Try the fruit drinks, too, *maracuay* (passion fruit), or *guanabana* (soursop).

Tierras Columbianas, 82-18 Roosevelt Ave. (☎718/426-8868). One of the most popular of the Jackson Heights Colombians—great food (wonderful soups and spicy meat dishes), decently priced and in large portions.

Victor's, 6909 Roosevelt Blvd. (☎718/651-9474). Filipino restaurant serving huge amounts of rice, beans, chicken, and beef for around $6 a main course.

Forest Hills, Jamaica, Bayside

Carmichael's Diner & Cocktail Lounge, 117-08 Gut R. Brewer Blvd. (☎718/723-6908). Fried chicken, chopped barbecue and black-eyed peas for around $10 a head.

Chalet Alpina, 98-35 Metropolitan Ave. (☎718/793-3774). Reasonably priced restaurant strong on meat and potato dishes.

Suzu, 39-32 Bell Blvd. (☎718/224-5622). Invent your own sushi for about $15.

Staten Island

Basilio Inn, 2-6 Galesville Court (☎718/720-6835). Homestyle Italian with a *bocci* court out the back.

La Fosse aux Loups, 11 Schuyler St. (☎718/442-9111). Once an inexpensive Mexican eatery, now a fairly expensive Belgian restaurant—though still, oddly enough, serving inexpensive Mexican food.

Just Omelettes, 150 Bay St. (☎718/273-7237). Serves 101 varieties of omelette. Within reasonable walk of the ferry terminal.

Tug's, 1115 Richmond Terrace (☎718/447-6369). Good for watching the water while you eat, and, on Sundays, a nice place for brunch.

CHAPTER NINE

NIGHTLIFE: ROCK, JAZZ, AND CLUBBING

Considering New York's everyday energy and diversity, its **music scene** can be disappointing. There is excellent **jazz**, traditional and contemporary and still concentrated in Greenwich Village, and around the clubs—and to a greater extent in the Outer Boroughs—you'll find a scattering of blues, Latin American, and hip hop. But straight **rock music** is currently something of a write-off—at least as far as originality goes. Since the early days of punk, which found an American focus here at Max's Kansas City (since closed) and the legendary CBGBs, American bands have drifted; if you see anyone interesting, they're likely to be a British import.

With **nightclubs**, New York is more in its element, though the recent trend toward so-called "supper clubs," where the emphasis is more on style and comfort than light shows and dancing, has deprived the city of some of its more spectacular places. That said, New York is as hung up on fashion as it ever was, and the scene just as capricious, clubs still furnished for a year or so of fame on multimillion-dollar budgets, and often with sound and light systems that are nowhere rivaled. If you just want to dance, there are countless places to do so, many charging prices that, while never cheap, won't break the bank. But the most interesting places are still by definition the most exclusive, their doors guarded against the unhip by fashion-sensitive bouncers.

The **sections** that follow give an account of the best of current places to go, though you should keep in mind that the music—and especially the club—scenes change continually; for the current **background**, check out the magazine *Details*, the city's eloquent and interesting manual of fashion and style. And for the best **listings**, pick up the *Village Voice*—better for music than clubs—or the more mainstream *New York Magazine*. And remember, also, to take some **ID** with you wherever you go: liquor laws have latterly been enforced more stringently and authorities have clamped down on entry and under-age drinking (ie under 21). Look anything around the magic age and you may well not get in at all.

> *For music-oriented bars see also the preceding chapter, and for clubs that host sporadic live music nights, see the* **Nightclubs** *section below.*

Rock music

New York's **rock music scene** has changed radically over recent years. It's more diffuse now, and rising rents and closing clubs have (as in just about every other field) forced many musicians out of Manhattan and into the Outer

Boroughs and New Jersey: if there is a scene at all now, it's one that has no clear center. That said, there are still plenty of bands around, playing many different kinds of music: there's an exciting off-Manhattan hub in Hoboken, New Jersey, centering on *Maxwell's* (see below); rap and hip hop, including house, are still big, both in the streets and in the recording studios, which put out a regular diet of cultish 12-inch singles; and, in Brooklyn and Queens at least, there's a huge Latin/South American and reggae contingent—though the clubs themselves are way off the average tourist circuit.

In Manhattan itself—principally in the East Village and Lower East Side—most of the energy is provided by a growing assortment of neighborhood bars which host a variety of new wave and (often) blues talent. Basically the listings below should point you to the bigger places; if you want to get more involved or listen to something more obscure, the *Village Voice* is hard to beat.

The big performance venues

Madison Square Garden, Seventh and Eighth Ave., W. 31st–33rd St. (☎465-6000). New York's principal large stage, hosting not only hockey and basketball but also a large proportion of the really big rock acts that visit the city. The arena, seating 20,000-plus, is not the most soulful place to see a band, but it may be the only chance you get.

Meadowlands Stadium, East Rutherford, New Jersey (☎201/935-8500). The city's other really big arena, again with room for around 20,000.

Radio City Music Hall, Sixth Ave. and 50th St. (☎247-4777). Not the place for rock it once was; most of the acts that play here now are firmly mainstream—although the building itself has as great a sense of occasion as it ever did.

Smaller venues

Abilene Café, 73 Eighth Ave. (☎255-7373). Blues acts nightly. $10 cover.

Apollo Theater, 253 W. 125th St. (☎749-5838). Regular black acts, as well as amateur nights (Wednesdays) and the odd dog show.

Beacon Theater, 2124 Broadway (☎496-7070). Irregular live bands.

The Bitter End, 147 Bleecker St. (☎673-7030). Young, fairly mainstream bands in an intimate cabaret club setting. Don't expect to see anyone famous. Cover around $5.

The Bottom Line, 15 W. 4th St. (☎228-7880). Not New York's most adventurous club but one of the better known—and the place where you're most likely to see established name bands. Cabaret setup, with tables crowding out any suggestion of a dance floor. Claim to fame: Bruce Springsteen supposedly started up the ladder here. Entrance $10–15.

Cat Club, 76 E. 13th St. (☎505-0090). Long-established club with a sumptuous art deco interior and live bands most nights of the week. Consisting of a large dance floor surrounded by tables, it's one of the nicest places for live music; admission $10–15.

CBGB (and OMFUG), 315 Bowery (☎982-4052). Deliberately sleazy, and despite a relative decline in influence still a great place to see (if not actually listen to) a band. Shows at 9:30pm (Fri/Sat 10:30pm); admission $5–10.

China Club, 2130 Broadway (☎877-1166). Music industry club peopled by celebs and aging rockers. Open nightly until 4am.

Dan Lynch's, 221 Second Ave. (☎677-0911). Blues and R&B bands nightly from 10pm. Free entrance.

Delta 88, 332 Eighth Ave. (☎924-3499). Live music—hosts everything from cajun to gospel to R&B. No cover Mon, Tues–Sun $5.

Kenny's Castaways, 157 Bleecker St. (☎473-9870). Showcase for local hopefuls. Live acts from 9pm nightly.

King Tut's Wah Wah Hut, 112 Ave. A (☎254-7772). Tiny bar that is an East Village institution. Punky crowd; cover varies, though it's usually under $5.

Lone Star Café Roadhouse, 240 W. 52nd St. (☎245-2950). The uptown outpost of the now defunct downtown rock'n'roll bastion, with a good variety of nightly acts, though fewer big names. Cheap drinks, good food (burgers, chicken, etc); still one of the city's better live clubs. Entrance around $10.

Manny's Car Wash, 1558 Third Ave. (☎369-2583). Smoky, Chicago-style blues bar with a small dance floor and and reasonable prices. Shows from 9:15pm. No cover Sundays for blues jams; Mondays women get in free. Otherwise, covers range from $3 to $10.

Marquee, 547 W. 21st St. (☎929-3257). Supposedly a sister club to its London namesake, the Marquee presents a mixture of blues, rock, and, especially, new British bands—if you're hoping to see the Inspiral Carpets, this could be the place. Admission $10–20.

Maxwell's, Washington and 11th St., Hoboken, New Jersey (☎201/798-4064). Neighborhood club hosting up to a dozen bands a week: some big names but really one of the best places to check out the current tri-state scene.

New World, 254 E. 2nd St. (☎677-5200). Club for visiting bands and host space to a broad array of specialized nights, from the Rock 'n' Roll Fag Bar (go-go boys and drag queens) to Sunday night's Girl World.

Nightingale Bar, Second Ave. at 13th St. (☎473-9398). Bar with blues and new wave bands nightly.

North River Bar, 145 Hudson St. (☎226-9411). Down-to-earth TriBeCa bar that books regular live—mostly rock—bands. Try the shots served in test tubes.

101 Avenue A, 101 Ave. A (☎420-1590). Formerly—and famously—The Pyramid Club and currently in a state of flux. Could be the next in place, or disappear: at any rate, one to watch out for in the listings.

The Ritz, W. 54th St. at Eighth Ave. (☎541-8900). Now in a new location in the old *Studio 54* building, this is the *Bottom Line*'s main rival for name acts. Limited seating; music at 9pm and 11pm most nights; admission $12–20.

SOB's ("Sounds of Brazil"), 204 Varick St. (☎243-4940). Disco/club/restaurant, with regular jazz, salsa-tinged, and World Music acts. Lively and fun, popular with a predominantly yuppie crowd. Two performances a night. Admission $15–20.

The Space at Chase, 98 Third Ave. (☎475-1407). A front room bar full of beefy collegiate types in baseball caps, with a room out back where bands play. A fun, sloppy place, perfect for seeing fun, sloppy bands. Music starts around 10pm; cover $3–5.

Sweetwater's, 170 Amsterdam Ave. (☎873-4100). Restaurant with R&B, jazz, and rock bands nightly. Cover $20.

Tramps, 54 W. 21st St. (☎727-7788). Blues and new wave bands almost nightly, from 9pm (weekends additional show at midnight). Entrance $10–15.

Wetlands, 161 Hudson St. (☎966-4225). A self-proclaimed "ecosaloon" that books regular live bands—particularly reggae—and circulates petitions among the patrons. Very 1960s. Admission $4–10.

Jazz and folk

There are few cities anywhere that are home to quite so many **jazz** clubs, festivals, jazz-related organizations, or, indeed, musicians—and if you're serious about jazz then this itself could be a good reason for visiting (even moving to) Manhattan.

There are around forty places in Manhattan presenting jazz nightly or at least regularly. Most clubs are located downtown, most often in **Greenwich Village** or **SoHo**; midtown clubs tend on the whole to be slick dinner-dance joints for businesspeople and as such are expensive and largely unexciting. The usual sources (notably the *Voice*) have listings of what's on. There's also *Hothouse*, a free monthly magazine that you can sometimes pick up from the clubs themselves, and the jazz **monthly**, *Downbeat*. Or simple listen to some of the city's jazz-oriented **radio stations**. Two of the best of these are *WBGO* (88.5 FM), a 24-hour jazz station, and *WKCR* (98.7 FM)—Columbia University's radio station. Failing that, phone **Jazz Line** (☎718/465-7500) for recorded information detailing the night's events.

Price policies vary from club to club, but at most there's a hefty **cover** ($10–12:50) and always a **minimum** charge for food and drinks. An evening out at a major club will set you back at least $15 per person, $25–30 if you want to eat. **Piano bars**—usually small and atmospheric—come cheaper with neither admission fee nor a minimum, though drinks are obviously still jacked up.

Jazz clubs

Angry Squire, 216 Seventh Ave. (☎242-9066). Nightly jazz and solid and affordable food and drink—including unlimited champagne brunch at weekends. Nights $5–8 cover, though no cover at all if you sit at the bar. Highly recommended.

Arthur's BeBop Cafe, 1 Charles St. (☎989-2339). Live jazz every weekend. No credit cards.

Arthur's Tavern, 57 Grove St. (☎675-6879). Small, amiable piano bar with some inspired performers and no cover or minimum—though drinks are predictably pricey. A good place for a night out as long as you're not into getting wrecked.

Birdland, 2745 Broadway (☎749-2228). Not the original place where Charlie Parker played, but an Upper West Side place for live jazz seven nights of the week. Music from 9pm (from 6pm on Sunday); cover $5–7—big names at weekends.

The Blue Note, 131 W. 3rd St. (☎475-8592). Big names mainly and with high prices—but good music and atmosphere. For all shows there's a $5 drinks minimum per person plus anything between $15 and $45 cover charge per table, depending on who's playing, $10 if you sit at the bar. Late-night shows—until 4am—are free if you've seen the previous set, $5 if you haven't.

Blue Willow, 644 Broadway (☎673-6480). Live jazz in a mellow setting.

Bradley's, 70 University Place (☎228-6440). Neighborhood bar that features well-known bass/piano duos and acts as meeting point for local jazz musicians. A good place to catch big names jamming with people they wouldn't normally play with. Plan to arrive late, as early evening the bar is too crowded with locals to actually hear anything. $8 minimum per person at the tables; $5–10 cover except Monday and Tuesday when it's free.

Condon's, 117 E. 15th St. (☎254-0960). A relatively new, small intimate club close to Union Square that stages big names. Cover $12.50, and a two-drink minimum; there's a cover at the bar but no minimum but—although the sound is good—the view is very restricted. Sets at 9/10pm and 11pm/midnight. If they're not too busy (most likely on Tuesday or Wednesday) they'll let you stay for the second set without paying again.

Fat Tuesday's, 190 Third Ave. (☎533-7902). Another of New York's principal jazz clubs, small and atmospheric in a mirrored basement with low ceilings. Prices vary according to who's on, but generally hover around the $12.50 cover, $7.50 minimum mark. Sets at 8pm and 10pm, so a better choice for early risers than some of the other clubs.

Fifty Five, 55 Christopher St. (☎929-9883). See "Bars" in Chapter Eight, *Drinking and Eating*.

Fortune Garden Pavillion, 209 E. 49th St. (☎753-0101). They call it "Dim sum and Jazz," and the music lives up to the food. $20 first set, $15 second set.

Greene Street Café, 101 Greene St. (☎925-2415). Huge converted warehouse, split between two levels and with dire acoustics. The music is generally excellent but views from the bar are so restricted you'll need either to pay for a balcony seat ($5 cover plus $5 minimum) or fork out for a dinner table.

J's, 2581 Broadway (☎666-3600). Intensely swinging jazz. Cover $5–10.

Knickerbocker's, 9th St. and University Place (☎228-8490). Just down the street from *Bradley's*, this is an excellent restaurant with high calibre bass/piano duos. $7 minimum at the tables—nothing at the bar (which has a better view of the performers); no cover.

The Knitting Factory, 47 E. Houston St. (☎219-3055). Small, vibrant club hosting regular live jazz and avant-garde rock. Shows at 9pm and 11pm. Entrance $5–10.

Michael's Pub, 211 E. 55th St. (☎758-2272). This slick midtown bar isn't so much known for the quality of its jazz as for the fact that Woody Allen plays clarinet here on occasional Monday nights. Cover $15–20.

Sweet Basil, 88 7th Ave. (☎242-1785). One of New York's major—and most crowded—jazz spots, particularly at weekends, when there's brunch and free jazz through the afternoon. For the best of the music, though, stick to weekday evenings. Shows usually start at 9pm. $15 cover and a $6 minimum at the tables, per set ($12 at the bar including a drink).

Village Corner, Bleecker St. at La Guardia Place (☎473-9762). Pleasant smoky bar with free admission—though don't go for the music which is generally lost in the din of conversation.

Village Gate, Bleecker St. at Thompson (☎475-5120). One of New York's oldest and largest surviving jazz clubs and still one of the best. Monday salsa nights are the current highlight, well worth the $10 entrance; other times, you can cut costs by taking a seat in the downstairs sidewalk café and listening to regular bass/piano duos for a $5 minimum.

Village Vanguard, 178 Seventh Ave. (☎255-4037). An NYC jazz landmark that celebrated its fiftieth anniversary a few years back and still pulls the big names. Admission around $10; $5 drink minimum at weekends.

Visiones, 125 Macdougal St. (☎673-5576). Spanish restaurant four doors down from *The Blue Note* that hosts a wide, more contemporary array of different acts. Two shows each night, at 9:30pm and 11:30pm. Often no cover charge, otherwise $5.

Wonderland Blues Bar, 519 Second Ave. (☎213-5098). Cosy jazz bar which caters to the after midnight crowd. No cover during the week, $5 weekends.

Zanzibar & Grill, 550 Third Ave. (☎779-0606). Restaurant (serving regional American food) and jazz club. Sets start at 9pm, Monday to Saturday, and on Sundays at 8pm.

Zinno, 126 W. 13th St. (☎924-5182). Supper and jazz club. $10 if you sit at the bar, $15 for a table.

Folk clubs

Eagle Tavern, 355 W. 14th St. (☎924-0275). Local and imported Irish folk and occasional poetry on selected weeknights. $7–12 cover.

O'Lunney's, 12 W. 44th St. (☎840-6688). Restaurant serving steaks, hamburgers, and the like to some traditional country 'n' western live sounds. $3 cover at the tables.

The Speakeasy, 107 Macdougal St. (☎598-9670). The only folk club in NYC with music seven nights a week. Something of a hangout for musicians and folkies. $5–10 cover; bland health-food menu.

Nightclubs and discos

New York—and especially Manhattan—**clublife** is a rapidly evolving creature. While many of the name DJs remain the same, clubs shift around and open and close according to the whims of fashion. Musically, house holds sway at the moment—with the emphasis on the deep, vocal style that's always been popular in the city—but Latin Freestyle, dancehall reggae, and rap all retain interest.

Having said that, the rundown below would be a fun one right now, but within weeks it's bound to have serious omissions. Always check, ask contacts for information, look in *Details* magazine, and hunt down flyers that advertise clubs and one-off events: you'll find them in bars and restaurants, record and clothes shops, even phone booths. Many offer substantial discounts on the cover charge, especially if you're prepared to turn up unfashionably early.

Bear in mind, too, that the hipness quotient of a club can go up or down at the drop of a hat, and that clubs can (and must if they want to survive) change rapidly. Many of the hipper clubs follow a pattern whereby the trendy, dressed-up, and predominantly white downtown crowd is targeted at the opening, waiting for the name to get established before letting the Spanish and black kids in from uptown—the people who prefer dancing to showing off.

The **procedure** of clubbing in New York is less likely to change its ways. Assuming you're curious (and in many cases rich) enough, these are the main points:

• Hippest (and cheapest) time to club is during the week. Weekends are favored by out-of-towners and so shunned by serious nightpeople. Admission to clubs at weekends is in any case invariably more expensive than during the week.

• Style is vital: don't expect to get in to some of the more exclusive places just because you can afford to.

• Nothing gets going much before midnight. Don't go before this. And when you do eventually stagger out (most clubs close around 4am), keep your wits about you.

• Don't reckon to beat bar prices by smuggling in a hip flask—the mixers are the same price as everything else: around $5. A night at any NYC club needs money.

> *Note that some of the city's* exclusively gay or lesbian *nightspots are detailed under* "Gay and Lesbian Bars" *in Chapter Eight, Drinking and Eating.*

Au Bar, 41 E. 58th St. (☎308-9455). "Supper club" full of European ex-pats and would-be American aristocrats. Best dress. Sun–Thurs admission $10, Fri and Sat $15.

Baja, 100 W. 72nd St. (☎724-8890). Yuppie Upper West Side club playing standard dance music to a fairly safe, smartly dressed clientele. $5 weeknights, $10 weekends.

The Building, 51 W. 26th St. (☎576-1890). Formerly an old Con Edison power station, The Building has been left with its original fittings, save for the introduction of a dance floor overlooked by two mezzanines. Open Wed–Sun 10pm–4am; entry $7–15. Wednesday and Sunday are gay nights, Thursday is drag queen night, Friday is given over to industrial music, and Saturday to retro disco and house. An exciting and original club.

Cave Canem, 24 First Ave. (☎529-9665). Restaurant/dance club housed on two floors of a former bathhouse that's decked out in decadent Roman empire and serves food based on Imperial Roman cuisine. Entrees in the restaurant run at $13–20. A wide range of music, no cover charge during the week, $5 at weekends.

The Crane Club, 201 W. 79th St. (☎877-3097). An upscale bar that plays loud contemporary rock and charges around $5 cover. Preppies galore.

Danceteria, 29 E. 29th St. (☎683-1046). Once one of NYC's great clubs, offering several floors of dancing. It's recently been reopened, though for how long remains a matter of conjecture.

Delia's, 197 E. 3rd St. (☎254-9184). Another supper club whose sleazy location satisfies Upper East Side desires to slum it downtown. And inside is anything but sleazy, the formidable Delia presiding over a plush environment designed to cater to the needs of leisurely diners and dancers alike. If the neighborhood doesn't appeal, Delia will book a car to take you home.

El Morocco, 307 E. 54th St. (☎570-1500). Flashy club restaurant once patronized by Errol Flynn, though it's not on the list of "in" places to be seen today.

Emerald City, 617 W. 57th St. (☎247-1530). A massive nightclub that likes to see itself as one of the city's more important new clubs. Definitely targeted downmarket, though, and for very young kids, with mainstream disco music and free entry for "ladies" before 11pm. After 11pm everyone pays $15 admission.

Island Club, 285 W. Broadway (☎226-4598). Wednesday, Thursday, and Sunday hard-core reggae music, Fridays and Saturdays salsa and Latin-edged sounds. Admission $5–10.

Jukebox, 304 E. 39th St. (☎685-1556). Club playing a mix of Fifties, Sixties, and Seventies music. Cover $5.

Kiliminjaro, W. 18th St. and Tenth Ave. Great club whose mixture of African jive, soul, soca, and reggae, not to mention the resident band "Ethiopia," attracts a mixed crowd. Try the rum swizzles (three rums and three fruit juices)—great value at $7 a throw. Open until 5am; entrance $18.

Limelight, 660 Sixth Ave. (☎807-7850). Housed in a converted Gothic church, this caused a storm of outrage when it opened, and is enjoying something of a renaissance after a lean period, particularly for its UK-influenced Thursday night sessions. Still no longer the exclusive hangout it was. Admission $18.

The Living Room, 154 E. 79th St. (☎772-8488). A preppy club with an attitude. Wear black and look suitably cool and you'll have no problem getting in.

Mars, 28–30 Tenth Ave. (☎691-6262). In the running for the hippest spot in town, a multi-level club that's the brainchild of Rudolph of erstwhile *Danceteria* fame. Each floor sports a different atmosphere and music, varying from a mocked-up Western saloon to rooms laid out to resemble a 1940s *film noir*. Admission $15–20.

Mission, 531 E. 5th St., between Aves. A and B (☎473-9096). East Village club specializing in Goth, Punk, and New Wave music—Jesus and Mary Chain, Psychedelic Furs, Sisters of Mercy, Cure, etc—and apparently a hangout for various members of the aforementioned groups. Open Thurs–Sat, from 10pm; admission is $6 and drinks are cheap.

Nell's, 246 W. 14th St. (☎675-1567). First of the so-called "supper clubs" and still going strong, although it's reputation as the city's most exclusive establishment has somewhat waned of late. Admission $5 weeknights, $10 weekends.

Nick's Grove, 209 E. 84th St. (☎744-5003). *Baja*-like dance place for the East Side. Cover $5.

Octagon, 555 W. 33rd St. (☎947-0400). Run-of-the-mill club playing top forty music, other than on Saturday nights, when Roger Sanchez' *Ego Trip* plays deep house, classics, and reggae. Admission runs from $5 on Thursday to $15 Friday and Saturday.

Palladium, 126 E. 14th St. (☎473-7171). Biggest and for some still among the best of New York clubs—though *Palladium*'s initial exclusivity was deliberately short-lived, and it now caters to a fairly mixed custom. Housed in an enormous old theater, the dance floor, light and sound system take some beating, as does the music, especially midweek. For no-nonsense dancing without the posing, still one of the best. Admission $20.

Private Eye's, 12 W. 21st St. (☎206-7770). Nowadays the city's premiere gay club, with a tiny dance floor, video screens, and some of the most spirited carousing you'll find. $15.

Red Zone, 440 W. 54th St. (☎582-2222). Popular with a young, mainly Latin crowd. David Morales plays on Saturdays; open Tues–Sun.

Roseland, 239 W. 52nd St. (☎247-0200). Ballroom dancing from lunchtime to midnight, Thursday to Sunday, just as it's been for the last 65 years. $10 admission.

Save the Robots, on Avenue C. East Village club that gets going when the other nightspots are winding down. Open Thurs, Fri, Sat from 4am until 8am, entrance $10. Can be difficult to get into....

Shelter, 157 Hudson St. (☎677 2582). At the time of writing one of the new hot spots: expect a lethal mixture of deep house and disco classics played over an awesome sound system to a mainly black crowd. Great atmosphere, with the emphasis on serious dancing. Saturday night is gay night.

Shout, 124 W. 43rd St. (☎869-2088). Rock 'n' Roll revival meetings for Manhattan's chicest Brylcreams and bobtails. Increasingly popular with those who remember the records from the first time around. Open early evening: before 8pm admission $5, after 8pm and on Saturdays $10.

Sound Factory, 27th St. between 10th and 11th aves. Two of NYC's most renowned DJs play here: Tony Humphries on Fridays, Frankie Knuckles on Saturdays.

Stringfellows, 35 E. 21st St. (☎254-2444). Slick, rather tacky New York branch of the London club. Primarily a singles crowd, and expensive at $15 weeknights, $25 on Saturdays.

Roxy, 515 W. 18th St. (☎645-5157). Dance music with the emphasis on house. Admission $15.

20 West, 27 W. 20th St. (☎924-0205). Fifties and Sixties-style dance club complete with dancing deejays, waiters, and bartenders. No cover Tuesday, Wednesday and Thursday $5, Friday and Saturday $10.

Wonderama, (☎517-0173). One of Manhattan's itinerant clubs: different location each Friday for a trendy crowd moving to a mix of house, hip hop, and reggae.

CHAPTER TEN

THE PERFORMING ARTS AND MOVIES

With Broadway, the Met, the New York Philharmonic, New York City can still supply glittering concert halls and glamorous events—but you may need to take out a mortgage to attend. **Theater** is fabulous, and fabulously expensive, with Broadway prices crippling, and even Off Broadway seats causing terminal damage. If you know where to look, though, there are a variety of ways to get tickets cheaper, and Off-Off Broadway prices approach the realistic. The best of these options are detailed below. **Dance, music**, and **opera** are also superbly represented: again the big mainstream events are extremely expensive; smaller ones are often equally as interesting as well as far cheaper. As for the **movies**, New York gets foreign ones with extremely limited distribution anywhere else.

What's on listings can be found in a number of places. Perhaps the most useful general source, clear and comprehensive, is *New York Magazine*, though the *Village Voice* is better for things downtown and anything vaguely "alternative." The *Sunday Times Weekly Guide* is also good, especially for mainstream events: the paper's *Weekend* section, on Fridays, lists "ticket availability" for the major shows not sold out for the weekend. Specific Broadway listings can be found in the free *Official Broadway Theater Guide*, available from theater and hotel lobbies or the New York Convention and Visitor's Bureau (see "Information, Maps, and Tours" in *Basics*).

Theater

New York is one of the great **theater** centers of the world. You can find just about any kind of production here, from lavish, over-the-top musicals to experimental productions in converted garages: the variety is endless. But it's not cheap. Indeed, the big budget Broadway blockbusters seem to be pricing themselves out of existence—with prices steadily spiraling and audience levels dropping, theaterland is in trouble. What follows is a guide to where to find the various types of production—and how to avoid paying through the nose for them.

Theaters in the city are referred to as **Broadway, Off Broadway**, or **Off-Off Broadway**, categories which represent a descending order of ticket price, production polish, elegance, and comfort (but don't necessarily have much to do with the address). They also represent an ascending order of innovation, experimentation, and theater for the sake of art rather than cash. **Broadway** offerings consist primarily of large-scale musicals, comedies and dramas with big-name actors, with the occasional classic and one-person show. **Off Broadway** theaters also tend to provide polished production qualities, but combine them with a greater willingness to experiment. It's in Off Broadway you'll find social and political drama, satire, ethnic plays, and repertory: in short, anything that Broadway wouldn't consider a sure-fire money-maker. Lower operating costs also mean that Off Broadway often serves as a proving ground for what sometimes ends up as a big Broadway production. **Off-Off Broadway** is drama on a shoestring, sometimes on subjects other theaters find too sensitive or not profitable enough to mount. Unlike Off Broadway, Off-Off doesn't have to use professional actors.

For the record, it's the size of the theater that technically determines the category it falls into: under 100 seats and a theater is Off-Off; 100 to 500 and it's Off. Most Broadway theaters are located in the blocks just east or west of Broadway between 40th and 52nd streets; Off and Off-Off Broadway theaters are sprinkled throughout Manhattan, with a concentration in the East and West Villages, Chelsea, and several in the 40s and 50s west of the Broadway theater district.

Tickets

Nowhere are regular **tickets** cheap on Broadway—a couple of orchestra seats for something like *Les Miserables* will set you back a cool $100. Off Broadway prices have risen recently, too, to as much as $35 in some cases, though most seats remain cheaper than anything you'll find along the Great White Way: in general, expect to pay from $15 Off Broadway and $6 Off-Off. If you know where and how to look, even these prices can be cut considerably. Basically there are two straightforward and well-practiced methods of **cutting costs**, the first of which requires a little patience.

• Stand in line on the day of the performance at the **TKTS booth** at Times Square, where at least one pair of tickets for every performance of every Broadway and Off Broadway show is available at half price (plus a $1.25 ticket service charge—altogether around $15–20). There's a single line for all shows, and the most popular sell out soonest: get here early if you're after the hit of the month. TKTS hours are Monday to Saturday 3 to 8pm, noon to 2pm for Wednesday and Saturday matinees, but the booth opens as early as 10:30am if a long line forms; on Sunday, matinee and evening performance tickets are on sale from noon until they run out. There's another TKTS booth in the lobby of 2 World Trade Center (useful to know if it's raining, and even more useful in that certain matinee tickets are sold here on the day *before* the performance) and one at Court and Montague streets near Borough Hall in Brooklyn (Mon–Fri 11am–5:30pm, Sat 11am–3:30pm), reputedly with the shortest lines of all, and which also sells tickets for matinees the following day on Tuesdays, Fridays, and Saturdays. All three booths take cash or travelers' checks only; best days for availability and short lines are Tuesday, Wednesday, and Thursday.

• Look for **twofer discount coupons** in either of the New York Convention and Visitor's bureaux and many shops, banks, restaurants, and hotel lobbies. These entitle two people to a hefty discount (though the days when they really offered two-for-the-price-of-one are long gone), and unlike TKTS it's possible to reserve ahead, though don't expect to find coupons for the latest shows. If you can't find a coupon for the production you want, the *Hit Show Club* (300 W. 43rd St., NYC 10036) will send a pair of discount slips for every Broadway show on receipt of a stamped addressed envelope—useful if you're around for any length of time.

• If you're prepared to pay the **full price** you can, of course, go directly to the theater, but rather easier *Tickets Central*, 406 W. 42nd St., sells tickets for fifty Off and Off-Off Broadway theaters from 1 to 8pm daily: expect to pay from $15 Off Broadway, $6 Off-Off. Finally, if lining up for tickets is below your dignity and your credit rating, *Ticketron* (☎399-4444) will book seats for those with credit cards; pick up the tickets at the theater on production of your card. A charge of $2.50 is added to the top ticket price you'll pay.

Off-Off Broadway and Repertory

AMAS Repertory, 1 E. 104th St. (☎369-8000). Multiracial showcase.

American Jewish Theater of the 92nd St. Y, 1395 Lexington Ave. (☎415-5440). Classical and contemporary plays in English on Jewish themes.

American Place Theater, 111 W. 46th St. (☎840-2960). New works by living Americans.

Circle In The Square Uptown, 1633 Broadway (☎307-2700). Classics and "potential classics."

Circle Repertory Company, 99 Seventh Ave. South (☎924-7100). Contemporary: has premiered many award winners.

Jean Cocteau Repertory, Bouwerie Lane Theater, 330 Bowery (☎677-0060). Aims at "dramatic poem" production style. Genet, Sophocles, Shaw, Strindberg, Sartre, Wilde, Williams, etc, along with unknowns.

Hudson Guild Theater, 441 W. 26th St. (☎760-9810). Introduces new American and European playwrights.

Steve McGraw's, 158 W. 72nd St. (☎595-7400). Cabaret satire and spoofs of Broadway hits.

Negro Ensemble Company, 155 W. 46th St. (☎575-5860). Plays about the black experience.

New Federal Theater of the Henry Street Settlement, 466 Grand St. (☎598-0400). Outlet for minority playwrights, performers, and production staff. Has premiered some award winners.

New York Shakespeare Festival, The Public Theater, 425 Lafayette St. (☎598-7150). Year-round, six performing areas stage new American plays and accommodate visiting artists and companies. In summer the Shakespeare Festival proper takes off at the open-air Delacorte Theater in Central Park (☎861-7277); performances are free but come early for the best places.

Ontological-Hysteric Theater Company, no permanent premises (☎941-8911). Avant-garde/destructionist productions.

Playwrights Horizons, 416 W. 42nd St. (☎279-4200). New works and new writers. Originated the controversial "Sister Mary Ignatius Explains It All to You," as well as "Sunday In The Park With George."

Royal Court Repertory, 301 W. 55th St. (☎956-3500). Many mystery plays; other drama and comedy.

Theater For the New City, 155 First Ave. (☎254-1109). Known for following the development of new playwrights and presenting integration of dance, music, and poetry with drama.

West Side Repertory, 252 W. 81st St. (☎874-7920). Small basement theater that puts on four productions a year: Shaw, Wilde, Pirandello. Professional producer-director; performers and staff are pros and talented amateurs.

The Wooster Group (Performing Garage), 33 Wooster St. (☎966-3651). Experimental/Multi-media/Abstract.

WPA Theater, 519 W. 23rd St. (☎206-0523). Neglected American classics and American Realist plays, acted in a style described as "derived from Stanislavski."

Off Broadway

Worth checking out for interesting productions are:

American Theater of Actors, 314 W. 54th St. (☎581-3044).

Apple Corps Theater Company, 336 W. 20th St. (☎929-2955).

Vivian Beaumont Theater, Lincoln Center, Broadway at 64th (☎239-6200).

Cherry Lane Theater, 38 Commerce St. (☎989-2020).

Chicago City Limits, 351 E. 74th St. (☎772-8707).

Cubicolo Theater, 414 W. 51st St. (☎265-2138).

Douglas Fairbanks Theater, 432 W. 42nd St. (☎532-8038).

Jan Hus Theater Company, 351 E. 74th St. (☎288-6743).

La Mama Theater Club, 74A E. 4th St. (☎475-7710).

Lucille Lortel Theater, 121 Christopher St. (☎924-8782).

Manhattan Theater Club, 131 W. 55th St. (☎645-5590).

Off Center Theater, no permanent location (☎766-3277).

Orpheum Theater, 126 Second Ave. (☎477-2477).

Promenade Theater, 216 Broadway (☎580-1313).

Provincetown Playhouse, 133 Macdougal St. (☎477-5048).

Ridiculous Theater Company, 1 Sheridan Square (☎691-2271).

Roundabout Theater Company, 100 E. 17th St. (☎420-1360).

Samuel Beckett Theater, 410 W. 42nd St. (☎594-2826).

Second Stage Theater, 2162 Broadway (☎787-8302).

78th Street Theater Lab, 238 W. 78th St. (☎362-1736).

SoHo Repertory Company, 80 Varick St. (☎226-5620).

St. Clements Theater, 423 W. 46th St. (☎246-7277).

Theater at St. Peter's Church, Lexington Ave. and 54th St. (☎935-2200).

13th St. Theater, 50 W. 13th St. (☎675-6677).

Westbeth Theater Center, 151 Bank St. (☎691-2272).

Dance

New York has five major ballet companies, dozens of modern troupes, and untold thousands of soloists. You would have to be very particular indeed in your tastes not to find something of interest. Events are listed in broadly the same places as for music and theater—if this is your particular interest, though, you might want also to pick up *Dance Magazine*. Half-price tickets, on a day-to-day basis only, are available from **The Music & Dance Booth** in Bryant Park (42nd St. between Fifth and Sixth avenues). This is open Tuesday to Friday noon to 2pm and 3pm to 7pm; Wednesday and Saturday 11am to 2pm and 3pm to 7pm; Sunday (for Monday tickets) noon to 6pm: call ☎382-2323 for details of ticket availability.

Theaters and companies

American Ballet Theater, 890 Broadway (☎477-3030). Under the direction of Mikhail Baryshnikov, the ABT is big, glamorous, and the epitome of the standard idea of ballet. The company has its studios and offices downtown near Union Square but performs at the Metropolitan Opera House (in Lincoln Center) from early May into July.

Brooklyn Academy of Music, 30 Lafayette St., Brooklyn (☎718/636-4100). Universally known as BAM, this is America's oldest performing arts academy and one of the busiest and most daring producers in New York. In the fall, BAM's *Next Wave* festival showcases the hottest international attractions in avant-garde dance and music; in winter visiting artists appear, and each spring there's a *Festival of Black Dance*—everything from ethnic authenticity to tap and body-popping. A great place and one definitely worth crossing the river for.

City Center, 131 W. 55th St. (☎246-8989). Rivaling Radio City Music Hall for tinges of exotic kitsch, five resident dance troupes hold seasons here lasting from two weeks to a month. Companies include modern ensembles led by America's two undisputed choreographic giants, the *Merce Cunningham Dance Company* and the *Paul Taylor Dance Company*. Also here are the *Alvin Ailey American Dance Theater* (glossy contemporary pizzazz with an emphasis on black dance), the *Joffrey* and *Dance Theater of Harlem* (see below), and occasionally the *Martha Graham Dance Company*. What's left of the year is devoted to a mix of visiting artists from the USA and abroad.

The Cunningham Studio, 11th floor, Westbeth, 463 West St. (☎691-9751). The home of the *Merce Cunningham Dance Company*, this rooftop studio is used as an evening performance space by young choreographers. The night-time views of the Manhattan skyline provide a stunning backdrop to performances.

Dance Theater of Harlem. The mostly black ensemble founded in 1971 has rapidly developed into a company of major standing. They perform annually at *City Center* (see above) in a mixed repertory that includes many classics along with short works devised specifically for their own company.

Dance Theater Workshop, down the block and around the corner from the Joyce at 219 W. 19th St. (☎924-0077). Alternative dance is king at DTW, with varied programs featuring the broadest range of the newest and brightest. The small space is located on the third floor of a former warehouse, has an unintimidating relaxed atmosphere, low ticket prices, and performances virtually every night of the year.

Emanu-El Midtown YM/YWHA, 344 E. 14th St. (☎673-2207). Has been presenting dance for decades. The facility is actually a gymnasium and can be stifling on even moderate days. Still, the range of talents seen here (and the budget-priced admission) make it a space to know about.

The Joffrey Ballet, At the *City Center* (see above). Famed for its interpretations of twentieth-century classics and contemporary works by the likes of Twyla Tharp and resident choreographer Gerald Arpino, the Joffrey divides its time between New York and Los Angeles.

The Joyce Theater, 175 Eighth Ave. (☎242-0800). Probably the most important middle-sized dance space in Manhattan, the Joyce has the *Eliot Feld Ballet* in residence plus short seasons of other top-notch companies.

New York City Ballet, Performs for six months of the year at Lincoln Center's New York State Theater (see below) and is considered by many to be the greatest dance company in existence.

P.S. 122, 150 First Ave. (☎228-4249). A converted school in an unfashionable downtown section of the city: tends to the radical and the new.

Riverside Church, This has a small theater in its complex on Riverside Drive at 122nd St. (☎864-2929). The annual *Riverside Dance Festival* (phone for dates) presents both ethnic and traditional modern dance.

Classical music and opera

New Yorkers take serious music seriously. Long lines form for anything popular, a good many concerts sell out, and summer evenings can see a quarter of a million people turning up in Central Park for free performances by the New York Philharmonic.

The range of what's on offer is wide, but it's big names at big concert halls that attract the crowds, leaving you with a good number of easily attended selections. **Tickets** for these are available half price (on the day) from the *Music & Dance Booth* in Bryant Park (see above for details).

Opera

Lincoln Center (Broadway at 64th St.; see Chapter Three, "Upper Manhattan"), New York's powerhouse of highbrow art, very much dominates the city's operatic scene. Its star turn is **The Metropolitan Opera House**, usually known as "The Met" (box office Mon–Fri 10am–8pm, Sun noon–6pm; ☎362-6000), with the *Metropolitan Opera Company* playing from September to late April and the *American Ballet Theater* (see "Dance") taking over in the spring. Tickets are outrageously expensive and difficult to get hold of, and while last minute cancellations and standing room tickets *can* be picked up from the box office, a line is likely to form the night before if the performance is a popular one. A much better option, still in Lincoln Center, is **The New York State Theater** (box office Mon 10am–7:30pm, Tue–Sat 10am–8:30pm, Sun 11:30am–7:30pm; ☎870-5770) where Beverley Sills' *New York City Opera* plays David to the Met's Goliath. Its wide and adventurous program varies wildly in quality—sometimes startlingly innovative, occasionally failing completely. Seats go for less than half the Met's prices, and standing room tickets are available if a performance sells out. Occasionally the students of the **Julliard School** (☎799-5000) take on opera productions under the control of a famous conductor, usually for low ticket prices.

Away from Lincoln Center productions come on a smaller scale with ticket prices to match. Quality will vary wildly from production to production, but companies are all pretty good and, importantly, often schedule works which are neglected in the Met's roster of familiar "top-of-the-charts" classics.

Amato Opera Theater, 319 Bowery (☎228-8200). This downtown group presents an ambitious and varied repertory of classics. Singers, designers, and conductors are young professionals on the way up. Weekends only.

Concert halls

The Avery Fisher Hall, in Lincoln Center (☎874-2424). Permanent home of the *New York Philharmonic* under Zubin Mehta, and temporary one to visiting orchestras and soloists. Ticket prices for the Philharmonic range from $10 to $45. An often fascinating bargain are the **NYP open rehearsals** at 9:45am on concert days. Tickets for these, non-reservable, cost just $5.

Alice Tully Hall (☎362-1911), also in Lincoln Center, is a smaller recital hall for chamber orchestras, string quartets, and instrumentalists. Prices similar to those in the Avery Fisher Hall.

Brooklyn Academy of Music, 30 Lafayette St., Brooklyn (☎718/636-4100). See "Dance."

Bargemusic, Fulton Ferry Landing, Brooklyn (☎718/624-4061). Jazz and chamber music. Admission around $10.

Carnegie Hall, 154 W. 57th St. (☎247-7800). The greatest names from all schools of music performed here in the past, from Tchaikovsky and Toscanini to Gershwin and Billie Holiday. The acoustics remain superb, and a patching-up operation is under way to amend years of structural neglect and restore the place to former glories. Expect music of just about any sort, and low to moderate prices.

Cooper Union, Third Ave. at 7th St. (☎254-6374).

Kaufman Concert Hall, in the 92nd St. Y at Lexington Ave. (☎427-6000).

Lehman Center for the Performing Arts, Bedford Park Boulevard, the Bronx (☎960-8833).

Merkin Concert Hall, Abraham Goodman House, 129 W. 67th St. (☎362-8719).

Town Hall, 123 W. 43rd St. (☎840-2824).

Cabaret and comedy

Comedy clubs and **cabaret spots** are rife in New York and often of an extraordinarily high standard. What you'll see varies from stand-up comics and improvised comedy (amazing if you've never been before—quick-fire wit is part of the city psyche) to singing waiters and waitresses, many of whom are "resting" professionals waiting for their big break. Most clubs have shows every night, usually two at weekends (at about 9pm and midnight) and usually charge a cover ($5 up) and a minimum that works out about equivalent to a couple of drinks. Those below are usually worth trying, but check *New York Magazine* for the fullest and most up-to-date listings.

The Ballroom, 253 W. 28th St. (☎244-3005). One of the largest stages around, with some of the city's most ambitious singers and comedians. Cover $15, two drink minimum. The bar and dining area also double as New York's best tapas bar; see Chapter Eight, "Drinking and Eating," for details.

Brandy's Piano Bar, 235 E. 84th St. (☎650-1944). Small, neighborhood bar featuring bar staff and waitresses who sing popular Broadway show hits as well as old theme tunes from TV shows like Mary Tyler Moore, even the Flintstones. No cover charge, though there's a minimum drinks charge at the tables.

Caroline's Comedy Club, 89 South St., Pier 17 (☎620-5971). Glitzy room that books some of the best acts in town. $7.50–10 cover during the week, $12.50–17.50 at weekends.

Catch a Rising Star, 1487 First Ave. (☎794-1906). New talent showcase twice nightly, three times on Saturday. Alumni include Pat Benatar. Cover around $10.

Chicago City Limits, 351 E. 74th St. (☎772-8707). Improvisation club playing one show nightly, two at weekends. From 8:30pm; cover $10–15.

Comedy Cellar, 117 Macdougal St. (☎254-3630). Comedy club with nightly shows and two or three at weekends. Cover around $7.

Comedy Stop at the Top, 160 Bleecker St. (☎982-9292). New comedy club situated above the *Village Gate* jazz bar. Weekend shows from 9:30pm; cover $7.

Comic Strip, 1568 Second Ave. (☎861-9386). Famed showcase for stand-up comics and young singers going for the big time. Nightly shows from 9pm, two shows at weekends. Cover $5–12.

Dangerfield's, 1118 First Ave. (☎593-1650). New talent showcase run by the established comedian, Rodney Dangerfield. Cover $10–15.

Don't Tell Mama, 343 W. 46th St. (☎757-0788). Lively, convivial piano bar and cabaret featuring rising stars. Shows at 8pm and 10pm. Cover $6–15, two-drink minimum.

Duplex, 61 Christopher St. (☎255-5438). Village cabaret popular with gays; it was here, too, that Joan Rivers was discovered. Two shows a night at 8pm and 10pm (Friday and Saturday 10pm and midnight), mainly comedy, previewing yet more up-and-coming New York talent. Cover $7–11. The rowdy piano bar downstairs is worth catching.

Eighty Eight, 228 W. 10th St. (☎924-0088). New addition to the local cabaret scene, owned by comedians and entertainers who have been playing the circuit for years. Cabaret upstairs, piano bar down; cover $10–15. Friday and Saturday are the best nights.

5 and 10 No Exaggeration, 77 Greene St. (☎925-7414). An antiques shop and bar in front; a cabaret and restaurant in the back.

Improvisation, 358 W. 44th St. (☎765-8268). Nightly new comic and singing talent—most, as the name suggests, improvised. Cover $7–8. Shows at 9pm during the week; two shows on Friday, three on Saturday.

The Late Show, 407 Amsterdam Ave. (☎724-6868). Club serving snacks and desserts to entertainment from Broadway professionals who double as singing waiters and waitresses between shows.

Manhattan Punch Line, 410 W. 42nd St., 3rd floor (☎239-0827). October–June. Satire, comedy, stand-up gagsters, revues.

Mostly Magic, 55 Carmine St. (☎924-1472). Intimate off-the-beaten-track club that hosts regular magic and comic acts. Cover $10–15.

Mrs. J.'s Sacred Cow, 228 W. 72nd St. (☎873-4067). Full-scale restaurant with performing waiters and waitresses.

Sing-a-long, 17 W. 19th St. (☎206-8660). You can win prizes at this bar with TV monitors that encourage you to follow the bouncing ball and sing and dance.

Stand Up New York, 236 W. 78th St. (☎595-0850). Upper West Side club that's not so much a showcase as a forum for established acts. Nightly shows, two sometimes three at weekends. Cover about $10.

Trixie's, 307 W. 47th St. (☎582-5498). Actually a restaurant, but it's not worth coming here just to eat—or outside a large crowd. Live entertainment varies from professional musicians to customers crooning old Fifties tunes; service is from an assorted cast of singing waitresses. A rowdy, fun night out. Reservations essential.

Movies

New Yorkers treat **movies** with an enthusiasm which borders on obsession: people stand in line hours to see obscure foreign movies; being literate in movie trivia is seen as equivalent to cultured sophistication; and Revival movie theaters do brisk business. Talk to a New Yorker and sooner or later the conversation will get around to their favorite line from a favorite scene of a favorite movie. If you want to be ahead of the crowds back home, flip though any newspaper (most critically Andrew Sarris in the *Village Voice* or Pauline Kael in the *New Yorker*) for details of which movie is showing where, and be warned that for the newest movies you'll need to line up for an hour just to buy your ticket, usually some time before it starts. Be sure you're in the right line for the showing you want, and expect to pay around $6 or $7.

If you're here mid-September to early October the **New York Film Festival** at Alice Tully Hall, Lincoln Center, is well worth catching: a showcase of serious cinema from around the world.

Otherwise there are far fewer specialist movie theaters than you might expect, though at those which do exist the choice is good. Titles change daily, so you'll need a keen eye to spot a favorite from what's on offer. The following regularly feature **Revival and Art movies**.

Anthology Film Archives, 32–34 Second Ave. (☎505-5181). Shows many movies you thought you'd never have the chance to see again.

Biograph, 225 W. 57th St. (☎582-4582). Revival house featuring all your favorite movie classics.

The New Cinema 12, 22 E. 12th St. (☎924-3363). Modern films (1950 onward) are standard here, plus the occasional festival.

Eighth Street Playhouse, 52 W. 8th St. (☎674-6515). Shows the *Rocky Horror Picture Show* Fridays and Saturdays at midnight.

The Museum of Modern Art, 11 W. 53rd St. (☎708-9490). Two new theaters devoted to a vast array of classic films. Archival material is available in MoMA's film library.

Museum of the Moving Image, 35th Ave. and 36th St., Queens (☎718/784-0077). Foreign and avant-garde movies.

Theater 80 St. Marks, 80 St. Mark's Place (☎254-7400). Also schedules classics. Don't miss the mini-Grauman's Chinese Theater collection of star footprints and autographs in the sidewalk outside.

CHAPTER ELEVEN

OUT FROM THE CITY

With characteristic chauvinism New Yorkers view the idea of traveling farther north than the Bronx with horror, and it's true that most
visitors find little time to escape from the obvious attractions of the
city. But within easy reach of Manhattan are surprisingly pastoral
destinations that offer the perfect antidote to Manhattan's hassle and heat. A
couple of days' time out can revive your waning enthusiasm, and there's no shortage of interesting places to head for.

The most obvious target if you don't want to leave the city for more than a day
or two is **Long Island**, which unfurls east of the city in over a hundred miles of
lush farmland and broad sandy beaches. This is where the city's wealthy (**The
South Fork**), not so wealthy (**Jones Beach**), and gay (**Fire Island**) head at
weekends, and it's not unusual for it to be crowded in places, particularly in high
season. But there are stretches that serve fewer trippers, the unfashionable
North Fork for example; and ferry links with Connecticut mean you're well
placed to travel on to New England.

North of the city, the **Hudson Valley** is no less accessible and certainly more
beautiful, its wooded banks winding their way north to the state capital **Albany**—
itself not of much interest but providing a possible overnighter before the angular
profile of the **Catskill Mountains**.

Practicalities

Getting around
Getting around is straightforward. The quickest way to Long Island is the **Long
Island Railroad** (departures from Penn Station in Manhattan: ☎718/454-LIRR or
☎718/990-7498 for details), though numerous **bus services** (operated by the
major companies and the local **Hampton Jitney**, ☎212/895-9336 or
☎516/283-4600) cover most destinations.

To the Hudson Valley and Albany, train services operate on a limited network
(from Grand Central Station in Manhattan), but more practical are the major bus
companies. For bus timetables and routes contact the appropriate office:
Greyhound, 625 Eighth Ave. (☎212/971-0492), or the Port Authority Terminal
(☎212/635-0800). The local bus company in the Hudson Valley and Catskills is
Shortline (☎212/736-4700).

Most convenient, of course, is travel by **car**, since the public transit network is
less than comprehensive, and even if you are going somewhere that has a bus or
train station it will often be several miles outside town, making a certain amount
of walking unavoidable.

If you haven't brought your own vehicle the Manhattan Yellow Pages are the
best place to locate inexpensive rental deals—or see our listings overleaf. Bear in
mind, though, that New York State law deems that you have to be 25 years of age

at least to rent a vehicle of any kind. Some agencies may bend the rules, but it costs, and the best thing to do is to travel to New Jersey or Connecticut on public transit, where 21 is the minimum age, and rent a car there. Assuming you are over 25, rates at the cheaper outlets start at $50 a day plus $9 collision damage insurance, and a small milage charge after the first 100 miles; weekly prices start at about $200 plus $56 collision insurance, with the milage rate levied after 850 miles. Alternatively there are the big chains, whose rates can be dramatically reduced by booking a week or so in advance.

CAR RENTAL OUTLETS

ABC, 200 E. 33rd St. (☎685-5955). Two-day packages available for $99, including 200 miles free.

Avis, 217 E. 43rd St. and elsewhere (☎800/331-1212).

Budget, 225 E. 43rd St. and other branches all over Manhattan (☎807-8700). $68 a day, unlimited milage.

East Side Rent a Car, 240 E. 92nd St. (☎410-3100). Three-day deals for $119.

Dollar, 235 W. 56th St. (☎399-3590). $70 a day with unlimited milage.

Hertz, 310 E. 48th St. and elsewhere (☎800/654-3131).

National 252 W. 40th St. (☎800/328-4567).

Rent a Wreck (☎800/421-7253 or ☎212/721-0080). Specialists in used car rental: $119 Friday–Sunday.

Tried & True, 241 W. 28th St. (☎268-9444). Three days for $139, including 300 free miles.

Accommodation

Accommodation choices range from youth hostels/YMCAs through bed and breakfast to more luxurious hotels. There are only a scattering of **youth hostels**, and **hotels** go for only a little less than in New York City. Cheap and handy stand-bys exist, however, in **motels**, whose prices hover around $40 for a double. The *Howard Johnson* and *Holiday Inn* hotel indexes, available from their hotels in New York and around the USA, give prices of their upstate hotels/motels (including the reductions made by squeezing several people into a room). Two further upstate possibilities are **bed and breakfasts** and **country inns**—basically European-style guesthouses. We've listed the best value and most practical of what's available, but for full details locally, contact the relevant **Chamber of Commerce** office—small information bureaux, open to the public at least Monday to Friday and often at weekends. Addresses and phone numbers are included in the guide. Alternatively, several **agencies** can help with bed and breakfast:

• **Long Island** *Alternate Lodgings*, Box 1782, E. Hampton, NY 11937 (☎513/324-9449; ☎212/686-7847); *A Reasonable Alternative*, 117 Spring St., Port Jefferson, NY 11777 (☎516/928-4034); *Bed & Breakfast of Long Island*, PO Box 312, Old Westbury, NY 11568 (☎516/334-6231); *Hampton Bed & Breakfast Registry*, Box 695, E. Moriches, NY 11940 (☎516/878-4439).

• **Hudson Valley & Catskills** *Bed & Breakfast USA*, PO Box 528, Croton-on-Hudson, NY 10521 (☎914/271-6228).

LONG ISLAND

Long Island, stretching some 125 miles to the east of Manhattan, is an obvious target for a quick break from the city. The western end, which includes the urban boroughs of Brooklyn and Queens, is little more than an extension of NYC. But as you head east, the population begin to thin out and a countryside takes over which, especially in the sandy reaches of the South Shore and the far-off North Fork, can get surprisingly remote. The **North and South Shores** differ greatly, too—the former more immediately beautiful, its cliffs topped with mansions and estates built by wealthy New Yorkers in America's boom years, while the South Shore is fringed by an almost continuous stretch of beach and dune, and in many places populous pockets of vacationers to match. **Jones Beach** and—for gays especially—**Fire Island** are the major resorts here. At its far end Long Island splits in two, the **North Fork** retaining a marked rural aspect while the **South Fork**, much of which is known as **The Hamptons**, has long been an enclave of New York's richest and finest.

For most of these places transport is no problem, and while a car is as ever the best way of getting around, the Long Island Railroad provides a reliable if rather grubby alternative. *Greyhound* plies longer routes or, for local connections, there are the *Hampton Jitney, Suffolk County*, and other bus services. Pick up schedules at local Chambers of Commerce or, for the LI Railroad, from Penn Station.

If you're driving there are a number of regulations covering Long Island's **beaches**. Permits for parking are issued only to residents of the nearby towns, and without one you face a steep daily rate (or even steeper fine) if you want to leave your car in any of the ordained parking lots. On the whole it comes out cheaper to head down to the beach on foot, or, if you have a car and want to use it, to either find a beach at which you can park for free or somewhere really out of the way where no one's likely to disturb you. For full information contact the local Chamber of Commerce.

The South Shore and Fire Island

The suburbs of Brooklyn and Queens straggle their way eastward, merging without break into the drab commuter towns of western Long Island. **GARDEN CITY** is as green (and as bland) as its name suggests, made up of long shady boulevards lined with grandiose stockbroker dwellings sitting behind obsessive lawns. Its 7th Street has been tagged "the Fifth Avenue of Long Island," dotted with fashion and specialty shops, and the town as a whole has an exclusive air. Other than the pricey ($160 and up) but pleasant *Garden City Hotel* at 45 Seventh St. (☎516/747-3000) there's nowhere **to stay**, and apart from the **Cradle of Aviation Museum** (daily 9am–5pm) out at Mitchel Field, little reason to stop at all. But if you do find yourself out here, **eating and drinking** are best at *Leo's* on the corner of Franklin Avenue and 7th Street. Five miles away, just off the Northern State Parkway, **OLD BETHPAGE VILLAGE** (March–Nov Tue–Sun 10am–5pm, Dec–Feb Tue–Sun 10am–4pm) forms the only possible target on this part of the island aside from the sea. A restored pre-Civil War village painstakingly assembled here from a variety of sites, it's billed as "a trip back in time," with craft demonstrations, animals, and the like helping to suspend your disbelief. Personally, I'd head straight on for the beach.

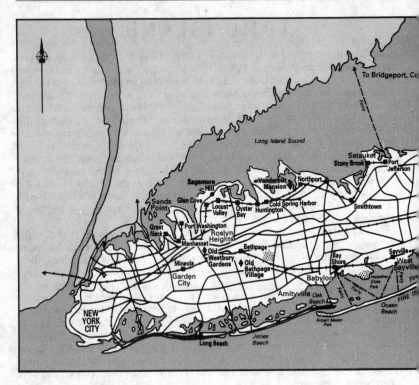

Long Island's **South Shore** merges gently with the wild Atlantic, shallow and open and slick with creamy sand that spawns luscious dune-filled beaches along its entire 125-mile length. First actual beach is **LONG BEACH**, easy to reach by regular train from Penn Station and consequently well favored by New Yorkers eager to escape the summer city heat. **JONES BEACH STATE PARK** (actually a series of beaches) lines a skinny spit of land a little farther along, the brainchild of Robert Moses who single-handedly masterminded so many of New York's parks, both in and out of the city, and whose desire to cover everything with asphalt has left him with a rather ambiguous reputation today. Jones Beach is probably his most successful creation, primarily because he decided to leave well alone, content to simply make it more accessible with a boardwalk and a handful of parking lots. Come here on warm summer weekends and you'll find yourself fighting for room; edge along a few hundred yards and the crowds begin to thin out, especially if you stroll up as far as **GILGO** or **OAK BEACH**, or cross the water to the **Robert Moses State Park** on the western tip of Fire Island. Unless you bring your own, the only alternative to fast **food** is the *Boardwalk Restaurant*, hard by the most populous section of Jones Beach, where you can eat seafood for $6 up and take in great views of the Atlantic at the same time. Those driving pay $3 for the privilege of a parking space; otherwise the best way of reaching Jones Beach from the city is to take a train from Penn Station to FREEPORT and a connecting bus from there.

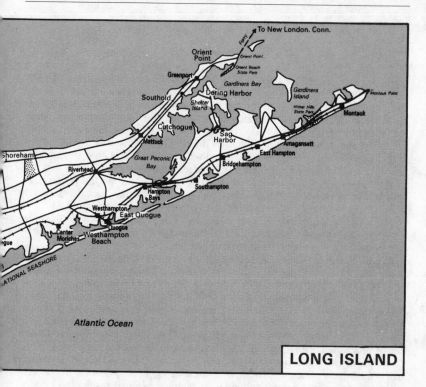

LONG ISLAND

From Jones Beach follow Ocean Parkway along the island to **CAPTREE**, best base for early morning fishing trips or whale-sighting expeditions (☎516/785-1600 if you're interested), and cross back to Long Island itself by way of the Robert Moses Causeway to **BAY SHORE**—of no interest for itself but definitely the best of the ferry terminals for FIRE ISLAND (which you can reach for around $4 one way). This way you miss out the sprawling mess of **BABYLON** and **AMITYVILLE**, the latter with a reputation founded on its famous "horror" of a decade or so ago—an event since popularized in a book and movie of the same name. The house on the hill, from which the family were driven in terror by some mysterious supernatural force, still stands.

Fire Island

In many ways **FIRE ISLAND**, a slim spit of land lying parallel to the south shore, is a microcosm of New York City. In summer half of Manhattan heads up here for the weekend, holing up in a series of tiny settlements that mirror the city in miniature. These days it's primarily a gay resort: young gays make for **CHERRY GROVE**; older and wealthier ones for **FIRE ISLAND PINES**; **KISMET** is the hangout of older Jews, **OCEAN BAY PARK** yuppie and jappie; while **POINT O WOODS** is probably the most exclusive enclave on the island, ringed by fences to keep out the riffraff. Whatever you think about this kind of strict demarcation, it's typically New York, and it's as well to remember that Fire Island isn't the kind of place people visit to experience something different; they go because they know what to expect.

Few people live on Fire Island in winter, when it's a wind-swept strip of desolation buffeted by Atlantic storms and only connected with the mainland by infrequent ferries. Most houses are holiday homes, or timeshare apartments bought up by syndicates of people so they can have at least one weekend in two out on the beach. Ferries dock at a number of villages but most frequently at trendy **OCEAN BEACH**, where the trippers dump supplies of groceries on boldly marked carts (cars aren't allowed on the island) and set off for their vacation pads. The season is as rigidly defined as the people: Memorial Day onward Fire Island hums with activity and is swamped with crowds; after Labor Day, though the weather may still be very warm, the throngs diminish dramatically and you may be able to find a space on the beach or a table in one of the restaurants. Needless to say it's better out of season, but if you can't come then it's still worth a trip, if only to taste the bizarre spirit of hedonism that infects the place for these few months. Bear in mind, too, that even when Fire Island is packed to the gills, it's still long enough to throw off the bulk of the crowds and offers some gorgeous wild walks along the dunes and beaches.

Accommodation should be booked in advance whenever you're coming, and reservations are essential in high season: *Jerry's*, 620 Bay Walk, Ocean Beach (☎516/583-8870) doles out rooms, and you can expect to pay roughly $45 per person, double that at weekends; *Flynn's*, in nearby Ocean Bay Park (☎516/583-8000), has doubles from $60. In Fire Island Pines—and thus more specifically for gays—best place to stay is the *Botal* (☎516/597-5600), or, much cheaper, *Buck 'n' Beau's Bed 'n' Board* (☎516/597-6833); and in Cherry Grove there's the *Cherry Grove Beach Hotel* (☎516/597-6600)—home also to the hi-tech and very popular *Ice Palace* discotheque. *Giovanni's*, directly opposite the Ocean Beach ferry terminal, is the best and most convivial place to eat for under $5; *Flynn's* is frequented with almost ritualistic determination by the younger summer residents—Fridays above all—while on Saturdays, *Leo's* on Bay Walk is good for riotous boozing and eating. *Skimmer's*, in Ocean Bay Park, is the place to go for hot hors d'oeuvres.

From Bay Shore route 27 hurries through a series of sprawling settlements, none of special interest. (Unless you're following an *alternative route to Fire Island*, in which case ferries leave from SAYVILLE—to Cherry Grove, Fire Island Pines, and PATCHOGUE—to Davis Park, Watch Hill. All cost around $4 one way.) Beaches continue all along here, emptier the farther you get away from the city, but if you're not intent on swimming or sunning, don't stop until you near the southern fork of Long Island and the area known as THE HAMPTONS.

The North Shore and North Fork

The **North Shore** is Long Island at its most rugged, dropping into the sea in a series of bluffs, coves, and wooded headlands, less developed than the South Shore and in many places with a more tangibly rural feel, especially up on the distant North Fork. Come off the Long Island Expressway beyond Queens and you're already on top of that part of the North Shore known as the **Gold Coast**— hunting-ground in the 1920s and 1930s of the rich and elegant, and even now dotted with palatial mansions hiding away in trees which sweep graciously down to the deeply indented shoreline. The first jut of land you reach—with the uninteresting town of GREAT NECK at its center—became F. Scott Fitzgerald's *West Egg* in *The Great Gatsby*, home of the narrator Nick and Gatsby himself. To this day it harbors some of the most expensive real estate in the country—so expensive that nowadays few people can afford to live here, and many of the large houses have either been demolished or stand empty and disused.

Sands Point and Old Westbury Gardens

SANDS POINT, on the sharp tip of the next peninsula, is one such place, a collection of turn-of-the-century buildings once owned by the Guggenheim family and now open to the public as a park and museum. It's a mixed estate, part Tudor revival, part turreted castle (**Castlegourd**), with, at its center, the Normandy-style manor house of **Falaise**. You can walk around the house, check out a display on American folk and applied art in the Castlegourd section of the complex, or just browse around the 209 acres of parkland—it's deliberately unkempt, and offers great views over what Fitzgerald called "the most domesticated body of salt water in the Western hemisphere, the great barnyard of Long Island Sound." (Open May–Oct Sat–Wed 10am–5pm. Tours—non-obligatory—of the park cost 50¢ and take 40 minutes; obligatory escorted tours of Falaise run all day Mon–Wed and take an hour, fee $2. Admission to estate $1.)

If Sands Point represents an attempt to recreate an entire pageant of past European architectural styles, then the estate of OLD WESTBURY GARDENS a few miles inland is more definite in its aims—a conscious and not entirely unsuccessful stab at reproducing an English country estate complete with stately mansion and acres of imaginatively ordered gardens. Built by one John S. Phipps to keep his English wife in the style to which she was accustomed, the English feel is enhanced by the furnishings of the house—oak panels, gilded mirrors, and crystal chandeliers—and a collection of paintings that is dominated by the works of Reynolds, Constable, and Gainsborough. All in all, a convincing charade, and a vivid indication of the degree of wealth it was possible to amass in America's boom years. (May–Oct Wed–Sun 10am–5pm. Admission to gardens $4.50; house and gardens $7.50. Look out for the jazz concerts on the lawns during the summer months.)

Roslyn Heights and Sagamore Hill

After Westbury Gardens you'll want to get away from Long Island's freeway-dominated center and head back to the coast. ROSLYN HEIGHTS is the first town you'll hit, quaintly centering on a dipping main street and flanked by towered and gabled clapboard houses. From here a road heads coastward via the newly refurbished town of GLEN COVE—an ugly combination of industrial estate and pedestrianized shopping mall—and some lushly wooded countryside. This is LOCUST VALLEY, home for many years to a localized accent that was distinguished by its lazy, rather affected drawl. Non-speakers claimed it was borne of the snobbery of the people who lived here and referred to it as "Locust Valley Lockjaw": even now it's occasionally contended that you can identify the languid tones of someone who has lived in Locust Valley all their life.

It's SAGAMORE HILL, though, that makes the road worth taking—ex-country retreat of Teddy Roosevelt and today one of Long Island's major tourist hangouts, swarmed over by thousands of eager schoolkids in Indian file every year (May–Oct daily 9:30am–5pm, Nov–April 9:30am–4:30pm; $1). Roosevelt lived here for 30-odd years—after cowboying for a while in the Dakotas and in between big game hunting in Africa—and the house has been very largely kept as it was then: 23 rooms in all, cosily furnished and adorned everywhere by the great man's trophies, sprouting horns from walls or grinning toothily up from the firesides. All of the furnishings, even the books, are original, in a sensitive and not overostentatious piece of preservation. The negligible price and gorgeous grounds, springing lawns falling down to Oyster Bay and the sea, make it a detour well worth making—though you'll need a car. Before you leave, be sure to take a look in at the **Old Orchard Museum** across the far side of the parking lot. This displays artifacts relating to Teddy's political and personal life, and shows a short biographical film.

Oyster Bay to Sunken Meadow

Push south from here to **OYSTER BAY** and **Raynham Hall** (20 West Main Street; Tues–Sun 1–5pm; £1), a heavily restored eighteenth-century mansion that was the Townsend family home during the Revolutionary war. British troops were quartered here for a time, and Townsend, who was Washington's chief spy in New York City, was able through some smart eavesdropping to foil Benedict Arnold's plot to betray West Point. These days it's a great deal less intriguing, but worth the entrance fee for the carefully renovated rooms and some neat formal gardens. Just outside town the **Planting Fields Arboretum** (daily 9am–5pm) on Planting Fields Road is an extensive network of botanical gardens that's worth a look if you're interested in such things, and includes the **Coe Mansion**, a mock-Tudor monstrosity which the marine-insurance magnate William Robertson Coe called home (Mon–Fri 1–3:30pm; entrance fee May–Sept and weekends, other times free).

COLD SPRING HARBOR lies across from here, one of Long Island's most attractive small towns though long since despoiled by a burgeoning tourist industry. It grew up as a whaling port, and the **Whaling Museum** on Main Street (Tues–Sun 11am–5pm) recaptures that era better than the town ever could now, its major features a fully equipped whaleboat and a 400-piece display of scrimshaw. Hourly films give the lowdown on the industry, which flourished here in the mid-nineteenth century and died almost as soon as it had begun. A few miles on, **HUNTINGTON** is a bustling little provincial town with a couple of minor excitements which could conceivably hold you for an hour or two. **Walt Whitman's birthplace** (Sat–Sun 10am–4pm, Wed–Fri 1–4pm), out at Huntington Station, has a handful of the poet's manuscripts; the **Historical Society** (Tues–Fri 10am–4pm) shows a set of eighteenth-century period rooms, and the **Heckscher Museum** holds a rather ordinary potpourri of American and European fine art (Tues–Fri 10am–5pm, Sat–Sun 1–5pm, closed Mon).

Less modest is the **VANDERBILT MANSION** (April–Oct Tues–Sat 10am–4pm, Sun noon–5pm; Nov–Mar Tues–Sun noon–4pm; $1) just outside CENTREPORT, a country estate once home to William K. Vanderbilt II and showing about as much taste as you will have come to expect if you've seen a Vanderbilt residence before. This one, in the style of a Baroque Spanish palace, is heavily ornate both outside and in, with marble-encased galleries, swirling staircases, and gaudily carved fireplaces. William K. hadn't the business brain of his great-grandfather Cornelius (the railroad tycoon), and he devoted himself instead to living it up and indulging his great passion, natural history. The fruits of this enthusiasm (all 17,000 of them) are on show in a building in another part of the grounds, and there's also a rather run-of-the-mill planetarium.

The Vanderbilt Mansion has a commanding view of **NORTHPORT BAY**, where the town of the same name—"achingly all-American," wrote Joyce Johnson in *Minor Characters*—sits bright and orderly by the water's edge. Its main street runs straight and wide to the placid harbor, a long stretch of wooden-fronted stores and houses that looked authentic enough to be used as a backdrop for shoot-outs in westerns in the 1920s and 1930s. A small **historical museum** (Tues–Sun 1–4:30pm), giving a resume of the town's shipbuilding past, may provide an excuse for the briefest of stops, but otherwise head straight on to **SUNKEN MEADOW**, which emerges through the trees as a free **beach**, nature and recreation reserve that's more remote and far less crowded than, say, Jones or Long Beach.

Stony Brook

Beyond, you pass through some of the most beautiful countryside on the island, leafy glades enfolding a road that winds its way around the tranquil inlets of Long Island Sound. **STONY BROOK** is generally regarded as the historic and cultural heart of the region, home to a *SUNY* campus and with a reconstructed center that stands as testament to the dream of wealthy 1940s philanthropist Ward Delville, who rescued the place from chronic decay and rebuilt it to its original Federal-style splendor. It's neatly done, and there's no denying the prettiness of the white clapboard houses, but for all the attention to detail you can't help feeling you're seeing a reconstruction, and its timbered storefronts remind more of a laundered shopping precinct.

You have to stroll half a mile or so down the road to find the town's real attraction—**The Museums at Stony Brook**, a concoction of three museums, one showing paintings and drawings, another a collection of carriages, and a third a historical collection. The *Art Museum* (Wed–Sat 10am–5pm, Sun noon–5pm; $5) is largely made up of the work of **William Sidney Mount**, an artist who lived in a house up the road (occasionally open to the public) and painted most of his life along the North Shore between here and Setauket. Mount is widely considered America's first true genre painter: he began painting European-influenced religious scenes but soon graduated to more original portrayals of local street and rural life, incorporating blacks and ethnic groups centrally and uncritically into pictures for the first time. Contemporary critics found this mildly outrageous but applauded Mount's skill, and his paintings were snapped up avidly in Europe, where aristocrats were delighted with what they saw as an exotic and faintly risque subject-matter. Among the best pictures in the museum's vast collection (they own virtually everything of Mount's) are the sensitive *Banjo Player* (1855), probably Mount's best-known painting, *Dance of the Haymakers* (1845), and *Farmers Nooning* (1836)—one of the most ambitious of his works, with a highly original attention to detail and landscape. Look out, too, for some of his local scenes—*The Mill at Stony Brook* (1855) for example, the model for which you can see by the pond in the center of town (June–Oct, Sun 1–4pm).

Setauket to Riverhead

From Stony Brook Route 25a follows the coast to Port Jefferson, taking in the ravishingly pretty village of **SETAUKET** on the way, where you could do worse than take a stroll around the churchyard of the eighteenth-century **Caroline Church** or just stop off to soak up the ordered peace of the manicured village green. **PORT JEFFERSON** is a mix of industrial working harbor and jazzed-up waterside buildings housing seafood restaurants and souvenir shops—pleasant enough, but too much a museum piece to enjoy for very long. Basically the reason for coming here is twofold: to call in at the **Mather Museum** on Prospect Street, which puts on a convincing show of local artifacts and Indian finds, and to wait for one of the frequent (four times daily in spring, more in summer) **ferries** to Bridgeport, Connecticut. The journey takes an hour and a half and costs around $10 one way, $14 one-day round trip for foot passengers.

SHOREHAM, farther down the coast, has for some time been the focus of a local controversy: nestling sinisterly behind the exuberant green, it's one of the largest nuclear reactors on the East Coast, finished a couple of years back but yet to produce any electricity. Pressure groups campaigned against the siting of the reactor from the beginning and now seem confident it will never come onstream, not least because—since construction went a cool $4 billion over budget—no one can afford its energy. Inland from Shoreham the leafy gentleness of the North Shore gives way to the sweeping plowland plains of Suffolk County's agricultural heartland—believe it or not, the North East's largest arable producer, with a climate mild enough to grow peaches, tomatoes, and grapes out of doors. At **RIVERHEAD**, an unattractive town where you can stop at the **Suffolk County Museum** (West Main Street; Mon–Sat 12:30–4:30pm), you branch south for the designer-chic of the Hamptons and Montauk, or take a more rustic path up Long Island's North Fork.

The North Fork

The **North Fork** has a strikingly different feel to its southern neighbor, and, indeed, to the rest of the island: not only is it more rural, but its landscapes are a great deal wilder. There are also far fewer tourists. Of its towns, **CUTCHOGUE** is the first of any real interest, a set of pre- and post-colonial houses grouped around a village green. It makes a good base for tours around the **Hargrave Vineyard** at the junction of Route 25 and Alvan's Lane—Long Island's only winery. These run regularly throughout the day between Memorial and Labor Day, at weekends only from Labor Day until Christmas.

Heading west, the North Fork takes on a decidedly New England air, primarily due to the fact that this region, together with a number of towns across Long Island Sound, once formed an independent colony. Its principal center is **SOUTHOLD**, where there's an **Archaeological Museum** which houses the most complete set of Indian finds of Long Island. Drop in during summer months between Friday and Sunday, 1:30–4:30pm and you'll find it open; otherwise carry straight on—the town has little else to detain you.

GREENPORT, five miles on, is probably this area's most picturesque town, a clutter of narrow streets and alleys leading down to a harbor pierced by the masts of visiting yachts. It also forms the best base for exploring this end of the island, with **accommodation** easy to find and relatively cheap (try *Bartlett House*, 503 Front Street (☎516/477-0371) which has inexpensive double rooms). There are regular 15-minute **ferry connections** to Shelter Island and hence the South Fork.

ORIENT POINT, just a few miles east, offers access to the gloriously untouched **Orient Point State Park** and frequent ferries (in summer six a day; last one leaves 2pm) to New London, Connecticut—a journey which takes 1 hour 30 minutes and costs $8 one way, $12 one-day round trip for foot passengers.

The South Fork: The Hamptons, Sag Harbor, and Montauk

Chic riviera or staid stockbroker country? Whatever you think of The Hamptons they're still very much the place to see and be seen. A string of small towns set in the green countryside of Long Island's fashionable South Fork, there are few more wealthy—or status-ridden—parts of America than this: huge palaces lurk in the trees or stand boldly on the flats behind the dunes, much of the property bought up greedily by affluent New Yorkers eager for a weekend retreat; cars are consciously prestigious British or German models; clothes, designer labels of the safest and most sedate kind. Nowhere, but nowhere, is consumption as deliberately conspicuous as in The Hamptons . . ..

Even though their moneyed reputation is less than a century old, **The Hamptons** have always been sought after, and the towns here are among the oldest in the state, settled by restless New Englanders in the mid-1650s. Until the late nineteenth century they remained relatively isolated farming communities, but as the rich became more mobile, turning up here in their motor cars, The Hamptons became their playground. In the 1920s and 1930s celebrities and ritzy New Yorkers flocked here in droves, starting a fashion that has never really died. Pollock and De Kooning came up in the 40s, Betty Friedan still lives in Sag Harbor, Gloria Vanderbilt has a house in Southampton, and Woody Allen and other big names are either residents or frequent visitors, all giving the area a gossip column cachet that you'll either love or hate. That it's expensive there can be no doubt, and the crowds that congregate here in summer may alone be enough to put you off. But if you come up on the Long Island Railroad, stay somewhere relatively cheap (for all the chic country clubs there are still plenty of shoe-string motels), and use local buses for getting around, you'll find you can survive without spending a fortune. And the beaches that line the nearby Atlantic are everywhere long enough to grab some space for yourself.

Westhampton

The Hampton farthest west, **WESTHAMPTON**, attracts a crowd markedly less studded with celebrities than its eastern counterparts and is, as a result, more commercial: discos jostling for space with loud pizza restaurants, and the singles set ("Groupers" to the locals) flooding into timeshares to swap sexual—or nowadays maybe real estate—experiences. There's little to do but swim by day and eat and drink by night, but if you're here in the first week of August you may want to see the annual open-air art show in nearby **WESTHAMPTON BEACH**. Quieter, and a good base for the fifteen-mile-long swathe of beach that rings nearby Shinnecook Bay, is **QUOGUE**, a mile or two farther on and accessible by bus. The same goes for **HAMPTON BAYS**, essentially a family-oriented resort but neatly placed for the nearby sheltered expanses of Shinnecook and Beconic Bays—both of which, if you're prepared to walk, have beach space for the asking. If, however, you want somewhere with a touch more style, forge on to Southampton.

Southampton

Largest of the towns, and the best situated for seeing the rest of the region, **SOUTHAMPTON** is one of the most famous havens of the rich on the entire eastern seaboard. And though it hasn't been totally overwhelmed by money, long association with the Long Island Smart Set has left it unashamedly cutesy: one glance at the clothes stores, galleries, and jewelry shops lining its pristine streets should be enough to give you some idea of the kind of people who visit here. That said, even if it isn't cheaper, accommodation is easier to find than in the other Hamptons, and the nearby beaches are quite superb—though like the town itself they can be obliterated with bodies at the season's height. If you don't have a car the beaches are just a short walk away and ideal for a day or so's basking; if you have, try somewhere more remote—like most of the beaches around here, only town residents are allowed to use the parking lots.

Things to see in town include an excellent local **Historical Museum** (17 Meeting House Lane; mid-June–Sept 14, Tues–Sun 11am–5pm), which gives a rundown on Southampton history from Indian times onward; the **Parrish Art Museum** (25 Job's Lane; Tues–Sat 10am–5pm, Sun 1–5pm), which puts on changing exhibitions and whose permanent collection includes a large set of works by William Merrit Chase; and the **Halsey Homestead**, the oldest English frame house in the state, built in 1648 and furnished in period style (South Main Street; mid-June–mid-Sept, Tues–Sun 11am–5pm).

For information, the *Chamber of Commerce* (daily 9am–5pm) is at 76 Main Street and gives out walking tours of the town and lists of B&B rooms; otherwise the cheapest bed in town is at the *Hill Guest House*, 535 Hill Street (☎516/283-9889). For **food**, *Joe's*, 23 Hill Street, does pizzas and pasta at rock-bottom prices, or, if you want something a little more exciting, try *Barrister's* on Main Street for marvelous soft-shell crabs; alternatively, the *Driver's Seat*, on Job's Lane, is younger, trendier, and marginally less expensive. **Bikes** can be rented by the hour or day from *Rotations* (☎516/283-2890), at the junction of Job's Lane and Hill Street. If you're here at the end of the summer, Labor Day weekend is highlighted by the **Pow-Wow** at the **Shinnecook Indian Reservation** on the outskirts of town, when the tribe opens its allotted lands to public gaze and sells ethnic foods and handicrafts and performs traditional dances. Other times, steer clear of the reservation; the Shinnecooks are said to discourage visitors.

Bridgehampton

The next Hampton east is **BRIDGEHAMPTON**, a migrant black workers' community turned comfortable escape for successful New York literary and artistic types, who have more or less banished the original locals by buying up all the property—a familiar tale around here. A drive down the main street will show you just about all there is to see. *Cato's* and *Bobby Van's* are the laid-back hangouts where Bridgehampton's novelists and playwrights drift in to eat after a hard day over a hot word processor. Give them a go if you're here for any length of time—you might even see someone famous (Kurt Vonnegut, Malcolm Morley, and Alan Alda are all local residents). And before you head on, hang a right at the war memorial, where a few miles down the road is another fine stretch of sandy **beach**, one that stays far less crowded than Southampton's.

East Hampton, Amagansett, and Sag Harbor

Five miles farther on, **EAST HAMPTON** was once voted the prettiest village in the entire USA by a newspaper poll, and it's easy to see why. Dark clapboard houses set around a wedge of village green, backed by a stolid Norman-style church and small cemetery make this small-town America at its most endearing. The house at 14 James Lane was the subject of John Howard Payne's *Home Sweet*

Home, a song the actor-dramatist wrote from Paris in the 1820s when homesick, and is now open to the public as a **museum** (Mon–Sat 10am–4pm, Sun 2–4pm, closed Tues & Wed Sept–June). A sharp precis of the town's history is given at an eighteenth-century **town house** on Main Street, but that aside there's little to keep you—only a still-working **Hook Mill** at the far end of Main Street and the palace-studded estates just south of town.

If you want to stay, be aware that rooms in East Hampton can work out prohibitively expensive. Far better to bed down in adjacent **AMAGANSETT**—less pretentious than East Hampton and another gathering place for the singles set, who swarm down to strut their stuff along the nearby **Atlantic Avenue Beach**. There's a good museum, too, the **East Hampton Town Marine Museum** (on Bluff Road: July–Aug Tues–Sun 10:30am–5pm, closed Mon; June and Sept Sat & Sun 10:30am–5pm), dedicated to the maritime history of this part of Long Island and with displays and dioramas on fishing, whaling, and other nautical activities. At bedtime try the *Gansett Green Manor* (☎516/267-3133) on Main Street, where you should be able to find doubles for around $60.

North of here, and administratively part of East Hampton, **SAG HARBOR** is one of the most historic of the South Fork towns. It was once a harbor second only to that of New York, which was designated first Port of Entry to the New Country by George Washington; the state's first **custom house** was established here and still stands (June–Sept Tues–Sun 10am–5pm). Nowadays Sag Harbor is becoming heavily touristed but, despite the encroaching designer clothes stores, it retains a feel which marks it out strikingly from its rather more sanitized neighbors to the south and west.

The town's prosperity was founded, albeit for a short period only, on whaling, and as at Cold Spring Harbor on Long Island's north shore there are a number of relics from those years. Best of these is the **Whaling Museum** on Main Street (May 15–Sept 30, Mon–Sat 10am–5pm, Sun 1–5pm), housed in an overblown Greek Revival mansion and containing whaling equipment and a collection of guns and scrimshaw. Nearby the **Whaler's Presbyterian Church** dates from the same era, once topped with a telescope-shaped spire (since lost) and crenellated with jutting rows of whale blubber spades. A more touching monument to the town's whaling antecedents is the **Oakland Cemetery**, where memorials remember young whalers, most of whom died in their twenties: one, in the shape of a broken mast, stands out in particular—beautifully reliefed and recalling horrific encounters with "the monsters of the deep."

There's no whaling done nowadays, of course, and the town focuses on a peaceful main street which curves elegantly down to a harbor where pleasure boats rock gently at their moorings, looking over to the privately owned estates of **NORTH HAVEN**. From here one Colonel Meigs routed the unfortunate English in the Revolutionary wars, destroying a dozen ships and making off with copious supplies of food and drink—a feat for which he's remembered in a monument on Union Street. Now the only reason to go to North Haven is to take one of the frequent ferries to **SHELTER ISLAND**, a short $4 trip across the bay. There's not much here unless you're into the wholesome joys of outdoor activities, but Route 114 takes you straight to DERING HARBOR from where you can catch another ferry to GREENPORT on Long Island's North Fork.

John Steinbeck lived in Sag Harbor for many years—it was from here that he set out on his *Travels with Charley*—and he's remembered by a plaque on the windmill in the harbor, which also offers **tourist information** in the summer months. There's hardly anywhere to **stay**—only the *Baron's Cove Inn* (☎516/725-2100) has rooms, and they're not cheap—but if you're after **something to eat** Main Street is lined with reasonably priced restaurants. Try the burgers at *Ryerson's* or the *Sandbar*, and have a drink in The Corner near the harbor, a well-frequented local haunt. The only other possibility of a room at realistic rates is the *Ram's Head Inn* (☎516/749-0811), overlooking Coecles Bay on Shelter Island, where you can sleep for around $30 per person.

Montauk

MONTAUK, up beyond Amagansett on the farthest tip of Long Island, is quite different from the rest of The Hamptons—indeed, few people ever lump them together. Untainted by social climbers, it sits bleakly among the dunes, a blustery, wind-battered place which, but for a hurricane and the Wall Street Crash of 1929, would have been a sizable resort. As it is, the entrepreneur who wanted to develop the place lost his money, and, a weird Florentine tower in the town center apart, Montauk stayed as it was—a not particularly attractive town with access to some enticingly undisturbed country, not least the dunes and free beaches of the **Hither Hills State Park** and the rocky toe of **Montauk Point** itself.

This area was originally, in the eighteenth century, little more than a summer pasture for grazing cattle, and the town's oldest buildings date from that time. Later it became better known as a quarantined campground for diseased veterans of the Spanish-American War—Teddy Roosevelt's Rough Riders & Co.—who were forced to bivouac on the wilds of Montauk Point after being refused entry by a hygiene-conscious New York City. Today this cape has a rare beauty that figures in all the tourist brochures, its **Lighthouse** (which you should be able to visit) forming an almost symbolic finale to this stretch of the American coast. Back in the town center there are a number of **motels** offering fairly priced rooms: try the *Oceanside Beach Resort* (☎516/668-9825), on the junction of the Old Montauk Highway and Main Street, whose doubles flicker between $30 and $70 depending on the time of year. For **sustenance** you'll do no better than *The Lobster Roll* on the Montauk Highway, a famous eatery in these parts, where you can feed on excellent fish and seafood, all freshly caught, for between $5 and $15.

THE HUDSON VALLEY AND THE CATSKILLS

To the average New Yorker, the **Hudson River Valley** is a wide, dirty stretch either passed under en route to Jersey City or over to reach Hackensack. But travel a few miles north, leaving Manhattan under its smog blanket, and you're in some of the most beautiful and easily accessible countryside in the state, a region lionized in the paintings of Thomas Cole and Frederick Church. The **Catskill Mountains** often formed the subject of their pictures and the timbered peaks of the Catskill Park are still one of the most attractive, most visited spots upstate. In the fall the region comes into its own with a kaleidoscopic variety of colors in the thick woodlands that rivals anything to be seen in New England. And always, below, is the Hudson, molasses brown as it forges its way to the ocean. Henry Hudson discovered the river in 1609, searching for the northwest passage—he failed, but the Dutch, French, and English settlements that sprung up in his wake have left a corridor of historic towns at the river's edge. These, and the surrounding countryside, form an ideal stretch for leisurely travel: otherwise a time-conscious circuit of the Hudson Valley will take about three days.

First stop on most explorations are the three **Tarrytown Restorations**, about 25 miles out of Manhattan: Washington Irving's former home is here, in idyllic surroundings which can be visited by train on a day trip from the city. Elsewhere the US Military Academy at **West Point** is an undying attraction, and beyond, the **West Bank** of the river leads through mountainsides of maple and a string of small towns like **New Paltz** and **Kingston**, both on *Greyhound* bus routes. *Amtrak* travel up the **East Bank** to **Albany**, the brutally if imaginatively modernized state capital, though this eastern rail route isn't going to help you see the mansions around Hyde Park: for these you just have to have a car.

Lower Hudson Valley: the Sleepy Hollow Restorations and Lyndhurst

Centering on **TARRYTOWN**, the **Sleepy Hollow Restorations** (Sunnyside, the Philipsburg and Van Cortland Manors) and the National Trust's **Lyndhurst** form the first stops on an exploration of the Hudson Valley, an easy day trip from NYC either by car or, less conveniently, the Hudson–Harlem commuter train from Grand Central. Tarrytown, leafy and residential, straddles the eastern end of the Tappan Zee Bridge and was made mildly famous as the village around which **Washington Irving** spun the tale of *The Legend of Sleepy Hollow*. Irving moved just south of the town in 1835, and rebuilt a farm cottage there as **Sunnyside**, "a little old fashioned stone mansion," he wrote, "all made up of gable ends, and as full of angles and corners as an old cocked hat." Tours squeeze around the rooms, and are enjoyable even if you've never read a word of Irving. To get there, turn off US-9 (Broadway) on to West Sunnyside Lane; tours run daily 10am–5pm, tickets $5, $8 for this and one other restoration, $12 for all three.

Lyndhurst

About a mile north of Sunnyside, **Lyndhurst** is as dapper a piece of nineteenth-century Gothic revivalism as you'll find anywhere, with spires and crockets and lapped by landscaped lawns. The conducted tours (daily except Mon May–Oct 10am–5pm, Nov, Jan, & March Sat–Sun 10am–5pm; admission charge) fill you in on Lyndhurst's collection of Victoriana and the lives of its previous owners, who included the hated Jay Gould. At the northern end of town the **Philipsburg Manor and Mill** (April–Dec daily 10am–5pm; Jan–March Sat–Sun 10am–5pm) was home to the Philipse family, Dutch settlers of 1600 who milled grain here and shipped it down river to New York and abroad. This made them a fabulous fortune, and their only mistake was to put their money on the wrong side in the Revolutionary War, after which their holdings were summarily confiscated. The **Manor House** restoration mimics that era in a too-good-to-be-true combination of bare floors and elegant furniture, though the **mill** itself is still real enough, grinding grain and lending the setting the charm of a Constable landscape. Sometimes it's possible to join group tours of the **Old Dutch Church of Sleepy Hollow**, across the road from the Manor House; or you can pick up a leaflet and explore the cemetery and its tombs of Washington Irving and Andrew Carnegie for yourself.

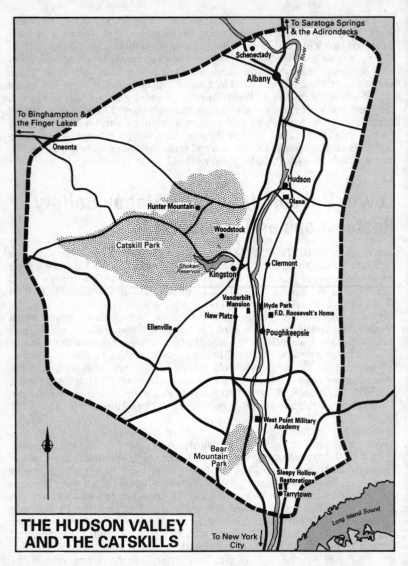

**THE HUDSON VALLEY
AND THE CATSKILLS**

Unlike the Philipse family, the Van Cortlands were staunch revolutionaries, and so hung on to the **Van Cortland Manor** (April–Dec daily, 10am–5pm; Jan–March Sat–Sun 10am–5pm) at **CROTON-ON-HUDSON** until 1945. This is the largest and most elaborate of the restorations, and the most ambitious—the house an immaculate representation of life in the late eighteenth century, with a pleasing contrast between the fripperies of the manor itself and the down-to-earth practicalities of its **Ferry House**. There are demonstrations of domestic arts and an ornamental garden, plus added ornaments in the shape of the becostumed staff. To get here, head north from Tarrytown on Route 9 for about 8 miles, exit on to Croton Point Avenue, then go one block east to South Riverside Avenue and turn right for the main entrance. Admission as Sunnyside.

Next stop for most will be West Point Military Academy, for which you cross the river at Peekskill; alternatively, if you're driving from Tarrytown it's possible to head over the bridge there and up through the closely wooded mountains of the **PALISADES INTERSTATE PARK** and **BEAR MOUNTAIN**: a gorgeous area for walking and sailing in summer, skiing in winter. Facilities congregate around the *Bear Mountain Inn* (☎914/786-2731) whose moderately priced rooms fill very quickly.

West Point

Some years after the end of the Revolutionary War, Congress realized that the ragged troops who had won the battles of the 1770s had been knocked into shape by officers and expertise almost exclusively European, and that homegrown skills needed to be cultivated in case foreign help wasn't so readily forthcoming again. Thus the **UNITED STATES MILITARY ACADEMY AT WEST POINT** was founded in 1802, and has been supplying the country with officers ever since—Generals Custer, Lee, MacArthur, Eisenhower, and Patton to name but a famous few. Today 4000-odd candidates fill the place, as resplendent and immaculately presented as the campus itself, which protectively overlooks the river from a wide bluff. A tough four-year regimen of intensive physical training accounts for the frighteningly fit physiques around, and the academic training is equally rigorous. In the **Visitors' Information Center** (daily 8:30am–4:15pm) a model cadet room and film detail the rigors of West Point life, and the **West Point Museum** (10:30am–4:15pm daily) shows their spoils: weapons, uniforms, and trophies from wars at home and abroad include General MacArthur's bathrobe, Hitler's pistol, Frank Borman's space suit, and, disturbingly, the removed safety catch from the Nagasaki atomic bomb. Root out the Vietnam section and all you find is a sub-Action Man Viet Cong uniform—army chiefs always felt the war could have been won, had the politicians not "tied their hands." No one's celebrating that war here. Gulf memorabilia to follow, no doubt.

Most of West Point's visitors come in search of patriotism rather than war memorabilia, and it's readily supplied on the **Parade Ground** where trainee officers and gentlepersons do their drilling, with much pomp and circumstance and a great deal of shouting. If this is your kind of thing—and it is impressive—phone ☎914/938-3507 or 938-2638 for a schedule of events, which are at their most frequent in spring and fall. Other than this there's not that much to see: a dismal cadet chapel styled in military Gothic, and the remains of **Fort Putnam** (May–Oct daily 10:30am–4pm), one of several built to keep control of the Hudson against the British, are all that might detain you.

If you're **coming from New York City** the *Day Line Ferry* leaves Pier 81 at the end of West 41st Street at 9:30am Tuesday to Sunday between late May and mid-September and returns at 3:30pm, arriving back in New York at 6:30pm. Costs for the round trip, via Bear Mountain, are around $16 per person.

Pushing **north** from West Point you're confronted with a choice: to the west of the river is a string of pleasant towns along Thruway 87; on the east side historic houses are the attraction—the homes of the Vanderbilts, Roosevelts, Livingstones, and the painter Frederick Henry Church point to just how long this has been a desirable stretch of riverside real estate. It's possible to zig-zag from one side to the other, but easier and more satisfying to attack each side individually—say the west bank heading north, the east coming back.

The West Bank: New Paltz, Kingston, and Catskill

Distinguished by what is carefully called "The oldest street in America with its original houses," **NEW PALTZ** sits prettily between Mohonk Mountain and the Hudson. In 1677 a small community of exiled Huguenots bought the land here from an Indian tribe, and named it after the Pfalz in the Rhineland where they'd found temporary refuge. At first they built log cabins but soon made lasting homes of stone, and it's these everyone comes to see today: six of the houses date from before 1720, and they're arranged around a village green worthy of any calendar photo. The oldest, the **Jean Hasbrouk Memorial House** is a folkish example of the simple Flemish style imported by the refugees, one that became increasingly elegant as the community thrived. A comprehensive **guided tour** traces the history of each house and shows the remodeled interiors, starting from the **Deyo House** at 10:30am and 1:30pm. The site is open Wednesday to Sunday from Memorial Day to the end of September.

For **food and a room**, KINGSTON farther on is a better bet, though there's no shortage of fast-food joints and delis in New Paltz: of the restaurants, *Barnaby's* has cheapish burgers and salads, and the *Wildflower Café* (☎914/255-0020) covers the health food/vegetarian market. Farther out—and the closest chance of a cheapish room—is the antique-furnished *Schoonmaker's House* (☎914/687-7946), on Route 213 between High Falls and Rosendale, $60 a double; or *Brodhead House* in High Falls itself (☎914/687-7700), $60 double.

Cut west out of New Paltz on Route 299 and you're heading through the pink and white laurels that blanket **Mount Mohonk**, whose outdoor facilities have been monopolized by the huge *Mohonk Mountain House*. But drive on to **Lake Minnewaska** and there's a relative wilderness to explore around the hemlock-rimmed lake. Admission is $5.

Kingston

KINGSTON comes billed as "the Williamsburg of the north," and while nothing so elaborate it lives up to the hype and expectations of a place that prides itself on its history. Dutch settlers established a trading post here only seven years after Hudson discovered the river, enjoying a peaceful relationship with the local Indians, which ended when they rose against the settlers, burning down the post and massacring most of its inhabitants. Governor Peter Stuyvesant ordered a stockade built, and a few of the farmhouses from this period survive, ensuring the town's popularity with tourists today. The **stockade** area at the end of town is the picturesque part that everyone comes to see, and **Green** and **Crown streets** are cluttered with well-preserved houses of the seventeenth and eighteenth centuries in a mix of styles. Pride of place goes to the low, rough-hewn **Senate House** (312 Fair Street, April–Dec Wed–Sat 10am–5pm, Sun 1–5pm; Jan–March Sat 10am–5pm, Sun 1–5pm; free). During the Revolutionary battles the Hudson Valley was the scene of much of the fighting, and as the British pushed the patriots and their embryonic government north, Kingston was hurriedly declared capital of the state. The state Senate met here from September until October, when the British troops began to get too close for comfort (eventually they sacked and burned much of the town). Inside the Senate House is a restoration of how the building might have looked then, and outside is an equally modest garden and museum (times as Senate House).

The Senate House is also the place to find out about the walking tours given by the *Friends of Historic Kingston* (☎914/338-5100) for a wider view of the old stockade and its architecture. While you're here, poke your head around the door of the **Volunteer Firemen's Hall and Museum** (265 Fair Street, April–Oct Sat–Sun 1–4pm; free) for some intricate and highly polished equipment.

The early nineteenth century saw the completion of the Delaware–Hudson canal a few miles out of town, which in its turn led to the development of **Roundout's Landing** nearby. Coal, bricks, and produce went down river to New York City, and ever-increasing numbers of tourists responded by heading for the Catskills via Kingston. The canal has long since fallen into disuse, but the **Hudson River Maritime Center** (daily, 10am–4pm; admission charge) preserves some of this history, with a selection of antique and antiquated boats, a working shipbuilding yard, and weekend trips to a lighthouse. There's also a **Trolley Museum** (summer, Sat–Sun 10am–4pm) here, offering rides in old-fashioned trolley cars.

For **accommodation** the choice is between the *Holiday Inn* at 503 Washington Avenue (☎914/338-0400)—doubles around $60—or there's a *Howard Johnson's Motor Lodge* (☎914/338-4200) at Route 28 North (exit 19 on Thruway 87). Inexpensive **food** isn't difficult to find: two restaurants are *Dallas Hot Weiners* at 51 North Street, for hamburgers, sandwiches, etc., or the *Pizza Place* at the corner of John and Wall streets. For a blow-out *Scheller's Restaurant*, 61 John Street, has German/Austrian grub with home-made wurst, hams, and strudels.

Catskill

It's about 27 miles from Kingston to **CATSKILL**—a prim, quaintish residential place along classic Main Street: what goes on in town goes on along this strip, and that probably doesn't amount to very much. Nearby, the leafy **Catskill Creek** draws a good number of the boating and fishing crowd into town, and though there's nothing in the way of "sights" the Federal, Gothic, and Greek Revival houses of the center are worth an amble; for a detailed account of the more characterful buildings—including the house of artist Thomas Cole, founder of the Hudson Valley School—pick up *A Guide to Catskill's Architectural History* from the County Court House (319 Main Street) or the **Green County Promotion Department** (290 Main Street; ☎518/622-3934) which can also help with accommodation.

From Catskill it's an easy trip across the Rip Van Winkle Bridge to OLANA and HUDSON (for which see the next but one section, "The East Bank") or west into the Catskill National Park.

The Catskills

> *Whoever has made a voyage up the Hudson must remember the Kaatskill moun-*
> *tains. They are a dismembered branch of the great Appalachian family, swelling up*
> *to a noble height, and lording it over the surrounding country. Every change of*
> *season, every change of weather, indeed, every hour of the day, produces some*
> *change in the magical hues and shapes of these mountains, and . . . sometimes,*
> *when the rest of the landscape is cloudless, they will gather a hood of gray vapors*
> *which, in the last rays of the setting sun, will glow and light up like a crown of*
> *glory.*

So wrote Washington Irving at the beginning of Rip Van Winkle, and beneath the purple his prose isn't far wrong. **The Catskills**, magnificent heights wooded with maple and beech which turn to shuffled embers of orange, gold, and bronze each fall, have a rich and ravishing beauty—one that can absorb any number of week-ending Manhattanites. It's inspiring country, and filled with all the amenities—campgrounds, hiking trails, canoeing, fishing, and, especially, skiing: both **Catskill** town and **Ellenville** are home to numerous ski-resort-cum-nightclub pleasure palaces. If you're not here for the sport, though, or the high prices scare you off, just stick within the limits of the Catskill Park and its majestic mountain heights—it is, as Thoreau said, "a landscape fit to entertain a traveling god."

Through the mountains to Woodstock

It's difficult to suggest any single route through the mountains: from Catskill Route 23/23A forms a neat circle, easily managed (easier still if you detour across Route 296) and giving breathtaking views across the mountains and the dramatic **gorge** between Hunter and Catskill—the mythical spot where Rip nodded off for twenty years. Out of Kingston you can loop past the lovely **Ashokan Reservoir** and **Woodstock** and head through the forested uplands to pick up Route 23A at Lexington. Really, there's an unlimited variety of byways to explore if you have time and transport on your side. A taste can be managed in a day if you have a car, but if you're touring the region in detail pick up the Green County Promotion Department's *Scenic Tours Map* in Catskill for a thorough selection of planned-out routes.

Though each of the Catskill's small villages has its charms, **WOODSTOCK** is the only town to spend any time in. It's not the place of the famed psychedelic picnic of the 1960s—that was about 60 miles west of here at White Lake—nor is it the hippy hangout usually imagined. Yet since the 1969 concert Woodstock has become a part of the international lexicon; people use the terms "before Woodstock" and "after Woodstock" with the hushed air of a religious event. The town that gave its name to the jamboree has itself become a cultural landmark—and one of the prettiest and most agreeable upstate spots.

Founded in the 1700s, Woodstock first gained fame as a major arts and crafts center at the turn of this century, when the Byrdcliffe Crafts Studios and the summer school of New York's Art Students' League were established here. The art connection flourished, and today's village abounds in artists of all disciplines, both struggling and successful. To the visitor it's a sort of drive-in arts colony, but many of New York's best and brightest now live in Woodstock or have second homes here. To be honest, with a few exceptions you'll need to search hard beneath the tourist facade to find the truly original or even artistic—but that's half the fun.

Best time to visit is a weekday, when the town is a lot less crowded. Perhaps surprisingly, it's possible to find **rooms** without busting your budget, but they're limited, and in the busy season an advance reservation is more or less essential. In the center of the village the *Twin Gables Guest House*, 77 Tinker Street (☎914/679-9479), is Woodstock's best bargain—from $30 single, $48 double—but has a devoted following so reserve well ahead. Down by the Old Mill Stream the *Millstream Motel*, 38 Tannery Brook Road (☎914/679-8211), is a neat and trim place with doubles from $60 including breakfast, and the *Pinecrest Lodge*, Country Club Lane (☎914/679-2814), at the edge of the village has doubles from $60, again with breakfast.

Budget **eating** is also well served: *Duey's*, 50 Mill Hill Road, is a good, inexpensive hangout, and *Misty's* on the Village Green is excellent for a bargain breakfast. For pizza, heroes, salads, and lasagne, *Woodstock Pizza*, also on the Green, is a nifty choice, and the deli section of the *Grand Union Supermarket* on Mill Hill Road offers sandwiches and takeout hot meals at rock-bottom prices. Though not the cheapest place to eat, *The Tinker Street Café*, 59 Tinker Street, was a hub during the 1960s and is still going strong with live music at weekends year round. What's more there's no cover charge, which makes the burgers and Italian dinner specialties quite reasonable.

Along with *Marty's*, *The Lake* on Mill Hill Road (☎914/679-9300) started life as one of Woodstock's choice **clubs**: it still features up-and-coming bands, a first-rate disco, and modest admission charges. **Theater** is mainly a summer event: though the noted *Woodstock Playhouse* burned down a few years back, the River Arts Repertory at the *Birdcliffe Theater* on Byrdcliffe Road (☎914/679-2100) can present stellar productions. There's **classical music** at the *Maverick Chamber Music Concerts* on Maverick Road (☎914/679-7558) each Sunday at 3pm in July and August. **Galleries**, of varying style and quality, are littered throughout Woodstock: as well as numerous commercial places take in the *Art Gallery of the Woodstock Artist's Association*, 28 Tinker Street; the gallery/shop of the *Woodstock Guild of Craftsmen*, 34 Tinker Street; and the *Catskill Center for Photography*, 59A Tinker Street. And don't miss *Garden of Eve's*, a junk/bookshop at 5 Tannery Brook Road. For **listings** of events (and much more) the *Woodstock Times* is packed with information on and insights into the community. Tuning in to *WDST* (100.1 FM), Woodstock's radio station, is another good way of finding out what's happening.

Skiing, Walking, and Sleeping—some practical details

The Catskill Park's facilities don't always come cheap: **Hunter Mountain Resort**, ski center of the region, draws in New York City's crowds to its 37 trails and slopes from the end of November till Easter—it can, and does, handle 14,000 skiers an hour. Use of the extensive facilities starts at $30 a day (2-, 3-, and 5-day reduced tickets available), plus there's full equipment rental. The very cheapest rooms go from $75 a double—ask at the *Hunter Mountain Lodging Bureau* opposite the entrance to the resort (10am–6pm daily; ☎518/263-4208).

Cross-country and mountain **walking** is understandably popular, and there are miles of well-organized trails to follow. Best way to start is with the Department of Environmental Conservation booklet, *Catskill Trails*, available from 439 Main Street, Catskill, which details thirty-odd routes and contains much useful advice. Whether you're walking or not the Catskills offer excellent **camping**. State campgrounds include the *Devil's Tombstone Ground* four miles south of Hunter on Route 214 (☎914/688-7160); the *North and Shore Lake Ground* three miles northeast of Haines Falls off Route 23A (☎518/589-5058); the *Kenneth Wilson Campground* five miles west of Woodstock on County Route 40 off Route 28, (☎914/679-7020); and, in the heart of the trails, the *Woodland Valley Ground*, six miles southwest of Phoenicia. Finally, if you want to cool off, it's possible to rent an inflated inner tube from *Town Tinker Tube Rental* on Bridge St., Phoenicia (☎914/688-5553) and ride the rapids down the Esopus river.

The East Bank: Hyde Park, Clermont, and Olana

The Hudson's eastern bank rises and falls in the low hummocks and parkland that run alongside the *Taconic State Parkway*, fastest if not most rewarding road to Hyde Park. Slower but more scenic is Route 9; and a good compromise is to take the Parkway and cross over to Route 9 via Route 84.

Finding a room on the east bank isn't as easy as on the west, something to bear in mind as you make your plans. For HYDE PARK best choice is a motel: most, like the *Colonial Motel*, 38 Albany Post Road (☎914/229-2444), start at around $50 for a double; the nearest **campground** is in the *Mills-Norrie State Park* (☎914/889-4646), four miles north of Hyde Park on Route 9. In RHINEBECK *Kallop's Bed and Breakfast* is small but inexpensive: around $20 single, $35 double.

Hyde Park and the Roosevelts

HYDE PARK is a peaceful plateau of land with magnificent views of the river and, marked off the Albany Post Road, the **homes of Franklin and Eleanor Roosevelt**. Though it's not nearly as rural as the home of the other President Roosevelt at Sagamore Hill, Long Island, the **house** (April–Oct daily 9am–5pm, Nov–March Thurs–Mon 9am–5pm; admission charge) where Franklin Delano Roosevelt was born and spent much of his adult life is pleasingly sited and well documented. It's not possible to see the whole place, as it was badly damaged by fire a few years ago, but the newish **museum** more than makes up for this with extensive information, documents, and photos of FDR's career. He was struck by polio in 1920, and the specially adapted car he drove is on show, along with photos from the war years, the plans for the New Deal, and the letter from Einstein that led to the development of the first atomic bomb.

Roosevelt lies buried in the grounds of his home beside his wife **Eleanor**, a gifted and influential politician without whose aid it's unlikely his political career would have survived. Born Anna Eleanor Roosevelt, she was the niece of Theodore and a distant cousin of Franklin, and became active in liberal Democratic affairs after her husband contracted polio. In the early 1930s she toured the country, reporting to FDR on the living conditions of the unemployed and poor—an act that influenced the framing of the New Deal. After Franklin's death in 1945 Eleanor moved to **Val-Kill**, a nearby retreat she had had built twenty years earlier, from here carrying on her work as US delegate to the United Nations General Assembly and Chairwoman of the Human Rights Commission, and receiving dignatories such as Khrushchev, Tito, Haile Selassie, and John F. Kennedy until her death in 1962. To tour the simple home of this remarkable woman, catch the half-hourly shuttle bus from the FDR house (May–Oct daily 10am–5pm, apart from March, April, Nov, & Dec weekends, 10am–4pm).

The Vanderbilt Mansion

If the Roosevelt homes are examples of urbane humility, then the **VANDERBILT MANSION** farther up Route 9 shows just how little taste big money can buy. Believe it or not, this was the smallest of the various Vanderbilt residences, built for Frederick, grandson of the railroad baron "Commodore" Cornelius. From the entrance to the extensive grounds, McKim, Mead, and White's Beaux-Arts building is pompously commanding. Inside, the mansion is gloomily elaborate, from the gilt and frills of the Rococo reception room to Louise Vanderbilt's gross recreation of a Louis XV boudoir. Because Frederick's marriage to Louise, a divorcee and socialite twelve years his senior, was disapproved of, he received the least inheritance among his siblings. On Louise's death he hid himself away in a small sanctuary here and set about increasing his inheritance to a fortune of $80 million. Tours of the mansion run throughout the day (April–Oct daily 9am–5pm, Nov–March Thurs–Mon 9am–5pm; admission charge).

Claremont

After these excesses you need some relief, and **CLAREMONT**, 22 miles north on Route 9 (turn west onto Route 6: the grounds are open 8am–sunset, the house May–Oct Wed–Sun 10am–4pm) is just the thing. Home to several generations of the Livingstone family, Claremont's dignified Federal interior is one of genteel restraint, and the surrounding park, rich with fragrant lilacs and locust trees, a delight. Inside the house is a portrait of **Robert Livingstone**, the man who negotiated one of the great bargain land deals of all time, the **Louisiana Purchase**. Back in 1803 Louisiana was the name given to a vast and vague territory covering roughly one-third of North America. These lands were controlled by the French, but Napoleon had already had his fingers burnt attempting to put down a revolt in the American colonies, and realized that the combined strength of a native and American fighting force would be impossible to match, so he sold Louisiana—for $16 million. Livingstone and President Thomas Jefferson could hardly believe it: the land area of the United States had effectively been doubled, and for a fraction of the price they'd been prepared to pay. It worked out at four cents an acre: no wonder Livingstone looks so pleased with himself.

Claremont is pretty, no argument; but the real treat comes just one mile south of the Rip Van Winkle bridge, hidden away on a hillside.

Olana

"About one hour this side of Albany is the center of the world. I own it," wrote the artist **Frederick Church** of **OLANA**, the home he designed and built. It's arguably the most attractive and certainly the best sited of all the Hudson Valley mansions: Church chose the spot above a bend in the river for its superlative views and the peculiar quality of light that he repeatedly sketched and painted. To improve on nature he relandscaped Olana's hillside, placing an artificial lake to balance and reflect the Hudson, choosing and siting every tree. And the house itself was Church's almost obsessive passion. Built in a joke-Persian style with the help of Calvert Vaux and Richard Morris Hunt, he made two hundred sketches of the staircase alone to fit it into his vision of a combined home, studio, and gallery. Much of the inspiration came from his trips to Persia and the Middle East (the name *Olana* is Arabic for "house on the hill"), and the colors and rich motifs all have an enthusiastic eastern feel. An (obligatory) conducted tour takes in the various rooms filled with the bric-a-brac Church accumulated on his travels and a good proportion of his romantic canvases: "Pictures as vivid and mellow as if painted by sunbeams," as one contemporary put it. The house is open from May 28 to Labor Day Wednesday to Saturday 10am to 4pm, Sunday noon to 4pm; Labor Day to October 30, Wednesday to Sunday noon to 4pm, and there's an admission charge. Tours are popular so phone in advance for a reservation—☎518/828-0135.

Heading north from Olana you pass through **HUDSON**, and to be honest that's the best thing to do—its restored clapboard Victorian houses can easily be taken in without making a stop. If you've seen the movie *Ironweed* you may recognize Main Street here: the 1930s storefronts were used to create a illusion of Albany during the depression years. Alternatively, if you're heading for ALBANY itself, it's quicker to cross over the Rip Van Winkle bridge to CATSKILL and pick up the 87 Thruway.

Albany

ALBANY made its money by controlling the east–west trade route of the Erie Canal, and its reputation by being state capital. The governor's official residence is here, and the wheelings and dealings of the state bureaucracy roll on in the glassy Empire State Plaza that gives the city its futuristic skyline and contemporary identity. It's not a place to spend more than a day or so (all you'll need to see are the civic buildings and a fine museum), but it forms a handy stop when heading up to Saratoga Springs and the Adirondacks, or Vermont and New England.

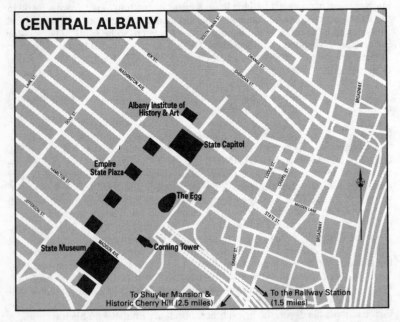

Arrive by *Greyhound* bus and it's a bearable walk or bus ride to the center; arrive by train and you're in RENSSELAER about two miles out of town—don't try and walk it, but catch a regular bus straight to the Plaza. Other than the small **youth hostel** at 46 Elm Street (☎518/434-4963), what budget **rooms** exist start at around $40 a double in out-of-center hotels: contact the **Albany Conventions and Visitors' Bureau**, 600 Broadway (☎518/434-1217 or 474-2418; closed at weekends), which may also know of vacancies in the State University dorms in the summer. Bear in mind, too, that Albany's hotels fill almost as swiftly as Saratoga's in the racing season (August). Cheap central **food** is on offer from snack bars in the concourse, burgers, etc, from *Jack's Diner*, 547 Central Avenue, pizzas from the *Little Antony* chain, 1095 Central Avenue or 128 Madison Avenue.

Piercing into the confusion of downtown Albany like an arrowhead, Nelson A. Rockefeller's **Empire State Plaza** is reminiscent of the earlier Rockefeller Center in New York City, the 42-story **Corning Tower** supported by a bodyguard of four subsidiary buildings. The billion-dollar blocks went up in the 1960s and 1970s to house the offices of the State Legislature—and, no doubt about it, add architectural prestige to a workaday town center. Ninety-eight acres of nineteenth-century Albany were torn down for this, and whatever you may think of that, the Empire State Plaza is a well-conceived piece of urban planning, at least marginally more likable than most. Come here by bus or car and you'll be delivered to the underground concourse, a sort of subterranean Main Street splattered with modern art. Information desks hand out maps, and the *Visitors' Assistance Center* (at the Capitol end of the concourse) coordinates conducted tours, but it's easy enough to follow the signs. For a panoramic view of the lie of the land, the Corning Tower **observation deck** (daily 9am–4pm) seems designed to make you feel like the conqueror of an invaded country, looking out across Albany's overpass to the Adirondack foothills, the Catskills, and the Massachusetts Berkshires.

For the locals, at least, Albany's number one target is the **New York State Museum** (10am–5pm daily, hourly tours; free), the whole state revealed in imaginative if static natural history tableaux. There's an excellent section on New York City—better in fact than anything you'll find in Manhattan itself—with histories of immigration and skyscraper building, storefronts and period rooms, the original set of *Sesame Street*, and a 1940 subway car to show you how much things haven't changed.

At the other end of the strip the **Capitol** building adds a little soul to the anti-human Plaza. A sandwich of Italian, French, and Flemish Gothic, it's a reminder of an earlier period of civic grandeur, built at the end of the nineteenth century for the then fantastic sum of $24 million—twice the bill for the Capitol in Washington DC. The **conducted tours** (on the hour 9am–4pm daily, half-hourly in summer; free) pick out the opulent highlights: the Senate Chamber rich in Siena marble and carved mahogany, and the "Million Dollar Staircase," festooned with carvings of governors, presidents, and sundry national heroes. Less ornate but more bizarre, another staircase busily interprets Darwin's theories of evolution.

A short walk from the Capitol the **Performing Arts Center** adds the only curves to the rigid angularity of the Plaza. Known as "The Egg," there's not a straight line in it. Even if you don't take in a play, it's worth peeking inside; ask at the concourse information desk for tour details.

Other than this Albany has but a couple of mainstream attractions. A twenty-minute walk or a #8 bus from the center, **Historic Cherry Hill** (532½ South Pearl Street—walk down Broadway and turn left on to South Pearl Street; Tues–Sat 10am–3pm, Sun 1–3pm, tours on the hour; admission charge) is a better-than-average mansion that housed five generations of the Van Rensselaer family from 1787 to 1963, a continuity that makes for some interesting leftovers in the house's decoration. Back toward town, the **Shuyler Mansion** (bus #6 or #8; 32 Catherine St, April–Dec Wed–Sat 10am–5pm, Sun 1–5pm; Jan–March Sat 10am–5pm, Sun 1–5pm; free) was the house of Revolutionary notable General Philip Shuyler and his daughter Elizabeth, until she married Alexander Hamilton here in 1780. All this is enough for anyone in a single day, but for devotees of the Hudson Valley school of painting the **Albany Institute of History and Art** at 125 Washington Avenue (one block east of the Capitol; Tues, Wed, Fri 10am–5pm, Thur 10am–8pm, Sat & Sun noon–5pm) has the best collection outside the Met.

PART THREE

THE

CONTEXTS

THE HISTORICAL FRAMEWORK

To Europe she was America, to America she was the gateway of the earth. But to tell the story of New York would be to write a social history of the world.

H.G. Wells

EARLY DAYS AND COLONIAL RULE

In the earliest times the area that is today New York City was populated by Native Americans. Each tribe had its own territory and lived a settled existence in villages of bark huts, gaining a livelihood from crop planting, hunting, trapping, and fishing. In the New York area the *Algonquin* tribe was the most populous. Survivors of this and other tribes can still be seen at Long Island's **Shinnecook reservation**—as well as remnants of native culture at the upstate Turtle Center for the Native American Indian.

The native lifestyle represented a continuum of several thousand years, one that was to end with the arrival of European explorers. In 1524 **Giovanni da Verrazano**, an Italian in the service of the French King Francis I, arrived, following in the footsteps of Christopher Columbus thirty-two years earlier. On his ship, the *Dauphane*, Verrazano had set out to find the legendary North West Passage to the Pacific; instead he discovered **Manhattan**. "We found a very agreeable situation located within two small prominent hills, in the midst of which flowed to the sea a very great river, which was deep within the mouth; and from the sea to the hills, with the rising of the tide, which we found eight feet, any laden ship might have passed." Verrazano returned, "leaving the said land with much regret because of its commodiousness and beauty, thinking it was not without some properties of value," to woo the court with tales of fertile lands and friendly natives, but oddly enough it was nearly a century before the powers of Europe were tempted to follow him.

In 1609 **Hendrik Hudson**, employed by the **Dutch East India Company**, landed at Manhattan and sailed his ship, the *Half-Moone*, as far as Albany. Hudson found that the river did not lead to the North West Passage he had been commissioned to discover—but in charting its course for the first time gave his name to the mighty river. "This is a very good land to fall with," noted the ship's mate, "and a pleasant land to see." In a series of skirmishes Hudson's men gave the native people a foretaste of what to expect from future adventurers. Hudson sailed home to England, where he was promptly reprimanded for working for the Dutch and sent on another expedition under the British flag: arriving in Hudson Bay, the temperature falling and the mutinous crew doubting his ability as a navigator, Hudson, his son, and several others were cast adrift in a small boat on the icy waters where, presumably, they froze to death.

The British fear that the Dutch had seized the initiative in the new found land proved well justified, for they had the commercial advantage and wasted no time in making the most of it. In the next few years the Dutch established a trading post at the most northerly point Hudson had reached, **Fort Nassau**. In 1624, four years after the Pilgrim Fathers had sailed to Massachusetts, thirty families left Holland to become New York's first Continental settlers, most sailing up to Fort Nassau but a handful—eight families in all—staying behind on a small island they called Nut Island because of the many walnut trees there: today's Governor's Island. Slowly the community grew as more settlers arrived, and the little island became crowded; the decision was made to move to the limitless spaces across the water, and **the settlement of Manhattan** (an Indian word whose meaning is uncertain) began.

The Dutch gave their new outpost the name **New Amsterdam**, and in 1626 **Peter Minuit** was sent out to govern the small community of just over three hundred. Among his first, and certainly more politically adroit, moves was to buy the whole of Manhattan Island from the Indians for trinkets worth 60 guilders (about $25 today); though the other side of the anecdote is even better—for the Indians Minuit dealt with didn't even come from Manhattan, let alone own it. As the colony slowly grew, a string of governors succeeded Minuit, the most famous of them **Peter Stuyvesant**—"Peg Leg Pete," a seasoned colonialist from the Dutch West Indies who'd lost his leg in a skirmish with the Portuguese. Under his leadership New Amsterdam doubled in size and population, protected from British settlers to the north by an encircling wall (**Wall Street** today follows its course) and defended by a rough-hewn fort on what is now the site of the Customs House. Stuyvesant also built himself a farm (a *bowerie* in Dutch) a little to the north, that gave its name to the **Bowery**.

Meanwhile the **British** were steadily and stealthily building up their presence to the north. Though initially preoccupied by Civil War at home, they maintained their claim that all of America's East Coast, from New England to Virginia, was theirs, and in 1664 sent a Colonel Richard Nicholls to claim the lands around the Hudson that King Charles II had granted to his brother, the Duke of York. To reinforce his sovereignty Charles sent along four warships and landed troops on Nut Island and Long Island. The Dutch settlers had by then had enough of Stuyvesant's increasingly dictatorial rule, especially the high taxes demanded by the nominal owners of the colony, the Dutch West India Company, and so refused to defend Dutch rule against the British. Captain Nicholls' men took New Amsterdam, renamed it **New York** in honor of the Duke and settled down to a hundred-odd years of British rule, interrupted only briefly in 1673 when the Dutch once more managed to gain the upper hand.

During this period not all was plain sailing. When King James II was forced to abdicate and flee Britain in 1689, a German merchant called **James Leisler** led a revolt against British rule. Unfortunately for Leisler it mustered little sympathy, and he was hanged for treason. Also, by now black slaves consti-

tuted a major part of New York's population, and though laws denied them weapons and the right of assembly, in 1712 a number of slaves set fire to a building near Maiden Lane and killed nine people who attempted to stop the blaze. When soldiers arrived, six of the incendiaries committed suicide and twenty-one others were captured and executed. In other areas civil rights were slowly being established. In 1734 **John Peter Zenger**, publisher of the *New York Weekly Journal*, was tried and acquitted of libeling the British government, establishing freedom of the press that would later be enshrined in the First Amendment to the Constitution.

REVOLUTION

By the 1750s the city had reached a population of 16,000, spread roughly as far north as Chambers Street. As the new community became more confident, so it realized that it could exist independently of the Crown in Britain. But in 1763 the **Treaty of Paris** concluded the Seven Years' War with France, which conceded sovereignty over most of explored North America. British rule was thus consolidated and the government decided to try throwing its weight around. Within a year, discontent over British rule escalated with the passage of the punitive **Sugar**, **Stamp**, **and Colonial Currency Acts**. Further resentment erupted over the **Quartering Act**, which permitted British troops to requisition private dwellings and inns, their rent to be paid by the colonies themselves. Ill-feeling steadily mounted and skirmishes between soldiers and the insurrectionist **Sons of Liberty** culminated in January 1770 with the killing of a colonist and the wounding of several others. **The Boston Massacre**, in which British troops fired upon taunting protestors, occurred a few weeks later and helped fan the embryonic flames of Revolution.

In a way, New York's role during the **War of Independence** was not crucial, for all the battles fought in and around the city were generally won by the side that lost the war. But they were the first military engagements between the British and American forces after the **Declaration of Independence** was proclaimed to the cheering crowds outside the site of today's **City Hall Park**, who then went off to pull down the statue of George III that stood on the Bowling Green. The British, driven from Boston the previous winter, resolved that New York should be the place where they would reassert their authority over the rebels, and in June and July of 1776 some two hundred ships under the command of **Lord Howe** arrived in New York Harbor. The troops made camp on Staten Island while the commander of the American forces, **George Washington**, consolidated his men, in the hope that the mouth of the harbor was suffi- ciently well defended to stop British ships from entering it and encircling his troops. But Howe managed to slip two frigates past Washington to moor north of the city and decided to make his assault on the city by land. On August 22 he landed 15,000 men, mainly Hessian mercenar- ies, on the southwest corner of Brooklyn. His plan was to occupy Brooklyn and launch an attack on Manhattan from there. In the **Battle of Long Island**, Howe's men penetrated the American forward lines at a number of points, the most important engagement taking place at what is today Prospect Park.

The Americans fell back to their positions, and as the British made preparations to attack the fortifications, Washington could see that his garrison would be easily defeated. On the night of August 29, under cover of rain and fog, he evacuated his men safely to Manhattan from the ferry slip beneath where the Brooklyn Bridge now stands, preserving the bulk of his forces. A few days later Howe's army set out in boats from Green Point and Newtown Creek in Brooklyn to land at what is now the 34th Street heliport site. The defenders of the city retreated north to make a stand at Harlem Heights, but were pushed back again to even- tual defeat in the **Battle of White Plains** in Westchester County (the Bronx), where Washington lost 1400 of his 4000 men. More tragic still was the defense of **Fort Washington**, perched on a rocky cliff 230 feet above the Hudson, near today's George Washington Bridge. Here, rather than evacuate the troops, the local commander made a deci- sion to stand and fight: trapped by the Hudson to the west it was a fatal mistake, and upward of 3000 men were killed or taken prisoner. Gathering more forces Washington retreated, and for the next seven years New York was occupied by the British as a garrison town. During this period many of the remaining inhab-

itants and most of the prisoners taken by the British slowly starved to death.

Lord Cornwallis's **surrender** to the Americans in October 1783 marked the end of the War of Independence, and a month later New York was finally relieved. Washington, the man who had held the American army together by sheer willpower, was there to cele- brate, riding in triumphal procession down Canal Street and saying farewell to his officers at **Fraunces Tavern**, a building that still stands at the end of Pearl Street. It was a tear- ful occasion for men who had fought through the worst of the war years together: "I am not only retiring from all public employments," he declared, "but am retiring within myself."

But that was not to be. New York was now the fledgling nation's **capital** and, as Thomas Jefferson *et al.* framed the Constitution and the role of President of the United States, it became increasingly clear that there was only one candidate for the position. On April 30 1789 Washington took the oath of President at the site of the **Federal Hall National Memorial** on Wall Street. The federal govern- ment was transferred to Philadelphia a year later.

IMMIGRATION AND CIVIL WAR

In 1790 the first official census of Manhattan put the population at around 33,000: business and trade were on the increase, with the market under a buttonwood tree on Wall Street being a forerunner to the New York Stock Exchange. A few years later, in 1807, **Robert Fulton** launched the *Clermont*, a steamboat that managed to splutter its way up the Hudson River from New York to Albany, pioneering trade with upstate areas. A year before his death in 1814 Fulton also started a ferry service between Manhattan and Brooklyn, and the dock at which it moored became a focus of trade and eventually a maritime center, taking its name from the inventor.

But it was the opening of the **Erie Canal** in 1825 that really allowed New York to develop as a port. The Great Lakes were suddenly opened to New York, and with them the rest of the country; goods manufactured in the city could be taken easily and cheaply to the American heartlands. It was on this prosperity, and the mass of **cheap labor** that flooded in throughout the nineteenth and early twentieth centuries, that New York—and to an extent the nation—became wealthy. The first waves of **immigrants**, mainly **German** and **Irish**, began to arrive in the mid-nineteenth century, the latter forced out by the Potato Famine of 1846, the former by the failed Revolution of 1848–9, which had left many German liberals, laborers, intellectuals, and businessmen dispossessed by political machinations. The city could not handle people arriving in such great numbers and epidemics of yellow fever and cholera were common, exacerbated by poor water supplies, insanitary conditions, and the poverty of most of the newcomers. But in the 1880s large-scale **Italian** immigration began, mainly of laborers and peasants from southern Italy and Sicily, while at the same time refugees from **Eastern Europe** started to arrive—many of them Jewish. The two communities shared a home on the **Lower East Side**, which became one of the worst slum areas of its day. On the eve of the Civil War the majority of New York's 750,000 population were immigrants; in 1890 one in four alone of the city's inhabitants was Irish.

During this period life for the well off was fairly pleasant and development in the city progressed rapidly. Despite a great fire in 1835 that destroyed most of the business district downtown, trade boomed and was celebrated in the opening of the **World's Fair** of 1835 at the Crystal Palace on the site of Bryant Park—an iron and glass building that fared no better than its London namesake, burning down in 1858. In the same year work began on clearing the shantytowns in the center of the island to make way for a newly landscaped open space—a marvelous design by Frederick Law Olmsted and Calvert Vaux that became **Central Park**.

Two years later the **Civil War** broke out, thanks to the growing differences between the northern and southern states, notably on the issue of slavery. New York sided with the Union against the Confederates, but had little experience of the hand-to-hand fighting that ravaged many parts of the country. It did however form a focus for much of the radical thinking behind the war, particularly with **Abraham Lincoln**'s influential "Might makes Right" speech from the **Cooper Union Building** in 1860. In 1863 a **conscription law** was passed that allowed the rich to buy themselves out of military service. Not surprisingly this was deeply unpopular, and New Yorkers rioted, burning buildings and looting shops: over a thousand people were killed in these **Draft Riots**. A sad footnote to the war was the assassination of Lincoln in 1865: when his body lay in state in New York's City Hall, 120,000 people filed past to pay their last respects.

THE LATE NINETEENTH CENTURY

The end of the Civil War saw much of the country devastated but New York intact, and it was fairly predictable that the city would soon become the wealthiest and most influential in the nation. Broadway developed into the main thoroughfare, with grand hotels, restaurants, and stores catering to the rich; newspaper editors **William Cullen Bryant** and **Horace Greeley** respectively founded the *Evening Post* and the *Tribune*; and the city became a magnet for writers and intellectuals, with **Washington Irving** and **James Fenimore Cooper** among its notable residents. By dint of its skilled immigrant workers, its facilities for marketing goods, and the wealth to build factories New York was also the greatest business, commercial, and manufacturing center in the country. **Cornelius Vanderbilt** controlled a vast shipping and railroad empire, and **J.P. Morgan**, the banking and investment wizard, was instrumental in organizing financial mergers that led to the formation of prototype corporate business. But even bigger in a way was a character who was not a businessman but a politician: **William Marcy Tweed**. From lowly origins Tweed worked his way up the Democratic Party ladder to the position of alderman at the age of twenty-one, eventually becoming chairman of the party's State Central Committee. Surrounded by his own men—the **Tweed Ring**—and aided by a paid-off mayor, "Boss" Tweed took total control of the city's government and finances. Anyone in a position to endanger his money-making schemes was bought off by cash extorted from the huge bribes given by contractors eager to carry out municipal services. In this way $160,000,000 found its way into Tweed and his cronies' pockets. Tweed stayed in power by organizing the speedy naturalization of aliens, who, in repayment, were expected to vote for Tweed and his sidekicks every so often. For his part, Tweed gave generously to the poor, who knew he was swindling the rich but saw him as a Robin Hood figure. As a contemporary observer remarked, "The government of the rich by the manipulation of the poor is a new phenomenon in the world." Tweed's swindles grew in audacity and greed until a determined campaign by **George Jones**, editor of the *New York Times*, and **Thomas Nast**, whose vicious portrayals of Tweed and his henchmen appeared in *Harper's Weekly*, brought him down. The people who kept Tweed in power may not have been able to read or write, but they could understand a cartoon—and Tweed's heyday was over. A committee was established to investigate corruption in City Hall and Tweed found himself in court. Despite a temporary escape to Spain he was returned to the US, and died in Ludlow Street Jail—by pleasing irony a building he had commissioned when Chief of Works.

The latter part of the nineteenth century, however, was for some the city's golden age: elevated railroads (the **Els**) sprang up to ferry people quickly and cheaply across the city, **Thomas Edison** lit the streets with his new electric light bulb, powered from the first electricity plant on Pearl Street, and in 1883, to the wonderment of New Yorkers, the **Brooklyn Bridge** was opened, Brooklyn itself along with Staten Island, Queens, and the part of Westchester that became the Bronx, becoming part of the city in 1898. All this commercial expansion stimulated the city's cultural growth, and **Walt Whitman** eulogized the city in his poems, **Henry James** recorded its manners and mores in novels like *Washington Square*. **Richard Morris Hunt** built palaces along Fifth Avenue for the wealthy Robber Barons, who plundered Europe to assemble art collections to furnish them—collections that would eventually find their way into the newly opened Metropolitan Museum of Art. For the "Four Hundred," the wealthy elite that reveled in and owned the city, New York in the "gay nineties" was a constant string of lavish balls and dinners that vied with each other until opulence became obscenity. At one banquet the millionaire guests arrived on horseback and ate their meals in the saddle; afterward the horses were fed gourmet-prepared fodder.

FURTHER IMMIGRATION AND BUILDING

At the same time, emigration of Europe's impoverished peoples continued unabated, and in 1884 new immigrants from the Orient settled in what became known as **Chinatown**; the following year saw a huge influx of southern Italians to the city. As the Vanderbilts, Astors, and Rockefellers basked in the glory of the mansions uptown, overcrowded tenements led to terrible living standards for the poor. Working conditions were little better, and were compassionately described by police reporter and photographer **Jacob Riis**, whose book *How the Other Half Lives* detailed the long working hours, exploitation, and child labor that kept the city's coffers full.

More Jewish immigrants arrived to cram the Lower East Side and in 1898 the population of New York reached over 3 million—the largest city in the world. Twelve years earlier Augustus Bartholdi's **Statue of Liberty** had been finished, holding a symbolic torch to guide the huddled masses; now pressure grew to limit immigration, but still people flooded in. **Ellis Island**, the depot which processed arrivals, was handling 2000 people a day, a total of 10 million by 1929, when laws were passed to curtail immigration. By the turn of the century, around half of the city's peoples were foreign-born, and a quarter of the population was made up of German and Irish migrants, most of them people living in slums. The section of Manhattan bounded by the East River, East 14th Street and Third Avenue, the Bowery and Catherine Street was probably the most densely populated area on earth, inhabited by a poor who lived under worse conditions and paid more rent than the inhabitants of any other big city in the world. Yet, in 1900, J.P. Morgan's United States Steel Company became the first billion-dollar corporation.

The early 1900s saw some of this wealth going into adventurous new architecture. SoHo had already utilized the **cast iron building** to mass produce classical facades, and the **Flatiron Building** of 1902 announced the arrival of what was to become the city's trade mark—the skyscraper. On the arts front **Stephen Crane**, **Theodore Dreiser**, and **Edith Wharton** used New York as the subject for their writing, **George M. Cohan** was the

Bright Young Man of Broadway, and in 1913 the **Armory exhibition** of Modernist painting by Picasso, Duchamp, and others caused a sensation. Meantime the skyscrapers were pushing higher and higher, and in the same year a building that many consider the *ne plus ultra* of the genre, the **Woolworth Building**, was formally opened. Also that year **Grand Central Terminal** celebrated New York as the gateway to the continent.

The first two decades of the century saw a further wave of immigration, made up chiefly of Jews. In that period one-third of all the Jews in Eastern Europe arrived in New York and some 1.5 million of them settled in New York City, primarily in the Lower East Side. Despite advances in public building, caused by the outcry that followed Jacob Riis's reports, the area could not cope with a population density of 640,000 per square mile, and the poverty and inhuman conditions reached their worst as people strove to better themselves by working in the sweatshops of Hester Street. Workers, especially those in trades dominated by Jewish immigrants from socialist backgrounds, began to strike to demand better wages and working conditions. Most of the garment manufacturers, for example, charged women workers for their needles and the rent of lockers, and handed out punitive fines for spoilage of fabrics. Strikes of 1910–11 achieved only limited success, and it took disaster to rouse public and civic conscience. On March 25, 1911, just before the **Triangle Shirtwaist Factory** at Washington Place was about to finish work for the day, a fire broke out. The workers were trapped on the tenth floor and 146 of them died (125 were women), mostly by leaping from the blazing building. Within months the State had passed fifty-six factory reform measures, and unionization spread through the city.

THE WAR YEARS: 1914–1945

With America's entry into World War I in 1917 New York benefited from wartime trade and commerce. At home, perhaps surprisingly, there was little conflict between the various European communities crammed into the city. Although Germans comprised roughly one-fifth of the city's population, there were few of the attacks on their lives or property that occurred elsewhere in the country.

The post-war years saw one law and one character dominating the New York scene: the law was **Prohibition**, passed in 1920 in an attempt to sober up the nation; the character was **Jimmy Walker**, elected mayor in 1925 and who led a far from sober lifestyle. "No civilized man," said Walker "goes to bed the same day he wakes up," and during his flamboyant career the Jazz Age came to the city. In speakeasies all over town the bootleg liquor flowed, and writers as diverse as **Damon Runyon**, **F. Scott Fitzgerald**, and **Ernest Hemingway** portrayed the excitement of the times. With the **Wall Street** crash of 1929 (see "The Financial District" in Chapter One, *Lower Manhattan*), however, the party came to an abrupt end. The Depression began, and Mayor Walker was flushed away along with the torrent of civic corruption and malpractice that the changing times had uncovered and abrogated.

By 1932 approximately one in four New Yorkers was unemployed, and shantytowns, blackly known as "Hoovervilles" after the then President, had sprung up in Central Park to house the workless and homeless. Yet during this period three of New York's most opulent—and most beautiful—skyscrapers were topped out: the **Chrysler Building** in 1930, the **Empire State Building** in 1931 (though it was to stand near-empty for years), and in 1932 the **Rockefeller Center**—all very impressive, but of little immediate help to those in Hooverville, Harlem, or other depressed parts of the city. It fell to **Fiorello LaGuardia**, Jimmy Walker's successor as mayor to take over the running of the crisis-strewn city. He did so with ruthless tax and rationalization programs that, surprisingly, won him the approval of the people in the street: Walker's good living had got the city into trouble, reasoned voters; hard-headed straight-talking LaGuardia would get it out. Moreover President Roosevelt's **New Deal** supplied funds for roads, houses, and parks, the latter undertaken by the controversial Parks Commissioner **Robert Moses**. Under LaGuardia and Moses, the most extensive public housing program in the country was undertaken; the Triborough, Whitestone, and Henry Hudson bridges completed; 50 miles of new expressway and 5000 acres of new parks opened. And, in 1939, Mayor LaGuardia opened the airport that carries his name.

LaGuardia was reelected three times, taking the city into the **war years**. The country's entry into World War II in 1941 had few direct effects on New York City: lights were dimmed, 200 Japanese were interned on Ellis Island, and guards placed on bridges and tunnels. But, more importantly, behind the scenes experiments taking place at Columbia University split the uranium atom, giving a name to the **Manhattan Project**—the creation of the first atomic weapon.

THE POST-WAR YEARS

Though the beleaguered black community of Harlem erupted into looting and violence in 1943, the city maintained its preeminent position in the fields of finance, art, and communications, both in America and the world, its intellectual and creative community swollen by refugees escaping the Nazi threat to Europe. When the **United Nations Organization** was seeking a permanent home, New York was the obvious choice: lured by Rockefeller-donated land the building of the Secretariat began in 1947.

The building of the United Nations, along with the boost to the economy that followed the war, brought about the development of Midtown Manhattan. First in the race to fill the once-residential Park Avenue with offices was the **Lever House** of 1952, quickly followed by skyscrapers like the **Seagram Building** that give the area its distinctive look. Downtown, the **Stuyvesant Town** and **Peter Cooper Village** housing projects went ahead, along with many others all over the city. As ever, there were plentiful scandals over the financing of the building, most famously concerning the **Manhattan Urban Renewal Project** on the Upper East Side.

A further scandal, this time concerning organized crime, ousted Mayor **William O'Dwyer** in 1950: he was replaced by a series of unremarkable characters who did little to stop the gradual **decline** that had begun in the early 1950s as a general stagnation set in among the country's urban centers. New York fared worst: immigration from Puerto Rico had once more crammed East Harlem and the Lower East Side, and the nationwide trend of black migration from poorer rural areas was also magnified here. Both groups were forced into the ghetto area of Harlem, unable to get a slice of the

city's wealth. Racial disturbances and riots occurred in what had for two hundred years been one of the more liberal of American cities. One response to the problem was a general exodus of the white middle classes—the **Great White Flight** as the media gleefully labeled it—out of New York. Between 1950 and 1970 over a million families left the city. Things went from bad to worse during the 1960s with **race riots** in Harlem, Bedford-Stuyvesant, and East Harlem.

The **World's Fair** of 1964 was a white elephant to boost the city's credit in the financial world, but on the streets the call for civil liberties for blacks and protest against US involvement in Vietnam were, if anything, stronger than in the rest of the country. What little new building went up during this period seemed willfully to destroy a lot of the best of earlier traditions: a new **Madison Square Garden** was built on the site of the grandly neo-Classical **Pennsylvania Station**, and the **Singer Building** in the Financial District was demolished for an ugly skyscraper. In Harlem municipal investment stopped altogether and the community stagnated.

THE 1970s AND 80s

Manhattan reached **crisis point** in 1975. By now the city was spending more than it received in taxes—billions of dollars more. In part, this could be attributed to the effects of the White Flight: companies closed their headquarters in the city when offered lucrative relocation deals elsewhere, and their white collar employees were usually glad to go with them, thus doubly eroding the city's tax base. Even after municipal securities were sold, New York ran up a debt of $13 billion. Essential services, long fragile through underfunding, were ready to collapse. The mayor who presided over this cataclysmic decline, **Abraham Beame**, was an accountant.

Essentially, three things saved the city: the **Municipal Assistance Corporation** (aka the **Big Mac**), which was formed to borrow the money the city could no longer get its hands on; the election of **Edward I. Koch** as mayor in 1978; and, in an indirect way, the plummeting of the dollar on the world currency market following the oil price rises of the 1970s. This last effect, combined with cheap transatlantic airfares, brought European tourists into the city *en masse* for the first time, and with them came money for the city's hotels and service industries. Mayor Koch, cheerfully saying "Isn't it terrible?" to whatever he could not immediately put right, and asking "How am I doing?" each time he scored a success, gained the appreciation of New Yorkers, ever eager to look to their civic leaders for help or blame.

The slow reversal of fortunes coincided with the completion of two face-saving building projects: though, like the Empire State Building it long remained half empty, the **World Trade Center** was a gesture of confidence by the Port Authority of New York and New Jersey, which financed it; and in 1977 the **Citicorp Center** added modernity and prestige to its environs on Third Avenue.

Since the mid-1970s slump the city in some respects went from strength to strength. Ed Koch managed simultaneously to offend liberal groups and win the electoral support of ethnic groups, and despite the death of his friend and supporter Queens Borough president **Donald Manes**, (who committed suicide when an investigation into the city's various debt collecting agencies was announced) he was probably the most popular mayor since LaGuardia—some measure of his adroitness as a politician.

INTO THE 1990s

A spate of building gave the city yet more fabulous architecture, notably **Battery City Park** downtown, while master builder Donald Trump provided housing for the super-wealthy. But the popularity of Ed Koch waned. Many middle-class constituents considered Koch to have only rich property-barons' interests at heart; he also alienated a number of minorities—particularly blacks—with off-the-cuff statements that he was unable to bluff away. And although he was not been directly implicated, the scandals in his administration, beginning with the suicide of Donald Manes and continuing with the indictment (although she was acquitted) for bribery of another prominent friend, former Arts Commissioner Bess Myerson, took their political toll.

In 1989, Koch lost the Democratic nomination for the mayoral elections to **David Dinkins**, a 61-year-old black ex-marine and borough president of Manhattan. In a tough election the same year, Dinkins beat

Republican Rudolph Giuliani, a hard-nosed US attorney (whose role as leader of the prosecution in a police corruption case was made into the film *Prince of the City*). But even before the votes were counted, pundits were forecasting that the condition of the city was beyond any mayoral healing.

By the end of the 1980s New York was slipping hard and fast into a **massive recession**: in 1989 the city's budget deficit ran at $500 million; of the 92 companies that had made the city their base in 1980, only 53 were left, the others having moved to cheaper pastures; one in four New Yorkers was officially classed as poor—a figure unequaled since the Depression. The first black to hold the office, David Dinkins oversaw his first year as mayor reasonably well: the city's **Board of Estimate** had been declared unconstitutional by the Supreme Court (it violated the one person, one vote principle), and was abolished and replaced by a beefier City Council. Dinkins used his powers to quell racial unrest that had seemed about to explode in the spring, and skillfully passed a complex budget through the Council.

The date from which Dinkins'—and to some extent the city's—slide commenced was during the first week of the US Open Tennis tournament in summer 1990. On his way to the match, Brian Watkins, a tennis fan from Utah was stabbed to death in a subway station by a group of muggers while trying to protect his mother. Instead of holding a Koch-style "what is this city coming to?" press conference, Dinkins issued a statement saying that the media were exaggerating the importance of the murder—and then boarded a police helicopter to fly to the tennis event. As was predictable, the press latched onto this immediately, and Dinkins fell swiftly, and seemingly irrevocably, from popular favor, becoming known as the man "to whom everything sticks but praise."

From the summer on, the city's fortunes went into freefall. The unions went on the offensive when it was learned the city intended to lay off 15,000 workers; crime—especially related to the sale of crack—escalated; businesses failed. By the end of the year the city's budget deficit had reached $1.5 billion, and city creditors were threatening to remove support for municipal borrowing unless the figure was reduced drastically.

Throughout 1991 the previous year's financial disasters started to have the repercussions on the city's **ordinary people**: homelessness increased as city aid was cut back, schools became no-go zones with armed police and metal detectors at the gates (less than half of high school kids in the city graduate, a far smaller proportion than elsewhere in the United States), and a garbage workers' strike in May left piles of waste rotting on the streets.

Once again, New York seems to have hit bottom, and though it's easy to assume that this is just another low point in the city's cyclic fortunes, this time there seems no obvious solution. Unlike 1976, the State government refuses to bail the city out with aid loans; and, as far as the Federal government is concerned, the coffers ran out for New York long ago. After a decade of Reaganite optimism and growth, New York faces one of the bitterest periods of its history.

ARCHITECTURAL CHRONOLOGY

1625	First permanent **Dutch settlement** on Manhattan.	No buildings remain of the period. **Wall Street** marks the northern boundary of the settlement defenses in 1653.
Late 18th c.	New York under **British colonial rule**.	**St. Paul's Chapel** (1766) built in Georgian style.
1812	British blockade of Manhattan.	**City Hall** built.
1825	Opening of **Erie Canal** increases New York's wealth.	**Fulton Street** dock and market area built. Greek Revival row houses popular—eg **Schermerhorn Row, Colonade Row, St. Mark's Place, Chelsea**. Of much Federal Style building, few examples remain: The **Abigail Adams Smith House**, the **Morris-Jumel Mansion**, and **Gracie Mansion** the most notable.
1830–50	First wave of **immigration**, principally German and Irish.	The **Lower East Side** developed. **Trinity Church** built (1846) in English Gothic style, **Federal Hall** (1842) in Greek revival.
1850–1900	**More immigrants** (more Irish and Germans, later Italians and East European Jews) settle in Manhattan. **Industrial development** brings extreme wealth to individuals. The **Civil War** (1861–65) has little effect on the city.	Cast iron architecture enables buildings to mimic grand Classical designs cheaply. Highly popular in the shops and factories of SoHo, eg the **Haughwout Building** (1859). Large, elaborate mansions built along Fifth Avenue for America's new millionaires. **Central Park** opened (1876). The **Brooklyn Bridge** (1883) links Gothic with industrial strength; **St. Patrick's Cathedral** (1879) and **Grace Church** (1846) show it at its most delicate. **Statue of Liberty** unveiled (1886).
Early 20th c.		The **Flatiron Building** (1902) is the first skyscraper. Much civic architecture in the Beaux Arts neo-Classical style: **Grand Central Terminal** (1919), **New York Public Library** (1911), **US Customs House** (1907), **General Post Office** (1913), and the **Municipal Building** (1914) are the finest examples. The **Woolworth Building** (1913) becomes Manhattan's "Cathedral of Commerce."
1915		The **Equitable Building** fills every square inch of its site on Broadway, causing the first zoning ordinances to ensure a degree of setback and allow light to reach the streets.
1920	Volstead Act enforces **prohibition**. Economic confidence of the 1920s brings the **Jazz Age**.	Art Deco influences show in the **American Standard Building** (1927) and the **Fuller Building** (1929).
1929	**Wall Street Crash**. America enters the **Great Depression**.	Many of the lavish buildings commissioned and begun in the 1920s reach completion. Skyscrapers combine the monumental with the decorative: **Chrysler Building** (1930), **Empire**

State Building (1930), **Waldorf Astoria Hotel** (1931), and the **General Electric Building** (1931). **Rockefeller Center**, the first exponent of the idea of a city-within-a-city, is built through the decade. The **McGraw-Hill Building** (1931) is self-consciously modern.

1930s The **New Deal** and **WPA** schemes attempt to reduce unemployment.	Little new building other than housing projects. WPA murals decorate buildings around town, notably in the **New York Public Library** and the **County Courthouse**.
1941 America goes to **war**.	New zoning regulations encourage the development of the setback skyscraper: but little is built during the war years.
1950 **United Nations Organization** established.	The **UN Secretariat** (1950) introduces the glass curtain wall to Manhattan. Similar Corbusier-influenced buildings include the **Lever House** (1952) and, most impressively, the **Seagram Building** (1958), whose plaza causes the zoning regulations to be changed in an attempt to encourage similar public spaces. The **Guggenheim Museum** (1959) opens.
1960s **Protest Movement** stages demonstrations against US involvement in Vietnam.	Much early-1960s building pallidly imitates the glass box skyscraper. The **Pan Am** (1963) building attempts something different; more successful is the **Ford Foundation building** (1967). In the hands of lesser architects, the plaza becomes a liability. New **Madison Square Garden** (1968) is built on the site of the old Penn Station. The minimalist **Verrazano Narrows Bridge** (1964) links Brooklyn to Staten Island.
1970s Mayor Abraham Beame presides over **New York's decline**. City financing reaches **crisis point** as businesses leave Manhattan.	The **World Trade Center Towers** (1970) add a soaring landmark to the Lower Manhattan skyline. The **Rockefeller Center Extensions** (1973-4) clone the glass box skyscraper. Virtually no new corporate development until the **Citicorp Center** (1977) adds new textures and profile to the city's skyline. Its popular atrium is adopted by later buildings.
1975 Investment in the city increases. **Ed Koch elected mayor**.	**One UN Plaza** adapts the glass curtain wall to skilled ends.
1978 **Corporate wealth returns** to Manhattan.	The **IBM Building** (1982) shows the conservative side of modern architecture; post-Modernist designs like the **AT&T Building** (1983) and **Federal Reserve Plaza** (1985) depart from convention to mix historical styles in the same building.
1980s **Ed Koch reelected mayor**.	**Statue of Liberty** restoration completed. The mixed-use **Battery City Park** opens to wide acclaim.
1986 Wall Street **crashes;** Dow Jones index plunges 500 points in a day.	Property market takes a dive. **Equitable Building** on 7th Ave opens.
1989 **Ed Koch** loses Democratic nomination to **David Dinkins**, who goes on to become NYC's first black mayor.	**Rockefeller Center** sold to Japanese. **RCA Building** renamed **General Electric Building**.
1990 Major **recession** hits New York.	**Ellis Island** Museum of Immigration opens to public.
1991 NYC's **budget deficit** reaches record proportions.	**Guggenheim** Museum reopens with new extension.

TWENTIETH-CENTURY AMERICAN ART

This is no more than a brief introduction to a handful of American painters; for more detailed appraisals, both of the century's major movements and specific painters, see "Books."

Twentieth-century American art begins with **The Eight**, otherwise known as the **Ashcan School**, a group of artists who were painting in New York in the first decade of this century. Led by Robert Henri, many of them worked as illustrators for city newspapers and they tried to depict modern American urban life—principally in New York City—as honestly and realistically as possible, in much the same way as earlier painters had depicted nature. Their exhibitions, in 1908 and 1910, were, however, badly received, and most of their work was scorned for representing subjects not seen as fit for painting. Paralleling the work of the Ashcan School was that of the group that met at the **Photo-Secession Gallery** of the photographer Alfred Stieglitz on Fifth Avenue. They were more individual, less concerned with social themes than expressing their own individual styles, but were equally unappreciated. Art, for Americans, even for American critics, was something that came from Europe, and in

the early years of the twentieth century attempts to Americanize it were regarded with suspicion.

Change came with the **Armory Show** of 1913: an exhibition, set up by the remaining Ashcan artists (members of the new *Association of American Painters and Sculptors*), to bring more than 1800 European works together and show them to the American public for the first time. The whole of the French nineteenth century was represented at the show, together with Cubist and Expressionist painters and, from New York, the work of the Ashcan painters and the Stieglitz circle. It was visited by over 85,000 people in its month-long run in New York, and plenty more caught it as it toured America. The immediate effect was uproar. Americans panned the European paintings, partly because they resented their influence but also because they weren't quite sure how to react; the indigenous American artists were criticized for being afraid to adopt a native style; and the press fanned the flames by playing up to public anxieties about the subversive nature of modern art. But there was a positive effect: the modern art of both Europe and America became known all over the continent, particularly abstract painting. From now on American artists were free to develop their own approach.

The paintings that followed were, however, far from abstract in style. The Great Crash of 1929 and subsequent Depression led to the school of **Social Realism** and paintings like **Thomas Hart Benton**'s *America Today* sequence (now in the Whitney Museum at the Equitable): a vast mural that covered, in realistic style, every aspect of contemporary American life. The New Deal and the attendant **Federal Art Project** of the WPA supported many artists through the lean years of the 1930s by commissioning them to decorate public buildings, and it became widely acknowledged that not only were work, workers, and public life fit subjects for art, but also that artists had some responsibility to push for social change. Artists like **Edward Hopper** and **Charles Burchfield** sought to recreate, in as precise a way as possible, American contemporary life, making the particular (in Hopper's case empty streets, lone buildings, solitary figures in diners) "epic and universal." Yet while Hopper and Burchfield can be called great artists in their own right, a great deal of the work of the time, particularly that commissioned as public works, was inevitably dull and conformist, and it wasn't long before movements were afoot to inject new life into American painting. It was the beginning of abstraction.

With these ideas the center of the visual art world gradually began to shift. The founding of the **Museum of Modern Art**, and also of the **Guggenheim Museum** some years later, combined with the arrival of many European artists throughout the 1930s (Gropius, Hans Hofmann, the Surrealists) to make New York a serious rival to Paris in terms of influence. **Hans Hofmann** in particular was to have considerable influence on New York painters, through both his art school and his own boldly Expressionistic works. Also, the many American artists who had lived abroad came back armed with a set of European experiences which they could couple with their native spirit to produce a new, indigenous, and wholly original style. First and most prominent of these was **Arshile Gorky**, a European-born painter who had imbibed the influences of Cézanne and Picasso—and, more so, the Surrealists. His technique, however, was different: not cold and dispassionate like the Europeans but expressive, his paintings textured and more vital. **Stuart Davis**, too, once a prominent member of the Ashcan School, was an important figure, his paintings using everyday objects as subject matter but jumbling them into abstract form—as in works like *Lucky Strike*, which hangs in the Museum of Modern Art. Another artist experimenting with abstract forms was **Georgia O'Keefe**, best known for her depictions of flowers, toned in pastel pinks and powder blues. These she magnified so they became no more than unidentified shapes, in their curves and ovular forms curiously erotic and suggestive of fertility and growth. The Whitney Museum holds a good stock of her work.

The **Abstract Expressionists**—or **The New York School** as they came to be known—were a fairly loose movement, and one which splits broadly into two groups: the first creating abstractions with increasing gusto and seemingly endless supplies of paint, while the rest employed a more ordered approach to their work. Best known among the first group is **Jackson Pollock**, a farmer's son from Wyoming who had studied under Thomas Hart Benton in New York and in the 1930s was painting Cubist works reminiscent of Picasso. Pollock considered the American art scene to be still under the thumb of Europe, and he deliberately set about creating canvases that bore little relation to anything that had gone before. For a start his paintings were huge, and it was difficult to tell where they ended; in fact Pollock would simply determine the edge of a composition by cutting the canvas wherever he happened to feel was appropriate at the time—a large-scale approach that was much imitated and in part determined by the large factory spaces and lofts where American artists worked. Also, it was a reaction against bourgeois (and therefore essentially European) notions of what a painting should be: the average Abstract Expressionist painting simply couldn't be contained in the normal collector's home, and as such was at the time impossible to classify. Often Pollock would paint on the floor, adding layers of paint apparently at random, building up a dense composition that said more about the action of painting than any specific subject matter: hence the term "action painting" which is invariably used to describe this technique. As a contemporary critic said: with Pollock the canvas became "an arena in which to act—rather than as a space in which to reproduce . . . ."

Similar to Pollock in technique, but less abstract in subject matter, was the Dutch-born artist **Willem de Kooning**, whose *Women* series clearly attempts to be figurative—as do a number of his other paintings, especially the earlier ones, many of which are in the Museum of Modern Art. Where he and Pollock are alike is in their exuberant use of paint and color, painted, splashed, dripped, or scraped on to the canvas with a palette knife. **Franz Kline** was also of this "gestural" school, though he cut down on color and instead covered his canvas with giant black shapes against a stark white background: bold images reminiscent of Chinese ideograms and Oriental calligraphy. **Robert Motherwell**, who some have called the leading light of the Abstract Expressionist movement (in so far as it had one), created a similar effect in his *Elegies to the Spanish Republic*, only here his symbols are drawn from Europe not the East—and unlike Abstract

Expressionist paintings they gain their inspiration from actual events. Again, for his work the Whitney and MoMA are good sources.

Preeminent among the second group of Abstract Expressionists was **Mark Rothko**, a Russian-born artist whose work is easy to recognize by its broad rectangles of color against a single-hued background. Rothko's paintings are more controlled than Pollock's, less concerned with exuding their own painterliness than with expressing, as Rothko put it, "a single tragic idea." Some have called his work mystic, religious even, and his paintings are imbued with a deep melancholy, their fuzzy-edged blocks of color radiating light and, in spite of an increasingly lightened palette, a potent sense of despair. Rothko, a deeply unhappy man, committed suicide in 1970, and it was left to one of his closest friends, **Adolf Gottlieb**, to carry on where he left off. With his *pictographs* Gottlieb spontaneously explored deep psychological states, covering his canvases with "Native" American signs. He also used a unique set of symbols of cosmos and chaos—discs of color above a blotchy earth—as in his *Frozen Sounds* series of the early 1950s, currently in the Whitney collection.

The Abstract Expressionists gave native American art stature worldwide and helped consolidate New York's position as center of the art world. But other painters weren't content to follow the emotional painting of Pollock and Rothko *et al.*, and toned down the technique of excessive and frenzied brushwork into impersonal representations of shapes within clearly defined borders—**Kenneth Noland**'s *Target* and the geometric (and later 3-dimensional) shapes of **Frank Stella** being good examples. **Ad Reinhardt**, too, honed down his style until he was using only different shades of the same color, taking this to its logical extreme by ultimately covering canvases with differing densities of black.

Barnett Newman is harder to classify, though he is usually associated with the Abstract Expressionists, not least because of the similarities to Rothko of his bold "fields" of color. But his controlled use of one striking tone, painted with only tiny variations in shade, and cut (horizontally or vertically) by only a single contrasting strip, give him more in common with the trends in art that followed. **Helen Frankenthaler** (and later **Morris Louis**) took this one stage farther with pictures like *Mountains and Sea*, which by staining the canvas rather than painting it lends blank areas the same importance as colored ones, making the painting seem as if created by a single stroke. With these two artists, color was the most important aspect of painting, and the canvas and the color were absorbed as one. In his mature period Louis began—in the words of a contemporary critic—"to think, feel and conceive almost exclusively in terms of open color." And as if to reject any other method, he destroyed most of his work of the previous two decades.

With the 1960s came **Pop Art**, which turned to America's popular media for subject—its films, TV, advertisements, and magazines—and depicted it in heightened tones and colors. **Jasper Johns**' *Flag* bridges the gap, cunningly transforming the Stars and Stripes into little more than a collection of painted shapes, but most Pop Art was more concerned with monumentalizing the tackier side of American culture: **Andy Warhol** did it with Marilyn Monroe and Campbell's Soup; **Claes Oldenburg** by recreating everyday objects (notably food) in soft fabrics and blowing them up to giant size; **Robert Rauschenberg** by making collages or "assemblages" of ordinary objects; **Roy Lichtenstein** by imitating the screen process of newspapers and cartoon strips; and **Ed Kienholz** through realistic tableaux of the sad, shabby, or just plain weird aspects of modern life. But what Pop Art really did was to make art accessible and fun. With it the commonplace became acceptable material for the twentieth-century artist, and as such paved the way for what was to follow. **Graffiti** has since been elevated to the status of art form, and New York painters like **Keith Haring** (who died in 1990) and **Kenny Scharf** were celebrities in their own right, regularly called in to decorate Manhattan nightclubs.

Ironically, over the last decade or so there has been a return to straight figurative depictions, either supra-realistically as in the poignant acetate figures of **Duane Hanson** and the more conventional nude studies of **Philip Pearlstein**, or in a minimal way as with the quasi-abstractions of **Robert Moskowitz**. There has even been a return by some artists to the conventions of nineteenth-century portraiture and history painting, seen in the work of **Mark Tansey** and **Robert Arneson**. Most exciting is the work of the KOS group, from the South Bronx. As for the future, things have never been more fluid. But New York remains, at least in terms of the marketplace, center of art worldwide—and the city to which everyone continues to look for inspiration.

WRITERS ON NEW YORK CITY

New York City is about reaction: its devotees are committed, so are its critics. Below are three pieces on the city: the first by Midwesterner Garrison Keillor; the second by resident New Yorker, Quentin Crisp, the third by David Widgery, who lives in London.

GARRISON KEILLOR

GARRISON KEILLOR *was born in Minnesota in 1942. From the mid-1970s to the late 1980s he hosted the live radio show* A Prairie Home Companion, *but his chief fame lies in creating Lake Wobegon, a small Midwestern town where, as he puts it, "All the women are strong and all the men are beautiful." His books are humorous, often autobiographical, collections of stories of characters from Lake Wobegon.*

Keillor now spends much of his time in New York City: the contrast between Manhattan and his native Midwest comes over clearly in his thoughts on a subject that has inspired numerous writers over the years—the New York subway.

SOLIDARITY FOREVER

When I moved from Minnesota to New York, so many New Yorkers warned me against setting foot in the subway that I naturally headed there first, and I've been riding it daily ever since. It's dirty, plagued with beggars, sometimes miserably slow, and yet, it's a *train* and that gives it grandeur, even with homeless people sleeping across the seats. When you grow up in a little town like Wobegon, next to a deserted railroad track rusting in the weeds, and you imagine a shiny train chugging in and carrying you away, it marks you for the rest of your life. When I stand in my dreary station on West 68th Street and see the C train's lights come around the tunnel bend and feel the rails shake, my heart smiles. I feel fulfilled.

You can tell I'm not a real New Yorker, by the way, when I call it the C train. The subway is such a part of the soul of the city, the mark of a native New Yorker is the way he refers to

the subway lines by their antique names—the BMT, the IRT, and the IND—the initials of transit companies dead 60 years or more. To us immigrants, they are the A train or the No 1, known by the letter or number on the sign in the train window.

The pace of life in New York tends to be stately, and tourists think of it as fast only because they're here at weekends, when there's less traffic. During the week, especially in Manhattan, the pace is so slow, you often feel that any mode of transportation might be as fast as any other—you could walk, drive, take a cab, or ride the subway, and get there about the same time—so we choose our transport more on aesthetic grounds. Like most older American men, I'm sentimental about trains, but my real love is the automobile. In a car, you can sing along with the Temptations or interview yourself ("Gar, you're 48 years old and yet you're the leading pitcher in the National League, what's your secret?"), or yell at your boss. The subway forces you to act reasonable and wear a public face. The automobile is the sweetest privacy a person gets in a day. But in New York, having a car of your own is a handicap, like having a hump of your own. At parties, you sometimes see clumps of car owners comparing costs of garage space, the merits of various routes out of town, discussing the hump. Taxis aren't much better. Traffic in New York ebbs more than it flows, and the narrow cross-streets go into coronary occlusion regularly. Sitting motionless in a cab for 15 minutes as pedestrians flow by, you feel a vibration from deep below. It is the subway. You should get out and go down and take it.

Life in New York is slow, but I feel my steps quicken when I take the handrail and climb down the steps to the subway station. The beggar who sits on the top step never gets a nickel from me. I hurry down and when I go through the turnstile I break into a slow trot down the next flight to the platform. I hurry because I don't want barely to miss a train, which feels logical, but of course, by hurrying, I sometimes barely miss a train that if I had walked slowly I wouldn't have been aware of. If I find the platform crowded, I'm happy. It means that some of the job of waiting has been done by others. If I find a train pulling out, its red lights disappearing into the dark, it's a sad moment, in a place that is forlorn already:

water dripping, garbage on the tracks, a raggedy man asleep on a bench. I stand and think of all the things I could have done differently this morning and shaved faster or toasted the bagel lighter. I could've skipped the editorial page of the *New York Times*. Once every few weeks, I come to the platform as the train is rolling in. It stops and I board it, as if it were my private subway. This is a great day, always.

A speed merchant it isn't, though the view from the front window of the Broadway Express as it races downtown from 96th Street, zooming through the turns at 40 miles an hour, is as exciting as the Coney Island roller coaster. Elegant it ain't either. In the stations and cars, none of the ads are for BMWs or ski resorts, they're for haemorrhoids and sore feet, bunions, bad skin, bad teeth, drug treatment. The movie ads show glamorous stars but subway riders like to draw on them, give them warts and pimples, black eyes, make them cry, make stuff come out of their noses and draw big balloons overhead where the stars confess to their homosexuality, their drug habits.

It takes a strong person to pursue elegance at street level in New York. A new sidewalk café, Chinese-Mexican, with six tables, opened in my neighborhood this summer, and every night I walked by and saw people eating Szechuan *tostados* and drinking Dos Equis or Tsing-tao beer, truck exhaust swirling around them, panhandlers leaning over their table, a homeless man curled up in the doorway, and the diners looked as cool as if they were at the Ballroom. I admire the resolution of people who can look reality in the face and deny it. People who are drawn to the romance of the subway, for example.

The subway is where you can study people, through discreet glances, and ponder their histories. The man in the expensive suit with the *Wall Street Journal* tucked under his arm: who he? A young black woman sits reading Thoreau's *Walden*, a woman who, if I saw her on the street, I'd never associate with Thoreau. Thoreau was a surburban guy who walked to work at his pond and who wrote, "Simplicity simplicity, simplicity! Our life is frittered away by detail. Let your affairs be as two or three, and keep your accounts on your thumbnail. In the midst of this chopping sea of civilized life, a man must live by dead reckoning if he would

not founder and go to the bottom. Simplify, simplify." Thoreau never lived in New York. He did not envision the subway.

The subway is where I stand, studying Spanish from the advertising placards such as the ad for Tide *detergente* with the phrase *blanquier tan blanco,* as a young man in a dark suit and a narrow black tie stands in the middle of the car, swaying and preaching the Gospel. I don't imagine that the Spanish for "whiter than white" is particularly useful phrase in New York but it describes how I feel sometimes: *too damn white.* But this is what the man is preaching, that ye must be washed in the blood of the lamb and be made spotless, whiter than snow. This is a message I grew up hearing, and I look at him and smile to show my agreement, but he reads something else in my expression, like spiritual need. He zeroes in on me. "There are two trains in this life and only two. One train to heaven and the other to hell. Which train are you on, brother?" he asks. His judgement is fierce, like my father's. Across the aisle is a young black woman wearing the biggest hair comb ever seen, with her name spelled out in rhinestones: MICHELLE. As if life is a show and here is her marquee. She needs the Gospel more than I do, but he comes and preaches it me. I avoid his eyes. I study the Spanish, such a graceful language. The phrase *No se apoye contra la puerta* (Don't lean against the door) sounds like an invitation to dance, compared to what they said where I come from ("What's the matter with you? For crying out loud. Quit leaning against the door!"). Spanish is the loving tongue, like the song says. My dad told me, "Get a job," *Aprenda una vocacion,* says the ad. He said, "Listen to what I'm telling you!" *Este atento a los instrucciones.* If my old man spoke Spanish, maybe I'd have listened to him. The preacher closes up his Bible and gets off at 14th Street. My stop, too, but I ride on to West 4th. I'll walk back.

The subway is a great cultural institution. It makes us New Yorkers stand close to each other, which we imagine we don't want to do, but really we want to be *made* to. We need an institution to bring us together and the subway does that in a big way. Life is constantly spinning, you see, and a powerful centrifugal force wants to hurl us apart, alone, into the darkness, to become recluses in cabins in Vermont. We need to get—in a crowd now and then to experience the pleasure of the city, a painful pleasure at first for those of us from the provinces—in the Midwest, a comfortable conversational distance is about four feet, and the first time a Midwesterner boards the subway, he reaches critical mass and implodes—but you get used to it. And then it seems lovely, like when we were kids, and were jammed together in a car. My aunts and uncles produced flocks of kids and believed that, no matter how many were in the back seat, you could always get one more in. If we could exhale enough to whisper, then there was room for another one. The subway operates on a similar principle. At Times Square, they pack into the cars and then more people get on. The train is so packed, you don't even need to hang on, you just ride in a loose human gel.

When people are squeezed tight, they become extremely courteous. No eye contact. No sudden moves. Nothing sudden. Nothing loud or rude. Ten of us stand in 12 square feet at the end of the car, ten people carefully balanced as the train starts, ten arms holding on to a bar so we don't lurch into each other, ten people trying to maintain a half-inch space between each other. Of the nine people around me, five are black, which is more black people than have come through Lake Wobegon in 20 years. To be packed in so close to black men and women seems like a privilege, if you consider that all systems of oppression and cruelty require distance to be maintained. Segregation means exactly that, and so does apartheid. So, to stand inches away from each other is liberating. I wouldn't say this to the woman standing next to me, whose hip I feel against the side of my leg, but it's true.

It occurs to me, riding the subway, that the Golden Rule is a matter of great practicality, reminding you to look at every situation from both sides because the person you are doing it to today can do it to you tomorrow: count on it. Our situations are easily reversed. The Rule means: whatever you do, don't be too arrogant—the person you sack today is the person you'll need tomorrow, the man you put in prison will someday be the warden, so resist the temptation to moral grandeur, because the world does turn. The people crowded around me, whose bodies touch mine, are the broadest slice of New York I'll see today and the closest neighbors I have. I am stunned by their civility. I

think of the Rule here because there is no place in New York where it is so assiduously applied. Packed in tight, you *feel* the social contract and sense its fragility. The train lurches and instantly we each rebalance so as not to break it. Solidarity forever, as the old song says, the subway makes us strong.

© Garrison Keillor 1991

This article was originally published in the Independent *Magazine.* Garrison Keillor's *books,* Lake Wobegon Days, Leaving Home, Happy to Be Here, *and* We are Still Married *are all published by Viking Penguin at $8.95.*

QUENTIN CRISP

There are few more active devotees of New York City than **QUENTIN CRISP**. *He has lived here—in a seedy boarding house in the East Village—for five years, making a living from writing and reviewing films and filling up on peanuts and champagne at literary launches, lunches, and previews across America: all part of what he calls the smiling and nodding racket. He's a well-known figure in his neighborhood, and he recently achieved his greatest ambition—to be given full American citizenship after four years as a "resident alien." "Now," says Crisp, "I am beyond deportation and able to commit my first murder." Though in his eighties, he has no desire to return to Britain: he would, he claims, rather live in New York than anywhere else in the world. What follows is a brief personal view of the city, specially written for this book, by one of its most diehard fans.*

I am now a twilight American.

In the days when I was only English , a full-time American, curling his lip as he spoke, said to me, "You British think that where the suburbs of New York end, the suburbs of Los Angeles begin." Actually our ignorance is even more profound than that. When we say "America" we mean New York and, when we say "New York," we are referring not to the state nor even to the Bronx or Brooklyn but only to Manhattan. Furthermore, if shown a map of The United States, we mistake Long Island for Manhattan whereas in fact the latter is merely a tiny rock, the shape of a date stone, crushed between Long Island and the rest of the continent. Nevertheless, in spite of its cramped situation and its relatively limited size, it cannot be denied that, when you are in this city, you feel you are at the heart of the world.

At a time when most people who crossed the Atlantic Ocean did so by boat, it was the skyline of New York that made the deepest impression. Returning home, the first things a traveler mentioned were the skyscrapers. They are still spectacular but nowadays, when most capital cities bristle with very tall buildings, this aspect of New York is no longer so remarkable. Indeed it would not be difficult to photograph London or Sydney to look like any American metropolis. For an English person, though not necessarily for an Australian, the uniqueness of New York lies not in its architecture nor in its climate but in its people.

Everybody here is your instant friend.

Strange to relate, it is the natives themselves who issue dire warnings concerning the coldness and the dangers of the place. Ignore what they say. Take exactly the same safety precautions that you would use as a visitor to any big modern city. Do not stroll, swaddled in furs and bristling with diamonds, along dim side streets after midnight. At all other times, wander whither you please. Even those denizens who wish to praise their habitat misguidedly tell you that you will love the bustle of New York. In truth, except during rush hours, it is a leisurely city in which anything goes. I have seen elderly gentlemen meandering through mid-Manhattan wearing nothing but their running shorts. In fact there is almost nothing that anyone could wear or say or do here that would cause anything like the shocked reaction that in England greets the slightest deviation from traditional dress or behavior.

See the sights if you must; go to the top of the Empire State Building or the World Trade Center if you are a born tourist, but spend most of your time in the streets where you will find you are perpetually welcome as though this teeming city were a village. It is not a good idea to travel on the subway. The system is very complicated and the situation is made worse by the fact that all maps have been disfigured beyond recognition. Moreover, the stations are bleak and the trains so noisy that conversation of any kind is impossible. Unless you are desperate, try not to take taxis. They are amazingly plentiful but the drivers, though friendly, have no more idea of the whereabouts

of your destination than you do. English cabbies, if you try to give them instructions, interrupt you angrily with the words, "D'yer wanna drive the damn thing yerself?" Their American counterparts expect a guided tour and, to complicate matters further, may not understand anything you say. As you look through the thick pane of glass that separates you from them, you will see they have names like Ascencio or Rodriguez so, if communications break down, try Spanish.

When your feet give out, take buses. They are frequent, air cooled in summer and warm in winter but unfortunately you must pay your fare (a dollar at the moment) in exactly the right amount of silver coinage. Bus drivers give no change. This is almost the only annoying quirk that mars the joy of metropolitan life.

Feel free to ask for street directions from anybody; you will get their life story. And though they look like gangsters, even the policemen are cozy.

New York is one vast carnival. The splendour and the squalor are woven together more closely and more conspicuously than in any other city that I, at any rate, have ever visited. At one moment you are treading sidewalks paved with the names of famous people; the next you are bouncing down avenues in such a state of disrepair that, if you are in a fast-moving vehicle, your head hits the roof. It is also a gloriously noisy place in which ambulances, police cars and fire engines never seem to sleep. Being in New York is like taking part in a Frank Capra movie—crazy, human, beautiful. You will notice as soon as you arrive that everyone is handsome, probably because of the dazzling mixtures of races that have made their homes here.

If there are any drawbacks to this earthly paradise, they are climatic and financial.

At a distance most parts of the world seem to have a climate; when you are in them, they only have weather. This is true of New York. Occasionally the seasons are as unpredictable as those of Southern England but I am happy to tell you that they are never as dreary. Speaking generally, the winters are short, as bright and bitter as one of Dorothy Parker's epigrams, but the summers seem long because they are so hot. Some years for most of July and all of August the temperature hovers at ninety degrees. If, during this time, there is a thunderstorm, do not expect any relief. Hot water pours from the sky, a torrid wind blows through the concrete canyons and the next day is as humid as the one before. To enjoy the city at its best, come in the autumn—like Mr. Columbus. This time of year is almost always clear, beautiful and dry.

The rigors of the financial climate are harder to evade. When you visit America, stay with friends however much you may come to dislike them before the end of your stay. Hotels are staffed by very obliging people and their managers make a great fuss of you but accommodation is far from cheap. All this happiness has to be paid for.

However, do not allow these minor disadvantages to deter you for a moment. Pack tonight; leave home tomorrow.

Books by Quentin Crisp include The Naked Civil Servant (NAL $6.95); How To Become a Virgin (St. Martin $6.95); *and* How To Go to the Movies (St. Martin $15.95).

DAVID WIDGERY

DAVID WIDGERY *combines a career as a general practitioner in London's East End with that of a writer and critic. He is a closet New York aficionado, and regards sunbathing on top of the World Trade Center and eating in Little Italy during the San Gennaro Festival as among the greatest pleasures of civilized life. "I love the United States," he says, "but it's the America of radicalism, muckraking and rhythm and blues which the establishment is at present so keen to deny."*

I first went to Manhattan twenty years ago; a terrified teenager clutching a "99 Day, $99" coach ticket. America seemed to be curling open like an old tin can before my eyes, the civil rights movement was spilling into the northern city ghettoes, the Berkeley students were discovering pot and "organizing within the knowledge factory" and a huge plume of smoke hung above Los Angeles from the gleeful riot in Watts. Sixties New York was fast, belligerent and scared. My strongest memories were the poster over the Students for a Democratic Society's HQ saying "No Vietnamese ever called me Nigger"; the smell of hot oil and rubber inside Greyhound Stations and lines of poor people with their parcels wrapped up with infinite patience and newly achieved dignity.

Back again in 1974, New York still felt, to a European, a radical city, a place of imminence, a mix of the older 1960s possibilities and the new spirit of the women's and gay movement which still meant change. The Watergate Tapes were on sale in supermarket checkouts, Vietnam was in every other sentence and the Movement was still moving. Political optimism was only temporarily stalled, the Empire was uneasy.

So the first shock of New York deep into the Reign of Reagan is its platitudinous self-confidence, its intellectual conformism and a social conservatism so profound it has ceased to be a cosmetic and has been absorbed into the very civic skin. Never mind the homeless sleeping out in the public parks, subways unfit for cattle, the poor hawking secondhand goods on the street corners and the plummeting stock exchange; there is a tennis clip on every mountain bike, a new restaurant on every intersection and if you don't *enjoy*, it's your own damn fault.

Typical is what's happened to the poor old Statue of Liberty, spruced up for its Centennial as the new brand image of capitalism, another product from the people who gave you freedom. The statue was a democratic gesture, its catchline was written by the socialist poet Emma Lazarus, and the French fund-raising effort was an act of defiance against absolutism. But its incessantly produced image now beams benignly over the aerial bombardment of Tripoli and the rolling up of the Contras, or whatever wheeze comes next from the patriots who now direct US foreign policy.

Inside Liberty's tower, a Museum of Immigration is now housed* (rather tough on Black Americans, who mostly arrived in shackles at the plantation posts), which even includes Samuel Gompers, George Grosz and Helen Keller. But the Museum is deserted while thousands stand in a line to photograph themselves looking out from Liberty's flame. While I read a panel on the rise of the No-Nothing-Party before the First World War and its campaign against dope fiends and alien gunmen, someone strides past in a studied "Don't Mess with the US" T-shirt shouting "All this history bores me." Indeed.

---

*Now moved to Ellis Island

History is now New York's enemy and if you inquire about Watergate, let alone Stonewall, people brought up on TV and leisure magazines look back with alarm. Being a European sentimentalist, I trot off to the usual shrines, eating a cold turkey sandwich on the spot John Lennon got shot; gawping at the Apollo and the Cedar Bar and visiting Trotsky's old print shop in St Mark's Place. While wading through throngs of New Yorkers lineing for "Vienna 1900" (a kind of Habitat catalogue for the Franz-Josef era) at the Museum of Modern Art to see the Pollocks and De Koonings I hear the gallery guide announcing that "the Post-Impressionists were like the European Romantics. That is they were alchoholics and committed suicide." But the real New York is a another time-space continuum. Now.

As a city it has lost none of its architectural exuberance and manic energy. The taxis still swerve rather than drive, the sign language is still imperative and muscular ("Don't block the box," "Touchbank Here," "Stop Cheap Steaks") and people throw frisbees as if their life depended on it. There is less English spoken, more babies with bald fathers and a lot more purple prose in the delis which now stick reviews over their midget vegetables and lake sturgeons and offer varietal grape juices. *Enjoy* is the supreme injunction.

If you think gentrification is people sticking brass door knockers on their Stoke Newington front doors, you should see the gentry in operation in New York. There a neighborhood can be razed, and replaced by yuppie Lego in a matter of months and gourmetified and art-galleried in the process.

Which is not to say all the cultural landmarks have been built over by sushi bars and designer bike shops. Despite AIDS, people still strip for charity, organize telephone sex link-ups which are shown on your telephone bill as long distance calls, and line to see "My Beautiful Launderette" which, along with Laura Ashley, muffins and antique clocks, was one of the few signs that the United Kingdom exists.

The US labor movement, once mighty but now organizing only 17 percent of the workforce, soldiers on, thank God, and the best day I spent in New York was being shown around the back of a power plant, Mafia-disposed toxic waste and all, by a rank and file organizer. And there is a Left, although in comparison with the movement of the 1960s and 1970s it is microscopic.

So I was delighted to meet Victor Navasky, the editor of the *Nation*, an organ of sensible liberalism which, in current circumstances, seems crypto-Bolshevik; to come across writers for the post-Murdoch *Village Voice* who are as appalled by Reaganism as most Europeans; and to meet people who are, ahem, Marxists.

What is surprising is the degree of self-delusion among those tyros of empiricism, the bankers themselves. Banker availability is a New York specialty, they are young, they are noisy and they are everywhere: restaurants, gallery openings, night clubs and all younger than oneself. I interrupt one who is discussing the investment potential of a Jamie Reid Sex Pistols daub at Reid's New York opening at the Josh Bauer Gallery.

"Does it matter to you that since Reaganomics, the USA is not only a net debtor, but the biggest debtor in the world? And why are all the farms going bust?"

He isn't worried, his art collection will see him through; if the Exchange busts, he has a Schnabel under the table.

Steve Mass, founder of the Mudd Club, is also delighted by the ironies of yuppies shelling out for Situationist off-cuts, but equally off-beam. "What we really needed in New York was someone like David Hebridge to tell us what it all *meant*." Hmmm. Was it like this in 1928, I wonder?

At the Palladium, which has less style than Stoke Newington's Three Crowns on Friday night, more bankers are waiting to meet the Eurythmics, whose co-leader's birthday we are celebrating. "Do you know any good bands in Britain? Up and coming and with investment potential?" asks one. I take a deep breath, "Well, there's this group called the Redskins. You seem to have plenty of statues that need kicking down."

This article was originally published in London, in City Limits *Magazine in October 1986; thanks to them for letting us reprint. David Widgery's works include* Beating Hearts, *a study of racism and anti-racism centering on the East London Bangladeshi community where he practices, and the introduction to the photobook* A Day in the Life of London.

BOOKS

TRAVEL/IMPRESSIONS

Mike Marqusee (ed.) *New York: An Illustrated Anthology* (Salem House Publishers $19.95). Pricey, but the best and most neatly packaged collection of writings on New York—from Walt Whitman to Kathy Acker—that you'll find.

B. Cohen, S. Chwast, and S. Heller (ed.) *New York Observed* (Abrams, $17.95). An anthology of writings on and illustrations of the city from 1650 to the present: a good alternative to the more literary Marqusee book.

Stephen Brook *New York Days, New York Nights* (Atheneum, 1985, $14.95). A witty and fairly penetrating account of the city, marred only by some remarkably sexist passages.

Jan Morris *Manhattan '45* (Oxford University Press $9.95) Morris's latest, and best, writings on Manhattan, reconstructing New York as it greeted returning GIs in 1945. Effortlessly written, fascinatingly anecdotal, marvelously warm about the city. See also *The Great Port* (Oxford University Press $8.95).

Brendan Behan *Brendan Behan's New York* (Geis, 1964). Behan's journey through the underbelly of New York City in the early 1960s, readably recounted in anecdotal style—and with some characterful sketches by Paul Hogarth.

Jerome Charyn *Metropolis* (Avon $8.95). A native of the Bronx, Charyn dives into current-day New York from every angle and comes up with a book that's sharp, sensitive, and refreshingly real: one of the best things you can read on the city, from one of its better contemporary writers. See "New York in fiction", below.

Florence Turner *At the Chelsea* (Harcourt Brace Jovanovich $8.95). 1960s memoir of the famed hotel and its various arty (and artless) transients, by a woman who lived there for a decade.

Edmund White *States of Desire: Travels in Gay America* (NAL-Dutton $8.95). A revealing account of life in gay communities across America, containing an informed if dispassionate chapter on New York. Good on Fire Island and the more lurid aspects of NYC gay bars.

Geoffrey Moorhouse *Imperial City: The Rise and Fall of New York* (H. Holt & Co. $21.95). Though not exactly packed full of penetrating insights, this has reasonably entertaining background on the Big Apple.

Bernard Levin *A Walk up Fifth Avenue* (Sceptre, UK). Pompous, rather banal account of Levin's self-congratulatory meander up NYC's greatest street, from the TV series of the same name.

Henry James *Lake George to Burlington* (Tragara Press, UK, 1981). Travels through the peaceful and often wild backwaters of New York State in the late 1800s. As ever, elegantly written.

Frederico Garcia Lorca *Poet in New York* (Grove Weidenfeld $4.95). The Andalusian poet and dramatist spent nine months in the city around the time of the Wall Street Crash. This collection of over 30 poems reveals his feelings on the brutality, loneliness, greed, corruption, racism, and mistreatment of the poor.

HISTORY, POLITICS, AND SOCIETY

Oliver E. Allen *New York New York* (Macmillan $27.50). Entertaining anecdotal illustrated history with good accounts of the Robber Barons and other eminent New Yorkers, along with a deft appraisal of the Koch era.

Edward Robb Ellis *The Epic of New York City* (Mabaro Boooks $24.95). Popularized history of the city in which its major historical figures—Peter Stuyvesant, William Tweed, and the rest—become a cast of characters as colorful as any historical novel. Interesting, but you wonder where Ellis gets some of his facts from.

Hugh Brogan *Penguin History of the United States* (Viking Penguin $7.95). Good, up-to-date and very complete general history of America.

Ron Rosenbaum *Manhattan Passions* (Viking Penguin $6.95). Rosenbaum lunches with the rich and powerful in New York—and writes about it with wit, style, and sometimes hardbitten contempt. Pieces on Donald Trump, Ed Koch, and the late Malcolm Forbes to name just a few.

ART, ARCHITECTURE, AND PHOTOGRAPHY

Paul Goldberger *The City Observed: A Guide to the Architecture of Manhattan* (Random $15.95). If you need an up-to-date, well-written, and erudite rundown on New York's premier buildings look no farther. Goldberger's book is hard to fault.

Gerard R. Wolfe *New York: A Guide to the Metropolis* (McGraw $14.95). This is more academic—and less opinionated—than Goldberger's book, but it does include some good stuff on the Outer Boroughs. Also informed historical background.

N. White and E. Willensky (ed.) *AIA Guide to New York* (Harcourt Brace $21.95). Standard guide to the city's architecture, more interesting than it sounds.

Richard Berenhurst *Manhattan Architecture* (Prentice Hall, $45). Magnificent coffee-table tome of lavish photos with an informed introductory essay on Manhattan's skyscrapers and other buildings.

Margot Gayle & Michele Cohen *Guide to Manhattan's Sculpture.* (Prentice Hall $15.95). The Art Commission and Municipal Art Society's very thorough illustrated guide to more or less every piece of standing sculpture on the island. Accessibly laid out and written.

W. Brown *American Art* (Abrams $49.50). Encyclopedic account of movements in the visual and applied arts in America from Colonial times to the present day.

Les Krantz *American Artists* (Facts on File, 1985). Alphabetic guide to American art after World War I. An attractive and indispensable reference.

Barbara Rose and Alexander Liberman *American Painting: The Twentieth Century* (Rizzoli International $25). Full and readable, with prints that more than justify the price.

Jacob Riis *How the Other Half Lives* (Hill & Wang $6.95). Republished photo-journalism

reporting life in the Lower East Side at the end of the nineteenth century. The original awakened many to the plight of New York's poor.

Philip S. Foner and Reinhard Schultz *The Other America* (Unwin Hyman $14.95). Art and images of poverty and the labor movement in the USA. Includes photographs of early twentieth century New York by Jacob Riis (see above) and Lewis W. Hine.

SPECIFIC GUIDES

Toby & Gene Glickman *The New York Red Pages* (Greenwood $12.95). Radical guide to the city taking in politically significant sites and points of interest. Covering Lower Manhattan only, if you can get hold of it it's an informing read.

Mark Leeds *Ethnic New York* (Passport Books $14.95). A guide to the city that details its major ethnic neighborhoods, with descriptions of restaurants, shops, and festivals. Though its maps are terrible, an excellent introduction to the city's ethnic locales, especially off Manhattan.

Myer Alperson and Mark Clifford *The Food Lover's Guide to the Real New York* (Prentice Hall $12.95). Complete illustrated guide to the edible ethnic delights of all five boroughs.

Deborah Jane Gardner *New York Art Guide* (Art Guide Publications $5.95). Pocket book detailing city galleries, museums, performance spaces, art and architectural associations, and more. Useful if you're touring private galleries.

Richard Alleman *The Movie Lover's Guide to New York* (Harper & Row $14.95). Over two hundred listings of corners of the city with cinematic associations. Interestingly written, painstakingly researched, and indispensable to anyone with even a remote interest in either New York or film history.

Bubbles Fisher *The Candy Apple: New York for Kids* (Prentice Hall $11.95). Written by a quintessential New York grandmother, this guide is fun for adults to read, and offers lots of good ideas about what to do with kids in the city.

James Stevenson *Uptown Local, Downtown Express* (Viking $15.75). Line drawings and droll commentary on some of the minutiae of New York's urban landscape by the *New Yorker* writer and cartoonist.

Judi Culbertson and Tom Randall *Permanent New Yorkers* (Chelsea Green $16.95). This unique guide to the cemeteries of New York includes the final resting-places of such notables as Herman Melville, Duke Ellington, Billie Holliday, Horace Greeley, Mae West, Judy Garland, and 350 others.

Barbara McMartin *Fifty Hikes in the Adirondacks* (Backcountry $11.95). Hiking guide to the national park. Backcountry also publishes hiking guides to the Hudson Valley and the Finger Lakes.

R. & P. Albright *Short Walks on Long Island* and **Phil Angellino** *Short Bike Rides on Long Island* (Globe-Pequot $5.95 and $8.95). By far the best books to buy if you're spending any length of time on Long Island.

NEW YORK IN FICTION

Martin Amis *Money* (Viking Penguin $8.95). Following the wayward moments of degenerate film director John Self between London and New York, a weirdly scatalogical novel that's a striking evocation of 1980s excess.

Paul Auster *The New York Trilogy: City of Glass, Ghosts,* and *The Locked Room* (Viking Penguin $9.95). Three Borgesian investigations into the mystery, madness, and murders of contemporary NYC. Using the conventions of the crime thriller, Auster unfolds a disturbed and disturbing picture of the city.

James Baldwin *Another Country* (Dell $5.95). Baldwin's best-known novel, tracking the feverish search for meaningful relationships among a group of 1960s New York bohemians. The so-called liberated era in the city has never been more vividly documented—nor its gut-level racism.

John Franklin Bardin *The Deadly Percheron; The Last of Philip Banter, Devil Take the Blue-Tail Fly* (Viking Penguin $5.95 each). These three unique tales are the only works by Bardin, who disappeared from literary life in 1948; paranoid, almost surreal mysteries that use 1940s New York as a vivid backdrop for intricate storylines.

Wilton Barnhardt *Emma Who Saved My Life* (St. Martin $4.95). Warm and witty novel about making it in New York in the 1970s. Full of sharply observed, satirical detail on city characters, locations, dilemmas, and situations, and funny enough to make you laugh out loud, it's perhaps the most perfect thing to take with you on a visit.

Madison S. Bell *The Year of Silence* (Viking Penguin $6.95). The story of an Upper West Side suicide, and the effects it has on everyone connected, from the woman's lover to the Broadway panhandler who discovers the body. Controlled, delicately paced writing, structured (almost) as a set of separate stories, and unsentimentally revealing the city and its people. See also Bell's collection of short stories, *Zero db* (Viking Penguin $6.95), and his *Waiting for the End of the World* (Viking Penguin $6.95), an earlier novel about a terrorist plot to plant a nuclear device in the subway tunnels under Times Square.

William Boyd *Stars and Bars* (Viking Penguin $6.95). Set partly in New York, part in the deep South, a well-observed novel that tells despairingly and hilariously of the unbridgeable gap between the British and Americans. Full of ringing home truths.

Peter Cameron *Leap Year* (Harper Collins $8.95). A delightful comic novel, somewhat in the mold of Armistead Maupin, set in New York and taking a gently satirical look at the lives of a number of interconnected Manhattanites in the late 1980s. Entertaining and perceptive.

Jerome Charyn *War Cries over Avenue C* (Viking Penguin $7.95). Alphabet City is the derelict backdrop for this novel of gang warfare among the Vietnam-crazed coke barons of New York City. An offbeat tale of conspiracy and suspense. His latest book, *Paradise Man* (Mysterious Press $4.95), is the violent story of a New York hit man.

John Cheever *The Stories of John Cheever* (Ballantine $6.95). These marvelous stories have a warmth, depth of understanding, and a narrative tension that make utterly compelling reading. And they are also a superb evocation of New York (city and state) in the 1950s and 60s.

E. L. Doctorow *Ragtime* (Bantam $4.95). America, and particularly New York, before World War I: Doctorow cleverly weaves together fact and fiction, historical figures, and invented characters, to create what ranks as biting indictment of the country and its racism. See also the earlier and equally skillful *Book of Daniel* (Fawcett $4.95); *World's Fair* (Fawcett $5.95)—a beautiful evocation of a Bronx boyhood in the 1930s; *Loon Lake* (Fawcett

$4.95), much of which is set in the Adirondacks; and his latest, *Billy Bathgate* (Harper Collins $5.95).

J.P. Donleavy *A Fairy Tale of New York* (Atlantic Monthly $7.95). Comic antics through the streets of New York in the well-worn Donleavy tradition.

Andrea Dworkin *Ice and Fire* (Grove Weidenfeld $14.95). An unpleasant and disturbing romp through the East Village by one of America's leading feminist writers.

Brett Easton Ellis *American Psycho* (Vintage $11.00) Arriving in a blaze of hype, Easton Ellis's profoundly unpleasant book studies the life of Patrick Bateman, who works on Wall Street by day and tortures women to death for sexual pleasure by night. Like his previous book, *Less than Zero* (set in LA), the protagonists' world is a vapid one where designer labels are more important signifiers than people's names. Reviled by critics, *Psycho* is, in the final analysis, not a profound enough literary vessel for the disturbing ideas it contains.

Ralph Ellison *Invisible Man* (Random $9.95). The definitive if sometimes long-winded novel of what it's like to be Black and American, using Harlem and the 1950s race riots as a background.

F. Scott Fitzgerald *The Great Gatsby* (Collier Macmillan $4.95). Fitzgerald's best and best-known novel, set among the estates, the parties, and hedonism of Long Island's Gold Coast in the twenties. Stylishly written detail on the city, too.

Helen Hanff *Apple of my Eye* (Moyer Bell Ltd $8.95). Deliberately ironic look at the city by a native New Yorker who found fame as the author of *84 Charing Cross Road*. At times irritatingly naive, but often insightful and gently penetrating.

Oscar Hijuelos *Our House in the Last World* (Pocket Books $7.95). A warmly evocative novel of immigrant Cuban life in New York from before the war to the present day.

Chester Himes *The Crazy Kill* (Random $6.95). Himes writes violent, fast-moving, and funny thrillers set in Harlem, of which this is just one.

Andrew Holleran *Dancer from the Dance* (NAL Dutton $8.95). Enjoyable account of the embryonic gay disco scene of the early 1970s. Interesting locational detail of Manhattan haunts and Fire Island, but suffers from over-exaltation of the central character.

Washington Irving *The Legend of Sleepy Hollow and Other Stories* (Airmont $2.65). Washington Irving's classic tale, set in the Hudson Valley and the Catskills.

Henry James *Washington Square* (Viking Penguin $2.95). Skillful examination of the codes and dilemmas of New York genteel society in the nineteenth century.

Tama Janowitz *Slaves of New York* (Pocket Books $3.95). Written by one of the so-called "brat-pack" of young American writers, this collection of short stories pokes gentle fun at New York in the 1980s. Janowitz's recurring cast of characters is colorful, shocking, sad, and endearing. Her most recent novel, *A Cannibal in Manhattan* ($7.95), is a far less fresh or original work.

Joyce Johnson *Minor Characters* (Pocket Books $7.95). Women were never a prominent feature of the Beat generation; its literature examined a male world through strictly male eyes. This book, written by the woman who lived for a short time with Jack Kerouac, redresses the balance superbly well. And there's no better novel available on the Beats in New York. See also her *In the Night Café* (Pocket Books $7.95), a novel which charts—again in part autobiographically—the relationship between a young woman and a struggling New York artist in the 1960s.

William Kennedy *The Albany Trilogy* (Viking Penguin, 3 volumes $4.50–7.95). The binding thread of these novels is Albany and the Catskills, in the first adeptly re-created during the Prohibition era and following the fugitive tracks of gangster Jack "Legs" Diamond.

Stephen Koch *The Bachelor's Bride* (Marion Boyars $18.95). Readable if slightly affected novel of art society in 1960s New York.

Joseph Koenig *Little Odessa* (Ballantine $3.95). An ingenious, twisting thriller set in Manhattan and Brooklyn's Russian community in Brighton Beach. A seriously readable, exciting novel, and a good contemporary view of New York City.

Larry Kramer *Faggots* (NAL-Dutton $7.55). Parody of the NYC gay scene, lewdly honest and raucously funny, by the author of the AIDS play *The Normal Heart*.

Edward Limonov *It's Me, Eddie* (Grove Weidenfeld $7.95). The Jewish-Russian emigre on welfare in NYC and ambivalent about why he ever came. Tries hard to be at once funny and meaningful, though it rarely succeeds on either level.

Mary McCarthy *The Group* (Avon $4.95). Eight Vassar graduates making their way in the New York of the thirties. Sad, funny, and satirical.

Jay McInerney *Bright Lights, Big City* (Vintage $5.95). A cult book, and one which made first-time novelist McInerney a mint, following a struggling New York yuppie from one cocaine-sozzled nightclub to another. See also McInerney's latest novel, *Story of My Life* (Vintage $6.95): easily his best work to date, a superbly observed social satire in which the heroine weaves her way through a Manhattan that's disturbingly (and sometimes hilariously) superficial, self-indulgent, and exhausted.

Ann Petry *The Street* (Houghton Mifflin $9.95). The story of a Black woman's struggle to rise from the slums of Harlem in the 1940s. Convincingly bleak.

Marge Piercy *Braided Lives* (Fawcett $5.95). More a novel of Detroit than New York but an excellent one, and with much 1950s detail on the city, its neighborhoods, and embryonic movements.

Thomas Pynchon *V* (Harper Collins $9.95). First novel by one of America's greatest living writers. The settings shift from Valletta to Namibia, but New York's Lower East Side is a key reference point. And there's a fantastic crocodile-hunt through the city sewers. Recommended.

Judith Rossner *Looking for Mr. Goodbar* (Pocket Books $3.95). A disquieting book, tracing the progress—and eventual demise—of a woman teacher through volatile and permissive New York in the 1960s. Good on evoking the feel of the city in the 1960s era, but on the whole a depressing read.

Henry Roth *Call It Sleep* (Avon $4.95). Roth's only work of any real note traces—presumably autobiographically—the awakening of a small immigrant child to the realities of life among the slums of the Jewish Lower East Side. Read more for the evocations of childhood than its social comment.

Paul Rudnick *Social Disease* (Ballantine $6.95). Hilarious, often incredible, send-up of Manhattan night-owls. Very New York, *very* funny.

Damon Runyon *Guys and Dolls* (River City Press $15.95). A collection of short stories drawn from the chatter of Lindy's Bar on Broadway and since made into the successful musical.

J.D. Salinger *The Catcher in the Rye* (Bantam $3.95). Salinger's brilliant novel of adolescence, following Holden Caulfield's sardonic journey of discovery through the streets of New York. Essential reading.

Sarah Schulman *The Sophie Horowitz Story* (Naiad Press $7.95) and *After Dolores* (Plume $7.95). Lesbian detective stories set in contemporary New York: dry, downbeat, and very funny. See also *Girls, Visions, and Everything* (Seal Press $8.95), a stylish and, again, humorous study of the lives of Lower East Side lesbians.

Hubert Selby Jr. *Last Exit to Brooklyn* (Grove Weidenfeld $9.95). First published in 1966 and even now it's a disturbing read, evoking the sex, the immorality, the drugs, the violence of downtown Brooklyn in the 1960s with fearsome clarity. An important book, the recent movie a little less so.

Dyan Sheldon *Dreams of an Average Man* (Crown $15.95). Dense, typically mordant novel of deceit, social manners, and mid-life crises among NYC yuppies. An insightful and frequently scary read.

Isaac Bashevis Singer, *Enemies* (Farrar Straus & Giroux $8.95). A Polish Jew settles in New York following the war and marries the woman who helped him escape the Nazis, only to find the wife he thought was dead has managed to escape, too. A bleak tale, suffused with guilt and regret, set in a Manhattan haunted by the horrific and seemingly everlasting shadow of the holocaust.

Betty Smith *A Tree Grows in Brooklyn* (Harper Collins $5.95). Something of a classic, and rightly so, in which a courageous Irish girl makes good against a vivid pre-war Brooklyn backdrop. Totally absorbing.

Rex Stout *The Doorbell Rang* (Viking Press, 1965). Stout's Nero Wolfe is perhaps the most intrinsically "New York" of all the literary detectives based in the city, a larger-than-life character who, with the help of his dashing assistant, Archie Goodwin, solves crimes—in this story and others—from the comfort of his sumptuous Midtown Manhattan brownstone. Compulsive reading, and wonderfully evocative of the city in the 1940s and 50s.

Lee Tulloch *Fabulous Nobodies* (Harper Collins $7.95). Latest in a line of novels simultaneously satirizing and celebrating New York's obsession with style. Tulloch writes with some wit, but the endless lists of designer labels in lieu of any real plot is wearying.

Edith Wharton *Old New York* (Scribner, o/p). A collection of short novels on the manners and mores of New York in the mid-nineteenth century, written with Jamesian clarity and precision. Scribner also publish her *Hudson River Bracketed*, and *The Mother's Recompense* ($10.95 each), both of which center around the lives of women in nineteenth-century New York.

Tom Wolfe *The Bonfire of the Vanities* (Bantam $5.95). Wolfe's first novel, which uses his skills of social observation to the full. Sherman McCoy is a Wall Street bond dealer who finds he can't live on $1 million a year, and meets his match when, while swooning at the monied spires of Manhattan, he inadvertently drives his Mercedes into the South Bronx. The best head-to-toe revelation of New York in the late 1980s you could wish for—and a fine racy read to boot, despite its recent appearance as a roundly criticized film (see below).

NEW YORK ON FILM

"There are eight million stories in the Naked City." So goes the line in the 1948 movie of the same name. Ever since the silent era, film makers have been mining some of those stories, hoping to turn them into cinematic gold. What follows is a selection, biased by our own tastes, of some of the more representative films set and/or shot in the city and its environs. For more details of the city in film, get hold of *The Movie Lover's Guide to New York* by Richard Alleman (see "Books").

After Hours (Martin Scorsese: 1985). Feverish nightmare comedy of young computer programer's overnight descent into hell—downtown New York. Lightweight but entertaining, thanks to game cast and Scorsese's at-his-fingertips technique.

All About Eve (Joseph L. Mankiewicz: 1950). Terrifically talky, overripe egos in Manhattan theater world. A script peppered with brilliantly artificial dialogue, delivered from the guts by Bette Davis as aging Broadway star Margo Channing.

All That Jazz (Bob Fosse: 1979). Broadway choreographer Roy Scheider's life and death viewed as a running, Felliniesque production number in Fosse's autobiographical ego-trip. What can be said about a musical whose highpoint is an open-heart surgery extravaganza?

Angel Heart (Alan Parker: 1987). Mickey Rourke runs up against destiny and one Louis Cyphre (Robert de Niro) in the New York of the 1950s: atmospheric shots of Harlem and Coney Island add to the ambience of evil, violence, and guilt.

Angels with Dirty Faces (Michael Curtiz: 1938). Action, comedy, and sentimentality expertly whipped up by Warner Brothers. Archetypal role for James Cagney as gangster who goes to the chair pretending to be a coward for the sake of idolizing slum boys (The Dead End Kids).

Angelo My Love (Robert Duvall: 1983). Actor-turned-director Duvall's neo-realist portrait of young city gypsy (a motion picture natural) and his milieu.

Annie Hall (Woody Allen: 1977). Oscar-winning autobiographical comic romance between neurotic Allen and scatty Diane Keaton is a Valentine to her and to the city. Simultaneously clever, bourgeois, and very winning. For place-spotters, Annie's apartment was on 70th Street between Lexington and Park avenues.

Batman (Tim Burton: 1989). After the campy tongue-in-cheek TV series of the 1960s, the celluloid Batman returns to his comic-strip origins, battling villains in a somber, psychologically intense Gotham City. Jack Nicholson steals the show as The Joker.

Blackboard Jungle (Richard Brooks: 1955). Idealistic teacher Glenn Ford tames violent young thugs in studio-bound NYC high school. Watchable, even though it's largely contrived Hollywood social realism. The sensation it caused had something to do with the use of Bill Haley and the Comets' song "Rock Around the Clock."

Bonfire of the Vanities (Brian de Palma: 1990). Disappointingly miscast version of Tom Wolfe's best seller (see "Books") with Tom Hanks as Wall Street dealer Sherman McCoy driving to disaster. Much use of Bronx/Brooklyn locations can't enhance an ill-starred big-budget attempt.

Breakfast at Tiffany's (Blake Edwards: 1961). Truman Capote's sophisticated novella somewhat softened to accommodate Audrey Hepburn as charmingly loose Manhattanite Holly Golightly.

Bright Lights, Big City (James Bridges: 1988). Adaptation of Jay McInerney's cult novel (see "Books") about a coked-out yuppie whose life disintegrates as he stumbles from club to club. Michael J. Fox does his best in the lead role, but fails to bring across the feverish cynicism of the character or the book.

Broadway Danny Rose (Woody Allen: 1974). Warm, engaging little showbiz fable with Allen as good-hearted, small-time agent on the run from loony Mafia family. Mia Farrow is the blond floozie catalyst. Scenes shot at Carnegie Deli, 55th and Broadway.

Coogan's Bluff (Don Siegel: 1968). First team-ing of *Dirty Harry* director and Clint Eastwood, as upright Arizona lawman showing NY's Finest how to corral criminals. Siegel's **Madigan**, made the same year, contrasts detective Richard Widmark's routine with police commissioner Henry Fonda's problems. Both pictures are stylish, tough character studies.

The Cool World (Shirley Clarke: 1964). This arty documentary-style scan of a Harlem teen-ager who longs to be gun-toting gang member doesn't coalesce, despite grippingly "real" moments. Three years earlier Clarke experi-mented with film forms in **The Connection**, in which a group of addicts awaiting their pusher are recorded by docu-film maker. Three years later she trained her camera on a monologuing black hustler in **Portrait of Jason**.

The Cotton Club (Francis Ford Coppola: 1984). Jazz and gangsters in costly, overplotted musi-cal melodrama starring Richard Gere.

Crossing Delancey (Joan Micklin Silver: 1989). Lovely if overdramatized story of a Jewish woman (Amy Irving) who lives uptown but visits her grandmother south of Delancey each week. The matchmaking scenes between the grandmother and the local *yenta* steal the show. An engaging view of contemporary life in the Jewish Lower East Side.

The Crowd (King Vidor: 1928). Downbeat, influential silent study of day-to-day lives of hard-luck office worker and wife. Mixes pathos, realism, and humor in just the right amounts.

Cruising (William Friedkin: 1980). Cop Al Pacino goes underground to smoke out killer of gays in tasteless, unbalanced thriller filmed on location. Salaciously stylized "realism."

Cry of the City (Robert Siodmak: 1948). Ruthless gangster Richard Conte pursued by boyhood friend turned cop Victor Mature. Made at a time when police sirens and rainsoaked sidewalks were the stuff of poetry.

Dead End (William Wyler: 1937). Highly enter-taining, stage-derived tragedy of the East Side's teeming poor, set on an impressive studio-built street set. With Humphrey Bogart as a mother-obsessed small-time gangster, and a pack of lippy adolescents who earned their own movie series as *The Dead End Kids*.

Desperately Seeking Susan (Susan Seidelman: 1985). Bored suburban housewife Rosanna Arquette becomes obsessed with mysterious Madonna in off-the-wall comedy. Effervescent and unpretentious with a feel for modern New York.

Dog Day Afternoon (Sidney Lumet: 1975). Outlandish but true story of man (Al Pacino, perfect) robbing bank so his lover (Chris Sarandon, ditto) can have a sex change.

Do the Right Thing (Spike Lee: 1989). Set over 24 hours in and around an Italian-owned pizza joint in Bedford-Stuyvesant, Brooklyn, Lee's best film to date skillfully moves from comedy to an adept exploration of the racial problems of that neighborhood and the city itself. Realistic, stylish, and with a great soundtrack.

Easter Parade (Charles Walters: 1948). Fred Astaire came out of retirement to partner Judy Garland in a musical festooned with 17 Irving Berlin songs. The title tune—featuring a stroll on Fifth Avenue—was, like everything else, shot on a Hollywood backlot.

Escape From New York (John Carpenter: 1981). In 1997 Manhattan has become a maxi-mum security prison from which anti-hero Kurt Russell must rescue the hijacked US President. Visually explosive thriller promises more than it delivers.

Eyes of Laura Mars (Irvin Kershner: 1978). Chic terror in surprisingly effective pulp thriller that uses NY locations cannily. Faye Dunaway is riveting as vulnerable fashion photographer with psychic vision.

Eyewitness (Peter Yates: 1981). Unsuccessfully updated 1940s-style melodrama benefits from Manhattan setting and comic-romantic by-play between janitor William Hurt and Sigorney Weaver as TV reporter investigat-ing a murder he supposedly saw.

Fame (Alan Parker: 1980). Collective, contemporary puttin'-on-a-show sort of musical-drama set against the background of Manhattan's High School for the Performing Arts. Some good scenes and acting, but end result is neither fish nor fowl.

Fort Apache, The Bronx (Daniel Petrie: 1981). Paul Newman in handsome form as veteran cop based in the city's most crime-infested and corrupt precinct. Tense, entertaining, and totally unbelievable.

42nd Street (Lloyd Bacon: 1933). Milestone backstage musical from Warner Bros., starring Ruby Keeler as the young chorine who has to replace the ailing leading lady: she goes out onstage as an unknown and, guess what, comes back a star. Corny and cheerful.

The French Connection (William Friedkin: 1971). Plenty of juicy atmosphere in extremely tense, sensationally made Oscar-winning cop thriller starring Gene Hackman, whose classic car chase takes place under the Bensonhurst Elevated Railroad.

The Godfather (Francis Ford Coppola: 1972) Oscar-winning epic about Mafia family, friends and enemies is superb movie opera. **Part Two**, two years later, developed and deepened its predecessor's themes and strengths. **Part Three** (1990) concluded the story, but was a disappointment to fans. A great triple bill.

Ghostbusters (Ivan Reitman: 1985). A trio of flaky paranormal investigators—Dan Ackroyd, Bill Murray, and Harold Rami—go into business flushing out the spooks and spirits of Manhattan. Some genuinely funny moments in the Public Library and the Upper West Side.

Gremlins II (Joe Dante: 1990). Hilarious sequel sees thousands of gremlins taking over a prestigious skyscraper, a move which threatens to ruin the business empire of a Trump-like figure. Worth seeing if only for the rendition of "New York, New York" by thousands of the little reptiles.

The Group (Sidney Lumet: 1966). A bevy of fine acting talent on display in ambitious, episodic adaptation of Mary McCarthy's novel about the personal/professional careers of a 1930s Vassar College clique. See "Books."

Guys and Dolls (Joseph L. Mankiewicz: 1955). Marlon Brando sings and dances in this overblown version of Broadway musical about

Damon Runyon-derived low-lifes. Jean Simmons is fetching as Salvation Army woman he woos, while Frank Sinatra walks amiably through.

Hannah and Her Sisters (Woody Allen: 1986). Allen in mellowed, Chekhovian mood. The human comedy on view is exceptionally well played and wryly observed, but it lacks depth.

Hello Dolly! (Gene Kelly: 1969). This elephantine nail in the movie musical's coffin was an extravagant showcase for Barbra Streisand, too young but dynamic anyway as widowed matchmaker Dolly Levi.

Hester Street (Joan Micklin Silver: 1975). Young, tradition-bound Russian-Jewish immigrant Carol Kane joins her husband in turn-of-the-century Lower East Side to find he's cast off Old World ways. Simple but appealing tale with splendid period feeling.

Insignificance (Nicholas Roeg: 1985). Marilyn Monroe, Albert Einstein, and Eugene McCarthy lookalikes play stagey games in the Roosevelt Hotel. Essentially empty, Roeg's movie is worth watching for Tony Curtis's boozy senator and the lyrical, terrifying last few minutes.

Ironweed (Hector Babenco: 1987). Based on William Kennedy's *Albany Trilogy* (see "Books"), this is a convincingly somber recreation of the Depression years, with Meryl Streep and Jack Nicholson in top form as the drink-sodden lovers. To capture the feeling of Albany in the 1930s scenes were shot upstate along the Hudson.

It's Always Fair Weather (Gene Kelly, Stanley Donen: 1955). *On the Town* gone sour. Trio of wartime buddies reunite ten years later to discover they loathe each other and themselves. Smart, cynical, and satirical musical that was—undeservedly but unsurprisingly—a box office flop.

King Kong (Merian C. Cooper/Ernest B. Schoedsack: 1933). A giant ape runs amok when taken from his jungle home to far less hospitable New York by a film producer. The scene where King Kong stands astride the Empire State Building, swatting passing planes while tending Fay Wray, has become part of the city myth.

King of Comedy (Martin Scorsese: 1983). Quirky, biting satire set on the fringes of the New York entertainment world mixes the familiar with the bizarre in the tale of talentless autograph hound Rupert Pupkin (Robert de Niro) who wants to be a celebrity on a par with his Johnny Carson-like idol Jerry Lewis.

Klute (Alan J. Pakula: 1971). Oscar winner Jane Fonda as Manhattan call-girl Bree Daniel, ably supported by titular detective Donald Sutherland, in taut, well-above-average damsel-in-distress thriller with modern twists.

Last Exit to Brooklyn (Uli Edel: 1989). As films-of-the-books go, not a bad version of Hubert Selby's *succès de scandale* (see "Books"). Partly set in Red Hook (see Chapter Four), the film is strong on period detail and just as shocking in its portrayal of sex and violence as the novel.

Looking For Mr. Goodbar (Richard Brooks: 1977). Diane Keaton plays Upper West Side school teacher by day, promiscuous coke-sniffing club-goer by night, until she winds up in the evil hands of Richard Gere. Violent and frightening—even more so once you know it was based on a true story. See "Books."

The Lost Weekend (Billy Wilder: 1945). Strong, enduring drama about dipso writer Ray Milland's DT-strewn path to Bellevue. One of the most famous scenes is his long trek down Third Avenue trying to sell his typewriter. Shot on location, including P.J. Clarke's bar (for more on which see Chapter Eight, "Drinking and Eating").

The Manchurian Candidate (John Frankenheimer: 1962). Enormously skillful critique of American politics (from Richard Condon's novel) culminates with brainwashed Laurence Harvey turning assassin in Madison Square Garden. With Frank Sinatra, Angela Lansbury, and Janet Leigh.

Manhattan (Woody Allen: 1979). A black-and-white masterpiece of middle-class intellectuals' self-absorptions, lifestyles, and romances, cued by a Gershwin soundtrack in what is probably the greatest eulogy to the city ever made. Essential viewing.

Manhattan Melodrama (W.S. Van Dyke: 1934). Clark Gable and William Powell as boyhood pals from the slums who grow up on opposite sides of the law. Mickey Rooney plays Gable aged 12, Myrna Loy is the love interest. The movie earned notoriety when Public Enemy Number 1 John Dillinger was shot down as he emerged from seeing it in a Chicago cinema.

Marathon Man (John Schlesinger: 1976). Ex-Nazi deathcamp doctor Laurence Olivier goes after student Dustin Hoffman's teeth—and life—in incredible, botched-up, brutal thriller.

Marty (Delbert Mann: 1955). Modest Oscar winner from Paddy Chayefsky's teleplay about fat, mother-dominated Bronx butcher Ernest Borgnine meeting equally shy schoolteacher Betsy Blair in a Brooklyn dance hall. Hailed as a breakthrough in the way in which it focused on "real" people, it looks rather tame today.

Mean Streets (Martin Scorsese: 1973). Scorsese's breakthrough film breathlessly follows small-time hood Harvey Keitel and his volatile, harum-scarum buddy Robert de Niro around Little Italy (actually Belmont in The Bronx) before reaching the inevitably violent climax.

Midnight Cowboy (John Schlesinger:1969). The love story between Jon Voight's naive hustler Joe Buck and Dustin Hoffman's touching city creep Ratso Rizzo is the core of this ground-breaking Oscar winner. The pair are superlative. Much of the rest of the picture is empty, flashy aggression.

Miracle on 34th Street (George Seaton: 1947). Macy's Santa Claus Edmund Gwenn tries to prove he's the genuine item to young Natalie Wood and the courtroom.

Mixed Blood (Paul Morrisey: 1984). Blithely amoral comedy about flamboyant drug-pushing "Godmother" Marilia Pera and her Alphabet City brood. Bloody cartoon action peppered with a hot salsa soundtrack.

Moonstruck (Norman Jewison: 1987). Romantic comedy with Cher in good form as a Brooklyn Italian princess finding love and excitement with a Brandoesque Nicolas Cage. Good views of Brooklyn Heights and the Metropolitan Opera.

Moscow on the Hudson (Paul Mazursky: 1984). Robin Williams as a Russian circus saxophonist who defects in this witty, sentimental comedy on the East/West divide. More schmaltzy propaganda for the US.

My Dinner With André (Louis Malle: 1981). Chamber version of the ultimate New York movie. It's all talk, analysis, philosophy, as playwright-actor Wallace Shawn and former *avant-garde* theater director André Gregory play scripted (by Shawn) versions of themselves. Unique.

My Favourite Year (Richard Benjamin: 1984). The year is 1954 and the film is based on Mel Brooks' real life, when as a rookie writer for Sid Caesar's *Your Show of Shows*, he had to keep Errol Flynn sober for a live TV broadcast. Locations include Radio City Music Hall, Central Park, and parts of Brooklyn.

New York, New York (Martin Scorsese: 1977). Intense performances from Robert de Niro and Liza Minelli in moody, impressive attempt to sour and splinter 1940s movie-musical conventions. The tone is dark, the narrative unbalanced, but occasionally it all really works. NY imaginatively re-created on studio soundstages.

Next Stop, Greenwich Village (Paul Mazursky: 1974). Brooklyn boy heads to the Village in 1953, hoping to become actor in endearing autobiographical comedy. Shelley Winters is outstandingly funny as his smothering, outrageous mother.

On the Town (Gene Kelly, Stanley Donen: 1949). Exhilarating, landmark musical, ballet-inspired, about three sailors' romantic adventures on 24-hour leave in NYC. With Gene Kelly, Frank Sinatra, and Ann Miller flashing her legs in the Museum of Natural History. Partly shot on location (from Brooklyn Navy Yard to the top of the Empire State), it's as much New York travelog as musical.

On the Waterfront (Elia Kazan: 1954). Oscar winner contains what is arguably Marlon Brando's greatest performance as anti-hero Terry Malloy, an inarticulate longshoreman reluctantly caught up in union racketeering. Superb location shooting. With Eva Marie Saint, Karl Malden, and Rod Steiger.

Once Upon a Time In America (Sergio Leone: 1984). Sprawling, self-indulgent, but often brilliantly atmospheric saga starring Robert de Niro. Spanning decades, it comes close to capturing some of the pulp pleasures of 1930s and 1940s movies.

The Out of Towners (Arthur Hiller: 1970). From the moment they set foot in the city, everything that can go wrong for Jack Lemmon and Sandy Dennis does in Neil Simon's fraught and rather unsympathetic comedy.

Panic in Needle Park (Jerry Schatzberg: 1971). Al Pacino and Kitty Winn give dedicated performances as pair of druggies in authentic-seeming downer.

The Pope of Greenwich Village (Stuart Rosenberg: 1984). Thin, shaky-footed retread of *Mean Streets*. Mickey Rourke and Eric Roberts are small-time thieves falling foul of the Mafia.

Radio Days (Woody Allen: 1987). Mia Farrow rises from cigarette girl to Manhattan personality in Allen's slender collection of vignettes from the days of 1930s radio. Some location shooting in Brooklyn and Times Square, but not a film to compare with his best work.

Ragtime (Milos Forman: 1981). Miscalculated adaptation of E. L. Doctorow's novel nevertheless has a fresh performance from Elizabeth McGovern as Evelyn Nesbit and an amusing one from James Cagney as the wily old police commissioner. See "Books."

Rear Window (Alfred Hitchcock: 1954). Broken-legged photographer James Stewart plays Peeping Tom and discovers one of his neighbors is a killer. Peerless Hitchcock comedy-thriller, notable for its backlot recreation of a NYC courtyard, and the sexual chemistry between Stewart and Grace Kelly.

The Roaring Twenties (Raoul Walsh; 1939). World War I veteran gets involved with NY bootleggers. James Cagney supported by Humphrey Bogart. Definitive Warner's gangster formula, and crackling entertainment.

Rosemary's Baby (Roman Polanski: 1968). Seminal urban Gothic from Ira Levin's best-seller, about pregnant young married Mia Farrow plagued by satanic cult. The building she lives in is the famed Dakota, 72nd Street and Central Park West (for more on which, see "The Upper West Side" in Chapter Three).

Saturday Night Fever (John Badham: 1977). Crudely scripted, shrewdly marketed flick that was a massive youth cult hit, with John Travolta as a sensitive stud using disco as his escape route over the Brooklyn Bridge to Manhattan. Not totally bad, unlike the 1983 sequel **Staying Alive**.

The Secret of my Success (Herbert Ross: 1987). Michael J. Fox plays the hick come to New York to make it whatever the costs, and becomes the bemused target of his boss's wife's advances. Scatty, funny, and with some great shots of NYC.

Serpico (Sidney Lumet: 1973). Al Pacino is on target as real-life NYC cop, atypically cultured and incorruptible, in fast-paced tribute to loner righteousness that teems with atmosphere.

The Seven Year Itch (Billy Wilder: 1955). When his wife and kid vacate humid Manhattan, Mitty-like pulp editor Tom Ewell is left guiltily leching over the innocent TV-toothpaste temptress upstairs—Marilyn Monroe, at her most wistfully comic. The sight of her pushing down her billowing skirt as she stands on a subway grate (at Lexington Ave. and 52nd St.) is one of the era's most resonant movie images.

Sid and Nancy (Alex Cox: 1986). The Chelsea Hotel is setting for the final scenes in the lives of punk's *enfants terribles*, Sid Vicious and Nancy Spungen. Their sad, shabby, and often sick story is handled with warmth and humor.

Skyline (Fernando Colomo: 1980). Warm and gentle comedy about a young Spanish photographer coping with culture shock in NYC.

Smithereens (Susan Seidelman: 1982). Cheaply and roughly made story of city's punks and dispossessed that has its moments. Very obviously a springboard for the same director's *Desperately Seeking Susan*.

Sophie's Choice (Alan J. Pakula: 1982). Meryl Streep sports a Polish accent as Jewish biologist Kevin Kline's mistress in this glum but honorable adaptation of William Styron's novel set in 1947 Flatbush Brooklyn. Guilt and retribution stirred with romantic melodrama.

Something Wild (Jonathan Demme: 1986) About the best of the yuppie-in-peril nouvelle vogue with Melanie Griffith hijacking mild Manhattan businessman Jeff Daniels for a ride into New Jersey and her colorful past. The skill of the film is its ability to change gear several times—from screwball comedy to high school nostalgia to something very wild and very nasty indeed.

The Sweet Smell of Success (Alexander Mackendrick: 1957). Broadway gossip columnist Burt Lancaster and sleazy press agent Tony Curtis are a great team in this biting study of showbiz corruption. British director Mackendrick handles the juicy on-location, night-time milieu with real flair.

Superman (Richard Donner: 1978). Chris Reeve struggles for Truth, Justice, and the American Way in contemporary Manhattan by way of the Planet Krypton and a lovingly filmed Midwest. Alter ego Clark Kent's offices are the *Daily News* building on 42nd Street. The sequel **Superman 2** has stunning nighttime vistas from atop the Verrazano Narrows Bridge.

Taxi Driver (Martin Scorsese: 1976). Superbly unsettling study of obsessive outsider Robert de Niro, with Jodie Foster as the pubescent hooker he tries to "save" in horrifying gory climax. Scorsese's NYC is hallucinatorily seductive, yet thoroughly repellent.

Tootsie (Sydney Pollack: 1982). Dustin Hoffman's performance as an intense, out-of-work New York actor who dons female drag and becomes a soap opera celebrity is a work of masterful comic talent.

A Tree Grows in Brooklyn (Elia Kazan: 1945). This touching working-class family saga, from a best seller set in the earlier years of this century, was Kazan's directorial debut. See "Books."

Up the Down Staircase (Robert Mulligan: 1967). Harren High School is the setting for screen version of Bel Kaufman's best seller about beleaguered teacher Sandy Dennis. *Blackboard Jungle* with a sex-change.

Wall Street (Oliver Stone: 1987). Facile tale of Good versus Evil in the wheeler-dealer corporate jungle of the late 1980s. Michael Douglas is convincingly wicked, and the views out of his office window are terrific. But as a movie it's almost laughably shallow.

West Side Story (Robert Wise, Jerome Robbins: 1961). Sex, Shakespeare, and singing in an overlauded, hypercinematic Oscar-winning musical (via Broadway) about rival street gangs. Certainly it's excitingly assembled and impressively packaged.

Yankee Doodle Dandy (Michael Curtiz: 1942). James Cagney's Oscar-winning performance as showbiz Renaissance man George M. Cohan is a big, spirited biopic with music. Of its kind, probably the best ever.

Year of the Dragon (Michael Cimino: 1985). Mickey Rourke is a racist Vietnam veteran cop out to clean up Chinatown from newly appointed smack baron John Lone. Ostensibly anti-racist, but in fact falling into standard traps with glamorized violence and the condoning of its hero.

A GLOSSARY OF NEW YORK PEOPLE

ALLEN Woody Writer, director, comedian. Many people's clichéd idea of the neurotic Jewish Upper East Side Manhattanite, his clever, crafted films *Annie Hall, Manhattan, Broadway Danny Rose, Hannah and Her Sisters* and *Radio Days* comment on, and have become part of, the New York myth.

ASTOR John Jacob (1822–1890) Robber baron, slum landlord, and, when he died, the richest man in the world. Astor made his packet from exacting extortionate rents from those living in abject squalor in his many tenements. By all accounts, a right bastard.

BEECHER Henry Ward (1813–1887) Revivalist preacher famed for his support of women's suffrage, the abolition of slavery—and as the victim of a scandalous accusation of adultery that rocked nineteenth-century New York. His sister, Harriet Beecher Stowe, wrote the best-selling novel *Uncle Tom's Cabin*, which contributed greatly to the anti-slavery cause.

BRADY James ("Diamond Jim") (1856–1917) Financier and bon vivant of the Gay 90s. Famed for bespattering himself with diamonds—hence the nickname. One of the good guys of the era, he gave much money to philanthropic causes.

BRESLIN Jimmy Bitter, Brit-hating but often brilliant columnist for *Newsday*. Once ran for mayor on a Secessionist ticket (declaring New York independent from the state) with Norman Mailer as running mate.

BRILL Diane Doyenne of the nightclub hangers-out and hangers-on.

BRYANT William Cullen (1794–1878) Poet, newspaper editor, and prime mover for Central Park and the Met. The small park that bears his name at 42nd St. and 5th Ave. is a semi-seedy and ill-fitting memorial to a nineteenth-century Wunderkind.

BURR Aaron (1756–1836) Fascinating politician whose action-packed career included a stint as Vice-President, a trial and acquittal for treason, and, most famously, the murder of Alexander Hamilton (qv) in a duel. His house, the Morris-Jumel Mansion, still stands.

CARNEGIE Andrew (1835–1919) Emigre Scottish industrialist who spent most of his life amassing a vast fortune and his final years giving it all away. Unlike most of his wealthy contemporaries he was not an ostentatious man—as his house, now the Cooper-Hewitt Museum, shows.

COHAN George M. (1878–1942) If you've seen the illustrious biopic *Yankee Doodle Dandy* you probably think this actor, dancer, composer, playwright, and Broadway producer was a wonderful chap; in reality Cohan was a dislikable and disreputable wheeler-dealer who ruined others for his success.

CRISP Quentin Writer (*The Naked Civil Servant*) and celebrated apologist for NYC, living in self-imposed exile from his native England. Frequently to be found giving readings.

CUOMO Mario Governor of New York State and ongoing contender for the Democratic Party presidential nomination. A liberalish politician whose main problem in achieving greater things will probably be his Italian ancestry.

DINKINS David, First black mayor of New York City. Elected in 1989 after a hard, mud-slinging mayoral campaign against Republican Rudolph Guliani, his term in office has so far left him seeming ineffectual and weak: "Everything sticks to him," said a pundit "– but praise."

FRICK Henry Clay (1849–1919) John Jacob Astor minus the likable side. Frick's single contribution to civilization was to use his inestimable wealth to plunder some of the finest art treasures of Europe, now on show at his onetime home on 5th Avenue.

FULTON Robert (1765–1815) Engineer, inventor, and painter who got suburban commuting going with his ferry service to Brooklyn. The point where it landed now marks the beginning of Fulton St. He did not, as you'll read everywhere else, invent the steamboat.

GARVEY Marcus (1887–1940) Activist who did much to raise the consciousness of blacks in the early part of the century (and is now a Rasta legend). When he started to become a credible political threat to the white-controlled government he was thrown in prison for fraud; pardoned but deported, he spent the last years of his life in London.

GILBERT Cass (1859–1934) Architect of two of the city's most beguiling landmarks—the Woolworth Building and the Customs House.

GOULD Jay (1836–1892) Robber baron extraordinaire. Using the telegraph network to be the first person in the know, Gould made his fortune during the Civil War, and went on to manipulate the stock market and make millions more. His most spectacular swindle cornered the gold market, netted him $11 million in a fortnight, and provoked the "Black Friday" crash of 1869.

GREELEY Horace (1811–1872) Campaigning founder-editor of the *New Yorker* magazine and *Tribune* newspaper who advised a protegee to "Go West, young man!." An advocate of women's rights, union rights, the abolition of slavery, and other worthy, liberal matters.

HAMILTON Alexander (1755–1804) Brilliant Revolutionary propagandist, fighter (battlefield aide to Washington), political thinker (drafted sections of the Constitution), and statesman (first Secretary to the Treasury). Shot and killed in a duel by Aaron Burr (qv). His house, Hamilton Grange, is preserved at the edge of Harlem.

HARING Keith Big-name artist who used crude animal forms for decoration/patterning. Designed bits of Palladium nightclub, sleeve to Malcolm McLaren's *Buffalo Girls*, etc. His recent early death prematurely removed one of America's most promising artists and designers.

HELMSLEY Harry Property-owning tycoon who, like Donald Trump (qv), had a penchant for slapping his name on all that fell into his grasp. Hence many old hotels are now Helmsley Hotels, and, more offendingly, the New York Central Building on Park Avenue has become the Helmsley Building. Since the trial of his wife Leona, Harry has apparently gone senile.

HELMSLEY Leona Wife of Harry, self-styled "Queen of New York" and majordomo of the Helmsley Palace Hotel. To the delight of many, the shit hit the fan for Leona in 1989, when she was found guilty of million-dollar tax evasion.

IRVING Washington (1783–1859) Satirist, biographer, short story writer (*The Legend of Sleepy Hollow*, *Rip Van Winkle*), and diplomat. His house, just outside the city at Tarrytown, is worth a visit.

JOHNSON Philip Architect. As henchman to Ludwig Mies Van der Rohe, high priest of the International Style glass box skyscraper, he designed the Seagram Building on Park Avenue. In later years he has moved from Modernism to Post-Modernism, with the AT&T Building on Third Avenue (passable), the Federal Reserve Plaza on Liberty Street (puerile), and the thing at 53rd Street and Third (unspeakable). Other claims to fame: a brief stint as token intellectual for quasi-fascist senator Huey Long in the 1930s, and his personal founding of the thoroughly fascist *Youth and The Nation* organization.

KOCH Ed The most popular mayor of New York since Fiorello LaGuardia (qv). Elected by a slender majority in 1978, Koch won New Yorkers over by his straight-talking, no bullshit approach—and by appeasing the loudest liberal/ethnic groups when, and only when, politically necessary. After three terms in office, he lost the Democratic nomination in 1989 to David Dinkins (qv) following scandals involving other council officils and his insensitive handling of black social problems.

LAGUARDIA Fiorello (1882–1947) NYC mayor who replaced Jimmy Walker (qv) and who gained great popularity with his honest and down-to-earth administration.

MAILER Norman The old sexist slugger still breezes in from Brooklyn between novels.

MONTAUG Haoui Doorman at the Tunnel club, important nightperson and discoverer of Madonna. To be on first-name terms with Haoui is the cool person's waking wish.

MORGAN J. Pierpoint (1837–1913) Top-of-the-pile industrialist and financier who bailed the country out of impending doom in 1907 and used a little of his spare cash to build the Morgan Library on 3rd Avenue. Morgan created a financial empire that was bigger even than the Gettys' and that enabled him to buy out Andrew Carnegie and Henry Frick.

MOSES Robert (1889–1981) Moses is perhaps more than anyone responsible for the way the city looks today. Holding all key planning and building posts from the 30s to the 60s, his philosophy of urban development was to tear down whatever was old and in the way, and slap concrete over the green bits in between.

OLMSTED Fredrick (1822–1903) Landscape designer and writer. Central Park and many others were the fruits of his partnership with architect Calvert Vaux.

O'NEILL Eugene (1888–1953) NYC's (and America's) most influential playwright. Many of the characters from plays like *Mourning Becomes Electra*, *The Iceman Cometh*, and *Long Day's Journey into Night* are based on his drinking companions in The Golden Swan bar.

PARKER Dorothy (1893–1967) Playwright, essayist, and acid wit. A founder member of the Round Table group.

RIIS Jacob (1849–1914) Photo-journalist. His compassionate account of the poor and the horrors of slum dwelling, *How the Other Half Lives*, was instrumental in hastening the destruction of the worst tenements.

ROCKEFELLER John D. (1839–1937) Multi-millionaire oil magnate and founder of the dynasty.

ROCKEFELLER John D. Jr (1874–1960) Unlike his tight-fisted dad, Rockefeller Junior gave away tidy sums for philanthropic ventures in New York. The Cloisters, The Museum of Modern Art, Lincoln Center, Riverside Church, and most famously Rockefeller Center were all (or mainly all) his doing.

ROCKEFELLER Nelson (1908–1979) Politician son of John D. Jr. Elected governor of New York State in 1958 he held on to the post until 1974, when he turned to greater things and sought the Republican Party presidential nomination. He didn't get it, but before his death served briefly as Vice-President under Gerald Ford.

RUBELL Steve (1946–1989) Entrepreneur. Founder and former owner of Studio 54, his last venture (with business partner Ian Shrager) was The Royalton Hotel, the last word in with-it luxury.

SABAN Steven Nightperson and writer. Chronicler of the after-hours in-crowd, Saban's column in *Details* magazine should be read by those who have to be in bed by midnight.

SIMON Neil Playwright. With a record of Broadway/film hits as big as his bank balance (*Brighton Beach Memoirs* the latest), Simon can lay claim to being the most popular MOR playwright today.

TRUMP Donald Property tycoon. When you shell out $30 for your shoebox room, reflect that Donald sits on top of a real estate empire worth, at its peak, $1,300 million. His creations include the glammed-out Trump Tower on 5th Avenue, Trump Plaza near Bloomingdale's, and Trump's Casino in Atlantic City, NJ. In 1990 his financial empire took a massive drumming and his personal life collapsed with a much-publicized divorce from his wife Ivana.

TWEED William Marcy "Boss" (1823–78) Top banana of the NY Democratic Party who fiddled city funds to the tune of $200 million and gave Democratic Party headquarters Tammanny Hall its bad name.

VANDERBILT Cornelius "Commodore" (1794–1877) Builder and owner of much of the nation's railroads in the nineteenth century. At his death he was the wealthiest-ever American.

VANDERBILT Cornelius (1843–1899) Commodore's son and another hard-nosed capitalist. He doubled the family wealth between his father's death and his own—a fortune that kept (and keeps) successive generations of Vanderbilts in spare change.

WALKER Jimmy (1881–1946) Professional songwriter who turned politician and was elected NYC mayor at the height of the jazz age. As a dapper-dressed man-about-town he reflected much of its fizz but with the Depression he lost popularity and office.

WARHOL Andy (?–1987) Artist and media maneuverist. Instigator of Pop Art, The Velvet Underground, The Factory, *Interview* magazine, and *Empire*—a 24-hour movie of the Empire State Building (no commentary, no gorillas, nothing but the building). Died, oddly enough, after a routine gallstone operation.

WHITE Stanford (1853–1906) Partner of the architectural firm McKim, Mead, and White, which designed such neo-Classical piles as the General Post Office, Washington Square Arch, the Municipal Building, and bits of Columbia University. Something of a *roué*, White's days were brought to an abrupt end with a bullet through the head from the gun of a cuckolded husband.

INDEX